A Complete Guide to Programming in C++

Ulla Kirch-Prinz

Peter Prinz

JONES AND BARTLETT PUBLISHERS

Sudbury, Massachusetts

BOSTON   TORONTO   LONDON   SINGAPORE

World Headquarters
Jones and Bartlett Publishers
40 Tall Pine Drive
Sudbury, MA 01776
978-443-5000
info@jbpub.com
www.jbpub.com

Jones and Bartlett Publishers
Canada
2406 Nikanna Road
Mississauga, ON L5C 2W6
CANADA

Jones and Bartlett Publishers
International
Barb House, Barb Mews
London W6 7PA
UK

Cover Image: Stones on shore-line and yellow leaf, Bjorkliden, Sweden, by Peter Lilja

Library of Congress Cataloging-in-Publication Data

Prinz, Peter.
    [C++ Lernen und professionell anwenden. English]
    A complete guide to programming in C++ / Peter Prinz, Ulla Kirch-Prinz; translated by Ian Travis.
      p.   cm.
    ISBN: 0-7637-1817-3
    1. C++ (Computer program language)   I. Kirch-Prinz, Ulla.   II. Title.

  QA76.73.C153 P73713 2001
  005.13'3—dc21   2001029617

Chief Executive Officer: Clayton Jones
Chief Operating Officer: Don W. Jones, Jr.
V.P., Managing Editor: Judith H. Hauck
V.P., Design and Production: Anne Spencer
V.P., Manufacturing and Inventory Control: Therese Bräuer
Editor-in-Chief: Michael Stranz
Development and Product Manager: Amy Rose
Marketing Manager: Nathan Schultz
Production Assistant: Tara McCormick
Cover Design: Night & Day Design
Composition: Northeast Compositors
Text Design: Mary McKeon
Printing and Binding: Courier Westford
Cover printing: John Pow Company, Inc.

This book was typeset in QuarkXpress 4.11 on a Macintosh G4. The font families used were Goudy, Gill Sans, Courier, Rubino Serif, and Seven Sans. The first printing was printed on 50 lb. Rolland Opaque.

Printed in the United States of America

05 04 03 02 01   10 9 8 7 6 5 4 3 2 1

Dedicated to our children, Vivi and Jeany

preface

This book was written for readers interested in learning the C++ programming language from scratch, and for both novice and advanced C++ programmers wishing to enhance their knowledge of C++. It was our goal from the beginning to design this text with the capabilities of serving dual markets, as a textbook for students and as a holistic reference manual for professionals.

The C++ language definition is based on the **A**merican **N**ational **S**tandards **I**nstitute *ANSI Standard* X3J16. This standard also complies with ISO norm 14882, which was ratified by the **I**nternational **S**tandardization **O**rganization in 1998. The C++ programming language is thus platform-independent in the main with a majority of C++ compilers providing ANSI support. New elements of the C++ language, such as exception handling and templates, are supported by most of the major compilers. Visit the Jones and Bartlett web site at www.jbpub.com for a listing of compilers available for this text.

The *chapters* in this book are organized to guide the reader from elementary language concepts to professional software development, with in-depth coverage of all the C++ language elements en route. The order in which these elements are discussed reflects our goal of helping the reader to create useful programs at every step of the way.

Each **double-page** spread in the book is organized to provide a description of the language elements on the right-hand page while illustrating them by means of graphics and sample programs on the left-hand page. This type of visual representation offered by each spread will provide students and professionals with an unmatched guide throughout the text. The sample programs were chosen to illustrate a typical application for each language element. In addition, filter programs and case studies introduce the reader to a wide range of application scenarios.

To gain command over a programming language, students need a lot of experience in developing programs. Thus, each chapter includes **exercises** followed by **sample solutions,** allowing the reader to test and enhance his or her performance and understanding of C++.

The **appendix** provides further useful information, such as binary number representation, pre-processor directives, and operator precedence tables, making this book a well-structured and intelligible reference guide for C++ programmers.

In order to test and expand your acquired knowledge, you can **download** sample programs and solutions to the exercises at:

http://completecpp.jbpub.com

Content Organization

Chapter 1 gives a thorough description of the fundamental characteristics of the object-oriented C++ programming language. In addition, students are introduced to the steps necessary for creating a fully functional C++ program. Many examples are provided to help enforce these steps and to demonstrate the basic structure of a C++ program.

Chapter 2 provides a complete introduction to the basic types and objects used by C++ programs. Integral types and constants, fundamental types, and Boolean constants are just a few of the topics discussed.

Chapter 3 describes how to declare and call standard functions. This chapter also teaches students to use standard classes, including standard header files. In addition, students work with string variables for the first time in this chapter.

Chapter 4 explains the use of streams for input and output, with a focus on formatting techniques. Formatting flags and manipulators are discussed, as are field width, fill characters, and alignment.

Chapter 5 introduces operators needed for calculations and selections. Binary, unary, relational, and logical operators are all examined in detail.

Chapter 6 describes the statements needed to control the flow of a program. These include loops with while, do-while, and for; selections with if-else, switch, and the conditional operator; and jumps with goto, continue, and break.

Chapter 7 provides a thorough introduction to the definition of symbolic constants and macros, illustrating their significance and use. Furthermore, a comprehensive examination of standard macros for character handling is included.

Chapter 8 introduces implicit type conversions, which are performed in C++ whenever different arithmetic types occur in expressions. Additionally, the chapter explores an operator for explicit type conversion.

Chapter 9 takes an in-depth look at the standard class string, which is used to represent strings. In addition to defining strings, the chapter looks at the various methods of string manipulation. These include inserting and erasing, searching and replacing, comparing, and concatenating strings.

Chapter 10 describes how to write functions of your own. The basic rules are covered, as are passing arguments, the definition of inline functions, overloading functions and default arguments, and the principle of recursion.

Chapter 11 gives a thorough explanation of storage classes for objects and functions. Object lifetime and scope are discussed, along with global, static, and auto objects. Namespaces and external and static functions are also included in the discussion.

Chapter 12 explains how to define references and pointers and how to use them as parameters and/or return values of functions. In this context, passing by reference and read-only access to arguments are introduced.

Chapter 13 provides a complete description of how classes are defined and how instances of classes, or objects, are used. In addition, structs and unions are introduced as examples of special classes.

Chapter 14 describes how constructors and destructors are defined to create and destroy objects. Also discussed are how inline methods, access methods, and read-only methods can be used. Furthermore, the chapter explains the pointer this, which is available for all methods, and what you need to pay attention to when passing objects as arguments or returning objects.

Chapter 15 gives a complete explanation of member objects and how they are initialized, and of data members that are created only once for all the objects in a class. In addition, this chapter describes constant members and enumerated types.

Chapter 16 takes an in-depth look at how to define and use arrays. Of particular interest are one-dimensional and multidimensional arrays, C strings, and class arrays.

Chapter 17 describes the relationship between pointers and arrays. This includes pointer arithmetic, pointer versions of functions, pointers as return values and read-only pointers, and pointer arrays. Students learn that operations that use C strings illustrate how to use pointers for efficient programming, and that string access via the command line of an application program is used to illustrate pointer arrays.

Chapter 18 explains sequential file access using file streams. Students will develop an understanding of how file streams provide simple and portable file handling techniques.

Chapter 19 provides a complete description of the various uses of overloaded operators. Arithmetic operators, comparisons, the subscript operator, and the shift operators for input and output are overloaded to illustrate the appropriate techniques. In addition, the concept of friend functions, which is introduced in this context, is particularly important for overloading operators. Students learn how overloading operators allows them to apply existing operators to objects of class type.

Chapter 20 discusses how implicit type conversion occurs in C++ when an expression cannot be compiled directly but can be compiled after applying a conversion rule. The programmer can stipulate how the compiler will perform implicit type conversion for classes by defining conversion constructors and functions. Finally, the chapter discusses ambiguity that occurs due to type conversion and how to avoid it.

Chapter 21 describes how a program can allocate and release memory dynamically in line with current memory requirements. Dynamic memory allocation is an important factor in many C++ programs, and the following chapters contain several case studies to help students review the subject.

Chapter 22 explains how to implement classes containing pointers to dynamically allocated memory. These include your own copy constructor definition and overloading the assignment operator. A class designed to represent arrays of any given length is used as a sample application.

Chapter 23 provides a thorough description of how derived classes can be constructed from existing classes by inheritance. In addition to defining derived classes, this chapter discusses how members are redefined, how objects are constructed and destroyed, and how access control to base classes can be realized.

Chapter 24 discusses implicit type conversion within class hierarchies, which occurs in the context of assignments and function calls. Explicit type casting in class hierarchies is also described, paying particular attention to upcasting and downcasting.

Chapter 25 gives a complete explanation of how to develop and manage polymorphic classes. In addition to defining virtual functions, dynamic downcasting in polymorphic class hierarchies is introduced.

Chapter 26 describes how defining pure virtual methods can create abstract classes and how you can use abstract classes at a polymorphic interface for derived classes. To illustrate this, an inhomogeneous list, that is, a linked list whose elements can be of various class types, is implemented.

Chapter 27 describes how new classes are created by multiple inheritance and explains their uses. Besides introducing students to the creation and destruction of objects in multiply-derived classes, virtual base classes are depicted to avoid ambiguity in multiple inheritance.

Chapter 28 explains how a C++ program uses error-handling techniques to resolve error conditions. In addition to throwing and catching exceptions, the chapter also examines how exception specifications are declared and exception classes are defined. In addition, the use of standard exception classes is discussed.

Chapter 29 examines random access to files based on file streams, and options for querying file state. Exception handling for files is discussed as well. The chapter illustrates how to make objects in polymorphic classes persistent, that is, how to save them in files. The applications introduced in this chapter include simple index files and hash tables.

Chapter 30 provides a thorough explanation of the advanced uses of pointers. These include pointers to pointers, functions with a variable number of arguments, and pointers to functions. In addition, an application that defines a class used to represent dynamic matrices is introduced.

Chapter 31 describes bitwise operators and how to use bit masks. The applications included demonstrate calculations with parity bits, conversion of lowercase and capital letters, and converting binary numbers. Finally, the definition of bit-fields is introduced.

Chapter 32 discusses how to define and use function and class templates. In addition, special options, such as default arguments, specialization, and explicit instantiation, are discussed. Students learn that templates allow the construction of functions and classes based on types that have not yet been stated. Thus, templates are a powerful tool for automating program code generation.

Chapter 33 explains standard class templates used to represent containers for more efficient management of object collections. These include sequences, such as lists and double ended queues; container adapters, such as stacks, queues, and priority queues; associative containers, such as sets and maps; and bitsets. In addition to discussing how to manage containers, the chapter also looks at sample applications, such as bitmaps for raster images, and routing techniques.

Additional Features

Chapter Goals   A concise chapter introduction, which contains a description of the chapter's contents, is presented at the beginning of each chapter. These summaries also provide students with an idea of the key points to look for throughout the chapter.

Chapter Exercises   Each chapter contains exercises, including programming problems, designed to test students' knowledge and understanding of the main ideas. The exercises also provide reinforcement for key chapter concepts. Solutions are included to allow students to check their work immediately and correct any possible mistakes.

Case Studies   Every chapter contains a number of case studies that were designed to introduce the reader to a wide range of application scenarios.

Notes   This feature provides students with helpful tips and information useful to learning C++. Important concepts and rules are highlighted for additional emphasis and easy access.

Hints   These are informative suggestions for easier programming. Also included are common mistakes and how to avoid making them.

Acknowledgements

Our thanks go out to everyone who helped produce this book, particularly to

Ian Travis, for his valuable contributions to the development of this book.
Alexa Doehring, who reviewed all samples and program listings, and gave many valuable hints from the American perspective.
Michael Stranz and **Amy Rose** at Jones and Bartlett Publishers, who managed the publishing agreement and the production process so smoothly.
Our children, **Vivi** and **Jeany**, who left us in peace long enough to get things finished!
And now all that remains is to wish you, Dear Reader, **lots of fun with C++**!

Ulla Kirch-Prinz
Peter Prinz

contents

chapter 1

Fundamentals

This chapter describes the fundamental characteristics of the object-oriented C++ programming language. In addition, you will be introduced to the steps necessary for creating a fully functional C++ program. The examples provided will help you retrace these steps and also demonstrate the basic structure of a C++ program.

■ DEVELOPMENT AND PROPERTIES OF C++

Characteristics

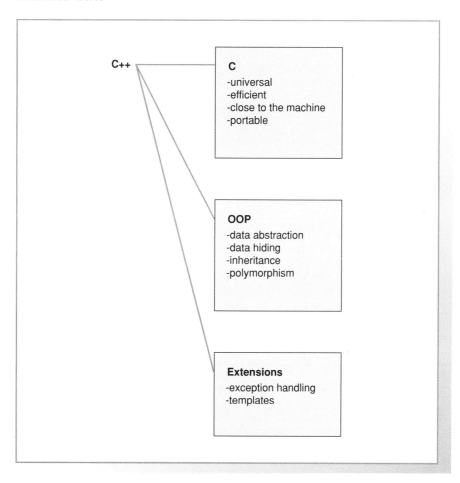

☐ Historical Perspective

The C++ programming language was created by Bjarne Stroustrup and his team at Bell Laboratories (AT&T, USA) to help implement simulation projects in an object-oriented and efficient way. The earliest versions, which were originally referred to as "C with classes," date back to 1980. As the name C++ implies, C++ was derived from the C programming language: ++ is the increment operator in C.

As early as 1989 an ANSI Committee (**A**merican **N**ational **S**tandards **I**nstitute) was founded to standardize the C++ programming language. The aim was to have as many compiler vendors and software developers as possible agree on a unified description of the language in order to avoid the confusion caused by a variety of dialects.

In 1998 the ISO (**I**nternational **O**rganization for **S**tandardization) approved a standard for C++ (ISO/IEC 14882).

☐ Characteristics of C++

C++ is not a purely object-oriented language but a hybrid that contains the functionality of the C programming language. This means that you have all the features that are available in C:

- ▪ universally usable modular programs
- ▪ efficient, close to the machine programming
- ▪ portable programs for various platforms.

The large quantities of existing C source code can also be used in C++ programs.

C++ supports the concepts of object-oriented programming (or OOP for short), which are:

- ▪ *data abstraction*, that is, the creation of classes to describe objects
- ▪ *data encapsulation* for controlled access to object data
- ▪ *inheritance* by creating derived classes (including multiple derived classes)
- ▪ *polymorphism* (Greek for multiform), that is, the implementation of instructions that can have varying effects during program execution.

Various language elements were added to C++, such as references, templates, and exception handling. Even though these elements of the language are not strictly object-oriented programming features, they are important for efficient program implementation.

■ OBJECT-ORIENTED PROGRAMMING

Traditional concept

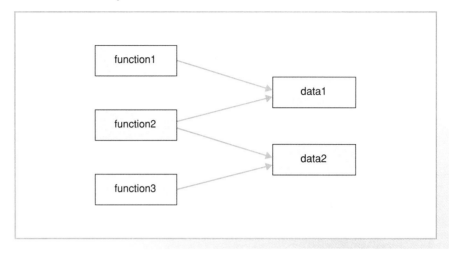

Object-oriented concept

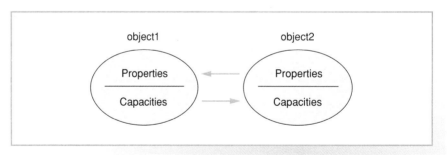

Traditional Procedural Programming

In traditional, procedural programming, data and functions (subroutines, procedures) are kept separate from the data they process. This has a significant effect on the way a program handles data:

- the programmer must ensure that data are initialized with suitable values before use and that suitable data are passed to a function when it is called
- if the data representation is changed, e.g. if a record is extended, the corresponding functions must also be modified.

Both of these points can lead to errors and neither support low program maintenance requirements.

Objects

Object-oriented programming shifts the focus of attention to the *objects*, that is, to the aspects on which the problem is centered. A program designed to maintain bank accounts would work with data such as balances, credit limits, transfers, interest calculations, and so on. An object representing an account in a program will have properties and capacities that are important for account management.

OOP objects combine data (properties) and functions (capacities). A class defines a certain object type by defining both the properties and the capacities of the objects of that type. Objects communicate by sending each other "messages," which in turn activate another object's capacities.

Advantages of OOP

Object-oriented programming offers several major advantages to software development:

- **reduced susceptibility to errors**: an object controls access to its own data. More specifically, an object can reject erroneous access attempts
- **easy re-use**: objects maintain themselves and can therefore be used as building blocks for other programs
- **low maintenance requirement**: an object type can modify its own internal data representation without requiring changes to the application.

■ DEVELOPING A C++ PROGRAM

Translating a C++ program

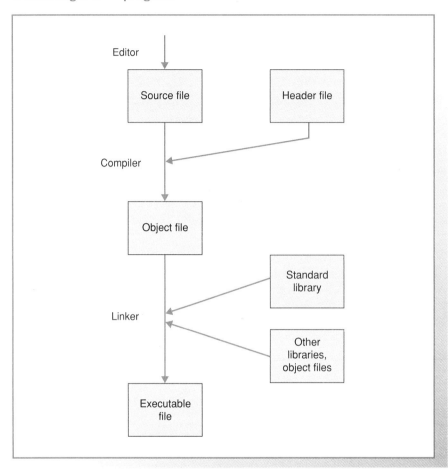

The following three steps are required to create and translate a C++ program:

1. First, a text editor is used to save the C++ program in a text file. In other words, the *source code* is saved to a *source file*. In larger projects the programmer will normally use *modular programming*. This means that the source code will be stored in several source files that are edited and translated separately.

2. The source file is put through a *compiler* for translation. If everything works as planned, an object file made up of *machine code* is created. The object file is also referred to as a *module*.

3. Finally, the *linker* combines the object file with other modules to form an *executable file*. These further modules contain functions from standard libraries or parts of the program that have been compiled previously.

It is important to use the correct file extension for the source file's *name*. Although the file extension depends on the compiler you use, the most commonly found file extensions are .cpp and .cc.

Prior to compilation, *header files*, which are also referred to as *include files*, can be copied to the source file. Header files are text files containing information needed by various source files, for example, type definitions or declarations of variables and functions. Header files can have the file extension .h, but they may not have any file extension.

The C++ *standard library* contains predefined and standardized functions that are available for any compiler.

Modern compilers normally offer an *integrated software development environment*, which combines the steps mentioned previously into a single task. A graphical user interface is available for editing, compiling, linking, and running the application. Moreover, additional tools, such as a debugger, can be launched.

✓ **NOTE**

If the source file contains just one *syntax error*, the compiler will report an *error*. Additional error messages may be shown if the compiler attempts to continue despite having found an error. So when you are troubleshooting a program, be sure to start with the first error shown.

In addition to error messages, the compiler will also issue *warnings*. A warning does not indicate a syntax error but merely draws your attention to a possible error in the program's logic, such as the use of a non-initialized variable.

■ A BEGINNER'S C++ PROGRAM

Sample program

```
#include <iostream>
using namespace std;

int main()
{
    cout <<  "Enjoy yourself with C++!"  << endl;
    return 0;
}
```

Screen output

```
Enjoy yourself with C++!
```

Structure of function main()

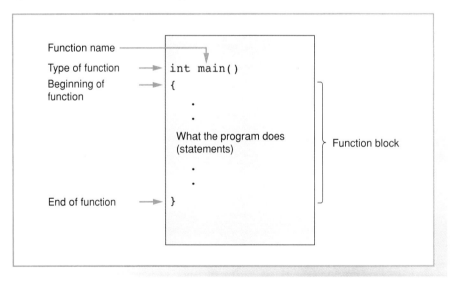

A C++ program is made up of objects with their accompanying *member functions* and *global functions*, which do not belong to any single particular class. Each function fulfills its own particular task and can also call other functions. You can create functions yourself or use ready-made functions from the standard library. You will always need to write the global function main() yourself since it has a special role to play; in fact it is the main program.

The short programming example on the opposite page demonstrates two of the most important elements of a C++ program. The program contains only the function main() and displays a message.

The first line begins with the number symbol, #, which indicates that the line is intended for the *preprocessor*. The preprocessor is just one step in the first translation phase and no object code is created at this time. You can type

```
#include <filename>
```

to have the preprocessor copy the quoted file to this position in the source code. This allows the program access to all the information contained in the header file. The header file iostream comprises conventions for input and output streams. The word *stream* indicates that the information involved will be treated as a flow of data.

Predefined names in C++ are to be found in the std (standard) namespace. The using directive allows direct access to the names of the std namespace.

Program execution begins with the first instruction in function main(), and this is why each C++ program must have a main function. The structure of the function is shown on the opposite page. Apart from the fact that the name cannot be changed, this function's structure is not different from that of any other C++ function.

In our example the function main() contains two *statements*. The first statement

```
cout << "Enjoy yourself with C++!" << endl;
```

outputs the text string Enjoy yourself with C++! on the screen. The name cout (console output) designates an object responsible for output.

The two less-than symbols, <<, indicate that characters are being "pushed" to the output stream. Finally endl (end of line) causes a line feed. The statement

```
return 0;
```

terminates the function main() and also the program, returning a value of 0 as an exit code to the calling program. It is standard practice to use the exit code 0 to indicate that a program has terminated correctly.

Note that statements are followed by a semicolon. By the way, the shortest statement comprises only a semicolon and does nothing.

■ STRUCTURE OF SIMPLE C++ PROGRAMS

A C++ program with several functions

```cpp
/*********************************************************
   A program with some functions and comments
*********************************************************/

#include <iostream>
using namespace std;

void line(), message();                // Prototypes

int main()
{
   cout << "Hello! The program starts in main()."
        << endl;
   line();
   message();
   line();
   cout << "At the end of main()." << endl;

   return 0;
}

void line()                            // To draw a line.
{
   cout << "--------------------------------" << endl;
}

void message()                 // To display a message.
{
   cout << "In function message()." << endl;
}
```

Screen output

```
Hello! The program starts in main().
--------------------------------
In function message().
--------------------------------
At the end of main().
```

The example on the opposite page shows the structure of a C++ program containing multiple functions. In C++, functions do not need to be defined in any fixed order. For example, you could define the function `message()` first, followed by the function `line()`, and finally the `main()` function.

However, it is more common to start with the `main()` function as this function controls the program flow. In other words, `main()` calls functions that have yet to be defined. This is made possible by supplying the compiler with a function *prototype* that includes all the information the compiler needs.

This example also introduces *comments*. Strings enclosed in `/*` . . . `*/` or starting with `//` are interpreted as comments.

EXAMPLES:

```
/* I can cover
   several lines */
// I can cover just one line
```

In single-line comments the compiler ignores any characters following the `//` signs up to the end of the line. Comments that cover several lines are useful when troubleshooting, as you can use them to mask complete sections of your program. Both comment types can be used to comment out the other type.

As to the *layout* of source files, the compiler parses each source file sequentially, breaking the contents down into tokens, such as function names and operators. Tokens can be separated by any number of whitespace characters, that is, by spaces, tabs, or new line characters. The order of the source code is important but it is not important to adhere to a specific layout, such as organizing your code in rows and columns. For example

```
void message
      (   ){ cout   <<
         "In function message()."   <<
   endl;}
```

might be difficult to read, but it is a correct definition of the function `message()`.

Preprocessor directives are one exception to the layout rule since they always occupy a single line. The number sign, #, at the beginning of a line can be preceded only by a space or a tab character.

To improve the legibility of your C++ programs you should adopt a consistent style, using indentation and blank lines to reflect the structure of your program. In addition, make generous use of comments.

exercises

■ EXERCISES

Program listing of exercise 3

```cpp
#include <iostream>
using namespace std;

void pause();          // Prototype

int main()
{
   cout << endl << "Dear reader, "
        << endl << "have a ";
   pause();
   cout << "!" << endl;

   return 0;
}

void pause()
{
   cout << "BREAK";
}
```

Write a C++ program that outputs the following text on screen:

```
Oh what
a happy day!
Oh yes,
what a happy day!
```

Use the manipulator `endl` where appropriate.

The following program contains several errors:

```cpp
*/ Now you should not forget your glasses //
#include <stream>
int main
{
  cout << "If this text",
  cout >> " appears on your display, ";
  cout << " endl;"
  cout << 'you can pat yourself on '
       << " the back!"  << endl.
  return 0;
)
```

Resolve the errors and run the program to test your changes.

What does the C++ program on the opposite page output on screen?

■ **SOLUTIONS**

Exercise 1

```cpp
// Let's go !

#include <iostream>
using namespace std;

int main()
{
   cout << " Oh what " << endl;
   cout << " a happy day! " << endl;
   cout << " Oh yes, " << endl;
   cout << " what a happy day! " << endl;

   return 0;
}
```

Exercise 2

The corrected places are underlined.

```cpp
/* Now you should not forget your glasses */
#include <iostream>
using namespace std;
int main()
{
   cout << " If this text ";
   cout << " appears on your display, ";
   cout << endl;
   cout << " you can pat yourself on "
        << " the back!" << endl;
   return 0;
}
```

Exercise 3

The screen output begins on a new line:

```
Dear reader,
have a BREAK!
```

chapter 2

Fundamental Types, Constants, and Variables

This chapter introduces you to the basic types and objects used by C++ programs.

■ FUNDAMENTAL TYPES

Overview*

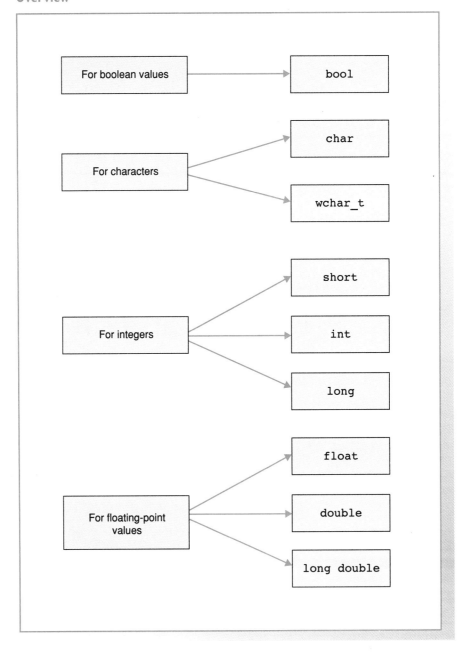

───────────────

* without type void, which will be introduced later.

A program can use several data to solve a given problem, for example, characters, integers, or floating-point numbers. Since a computer uses different methods for processing and saving data, the data *type* must be known. The type defines

1. the internal representation of the data, and

2. the amount of memory to allocate.

A number such as `-1000` can be stored in either 2 or 4 bytes. When accessing the part of memory in which the number is stored, it is important to read the correct number of bytes. Moreover, the memory content, that is the bit sequence being read, must be interpreted correctly as a signed integer.

The C++ compiler recognizes the *fundamental types*, also referred to as *built-in types*, shown on the opposite page, on which all other types (vectors, pointers, classes, ...) are based.

☐ The Type `bool`

The result of a comparison or a logical association using AND or OR is a *boolean* value, which can be true or false. C++ uses the `bool` type to represent boolean values. An expression of the type `bool` can either be `true` or `false`, where the internal value for `true` will be represented as the numerical value 1 and `false` by a zero.

☐ The `char` and `wchar_t` Types

These types are used for saving character codes. A *character code* is an integer associated with each character. The letter A is represented by code 65, for example. The *character set* defines which code represents a certain character. When displaying characters on screen, the applicable character codes are transmitted and the "receiver," that is the screen, is responsible for correctly interpreting the codes.

The C++ language does not stipulate any particular characters set, although in general a character set that contains the *ASCII code* (**A**merican **S**tandard **C**ode for **I**nformation Interchange) is used. This 7-bit code contains definitions for 32 control characters (codes 0 – 31) and 96 printable characters (codes 32 – 127).

The `char` (character) type is used to store character codes in one byte (8 bits). This amount of storage is sufficient for extended character sets, for example, the ANSI character set that contains the ASCII codes and additional characters such as German umlauts.

The `wchar_t` (wide character type) type comprises at least 2 bytes (16 bits) and is thus capable of storing modern Unicode characters. *Unicode* is a 16-bit code also used in Windows NT and containing codes for approximately 35,000 characters in 24 languages.

■ FUNDAMENTAL TYPES (CONTINUED)

Integral types

Type	Size	Range of Values (decimal)
char	1 byte	—128 to +127 or 0 to 255
unsigned char	1 byte	0 to 255
signed char	1 byte	—128 to +127
int	2 byte resp. 4 byte	—32768 to +32767 resp. —2147483648 to +2147483647
unsigned int	2 byte resp. 4 byte	0 to 65535 resp. 0 to 4294967295
short	2 byte	—32768 to +32767
unsigned short	2 byte	0 to 65535
long	4 byte	—2147483648 to +2147483647
unsigned long	4 byte	0 to 4294967295

Sample program

```
#include <iostream>
#include <climits>        // Definition of INT_MIN, ...
using namespace std;

int main()
{
  cout << "Range of types int and unsigned int"
       << endl << endl;
  cout << "Type              Minimum           Maximum"
       << endl
       << "-------------------------------------------"
       << endl;

  cout << "int            " <<   INT_MIN << "          "
                            <<   INT_MAX << endl;

  cout << "unsigned int   " <<   "            0         "
                            << UINT_MAX << endl;
  return 0;
}
```

☐ Integral Types

The types short, int, and long are available for operations with integers. These types are distinguished by their ranges of values. The table on the opposite page shows the integer types, which are also referred to as *integral types,* with their typical storage requirements and ranges of values.

The int (integer) type is tailor-made for computers and adapts to the length of a register on the computer. For 16-bit computers, int is thus equivalent to short, whereas for 32-bit computers int will be equivalent to long.

C++ treats character codes just like normal integers. This means you can perform calculations with variables belonging to the char or wchar_t types in exactly the same way as with int type variables. char is an integral type with a size of one byte. The range of values is thus –128 to +127 or from 0 to 255, depending on whether the compiler interprets the char type as signed or unsigned. This can vary in C++.

The wchar_t type is a further integral type and is normally defined as unsigned short.

☐ The signed and unsigned Modifiers

The short, int, and long types are normally interpreted as signed with the highest bit representing the sign. However, integral types can be preceded by the keyword unsigned. The amount of memory required remains unaltered but the range of values changes due to the highest bit no longer being required as a sign. The keyword unsigned can be used as an abbreviation for unsigned int.

The char type is also normally interpreted as signed. Since this is merely a convention and not mandatory, the signed keyword is available. Thus three types are available: char, signed char, and unsigned char.

✓ NOTE

In ANSI C++ the size of integer types is not preset. However, the following order applies:

```
char <= short <= int <= long
```

Moreover, the short type comprises at least 2 bytes and the long type at least 4 bytes.

The current value ranges are available in the climits header file. This file defines constants such as CHAR_MIN, CHAR_MAX, INT_MIN, and INT_MAX, which represent the smallest and greatest possible values. The program on the opposite page outputs the value of these constants for the int and unsigned int types.

■ FUNDAMENTAL TYPES (CONTINUED)

Floating-point types

Type	Size	Range of Values	Lowest Positive Value	Accuracy (decimal)
float	4 bytes	−3.4E+38	1.2E—38	6 digits
double	8 bytes	−1.7E+308	2.3E—308	15 digits
long double	10 bytes	−1.1E+4932	3.4E—4932	19 digits

✓ **NOTE**

IEEE format (IEEE = Institute of Electrical and Electronic Engineers) is normally used to represent floating-point types. The table above makes use of this representation.

Arithmetic types

Integral types
```
    bool
    char, signed char, unsigned char, wchar_t
    short, unsigned short
    int, unsigned int
    long, unsigned long
```

Floating-point types
```
    float
    double
    long double
```

✓ **NOTE**

Arithmetic operators are defined for arithmetic types, i.e. you can perform calculations with variables of this type.

☐ Floating-Point Types

Numbers with a fraction part are indicated by a decimal point in C++ and are referred to as floating-point numbers. In contrast to integers, floating-point numbers must be stored to a preset accuracy. The following three types are available for calculations involving floating-point numbers:

```
float          for simple accuracy
double         for double accuracy
long double    for high accuracy
```

The value range and accuracy of a type are derived from the amount of memory allocated and the internal representation of the type.

Accuracy is expressed in decimal places. This means that "six decimal places" allows a programmer to store two floating-point numbers that differ within the first six decimal places as separate numbers. In reverse, there is no guarantee that the figures 12.3456 and 12.34561 will be distinguished when working to a accuracy of six decimal places. And remember, it is not a question of the position of the decimal point, but merely of the numerical sequence.

If it is important for your program to display floating-point numbers with an accuracy supported by a particular machine, you should refer to the values defined in the `cfloat` header file.

Readers interested in additional material on this subject should refer to the Appendix, which contains a section on the representation of binary numbers on computers for both integers and floating-point numbers.

☐ The `sizeof` Operator

The amount of memory needed to store an object of a certain type can be ascertained using the `sizeof` operator:

```
sizeof(name)
```

yields the size of an object in bytes, and the parameter `name` indicates the object type or the object itself. For example, `sizeof(int)` represents a value of 2 or 4 depending on the machine. In contrast, `sizeof(float)` will always equal 4.

☐ Classification

The fundamental types in C++ are *integer types, floating-point types,* and the `void` type. The types used for integers and floating-point numbers are collectively referred to as *arithmetic types,* as arithmetic operators are defined for them.

The `void` type is used for expressions that do not represent a value. A function call can thus take a `void` type.

▪ CONSTANTS

Examples for integral constants

Decimal	Octal	Hexadecimal	Type
16	020	0x10	int
255	0377	OXff	int
32767	077777	0x7FFF	int
32768U	0100000U	0x8000U	unsigned int
100000	0303240	0x186A0	int (32 bit-) long (16 bit- CPU)
10L	012L	0xAL	long
27UL	033UL	0x1bUL	unsigned long
2147483648	020000000000	0x80000000	unsigned long

✓ **NOTE**

In each line of the above table, the same value is presented in a different way.

Sample program

```cpp
// To display hexadecimal integer literals and
// decimal integer literals.
//
#include <iostream>
using namespace std;

int main()
{
  // cout outputs integers as decimal integers:
  cout << "Value of 0xFF = " << 0xFF << " decimal"
       << endl;                     // Output: 255 decimal
  // The manipulator hex changes output to hexadecimal
  // format (dec changes to decimal format):
  cout << "Value of 27 = " << hex << 27 <<" hexadecimal"
       << endl;                     // Output: 1b hexadecimal
  return 0;
}
```

The boolean keywords `true` and `false`, a number, a character, or a character sequence (*string*) are all constants, which are also referred to as a *literals*. Constants can thus be subdivided into

- *boolean constants*
- *numerical constants*
- *character constants*
- *string constants*.

Every constant represents a value and thus a type—as does every expression in C++. The type is defined by the way the constant is written.

☐ Boolean Constants

A boolean expression can have two values that are identified by the keywords `true` and `false`. Both constants are of the `bool` type. They can be used, for example, to set flags representing just two states.

☐ Integral Constants

Integral numerical constants can be represented as simple decimal numbers, octals, or hexadecimals:

- a *decimal constant* (base 10) begins with a decimal number other than zero, such as 109 or 987650
- an *octal constant* (base 8) begins with a leading 0, for example 077 or 01234567
- a *hexadecimal constant* (base 16) begins with the character pair 0x or 0X, for example 0x2A0 or 0X4b1C. Hexadecimal numbers can be capitalized or non-capitalized.

Integral constants are normally of type `int`. If the value of the constant is too large for the `int` type, a type capable of representing larger values will be applied. The ranking for decimal constants is as follows:

```
int, long, unsigned long
```

You can designate the type of a constant by adding the letter L or l (for `long`), or U or u (for `unsigned`). For example,

12L	and	12l	correspond to the type `long`
12U	and	12u	correspond to the type `unsigned int`
12UL	and	12ul	correspond to the type `unsigned long`

■ CONSTANTS (CONTINUED)

Examples for floating-point constants

5.19	12.	0.75	0.00004
0.519E1	12.0	.75	0.4e-4
0.0519e2	.12E+2	7.5e-1	.4E-4
519.OE-2	12e0	75E-2	4E-5

Examples for character constants

Constant	Character	Constant Value (ASCII code decimal)
'A'	Capital A	65
'a'	Lowercase a	97
' '	Blank	32
'.'	Dot	46
'0'	Digit 0	48
'\0'	Terminating null character	0

Internal representation of a string literal

String literal: "Hello!"

Stored byte sequence: | 'H' | 'e' | 'l' | 'l' | 'o' | '!' | '\0' |

☐ Floating-Point Constants

Floating-point numbers are always represented as decimals, a decimal point being used to distinguish the fraction part from the integer part. However, exponential notation is also permissible.

EXAMPLES: `27.1`   `1.8E-2`   `// Type: double`

Here, `1.8E-2` represents a value of $1.8*10^{-2}$. `E` can also be written with a small letter e. A decimal point or `E` (`e`) must always be used to distinguish floating-point constants from integer constants.

Floating-point constants are of type `double` by default. However, you can add `F` or `f` to designate the `float` type, or add `L` or `l` for the `long double` type.

☐ Character Constants

A character constant is a character enclosed in *single* quotes. Character constants take the type `char`.

EXAMPLE: `'A'`   `// Type: char`

The numerical value is the character code representing the character. The constant `'A'` thus has a value of `65` in ASCII code.

☐ String Constants

You already know string constants, which were introduced for text output using the `cout` stream. A string constant consists of a sequence of characters enclosed in *double* quotes.

EXAMPLE: `"Today is a beautiful day!"`

A string constant is stored internally without the quotes but terminated with a *null character*, `\0`, represented by a byte with a numerical value of `0` — that is, all the bits in this byte are set to `0`. Thus, a string occupies one byte more in memory than the number of characters it contains. An *empty string*, `""`, therefore occupies a single byte.

The terminating null character `\0` is not the same as the number zero and has a different character code than zero. Thus, the string

EXAMPLE: `"0"`

comprises two bytes, the first byte containing the code for the character zero `0` (ASCII code 48) and the second byte the value `0`.

The terminating null character `\0` is an example of an escape sequence. Escape sequences are described in the following section.

■ ESCAPE SEQUENCES

Overview

Single character	Meaning	ASCII code (decimal)
\a	alert (BEL)	7
\b	backspace (BS)	8
\t	horizontal tab (HT)	9
\n	line feed (LF)	10
\v	vertical tab (VT)	11
\f	form feed (FF)	12
\r	carriage return (CR)	13
\"	" (double quote)	34
\'	' (single quote)	39
\?	? (question mark)	63
\\	\ (backslash)	92
\0	string terminating character	0
\ooo (up to 3 octal digits)	numerical value of a character	ooo (octal!)
\xhh (hexadecimal digits)	numerical value of a character	hh (hexadecimal!)

Sample program

```
#include <iostream>
using namespace std;
int main()
{
   cout << "\nThis is\t a string\n\t\t"
           " with \"many\" escape sequences!\n";
   return 0;
}
```

Program output:

```
This is        a string
               with "many" escape sequences!
```

ESCAPE SEQUENCES ∎ 27

☐ Using Control and Special Characters

Nongraphic characters can be expressed by means of *escape sequences*, for example \t, which represents a tab.

The effect of an escape sequence will depend on the device concerned. The sequence \t, for example, depends on the setting for the tab width, which defaults to eight blanks but can be any value.

An escape sequence always begins with a \ (backslash) and represents a single character. The table on the opposite page shows the standard escape sequences, their decimal values, and effects.

You can use octal and hexadecimal escape sequences to create any character code. Thus, the letter A (decimal 65) in ASCII code can also be expressed as \101 (three octals) or \x41 (two hexadecimals). Traditionally, escape sequences are used only to represent non-printable characters and special characters. The control sequences for screen and printer drivers are, for example, initiated by the ESC character (decimal 27), which can be represented as \33 or \x1b.

Escape sequences are used in character and string constants.

EXAMPLES: '\t'   "\tHello\n\tMike!"

The characters ', ", and \ have no special significance when preceded by a backslash, i.e. they can be represented as \', \", and \\ respectively.

When using octal numbers for escape sequences in strings, be sure to use three digits, for example, \033 and not \33. This helps to avoid any subsequent numbers being evaluated as part of the escape sequence. There is no maximum number of digits in a hexadecimal escape sequence. The sequence of hex numbers automatically terminates with the first character that is not a valid hex number.

The sample program on the opposite page demonstrates the use of escape sequences in strings. The fact that a string can occupy two lines is another new feature. String constants separated only by white spaces will be concatenated to form a *single* string.

To continue a string in the next line you can also use a backslash \ as the last character in a line, and then press the Enter key to begin a new line, where you can continue typing the string.

EXAMPLE: "I am a very, very \
            long string"

Please note, however, that the leading spaces in the second line will be evaluated as part of the string. It is thus generally preferable to use the first method, that is, to terminate the string with " and reopen it with ".

■ NAMES

Keywords in C++

asm	do	inline	short	typeid
auto	double	int	signed	typename
bool	dynamic_cast	long	sizeof	union
break	else	mutable	static	unsigned
case	enum	namespace	static_cast	using
catch	explicit	new	struct	virtual
char	extern	operator	switch	void
class	false	private	template	volatile
const	float	protected	this	wchar_t
const_cast	for	public	throw	while
continue	friend	register	true	
default	goto	reinterpret_cast	try	
delete	if	return	typedef	

Examples for names

```
valid:
    a           US          us      VOID
    _var        SetTextColor
    B12         top_of_window
    a_very_long_name123467890

invalid:
    goto    586_cpu     object-oriented
    US$     true        écu
```

☐ Valid Names

Within a program *names* are used to designate variables and functions. The following rules apply when creating names, which are also known as *identifiers*:

- a name contains a series of letters, numbers, or underscore characters (_). German umlauts and accented letters are invalid. C++ is case sensitive; that is, upper- and lowercase letters are different.
- the first character must be a letter or underscore
- there are no restrictions on the length of a name and all the characters in the name are significant
- C++ keywords are reserved and cannot be used as names.

The opposite page shows C++ keywords and some examples of valid and invalid names.

The C++ compiler uses internal names that begin with one or two underscores followed by a capital letter. To avoid confusion with these names, avoid use of the underscore at the beginning of a name.

Under normal circumstances the linker only evaluates a set number of characters, for example, the first 8 characters of a name. For this reason names of global objects, such as functions, should be chosen so that the first eight characters are significant.

☐ Conventions

In C++ it is standard practice to use small letters for the names of variables and functions. The names of some variables tend to be associated with a specific use.

EXAMPLES:

c, ch	for characters
i, j, k, l, m, n	for integers, in particular indices
x, y, z	for floating-point numbers

To improve the readability of your programs you should choose longer and more self-explanatory names, such as `start_index` or `startIndex` for the first index in a range of index values.

In the case of software projects, naming conventions will normally apply. For example, prefixes that indicate the type of the variable may be assigned when naming variables.

■ VARIABLES

Sample program

```
// Definition and use of variables
#include <iostream>
using namespace std;

int gVar1;                    // Global variables,
int gVar2 = 2;                // explicit initialization

int main()
{
   char ch('A');  // Local variable being initialized
                  // or:  char ch = 'A';

   cout << "Value of gVar1:    " << gVar1  << endl;
   cout << "Value of gVar2:    " << gVar2  << endl;
   cout << "Character in ch:   " << ch     << endl;

   int sum, number = 3; // Local variables with
                        // and without initialization
   sum = number + 5;
   cout << "Value of sum:      " << sum  << endl;

   return 0;
}
```

✔ HINT

Both strings and all other values of fundamental types can be output with cout. Integers are printed in decimal format by default.

Screen output

```
Value of gVar1:   0
Value of gVar2:   2
Character in ch: A
Value of sum:     8
```

Data such as numbers, characters, or even complete records are stored in *variables* to enable their processing by a program. Variables are also referred to as *objects*, particularly if they belong to a class.

☐ Defining Variables

A variable must be defined before you can use it in a program. When you *define* a variable the type is specified and an appropriate amount of memory reserved. This memory space is addressed by reference to the name of the variable. A simple definition has the following syntax:

SYNTAX: `typ name1 [name2 ... ];`

This defines the names of the variables in the list `name1 [, name2 ...]` as variables of the type `type`. The parentheses `[ ... ]` in the syntax description indicate that this part is optional and can be omitted. Thus, one or more variables can be stated within a single definition.

EXAMPLES:
```
char c;
int i, counter;
double x, y, size;
```

In a program, variables can be defined either within the program's functions or outside of them. This has the following effect:

- a variable defined outside of each function is *global*, i.e. it can be used by all functions
- a variable defined within a function is *local*, i.e. it can be used only in that function.

Local variables are normally defined immediately after the first brace—for example at the beginning of a function. However, they can be defined wherever a statement is permitted. This means that variables can be defined immediately before they are used by the program.

☐ Initialization

A variable can be initialized, i.e. a value can be assigned to the variable, during its definition. Initialization is achieved by placing the following immediately after the name of the variable:

- an equals sign (=) and an initial value for the variable or
- round brackets containing the value of the variable.

EXAMPLES:
```
char c = 'a';
float x(1.875);
```

Any *global* variables not explicitly initialized default to zero. In contrast, the initial value for any local variables that you fail to initialize will have an undefined initial value.

■ THE KEYWORDS const AND volatile

Sample program

```cpp
// Circumference and area of a circle with radius 2.5

#include <iostream>
using namespace std;

const double pi = 3.141593;

int main()
{
    double area, circuit, radius = 1.5;

    area = pi * radius * radius;
    circuit = 2 * pi * radius;

    cout << "\nTo Evaluate a Circle\n" << endl;

    cout << "Radius:        " << radius    << endl
         << "Circumference: " << circuit   << endl
         << "Area:          " << area      << endl;

    return 0;
}
```

✓ **NOTE**

By default cout outputs a floating-point number with a maximum of 6 decimal places without trailing zeros.

Screen output

```
To Evaluate a Circle

Radius:        1.5
Circumference: 9.42478
Area:          7.06858
```

A type can be modified using the const and volatile keywords.

☐ Constant Objects

The const keyword is used to create a "read only" object. As an object of this type is constant, it cannot be modified at a later stage and must be initialized during its definition.

EXAMPLE: `const double pi = 3.1415947;`

Thus the value of pi cannot be modified by the program. Even a statement such as the following will merely result in an error message:

```
pi = pi + 2.0;                      // invalid
```

☐ Volatile Objects

The keyword volatile, which is rarely used, creates variables that can be modified not only by the program but also by other programs and external events. Events can be initiated by interrupts or by a hardware clock, for example.

EXAMPLE: `volatile unsigned long  clock_ticks;`

Even if the program itself does not modify the variable, the compiler must assume that the value of the variable has changed since it was last accessed. The compiler therefore creates machine code to read the value of the variable whenever it is accessed instead of repeatedly using a value that has been read at a prior stage.

It is also possible to combine the keywords const and volatile when declaring a variable.

EXAMPLE: `volatile const unsigned time_to_live;`

Based on this declaration, the variable time_to_live cannot be modified by the program but by external events.

exercises

■ EXERCISES

Screen output for exercise 2

```
    I
            "RUSH"
                       \TO\
              AND
    /FRO/
```

For exercise 3

Defining and initializing variables:

```
int a(2.5);              const long large;
int b = '?';             char c('\'');
char z(500);             unsigned char ch = '\201';
int big = 40000;         unsigned size(40000);
double he's(1.2E+5);     float val = 12345.12345;
```

Exercise 1

The `sizeof` operator can be used to determine the number of bytes occupied in memory by a variable of a certain type. For example, `sizeof(short)` is equivalent to 2.

Write a C++ program that displays the memory space required by each fundamental type on screen.

Exercise 2

Write a C++ program to generate the screen output shown on the opposite page.

Exercise 3

Which of the variable definitions shown on the opposite page is invalid or does not make sense?

Exercise 4

Write a C++ program that two defines variables for floating-point numbers and initializes them with the values

`123.456` and `76.543`

Then display the sum and the difference of these two numbers on screen.

solutions

■ SOLUTIONS

Exercise 1

```cpp
#include <iostream>
using namespace std;

int main()
{
   cout << "\nSize of Fundamental Types\n"
        << " Type              Number of Bytes\n"
        << "--------------------------------" << endl;
   cout << " char:            " << sizeof(char) << endl;
   cout << " short:           " << sizeof(short)<< endl;
   cout << " int:             " << sizeof(int)  << endl;
   cout << " long:            " << sizeof(long) << endl;
   cout << " float:           " << sizeof(float)<< endl;
   cout << " double:          " << sizeof(double)<<endl;
   cout << " long double:     " << sizeof(long double)
        << endl;

   return 0;
}
```

Exercise 2

```cpp
// Usage of escape sequences

#include <iostream>
using namespace std;

int main()
{
   cout << "\n\n\t I"              // Instead of tabs
           "\n\n\t\t \"RUSH\""     // you can send the
           "\n\n\t\t\t \\TO\\"     // suited number
           "\n\n\t\t AND"          // of blanks to
           "\n\n\t /FRO/" << endl; // the output.

   return 0;
}
```

Exercise 3
Incorrect:

```
int a(2.5);                // 2.5 is not an integer value
const long large;          // Without initialization
char z(500);               // The value 500 is too large
                           // to fit in a byte
int big = 40000;           // Attention! On 16-bit systems
                           // int values are <= 32767
double he's(1.2E+5);       // The character ' is not
                           // allowed in names
float val = 12345.12345;   // The accuracy of float
                           // is only 6 digits
```

Exercise 4

```
// Defining and initializing variables

#include <iostream>
using namespace std;

int main()
{
   float x = 123.456F,              // or double
         y = 76.543F,
         sum;

   sum = x + y;

   cout << "Total:        "
        << x << " + " << y << " = " << sum << endl;

   cout << "Difference:   "
        << x << " − " << y << " = " << (x − y) << endl;

   return 0;
}
```

chapter 3

Using Functions and Classes

This chapter describes how to

- declare and call standard functions and
- use standard classes.

This includes using standard header files. In addition, we will be working with string variables, i.e. objects belonging to the standard class `string` for the first time.

Functions and classes that you define on your own will not be introduced until later in the book.

■ DECLARING FUNCTIONS

Example of a function prototype

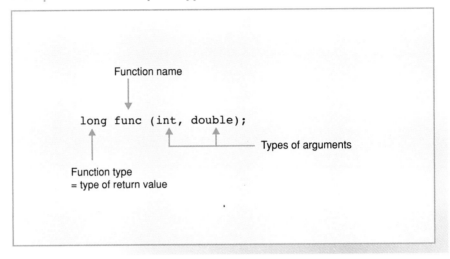

The prototype above yields the following information to the compiler:

- func is the function name
- the function is called with two arguments: the first argument is of type int, the second of type double
- the return value of the function is of type long.

Mathematical standard functions

```
double sin (double);          // Sine
double cos (double);          // Cosine
double tan (double);          // Tangent
double atan (double);         // Arc tangent
double cosh (double);         // Hyperbolic Cosine
double sqrt (double);         // Square Root
double pow (double, double);  // Power
double exp (double);          // Exponential Function
double log (double);          // Natural Logarithm
double log10 (double);        // Base-ten Logarithm
```

☐ Declarations

Each name (*identifier*) occurring in a program must be known to the compiler or it will cause an error message. That means any names apart from keywords must be *declared*, i.e. introduced to the compiler, before they are used.

Each time a variable or a function is defined it is also declared. But conversely, not every declaration needs to be a definition. If you need to use a function that has already been introduced in a library, you must declare the function but you do not need to redefine it.

☐ Declaring Functions

A function has a name and a type, much like a variable. The function's type is defined by its *return value*, that is, the value the function passes back to the program. In addition, the type of arguments required by a function is important. When a function is declared, the compiler must therefore be provided with information on

- the name and type of the function and
- the type of each argument.

This is also referred to as the function *prototype*.

Examples: `int toupper(int);`

`double pow(double, double);`

This informs the compiler that the function `toupper()` is of type `int`, i.e. its return value is of type `int`, and it expects an argument of type `int`. The second function `pow()` is of type `double` and two arguments of type `double` must be passed to the function when it is called. The types of the arguments may be followed by names, however, the names are viewed as a comment only.

Examples: `int toupper(int c);`

`double pow(double base, double exponent);`

From the compiler's point of view, these prototypes are equivalent to the prototypes in the previous example. Both junctions are standard junctions.

Standard function prototypes do not need to be declared, nor should they be, as they have already been declared in standard header files. If the header file is included in the program's source code by means of the `#include` directive, the function can be used immediately.

Example: `#include <cmath>`

Following this directive, the mathematical standard functions, such as `sin()`, `cos()`, and `pow()`, are available. Additional details on header files can be found later in this chapter.

■ FUNCTION CALLS

Sample program

```cpp
//  Calculating powers with
//  the standard function pow()

#include <iostream>      // Declaration of cout
#include <cmath>         // Prototype of pow(), thus:
                         // double pow( double, double);
using namespace std;

int main()
{
  double x = 2.5, y;

  // By means of a prototype, the compiler generates
  // the correct call or an error message!

  // Computes x raised to the power 3:
  y = pow("x", 3.0);     // Error! String is not a number
  y = pow(x + 3.0);      // Error! Just one argument
  y = pow(x, 3.0);       // ok!
  y = pow(x, 3);         // ok! The compiler converts the
                         // int value 3 to double.

  cout << "2.5 raised to 3 yields:        "
       << y << endl;

  // Calculating with pow() is possible:
  cout << "2 + (5 raised to the power 2.5) yields: "
       <<   2.0 + pow(5.0, x) << endl;

  return 0;
}
```

Screen output

```
2.5 raised to the power 3 yields:        15.625
2 + (5 raised to the power 2.5) yields:  57.9017
```

☐ Function Calls

A *function call* is an expression of the same type as the function and whose value corresponds to the return value. The return value is commonly passed to a suitable variable.

Example: `y = pow( x, 3.0);`

In this example the function `pow()` is first called using the arguments `x` and `3.0`, and the result, the power x^3, is assigned to `y`.

As the function call represents a value, other operations are also possible. Thus, the function `pow()` can be used to perform calculations for `double` values.

Example: `cout << 2.0 + pow( 5.0, x);`

This expression first adds the number `2.0` to the return value of `pow(5.0,x)`, then outputs the result using `cout`.

Any expression can be passed to a function as an *argument*, such as a constant or an arithmetical expression. However, it is important that the types of the arguments correspond to those expected by the function.

The compiler refers to the prototype to check that the function has been called correctly. If the argument type does not match exactly to the type defined in the prototype, the compiler performs type conversion, if possible.

Example: `y = pow( x, 3);`   `// also ok!`

The value 3 of type `int` is passed to the function as a second argument. But since the function expects a `double` value, the compiler will perform type conversion from `int` to `double`.

If a function is called with the wrong number of arguments, or if type conversion proves impossible, the compiler generates an error message. This allows you to recognize and correct errors caused by calling functions at the development stage instead of causing runtime errors.

Example: `float x = pow(3.0 + 4.7);`   `// Error!`

The compiler recognizes that the number of arguments is incorrect. In addition, the compiler will issue a warning, since a `double`, i.e. the return value of `pow()`, is assigned to a `float` type variable.

■ TYPE void FOR FUNCTIONS

Sample program

```cpp
// Outputs three random numbers

#include <iostream>   // Declaration of cin and cout
#include <cstdlib>    // Prototypes of srand(), rand():
                      // void srand( unsigned int seed );
                      // int rand( void );
using namespace std;
int main()
{
   unsigned int seed;
   int z1, z2, z3;

   cout << "    --- Random Numbers  --- \n" << endl;
   cout << "To initialize the random number generator, "
        << "\n please enter an integer value: ";
   cin  >> seed;        // Input an integer

   srand( seed);        // and use it as argument for a
                        // new sequence of random numbers.

   z1 = rand();         // Compute three random numbers.
   z2 = rand();
   z3 = rand();

   cout << "\nThree random numbers: "
        << z1 << "    " << z2 << "    " << z3 << endl;

   return 0;
}
```

✓ **NOTE**

The statement cin >> seed; reads an integer from the keyboard, because seed is of the unsigned int type.

Sample screen output

```
--- Random Numbers   ---

To initialize the random number generator,
please enter an integer value: 7777

Three random numbers: 25435    6908    14579
```

☐ Functions without Return Value

You can also write functions that perform a certain action but do not return a value to the function that called them. The type void is available for functions of this type, which are also referred to as procedures in other programming languages.

Example: `void srand( unsigned int seed );`

The standard function `srand()` initializes an algorithm that generates random numbers. Since the function does not return a value, it is of type void. An unsigned value is passed to the function as an argument to seed the random number generator. The value is used to create a series of random numbers.

☐ Functions without Arguments

If a function does not expect an argument, the function prototype must be declared as void or the braces following the function name must be left empty.

Example: `int rand( void );      // or   int rand();`

The standard function `rand()` is called without any arguments and returns a random number between 0 and 32767. A series of random numbers can be generated by repeating the function call.

☐ Usage of `srand()` and `rand()`

The function prototypes for `srand()` and `rand()` can be found in both the cstdlib and stdlib.h header files.

Calling the function `rand()` without previously having called `srand()` creates the same sequence of numbers as if the following statement would have been proceeded:

`srand(1);`

If you want to avoid generating the same sequence of random numbers whenever the program is executed, you must call `srand()` with a different value for the argument whenever the program is run.

It is common to use the current time to initialize a random number generator. See Chapter 6 for an example of this technique.

■ HEADER FILES

Using header files

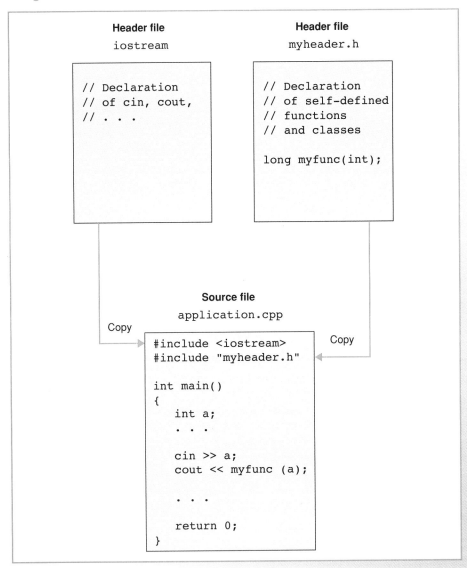

☐ Using Header Files

Header files are text files containing declarations and macros. By using an `#include` directive these declarations and macros can be made available to any other source file, even in other header files.

Pay attention to the following points when using header files:

- header files should generally be included at the start of a program before any other declarations
- you can only name *one* header file per `#include` directive
- the file name must be enclosed in angled brackets `< ... >` or double quotes `" ... "`.

☐ Searching for Header Files

The header files that accompany your compiler will tend to be stored in a folder of their own—normally called `include`. If the name of the header file is enclosed by angled brackets `< ... >`, it is common to search for header files in the `include` folder only. The current directory is not searched to increase the speed when searching for header files.

C++ programmers commonly write their own header files and store them in the current project folder. To enable the compiler to find these header files, the `#include` directive must state the name of the header files in double quotes.

Example: `#include "project.h"`

The compiler will then also search the current folder. The file suffix `.h` is normally used for user-defined header files.

☐ Standard Class Definitions

In addition to standard function prototypes, the header files also contain standard class definitions. When a header file is included, the classes defined and any objects declared in the file are available to the program.

Example: `#include <iostream>`
            `using namespace std;`

Following these directives, the classes `istream` and `ostream` can be used with the `cin` and `cout` streams. `cin` is an object of the `istream` class and `cout` an object of the `ostream` class.

■ STANDARD HEADER FILES

Header files of the C++ standard library

algorithm	ios	map	stack
bitset	iosfwd	memory	stdexcept
complex	iostream	new	streambuf
dequeue	istream	numeric	string
exception	iterator	ostream	typeinfo
fstream	limits	queue	utility
functional	list	set	valarray
iomanip	locale	sstream	vector

✓ **NOTE**

Some IDE's put the old-fashioned `iostream.h` and `iomanip.h` header files at your disposal. Within these header files the identifiers of `iostream` and `iomanip` are not contained in the `std` namespace but are declared globally.

Header files of the C standard library

assert.h	limits.h	stdarg.h	time.h
ctype.h	locale.h	stddef.h	wchar.h
errno.h	math.h	stdio.h	wctype.h
float.h	setjmp.h	stdlib.h	
iso646.h	signal.h	string.h	

The C++ standard library header files are shown opposite. They are *not* indicated by the file extension `.h` and contain all the declarations in their own namespace, `std`. Namespaces will be introduced in a later chapter. For now, it is sufficient to know that identifiers from other namespaces cannot be referred to directly. If you merely stipulate the directive

Example: `#include <iostream>`

the compiler would not be aware of the `cin` and `cout` streams. In order to use the identifiers of the `std` namespace globally, you must add a *using* directive.

Example: `#include <iostream>`
            `#include <string>`
            `using namespace std;`

You can then use `cin` and `cout` without any additional syntax. The header file `string` has also been included. This makes the `string` class available and allows user-friendly string manipulations in C++. The following pages contain further details on this topic.

☐ Header Files in the C Programming Language

The header files standardized for the C programming language were adopted for the C++ standard and, thus, the complete functionality of the standard C libraries is available to C++ programs.

Example: `#include <math.h>`

Mathematical functions are made available by this statement.

The identifiers declared in C header files are globally visible. This can cause name conflicts in large programs. For this reason each C header file, for example `name.h`, is accompanied in C++ by a second header file, `cname`, which declares the same identifiers in the `std` namespace. Including the file `math.h` is thus equivalent to

Example: `#include <cmath>`
            `using namespace std;`

The `string.h` or `cstring` files must be included in programs that use standard functions to manipulate C strings. These header files grant access to the functionality of the C string library and are to be distinguished from the `string` header file that defines the `string` class.

Each compiler offers additional header files for platform dependent functionalities. These may be graphics libraries or database interfaces.

■ USING STANDARD CLASSES

Sample program using class `string`

```
// To use strings.

#include <iostream>    // Declaration of cin, cout
#include <string>      // Declaration of class string
using namespace std;

int main()
{
   // Defines four strings:
   string prompt("What is your name:  "),
          name,                  // An empty
          line( 40, '-'),        // string with 40 '-'
          total = "Hello ";      // is possible!

   cout << prompt;           // Request for input.
   getline( cin, name);      // Inputs a name in one line

   total = total + name;     // Concatenates and
                             // assigns strings.

   cout << line << endl      // Outputs line and name
        << total << endl;
   cout << " Your name is "  // Outputs length
        << name.length() << " characters long!" << endl;
   cout << line << endl;
   return 0;
}
```

✓ **NOTE**

Both the operators + and += for concatenation and the relational operators <, <=, >, >=, ==, and != are defined for objects of class `string`. Strings can be printed with `cout` and the operator <<.
The class `string` will be introduced in detail later on.

Sample screen output

```
What is your name: Rose Summer
----------------------------------------
Hello Rose Summer
Your name is 11 characters long!
----------------------------------------
```

Several classes are defined in the C++ standard library. These include stream classes for input and output, but also classes for representing strings or handling error conditions.

Each class is a type with certain properties and capacities. As previously mentioned, the properties of a class are defined by its *data members* and the class's capacities are defined by its *methods*. Methods are functions that belong to a class and cooperate with the members to perform certain operations. Methods are also referred to as *member functions*.

☐ Creating Objects

An *object* is a variable of a class type, also referred to as an *instance* of the class. When an object is created, memory is allocated to the data members and initialized with suitable values.

Example: `string s("I am a string");`

In this example the object s, an instance of the standard class `string` (or simply a *string*), is defined and initialized with the string constant that follows. Objects of the `string` class manage the memory space required for the string themselves.

In general, there are several ways of initializing an object of a class. A string can thus be initialized with a certain number of identical characters, as the example on the opposite page illustrates.

☐ Calling Methods

All the methods defined as *public* within the corresponding class can be called for an object. In contrast to calling a global function, a method is always called for *one particular object*. The name of the object precedes the method and is separated from the method by a period.

Example: `s.length();          // object.method();`

The method `length()` supplies the length of a string, i.e. the number of characters in a string. This results in a value of 13 for the string s defined above.

☐ Classes and Global Functions

Globally defined functions exist for some standard classes. These functions perform certain operations for objects passed as arguments. The global function `getline()`, for example, stores a line of keyboard input in a string.

Example: `getline(cin, s);`

The keyboard input is terminated by pressing the return key to create a new-line character, `'\n'`, which is not stored in the string.

EXERCISES

Screen output for exercise 1

```
Number        Square Root

  4           2
12.25         3.5
 0.0121       0.11
```

Listing for exercise 2

```cpp
// A program containing errors!
# include <iostream>, <string>
# include <stdlib>
# void srand( seed);

int main()
{
    string message "\nLearn from your mistakes!";
    cout << message << endl;

    int len = length( message);
    cout << "Length of the string: " << len << endl;

    // And a random number in addition:
    int a, b;
    a = srand(12.5);
    b = rand( a );
    cout << "\nRandom number: " << b << endl;

    return 0;
}
```

Exercise 1

Create a program to calculate the square roots of the numbers

4   12.25   0.0121

and output them as shown opposite. Then read a number from the keyboard and output the square root of this number.

To calculate the square root, use the function sqrt(), which is defined by the following prototype in the math.h (or cmath) header file:

```
double sqrt( double x);
```

The return value of the sqrt() function is the square root of x.

Exercise 2

The program on the opposite page contains several **errors**! Correct the errors and ensure that the program can be executed.

Exercise 3

Create a C++ program that defines a string containing the following character sequence:

```
I have learned something new again!
```

and displays the length of the string on screen.

Read two lines of text from the keyboard. Concatenate the strings using " * " to separate the two parts of the string. Output the new string on screen.

■ **SOLUTIONS**

Exercise 1

```cpp
// Compute square roots

#include <iostream>
#include <cmath>
using namespace std;

int main()
{
   double x1 = 4.0, x2 = 12.25, x3 = 0.0121;

   cout << "\n   Number  \t Square Root" << endl;
   cout << "\n    " << x1 << "    \t " << sqrt(x1)
        << "\n    " << x2 << "    \t " << sqrt(x2)
        << "\n    " << x3 << "    \t " << sqrt(x3) << endl;

   cout << "\nType a number whose square root is to be"
                                    " computed. ";
   cin  >> x1;

   cout << "\n   Number  \t Square Root" << endl;
   cout << "\n  " << x1 << "  \t " << sqrt(x1) << endl;

   return 0;
}
```

Exercise 2

```cpp
// The corrected program:

#include <iostream>      // Just one header file in a line
#include <string>

#include <cstdlib>       // Prototypes of functions
                         // void srand( unsigned int seed);
                         // int rand(void);
// or:
// #include <stdlib.h>

using namespace std;   // Introduces all names of namespace
                       // std into the global scope.

int main()
{
   string message = "\nLearn from your mistakes!";...// =
   cout << message << endl;
```

```
      int len = message.length();
                              // instead of: length(message);
      cout << "Length of the string: " << len << endl;

      // And another random number:
      int b;                      // Variable a is not needed.
      srand(12);                  // instead of:  a = srand(12.5);
      b = rand();                 // instead of:  b = rand(a);
      cout << "\nRandom number: " << b << endl;
      return 0;
}
```

Exercise 3

```
#include <iostream>     // Declaration of cin, cout
#include <string>       // Declaration of class string
using namespace std;

int main()
{
   string message("I have learned something new again!\n"),
          prompt("Please input two lines of text:"),
          str1, str2, sum;

   cout << message << endl;    // Outputs the message

   cout << prompt << endl;     // Request for input

   getline( cin, str1);        // Reads the first
   getline( cin, str2);        // and the second line of text

   sum = str1 + " * " + str2;  // Concatenates, assigns
   cout << sum << endl;        // and outputs strings.

   return 0;
}
```

chapter 4

Input and Output with Streams

This chapter describes the use of streams for input and output, focusing on formatting techniques.

■ STREAMS

Stream classes for input and output

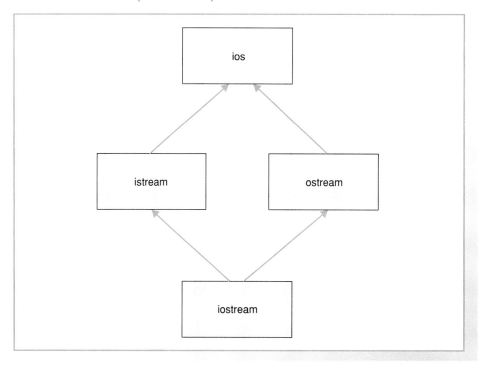

The four standard streams

- **cin**   Object of class istream to control standard input
- **cout**   Object of class ostream to control standard output
- **cerr**   Object of class ostream to control unbuffered error output
- **clog**   Object of class ostream to control buffered error output

☐ I/O Stream Classes

During the development of C++ a new class-based input/output system was implemented. This gave rise to the *I/O stream classes*, which are now available in a library of their own, the so-called *iostream library*.

The diagram on the opposite page shows how a so-called class hierarchy develops due to inheritance. The class `ios` is the base class of all other stream classes. It contains the attributes and abilities common to all streams. Effectively, the `ios` class

- manages the connection to the physical data stream that writes your program's data to a file or outputs the data on screen
- contains the basic functions needed for formatting data. A number of flags that determine how character input is interpreted have been defined for this purpose.

The `istream` and `ostream` classes derived from `ios` form a user-friendly interface for stream manipulation. The `istream` class is used for reading streams and the `ostream` class is used for writing to streams. The operator `>>` is defined in `istream` and `<<` is defined in `ostream`, for example.

The `iostream` class is derived by multiple inheritance from `istream` and `ostream` and thus offers the functionality of both classes.

Further stream classes, a file management class, for example, are derived from the classes mentioned above. This allows the developer to use the techniques described for file manipulation. These classes, which also contain methods for opening and closing files, will be discussed in a later chapter.

☐ Standard Streams

The streams `cin` and `cout`, which were mentioned earlier, are instances of the `istream` or `ostream` classes. When a program is launched these objects are automatically created to read *standard input* or write to *standard output*.

Standard input is normally the keyboard and standard output the screen. However, standard input and output can be redirected to files. In this case, data is not read from the keyboard but from a file, or data is not displayed on screen but written to a file.

The other two standard streams `cerr` and `clog` are used to display messages when errors occur. Error messages are displayed on screen even if standard output has been redirected to a file.

■ FORMATTING AND MANIPULATORS

Example: Calling a manipulator

Here the manipulator showpos is called.

```
cout << showpos << 123;    // Output:  +123
```

The above statement is equivalent to

```
cout.setf( ios::showpos);
cout << 123;
```

The other positive numbers are printed with their sign as well:

```
cout << 22;                        // Output:  +22
```

The output of a positive sign can be canceled by the manipulator noshowpos:

```
cout << noshowpos << 123;  // Output:   123
```

The last statement is equivalent to

```
cout.unsetf( ios::showpos);
cout << 123;
```

✓ **HINTS**

- The operators >> and << format the input and/or output according to how the flags in the base class ios are set

- The manipulator showpos is a function that calls the method cout.setf(ios::showpos);, ios::showpos being the flag showpos belonging to the ios class

- Using manipulators is easier than directly accessing flags. For this reason, manipulators are described in the following section, whereas the methods setf() and unsetf() are used only under exceptional circumstances.

- Old compilers only supply some of the manipulators. In this case, you have to use the methods setf() and unsetf().

☐ Formatting

When reading keyboard input, a valid input format must be used to determine how input is to be interpreted. Similarly, screen output adheres to set of rules governing how, for example, floating-point numbers are displayed.

The stream classes `istream` and `ostream` offer various options for performing these tasks. For example, you can display a table of numeric values in a simple way.

In previous chapters we have looked at the `cin` and `cout` streams in statements such as:

```
cout << "Please enter a number: ";
cin  >> x;
```

The following sections systematically describe the abilities of the stream classes. This includes:

- the `>>` and `<<` operators for formatted input and output. These operators are defined for expressions with fundamental types—that is, for characters, boolean values, numbers and strings.
- manipulators, which can be inserted into the input or output stream. Manipulators can be used to generate formats for subsequent input/output. One manipulator that you are already familiar with is `endl`, which generates a line feed at the end of a line.
- other methods for determining or modifying the state of a stream and unformatted input and output.

☐ Flags and Manipulators

Formatting flags defined in the parent class `ios` determine how characters are input or output. In general, flags are represented by individual bits within a special integral variable. For example, depending on whether a bit is set or not, a positive number can be output with or without a plus sign.

Each flag has a *default* setting. For example, integral numbers are output as decimals by default, and positive numbers are output without a plus sign.

It is possible to modify individual formatting flags. The methods `setf()` and `unsetf()` can be used for this purpose. However, the same effect can be achieved simply by using so-called *manipulators*, which are defined for all important flags. Manipulators are functions that can be inserted into the input or output stream and thus be called.

■ FORMATTED OUTPUT OF INTEGERS

Manipulators formatting integers

Manipulator	Effects
oct	Octal base
hex	Hexadecimal base
dec	Decimal base (by default)
showpos	Generates a + sign in non-negative numeric output.
noshowpos	Generates non-negative numeric output without a + sign (by default).
uppercase	Generates capital letters in hexadecimal output.
nouppercase	Generates lowercase letters in hexadecimal output (by default).

Sample program

```
// Reads integral decimal values and
// generates octal, decimal, and hexadecimal output.

#include <iostream>      // Declarations of cin, cout and
using namespace std;     // manipulators oct, hex, ...

int main()
{
   int number;
   cout << "Please enter an integer: ";
   cin >> number;
   cout << uppercase                 // for hex-digits
        << " octal  \t decimal  \t hexadecimal\n "
        << oct << number << "        \t "
        << dec << number << "        \t "
        << hex << number << endl;
   return 0;
}
```

☐ Formatting Options

The `<<` operator can output values of type `short`, `int`, `long` or a corresponding `unsigned` type. The following formatting options are available:

- define the numeric system in which to display the number: decimal, octal, or hexadecimal
- use capitals instead of small letters for hexadecimals
- display a sign for positive numbers.

In addition, the field width can be defined for the above types. The field width can also be defined for characters, strings, and floating-point numbers, and will be discussed in the following sections.

☐ Numeric System

Integral numbers are displayed as decimals by default. The manipulators `oct`, `hex`, and `dec` can be used for switching from and to decimal display mode.

Example: `cout << hex << 11;`   `// Output: b`

Hexadecimals are displayed in small letters by default, that is, using `a`, `b`, ..., `f`. The manipulator `uppercase` allows you to use capitals.

Example: `cout << hex << uppercase << 11;` `//Output: B`

The manipulator `nouppercase` returns the output format to small letters.

☐ Negative Numbers

When negative numbers are output as decimals, the output will always include a sign. You can use the `showpos` manipulator to output signed positive numbers.

Example: `cout << dec << showpos << 11;` `//Output: +11`

You can use `noshowpos` to revert to the original display mode.

When *octal* or *hexadecimal* numbers are output, the bits of the number to be output are always interpreted as unsigned! In other words, the output shows the bit pattern of a number in octal or hexadecimal format.

Example: `cout << dec << -1 << "    " << hex << -1;`

This statement causes the following output on a 32-bit system:

```
 -1    ffffffff
```

■ FORMATTED OUTPUT OF FLOATING-POINT NUMBERS

Manipulators formatting floating-point numbers

Manipulator	Effects
showpoint	Generates a decimal point character shown in floating-point output. The number of digits after the decimal point corresponds to the used precision.
noshowpoint	Trailing zeroes after the decimal point are not printed. If there are no digits after the decimal point, the decimal point is not printed (by default).
fixed	Output in fixed point notation
scientific	Output in scientific notation
setprecision (int n)	Sets the precision to n.

Methods for precision

Manipulator	Effects
int precision (int n);	Sets the precision to n.
int precision() const;	Returns the used precision.

 NOTE

The key word const within the prototype of precision() signifies that the method performs only read operations.

Sample program

```
#include <iostream>
using namespace std;
int main()
{
   double x = 12.0;
   cout.precision(2);                     // Precision 2
   cout << " By default:   " << x << endl;
   cout << " showpoint:   " << showpoint  << x << endl;
   cout << " fixed:       " << fixed      << x << endl;
   cout << " scientific: " << scientific << x << endl;
   return 0;
}
```

□ Standard Settings

Floating-points are displayed to six digits by default. Decimals are separated from the integral part of the number by a decimal point. Trailing zeroes behind the decimal point are not printed. If there are no digits after the decimal point, the decimal point is not printed (by default).

Examples:
```
cout << 1.0;        // Output: 1
cout << 1.234;      // Output: 1.234
cout << 1.234567;   // Output: 1.23457
```

The last statement shows that the seventh digit is not simply truncated but rounded. Very large and very small numbers are displayed in *exponential notation*.

Example:
```
cout << 1234567.8;  // Output: 1.23457e+06
```

□ Formatting

The standard settings can be modified in several ways. You can

- change the precision, i.e. the number of digits to be output
- force output of the decimal point and trailing zeroes
- stipulate the display mode (fixed point or exponential).

Both the manipulator `setprecision()` and the method `precision()` can be used to redefine precision to be used.

Example:
```
cout << setprecision(3);  // Precision: 3
// or:  cout.precision(3);
cout   << 12.34;          // Output: 12.3
```

Note that the header file `iomanip` must be included when using the manipulator `setprecision()`. This also applies to all standard manipulators called with at least one argument.

The manipulator `showpoint` outputs the decimal point and trailing zeroes. The number of digits being output (e.g. 6) equals the current precision.

Example:
```
cout << showpoint << 1.0; // Output: 1.00000
```

However, *fixed point* output with a predetermined number of decimal places is often more useful. In this case, you can use the `fixed` manipulator with the precision defining the number of decimal places. The default value of 6 is assumed in the following example.

Example:
```
cout << fixed << 66.0;    // Output: 66.000000
```

In contrast, you can use the `scientific` manipulator to specify that floating-point numbers are output as exponential expressions.

▪ OUTPUT IN FIELDS

Element functions for output in fields

Method	Effects
`int width() const;`	Returns the minimum field width used
`int width(int n);`	Sets the minimum field width to n
`int fill() const;`	Returns the fill character used
`int fill(int ch);`	Sets the fill character to ch

Manipulators for output in fields

Manipulator	Effects
`setw(int n)`	Sets the minimum field width to n
`setfill(int ch)`	Sets the fill character to ch
`left`	Left-aligns output in fields
`right`	Right-aligns output in fields
`internal`	Left-aligns output of the sign and right-aligns output of the numeric value

✓ **NOTE**

The manipulators `setw()` and `setfill()` are declared in the header file `iomanip`.

Examples

```
#include <iostream>       // Obligatory
#include <iomanip>        // declarations
using namespace std;
```

1st Example: `cout << '|' << setw(6) << 'X' << '|';`
Output: `|     X|`   `// Field width 6`
2nd Example: `cout << fixed << setprecision(2)`
                `<< setw(10) << 123.4 << endl`
                `<< "1234567890" << endl;`
Output: `     123.40`   `// Field width 10`
            `1234567890`

The << operator can be used to generate formatted output in fields. You can

- specify the *field width*
- set the alignment of the output to right- or left-justified
- specify a *fill-character* with which to fill the field.

☐ Field Width

The field width is the number of characters that can be written to a field. If the output string is larger than the field width, the output is not truncated but the field is extended. The output will always contain at least the number of digits specified as the field width.

You can either use the width() method or the setw() manipulator to define field width.

Example: `cout.width(6);     // or:  cout << setw(6);`

One special attribute of the field width is the fact that this value is non-permanent: the field width specified applies to the next output only, as is illustrated by the examples on the opposite page. The first example outputs the character 'X' to a field with width of 6, but does not output the '|' character.

The default field width is 0. You can also use the width() method to get the current field width. To do so, call width() without any other arguments.

Example: `int fieldwidth = cout.width();`

☐ Fill Characters and Alignment

If a field is larger than the string you need to output, blanks are used by default to fill the field. You can either use the fill() method or the setfill() manipulator to specify another fill character.

Example: `cout << setfill('*') << setw(5) << 12;`
`// Output: ***12`

The fill character applies until another character is defined.

As the previous example shows, output to fields is normally right-aligned. The other options available are left-aligned and internal, which can be set by using the manipulators left and internal. The manipulator internal left-justifies the sign and right-justifies the number within a field.

Example: `cout.width(6); cout.fill('0');`
`cout << internal << -123; // Output: -00123`

■ OUTPUT OF CHARACTERS, STRINGS, AND BOOLEAN VALUES

Sample program

```cpp
// Enters a character and outputs its
// octal, decimal, and hexadecimal code.

#include <iostream>    // Declaration of cin, cout
#include <iomanip>     // For manipulators being called
                       // with arguments.
#include <string>
using namespace std;

int main()
{
   int number = ' ';

   cout << "The white space code is as follows: "
        << number << endl;

   char ch;
   string prompt =
          "\nPlease enter a character followed by "
                                 " <return>: ";

   cout << prompt;

   cin >> ch;                         // Read a character
   number = ch;

   cout << "The character " << ch
        << " has code" << number << endl;

   cout << uppercase              // For hex-digits
        << "     octal  decimal  hexadecimal\n "
        << oct << setw(8) << number
        << dec << setw(8) << number
        << hex << setw(8) << number << endl;

   return 0;
}
```

☐ Outputting Characters and Character Codes

The >> operator interprets a number of type char as the character code and outputs the corresponding character:

Example:
```
char ch = '0';
cout << ch << ' ' << 'A';
// Outputs three characters: 0 A
```

It is also possible to output the character code for a character. In this case the character code is stored in an int variable and the variable is then output.

Example:
```
int code = '0';
cout << code;            // Output: 48
```

The '0' character is represented by ASCII Code 48. The program on the opposite page contains further examples.

☐ Outputting Strings

You can use the >> operator both to output string literals, such as "Hello", and string variables, as was illustrated in previous examples. As in the case of other types, strings can be positioned within output fields.

Example:
```
string s("spring flowers ");
cout << left              // Left-aligned
     << setfill('?')      // Fill character ?
     << setw(20) << s ;   // Field width 20
```

This example outputs the string "spring   flowers??????". The manipulator right can be used to right-justify the output within the field.

☐ Outputting Boolean Values

By default the << operator outputs boolean values as integers, with the value 0 representing false and 1 true. If you need to output the strings true or false instead, the flag ios::boolalpha must be set. To do so, use either the setf() method or the manipulator boolalpha.

Example:
```
bool ok = true;
cout << ok << endl                    // 1
     << boolalpha << ok << endl;  // true
```

You can revert this setting using the noboolalpha manipulator.

∎ FORMATTED INPUT

Sample program

```
// Inputs an article label and a price

#include <iostream>      // Declarations of cin, cout,...
#include <iomanip>       // Manipulator setw()
#include <string>
using namespace std;

int main()
{
   string label;
   double price;

   cout << "\nPlease enter an article label: ";

   // Input the label (15 characters maximum):
   cin >> setw(16);          // or:  cin.width(16);
   cin >> label;

   cin.sync();    // Clears the buffer and resets
   cin.clear();   // any error flags that may be set

   cout << "\nEnter the price of the article: ";
   cin >> price;              // Input the price

   // Controlling output:
   cout << fixed << setprecision(2)
        << "\nArticle:"
        << "\n  Label:  " << label
        << "\n  Price:  " << price << endl;

   // ... The program to be continued

   return 0;
}
```

✓ NOTE

The input buffer is cleared and error flags are reset by calling the sync() and clear() methods. This ensures that the program will wait for new input for the price, even if more than 15 characters have been entered for the label.

The >> operator, which belongs to the istream class, takes the current number base and field width flags into account when reading input:

- the number base specifies whether an integer will be read as a decimal, octal, or hexadecimal
- the field width specifies the maximum number of characters to be read for a string.

When reading from standard input, cin is buffered by lines. Keyboard input is thus not read until confirmed by pressing the <Return> key. This allows the user to press the backspace key and correct any input errors, provided the return key has not been pressed. Input is displayed on screen by default.

☐ Input Fields

The >> operator will normally read the next *input* field, convert the input by reference to the type of the supplied variable, and write the result to the variable. Any white space characters (such as blanks, tabs, and new lines) are ignored by default.

Example:
```
char ch;
cin >> ch;        // Enter a character
```

When the following keys are pressed

```
<return> <tab> <blank> <X> <return>
```

the character 'X' is stored in the variable ch.

An input field is terminated by the first white space character or by the first character that cannot be processed.

Example:
```
int i;
cin >> i;
```

Typing 123FF<Return> stores the decimal value 123 in the variable i. However, the characters that follow, FF and the newline character, remain in the input buffer and will be read first during the next read operation.

When reading strings, only one word is read since the first white space character will begin a new input field.

Example:
```
string city;
cin >> city;      // To read just one word!
```

If Lao Kai is input, only Lao will be written to the city string. The number of characters to be read can also be limited by specifying the field width. For a given field width of n, a maximum of n-1 characters will be read, as one byte is required for the null character. Any initial white space will be ignored. The program on the opposite page illustrates this point and also shows how to clear the input buffer.

■ FORMATTED INPUT OF NUMBERS

Sample program

```cpp
// Enter hexadecimal digits and a floating-point number
//
#include <iostream>
#include <iomanip>
using namespace std;

int main()
{
   int number = 0;

   cout << "\nEnter a hexadecimal number: "
        << endl;
   cin >> hex >> number;        // Input hex-number

   cout << "Your decimal input: " << number << endl;

   // If an invalid input occurred:
   cin.sync();                  // Clears the buffer
   cin.clear();                 // Reset error flags

   double x1 = 0.0, x2 = 0.0;

   cout << "\nNow enter two floating-point values: "
        << endl;

   cout << "1. number: ";
   cin  >> x1;                  // Read first number
   cout << "2. number: ";
   cin  >> x2;                  // Read second number

   cout << fixed << setprecision(2)
        << "\nThe sum of both numbers:    "
        << setw(10) << x1 + x2 << endl;

   cout << "\nThe product of both numbers: "
        << setw(10) << x1 * x2 << endl;

   return 0;
}
```

☐ Inputting Integers

You can use the `hex`, `oct`, and `dec` manipulators to stipulate that any character sequence input is to processed as a hexadecimal, octal, or decimal number.

Example:
```
int n;
cin >> oct >> n;
```

An input value of `10` will be interpreted as an octal, which corresponds to a decimal value of `8`.

Example:
```
cin >> hex >> n;
```

Here, any input will be interpreted as a hexadecimal, enabling input such as `f0a` or `-F7`.

☐ Inputting Floating-Point Numbers

The `>>` operator interprets any input as a decimal floating-point number if the variable is a floating-point type, i.e. `float`, `double`, or `long double`. The floating-point number can be entered in fixed point or exponential notation.

Example:
```
double x;
cin >> x;
```

The character input is converted to a `double` value in this case. Input, such as `123`, `-22.0`, or `3e10` is valid.

☐ Input Errors

But what happens if the input does not match the type of variable defined?

Example:
```
int i, j;    cin >> i >> j;
```

Given input of `1A5` the digit `1` will be stored in the variable `i`. The next input field begins with `A`. But since a decimal input type is required, the input sequence will not be processed beyond the letter `A`. If, as in our example, no type conversion is performed, the variable is not written to and an internal error flag is raised.

It normally makes more sense to read numerical values individually, and clear the input buffer and any error flags that may have been set after each entry.

Chapter 6, "Control Flow," and Chapter 28, "Exception Handling," show how a program can react to input errors.

■ UNFORMATTED INPUT/OUTPUT

Sample program

```
//  Reads a text with the operator >>
//  and the function getline().

#include <iostream>
#include <string>
using namespace std;

string header =
"    --- Demonstrates Unformatted Input ---";

int main()
{
   string word, rest;

   cout << header
        << "\n\nPress <return> to go on" << endl;


   cin.get();                     // Read the new line
                                  // without saving.

   cout << "\nPlease enter a sentence with several words!"
        << "\nEnd with <!> and <return>."
        << endl;

   cin >> word;              // Read the first word
   getline( cin, rest, '!');  // and the remaining text
                              // up to the character !

   cout << "\nThe first word:    " << word
        << "\nRemaining text: " << rest << endl;

   return 0;
}
```

✓ **NOTE**

1. A text of more than one line can be entered.
2. The sample program requires that at least one word and a following white space are entered.

Unformatted input and output does not use fields, and any formatting flags that have been set are ignored. The bytes read from a stream are passed to the program "as is." More specifically, you should be aware that any white space characters preceding the input will be processed.

☐ Reading and Writing Characters

You can use the methods `get()` and `put()` to read or write single characters. The `get()` method reads the next character from a stream and stores it in the given `char` variable.

Example:
```
char ch;
cin.get(ch);
```

If the character is a white space character, such as a newline, it will still be stored in the `ch` variable. To prevent this from happening you can use

```
cin >> ch;
```

to read the first non-white space character.

The `get()` method can also be called without any arguments. In this case, `get()` returns the character code of type `int`.

Example: `int c = cin.get();`

The `put()` method can be used for unformatted output of a character. The character to be output is passed to `put()` as an argument.

Example: `cout.put('A');`

This statement is equivalent to `cout << 'A';`, where the field width is undefined or has been set to 1.

☐ Reading a Line

The `>>` operator can only be used to read one word into a string. If you need to read a whole line of text, you can use the global function `getline()`, which was introduced earlier in this chapter.

Example: `getline(cin, text);`

This statement reads characters from `cin` and stores them in the string variable `text` until a new line character occurs. However, you can specify a different delimiting character by passing the character to the `getline()` function as a third argument.

Example: `getline(cin, s, '.');`

The delimiting character is read, but not stored in the string. Any characters subsequent to the first period will remain in the input buffer of the stream.

▨ **EXERCISES**

Screen output for exercise 3

```
Article Number    Number of Pieces  Price per piece
  .......             ......           ...... Dollar
```

Program listing for exercise 5

```cpp
// A program with resistant mistakes

#include <iostream>
using namespace std;

int main()
{
   char ch;
   string word;

   cin >> "Let's go! Press the return key: " >> ch;

   cout << "Enter a word containing
           three characters at most: ";

   cin  >> setprecision(3) >> word;

   cout >> "Your input: " >> ch >> endl;

   return 0;
}
```

Exercise 1

What output is generated by the program on the page entitled "*Formatted output of floating-point numbers*" in this chapter?

Exercise 2

Formulate statements to perform the following:

  a. Left-justify the number 0.123456 in an output field with a width of 15.
  b. Output the number 23.987 as a fixed point number rounded to two decimal places, right-justifying the output in a field with a width of 12.
  c. Output the number −123.456 as an exponential and with four decimal spaces. How useful is a field width of 10?

Exercise 3

Write a C++ program that reads an article number, a quantity, and a unit price from the keyboard and outputs the data on screen as displayed on the opposite page.

Exercise 4

Write a C++ program that reads any given character code (a positive integer) from the keyboard and displays the corresponding character and the character code as a decimal, an octal, and a hexadecimal on screen.

 TIP

The variable type defines whether a character or a number is to be read or output.

Why do you think the character P is output when the number 336 is entered?

Exercise 5

Correct the mistakes in the program on the opposite page.

■ **SOLUTIONS**

Exercise 1

Output of a sample program formatting floating-point numbers:

```
By default: 12
showpoint:  12.
fixed:      12.00
scientific: 1.20e+001
```

Exercise 2

```cpp
#include <iostream>
#include <iomanip>      // For setw() and setprecision()
using namespace std;

int main()
{
    double x1 = 0.123456,  x2 = 23.987,  x3 = -123.456;
// a)
    cout << left << setw(15) << x1 << endl;
// b)
    cout << fixed << setprecision(2) << right << setw(12)
         << x2 << endl;
// c)
    cout << scientific << setprecision(4) << x3 << endl;
    // Output: -1.2346e+002
    // A field width of 12 or more would be convenient!

    return 0;
}
```

Exercise 3

```cpp
// Input and formatted output of article characteristics.
#include <iostream>
#include <iomanip>
using namespace std;
int main()
{
    long number = 0;
    int  count = 0;
    double price = 0.0;
                                            // Input:
    cout << "\nPlease enter article characteristics.\n";
    cout << "Article number:  ";
    cin  >> number;
```

```cpp
   cout << "Number of pieces:      ";
   cin  >> count;

   cout << "Price per piece:     ";
   cin  >> price;

                                           // Output:
   cout <<
   "\n\tArticle Number   Quantity   Price per piece ";

   cout << "\n\t"
        << setw(8)  << number
        << setw(16) << count
        << fixed    << setprecision(2)
        << setw(16) << price << " Dollar" << endl;

   return 0;
}
```

Exercise 4

```cpp
#include <iostream>
#include <iomanip>          // Manipulator setw()
using namespace std;

int main()
{
   unsigned char c = 0;
   unsigned int  code = 0;

   cout << "\nPlease enter a decimal character code: ";
   cin  >> code;

   c = code;                               // Save for output

   cout << "\nThe corresponding character: " << c << endl;

   code = c;              // Character code. Is only
                          // necessary, if input is > 255.
   cout << "\nCharacter codes"
        << "\n  decimal:     " << setw(3) << dec << code
        << "\n  octal:       " << setw(3) << oct << code
        << "\n  hexadecimal: " << setw(3) << hex << code
        << endl;

   return 0;
}
```

When entering 336, the value 80 is stored in the low byte of variable code (336 = 256 + 80). Thus after the assignment, the variable c contains the value 80, representing the character P.

Exercise 5

The corrected program:

```cpp
// Corrections are commented.
//
#include <iostream>
#include <iomanip>        // Manipulator setw()
#include <string>         // Class string
using namespace std;

int main()
{
   string word;           // To read a word.
                          // char ch; is not needed.

                          // cout << ...instead of  cin >> .
   cout << "Let's go! Press the return key: ";

   cin.get();             // Input newline character

   cout << " Enter a word "                            // "
        "containing three characters at the most: ";// "

   cin  >> setw(3) >> word;             // setw(3) instead of
                                        // setprecision(3)

   cout << "Your input: "               // <<
        << word << endl;                // instead of  >> ch

   return 0;
}
```

5

Operators for Fundamental Types

In this chapter, operators needed for calculations and selections are introduced. Overloading and other operators, such as those needed for bit manipulations, are introduced in later chapters.

■ BINARY ARITHMETIC OPERATORS

Binary operator and operands

```
                              Operator
                                 │
                                 ↓
                              a  +  b
                              ↑     ↑
        Left operand ─────────┘     └───── Right operand
```

The binary arithmetic operators

Operator	Significance
+	Addition
–	Subraction
*	Multiplication
/	Division
%	Remainder

Sample program

```cpp
#include <iostream>
using namespace std;
int main()
{
    double x, y;
    cout << "\nEnter two floating-point values: ";
    cin >> x >> y;
    cout << "The average of the two numbers is: "
         << (x + y)/2.0 << endl;
    return 0;
}
```

Sample output for the program

```
Enter two floating-point values: 4.75    12.3456
The average of the two numbers is: 8.5478
```

If a program is to be able to process the data input it receives, you must define the operations to be performed for that data. The operations being executed will depend on the type of data — you could add, multiply, or compare numbers, for example. However, it would make no sense at all to multiply strings.

The following sections introduce you to the most important operators that can be used for arithmetic types. A distinction is made between *unary* and *binary* operators. A unary operator has only one operand, whereas a binary operator has two.

☐ Binary Arithmetic Operators

Arithmetic operators are used to perform calculations. The opposite page shows an overview. You should be aware of the following:

- ▪ *Divisions* performed with integral operands will produce integral results; for example, 7/2 computes to 3. If at least one of the operands is a floating-point number, the result will also be a floating-point number; e.g., the division 7.0/2 produces an exact result of 3.5.
- ▪ *Remainder division* is only applicable to integral operands and returns the remainder of an integral division. For example, 7%2 computes to 1.

☐ Expressions

In its simplest form an expression consists of only one constant, one variable, or one function call. Expressions can be used as the operands of operators to form more complex expressions. An expression will generally tend to be a combination of operators and operands.

Each expression that is not a `void` type returns a value. In the case of arithmetic expressions, the operands define the type of the expression.

```
Examples:  int a(4);  double x(7.9);
           a * 512        // Type int
           1.0 + sin(x)   // Type double
           x - 3          // Type double, since one
                          // operand is of type double
```

An expression can be used as an operand in another expression.

```
Example:   2 + 7 * 3                // Adds 2 and 21
```

Normal *mathematical rules* (multiplication before addition) apply when evaluating an expression, i.e. the *, /, % operators have higher precedence than + and -. In our example, 7*3 is first calculated before adding 2. However, you can use parentheses to apply a different precedence order.

```
Example:   (2 + 7) * 3           // Multiplies 9 by 3.
```

■ UNARY ARITHMETIC OPERATORS

The unary arithmetic operators

Operator	Significance
+ -	Unary sign operators
++	Increment operator
--	Decrement operator

Precedence of arithmetic operators

Precedence	Operator	Grouping
High	++ -- (postfix)	left to right
	++ -- (prefix) + - (sign)	right to left
	* / %	left to right
Low	+ (addition) - (subtraction)	left to right

Effects of prefix and postfix notation

```
#include <iostream>
using namespace std;
int main()
{
   int i(2), j(8);

   cout << i++ << endl;      // Output:  2
   cout << i   << endl;      // Output:  3
   cout << j-- << endl;      // Output:  8
   cout << --j << endl;      // Output:  6

   return 0;
}
```

There are four unary arithmetic operators: the sign operators **+** and **-**, the increment operator **++**, and the decrement operator **--**.

☐ Sign Operators

The *sign operator* **-** returns the value of the operand but inverts the sign.

Example: `int n = -5;    cout << -n;      // Output: 5`

The *sign operator* **+** performs no useful operation, simply returning the value of its operand.

☐ Increment / Decrement Operators

The increment operator **++** modifies the operand by adding 1 to its value and cannot be used with constants for this reason.

Given that i is a variable, both i++ (*postfix notation*) and ++i (*prefix notation*) raise the value of i by 1. In both cases the operation i = i + 1 is performed.

However, prefix **++** and postfix **++** are two different operators. The difference becomes apparent when you look at the value of the expression; ++i means that the value of i has already been incremented by 1, whereas the expression i++ retains the original value of i. This is an important difference if ++i or i++ forms part of a more complex expression:

`++i`   i is incremented first and the new value of i is then applied,

`i++`   the original value of i is applied before i is incremented.

The decrement operator **--** modifies the operand by reducing the value of the operand by 1. As the sample program opposite shows, prefix or postfix notation can be used with **--**.

☐ Precedence

How is an expression with multiple operators evaluated?

Example: `float val(5.0);   cout << val++ - 7.0/2.0;`

Operator precedence determines the order of evaluation, i.e. how operators and operands are grouped. As you can see from the table opposite, ++ has the highest precedence and / has a higher precedence than -. The example is evaluated as follows: `(val++) - (7.0/2.0)`. The result is `1.5`, as val is incremented later.

If two operators have equal precedence, the expression will be evaluated as shown in column three of the table.

Example: `3 * 5 % 2`   is equivalent to   `(3 * 5) % 2`

■ ASSIGNMENTS

Sample program

```cpp
// Demonstration of compound assignments

#include <iostream>
#include <iomanip>
using namespace std;

int main()
{
   float x, y;

   cout << "\n Please enter a starting value:    ";
   cin >> x;

   cout << "\n Please enter the increment value: ";
   cin >> y;

   x += y;

   cout << "\n And now multiplication! ";
   cout << "\n Please enter a factor:   ";
   cin >> y;

   x *= y;

   cout << "\n Finally division.";
   cout << "\n Please supply a divisor: ";
   cin >> y;

   x /= y;

   cout << "\n And this is "
        << "your current lucky number: "
                             // without digits after
                             // the decimal point:
        << fixed << setprecision(0)
        << x << endl;

   return 0;
}
```

☐ Simple Assignments

A *simple* assignment uses the assignment operator = to assign the value of a variable to an expression. In expressions of this type the variable must be placed on the left and the assigned value on the right of the assignment operator.

Examples: z = 7.5;
           y = z;
           x = 2.0 + 4.2 * z;

The assignment operator has low precedence. In the case of the last example, the right side of the expression is first evaluated and the result is assigned to the variable on the left.

Each assignment is an expression in its own right, and its value is the value assigned.

Example: sin(x = 2.5);

In this assignment the number 2.5 is assigned to x and then passed to the function as an argument.

Multiple assignments, which are always evaluated from right to left, are also possible.

Example: i = j = 9;

In this case the value 9 is first assigned to j and then to i.

☐ Compound Assignments

In addition to simple assignment operators there are also compound assignment operators that simultaneously perform an arithmetic operation and an assignment, for example.

Examples. i += 3;   is equivalent to i = i + 3;
           i *= j + 2;   is equivalent to i = i * (j+2);

The second example shows that compound assignments are implicitly placed in parentheses, as is demonstrated by the fact that the precedence of the compound assignment is just as low as that of the simple assignment.

Compound assignment operators can be composed from any binary arithmetic operator (and, as we will see later, with bit operators). The following compound operators are thus available: +=, -=, *=, /=, and %=.

You can modify a variable when evaluating a complex expression by means of an assignment or the ++, -- operators. This technique is referred to as a *side effect*. Avoid use of side effects if possible, as they often lead to errors and can impair the readability of your programs.

■ RELATIONAL OPERATORS

The relational operators

Operator	Significance
<	less than
<=	less than or equal to
>	greater than
>=	geater than or equal to
==	equal
!=	unequal

Precedence of relational operators

Precedence	Operator
High	arithmetic operators
	< <= > >=
	== !=
Low	assignment operators

Examples for comparisons:

Comparison	Result
5 >= 6	false
1.7 < 1.8	true
4 + 2 == 5	false
2 * 4 != 7	true

The Result of Comparisons

Each comparison in C++ is a `bool` type expression with a value of `true` or `false`, where `true` means that the comparison is correct and `false` means that the comparison is incorrect.

Example: `length == circuit   // false or true`

If the variables `length` and `circuit` contain the same number, the comparison is `true` and the value of the relational expression is `true`. But if the expressions contain different values, the value of the expression will be `false`.

When individual characters are compared, the character codes are compared. The result therefore depends on the character set you are using. The following expression results in the value `true` when ASCII code is used.

Example: `'A' < 'a'    // true, since 65 < 97`

Precedence of Relational Operators

Relational operators have lower precedence than arithmetic operators but higher precedence than assignment operators.

Example: `bool flag = index < max - 1;`

In our example, `max − 1` is evaluated first, then the result is compared to `index`, and the value of the relational expression (`false` or `true`) is assigned to the `flag` variable. Similarly, in the following

Example:
```
int result;
result = length + 1 == limit;
```

`length + 1` is evaluated first, then the result is compared to `limit`, and the value of the relational expression is assigned to the `result` variable. Since `result` is an `int` type, a numerical value is assigned instead of `false` or `true`, i.e. 0 for `false` and 1 for `true`.

It is quite common to assign a value before performing a comparison, and parentheses must be used in this case.

Example: `(result = length + 1) == limit`

Our example stores the result of `length + 1` in the variable `result` and then compares this expression with `limit`.

 NOTE

You cannot use the assignment operator = to compare two expressions. The compiler will not generate an error message if the value on the left is a variable. This mistake has caused headaches for lots of beginners when troubleshooting their programs.

■ LOGICAL OPERATORS

"Truth" table for logical operators

A	B	A && B	A || B
true	true	true	true
true	false	false	true
false	true	false	true
false	false	false	false

A	!A
true	false
false	true

Examples for logical expressions

x	y	Logical Expression	Result
1	-1	x <= y || y >=0	false
0	0	x > -2 && y == 0	true
-1	0	x && !y	true
0	1	!(x+1) || y - 1 > 0	false

✓ **NOTE**

A numeric value, such as x or x+1, is interpreted as "false" if its value is 0. Any value other than 0 is interpreted as "true."

The logical operators comprise the *boolean operators* && (AND), || (OR), and ! (NOT). They can be used to create compound conditions and perform conditional execution of a program depending on multiple conditions.

A logical expression results in a value false or true, depending on whether the logical expression is correct or incorrect, just like a relational expression.

☐ Operands and Order of Evaluation

The operands for boolean type operators are of the bool type. However, operands of any type that can be converted to bool can also be used, including any arithmetic types. In this case the operand is interpreted as false, or converted to false, if it has a value of 0. Any other value than 0 is interpreted as true.

The **OR** operator || will return true only if at least one operand is true, so the value of the expression

Example: (length < 0.2) || (length > 9.8)

is true if length is less than 0.2 or greater than 9.8.

The **AND** operator && will return true only if both operands are true, so the logical expression

Example: (index < max) && (cin >> number)

is true, provided index is less than max and a number is successfully input. If the condition index < max is not met, the program will not attempt to read a number! One important feature of the logical operators && and || is the fact that there is a fixed order of evaluation. The left operand is evaluated first and if a result has already been ascertained, the right operand will not be evaluated!

The **NOT** operator ! will return true only if its operand is false. If the variable flag contains the value false (or the value 0), !flag returns the boolean value true.

☐ Precedence of Boolean Operators

The && operator has higher precedence than ||. The precedence of both these operators is higher than the precedence of an assignment operator, but lower than the precedence of all previously used operators. This is why it was permissible to omit the parentheses in the examples earlier on in this chapter.

The ! operator is a unary operator and thus has higher precedence. Refer to the table of precedence in the Appendix for further details.

■ **EXERCISES**

Program listing for exercise 4

```cpp
// Evaluating operands in logical expressions.

#include <iostream>
using namespace std;
int main()
{
   cout << boolalpha; // Outputs boolean values
                      // as true or false
   bool res = false;

   int y = 5;
   res = 7 || (y = 0);
   cout << "Result of (7 || (y = 0)): " << res
        << endl;
   cout << "Value of y: " << y << endl;

   int  a, b, c;

   a = b = c = 0;
   res = ++a || ++b && ++c;
   cout << '\n'
        << "  res = " << res
        << ",   a = " << a
        << ",   b = " << b
        << ",   c = " << c << endl;

   a = b = c = 0;
   res = ++a && ++b || ++c;
   cout << "  res = " << res
        << ",   a = " << a
        << ",   b = " << b
        << ",   c = " << c << endl;
   return 0;
}
```

exercises

Exercise 1

What values do the following arithmetic expressions have?

a. `3/10`   b. `11%4`   c. `15/2.0`
d. `3 + 4 % 5`   e. `3 * 7 % 4`   f. `7 % 4 * 3`

Exercise 2

a. How are operands and operators in the following expression associated?

`x = -4 * i++ - 6 % 4;`

Insert parentheses to form equivalent expressions.
b. What value will be assigned in part a to the variable x if the variable i has a value of –2?

Exercise 3

The `int` variable x contains the number 7. Calculate the value of the following logical expressions:

a. `x < 10 && x >= -1`
b. `!x && x >= 3`
c. `x++ == 8 || x == 7`

Exercise 4

What screen output does the program on the opposite page generate?

solutions

▨ SOLUTIONS

Exercise 1

a. `0`   b. `3`   c. `7.5`

d. `7`   e. `1`   f. `9`

Exercise 2

a. `x = ( ((-4) * (i++)) - (6 % 4) )`

b. The value `6` will be assigned to the variable `x`.

Exercise 3

a. `true`

b. `false`

c. `false`

Exercise 4

```
Result of (7 || (y = 0)): true
Value of y: 5

res = true,    a = 1,    b = 0,    c = 0
res = true,    a = 1,    b = 1,    c = 0
```

chapter

Control Flow

This chapter introduces the statements needed to control the flow of a program. These are

- loops with `while`, `do-while`, and `for`
- selections with `if-else`, `switch`, and the conditional operator
- jumps with `goto`, `continue`, and `break`.

■ THE while STATEMENT

Structogram for while

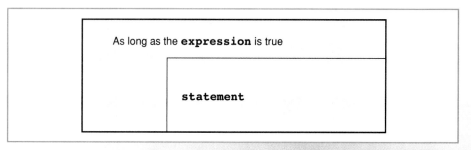

Sample program

```cpp
// average.cpp
// Computing the average of numbers

#include <iostream>
using namespace std;

int main()
{
    int x, count = 0;
    float sum = 0.0;

    cout << "Please enter some integers:\n"
            "(Break with any letter)"
         << endl;
    while( cin >> x )
    {
        sum += x;
        ++count;
    }
    cout << "The average of the numbers: "
         << sum / count << endl;
    return 0;
}
```

Sample output from the above program

```
Please enter some integers:
(Break with any letter)
9  10  12q
The average of the numbers: 10.3333
```

Loops are used to perform a set of instructions repeatedly. The set of instructions to be iterated is called the *loop body*. C++ offers three language elements to formulate iteration statements: while, do-while, and for. The number of times a loop is repeated is defined by a *controlling expression*. In the case of while and for statements this expression is verified before the loop body is executed, whereas a do-while loop is performed once before testing.

The while statement takes the following format:

Syntax:
```
while ( expression )
    statement          // loop body
```

When entering the loop, the controlling expression is verified, i.e. the expression is evaluated. If this value is true, the loop body is then executed before the controlling expression is evaluated once more.

If the controlling expression is false, i.e. expression evaluates to false, the program goes on to execute the statement following the while loop.

It is common practice to place the loop body in a new line of the source code and to indent the statement to improve the readability of the program.

Example:
```
int count = 0;
while ( count < 10 )
    cout << ++count << endl;
```

As this example illustrates, the controlling expression is normally a boolean expression. However, the controlling expression might be any expression that can be converted to the bool type including any arithmetic expressions. As we already learned from the section on boolean operators, the value 0 converts to false and all other values convert to true.

☐ Building Blocks

If you need to repeat more than one statement in a program loop, you must place the statements in a *block* marked by parentheses { }. A block is syntactically equivalent to a statement, so you can use a block wherever the syntax requires a statement.

The program on the opposite page calculates the average of a sequence of integers input via the keyboard. Since the loops contains two statements, the statements must be placed in a block.

The controlling expression cin >> x is true provided the user inputs an integer. The result of converting the expression cin >> x to a bool type will be true for any valid input and false in any other case. Invalid input, if the user types a letter instead of an integer, for example, terminates the loop and executes the next statement.

■ THE for STATEMENT

Structogram for `for`

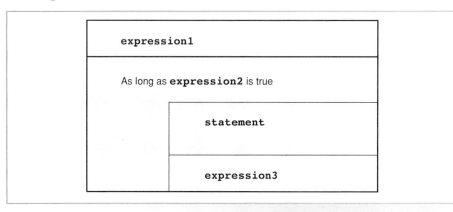

Sample program

```cpp
// Euro1.cpp
#include <iostream>
#include <iomanip>
using namespace std;

int main()
{
   double rate = 1.15;   // Exchange rate:
                         // one Euro to one Dollar
   cout << fixed << setprecision(2);

   cout << "\tEuro \tDollar\n";

   for( int euro = 1; euro <= 5; ++euro)
     cout << "\t " << euro
          << "\t " << euro*rate << endl;

   return 0;
}
```

Screen output

```
Euro    Dollar
 1       0.95
 2       1.90
 3       2.85
 4       3.80
 5       4.75
```

☐ Initializing and Reinitializing

A typical loop uses a *counter* that is initialized, tested by the controlling expression and reinitialized at the end of the loop.

Example:
```
int count = 1;              // Initialization
while( count <= 10)         // Controlling
{                           // expression
   cout << count
        << ". loop" << endl;
   ++count;                 // Reinitialization
}
```

In the case of a `for` statement the elements that control the loop can be found in the loop header. The above example can also be expressed as a `for` loop:

Example:
```
int count;
for( count = 1; count <= 10; ++count)
   cout << count
        << ". loop" << endl;
```

Any expression can be used to initialize and reinitialize the loop. Thus, a `for` loop has the following form:

Syntax:
```
for( expression1; expression2; expression3 )
   statement
```

expression1 is executed first and only once to initialize the loop. expression2 is the controlling expression, which is always evaluated prior to executing the loop body:

- if expression2 is `false`, the loop is terminated
- if expression2 is `true`, the loop body is executed. Subsequently, the loop is reinitialized by executing expression3 and expression2 is re-tested.

You can also define the loop counter in expression1. Doing so means that the counter can be used within the loop, but not after leaving the loop.

Example:
```
for( int i = 0; i < 10; cout << i++ )
   ;
```

As this example illustrates, the loop body can be an empty statement. This is always the case if the loop header contains all necessary statements. However, to improve readability, even the empty statement should occupy a line of its own.

■ THE for STATEMENT (CONTINUED)

Sample program

```cpp
// EuroDoll.cpp
// Outputs a table of exchange:  Euro and US-$

#include <iostream>
#include <iomanip>
using namespace std;

int main()
{
   long    euro, maxEuro;     // Amount in Euros
   double rate;               // Exchange rate Euro <-> $

   cout << "\n* * * TABLE OF EXCHANGE "
        << " Euro - US-$ * * *\n\n";

   cout << "\nPlease give the rate of exchange: "
           " one Euro in US-$: ";
   cin >> rate;
   cout << "\nPlease enter the maximum euro: ";
   cin >> maxEuro;

   //  --- Outputs the table   ---
                             // Titles of columns:
   cout << '\n'
        << setw(12) << "Euro" << setw(20) << "US-$"
        << "\t\tRate: " << rate << endl;

                             // Formatting US-$:
   cout << fixed << setprecision(2) << endl;

   long lower, upper,        // Lower and upper limit
        step;                // Step width

        // The outer loop determines the actual
        // lower limit and the step width:
   for( lower=1, step=1; lower <= maxEuro;
                         step*= 10, lower = 2*step)
        // The inner loop outputs a "block":
     for( euro = lower, upper = step*10;
          euro <= upper && euro <= maxEuro; euro+=step)
       cout << setw(12) << euro
            << setw(20) << euro*rate << endl;
   return 0;
}
```

Any of the three expressions in a `for` statement can be omitted, however, you must type at least two semicolons. The shortest loop header is therefore:

Example: `for(;;)`

This statement causes an infinite loop, since the controlling expression is assumed to be true if `expression2` is missing. In the following

Example: `for( ; expression; )`

the loop header is equivalent to `while(expression)`. The loop body is executed as long as the test expression is true.

☐ The Comma Operator

You can use the comma operator to include several expressions where a single expression is syntactically correct. For example, several variables can be initialized in the loop header of a `for` statement. The following syntax applies for the comma operator

Syntax: `expression1, expression2 [, expression3 ...]`

The expressions separated by commas are evaluated from left to right.

Example:
```
int x, i, limit;
for( i=0, limit=8;  i < limit;  i += 2)
    x = i * i,   cout << setw(10) << x;
```

The comma operator separates the assignments for the variables `i` and `limit` and is then used to calculate and output the value of `x` in a *single* statement.

The comma operator has the lowest precedence of all operators — even lower than the assignment operators. This means you can leave out the parentheses in the above example.

Like any other C++ expression, an expression containing the comma operator has a value and belongs to a certain type. The type and value are defined by the last expression in a statement separated by commas.

Example: `x = (a = 3, b = 5, a * b);`

In this example the statements in brackets are executed before the value of the product of `a * b` is assigned to `x`.

■ THE do-while STATEMENT

Structogram for do-while

```
┌─────────────────────────────────────────────────────────┐
│        ┌──────────────────────────────────────────┐      │
│        │                                          │      │
│        │              statement                   │      │
│        │                                          │      │
│        ├──────────────────────────────────────────┤      │
│        As long as the expression is true          │      │
│        │                                          │      │
└─────────────────────────────────────────────────────────┘
```

Sample program

```cpp
// tone.cpp
#include <iostream>
using namespace std;

const long delay = 10000000L;

int main()
{
   int tic;
   cout << "\nHow often should the tone be output? ";
   cin >> tic;

   do
   {
     for( long i = 0; i < delay; ++i )
         ;
     cout << "Now the tone!\a" << endl;
   }
   while( --tic > 0 );

   cout << "End of the acoustic interlude!\n";

   return 0;
}
```

In contrast to while and for loops, which are controlled by their headers, the do-while loop is controlled by its footer, i.e. the controlling expression is evaluated after executing the first loop. This results in the loop body being performed *at least once*.

Syntax:
```
do
    statement
while( expression);
```

When a do-while loop is executed, the loop body is processed first. Only then is the controlling expression evaluated. The loop body is iterated again if the result is true, otherwise the loop is terminated.

 NOTE

The do-while loop must be followed by a semicolon.

☐ Nesting Loops

Loops can be nested, that is, the loop body can also contain a loop. The ANSI standard stipulates a maximum depth of 256 nested loops.

The program on the opposite page outputs a number of tones with the number being defined by user input.

The program contains two loops — one of which is nested in the other. Each time the outer do-while loop is repeated a short break occurs. The break is caused by the inner for loop where the variable i is incremented from 0 to the value of delay.

Text and a tone are subsequently output. The tone is generated by outputting the control character BELL (ASCII code 7), which is represented by the escape sequence \a.

Since a do-while statement is used, the program outputs a tone even if the user types 0 or a negative number.

■ SELECTIONS WITH if-else

Structogram for the if-else statement

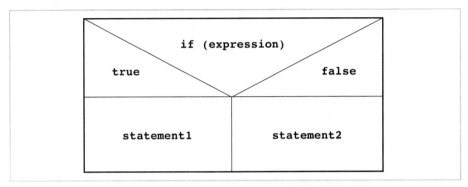

Sample program

```
// if_else.cpp
// Demonstrates the use of if-else statements

#include <iostream>
using namespace std;
int main()
{
   float x, y, min;

   cout << "Enter two different numbers:\n";
   if( cin >> x && cin >> y)  // If both inputs are
   {                          // valid, compute
     if( x < y )              // the lesser.
        min = x;
     else
       min = y;
     cout << "\nThe smaller number is: " << min << endl;
   }
   else
     cout << "\nInvalid Input!" << endl;

   return 0;
}
```

Sample output for this program

```
Enter two different numbers:
7.5  5.7
The smaller number is: 5.7
```

The if-else statement can be used to choose between two conditional statements.

Syntax: if(expression)
                statement1
            [else
                statement2]

When the program is run, expression is first evaluated and the program control branches accordingly. If the result is true, statement1 is executed and statement2 is executed in all other cases, provided an else branch exists. If there is no else and expression is false, the control jumps to the statement following the if statement.

☐ Nested if-else Statements

As the program opposite illustrates, multiple if-else statements can be nested. But not every if statement has an else branch. To solve the resulting problem, an else branch is always associated with the nearest preceding if statement that does not have an else branch.

Example: if(n > 0)
                if(n%2 == 1)
                    cout << " Positive odd number ";
                else
                    cout << "Positive even number";

In this example, the else branch belongs to the second if, as is indicated by the fact that the statement has been indented. However, you can use a code block to redefine the association of an else branch.

Example: if(n > 0)
            {   if(n%2 == 1)
                    cout << " Positive odd number \n";
            }
            else
                cout << " Negative number or zero\n";

☐ Defining Variables in if Statements

You can define and initialize a variable within an if statement. The expression is true if converting the variable's value to a bool type yields true. In this case the variable is available within the if statement.

Example: if(int x = func())
                { . . . }   // Here to work with x.

The return value of the function, func(), is used to initialize the variable x. If this value is not 0, the statements in the next block are executed. The variable x no longer exists after leaving the if statement.

■ Else-if CHAINS

Structogram for an else-if chain

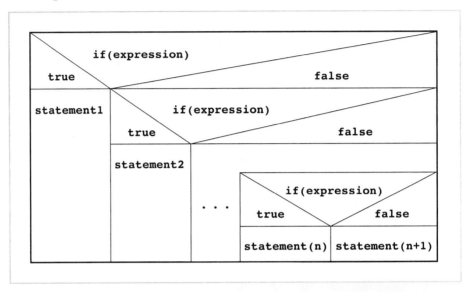

Sample program

```cpp
// speed.cpp
// Output the fine for driving too fast.

#include <iostream>
using namespace std;

int main()
{
   float limit, speed, toofast;
   cout << "\nSpeed limit: ";
   cin >> limit;
   cout << "\nSpeed: ";
   cin >> speed;

   if( (toofast = speed - limit ) < 10)
     cout << "You were lucky!" << endl;
   else if( toofast < 20)
     cout << "Fine payable: 40,-. Dollars" << endl;
   else if( toofast < 30)
     cout << "Fine payable: 80,-. Dollars" << endl;
   else
     cout << "Hand over your driver's license!" << endl;
   return 0;
}
```

☐ Layout and Program Flow

You can use an `else-if` chain to selectively execute one of several options. An `else-if` chain implies a series of embedded `if-else` statements whose layout is normally as follows:

```
if ( expression1 )
    statement1
else if( expression2 )
    statement2
        .
        .
        .
else if( expression(n) )
    statement(n)
[ else statement(n+1)]
```

When the `else-if` chain is executed, `expression1`, `expression2`, ... are evaluated in the order in which they occur. If one of the expressions proves to be true, the corresponding statement is executed and this terminates the `else-if` chain.

If none of the expressions are true, the `else` branch of the last `if` statement is executed. If this `else` branch is omitted, the program executes the statement following the `else-if` chain.

☐ The Sample Program

The program opposite uses an `else-if` chain to evaluate the penalty for driving too fast and outputs the fine on screen.

The speed limit and the actual speed are read from the keyboard. If the user types 60 as the speed limit and 97.5 as the actual speed, the first three expressions are not true, and the last `else` branch is executed. This outputs the message `"Hand over your driver's license!"` on a new line.

■ CONDITIONAL EXPRESSIONS

Structogram for a conditional expression

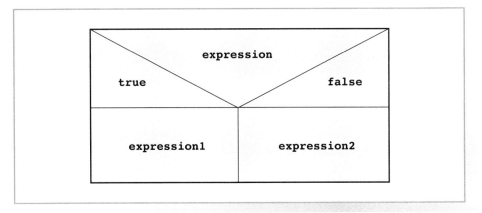

Sample program

```cpp
// greater.cpp
#include <iostream>
using namespace std;

int main()
{
   float x, y;

   cout << "Type two different numbers:\n";
   if( !(cin >> x && cin >> y) ) // If the input was
   {                             // invalid.
      cout << "\nInvalid input!" << endl;
   }
   else
   {
      cout << "\nThe greater value is: "
           << (x > y ? x : y)   << endl;
   }

   return 0;
}
```

Sample output for this program

```
Type two different numbers:
173.2
216.7
The greater value is: 216.7
```

Conditional Operator

The conditional operator `?:` is used to form an expression that produces either of two values, depending on the value of some condition. Because the value produced by such an expression depends on the value of a condition, it is called *conditional expression*.

In contrast to the `if-else` statement the selection mechanism is based on expressions: one of two possible expressions is selected. Thus, a conditional expression is often a concise alternative to an `if-else` statement.

Syntax: `expression ? expression1 : expression2`

`expression` is evaluated first. If the result is `true`, `expression1` is evaluated; if not `expression2` is executed. The value of the conditional expression is therefore either the value of `expression1` or `expression2`.

Example: `z = (a >= 0) ? a : -a;`

This statement assigns the absolute value of `a` to the variable `z`. If `a` has a positive value of `12`, the number `12` is assigned to `z`. But if `a` has a negative value, for example `-8`, the number `8` is assigned to `z`.

Since this sample program stores the value of the conditional expression in the variable `z`, the statement is equivalent to

```
if( a > 0 )
   z = a;
else
   z = -a;
```

Precedence

The conditional operator is the only C++ operator with three operands. Its precedence is higher than that of the comma and assignment operators but lower than all other operators. In other words, you could omit the brackets in the first example.

You can use the result of a conditional evaluation without assigning it, as the sample program on the opposite page shows. In this example, `x` is printed on screen if `x` is greater than `y`, and `y` is printed otherwise.

However, you should assign the result of complex expressions to a variable explicitly to improve the readability of your program.

■ SELECTING WITH switch

Structogram for the switch statement

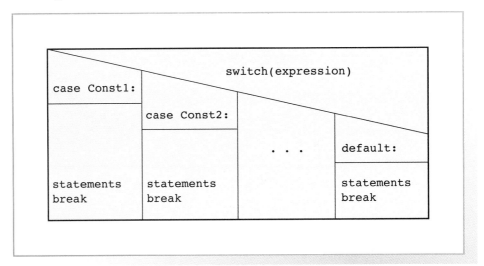

Example

```
// Evaluates given input.

int command = menu();      // The function menu() reads
                           // a command.
switch( command )          // Evaluate command.
{
  case 'a':
  case 'A':
          action1();       // Carry out 1st action.
          break;
  case 'b':
  case 'B':
          action2();       // Carry out 2nd action.
          break;
  default:
          cout << '\a' << flush; // Beep on
                                 // invalid input
}
```

☐ The `switch` Statement

Just like the `else-if` chain, the `switch` statement allows you to choose between multiple alternatives. The `switch` statement compares the value of *one* expression with multiple constants.

```
switch( expression )
{
   case const1: [ statement ]
               [ break; ]
   case const2: [ statement ]
               [ break; ]

     .
     .
     .

   [default:  statement ]
}
```

First, the `expression` in the `switch` statement is evaluated. It must be an integral type. The result is then compared to the constants, `const1`, `const2`, ..., in the `case` labels. The constants must be different and can only be integral types (boolean values and character constants are also integral types).

If the value of an expression matches one of the `case` constants, the program branches to the appropriate case label. The program then continues and the `case` labels lose their significance.

You can use `break` to leave the `switch` statement unconditionally. The statement is necessary to avoid executing the statements contained in any `case` labels that follow.

If the value of the expression does not match any of the `case` constants, the program branches to the `default` label, if available. If you do not define a `default` label, nothing happens. The `default` does not need to be the last label; it can be followed by additional `case` labels.

☐ Differences between `switch` and `else-if` Chains

The `else-if` chain is more versatile than the `switch` statement. Every selection can be programmed using an `else-if` chain. But you will frequently need to compare the value of an integral expression with a series of possible values. In this case (and only this case), you can use a `switch` statement.

As the example opposite shows, a `switch` statement is more easily read than an equivalent `else-if` chain, so use the `switch` statement whenever possible.

■ JUMPS WITH break, continue, AND goto

Structogram for break **within a** while **statement**

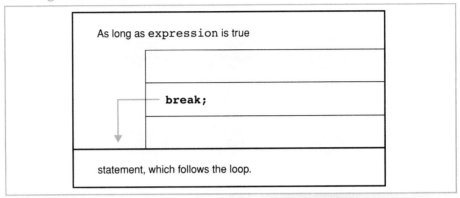

Sample program containing a break **statement**

```cpp
// ascii.cpp : To output an ASCII Code Table
#include <iostream>
#include <iomanip>
using namespace std;
int main()
{
   int ac = 32;              // To begin with ASCII Code 32
                             // without control characters.
   while(true)
   { cout << "\nCharacter   Decimal   Hexadecimal\n\n";
     int upper;

     for( upper =ac + 20; ac < upper && ac < 256; ++ac)
        cout << "        " << (char)ac      // as character
             << setw(10) << dec << ac
             << setw(10) << hex << ac << endl;
     if( upper >= 256)   break;
     cout <<"\nGo on -> <return>,Stop -> <q>+<return>";
     char answer;
     cin.get(answer);
     if( answer == 'q' || answer == 'Q' )
       break;
     cin.sync();                 // Clear input buffer
   }
   return 0;
}
```

✓ **NOTE**

The expression (char)ac yields the value ac of type char.

□ break

The break statement exits from a switch or loop immediately. You can use the break keyword to jump to the first statement that follows the switch or loop.

   The program on the opposite page, which outputs a group of 20 ASCII characters and their corresponding codes, uses the break keyword in two places. The first break exits from an infinite while(true) { ... } loop when a maximum value of 256 has been reached. But the user can also opt to continue or terminate the program. The second break statement is used to terminate the while loop and hence the program.

□ continue

The continue statement can be used in loops and has the opposite effect to break, that is, the next loop is begun immediately. In the case of a while or do-while loop the program jumps to the test expression, whereas a for loop is reinitialized.

Example:
```
for( int i = 0; i < 100; i++ )
{
    . . . // Processes all integers.
    if( i % 2 == 1)
      continue;
    . . .                 // Process even
                          // numbers only.
}
```

□ goto and Labels

C++ also offers a goto statement and labels. This allows you to jump to any given point marked by a label within a function. For example, you can exit from a deeply embedded loop construction immediately.

Example:
```
for( . . . )
    for( . . . )
      if (error) goto errorcheck;
    . . .
    errorcheck: . . .          // Error handling
```

A *label* is a name followed by a colon. Labels can precede any statement.

   Any program can do without goto statements. If you need to use a goto statement, do so to exit from a code block, but avoid entering code blocks by this method.

exercises

EXERCISES

Screen output for exercise 2

```
            ****** MULTIPLICATION TABLE ******

         1    2    3    4    5    6    7    8    9   10

   1  |  1    2    3    .    .    .    .    .    .   10
   2  |  2    4    6                                 20
   3  |  .    .    .                                  .
   4  |  .    .    .                                  .
   5  |  .    .    .                                  .
   6  |
   7  |
   8  |
   9  |
  10  | 10   20   30    .    .    .    .    .    .  100
```

Note on exercise 4

Use the function `time()` to initialize the random number generator:

```
#include <time.h>         // Prototype of time()
#include <stdlib.h>       // Prototypes of srand()
                          // and rand()
long sec;
time( &sec );             // Take the number of seconds and
srand( (unsigned)sec );   // use it to initialize.
```

Exercise 1

Rewrite the `EuroDoll.cpp` program in this chapter to replace both the `for` loops with `while` loops.

Exercise 2

Write a C++ program that outputs a complete multiplication table (as shown opposite) on screen.

Exercise 3

Write a C++ program that reads an integer between 0 and 65535 from the keyboard and uses it to seed a random number generator. Then output 20 random numbers between 1 and 100 on screen.

Exercise 4

Write a program for the following numerical game:

The computer stores a random number between 1 and 15 and the player (user) attempts to guess it. The player has a total of three attempts. After each wrong guess, the computer tells the user if the number was too high or too low. If the third attempt is also wrong, the number is output on screen.

The player wins if he or she can guess the number within three attempts. The player is allowed to repeat the game as often as he or she wants.

NOTE

Use the system time to seed the random number generator as shown opposite. The `time()` function returns the number of seconds since 1/1/1970, 0:0. The `long` value of the `sec` variable is converted to `unsigned` by `unsigned(sec)` and then passed to the `srand()` function.

■ **SOLUTIONS**

Exercise 1

The for loops of program EuroDoll.cpp are equivalent to the following while loops:

```
                    // The outer loop sets the lower
                    // limit and the step width used:
   lower=1, step=1;
   while( lower <= maxEuro)
   {
                    // The inner loop outputs a block:
     euro = lower;
     upper = step*10;
     while( euro <= upper && euro <= maxEuro)
     {
       cout << setw(12) << euro
            << setw(20) << euro*rate << endl;
       euro += step;
     }
     step *= 10, lower = 2*step;
   }
```

Exercise 2

```
//  MultTable.cpp
//  Outputs a multiplication table.

#include <iostream>
#include <iomanip>
using namespace std;
int main()
{
    int  factor1, factor2;

    cout << "\n\n                   "
         << "  ****** MULTIPLICATION TABLE  ******"
         << endl;

    // Outputs the first and second line:
    cout << "\n\n\n          ";                    // 1. line
    for( factor2 = 1 ; factor2 <= 10 ; ++factor2 )
       cout << setw(5) << factor2;

    cout << "\n          "                          // 2. line
         << "-------------------------------------------"
         << endl;
```

```
    //  Outputs the remaining lines of the table:

    for( factor1 = 1 ; factor1 <= 10 ; ++factor1 )
    {
        cout << setw(6) << factor1 << " |";
        for( factor2 = 1 ; factor2 <= 10 ; ++factor2 )
          cout << setw(5) << factor1 * factor2;
        cout << endl;
    }
    cout << "\n\n\n";                    // To shift up the table

    return 0;
}
```

Exercise 3

```
// random.cpp
// Outputs 20 random numbers from 1 to 100.

#include <stdlib.h>   // Prototypes of srand() and rand()
#include <iostream>
#include <iomanip>
using namespace std;

int main()
{
    unsigned int  i, seed;

    cout << "\nPlease type an integer between "
            "0 and 65535: ";

    cin >> seed;      // Reads an integer.
    srand( seed);     // Seeds the random
                      // number generator.

    cout << "\n\n                "
            "******   RANDOM NUMBERS   ******\n\n";

    for( i = 1 ; i <= 20 ; ++i)
       cout << setw(20) << i << ". random number = "
            << setw(3)  << (rand() % 100 + 1) << endl;

    return 0;
}
```

Exercise 4

```cpp
// NumGame.cpp  :  A numerical game against the computer
#include <cstdlib>    // Prototypes of srand() and rand()
#include <ctime>      // Prototype of time()
#include <iostream>
using namespace std;
int main()
{
   int  number, attempt;
   char wb = 'r';              // Repeat or finish.
   long sec;
   time( &sec);                // Get the time in seconds.
   srand((unsigned)sec);       // Seeds the random
                               // number generator
   cout << "\n\n            "
        << " *******   A NUMERICAL GAME   *******" << endl;
   cout << "\n\nRules of the game:" << endl;
   while( wb == 'r')
   {
     cout << "I have a number between 1 and 15 in mind \n"
          << "You have three chances to guess correctly!\n"
          << endl;
     number = (rand() % 15) + 1;
     bool found = false;     int count = 0;
     while( !found  && count < 3 )
     {
        cin.sync();               // Clear input buffer
        cin.clear();
        cout << ++count << ". attempt:    ";
        cin >> attempt;
        if(attempt < number)   cout << "too small!"<< endl;
        else if(attempt > number) cout <<"too big!"<< endl;
        else                      found = true;
     }
     if( !found)
       cout << "\nI won!"
            << " The number in question was: "
            << number << endl;
     else
       cout << "\nCongratulations! You won!" << endl;
     cout << "Repeat -> <r>    Finish -> <f>\n";
     do
       cin.get(wb);
     while( wb != 'r' &&  wb != 'f');
   }
   return 0;
}
```

chapter 7

Symbolic Constants and Macros

This chapter introduces you to the definition of symbolic constants and macros illustrating their significance and use. In addition, standard macros for character handling are introduced.

■ MACROS

Sample program

```cpp
// sintab.cpp
// Creates a sine function table

#include <iostream>
#include <iomanip>
#include <cmath>
using namespace std;

#define PI        3.1415926536
#define START     0.0              // Lower limit
#define END    (2.0 * PI)          // Upper limit
#define STEP  (PI / 8.0)           // Step width
#define HEADER   (cout << \
  "  *****  Sine Function Table *****\n\n")

int main()
{
  HEADER;                          // Title
                                   // Table Head:
  cout << setw(16) << "x" << setw(20) << "sin(x)\n"
       << "   ---------------------------------------"
       << fixed << endl;

  double x;
  for( x = START; x < END + STEP/2; x += STEP)
     cout << setw(20) << x << setw(16) << sin(x)
          << endl;

  cout << endl << endl;
  return 0;
}
```

Screen output

```
 *****  Table for the Sine Function  *****

           x                sin(x)
-------------------------------------------
       0.000000          0.000000
       0.392699          0.382683
       0.785398          0.707107

           .                  .
           .                  .
           .                  .
```

C++ has a simple mechanism for naming constants or sequences of commands, that is for defining *macros*. You simply use the preprocessor's #define directive.

Syntax: #define   name   substitutetext

This defines a macro called name. The preprocessor replaces name with substitute-text throughout the subsequent program. For example, in the program on the opposite page, the name PI is replaced by the number 3.1415926536 throughout the program in the first phase of compilation.

There is one exception to this general rule: substitution does not take place within strings. For example, the statement

```
cout << "PI";
```

outputs only PI and not the numerical value of PI.

☐ Symbolic Constants

Macros that are replaced by constants, such as the PI macro, are also known as *symbolic constants*. You should note that neither an equals sign nor a semicolon is used, as these would become part of the substitute text.

You can use any macros you have previously defined in subsequent #define directives. The program opposite uses the symbolic constant PI to define other constants.

☐ More about Working with Macros

Any preprocessor directive, and this includes the #define directive, must be placed in a line of its own. If the substitute text is longer than one line, you can terminate the line with a backslash \ and continue the substitute text in the next line, as is illustrated by the macro HEADER on the opposite page.

The rules that apply to naming variables also apply to naming macros. However, it is standard practice to capitalize symbolic constants to distinguish them from the names of variables in a program.

Using macros makes a C++ program more transparent and flexible. There are two main advantages:

1. *good readability:* You can name a macro to indicate the use of the macro

2. *easy to modify:* If you need to change the value of a constant throughout a program, you simply change the value of the symbolic constant in the #define directive.

■ MACROS WITH PARAMETERS

Sample program

```cpp
//  ball1.cpp
//  Simulates a bouncing ball
// ---------------------------------------------------
#include <iostream>
#include <string>
using namespace std;

#define DELAY  10000000L            // Output delay
#define CLS    (cout << "\033[2J")  // Clear screen
#define LOCATE(z,s) (cout <<"\033["<< z <<';'<< s <<'H')
        // Position the cursor in row z and column s

void main()
{
   int x = 2, y = 3, dx = 1, speed = 0;
   string floor(79, '-'),
          header = "****  JUMPING BALL  ****";

   CLS;
   LOCATE(1,25);  cout << header;
   LOCATE(25,1);  cout << floor;

   while(true)      // Let the ball "always" bounce
   {                // Terminate by interrupt key (^C)
     LOCATE(y,x);  cout << 'o' << endl; // Show the ball
     for( long wait = 0; wait < DELAY; ++wait)
       ;
     if(x == 1 || x == 79) dx = -dx;    // Bounce off
                                        // a wall?
     if( y == 24 )                      // On the floor?
     {
       speed = - speed;
       if( speed == 0 ) speed = -7;     // Restart
     }
     speed += 1;                        // Acceleration = 1
     LOCATE(y,x); cout <<  ' ';         // Clear output
     y += speed;   x += dx;             // New Position
   }
}
```

It is possible to call macros with arguments. To do so, you must supply the appropriate parameters when defining the macro. The parameters are replaced by valid arguments at run time.

Example: `#define SQUARE(a)    ((a) * (a))`

This defines a macro called `SQUARE()` with a parameter a. The name of the macro must be followed immediately by a left bracket. When the macro is *called*, for example

Example: `z = SQUARE(x+1);`

the preprocessor inserts the substitute text with the current arguments, which will be *expanded* as follows, in this case

```
z = ((x+1) * (x+1));
```

This example also shows that you must be careful when using brackets to indicate parameters for macros. Omitting the brackets in the previous example, `SQUARE`, would cause the expression to be expanded as follows `z = x + 1 * x + 1`.

The outer brackets in the definition ensure that even when the macro is used in a complex expression, the square is calculated before the result can be used for any further calculations.

☐ Macros for Screen Control

The program opposite uses macros to change the appearance of the screen. Peripheral devices, such as the screen or printers, can be controlled by special character sequences that normally begin with the ESC character (decimal 27, octal 033) and are thus known as *escape sequences*. A number of ANSI standard escape sequences exists for screen control.[1] See the appendix on *Escape Sequences for Screen Control* for an overview of the most important sequences.

`CLS` is a macro without any parameters that uses the escape sequence `\033[2J` to clear the screen. `LOCATE` is just one example of a macro with two parameters. `LOCATE` uses the escape sequence `\033[z;sH` to place the cursor at the position of the next screen output. The values z for the line and s for the column require decimal input with z = 1, s = 1 representing the top left corner of the screen or window.

The ball is "thrown in" at the coordinates x = 2, y = 3 and bounces off the "floor" and the "walls." In direction x (horizontally) the ball has a constant speed of dx = 1 or -1. In direction y (vertically) the ball is subject to a constant acceleration of 1, expressed as `speed += 1`.

---

[1]These escape sequences are valid for all standard UNIX terminals. The driver `ansi.sys` must be loaded for DOS or a DOS box in Win95 or Win98. For Win NT and Win 2000, corresponding functions based on system calls are offered for download.

■ WORKING WITH THE #define DIRECTIVE

Using macros in different source files

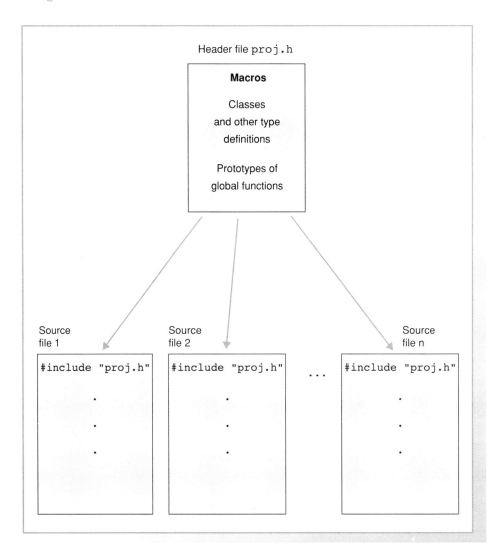

You can place the #define directive in any line of a program as long as it is placed prior to using the macro. However, it is recommended to place all definitions at the beginning of the source file for ease of location and modification.

If you need to use the same macros in different source files, it makes sense to create a header file. You can then include the header file in your source files. This method also lends itself to large-scale software projects. The programmers working on the project then have access to the same set of macro definitions and other declarations. This concept is illustrated opposite using the header file proj.h as an example.

Macros with parameters can be called just like functions. You should note the following important differences, however:

- **Macros**: A macro definition must be *visible* to the compiler. The substitute text is inserted and re-compiled each time the macro is called. For this reason, a macro should contain only a few statements to avoid inflating the object file each time the macro is called. The speed of program execution will, however, improve since the program does not need to branch to sub-routines in contrast to normal function calls. This can become apparent when macros are used within loops, for example.

  Side effects of macros are possible if the substitute text contains multiple instances of a parameter. The statement SQUARE(++x) expands to ((++x) * (++x)), for example. The variable x is incremented twice and the product does not represent the square of the incremented number.

- **Functions**: Functions are compiled independently. The linker then links them into the executable file. The program *branches* to the function whenever it is called, and this can reduce the speed of execution in comparison to a macro. However, the executable file will be shorter as it contains only one instance of the function code.

  The compiler checks the argument types, and the side effects seen with macros cannot occur.

Inline functions, which are introduced in the chapter on functions, are an alternative to macros.

■ CONDITIONAL INCLUSION

Multiple inclusions of header files

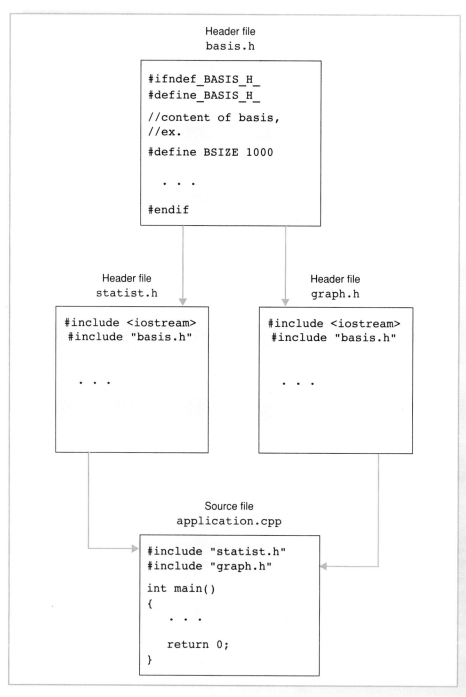

☐ Redefining Macros

A macro cannot simply be redefined. A macro definition is valid until it is removed by using an #undef directive. However, you do not need to supply the parameter list of a macro with parameters.

Example:
```
#define MIN(a,b)  ((a)<(b)? (a) : (b))
   . . .          // Here MIN can be called
#undef MIN
```

The macro MIN cannot be used after this point, but it can be defined again, possibly with a different meaning, using the #define directive.

☐ Conditional Inclusion

You can use the preprocessor directives #ifdef and #ifndef to allow the compiler to check whether a macro has been defined.

Syntax:
```
#ifdef name
   . . .          // Block, which will be compiled
                  // if name is defined.
#endif
```

In the case of the #ifndef directive, the code block is compiled up to the next #endif only if the macro name has **not** been previously defined.

On conditional inclusion else branching and nesting is also permissible. See *Preprocessor Directives* in the appendix for further information.

A macro definition does not need to include a substitute text to be valid.

Example: #define MYHEADER

A symbol without a substitute text is often used to identify header files and avoid multiple inclusion.

If you have a header file named "article.h", you can identify the header by defining a symbol, such as _ARTICLE_, within that file.

Example:
```
#ifndef _ARTICLE_
#define _ARTICLE_
   . . .          // Content of the header file
#endif
```

If you have already included the header, _ARTICLE_ will already be defined, and the contents of the header file need not be compiled. This technique is also employed by standard header files.

■ STANDARD MACROS FOR CHARACTER MANIPULATION

Sample program

```cpp
//  toupper.cpp: A filter that converts to capitals.
//  --------------------------------------------------
#include <iostream>
#include <cctype>
using namespace std;
int main()
{
   char c;
   long nChar = 0,         // Counts all characters
        nConv = 0;          // and converted characters
   while ( cin.get(c) )    // As long as a character
   {  ++nChar;             // can be read, to increment.
      if( islower(c))      // Lowercase letter?
      { c = toupper(c);    // Converts the character
        ++nConv;           // and counts it.
      }
      cout.put(c);         // Outputs the character.
   }
   clog << "\nTotal of characters:      " << nChar
        << "\nTotal of converted characters: " << nConv
        << endl;
   return 0;
}
```

✓ NOTE

The program reads characters from a file until end-of-file. When reading keyboard input, end-of-file is simulated by Ctrl+Z (DOS) or Ctrl+D (UNIX).

Macros for character classification

Macro	Return value true means:
isalpha(c)	c is a letter
islower(c)	c is a small letter
isupper(c)	c is a capital letter
isdigit(c)	c is a decimal digit
isalnum(c)	c is a letter or a digit
isspace(c)	c is a space letter
isprint(c)	c is a printable letter

The following section introduces macros that classify or convert single characters. The macros are defined in the header files `ctype.h` and `cctype`.

☐ Case Conversion

You can use the macro `toupper` to convert lowercase letters to uppercase. If `c1` and `c2` are variables of type `char` or `int` where `c1` contains the code for a lowercase letter, you can use the following statement

Example: `c2 = toupper(c1);`

to assign the corresponding uppercase letter to the variable `c2`. However if `c1` is not a lowercase letter, `toupper(c1)` returns the character "as is."

The sample program on the opposite page reads standard input, converts any letters from lower- to uppercase, and displays the letters. As `toupper` only converts the letters of the English alphabet by default, any national characters, such as accentuated characters in other languages, must be dealt with individually. A program of this type is known as a *filter* and can be applied to files. Refer to the next section for details.

The macro `tolower` is available for converting uppercase letters to lowercase.

☐ Testing Characters

A number of macros, all of which begin with `is...`, are available for classifying characters. For example, the macro `islower(c)` checks whether c contains a lowercase letter returning the value `true`, in this case, and `false` in all other cases.

```
Example:   char c;   cin >> c;        // Reads and
                                       // classifies
         if( !isdigit(c) )             // a character.
            cout << "The character is no digit \n";
```

The following usage of `islower()` shows a possible definition of the `toupper()` macro:

```
Example:   #define toupper(c) \
                (islower(c) ? ((c)-'a'+'A') : (c))
```

This example makes use of the fact that the codes of lower- and uppercase letters differ by a constant, as is the case for all commonly used character sets such as ASCII and EBCDIC.

The opposite page contains an overview of macros commonly used to classify characters.

■ REDIRECTING STANDARD INPUT AND OUTPUT

Sample program

```
// lines.cpp
// A filter that numbers lines.

#include <iostream>
#include <iomanip>
#include <string>
using namespace std;

int main()
{
   string line;
   int number = 0;

   while( getline( cin, line))    // As long as a line
   {                              // can be read.
     cout << setw(5) << ++number << ": "
          << line << endl;
   }
   return 0;
}
```

How to call the program

1. Redirecting the standard input:

   ```
   lines < text.dat | more
   ```

   This outputs the text file text.dat with line numbers. In addition, the data
   stream is sent to the standard filter more, which pauses screen output if the page
   is full.

2. Redirecting the standard output:

   ```
   lines > new.dat
   ```

   Here the program reads from the keyboard and adds the output to the new file
   new.dat. Please note, if the file already exists, it will be overwritten!
      You can use

   ```
   lines >> text.dat
   ```

   to *append* program output to the file text.dat. If the file text.dat does not
   already exist, it will be created.
      Type Ctrl+Z (DOS) or Ctrl+D (UNIX) to terminate keyboard input.

☐ Filter Programs

The previous program, `toupper.cpp`, reads characters from standard input, processes them, and sends them to standard output. Programs of this type are known as *filters*.

In the program `toupper.cpp`, the loop

```
while( cin.get(c)) { ... }
```

is repeated while the test expression `cin.get(c)` yields the value `true`, that is, as long as a valid character can be read for the variable `c`. The loop is terminated by end-of-file or if an error occurs since the test expression `cin.get(c)` will then be `false`.

The program on the opposite page, `lines.cpp`, is also a filter that reads a text and outputs the same text with line numbers. But in this case standard input is read line by line.

```
while( getline(cin,line)) { ... }
```

The test expression `getline(cin,line)` is `true` while a line can be read.

☐ Using Filter Programs

Filter programs are extremely useful since various operating systems, such as DOS, Win**, WinNT, and UNIX are capable of redirecting standard input and output. This allows easy data manipulation.

For example, if you need to output `text.dat` with line numbers on screen, you can execute the program `lines` by typing the following command:

Example: `lines < text.dat`

This syntax causes the program to read data from a file instead of from the keyboard. In other words, the standard input is redirected.

The opposite page contains additional examples. You can redirect input and output simultaneously:

Example: `lines < text.dat > new.dat`

In this example the contents of `text.dat` and the line numbers are stored in `new.dat`. The program does not generate any screen output.

 NOTE

These examples assume that the compiled program `lines.exe` is either in the current directory or in a directory defined in your system's PATH variable.

exercises

▪ EXERCISES

Hints for Exercise 2

You can use the function `kbhit()` to test whether the user has pressed a key. If so, the function `getch()` can be used to read the character. This avoids interrupting the program when reading from the keyboard.

These functions have not been standardized by ANSI but are available on almost every system. Both functions use operating system routines and are declared in the header file `conio.h`.

The function `kbhit()`

Prototype: `int kbhit();`
Returns: `0`, if no key was pressed, otherwise `!= 0`.

When a key has been pressed, the corresponding character can be read by `getch()`.

The function `getch()`

Prototype: `int getch();`
Returns: The character code. There is no special return value on reaching end-of-file or if an error occurs.

In contrast to `cin.get()`, `getch()` does not use an input buffer when reading characters, that is, when a character is entered, it is passed directly to the program and not printed on screen. Additionally, control characters, such as return (= 13), Ctrl+Z (= 26), and Esc (= 27), are passed to the program "as is."

```
Example:   int c;
           if( kbhit() != 0)  // Key was pressed?
           {
              c = getch();     // Yes -> Get character
              if( c == 27 )    // character == Esc?
              // . . .
           }
```

✔ NOTE

When a function key, such as F1, F2, ..., Ins, Del, etc. was pressed, the function `getch()` initially returns 0. A second call yields the key number.

Exercise 1

Please write

    a.   the macro ABS, which returns the absolute value of a number,

    b.   the macro MAX, which determines the greater of two numbers.

In both cases use the conditional operator ? : .

    Add these macros and other macros from this chapter to the header file myMacros.h and then test the macros.

    If your system supports screen control macros, also add some screen control macros to the header. For example, you could write a macro named COLOR(f,b) to define the foreground and background colors for the following output.

Exercise 2

Modify the program ball1.cpp to

    a.   display a white ball on a blue background,

    b.   terminate the program when the Esc key is pressed,

    c.   increase the speed of the ball with the + key and decrease the speed with the − key.

You will need the functions kbhit() and getch() (shown opposite) to solve parts b and c of this problem.

Exercise 3

Write a filter program to display the text contained in any given file. The program should filter any control characters out of the input with the exception of the characters \n (end-of-line) and \t (tabulator), which are to be treated as normal characters for the purpose of this exercise. Control characters are defined by codes 0 to 31.

    A sequence of control characters is to be represented by a single space character.

    A single character, that is, a character appearing between two control characters, is not to be output!

 NOTE

Since the program must not immediately output a single character following a control character, you will need to store the predecessor of this character. You may want to use two counters to count the number of characters and control characters in the current string.

SOLUTIONS

Exercise 1

```cpp
// ----------------------------------------------------------
// myMacros.h
// Header file contains the Macros
// ABS, MIN, MAX, CLS, LOCATE, COLOR, NORMAL, INVERS
// and symbolic constants for colors.
// ----------------------------------------------------------
#ifndef _MYMACROS_
#define _MYMACROS_

#include <iostream>
using namespace std;

// ----------------------------------------------------------
// Macro ABS
// Call:  ABS( val)
// Returns the absolute value of val
#define ABS(a) ( (a) >= 0 ? (a) : -(a))


// ----------------------------------------------------------
// Macro MIN
// Call:  MIN(x,y)
// Returns the minimum of x and y
#define MIN(a,b) ( (a) <= (b) ? (a) : (b))

// ----------------------------------------------------------
// Macro MAX
// Call:  MAX(x,y)
// Returns the maximum of x and y
#define MAX(a,b) ( (a) >= (b) ? (a) : (b))

// ----------------------------------------------------------
// Macros for controlling the screen
// ----------------------------------------------------------
// Macro CLS
// Call:  CLS;
// Clears the screen
#define CLS    (cout << "\033[2J")

// ----------------------------------------------------------
// Macro LOCATE
// Call:  LOCATE(row, column);
// Positions the cursor to (row,column).
// (1,1) is the upper left corner.
#define LOCATE(r,c) (cout <<"\033["<< (r) <<';'<<(c)<<'H')
```

```
// ----------------------------------------------------
// Macro COLOR
// Call:  COLOR(foreground, background);
// Sets the foreground and background color
// for the following output.
#define COLOR( f, b) (cout << "\033[1;3"<< (f) \
                               <<";4"<< (b) <<'m' << flush)
//  1: light foreground
// 3x: foreground x
// 4x: background x

// Color values for the macro COLOR
// To call ex.: COLOR( WHITE,BLUE);
#define BLACK   0
#define RED        1
#define GREEN      2
#define YELLOW     3
#define BLUE       4
#define MAGENTA    5
#define CYAN       6
#define WHITE      7


// ----------------------------------------------------
// Macro INVERS
// Call:  INVERS;
// The following output is inverted.
#define INVERS  (cout << "\033[7m")


// ----------------------------------------------------
// Macro NORMAL
// Call:  NORMAL;
// Sets the screen attributes on default values.
#define NORMAL  (cout << "\033[0m")

#endif      // _MYMACROS_
```

Exercise 2

```
// ----------------------------------------------------
//  ball2.cpp
//  Simulates a bouncing ball
// ----------------------------------------------------

#include <iostream>
#include <string>
using namespace std;
#include <conio.h>              // For kbhit() and getch()
#include "myMacros.h"
```

```
#define  ESC   27            // ESC terminates the program
unsigned long delay = 5000000;           // Delay for output

int main()
{
   int x = 2, y = 2, dx = 1, speed = 0;
   bool end = false;
   string floor(80, '-'),
          header   = "****  BOUNCING BALL ****",
          commands = "[Esc] = Terminate       "
                     "[+] = Speed up     [-] = Slow down";

   COLOR(WHITE,BLUE);     CLS;
   LOCATE(1,25);   cout << header;
   LOCATE(24,1);   cout << floor;
   LOCATE(25,10); cout << commands;

   while( !end)           // As long as the flag is not set
   {
     LOCATE(y,x);   cout << 'o';          // Show the ball
     for( long wait = 0; wait < delay; ++wait)
        ;
     if(x == 1 || x == 79) dx = -dx;  // Bounce off a wall?
     if( y == 23 )                        // On the floor?
     {
       speed = - speed;
       if( speed == 0 ) speed = -7;     // Kick
     }
     speed += 1;                          // Speed up = 1

     LOCATE(y,x); cout <<  ' ';          // Clear screen
     y += speed;   x += dx;              // New position

     if( kbhit() != 0 )                  // Key pressed?
     {
        switch(getch())                  // Yes
        {
          case '+':  delay -= delay/5;   // Speed up
                     break;
          case '-':  delay += delay/5;   // Slow down
                     break;
          case ESC:  end = true;         // Terminate
        }
     }
   }
   NORMAL;  CLS;
   return 0;
}
```

Exercise 3

```cpp
// -------------------------------------------------
//  NoCtrl.cpp
//  Filter to ignore control characters
//  To call e.g.:  NoCtrl < file
// -------------------------------------------------

#include <iostream>
using namespace std;

#define isCtrl(c)    ( c >= 0  &&  c <= 31  \
                                && c != '\n' && c != '\t')

int main()
{
   char c, prec = 0;           // Character and predecessor
   long nCtrl = 0, nChar = 0;  // Number of the following
                               // control characters or
                               // other characters
   while( cin.get(c))
   {
     if( isCtrl(c))            // Control characters
     {
         ++nCtrl;
         nChar = 0;
     }
     else                      // Normal character
     {
        if( nCtrl > 0)
        {
           cout.put(' ');
           nCtrl = 0;
        }
        switch( ++nChar)
        {
           case 1:   break;
           case 2:   cout.put(prec);  // Predecessor and
           default:  cout.put(c);     // current character
        }
        prec = c;
     }
   }
   return 0;
}
```

chapter **8**

Converting Arithmetic Types

This chapter introduces implicit type conversions, which are performed in C++ whenever different arithmetic types occur in expressions.

Additionally, an operator for explicit type conversion is introduced.

■ IMPLICIT TYPE CONVERSIONS

Integer promotions

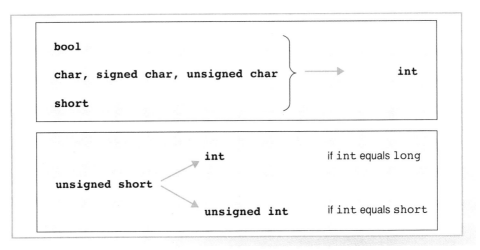

Type hierarchy

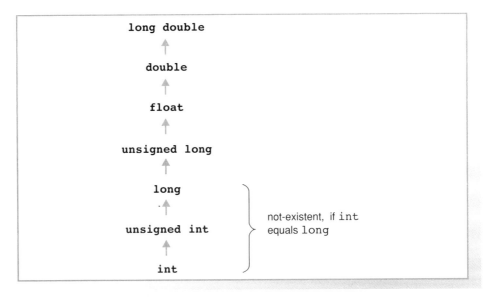

Example

```
short size(512);  double res, x = 1.5;
res = size / 10 * x;    // short -> int -> double
       ‾‾‾‾‾‾‾‾‾
          int
```

C++ allows you to mix arithmetic types in a single expression — in other words, the operands of an operator can belong to different types. The compiler automatically performs *implicit type conversion*, where a common type, which allows the operation in question to be performed, is assigned for the values of both operands. You can generally assume that the "smaller" type will be converted to the "larger" type. The assignment operator is an exception to this rule and will be discussed separately.

The result of an arithmetic operation belongs to the common type used to perform the calculation. However, comparison expressions will be `bool` types no matter what type of operands are involved.

☐ Integer Promotion

Integer promotion is first performed for any expression:

- ▦ `bool`, `char`, `signed char`, `unsigned char`, and `short` are converted to `int`
- ▦ `unsigned short` is also converted to `int` if the `int` type is greater than `short`, and to `unsigned int` in all other cases.

This type conversion is performed so as to preserve the original values. The boolean value `false` is converted to `0` and `true` is converted to `1`.

Thus, C++ will always use `int` type values or greater when performing calculations. Given a `char` variable `c`, the values of `c` and `'a'` in the expression

Example: `c < 'a'`

will be converted to `int` before being compared.

☐ Usual Arithmetic Type Conversions

If operands of different arithmetic types still occur after integer promotion, further implicit type conversions along the lines of the hierarchy on the opposite page will be necessary. In this case, the type of the operand with the highest rank in the hierarchy is applied. These type conversions and integer promotions are collectively known as *usual arithmetic type conversions*.

In our example, `size/10 * x`, the value of `size` is first promoted to `int` before an integer division `size/10` is performed. The interim result `50` is then converted to `double` and multiplied by `x`.

Usual arithmetic type conversions are performed for all binary operators and the conditional operator `?:` provided the operands belong to an arithmetic type, the only exceptions being the assignment operator and the logical operators `&&` and `||`.

■ PERFORMING USUAL ARITHMETIC TYPE CONVERSIONS

Converting signed integers

a) Converting a positive number

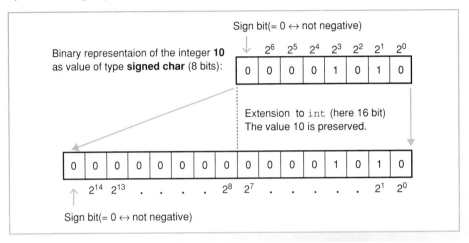

b) Converting a negative number

The bit pattern of **−10** is computed by starting with the bit pattern of **10** and generating the binary complement (see *Binary Representation of Numbers* in the appendix).

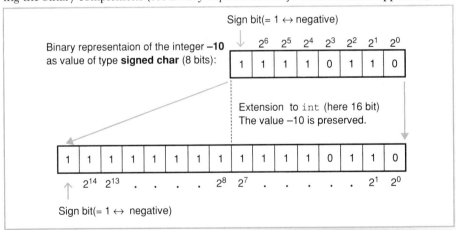

✓ **NOTE**

The value of a negative number changes if the bit pattern is interpreted as `unsigned`. The bit pattern 1111 0110 of −10, for example, corresponds to the `unsigned char` value

$246 == 0*2^0 + 1*2^1 + 1*2^2 + 0*2^3 + 1*2^4 + 1*2^5 + 1*2^6 + 1*2^7$

Usual arithmetic type conversions retain the value of a number provided it can be represented by the new type. The procedure for type conversion depends on the types involved:

1. **Conversion of an unsigned type to a larger integral type**

   Examples: `unsigned char` to `int` or `unsigned int`

   Zero extension is performed first. During this process, the bit pattern of the number to be converted is expanded to match the length of the new type by adding zeros from the left.

2. **Conversion of a signed type to a larger integral type**

   ▪ The new type is also `signed`

   Examples: `char` to `int`, `short` to `long`

   Signed integers are represented by generating the *binary complement*. The value is retained by performing *sign extension*. As shown in the example on the opposite page, the original bit pattern is expanded to match the length of the new type by padding the sign bit from the left.

   ▪ The new type is `unsigned`

   Examples: `char` to `unsigned int`, `long` to `unsigned long`

   In this case the value of negative numbers is not retained. If the new type is of the same length, the *bit pattern is retained*. However, the bit pattern will be interpreted differently. The sign bit loses its significance (see the note opposite).

   If the new type is longer, sign extension is performed first and the new bit pattern is then interpreted as unsigned.

3. **Conversion of an integral type to a floating-point type**

   Examples: `int` to `double`, `unsigned long` to `float`

   The number is converted to an exponential floating-point type and the value retained. When converting from `long` or `unsigned long` to `float`, some rounding may occur.

4. **Conversion of a floating-point type to a larger floating-point type**

   Examples: `float` to `double`, `double` to `long double`

   The value is retained during this type conversion.

■ IMPLICIT TYPE CONVERSIONS IN ASSIGNMENTS

Example 1:
```
int i = 100;
long lg = i + 50;    // Result of type int is
                     // converted to long.
```

Example 2:
```
long lg = 0x654321;   short st;
st = lg;        //0x4321 is assigned to st.
```

Example 3:
```
int i = -2;   unsigned int ui = 2;
i = i * ui;
// First the value contained in i is converted to
// unsigned int (preserving the bit pattern) and
// multiplied by 2 (overflow!).
// While assigning the bit pattern the result
// is interpreted as an int value again,
// i.e. -4  is stored in i.
```

Example 4:
```
double db = -4.567;
int i;   unsigned int ui;
i = db;          // Assigning -4.
i = db - 0.5;    // Assigning -5.
ui = db;         // -4 is incompatible with ui.
```

Example 5:
```
double d = 1.23456789012345;
float f;
f = d;           // 1.234568 is assigned to f.
```

Arithmetic types can also be mixed in *assignments*. The compiler adjusts the type of the value on the right of the assignment operator to match the type of the variable on the left.

In the case of *compound* assignments, calculations using normal arithmetic type conversions are performed first before type conversion is performed following the rule for simple assignments.

Two different cases can occur during type conversion in assignments:

1. If the type of the variable is larger than the type of the value to be assigned, the type of the value must be promoted. The rules for usual arithmetic type conversions are applied in this case (see Example 1).

2. If the type of the value to be assigned is larger, this type must be "demoted." The following procedures are followed depending on individual circumstances:

   a. **Conversion of an integral type to a smaller type:**

      - the type is converted to a smaller type by removing the most significant byte(s). The bit pattern that remains will be interpreted as unsigned, if the new type is also `unsigned`, and as signed in all other cases. The value can only be retained if it can be represented by the new type (see Example 2).

      - when converting an `unsigned` type to a `signed` type of the same scale, the bit pattern is retained and will be interpreted as signed (see Example 3).

   b. **Conversion of a floating-point type to an integral type**

      The decimal part of the floating-point number is removed. For example, `1.9` converts to the integer `1`. Rounding can be achieved by adding `0.5` to a positive floating-point number or subtracting `0.5` from a negative floating-point number. This would allow for converting (`1.9 + 0.5`) to `2`.

      If the resulting integer is too large or too small for the new type, the result is unpredictable. This particularly applies to converting negative floating-point numbers to `unsigned` integers (see Example 4).

   c. **Conversion of a floating-point type to a smaller type**

      If the floating-point number falls within the range of the new type, the value will be retained, although the accuracy may be compromised. If the value is too large to be represented by the new type, the result is unpredictable (see Example 5).

■ MORE TYPE CONVERSIONS

Sample program

```cpp
// Ellipse.cpp
// The program draws an ellipse.
// The points (x,y) on an ellipse with center (0,0)
// and axes A and B satisfy:
//    x = A*cos(t), y = B*sint(t)   for 0 <= t <= 2*PI .
//------------------------------------------------------

#include <iostream>
#include <cmath>          // Prototypes of sin() and cos()
using namespace std;

#define CLS          (cout << "\033[2J")
#define LOCATE(z,s)  (cout <<"\033["<<(z)<<';'<<(s)<<'H')
#define DOT(x,y)     (LOCATE(y,x) << '*')

#define  PI  3.1416
#define  Mx  40                // The point (Mx, My) is the
#define  My  12                // center of the ellipse.
#define  A   25                // Length of main axis
#define  B   10                // Length of subsidiary axis

int main()
{
    int x, y;              // Screen coordinates.

    CLS;
                    // 0 <= t <= PI/2 is a 1/4-circle:
    for( double t = 0.0 ; t <= PI/2 ; t += 0.03)
    {
        x = (int) (A * cos(t) + 0.5);
        y = (int) (B * sin(t) + 0.5);
        DOT( x+Mx, y+My);
        DOT( x+Mx,-y+My);
        DOT(-x+Mx, y+My);
        DOT(-x+Mx,-y+My);
    }
    LOCATE(24,0);
    return 0;
}
```

☐ Implicit Type Conversions in Function Calls

In the case of *function calls*, arguments with arithmetic types are converted to the types of the corresponding parameters, similarly to conversions in assignments.

Example:
```
void func( short, double);      // Prototype
int size = 1000;
// . . .
func( size, 77);                // Call
```

The function func() has two parameters belonging to the short and double types. However, the function is called using two int arguments. This leads to implicit conversion of the value of size to short and the integer 77 to double.

   When an int is converted to short the compiler issues a warning, since some data loss may occur. You can use explicit type conversion to avoid warnings during type conversion.

☐ Explicit Type Conversion

It is possible to convert the type of an expression explicitly using the *cast operator* (type).

Syntax: (type) expression

This converts the value of an expression to the given type. Explicit type conversion is also known as *casting*.

   The cast operator (type) is a unary operator and thus has a higher precedence than the arithmetic operators.

Example:
```
int a = 1, b = 4;
double x;
x = (double)a/b;
```

In this example the value of a is explicitly converted to a double. Following the conventions of usual implicit type conversion, b is also converted to double and a floating-point division is performed. The exact result, 0.25, is assigned to the variable x. Without casting, an integer division with a result of 0 would have occurred.

   C++ has additional operators for explicit type conversion—the cast operator dynamic_cast<>, for example. These operators, which are described in later chapters, are required for special circumstances, for example, to perform type checking at runtime when converting classes.

exercises

■ EXERCISES

Program listing for exercise 3

```cpp
// Convert.cpp -> Demonstrates type conversions.
#include <iostream>
#include <iomanip>
using namespace std;
int main()
{
    char v_char = 'A';
    cout << "v_char:        " << setw(10) << v_char
                              << setw(10) << (int)v_char
                              << endl;

    short v_short = -2;
    cout << "v_short:       " << dec << setw(10) << v_short
                              << hex << setw(10) << v_short
                              << endl;
    unsigned short  v_ushort = v_short;
    cout << "v_ushort:      " << dec << setw(10) << v_ushort
                              << hex << setw(10) << v_ushort
                              << endl;

    unsigned long  v_ulong = v_short;
    cout << "v_ulong:       " << hex << setw(20) << v_ulong
         << endl;
    float  v_float = -1.99F;
    cout << "v_float:       " << setw(10) << v_float << endl;
    cout << "(int)v_float: " << setw(10)
                              << dec << (int)v_float << endl;

    return 0;
}
```

Graphic for exercise 4

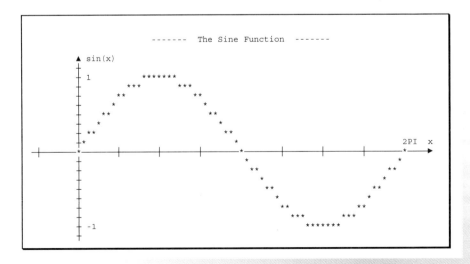

Exercise 1

A function has the following prototype

```
void func( unsigned int n);
```

What happens when the function is called with −1 as an argument?

Exercise 2

How often is the following loop executed?

```
unsigned int limit = 1000;
for (int i = -1; i < limit; i++)
//   . . .
```

Exercise 3

What is output when the program opposite is executed?

Exercise 4

Write a C++ program to output the sine curve on screen as in the graphic shown on the opposite page.

✓ **NOTE**

1. Plot one point of the curve in columns 10, 10+1, ..., 10+64 respectively. This leads to a step value of 2*PI/64 for x.

2. Use the following extended ASCII code characters to draw the axes:

Character	Decimal	Octal
−	196	304
+	197	305
▲	16	020
▶	30	036

Example: `cout << '\020';`   `// up arrowhead`

■ SOLUTIONS

Exercise 1

When called, the value −1 is converted to parameter n, i.e. to `unsigned int`. The pattern of −1 is interpreted as unsigned, which yields the greatest `unsigned` value.

On a 32-bit system, −1 has the bit pattern `0xFFFFFFFF`, which, when interpreted as unsigned, corresponds to the decimal value **4 294 967 295**.

Exercise 2

The statement within the loop is not executed at all! In the expression

```
i < limit
```

the value of variable `i`, −1, is implicitly converted to `unsigned int` and thus it represents the greatest `unsigned` value (see Exercise 1).

Exercise 3

The screen output of the program

```
v_char:                 A          65
v_short:               -2        fffe
v_ushort:           65534        fffe
v_ulong:                    fffffffe
v_float:            -1.99
(int)v_float:          -1
```

Exercise 4

```
// -------------------------------------------------------
//    sinCurve.cpp
//    Outputs a sine curve
// -------------------------------------------------------

#include <iostream>
#include <cmath>                     // Prototypes of sin()
using namespace std;

#define CLS         (cout << "\033[2J")
#define LOCATE(z,s) (cout <<"\033["<<(z)<<';'<<(s)<<'H')
#define PI          3.1415926536
#define START       0.0                 // Lower limit
#define END         (2.0 * PI)          // Upper limit
```

```
#define PNT        64         // Number of points on the curve
#define STEP    ((END-START)/PNT)
#define xA         14                     // Row  of x-axis
#define yA         10                     // Column of y-axis

int main()
{
    int  row, column;

    CLS;
    LOCATE(2,25);
    cout << "-------  The Sine Function  -------";

    //     --- Draws the coordinate system: ---

    LOCATE(xA,1);                                    // x-axis
    for( column = 1 ; column < 78  ; ++column)
    {
        cout << ((column - yA) % 8  ?  '\304' : '\305');
    }
    cout << '\020';                                  // top
    LOCATE(xA-1, yA+64);  cout << "2PI  x";

    for( row = 5 ; row < 24 ; ++row)          // y-axis
    {
        LOCATE(row, yA);  cout << '\305';
    }
    LOCATE( 4, yA);  cout << "\036 sin(x)";     // top

    LOCATE( xA-8, yA+1);  cout << " 1";
    LOCATE( xA+8, yA+1);  cout << " -1";

    //      --- Displays the sine function:  ---

    int begpt = yA,
        endpt = begpt + PNT;

    for( column = begpt ;  column <= endpt  ;  ++column)
    {
        double x = (column-yA) * STEP;
        row = (int)(xA - 8 * sin(x) + 0.5);
        LOCATE( row, column);  cout << '*';
    }

    LOCATE(25,1);                     // Cursor to the last row

    return 0;
}
```

chapter 9

The Standard Class
string

This chapter introduces the standard class `string`, which is used to represent strings. Besides defining strings we will also look at the various methods of string manipulation. These include inserting and erasing, searching and replacing, comparing, and concatenating strings.

■ DEFINING AND ASSIGNING STRINGS

Initializing

```
string message = "Good Morning!";
```

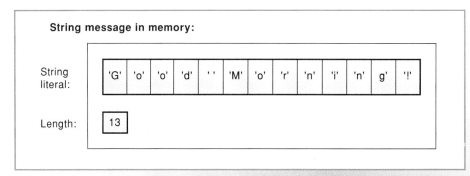

> **✓ NOTE**
>
> Objects of class string do not necessarily contain the string terminating character '\0', as is the case with C strings.

Sample program

```cpp
// string1.cpp: Using strings
#include <iostream>
#include <string>
using namespace std;
string prompt("Enter a line of text: "),     // Global
       line( 50, '*');                        // strings
int main()
{
   string text;                          // Empty string
   cout << line << endl << prompt << endl;
   getline( cin, text);         // Reads a line of text
   cout << line << endl
        << "Your text is " << text.size()
        << " characters long!" << endl;
                                   // Two new strings:
   string copy(text),            // a copy and the
          start(text,0,10);      // first 10 characters
                                 // starting with
                                 // position 0.
   cout << "Your text:\n" << copy << endl;
   text = "1234567890";          // Assignment
   cout << line << endl
        << "The first 10 characters:\n" << start << endl
        << text << endl;
   return 0;
}
```

C++ uses the standard class `string` to represent and manipulate strings allowing for comfortable and safe string handling. During string operations the required memory space is automatically reserved or modified. The programmer does not need to concern himself or herself with internal memory allocation.

The `string` class is defined in the `string` header file and was mentioned in Chapter 3 as an example for the use of classes. Several operators are overloaded for strings, that is, they were also defined for the `string` class. This allows for easy copying, concatenation, and comparison. Additionally, various methods for string manipulation such as insertion, erasing, searching, and replacing are available.

☐ Initializing Strings

A string, that is, an object belonging to the `string` class, can be initialized when you define it using

- a predefined string constant
- a certain number of characters
- a predefined string or part of a string.

If a string is not initialized explicitly, an empty string with a length of 0 is created. The length of a string, that is, the current number of characters in the string, is stored internally and can be accessed using the `length()` method or its equivalent `size()`.

Example:
```
string message("Good morning!");
cout << message.length();    // Output: 13
```

☐ String Assignments

When you assign a value to a string, the current contents are replaced by a new character sequence. You can assign the following to a `string` object:

- another string
- a string constant or
- a single character.

The memory space required is adjusted automatically.

The program on the opposite page uses the function `getline()`, which was introduced in an earlier chapter, to store a line of text from the keyboard in a string. In contrast, the `>>` operator reads only one word, ignoring any leading white space. In both cases the original content of the string is lost.

■ CONCATENATING STRINGS

Sample program

```cpp
// string2.cpp: Reads several lines of text and
//              outputs in reverse order.
#include <iostream>
#include <string>
using namespace std;
string prompt("Please enter some text!\n"),
       line( 50, '-');
int main()
{
   prompt+="Terminate the input with an empty line.\n ";
   cout << line << '\n' << prompt << line << endl;
   string text, line;          // Empty strings
   while( true)
   {
      getline( cin, line);     // Reads a line of text
      if( line.length() == 0)  // Empty line?
        break;                 // Yes ->end of the loop

      text = line + '\n' + text;   // Inserts a new
                                   // line at the beginning.
   }
                               // Output:
   cout << line << '\n'
        << "Your lines of text in reverse order:"
        << '\n' << line << endl;
   cout << text << endl;
   return 0;
}
```

Sample output for this program

```
----------------------------------------
Please enter some text!
Terminate the input with an empty line.
----------------------------------------
Babara, Bobby, and Susan
will go to the movies today


----------------------------------------
Your lines of text in reverse order:
----------------------------------------
will go to the movies today
Babara, Bobby, and Susan
```

Within the `string` class the operators + and += are defined for concatenating, and the operators ==, !=, <, <=, >, and >= are defined for comparing strings. Although these operators are being applied to strings, the well-known rules apply: the + has precedence over the comparative operators, and these in turn have higher precedence than the assignment operators = and +=.

Using + to Concatenate Strings

You can use the + operator to concatenate strings, that is, to join those strings together.

Example:
```
string sum, s1("sun"), s2("flower");
sum = s2 + s3;
```

This example concatenates the strings s1 and s2. The result, `"sunflower"` is then assigned to sum.

Two strings concatenated using the + operator will form an expression of the `string` type. This expression can in turn be used as an operand in a more complex expression.

Example:
```
string s1("sun"),s2("flower"),s3("seed");
cout << s1 + s2 + s3;
```

Since the + operator has precedence over the << operator, the strings are concatenated before the "sum" is output. Concatenation takes place from left to right. String constants and single characters are also valid as operands in expressions containing strings:

Example:
```
string s("Good morning ");
cout << s + "mister X" + '!';
```

 NOTE

At least one operand must be a `string` class object. The expression "Good morning " + "mister X" would be invalid!

Using += to Concatenate Strings

Strings can also be concatenated by first performing concatenation and then assigning the result.

Example:
```
string s1("Good "),s2("luck!");
s1 = s1 + s2;            // To concatenate s2 and s1
```

This example creates a temporary object as a result of s1 + s2 and then assigns the result to s1. However, you can obtain the same result using the assignment operator += , which is far more efficient.

Example:
```
s1 += s2;            // To concatenate s2 and s1.
s1 += "luck!";       // Also possible
```

This adds the content of the second string directly to s1. Thus, the += operator is preferable to a combination of the + and = operators.

■ COMPARING STRINGS

Sample program

```cpp
// string3.cpp: Inputs and compares lines of text.
#include <iostream>
#include <string>
using namespace std;
string prompt = "Please enter two lines of text!\n",
       line( 30, '-');
int main()
{
   string line1, line2, key = "y";
   while( key == "y" || key == "Y")
   {
     cout << line << '\n' << prompt << line << endl;
     getline( cin, line1);          // Read the first
     getline( cin, line2);          // and second line.

     if( line1 == line2)
       cout << " Both lines are the same!" << endl;
     else
     {
       cout << "The smaller line is:\n\t";
       cout << (line1 < line2 ? line1 : line2)
            << endl;
       int len1 = line1.length(),
           len2 = line2.length();
       if( len1 == len2)
         cout << "Both lines have the same length! \n";
       else
       { cout << "The shorter line is:\n\t";
         cout << (len1 < len2 ? line1 : line2)
              << endl;
       }
     }
     cout << "\nRepeat? (y/n) ";
     do
       getline( cin, key);
     while(    key != "y" && key != "Y"
           && key != "n" && key != "N");
   }
   return 0;
}
```

✓ **NOTE**

The relational operators yield the desired result for strings only if at least one operand is an object of class `string`. See Chapter 17, *Pointers and Arrays*, for more information.

The comparative operators

```
==    !=    <    <=    >    >=
```

were overloaded in the string class to allow easy comparison of strings. This also allows you to use strings to formulate the conditions for branches and loops.

Example:
```
// str1 and str2 are objects of type string
if( str1 < str2)   // str1 is less than str2?
   . . .
```

☐ Results of Comparisons

Strings are compared lexicographically, that is *character by character*, beginning at the first character. To decide whether a single character is smaller, greater, or identical to another character, the character codes of the character set are compared. Thus, if you are using the ASCII character set, the letter 'A' (ASCII code 65) is smaller than the letter 'a' (ASCII code 97).

A comparison results in a bool type value. Given two strings s1 and s2:

s1 == s2   is true only if both strings are identical; this requires that both strings are exactly the same length.

s1 < s2   is true only if the first character in s1 that differs from the corresponding character in s2 is smaller than the corresponding character in s2, or if s2 is simply an extension of s1.

All other comparative operations can be deduced from the above rules. For example, the expression s1 > s2 is true only if s2 < s1 is also true.

In an expression comparing strings, one operand can again be a string constant or a single character.

Example:
```
while( key == 'y' ) { . . . }
```

This example compares the string key with the single character 'y'. This is an alternative method of expressing the comparison key == "y".

String comparisons can also be combined to form more complex expressions.

Example:
```
while( key == "y" || key == "Y")
      { . . . }
```

The controlling expression is valid if the string key contains only the letter 'Y' or 'y'. Due to the higher precedence of the comparative operator versus the || operator, no parentheses are required in this example.

▪ INSERTING AND ERASING IN STRINGS

☐ Inserting a string

```
string s1("Miss Summer");
s1.insert(5, "Ashley "); // Insert at position: 5
```

Effect of the statement:

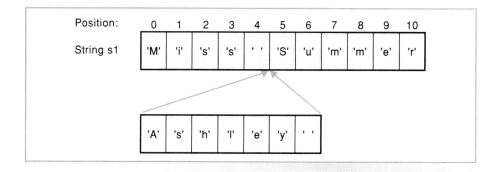

Erasing a substring

```
string s("The summer-time");
s.erase(4,7);      // Start position: 4, Quantity: 7
```

Effect of the statement:

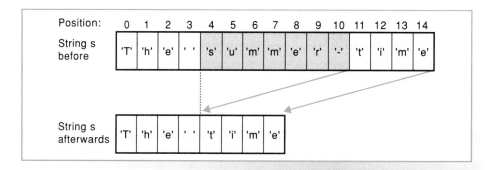

The `string` class contains numerous methods for performing string manipulations. A method exists for each operation, such as inserting, erasing, searching, and replacing. These methods generally allow passing a string constant instead of a second string. A single character can also be used wherever appropriate.

☐ Insertion

The method `insert()` inserts a string at a certain position of another string. The position is passed as the first argument and defines the character before which to insert the string. The first character in a string occupies position 0, the second character position 1, and so on.

Example:
```
string s1("Miss Summer");
s1.insert(5, "Ashley ");
```

The string `"Ashley "` is inserted into the string `s1` at position 5, that is in front of the `'S'` character in `"Summer"`. Following this, the string `"Miss Ashley Summer"` is assigned to `s1`.

If you need to insert only part of a string into another string, you can pass two additional arguments to the `insert()` method, the starting position and the length of the string.

Example:
```
string s1("Ashley is a devil"),
       s2(" sweetheart");
s1.insert(12, s2, 0, 12);
```

This example inserts the first 12 characters from the string `s2` at position 13 in string `s1`. String `s1` then contains the string "Ashley is a sweetheart".

☐ Erasing

You can use the `erase()` method to delete a given number of characters from a string. The starting position is supplied as the first argument and the number of characters to be erased is the second argument.

Example:
```
string s("The summer-time");
s.erase(4,6);      // Result: "The time"
```

This statement deletes 7 characters from string `s` starting at position 4. The `erase()` method can also be called without specifying a length and will then delete all the characters in the string up to the end of the string.

Example:
```
string s("winter-story");
s.erase(6);        // s now contains "winter"
```

You can also call `erase()` without any arguments to delete all the characters in a string.

■ SEARCHING AND REPLACING IN STRINGS

☐ **Replacing substrings**

   a. Example "Bob and Bill"

```
string s1("There they go again!"),
       s2("Bob and Bill");
s1.replace(6, 4, s2);
```

Effect of the statement:

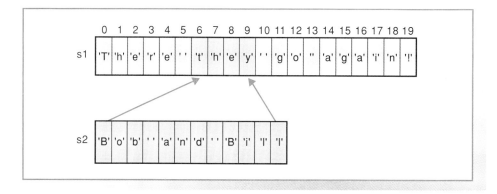

   b. Example "my love"

```
string s1("Here comes Mike!"), s2("my love?");
s1.replace(11, 4, s2, 0, 7);
```

Effect of the statement:

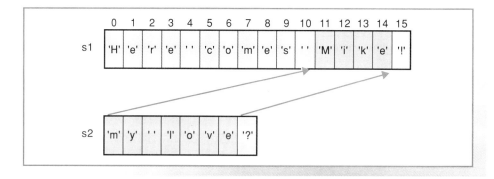

☐ Searching

You can search strings to find the first or last instance of a substring. If the string contains the required substring, the position of the substring found by the search is returned. If not, a pseudo-position npos, or −1, is returned. Since the npos constant is defined in the string class, you can reference it as string::npos.

The find() method returns the position at which a substring was first found in the string. The method requires the substring to be located as an argument.

Example:
```
string youth("Bill is so young, so young");
int first = youth.find("young");
```

The variable first has a value of 11 in this example.

You can use the "right find" method rfind() to locate the last occurrence of a substring in a string. This initializes the variable last with a value of 21 in our example.

Example:
```
int last = youth.rfind("young");
```

☐ Replacing

When replacing in strings, a string overwrites a substring. The string lengths need not be identical.

You can use the replace() method to perform this operation. The first two arguments supply the starting position and the length of the substring to be replaced. The third argument contains the replacement string.

Example:
```
string s1("There they go again!"),
       s2("Bob and Bill");
int pos = s1.find("they");       // pos == 6
if( pos != string::npos )
   s1.replace(pos, 2, s2);
```

This example uses the string s2 to replace 4 characters, "they", starting at position 6 in s1. After this operation s1 contains the string "There Bob and Bill go again!".

If you only need to insert part of a string, you can use the fourth argument to define the starting position and the fifth to define the length of the substring.

Example:
```
string s1("Here comes Mike!"),
          s2("my love?");
       s1.replace(11, 4, s2, 0, 7);
```

The string s1 is changed to "Here comes my love!".

■ ACCESSING CHARACTERS IN STRINGS

Sample program

```cpp
//   string4.cpp
//   The program counts words and white space characters.
// (A word is the maximum sequence of characters
//   containing no white space characters.)
//----------------------------------------------------------------
#include <iostream>
#include <string>
#include <cctype>                // Macro isspace()
using namespace std;

int main()
{
   string header("     **** Counts words    ****\n"),
          prompt("Enter a text and terminate"
                  " with a period and return:"),
          line( 60, '-'),
          text;                   // Empty string

   cout << header << endl << prompt << endl
        << line  << endl;
   getline( cin, text, '.');      // Reads a text up to
                                  // the first '.'

   // Counts words and white space characters
   int  i,              // Index
        nSpace = 0,      // Number of white spaces
        nWord  = 0;      // Number of words
   bool fSpace = true;   // Flag for white space

   for( i = 0; i < text.length(); ++i)
   {
      if( isspace( text[i]) )   // white space?
      {
         ++nSpace;   fSpace = true;
      }
      else if( fSpace)      // At the beginning of a word?
      {
         ++nWord;    fSpace = false;
      }
   }
   cout << line                    // Outputs the result.
        << "\nYour text contains (without periods)"
        << "\n             characters: " << text.length()
        << "\n                  words: " << nWord
        << "\n           white spaces: " << nSpace
        << endl;
   return 0;
}
```

When manipulating strings it is often important to access the individual characters that form the string. C++ has the operator `[]` and the method `at()` for this purpose. An individual character is always identified by its *index*, also referred to as *subscript*, that is, its position in the string. The first character will always have an index value of `0`, the second an index of `1`, and so on.

☐ Subscript Operator

The easiest way to access a single character in the string is to use the subscript operator `[]`. If you define a string as follows,

Example: `string s = "Let";`

the individual characters in the string are:

`s[0] == 'L',   s[1] == 'e',   s[2] == 't'`

The last character in a string always has an index of `s.length() - 1`. You can use the subscript operator to read any character in a string and also to overwrite a character, provided the string was not defined as a constant.

Example: `char c = s[0];`

This statement copies the first character from `s` to the variable `c`. In contrast

Example: `s[s.length() -1] = 'g';`

overwrites the last character in the string `s`. Following this, `s` will contain the string `"Leg"`.

☐ Invalid Indices

Any integral expression can be used as an index. However, no error message occurs if the boundaries of a valid index are overstepped.

Example: `cout << s[5];`   `// Error`

Your program's reaction to an invalid index is undefined; this requires careful attention by the programmer! You can call the `at()` method if you need to perform range checks.

☐ The `at()` method

You can also use the `at()` method to access a single character.

Example: `s.at(i) = 'X';`   is equivalent to   `s[i] = 'X';`

In contrast to the subscript operator, the `at()` method performs range checking. If an invalid index is found an *exception* occurs and the program will normally be terminated at this point. However, you can specify how a program should react to an exception.

EXERCISES

For exercise 3

```
// timeStr.cpp
// Demonstrates operations on a string containing
// the present time.

#include <iostream>
#include <string>
#include <ctime>             // For time(), ctime(), ...
using namespace std;

int main()
{
   long sec;
   time( &sec);             // Reads the present time
                            // (in seconds) into sec.
   string tm = ctime( &sec);    // Converts the
                                // seconds to a string.

   cout << "Date and time: " << tm << endl;

   string hr(tm, 11, 2);  // Substring of tm starting at
                          // position 11, 2 characters long.
   string greeting("Have a wonderful ");

   if( hr < "10")               // Compares strings
       greeting += "Morning!";
   else if( hr < "17")
       greeting += "Day!";
   else
       greeting += "Evening!";

   cout << greeting << endl;

   return 0;
}
```

Exercise 1

Write a C++ program to

- initialize a string s1 with the string `"As time by ..."` and a second string s2 with the string `"goes"`,
- insert string s2 in front of `"by"` in string s1,
- erase the remainder of string s1 after the substring `"by"`,
- replace the substring `"time"` in s1 with `"Bill"`.

In each case, your program should determine the position of the substring.

Output string s1 on screen at the beginning of the program and after every modification.

Exercise 2

Write a C++ program that reads a word from the keyboard, stores it in a string, and checks whether the word is a palindrome. A palindrome reads the same from left to right as from right to left. The following are examples of palindromes: "OTTO, " "deed, " and "level."

Use the subscript operator `[]`. Modify the program to continually read and check words.

Exercise 3

Write down the screen output for the program on the opposite page.

 NOTE

The function `time()` returns the current time as the number of seconds since 1/1/1970, 0:0. The number of seconds is stored in the variable `sec`, whose address was supplied as `&sec` when the function was called.

The function `ctime()` converts the number of seconds to a string with a date and time and returns this string. The string comprises exactly 26 characters including the null character `\0` and has the following format:

```
Weekday Month Day Hr:Min:Sec Year\n\0
```

Example: `Wed Jan 05 02:03:55 2000\n\0`

■ **SOLUTIONS**

Exercise 1

```cpp
// ------------------------------------------------------
// strDemo.cpp: Insert, search, and replace in strings.
// ------------------------------------------------------
#include <iostream>
#include <string>
using namespace std;

string header = "Demonstrating the use of strings\n",
       s1 = "As time by ...",
       s2 = "goes ";

int main()
{
   int pos = 0;

   cout << header << endl;
   cout << "s1 : " << s1 << endl;

   // To insert:
   cout << "\nInserting in string \"" << s2 <<"\""<< endl;

   pos = s1.find("by");
   if( pos != string::npos )
      s1.insert(pos,s2);
   cout << "s1 : " << s1 << endl;           // Result

   // To erase:
   cout << "\nTo erase remaining characters behind \"by\":"
        << endl;

   pos = s1.find("by");
   if( pos != string::npos )
      s1.erase(pos + 3);
   cout << "s1 : " << s1 << endl;           // Result

   // To replace:
   cout << "\nTo replace \"time\" by \"Bill\":"
        << endl;

   pos = s1.find("time");
   if( pos != string::npos )
      s1.replace(pos, 4, "Bill");
   cout << "s1 : " << s1 << endl;           // Result
   return 0;
}
```

Exercise 2

```cpp
// ----------------------------------------------------
// palindrome.cpp: Reads and compares lines of text.
// ----------------------------------------------------

#include <iostream>
#include <string>
using namespace std;

string header = " * * * Testing palindromes * * * ",
       prompt = "Enter a word: ",
       line( 50, '-');

int main()
{
   string word;                             // Empty string
   char key = 'y';

   cout << "\n\t" << header << endl;
   while( key == 'y' || key == 'Y')
   {
      cout << '\n' << line  << '\n'
           << prompt;

      cin >> word;

      // Compares the first and last character,
      // the second and the second to last etc.
      int i = 0, j = word.length() - 1;
      for( ; i <= j ; ++i, --j)
        if( word[i] != word[j] )
           break;

      if( i > j)                     // All characters equal?
         cout << "\nThe word " << word
              << " is a P A L I N D R O M E !" << endl;
      else
         cout << "\nThe word " << word
              << " is not a palindrome" << endl;

      cout << "\nRepeat? (y/n) ";
      do
        cin.get(key);
      while(    key != 'y' && key != 'Y'
             && key != 'n' && key != 'N');
      cin.sync();
   }
   return 0;
}
```

Exercise 3

The program outputs the date and time first. Then a greeting is printed according the time of day. For example:

```
Date and time: Thu Nov 28 09:01:37 2001

Have a wonderful morning!
```

chapter 10

Functions

This chapter describes how to write functions of your own. Besides the basic rules, the following topics are discussed:

- passing arguments
- definition of `inline` functions
- overloading functions and default arguments
- the principle of recursion.

■ SIGNIFICANCE OF FUNCTIONS IN C++

Elements of a C++ program

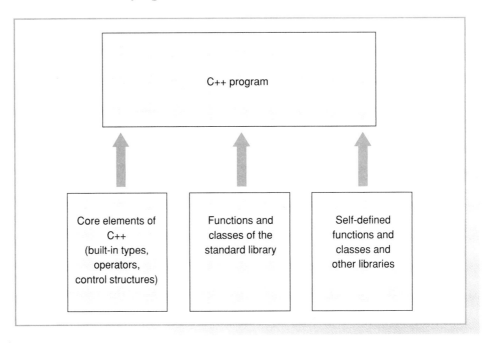

C++ supports efficient software development on the lines of the top-down principle. If you are looking to provide a solution for a more complex problem, it will help to divide the problem into smaller units. After identifying objects you will need to define classes that describe these objects. You can use available classes and functions to do so. In addition, you can make use of inheritance to create specialized classes without needing to change any existing classes.

When implementing a class you must define the capacities of those objects, that is, the member functions, in your program. However, not every function is a member function.

Functions can be defined globally, such as the function main() for example. Functions of this type do not belong to any particular class but normally represent algorithms of a more general nature, such as the search or sort functions of the standard library.

☐ Libraries

You will not need to program each "building block" yourself. Many useful global functions and classes are available from the C++ standard library. In addition, you can use other libraries for special purposes. Often a compiler package will offer commercial class libraries or graphical user interfaces. Thus, a C++ program will be made up of

- language elements of the C++ core
- global functions and classes from the C++ standard library
- functions and classes you have programmed yourself and other libraries.

Classes and functions that belong together are normally compounded to form separate source files, which can be compiled and tested independently. Using software components that you have already tested makes programming a complex solution much easier and improves the reliability of your programs. You can enhance the reusability of your source code by compiling your own libraries, but be sure to include comments for ease of readability.

Compiled source files, also known as *modules*, are compounded by the linker to an executable file by reference to the libraries you include. If you modify a source file, you may also need to recompile other files. In large scale projects it is recommended to use the *MAKE* utility for module management. An integrated developer environment will offer the functionality of this utility when you create a new project. This includes your own source files, the libraries used, and the compiler/linker settings for program compilation.

■ DEFINING FUNCTIONS

Example of a function definition

```cpp
// func1.cpp
#include <iostream>
using namespace std;

void test( int, double );                   // Prototype

int main()
{
  cout << "\nNow function test() will be called.\n";
  test( 10, -7.5);                          // Call
  cout << "\nAnd back again in main()." << endl;

  return 0;
}

void test(int arg1, double arg2 )          // Definition
{
    cout << "\nIn function test()."
         << "\n  1. argument: " << arg1
         << "\n  2. argument: " << arg2 << endl;
}
```

General form of a function

```
[type] name([declaration_list]) // Function header
{                                // Beginning

   .
   .
   What will be done             // Function block
   .
   .
}                                // End
```

The following section describes how to program global functions. Chapter 13, Defining Classes, describes the steps for defining member functions.

☐ Definition

Functions can be defined in any order, however, the first function is normally `main`. This makes the program easier to understand, since you start reading at the point where the program starts to execute.

The function `test()` is shown opposite as an example and followed by the general form of a function. The example can be read as follows:

`type`	is the function type, that is, the type of the return value.
`name`	is the function name, which is formed like a variable name and should indicate the purpose of the function.
`declaration_list`	contains the names of the parameters and declares their types. The list can be empty, as for the function `main()`, for example. A list of declarations that contains only the word `void` is equivalent to an empty list.

The *parameters* declared in a list are no more than local variables. They are created when the function is called and initialized by the values of the arguments.

Example: When `test( 10, -7.5);` is called, the parameter `arg1` is initialized with a value of `10` and `arg2` with `-7.5`.

The left curved bracket indicates the start of a *function block*, which contains the statements defining what the function does.

☐ Prototype and Definition

In a function definition the function header is similar in form to the prototype of a function. The only difference when a function is defined is that the name and declaration list are *not* followed by a semicolon but by a function code block.

The prototype is the declaration of the function and thus describes only the formal interface of that function. This means you can omit parameter names from the prototype, whereas compiling a function definition will produce machine code.

■ RETURN VALUE OF FUNCTIONS

Defining and calling the function `area()`

```cpp
// area.cpp
// Example for a simple function returning a value.
//----------------------------------------------------
#include <iostream>
#include <iomanip>
using namespace std;

double area(double, double);          // Prototype

int main()
{
    double  x = 3.5, y = 7.2,  res;

    res = area( x, y+1);               // Call

   // To output to two decimal places:
    cout << fixed << setprecision(2);
    cout << "\n The area of a rectangle "
         << "\n with width  " << setw(5)  << x
         << "\n and length  " << setw(5) << y+1
         << "\n is          " << setw(5) << res
         << endl;
    return 0;
}

// Defining the function area():
// Computes the area of a rectangle.
double area( double width, double len)
{
    return (width * len);   // Returns the result.
}
```

Screen output:

```
The area of a rectangle
with width   3.50
and length   8.20
is          28.70
```

The program opposite shows how the function `area()` is defined and called. As previously mentioned, you must declare a function before calling it. The *prototype* provides the compiler with all the information it needs to perform the following actions when a function is called:

- check the number and type of the arguments
- correctly process the return value of the function.

A function declaration can be omitted only if the function is defined within the same source file immediately before it is called. Even though simple examples often define and call a function within a single source file, this tends to be an exception. Normally the compiler will not see a function definition as it is stored in a different source file.

When a function is called, an argument of the same type as the parameter must be passed to the function for each parameter. The arguments can be any kind of expressions, as the example opposite with the argument `y+1` shows. The value of the expression is always copied to the corresponding parameter.

☐ Return Statement

When the program flow reaches a *return statement* or the end of a function code block, it branches back to the function that called it. If the function is any type other than `void`, the `return` statement will also cause the function to return a value to the function that called it.

Syntax: `return [expression]`

If `expression` is supplied, the value of the expression will be the return value. If the type of this value does not correspond to the function type, the function type is converted, where possible. However, functions should always be written with the `return` value matching the function type.

The function `area()` makes use of the fact that the `return` statement can contain any expression. The `return` expression is normally placed in parentheses if it contains operators.

If the expression in the `return` statement, or the `return` statement itself, is missing, the return value of the function is undefined and the function type must be `void`. Functions of the `void` type, such as the standard function `srand()`, will perform an action but not return any value.

■ PASSING ARGUMENTS

Calling function and called function

```
long func2(int, double);          // Prototype
//  . . .
void func1()
{
   int x = 1.1;
   double y;
   . . .
   long a = func2(x,y);            // Call of func2().
   . . .
}                                  // Pass by value

         long func2(int a, double b) // Definition
         {
            double x = 2.2;
            long result;
            .               // Here the result
            .               // is computed.
            .
            return result;
         }
```

Stack content after calling a function

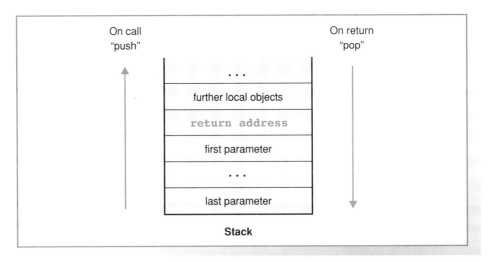

Stack

☐ Passing by Value

Passing values to a function when the function is called is referred to as *passing by value*. Of course the called function cannot change the values of the arguments in the calling function, as it uses copies of the arguments.

However, function arguments can also be *passed by reference*. In this case, the function is passed a reference to an object as an argument and can therefore access the object directly and modify it.

An example of passing by reference was provided in the example containing the function `time()`. When `time(&sek);` is called, the address of the variable `sek` is passed as an argument, allowing the function to store the result in the variable. We will see how to create functions of this type later.

Passing by value does, however, offer some important advantages:

- function arguments can be any kind of expression, even constants, for example
- the called function cannot cause accidental modifications of the arguments in the calling function
- the parameters are available as suitable variables within the functions. Additional indirect memory access is unnecessary.

However, the fact that copying larger objects is difficult can be a major disadvantage, and for this reason vectors are passed by reference to their starting address.

☐ Local Objects

The scope of function parameters and the objects defined within a function applies only to the function block. That is, they are valid within the function only and not related to any objects or parameters of the same name in any other functions.

For example, the program structure opposite contains a variable `a` in the function `func1()` and in the function `func2()`. The variables do not collide because they reference different memory addresses. This also applies to the variables `x` in `func1()` and `func2()`.

A function's local objects are placed on the *stack*—the parameters of the function are placed first and in reverse order. The stack is an area of memory that is managed according to the LIFO (*last in first out*) principle. A stack of plates is a good analogy. The last plate you put on the stack has to be taken off first. The LIFO principle ensures that the last local object to be created is destroyed first.

■ INLINE FUNCTIONS

Call to a function not defined as inline

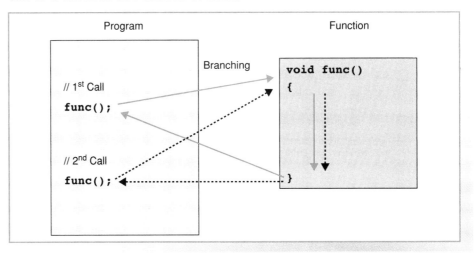

Call to an inline function

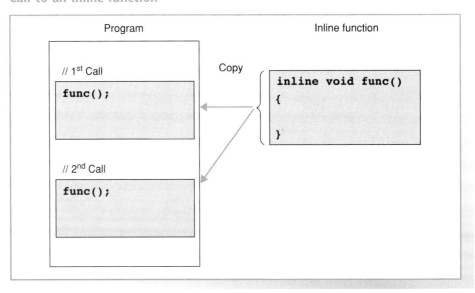

☐ Jumping to Sub-Routines

When a function is called, the program jumps to a *sub-routine*, which is executed as follows:

- the function parameters are placed on the stack and initialized with appropriate arguments
- the so-called *return address*, that is, the place where the function was called, is stored on the stack and the program flow branches to the function
- after executing the function the program uses the return address it stored previously to return to the calling function. The part of the stack occupied by the function is then released.

All this jumping back and forth can affect the run time of your program, especially if the function contains only a few instructions and is called quite often. The time taken to branch to a small function can be greater than the time needed to execute the function itself. However, you can define `inline` functions to avoid this problem.

☐ Inline Definition

The compiler inserts the code of an inline function at the address where the function is called and thus avoids jumping to a sub-routine. The *definition* of an inline function is introduced by the `inline` keyword in the function header.

Example:
```
inline int max( int x, int y)
{  return  (x >= y ? x : y );  }
```

The program code will expand each time an `inline` function is called. This is why `inline` functions should contain no more than one or two instructions. If an inline function contains too many instructions, the compiler may ignore the `inline` keyword and issue a warning.

An `inline` function must be defined in the source file in which it is called. You cannot simply supply a prototype of the function. The code containing the instructions must also be available to the compiler. It therefore makes sense to define `inline` functions in header files, in contrast to "normal" functions. This means the function will be available in several source files.

☐ Inline Functions and Macros

Inline functions are an alternative to macros with parameters. When a macro is called, the preprocessor simply replaces a block of text. In contrast, an `inline` function behaves like a normal function, although the program flow is not interrupted by the function branching. The compiler performs a type check, for example.

■ DEFAULT ARGUMENTS

Defining the function `capital()`

```
// Computes the final capital with interest and
// compound interest.
// Formula:  capital = k0 * (1.0 + p/100)^n
// where  k0 = start capital, p = rate, n = run time
// ---------------------------------------------------
 #include <math.h>
 double capital( double k0, double p, double n)
 {
    return (k0 * pow(1.0+p/100, n));
 }
```

Possible calls

```
// Function capital() with two default arguments
// Prototype:
double capital( double k0, double p=3.5, double n=1.0);

double endcap;

endcap = capital( 100.0, 3.5, 2.5);   // ok
endcap = capital( 2222.20, 4.8);      // ok
endcap = capital( 3030.00);           // ok

endcap = capital( );                  // not ok
// The first argument has no default value.

endcap = capital( 100.0, , 3.0);      // not ok
// No gap!

endcap = capital( , 5.0);             // not ok
// No gap either.
```

✓ **NOTE**

A function defined with default arguments is always called with the full number of arguments. For reasons of efficiency it may be useful to define several versions of the same function.

So-called *default arguments* can be defined for functions. This allows you to omit some arguments when calling the function. The compiler simply uses the default values for any missing arguments.

☐ Defining Default Arguments

The default values of a function's arguments must be known when the function is called. In other words, you need to supply them when you declare the function.

Example: `void moveTo( int x = 0, int y = 0);`

Parameter names can be omitted, as usual.

Example: `void moveTo( int = 0, int = 0);`

The function `moveTo()` can then be called with or without one or two arguments.

Example: `moveTo ();    moveTo (24); moveTo(24, 50);`

The first two calls are equivalent to `moveTo(0,0);` or `moveTo(24,0); .`
   It is also possible to define default arguments for only some of the parameters. The following general rules apply:

   ▪ the default arguments are defined in the function prototype. They can also be supplied when the function is defined, if the definition occurs in the same source file and before the function is called
   ▪ if you define a default argument for a parameter, all following parameters must have default arguments
   ▪ default arguments must not be redefined within the prototype scope (the next chapter gives more details on this topic).

☐ Possible Calls

When calling a function with default arguments you should pay attention to the following points:

   ▪ you must first supply any arguments that do not have default values
   ▪ you can supply arguments to replace the defaults
   ▪ if you omit an argument, you must also omit any following arguments.

You can use default arguments to call a function with a different number of arguments without having to write a new version of the function.

■ OVERLOADING FUNCTIONS

Sample program

```cpp
// random.cpp
// To generate and output random numbers.
//-------------------------------------------------------
#include <iostream>
#include <iomanip>
#include <cstdlib>      // For rand(), srand()
#include <ctime>        // For time()
using namespace std;

bool setrand = false;
inline void init_random()  // Initializes the random
{                          // number generator with the
                           // present time.
   if( !setrand )
   {  srand((unsigned int)time(NULL));
      setrand = true;
   }
}
inline double myRandom()      // Returns random number x
{                             // with  0.0 <= x <= 1.0
   init_random();
   return   (double)rand() / (double)RAND_MAX;
}
inline int myRandom(int start, int end)  // Returns the
{                                // random number n with
   init_random();               // start <= n <= end
   return (rand() % (end+1 - start) + start);
}

// Testing myRandom() and myRandom(int,int):
int main()
{
   int i;
   cout << "5 random numbers between 0.0 and 1.0 :"
        << endl;
   for( i = 0; i < 5; ++i)
      cout << setw(10) << myRandom();
   cout << endl;
   cout << "\nAnd now 5 integer random numbers "
           "between -100 and +100 :" << endl;
   for( i = 0; i < 5; ++i)
      cout << setw(10) << myRandom(-100, +100);
   cout << endl;
   return 0;
}
```

Functions in traditional programming languages, such as C, which perform the same task but have different arguments, must have different names. To define a function that calculated the maximum value of two integers and two floating-point numbers, you would need to program two functions with different names.

Example:
```
int    int_max( int x, int y);
double dbl_max( double x, double y);
```

Of course this is detrimental to efficient naming and the readability of your program—but luckily, this restriction does not apply to C++.

☐ Overloading

C++ allows you to overload functions, that is, different functions can have the same name.

Example:
```
int    max( int x, int y);
double max( double x, double y);
```

In our example two different function share the same name, `max`. The function `max()` was overloaded for `int` and `double` types. The compiler uses a function's signature to differentiate between overloaded functions.

☐ Function Signatures

A function signature comprises the number and type of parameters. When a function is called, the compiler compares the arguments to the signature of the overloaded functions and simply calls the appropriate function.

Example:
```
double maxvalue, value = 7.9;
maxvalue = max( 1.0, value);
```

In this case the `double` version of the function `max()` is called.

When overloaded functions are called, implicit type conversion takes place. However, this can lead to ambiguities, which in turn cause a compiler error to be issued.

Example:
```
maxvalue = max( 1, value);    // Error!
```

The signature does not contain the function type, since you cannot deduce the type by calling a function. It is therefore impossible to differentiate between overloaded functions by type.

Example:
```
int    search(string key);
string search(string name);
```

Both functions have the same signature and cannot be overloaded.

■ RECURSIVE FUNCTIONS

Using a recursive function

```cpp
// recursive.cpp
// Demonstrates the principle of recursion by a
// function, which reads a line from the keyboard
// and outputs it in reverse order.
// --------------------------------------------------
#include <iostream>
using namespace std;

void getput(void);

int main()
{
   cout << "Please enter a line of text:\n";
   getput();
   cout << "\nBye bye!" << endl;
   return 0;
}

void getput()
{
   char c;
   if( cin.get(c)   &&   c != '\n')
      getput();
   cout.put(c);
}
```

Program flow after typing ok<return>

	1st Execution	2nd Execution	3rd Execution

main()
{
   ...
   getput();
}
	getput()
	{
	   ...
	   // c = 'o'
	   getput();
	   cout.put(c);
	}
		getput()
		{
		   ...
		   // c = 'k'
		   getput();
		   cout.put(c);
		}
			getput()
			{
			   ...
			   // c = '\n'
			   // No call of
			   // getput()
			   cout.put(c);
			}

☐ Recursion

A function that calls itself is said to be *recursive*. This process can also be performed indirectly if the function first calls another function or multiple functions before it is called once more. But a break criterion is always necessary to avoid having the function call itself infinitely.

The concept of local objects makes it possible to define recursive functions in C++. Recursion requires local objects to be created each time the function is called, and these objects must not have access to any other local objects from other function calls. What effectively happens is that the local objects are placed on the stack, and thus the object created last is destroyed first.

☐ A Sample Program

Let's look at the principle of recursion by referring to the sample program opposite. The program contains the recursive function `getput()` that reads a line of text from the keyboard and outputs it in reverse order.

The function `getput()` is first called by `main()` and reads a character from the keyboard, storing it in the local variable `c`. If the character is not `'\n'`, the function `getput()` calls itself again and thus reads a further character from the keyboard before storing it in the local variable `c`.

The chain of recursive function calls is terminated by the user pressing the Return key. The last character to be read, `'\n'` (line feed), is output and the program flow branches to the previous `getput()` instance. This outputs the second to last character, and so on. When the first character to have been read has finally been output, the program flow is handed back to `main()`.

☐ Practical Usage

The logic of various solutions to common problems results in a recursive structure, for example, browsing directory trees, using binary trees for data management, or some sorting algorithms, such as the quick sort algorithm. Recursive functions allow you to formulate this kind of logic in an efficient and elegant manner. However, always make sure that sufficient memory is available for the stack.

exercises

■ EXERCISES

Working with several source files:

Within an integrated development environment a project, containing all source files of the program, first has to be created. This ensures that all the source files will be compiled and linked automatically.

However, when calling the compiler/linker from the command line, it is sufficient to declare the source files, for example:

```
cc  sum_t.cpp  sum.cpp
```

Screen output for exercise 3

n	Factorial of n
0	1
1	1
2	2
3	6
4	24
5	120
6	720
7	5040
.	. . .
.	. . . .
.	. . . . . .
19	121645100408832000
20	2432902008176640000

Exercise 1

a. Write the function `sum()` with four parameters that calculates the arguments provided and returns their sum.

    Parameters: Four variables of type `long`.

    Returns: The sum of type `long`.

    Use the default argument 0 to declare the last two parameter of the function `sum()`. Test the function `sum()` by calling it by all three possible methods. Use random integers as arguments.

b. Now restructure your program to store the functions `main()` and `sum()` in individual source files, for example, `sum_t.cpp` and `sum.cpp` .

Exercise 2

a. Write an `inline` function, `Max(double x, double y)`, which returns the maximum value of `x` and `y`. (Use `Max` instead of `max` to avoid a collision with other definitions of `max`.) Test the function by reading values from the keyboard.

    Can the function `Max()` also be called using arguments of the types `char`, `int`, or `long`?

b. Now overload `Max()` by adding a further `inline` function `Max(char x, char y)` for arguments of type `char` .

    Can the function `Max()` still be called with two arguments of type `int`?

Exercise 3

The *factorial* `n!` of a positive integer `n` is defined as

```
n! = 1*2*3 . . . * (n-1) * n
```
Where   `0! = 1`

Write a function to calculate the factorial of a number.

Argument: A number n of type `unsigned int`.
Returns: The factorial `n!` of type `long double`.

Formulate two versions of the function, where the factorial is

a. calculated using a loop
b. calculated recursively

Test both functions by outputting the factorials of the numbers 0 to 20 as shown opposite on screen.

Exercise 4

Write a function `pow(double base, int exp)` to calculate integral powers of floating-point numbers.

Arguments: The base of type `double` and the exponent of type `int`.
Returns: The power base^{exp} of type `double`.

For example, calling `pow(2.5, 3)` returns the value

$$2.5^3 \;=\; 2.5 * 2.5 * 2.5 \;=\; 15.625$$

This definition of the function `pow()` means overloading the standard function `pow()`, which is called with two `double` values.

Test your function by reading one value each for the base and the exponent from the keyboard. Compare the result of your function with the result of the standard function.

✓ NOTE

1. The power x^0 is defined as `1.0` for a given number `x`.
2. The power x^n is defined as $(1/x)^{-n}$ for a negative exponent `n`.
3. The power 0^n where `n > 0` will always yield `0.0`.

   The power 0^n is not defined for `n < 0`. In this case, your function should return the value `HUGE_VAL`. This constant is defined in `math.h` and represents a large `double` value. Mathematical functions return `HUGE_VAL` when the result is too large for a `double`.

■ SOLUTIONS

Exercise 1

```cpp
// -------------------------------------------------------
// sum_t.cpp
// Calls function sum() with default arguments.
// -------------------------------------------------------

#include <iostream>
#include <iomanip>
#include <ctime>
#include <cstdlib>
using namespace std;

long sum( long a1, long a2, long a3=0, long a4=0);

int main()                   // Several calls to function sum()
{
   cout << "  **** Computing sums  ****\n"
        << endl;

   srand((unsigned int)time(NULL));  // Initializes the
                                     // random number generator.
   long res, a = rand()/10, b = rand()/10,
           c = rand()/10, d = rand()/10;

   res = sum(a,b);
   cout << a << " + " << b << " = " << res << endl;

   res = sum(a,b,c);
   cout << a << " + " << b << " + " << c
        << " = " << res << endl;

   res = sum(a,b,c,d);
   cout << a << " + " << b << " + " << c << " + " << d
        << " = " << res << endl;

   return 0;
}
// -------------------------------------------------------
// sum.cpp
// Defines the function sum()
// -------------------------------------------------------

long sum( long a1, long a2, long a3, long a4)
{
   return (a1 + a2 + a3 + a4);
}
```

Exercise 2

```cpp
// ---------------------------------------------------
// max.cpp
// Defines and calls the overloaded functions Max().
// ---------------------------------------------------

// As long as just one function Max() is defined, it can
// be called with any arguments that can be converted to
// double, i.e. with values of type char, int or long.
// After overloading no clear conversion will be possible.

#include <iostream>
#include <string>
using namespace std;

inline double Max(double x, double y)
{
   return (x < y ? y : x);
}

inline char Max(char x, char y)
{
   return (x < y ? y : x);
}

string header(
        "To use the overloaded function Max().\n"),
      line(50,'-');

int main()     // Several different calls to function Max()
{
   double x1 = 0.0, x2 = 0.0;

   line += '\n';
   cout << line << header << line << endl;

   cout << "Enter two floating-point numbers:"
       << endl;
   if( cin >> x1  &&  cin >> x2)
   {
      cout << "The greater number is " << Max(x1,x2)
           << endl;
   }
   else
      cout << "Invalid input!" << endl;

   cin.sync(); cin.clear();   // Invalid input
                              // was entered.
```

```
    cout << line
        << "And once more with characters!"
        << endl;

    cout << "Enter two characters:"
        << endl;

    char c1, c2;
    if( cin >> c1  &&  cin >> c2)
    {
        cout << "The greater character is " << Max(c1,c2)
            << endl;
    }
    else
        cout << "Invalid input!" << endl;

    cout << "Testing with int arguments." << endl;
    int  a = 30, b = 50;
    cout << Max(a,b) << endl;        // Error! Which
                                     // function Max()?

    return 0;
}
```

Exercise 3

```
// ----------------------------------------------------
// factorial.cpp
// Computes the factorial of an integer iteratively,
// i.e. using a loop, and recursively.
// ----------------------------------------------------
#include <iostream>
#include <iomanip>
using namespace std;

#define N_MAX   20

long double fact1(unsigned int n);  // Iterative solution
long double fact2(unsigned int n);  // Recursive solution

int main()
{
    unsigned int n;

    // Outputs floating-point values without
    // decimal places:
    cout << fixed << setprecision(0);
```

```cpp
        // ---  Iterative computation of factorial  ---

        cout << setw(10) << "n" << setw(30) << "Factorial of n"
             << "              (Iterative solution)\n"
             << "       --------------------------------------"
             << endl;

        for( n = 0; n <= N_MAX;  ++n)
           cout << setw(10) << n << setw(30) << fact1(n)
                << endl;

        cout << "\nGo on with <return>";
        cin.get();

        // ---  Recursive computation of factorial  ----

        cout << setw(10) << "n" << setw(30) << "Factorial of n"
             << "              (Recursive solution)\n"
             << "       --------------------------------------"
             << endl;

        for( n = 0; n <= N_MAX;  ++n)
           cout << setw(10) << n << setw(30) << fact2(n)
                << endl;

        cout << endl;

        return 0;
}

long double fact1(unsigned int n)        // Iterative
{                                        // solution.
   long double result = 1.0;
   for( unsigned int i = 2; i <= n; ++i)
      result *= i;

   return result;
}

long double fact2(unsigned int n)        // Recursive
{                                        // solution.
   if( n <= 1)
      return 1.0;
   else
      return fact2(n-1) * n;
}
```

Exercise 4

```cpp
// ----------------------------------------------------
// power.cpp
// Defines and calls the function pow() to
// compute integer powers of a floating-point number.
// Overloads the standard function pow().
// ----------------------------------------------------
#include <iostream>
#include <cmath>
using namespace std;

double pow(double base, int exp);

int main()      // Tests the self-defined function pow()
{
   double base    = 0.0;
   int    exponent = 0;

   cout << "  **** Computing Integer Powers ****\n"
        << endl;

   cout << "Enter test values.\n"
        << "Base (floating-point): ";  cin >> base;
   cout << "Exponent (integer):      ";  cin >> exponent;

   cout << "Result of " << base << " to the power of "
        << exponent << " = " << pow( base, exponent)
        << endl;

   cout << "Computing with the standard function: "
        << pow( base, (double)exponent) << endl;
   return 0;
}
double pow(double base, int exp)
{
    if( exp == 0)       return 1.0;
    if( base == 0.0)
        if( exp > 0)  return 0.0;
        else           return HUGE_VAL;
    if( exp < 0)
    {
       base = 1.0 / base;
       exp = -exp;
    }
    double power = 1.0;
    for( int n = 1; n <= exp; ++n)
        power *= base;
    return power;
}
```

chapter 11

Storage Classes and Namespaces

This chapter begins by describing storage classes for objects and functions. The storage class is responsible for defining those parts of a program where an object or function can be used. Namespaces can be used to avoid conflicts when naming global identifiers.

■ STORAGE CLASSES OF OBJECTS

☐ Availability of Objects

C++ program

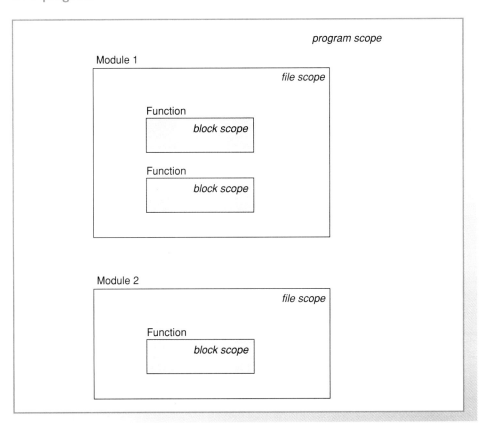

☐ Storage Class Specifiers

The storage class of an object is determined by

- the position of its declaration in the source file
- the storage class specifier, which can be supplied optionally.

The following storage class specifiers can be used

extern   static   auto   register

When an object is declared, not only are the object's type and name defined but also its *storage class*. The storage class specifies the *lifetime* of the object, that is, the period of time from the construction of the object until its destruction. In addition, the storage class delimits the part of the program in which the object can be accessed directly by its name, the so-called object *scope*.

Essentially, an object is only available after you have declared it within a *translation unit*. A translation unit, also referred to as *module*, comprises the source file you are compiling and any header files you have included.

As a programmer, you can define an object with:

▪ block scope	The object is only available in the code block in which it was defined. The object is no longer visible once you have left the code block.
▪ file scope	The object can be used within a *single* module. Only the functions within this module can reference the object. Other modules cannot access the object directly.
▪ program scope	The object is available throughout the program, providing a common space in memory that can be referenced by any program function. For this reason, these objects are often referred to as *global*.

Access to an object as defined by the object's storage class is independent of any access controls for the elements of a class. Namespaces that subdivide program scope and classes will be introduced at a later stage.

☐ Lifetime

Objects with block scope are normally created automatically within the code block that defines them. Such objects can only be accessed by statements within that block and are called *local* to that block. The memory used for these objects is freed after leaving the code block. In this case, the lifetime of the objects is said to be *automatic*.

However, it is possible to define objects with block scope that are available throughout the runtime of a program. The lifetime of these objects is said to be *static*. When the program flow re-enters a code block, any pre-existing conditions will apply.

Objects with program and file scope are always static. These objects are created when a program is launched and are available until the program is terminated.

Four storage classes are available for creating objects with the scope and lifetime you need. These storage classes will be discussed individually in the following sections.

■ THE STORAGE CLASS extern

Source file 1

```
// Cutline1.cpp
// A filter to remove white-space characters
// at the ends of lines.
// -------------------------------------------------
#include <iostream>
#include <string>
using namespace std;

void cutline( void );          // Prototype
string line;                   // Global string

int main()
{
   while( getline(cin, line)) // As long as a line
   {                          // can be read.
     cutline();               // Shorten the line.
     cout << line << endl;    // Output the line.
   }
   return 0;
}
```

Source file 2

```
// Cutline2.cpp
// Containing the function cutline(), which removes
// tabulator characters at the end of the string line.
// The string line has to be globally defined in another
// source file.
// -------------------------------------------------

#include <string>
using namespace std;

extern string line;                 // extern declaration

void cutline()
{
   int i = line.size();        // Position after the
                               // last character.
   while( i-- >= 0 )
     if(   line[i] != ' '      // If no blank and
        && line[i] != '\t' )   // no tab ->
       break;                  // stop the loop.

   line.resize(++i);           // Fix new length.
}
```

☐ Defining Global Objects

If an object is not defined within a function, it belongs to the *extern* storage class. Objects in this storage class have program scope and can be read and, provided they have not been defined as `const`, modified at any place in the program. External objects thus allow you to exchange information between any functions without passing any arguments. To demonstrate this point, the program on the opposite page has been divided into two separate source files. The string `line`, which has a global definition, is used to exchange data.

Global objects that are not explicitly initialized during definition receive an initial value of 0 (that is, all bits = 0) by default. This also applies to objects belonging to class types, if not otherwise stipulated by the class.

☐ Using Global Objects

An object belonging to the `extern` storage class is initially only available in the source file where it was defined. If you need to use an object before defining it or in another module, you must first declare the object. If you do not declare the object, the compiler issues a message stating that the object is unknown. The declaration makes the name and type of the object known to the compiler.

In contrast to a definition, the storage class identifier `extern` precedes the object name in a declaration.

Example: `extern long position;     // Declaration`

This statement declares `position` as an external object of type `long`. The `extern` declaration thus allows you to "import" an object from another source file.

A global object must be defined once, and once only, in a program. However, it can be declared as often as needed and at any position in the program. You will normally declare the object before the first function in a source file or in a header file that you can include when needed. This makes the object available to any functions in the file. Remember, if you declare the object within a code block, the object can only be used within the same block.

An `extern` declaration only refers to an object and should therefore not be used to initialize the object. If you do initialize the object, you are defining that object!

 NOTE

Global objects affect the whole program and should be used sparingly. Large programs in particular should contain no more than a few central objects defined as `extern`.

■ THE STORAGE CLASS static

```cpp
// Passw1.cpp
// The functions getPassword() and timediff()
// to read and examine a password.
// -------------------------------------------------------
#include <iostream>
#include <iomanip>
#include <string>
#include <ctime>
using namespace std;

long timediff(void);                        // Prototype
static string secret = "ISUS";              // Password
static long  maxcount = 3, maxtime = 60;    // Limits

bool getPassword()      // Enters and checks a password.
{               // Return value: true, if password is ok.
   bool ok_flag = false;        // For return value
   string word;                 // For input
   int count = 0, time = 0;
   timediff();                  // To start the stop watch
   while( ok_flag != true &&
          ++count <= maxcount)    // Number of attempts
   {
      cout << "\n\nInput the password:  ";
      cin.sync();               // Clear input buffer
      cin >> setw(20) >> word;
      time += timediff();
      if( time >= maxtime )      // Within time limit?
         break;                  // No!
      if( word != secret)
         cout << "Invalid password!" << endl;
      else
         ok_flag = true;         // Give permission
   }
   return ok_flag;               // Result
}

long timediff()         // Returns the number of
{                       // seconds after the last call.
   static long  sec = 0;      // Time of last call.
   long  oldsec = sec;        // Saves previous time.
   time( &sec);               // Reads new time.
   return (sec - oldsec);     // Returns the difference.
}
```

☐ Static Objects

If an object definition is preceded by the `static` keyword, the object belongs to the *static storage class*.

Example: `static int count;`

The most important characteristic of static objects is their *static* (or permanent) lifetime. Static objects are not placed on the stack, but are stored in the data area of a program just like external objects.

However, in contrast to external objects, access to static objects is restricted. Two conditions apply, depending on where the object is defined:

1. **Definition external to all program functions**

   In this case, the object is *external static*, that is, the object can be designated using its name within the module only, but will not collide with any objects using the same name in other modules.

 NOTE

In contrast to objects with an `extern` definition, the name of an external static object is unknown to the linker and thus retains its private nature within a module.

2. **Definition within a code block**

   This means that the object is *internal static*, that is, the object is only visible within a single block. However, the object is created only once and is not destroyed on leaving the block. On re-entering the block, you can continue to work with the original object.

The same rules apply to initializing static objects as they do to external objects. If the object is not initialized explicitly, a default value of 0 applies.

☐ Notes on the Sample Programs Opposite

The function `getPassword()` checks a password that is entered. Permission is refused following three unsuccessful attempts or when 60 seconds have elapsed. You could use the following instructions to call the function in another source file:

Example:
```
if( !getPassword() )
     cout << "No authorization!\n"; exit(1);
```

The string `secret` and the thresholds `maxcount` and `maxtime` are external static, whereas the variable `sec` in the function `timediff()` is internal static. Its value is zero only when the function is first called.

It makes sense to add a further function to these source files providing for password changes.

■ THE SPECIFIERS auto AND register

Sample function with a register variable

```cpp
// StrToL.cpp
// The function strToLong() converts a string containing
// a leading integer into an integer of type long.
// Argument:      A string.
// Return value: An integer of type long.
// --------------------------------------------------
// The digits are interpreted with base 10. White spaces
// and a sign can precede the sequence of digits.
// The conversion terminates when the end of the string is
// reached or when a character that cannot be converted is
// reached.
// --------------------------------------------------

#include <string>           // Type string
#include <cctype>           // isspace() and isdigit()
using namespace std;

long strToLong( string str)
{
   register int i = 0;            // Index
   long vz = 1, num = 0;          // Sign and number

   // Ignore leading white spaces.
   for(i=0; i < str.size() && isspace(str[i]); ++i)
       ;

   // Is there a sign?
   if( i < str.size())
   {
       if( str[i] == '+' ) { vz = 1;   ++i; }
       if( str[i] == '-' ) { vz = ---1; ++i; }
   }

   // Sequence of digits -> convert to integer
   for( ; i < str.size() && isdigit(str[i]); ++i)
      num = num * 10 + (str[i] - '0');

   return vz * num;
}
```

☐ auto **Objects**

The storage class auto (automatic) includes all those objects defined within a function but without the static keyword. The parameters of a function are also auto objects. You *can* use the auto keyword during a definition.

Example: auto float radius; // Equivalent to:
                            // float radius;

When the program flow reaches the definition, the object is created on the stack, but in contrast to a static type object, the object is destroyed on leaving the block.

auto objects have no specific initial value if they are not initialized explicitly. However, objects belonging to a class type are normally initialized with default values, which can be specified in the class definition.

☐ **Using CPU Registers**

To increase the speed of a program, commonly used auto variables can be stored in CPU *registers* instead of on the stack. In this case, the register keyword is used to declare the object.

A register is normally the size of an int variable. In other words, it only makes sense to define register variables if the variable is not too large, as in the case of types such as char, short, int or pointers. If you omit the type when defining a register variable, an int is assumed.

However, the compiler can ignore the register keyword. The number of registers available for register variables depends on your hardware, although two registers are normally available. If a program defines too many register variables in a code block, the superfluous variables are placed in the auto storage class.

☐ **Sample Function**

The function strToLong() illustrates an algorithm that converts a sequence of digits to a binary number. This is useful if you need to perform calculations with a number contained in a string.

The algorithm using the string "37" and the long variable num:

Step 0:   num = 0;
Step 1:   1st character '3' → number 3 = ('3'-'0')
              num = num * 10 + 3;   // = 3
Step 2:   2nd character '7' → number 7 = ('7'-'0')
              num = num * 10 + 7;   // = 37

This pattern is followed for every number in a longer string.

▪ THE STORAGE CLASSES OF FUNCTIONS

☐ Example of a Program Structure

Source file 1

```
extern bool getPassword(void);        // Prototype

int main()
{
   // The function permission(),
   // but not the function timediff()
   // can be called here.
      .
      .
      .
}
```

Source file 2

```
static long timediff(void);       // Prototype

bool getPassword(void)            // Definition
{
    // timediff() can be called here.
        .
        .
        .
}

static long timediff(void)        // Definition
{
        .
        .
        .
}
```

Only two storage classes are available for functions: `extern` and `static`. Functions with block scope are invalid: you cannot define a function within another function.

The storage class of a function defines access to the function, as it does for an object. External functions have program scope, whereas static functions have file scope.

☐ External Functions

If the keyword `static` is not used when defining a function, the function must belong to the `extern` storage class.

In a similar manner to external objects, external functions can be used at any position in a program. If you need to call a function before defining it, or in another source file, you will need to declare that function.

Example: `extern bool getPassword(void); // Prototype`

As previously seen, you can omit the `extern` keyword, since functions belong to the `extern` storage class by default.

☐ Static Functions

To define a static function, simply place the keyword `static` before the function header.

Example:
```
static long timediff()
        {  . . .  }
```

Functions in the `static` storage class have "private" character: they have file scope, just like external static objects. They can only be called in the source file that defines them. The name of a `static` function will not collide with objects and functions of the same name in other modules.

If you need to call a `static` function before defining it, you must first declare the function in the source file.

Example: `static long timediff( void );`

The program structure opposite takes up the example with the functions `getPassword()` and `timediff()` once more. The function `timediff()` is an auxiliary function and not designed to be called externally. The function is declared as `static` for this reason.

■ NAMESPACES

Defining namespaces

```cpp
// namesp1.cpp
// Defines and tests namespaces.
// ----------------------------------------------------
#include <string>           // Class string defined within
                            // namespace std
namespace MySpace
{
   std::string mess = "Within namespace MySpace";
   int count = 0;          // Definition: MySpace::count
   double f( double);       // Prototype:   MySpace::f()
}
namespace YourSpace
{
   std::string mess = "Within namespace YourSpace";
   void f( )                     // Definition of
   {                             // YourSpace::f()
     mess += '!';
   }
}
namespace MySpace                     // Back in MySpace.
{
   int g(void);             // Prototype of MySpace::g()
   double f( double y)             // Definition of
   {                              // MySpace::f()
     return y / 10.0;
   }
}
int MySpace::g( )                  // Separate definition
{                                  // of MySpace::g()
   return ++count;
}

#include <iostream>   // cout, ... within namespace std
int main()
{
  std::cout << "Testing namespaces!\n\n"
            << MySpace::mess << std::endl;
  MySpace::g();
  std::cout << "\nReturn value g(): " << MySpace::g()
            << "\nReturn value f(): " << MySpace::f(1.2)
            << "\n--------------------" << std::endl;
  YourSpace::f();
  std::cout << YourSpace::mess << std::endl;
  return 0;
}
```

Using global names in large-scale software projects can lead to conflicts, especially when multiple class libraries are in operation.

C++ provides for the use of namespaces in order to avoid naming conflicts with global identifiers. Within a namespace, you can use identifiers without needing to check whether they have been defined previously in an area outside of the namespace. Thus, the global scope is subdivided into isolated parts.

A normal namespace is identified by a name preceded by the `namespace` keyword. The elements that belong to the namespace are then declared within braces.

Example:
```
namespace myLib
{
    int count;
    double calculate(double, int);
    // . . .
}
```

This example defines the namespace `myLib` that contains the variable `count` and the function `calculate()`.

Elements belonging to a namespace can be referenced directly by name *within* the namespace. If you need to reference an element from *outside* of the namespace, you must additionally supply the namespace. To do so, place the scope resolution operator, `::`, before the element name.

Example:
```
myLib::count = 7;       // Outside of myLib
```

This allows you to distinguish between identical names in different namespaces. You can also use the scope resolution operator `::` to reference global names, that is, names declared outside of any namespaces. To do so, simply omit the name of the namespace. This technique is useful when you need to access a global name that is hidden by an identical name defined in the current namespace.

Example:
```
::demo();   // Not belonging to any namespace
```

Be aware of the following when using namespaces:

- namespaces do not need to be defined contiguously. You can reopen and expand a namespace you defined previously at any point in the program
- namespaces can be nested, that is, you can define a namespace within another namespace.

Global identifiers belonging to the C++ standard library automatically belong to the *standard namespace* `std`.

■ THE KEYWORD using

Sample program

```cpp
// namesp2.cpp
// Demonstrates the use of using-declarations and
// using-directives.
// -------------------------------------------------
#include <iostream>        // Namespace std

void message()             // Global function ::message()
{
   std::cout << "Within function ::message()\n";
}

namespace A
{
   using namespace std; // Names of std are visible here
   void message()          // Function A::message()
   {
     cout << "Within function A::message()\n";
   }
}

namespace B
{
   using std::cout;        // Declaring cout of std.
   void message(void);     // Function B::message()
}
void B::message(void)      // Defining B::message()
{
   cout << "Within function B::message()\n";
}

int main()
{
   using namespace std;   // Names of namespace std
   using B::message;       // Function name without
                           // braces!
   cout << "Testing namespaces!\n";
   cout << "\nCall of A::message()" << endl;
   A::message();
   cout << "\nCall of B::message()" << endl;
   message();              // ::message() is hidden because
                           // of the using-declaration.
   cout << "\nCall of::message()" << endl;
   ::message();                // Global function
   return 0;
}
```

You can simplify access to the elements of a namespace by means of a *using declaration* or *using directive*. In this case, you do not need to repeatedly quote the namespace. Just like normal declarations, using declarations and using directives can occur at any part of the program.

☐ using **Declarations**

A using declaration makes an identifier from a namespace visible in the current scope.

Example: `using myLib::calculate;    // Declaration`

You can then call the function `calculate()` from the `myLib` namespace.

```
double erg = calculate( 3.7, 5);
```

This assumes that you have not previously used the name `calculate` in the same scope.

☐ using **Directive**

The *using directive* allows you to import *all* the identifiers in a namespace.

Example: `using namespace myLib;`

This statement allows you to reference the identifiers in the `myLib` namespace directly. If `myLib` contains an additional namespace and a using directive, this namespace is also imported.

   If identical identifiers occur in the current namespace and an imported namespace, the using directive does not automatically result in a conflict. However, referencing an identifier can lead to ambiguities. In this case, you should use the scope resolution operator to resolve the situation.

   C++ header files without file extensions are used to declare the global identifiers in the standard namespace `std`. The using directive was used in previous examples to import any required identifiers to the global scope:

Example: `#include <string>`
          `using namespace std;`

When developing large-scale programs or libraries, it is useful to declare the elements of any proprietary namespaces in header files. Normal source files are used to define these elements.

■ EXERCISES

Program listing for exercise 1

```
// scope.cpp
// Accessing objects with equal names
// ----------------------------------------------------

#include <iostream>
#include <iomanip>
using namespace std;

int var = 0;

namespace Special {   int var = 100; }

int main()
{
   int var = 10;
   cout << setw(10) << var;                     // 1.
   {
      int var = 20;
      cout << setw(10) << var << endl;          // 2.
      {
        ++var;
        cout << setw(10) << var;                // 3.
        cout << setw(10) << ++ ::var;           // 4.
        cout << setw(10) << Special::var * 2    // 5.
              << endl;
      }
        cout << setw(10) << var - ::var;        // 6.
   }
   cout << setw(10) << var << endl;             // 7.

   return 0;
}
```

Exercise 1

In general, you should use different names for different objects. However, if you define a name for an object within a code block and the name is also valid for another object, you will reference only the new object within the code block. The new declaration hides any object using the same name outside of the block. When you leave the code block, the original object once more becomes visible.

The program on the opposite page uses identical variable names in different blocks. What does the program output on screen?

Exercise 2

You are developing a large-scale program and intend to use two commercial libraries, `tool1` and `tool2`. The names of types, functions, macros, and so on are declared in the header files `tool1.h` and `tool2.h` for users of these libraries.

Unfortunately, the libraries use the same global names in part. In order to use both libraries, you will need to define namespaces.
Write the following program to simulate this situation:

- Define an inline function called `calculate()` that returns the sum of two numbers for the header file `tool1.h`. The function interface is as follows:

  ```
  double calculate(double num1, double num2);
  ```

- Define an inline function called `calculate()` that returns the product of two numbers for a second header file `tool2.h`. This function has the same interface as the function in `tool1.h`.

- Then write a source file containing a `main` function that calls both functions with test values and outputs the results.

  To resolve potential naming conflicts, define the namespaces `TOOL1` and `TOOL2` that include the relevant header files.

Program listing for exercise 3

```cpp
// static.cpp
// Tests an internal static variable
// ---------------------------------------------------
#include <iostream>
#include <iomanip>
using namespace std;

double x = 0.5,
       fun(void);

int main()
{
   while( x < 10.0 )
   {
      x += fun();
      cout << "     Within main(): "
           << setw(5) << x << endl;
   }
   return 0;
}

double fun()
{
   static double x = 0;

   cout << "     Within fun():"
        << setw(5) << x++;
   return x;
}
```

Exercise 3

Test your knowledge of external and static variables by reference to the program on the opposite page. What screen output does the program generate?

Exercise 4

a. The function getPassword(), which checks password input, was introduced previously as an example of the use of static variables. Modify the source file Passw1.cpp, which contains the function getPassword(), by adding the function changePassword(). This function allows the user to change his or her password. Save the modified source file as Passw2.cpp.

b. A large-scale program with several users is used to perform bookings. Only authorized users, that is, users that have access to the password, are allowed to perform bookings.

In the initial stages of program development, you need to test the functionality of the source file, Passw2.cpp. To do so, create a new source file with a main function that contains only the following menu items in its main loop:

```
B = Booking
E = End of program
```

When B is typed, the password is first checked. If the user enters the correct password, he or she can change the password. The program does not need to perform any real bookings.

NOTE

The modified password is only available during runtime as it is not stored permanently.

SOLUTIONS

Exercise 1

Screen output of the program

```
10          20
21           1           200
20          10
```

Exercise 2

```cpp
// ----------------------------------------------------
// tool1.h
// Defining first function calculate() inline.
// ----------------------------------------------------

#ifndef _TOOL1_H_
#define _TOOL1_H_

inline double calculate( double num1, double num2)
{
   return num1 + num2;
}

#endif  // End of _TOOL1_H_

// ----------------------------------------------------
// tool2.h
// Defining second function calculate() inline.
// ----------------------------------------------------

#ifndef _TOOL2_H_
#define _TOOL2_H_

inline double calculate( double num1, double num2)
{
   return num1 * num2;
}

#endif  // End of _TOOL2_H_
```

```
// -----------------------------------------------------
// tool_1_2.cpp
// Uses two "libraries" and tests name lookup conflicts.
// -----------------------------------------------------

#include <iostream>

namespace TOOL1
{
  #include "tool1.h"
}
namespace TOOL2
{
  #include "tool2.h"
}

#include <iostream>
int main()
{
   using namespace std;
   double x = 0.5, y = 10.5, res = 0.0;

   cout << "Calling function of Tool1!" << endl;
   res = TOOL1::calculate( x, y);
   cout << "Result:   " << res
        << "\n-------------------------------" << endl;

   cout << "Calling function of Tool2!" << endl;
   res = TOOL2::calculate( x, y);
   cout << "Result:   " << res << endl;

   return 0;
}
```

Exercise 3

Screen output of the program

```
In fun():    0     In main():    1.5
In fun():    1     In main():    3.5
In fun():    2     In main():    6.5
In fun():    3     In main():   10.5
```

Exercise 4

```
// ----------------------------------------------------
// Passw2.cpp
// Defines the functions getPassword(), timediff() and
// changePassword() to examine and change a password.
// ----------------------------------------------------
#include <iostream>
#include <iomanip>
#include <string>
#include <ctime>
using namespace std;

static long timediff(void);              // Prototype
static string secret = "guest";          // Password
static long  maxcount = 3, maxtime = 60; // Limits

bool getPassword()  // Read and verify a password.
{
   // As before.
   // . . .
}

// Auxiliary function timediff() --> defining static
static long timediff()   // Returns the number of seconds
{                        // since the last call.
   // As before.
   // . . .
}

bool changePassword()    // Changes password.
{                        // Returns: true, if the
                         // password has been changed
   string word1,word2;        // For input

   // To read a new password

   cout <<"\nEnter a new password (2 - 20 characters): ";
   cin.sync();                    // Discards former input
   cin >> setw(20) >> word1;
```

```
      if( word1.size() > 1)
      {
         cout << "\nEnter the password once more: ";
         cin >> setw(20) >> word2;
         if( word1 == word2)        // Password confirmed?
         {                          // Yes!
            secret = word1;
            return true;
         }
      }
      return false;               // No new password
}

// --------------------------------------------------------
// Password.cpp
// Testing the functions getPassword() and
// changePassword().
//
// After entering the password correctly (max. three
// attempts within 60 seconds), the user can change it.
// --------------------------------------------------------
#include <iostream>
#include <iomanip>
#include <string>
#include <cctype>
using namespace std;

bool getPassword(void);           // Read a password.
bool changePassword(void);        // Change a password.
// Inline functions:
inline void cls()  { cout << "\033[2J"; }
inline void go_on()
{
   cout << "\n\nGo on with return! ";
   cin.sync();  cin.clear();        // Only new input
   while( cin.get() != '\n')
        ;
}
inline char getYesOrNo()    // Read character Y or N.
{
   char c = 0;
   cin.sync();  cin.clear();         // Just new input
   do
   {
     cin.get(c);
     c = toupper(c); // Permitting lower case letters also.
   }
   while( c != 'Y'  && c != 'N');
   return c;
}
```

```
static string header =
"\n\n      ****  Test password handling  ****\n\n";

static string menu =
"\n\n              B = Booking "
"\n\n              E = End of program"
"\n\n Your choice:    ";

int main()
{
   char choice = 0;
   while( choice != 'E')
   {
     cls();   cout << header << menu;  // Header and Menu
     cin.get(choice);   choice = toupper(choice);
     cls();   cout << header << endl;  // Header
     switch( choice)
     {
       case 'B':                      // Booking
         if( !getPassword() )
         {
            cout << "Access denied!" << endl;
            go_on();
         }
         else
         { cout << "Welcome!\n\n"
            << "Do you want to change the password? (y/n)";
         if( getYesOrNo() == 'Y')
            {
              if( changePassword() )
                cout << "Password changed!" << endl;
              else
                cout << "Password unchanged!" << endl;
              go_on();
            }
            // Place statements for booking here.
         }
         break;
       case 'E':
         cls();  cout << "\n    Bye Bye!" << endl;
         break;
     }
   } // End of while
   return 0;
}
```

References and Pointers

This chapter describes how to define references and pointers and how to use them as parameters and/or return values of functions. In this context, passing by reference and read-only access to arguments are introduced.

■ DEFINING REFERENCES

Example

```
float x = 10.7,   &rx = x;
```

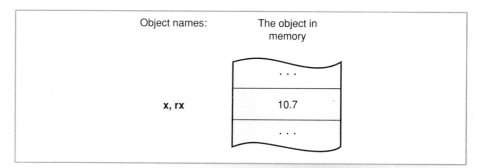

Sample program

```cpp
// Ref1.cpp
// Demonstrates the definition and use of references.
// -------------------------------------------------
#include <iostream>
#include <string>
using namespace std;

float x = 10.7F;                           // Global

int main()
{
   float   &rx = x;            // Local reference to x
// double &ref = x;            // Error: different type!

   rx *= 2;

   cout << "    x = " <<   x << endl     //  x = 21.4
        << "   rx = " << rx << endl;     // rx = 21.4
   const float& cref = x;      // Read-only reference
   cout << "cref = " <<   cref << endl;    // ok!
// ++cref;                       // Error: read-only!
   const string str = "I am a constant string!";
// str = "That doesn't work!";  // Error: str constant!
// string& text = str;          // Error: str constant!
   const string& text = str;    // ok!
   cout << text << endl;        // ok! Just reading.
   return 0;
}
```

A reference is another name, or alias, for an object that already exists. Defining a reference does not occupy additional memory. Any operations defined for the reference are performed with the object to which it refers. References are particularly useful as parameters and return values of functions.

☐ Definition

The ampersand character, &, is used to define a reference. Given that T is a type, T& denotes a reference to T.

Example:
```
float x = 10.7;
float& rx = x;   // or:  float &rx = x;
```

rx is thus a different way of expressing the variable x and belongs to the type "reference to float". Operations with rx, such as

Example:
```
--rx;              // equivalent to  --x;
```

will automatically affect the variable x. The & character, which indicates a reference, only occurs in declarations and is not related to the address operator &! The address operator returns the address of an object. If you apply this operator to a reference, it returns the address of the referenced object.

Example:
```
&rx    // Address of x, thus is equal to &x
```

A reference must be *initialized* when it is declared, and cannot be modified subsequently. In other words, you cannot use the reference to address a different variable at a later stage.

☐ Read-Only References

A reference that addresses a constant object must be a constant itself, that is, it must be defined using the const keyword to avoid modifying the object by reference. However, it is conversely possible to use a *reference to a constant* to address a non-constant object.

Example:
```
int a;    const int& cref = a;  // ok!
```

The reference cref can be used for read-only access to the variable a, and is said to be a *read-only identifier*.

A read-only identifier can be initialized by a constant, in contrast to a normal reference:

Example:
```
const double& pi = 3.1415927;
```

Since the constant does not take up any memory space, the compiler creates a temporary object which is then referenced.

■ REFERENCES AS PARAMETERS

Sample program

```cpp
// Ref2.cpp
// Demonstrating functions with parameters
// of reference type.
// -------------------------------------------------

#include <iostream>
#include <string>
using namespace std;
                                        // Prototypes:
bool getClient( string& name, long& nr);
void putClient( const string& name, const long& nr);

int main()
{
    string clientName;
    long    clientNr;

    cout << "\nTo input and output client data \n"
         << endl;
    if( getClient( clientName, clientNr))    // Calls
      putClient( clientName, clientNr);
    else
      cout << "Invalid input!" << endl;

    return 0;
}

bool getClient( string& name, long& nr)      // Definition
{
    cout << "\nTo input client data!\n"
         << " Name:    ";
    if( !getline( cin, name))  return false;

    cout << " Number: ";
    if( !( cin >> nr))  return false;

    return true;
}

                                          // Definition
void putClient( const string& name, const long& nr)
{                          // name and nr can only be read!

    cout << "\n-------- Client Data ---------\n"
         << "\n Name:    ";  cout << name
         << "\n Number: ";  cout << nr << endl;
}
```

☐ Passing by Reference

A *pass by reference* can be programmed using references or pointers as function parameters. It is syntactically simpler to use references, although not always permissible.

A parameter of a reference type is an alias for an argument. When a function is called, a reference parameter is initialized with the object supplied as an argument. The function can thus directly manipulate the argument passed to it.

Example: `void test( int& a) { ++a; }`

Based on this definition, the statement

```
test( var);      // For an int variable var
```

increments the variable `var`. Within the function, any access to the reference a automatically accesses the supplied variable, `var`.

If an object is passed as an argument when passing by reference, the object is not copied. Instead, the address of the object is passed to the function internally, allowing the function to access the object with which it was called.

☐ Comparison to Passing by Value

In contrast to a normal *pass by value* an expression, such as a+b, cannot be used as an argument. The argument must have an address in memory and be of the correct type.

Using references as parameters offers the following *benefits*:

- arguments are not copied. In contrast to passing by value, the run time of a program should improve, especially if the arguments occupy large amounts of memory
- a function can use the reference parameter to return *multiple* values to the calling function. Passing by value allows only one result as a return value, unless you resort to using global variables.

If you need to read arguments, but not copy them, you can define a *read-only reference* as a parameter.

Example: `void display( const string& str);`

The function `display()` contains a string as an argument. However, it does not generate a new string to which the argument string is copied. Instead, `str` is simply a reference to the argument. The caller can rest assured that the argument is not modified within the function, as `str` is declared as a `const`.

■ REFERENCES AS RETURN VALUE

Sample program

```cpp
// Ref3.cpp
// Demonstrates the use of return values with
// reference type.
// ---------------------------------------------------

#include <iostream>
#include <string>
using namespace std;
                                        // Returns a
double& refMin( double&, double&);      // reference to
                                        // the minimum.
int main()
{
   double x1 = 1.1,  x2 = x1 + 0.5,  y;

   y = refMin( x1, x2);    // Assigns the minimum to y.
   cout << "x1 = " << x1 << "        "
        << "x2 = " << x2 << endl;
   cout << "Minimum: " << y  << endl;

   ++refMin( x1, x2);            // ++x1, as x1 is minimal
   cout << "x1 = " << x1 << "        "        // x1 = 2.1
        << "x2 = " << x2 << endl;             // x2 = 1.6
   ++refMin( x1, x2);                  // ++x2, because x2 is
                                       // the minimum.
   cout << "x1 = " << x1 << "        "        // x1 = 2.1
        << "x2 = " << x2 << endl;             // x2 = 2.6
   refMin( x1, x2) = 10.1;        // x1 = 10.1, because
                                  // x1 is the minimum.
   cout << "x1 = " << x1 << "        "        // x1 = 10.1
        << "x2 = " << x2 << endl;             // x2 = 2.6
   refMin( x1, x2) += 5.0;        // x2 += 5.0, because
                                  // x2 is the minimum.
   cout << "x1 = " << x1 << "        "        // x1 = 10.1
        << "x2 = " << x2 << endl;             // x2 = 7.6
   return 0;
}

double& refMin( double& a, double& b)   // Returns a
{                                       // reference to
    return a <= b ? a : b;              // the minimum.
}
```

✓ **NOTE**

The expression refMin(x1,x2) represents either the object x1 or the object x2, that is, the object containing the smaller value.

☐ Returning References

The return type of a function can also be a reference type. The function call then represents an object, and can be used just like an object.

Example:
```
string& message()              // Reference!
{
    static string str = "Today only cold cuts!";
    return str;
}
```

This function returns a reference to a *static* string, `str`. Pay attention to the following point when returning references and pointers:

The object referenced by the return value must exist after leaving the function.

It would be a critical error to declare the string `str` as a normal `auto` variable in the function `message()`. This would destroy the string on leaving the function and the reference would point to an object that no longer existed.

☐ Calling a Reference Type Function

The function `message()` (mentioned earlier in this section) is of type "reference to string." Thus, calling

```
message()
```

represents a `string` type object, and the following statements are valid:

```
message() = "Let's go to the beer garden!";
message() += " Cheers!";
cout << "Length: " << message().length();
```

In these examples, a new value is first assigned to the object referenced by the function call. Then a new string is appended before the length of the referenced string is output in the third statement.

If you want to avoid modifying the referenced object, you can define the function type as a read-only reference.

Example: `const string& message();      // Read-only!`

References are commonly used as return types when overloading operators. The operations that an operator has to perform for a user-defined type are always implemented by an appropriate function. Refer to the chapters on overloading operators later in this book for more details. However, examples with operators from standard classes can be provided at this point.

■ EXPRESSIONS WITH REFERENCE TYPE

Example: Operator `<<` **of class** `ostream`

```
cout << "Good morning" << '!';
```

```
                    ┌──────────────────────────┐
                    │  cout << "Good morning"   │
                    └──────────────────────────┘
                    ╲_____╱

                         Reference to cout        ┌──────────┐
                                                  │  <<'!';  │
                                                  └──────────┘
```

Sample assignments of class `string`

```cpp
// Ref4.cpp
// Expressions with reference type exemplified by
// string assignments.
// ------------------------------------------------
#include <iostream>
#include <string>
#include <cctype>                    // For toupper()
using namespace std;
void strToUpper( string& );        // Prototype
int main()
{
   string text("Test with assignments \n");

   strToUpper(text);
   cout << text << endl;

   strToUpper( text = "Flowers");
   cout << text << endl;

   strToUpper( text += " cheer you up!\n");
   cout << text << endl;
   return 0;
}

void strToUpper( string& str)   // Converts the content
{                               // of str to uppercase.
   int len = str.length();
   for( int i=0; i < len; ++i)
     str[i] = toupper( str[i]);
}
```

Every C++ expression belongs to a certain type and also has a value, if the type is not void. Reference types are also valid for expressions.

☐ The Stream Class Shift Operators

The << and >> operators used for stream input and output are examples of expressions that return a reference to an object.

Example: `cout << " Good morning "`

This expression is not a void type but a reference to the object cout, that is, it represents the object cout. This allows you to repeatedly use the << on the expression:

```
cout << "Good morning" << '!'
```

The expression is then equivalent to

```
(cout << " Good morning ") << '!'
```

Expressions using the << operator are composed from left to right, as you can see from the table of precedence contained in the appendix.

Similarly, the expression `cin >> variable` represents the stream cin. This allows repeated use of the >> operator.

Example:
```
int a;   double x;
cin >> a >> x;        // (cin >> a) >> x;
```

☐ Other Reference Type Operators

Other commonly used reference type operators include the simple assignment operator = and compound assignments, such as += and *=. These operators return a reference to the operand on the left. In an expression such as

```
a = b  or  a += b
```

a must therefore be an object. In turn, the expression itself represents the object a. This also applies when the operators refer to objects belonging to class types. However, the class definition stipulates the available operators. For example, the assignment operators = and += are available in the standard class string.

Example:
```
string name("Jonny ");
name += "Depp";          //Reference to name
```

Since an expression of this type represents an object, the expression can be passed as an argument to a function that is called by reference. This point is illustrated by the example on the opposite page.

■ DEFINING POINTERS

Sample program

```cpp
// pointer1.cpp
// Prints the values and addresses of variables.
// ------------------------------------------------
#include <iostream>
using namespace std;

int var, *ptr;        // Definition of variables var and ptr

int main()            // Outputs the values and addresses
{                     // of the variables var and ptr.
   var = 100;
   ptr = &var;

   cout << " Value of var:       " <<  var
        << "   Address of var: " <<  &var
        << endl;
   cout << " Value of ptr: "       <<  ptr
        << "   Address of ptr: " <<  &ptr
        << endl;
   return 0;
}
```

Sample screen output

```
Value of var:        100    Address of var: 00456FD4
Value of ptr: 00456FD4    Address of ptr: 00456FD0
```

The variables `var` and `ptr` in memory

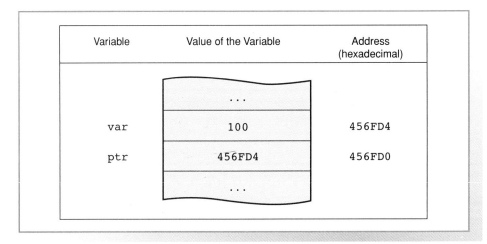

Variable	Value of the Variable	Address (hexadecimal)
	. . .	
var	100	456FD4
ptr	456FD4	456FD0
	. . .	

Efficient program logic often requires access to the memory addresses used by a program's data, rather than manipulation of the data itself. Linked lists or trees whose elements are generated dynamically at runtime are typical examples.

☐ Pointers

A *pointer* is an expression that represents both the *address* and *type* of another object. Using the address operator, &, for a given object creates a pointer to that object. Given that var is an int variable,

Example: `&var        // Address of the object var`

is the address of the int object in memory and thus a pointer to var. A pointer points to a memory address and simultaneously indicates by its type how the memory address can be read or written to. Thus, depending on the type, we refer to *pointers to char, pointers to int*, and so on, or use an abbreviation, such as *char pointer, int pointer*, and so on.

☐ Pointer Variables

An expression such as &var is a constant pointer; however, C++ allows you to define *pointer variables*, that is, variables that can store the address of another object.

Example: `int *ptr;              // or:  int* ptr;`

This statement defines the variable ptr, which is an int* type (in other words, *a pointer to int*). ptr can thus store the address of an int variable. In a declaration, the star character * always means "pointer to."

Pointer types are derived types. The general form is T*, where T can be any given type. In the above example T is an int type.

Objects of the same base type T can be declared together.

Example: `int a, *p, &r = a;  // Definition of a, p, r`

After declaring a pointer variable, you must point the pointer at a memory address. The program on the opposite page does this using the statement

`ptr = &var;` .

☐ References and Pointers

References are similar to pointers: both refer to an object in memory. However, a pointer is not merely an alias but an individual object that has an identity separate from the object it references. A pointer has its own memory address and can be manipulated by pointing it at a new memory address and thus referencing a different object.

■ THE INDIRECTION OPERATOR

Using the indirection operator

```
double x, y, *px;

px = &x;           // Let px point to x.
*px = 12.3;        // Assign the value 12.3 to x
*px += 4.5;        // Increment x by 4.5.
y  = sin(*px);     // To assign sine of x to y.
```

Address and value of the variables x **and** px

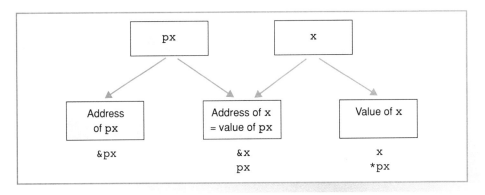

Notes on addresses in a program

- Each pointer variable occupies the same amount of space, independent of the type of object it references. That is, it occupies as much space as is necessary to store an address. On a 32-bit computer, such as a PC, this is four bytes.

- The addresses visible in a program are normally logic addresses that are allocated and mapped to physical addresses by the system. This allows for efficient storage management and the swapping of currently unused memory blocks to the hard disk.

- C++ guarantees that any valid address will not be equal to 0. Thus, the special value 0 is used to indicate an error. For pointers, the symbolic constant NULL is defined as 0 in standard header files. A pointer containing the value NULL is also called NULL pointer.

Using Pointers to Access Objects

The *indirection operator* * is used to access an object referenced by a pointer:

Given a pointer, `ptr`, `*ptr` is the object referenced by `ptr`.

As a programmer, you must always distinguish between the pointer `ptr` and the addressed object `*ptr`.

Example:
```
long  a = 10, b,        // Definition of a, b
          *ptr;         // and pointer ptr.
      ptr = &a;         // Let ptr point to a.
      b = *ptr;
```

This assigns the value of a to b, since `ptr` points to a. The assignment `b = a;` would return the same result. The expression `*ptr` represents the object a, and can be used wherever a could be used.

The star character * used for defining pointer variables is not an operator but merely imitates the later use of the pointer in expressions. Thus, the definition

```
long *ptr;
```

has the following meaning: `ptr` is a `long*` (pointer to `long`) type and `*ptr` is a `long` type.

The indirection operator * has high precedence, just like the address operator &. Both operators are unary, that is, they have only one operand. This also helps distinguish the redirection operator from the binary multiplication operator *, which always takes two operands.

L-values

An expression that identifies an object in memory is known as an *L-value* in C++. The term L-value occurs commonly in compiler error messages and is derived from the assignment. The *left* operand of the = operator must always designate a memory address. Expressions other than an L-value are often referred to as *R-values*.

A variable name is the simplest example of an L-value. However, a constant or an expression, such as x + 1, is an R-value. The indirection operator is one example of an operator that yields L-values. Given a pointer variable p, both p and *p are L-values, as *p designates the object to which p points.

■ POINTERS AS PARAMETERS

Sample function

```
// pointer2.cpp
// Definition and call of function swap().
// Demonstrates the use of pointers as parameters.
// -----------------------------------------------------
#include <iostream>
using namespace std;

void swap( float *, float *);    // Prototype of swap()

int main()
{
   float x = 11.1F;
   float y = 22.2F;
      .
      .
      .
   swap( &x, &y );
      .                  // p2 = &y
      .
      .
}              // p1 = &x
void swap( float *p1, float *p2)
{
   float temp;            // Temporary variable

   temp = *p1;            // At the above call p1 points
   *p1  = *p2;            // to x and p2 to y.
   *p2  = temp;
}
```

☐ Objects as Arguments

If an object is passed as an argument to a function, two possible situations occur:

- the parameter in question is the same type as the object passed to it. The function that is called is then passed a copy of the object (passing by value)
- the parameter in question is a reference. The parameter is then an alias for the argument, that is, the function that is called manipulates the object passed by the calling function (passing by reference).

In the first case, the argument passed to the function cannot be manipulated by the function. This is not true for passing by reference. However, there is a third way of passing by reference—passing pointers to the function.

☐ Pointers as Arguments

How do you declare a function parameter to allow an address to be passed to the function as an argument? The answer is quite simple: The parameter must be declared as a *pointer variable*.

If, for example, the function `func()` requires the address of an `int` value as an argument, you can use the following statement

Example:
```
long func( int *iPtr )
{
    // Function block
}
```

to declare the parameter `iPtr` as an `int` pointer. If a function knows the address of an object, it can of course use the indirection operator to access and manipulate the object.

In the program on the opposite page, the function `swap()` swaps the values of the variables `x` and `y` in the calling function. The function `swap()` is able to access the variables since the addresses of these variables, that is `&x` and `&y`, are passed to it as arguments.

The parameters `p1` and `p2` in `swap()` are thus declared as `float` pointers. The statement

```
swap( &x, &y);
```

initializes the pointers `p1` and `p2` with the addresses of `x` or `y`. When the function manipulates the expressions `*p1` and `*p2`, it really accesses the variables `x` and `y` in the calling function and exchanges their values.

exercises

■ EXERCISES

Listing for exercise 3

```
// A version of swap() with incorrect logic.
// Find the error!

void swap(float *p1, float *p2)
{
  float *temp;                      // Temporary variable

  temp = p1;
  p1   = p2;
  p2   = temp;
}
```

Solutions of quadratic equations

The quadratic equation: $a*x^2 + b*x + c = 0$ has real solutions:

$$x_{12} = (-b \pm \sqrt{(b^2 - 4ac)}) / 2a$$

if the discriminant satisfies: $b^2 - 4ac >= 0$
  If the value of $(b^2 - 4ac)$ is negative, no real solution exists.

Test values

Quadratic Equation	Solutions
$2x^2 - 2x - 1.5 = 0$	$x_1 = 1.5,\quad x_2 = -0.5$
$x^2 - 6x + 9 = 0$	$X_1 = 3.0,\quad x_2 = 3.0$
$2x^2 + 2 = 0$	none

Exercise 1

What happens if the parameter in the sample function `strToUpper()` is declared as a `string&` instead of a `string`?

Exercise 2

Write a `void` type function called `circle()` to calculate the circumference and area of a circle. The radius and two variables are passed to the function, which therefore has three parameters:

Parameters: A read-only reference to `double` for the radius and two references to `double` that the function uses to store the area and circumference of the circle.

 NOTE

Given a circle with radius r:

Area = π * r * r and circumference = 2 * π * r where π = 3.1415926536

Test the function `circle()` by outputting a table containing the radius, the circumference, and the area for the radii `0.5, 1.0, 1.5, . . . , 10.0`.

Exercise 3

a. The version of the function `swap()` opposite can be compiled without producing any error messages. However, the function will not swap the values of `x` and `y` when `swap(&x, &y);` is called. What is wrong?

b. Test the correct pointer version of the function `swap()` found in this chapter. Then write and test a version of the function `swap()` that uses references instead of pointers.

Exercise 4

Create a function `quadEquation()` that calculates the solutions to quadratic equations. The formula for calculating quadratic equations is shown opposite.

Arguments: The coefficients `a, b, c` and two pointers to both solutions.

Returns: `false`, if no real solution is available, otherwise `true`.

Test the function by outputting the quadratic equations on the opposite page and their solutions.

■ SOLUTIONS

Exercise 1

The call to function strToUpper() is left unchanged. But instead of passing by reference, a passing by value occurs, i.e., the function manipulates a local copy. Thus, only a local copy of the string is changed in the function, but the string in the calling function remains unchanged.

Exercise 2

```cpp
// -----------------------------------------------------
// circle.cpp
// Defines and calls the function circle().
// -----------------------------------------------------
#include <iostream>
#include <iomanip>
#include <string>
using namespace std;

// Prototype of circle():
void circle( const double& rad, double& um, double& fl);

const double startRadius =  0.5,      // Start, end and
             endRadius    = 10.0,     // step width of
             step         =  0.5;     // the table

string header = "\n      ***** Computing Circles ***** \n",
       line( 50, '-');

int main()
{
    double rad, circuit, plane;

    cout << header << endl;
    cout << setw(10) << "Radius"
         << setw(20) << "Circumference"
         << setw(20) << "Area\n" << line << endl;

    cout << fixed;               // Floating point presentation
    for( rad = startRadius;
         rad < endRadius + step/2;  rad += step)
    {
      circle( rad, circuit, plane);
      cout << setprecision(1)<< setw(8)  << rad
           << setprecision(5)<< setw(22) << circuit
                             << setw(20) << plane <<endl;
    }
    return 0;
}
```

```
// Function circle(): Compute circumference and area.
void circle( const double& r, double& u, double& f)
{
   const double pi = 3.1415926536;
   u = 2 * pi * r;
   f = pi * r * r;
}
```

Exercise 3

```
// ----------------------------------------------------
// swap.cpp
// Definition and call of the function swap().
// 1. version: parameters with pointer type,
// 2. version: parameters with reference type.
// ----------------------------------------------------
#include <iostream>
using namespace std;

void swap( float*, float*);        // Prototypes of swap()
void swap( float&, float&);

int main()
{
   float x = 11.1F;
   float y = 22.2F;

   cout << "x and y before swapping:    "
        << x << "    " << y << endl;

   swap( &x, &y);               // Call pointer version.

   cout << "x and y after 1. swapping: "
        << x << "    " << y << endl;

   swap( x, y);                 // Call reference version.

   cout << "x and y after 2. swapping: "
        << x << "    " << y << endl;

   return 0;
}

void swap(float *p1, float *p2)      // Pointer version
{
  float temp;                        // Temporary variable

   temp = *p1;                       // Above call points p1
   *p1  = *p2;                       // to x and p2 to y.
   *p2  = temp;
}
```

```cpp
void swap(float& a, float& b)        // Reference version
{
  float temp;                        // Temporary variable

  temp = a;                          // For above call
  a    = b;                          // a equals x and b equals y
  b    = temp;
}
```

Exercise 4

```cpp
// ----------------------------------------------------
// quadEqu.cpp
// Defines and calls the function quadEquation(),
// which computes the solutions of quadratic equations
//           a*x*x + b*x + c = 0
// The equation and its solutions are printed by
// the function printQuadEquation().
// ----------------------------------------------------

#include <iostream>
#include <iomanip>
#include <string>
#include <cmath>                     // For the square root sqrt()
using namespace std;

string header =
      " *** Solutions of Quadratic Equations ***\n",
      line( 50, '-');

// -----   Prototypes -----
// Computing solutions:
bool quadEquation( double a, double b, double c,
                   double* x1Ptr, double* x2Ptr);

// Printing the equation and its solutions:
void printQuadEquation( double a, double b, double c);

int main()
{
   cout << header << endl;
   printQuadEquation( 2.0, -2.0, -1.5);
   printQuadEquation( 1.0, -6.0, 9.0);
   printQuadEquation( 2.0,  0.0, 2.0);

   return 0;
}
```

```
// Prints the equation and its solutions:
void printQuadEquation( double a, double b, double c)
{
   double x1 = 0.0, x2 = 0.0;              // For solutions

   cout << line << '\n'
        << "\nThe quadratic equation:\n\t "
        << a << "*x*x + " << b << "*x + " <<  c << " = 0"
        << endl;

   if( quadEquation( a, b, c, &x1, &x2) )
   {
     cout << "has real solutions:"
          << "\n\t x1 = " << x1
          << "\n\t x2 = " << x2 << endl;
   }
   else
     cout << "has no real solutions!" << endl;

   cout << "\nGo on with return. \n\n";
   cin.get();
}


bool quadEquation( double a, double b, double c,
                   double* x1Ptr, double* x2Ptr)
// Computes the solutions of the quadratic equation:
//            a*x*x + b*x + c = 0
// Stores the solutions in the variables to which
// x1Ptr and x2Ptr point.
// Returns: true, if a solution exists,
//                otherwise false.
{
    bool return_flag = false;

    double help = b*b - 4*a*c;

    if( help >= 0)                // There are real solutions.
    {
      help = sqrt( help);

      *x1Ptr = (-b + help) / (2*a);
      *x2Ptr = (-b - help) / (2*a);

      return_flag = true;
    }
    return return_flag;
}
```

13

Defining Classes

This chapter describes how classes are defined and how instances of classes, that is, objects, are used. In addition, structs and unions are introduced as examples of special classes.

■ THE CLASS CONCEPT

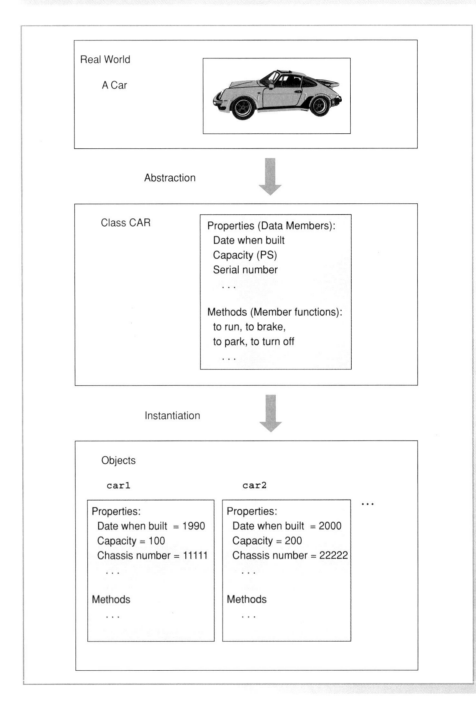

Classes are the language element in C++ most important to the support object-oriented programming (OOP). A class defines the properties and capacities of an object.

☐ Data Abstraction

Humans use *abstraction* in order to manage complex situations. Objects and processes are reduced to basics and referred to in generic terms. Classes allow more direct use of the results of this type of abstraction in software development.

The first step towards solving a problem is *analysis*. In object-oriented programming, analysis comprises identifying and describing objects and recognizing their mutual relationships. Object descriptions are the building blocks of classes.

In C++, a class is a user-defined type. It contains *data members*, which describe the properties of the class, and *member functions*, or *methods*, which describe the capacities of the objects. Classes are simply patterns used to instantiate, or create, objects of the class type. In other words, an object is a variable of a given class.

☐ Data Encapsulation

When you define a class, you also specify the private members, that is, the members that are not available for external access, and the public members of that class. An application program accesses objects by using the public methods of the class and thus activating its capacities.

Access to object data is rarely direct, that is, object data is normally declared as private and then read or modified by methods with public declarations to ensure correct access to the data.

One important aspect of this technique is the fact that application programs need not be aware of the internal structure of the data. If needed, the internal structure of the program data can even be modified. Provided that the interfaces of the public methods remain unchanged, changes like these will not affect the application program. This allows you to enhance an application by programming an improved class version without changing a single byte of the application.

An object is thus seen to encapsulate its private structure, protecting itself from external influences and managing itself by its own methods. This describes the concept of data encapsulation concisely.

■ DEFINING CLASSES

Definition scheme

```
class Demo
{
   private:

            // Private data members and methods here

   public:

            // Public data members and methods here

};
```

Example of a class

```
// account.h
// Defining the class Account.
// ---------------------------------------------------
#ifndef _ACCOUNT_          // Avoid multiple inclusions.
#define _ACCOUNT_

#include <iostream>
#include <string>
using namespace std;

class Account
{
   private:               // Sheltered members:
      string name;            // Account holder
      unsigned long nr;       // Account number
      double balance;         // Account balance

   public:                    //Public interface:
      bool init( const string&, unsigned long, double);
      void display();
};

#endif   //  _ACCOUNT_
```

A class definition specifies the name of the class and the names and types of the class *members*.

The definition begins with the keyword `class` followed by the class name. The data members and methods are then declared in the subsequent code block. Data members and member functions can belong to any valid type, even to another previously defined class. At the same time, the class members are divided into:

▪ `private` members, which cannot be accessed externally
▪ `public` members, which are available for external access.

The `public` members form the so-called *public interface* of the class.

The opposite page shows a schematic definition of a class. The `private` section generally contains data members and the `public` section contains the access methods for the data. This provides for data encapsulation.

The following example includes a class named `Account` used to represent a bank account. The data members, such as the name of the account holder, the account number, and the account balance, are declared as `private`. In addition, there are two public methods, `init()` for initialization purposes and `display()`, which is used to display the data on screen.

The labels `private:` and `public:` can be used at the programmer's discretion within a class:

▪ you can use the labels as often as needed, or not at all, and in any order. A section marked as `private:` or `public:` is valid until the next `public:` or `private:` label occurs
▪ the default value for member access is `private`. If you omit both the `private` and `public` labels, all the class members are assumed to be `private`.

☐ Naming

Every piece of software uses a set of naming rules. These rules often reflect the target platform and the class libraries used. For the purposes of this book, we decided to keep to standard naming conventions for distinguishing classes and class members. Class names begin with an uppercase letter and member names with a lowercase letter.

Members of different classes can share the same name. A member of another class could therefore also be named `display()`.

■ DEFINING METHODS

Methods of class Account

```cpp
// account.cpp
// Defines methods init() and display().
// --------------------------------------------------
#include "account.h"                    // Class definition
#include <iostream>
#include <iomanip>
using namespace std;

// The method init() copies the given arguments
// into the private members of the class.
bool Account::init(const string& i_name,
                   unsigned long i_nr,
                   double        i_balance)
{
   if( i_name.size() < 1)                // No empty name
        return false;
   name    = i_name;
   nr      = i_nr;
   balance = i_balance;
   return true;
}

// The method display() outputs private data.
void Account::display()
{
   cout << fixed << setprecision(2)
        << "------------------------------------\n"
        << "Account holder:    " << name  << '\n'
        << "Account number:    " << nr    << '\n'
        << "Account balance:   " << balance << '\n'
        << "------------------------------------\n"
        << endl;
}
```

A class definition is not complete without method definitions. Only then can the objects of the class be used.

☐ Syntax

When you define a method, you must also supply the class name, separating it from the function name by means of the scope resolution operator `::`.

Syntax:
```
type class_name::function_name(parameter_list)
{           . . .        }
```

Failure to supply the class name results in a global function definition.

Within a method, *all* the members of a class can be designated directly using their names. The class membership is automatically assumed. In particular, methods belonging to the same class can call each other directly.

Access to private members is only possible within methods belonging to the same class. Thus, `private` members are completely controlled by the class.

Defining a class does not automatically allocate memory for the data members of that class. To allocate memory, you must define an object. When a method is called for a given object, the method can then manipulate the data of this object.

☐ Modular Programming

A class is normally defined in several source files. In this case, you will need to place the class definition in a *header file*. If you place the definition of the class `Account` in the file `Account.h`, any source file including the header file can use the class `Account`.

Methods must always be defined within a source file. This would mean defining the methods for the class `Account` in a source file named `Account.cpp`, for example.

The source code of the application program, for example, the code containing the function `main`, is independent of the class and can be stored in separate source files. Separating classes from application programs facilitates re-use of classes.

In an integrated development environment, a programmer will define a *project* to help manage the various program modules by inserting all the source files into the project. When the project is compiled and linked, modified source files are automatically re-compiled and linked to the application program.

▪ DEFINING OBJECTS

The objects current and savings in memory

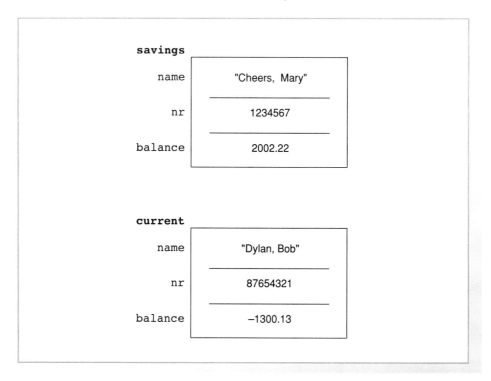

Defining a class also defines a new type for which variables, that is, objects, can be defined. An object is also referred to as an *instance* of a class.

☐ Defining Objects

An object is defined in the usual way by supplying the type and the object name.

Syntax: `class_name object_name1 [, object_name2,...]`

The following statement defines an object `current` of type `Account`:

Example: `Account current;   // or: class Account ...`

Memory is now allocated for the data members of the `current` object. The `current` object itself contains the members `name`, `nr`, and `balance`.

☐ Objects in Memory

If multiple objects of the same class type are declared, as in

Example: `Account current, savings;`

each object has its own data members. Even the object `savings` contains the members `name`, `nr`, and `balance`. However, these data members occupy a different position in memory than the data members belonging to `current`.

The same methods are called for both objects. Only one instance of the machine code for a method exists in memory—this applies even if no objects have been defined for the class.

A method is always called for a particular instance and then manipulates the data members of *this* object. This results in the memory content as shown on the opposite page, when the method `init()` is called for each object with the values shown.

☐ Initializing Objects

The objects belonging to the `Account` class were originally defined but not initialized. Each member object is thus defined but not explicitly initialized. The string `name`, is empty, as it is thus defined in the class `string`. The initial values of the members `nr` and `balance` are unknown, however. As is the case for other variables, these data members will default to 0 if the object is declared global or `static`.

You can define exactly how an object is created and destroyed. These tasks are performed by *constructors* and *destructors*. Constructors are specifically responsible for initializing objects—more details are given later.

■ USING OBJECTS

Sample program

```cpp
// account_t.cpp
// Uses objects of class Account.
// -------------------------------------------------

#include "Account.h"

int main()
{
   Account current1, current2;

   current1.init("Cheers, Mary", 1234567, -1200.99);
   current1.display();

//   current1.balance += 100;  // Error: private member

   current2 = current1;         // ok: Assignment of
                                // objects is possible.
   current2.display();          // ok

                                // New values for current2
   current2.init("Jones, Tom", 3512347, 199.40);

   current2.display();
                                // To use a reference:
   Account& mtr = current1;     // mtr is an alias name
                                // for object current1.
   mtr.display();               // mtr can be used just
                                // as object current1.

   return 0;
}
```

☐ Class Member Access Operator

An application program that manipulates the objects of a class can access only the public members of those objects. To do so, it uses the *class member access operator* (in short: *dot operator*).

Syntax: `object.member`

Where `member` is a data member or a method.

Example:
```
Account current;
current.init("Jones, Tom",1234567,-1200.99);
```

The expression `current.init` represents the `public` method `init` of the `Account` class. This method is called with three arguments for `current`.

The `init()` call cannot be replaced by direct assignments.

Example:
```
current.name    = "Dylan, Bob";    // Error:
current.nr      = 1234567;         // private
current.balance = -1200.99;        // members
```

Access to the `private` members of an object is not permissible outside the class. It is therefore impossible to display single members of the `Account` class on screen.

Example:
```
cout << current.balance;           // Error
current.display();                 // ok
```

The method `display()` displays all the data members of `current`. A method such as `display()` can only be called for one object. The statement

```
display();
```

would result in an error message, since there is no global function called `display()`. What data would the function have to display?

☐ Assigning Objects

The assignment operator = is the only operator that is defined for all classes by default. However, the source and target objects must both belong to the same class. The assignment is performed to assign the individual data members of the source object to the corresponding members of the target object.

Example:
```
Account current1, current2;
current2.init("Marley, Bob",350123, 1000.0);
current1 = current2;
```

This copies the data members of `current2` to the corresponding members of `current1`.

■ POINTERS TO OBJECTS

Sample program

```cpp
// ptrObj.cpp
// Uses pointers to objects of class Account.
// ---------------------------------------------------
#include "Account.h"    // Includes <iostream>, <string>
bool getAccount( Account *pAccount);        // Prototype
int main()
{
   Account current1, current2, *ptr = &current1;

   ptr->init("Cheer, Mary",          // current1.init(...)
            3512345, 99.40);
   ptr->display();                   // current1.display()

   ptr = &current2;         // Let ptr point to current2
   if( getAccount( ptr))    // Input and output a new
     ptr->display();        // account.
   else
      cout << "Invalid input!" << endl;
   return 0;
}
// ---------------------------------------------------
// getAccount() reads data for a new account
// and adds it into the argument.
bool getAccount( Account *pAccount )
{
   string name, line(50,'-');          // Local variables
   unsigned long nr;
   double startcapital;

   cout << line << '\n'
        << "Enter data for a new account: \n"
        << "Account holder: ";
   if( !getline(cin,name) || name.size() == 0)
     return false;
   cout << "Account number:   ";
   if( !(cin >> nr))             return false;
   cout << "Starting capital: ";
   if( !(cin >> startcapital)) return false;
   // All input ok
   pAccount->init( name, nr, startcapital);
   return true;
}
```

An object of a class has a memory address—just like any other object. You can assign this address to a suitable pointer.

Example: `Account savings("Mac, Rita",654321, 123.5);`
            `Account *ptrAccount = &savings;`

This defines the object `savings` and a pointer variable called `ptrAccount`. The pointer `ptrAccount` is initialized so that it points to the object `savings`. This makes `*ptrAccount` the object `savings` itself. You can then use the statement

Example: `(*ptrAccount).display();`

to call the method `display()` for the object `savings`. Parentheses must be used in this case, as the operator `.` has higher precedence than the `*` operator.

☐ Arrow Operator

You can use the class member access operator `->` (in short: *arrow operator*) instead of a combination of `*` and `.` .

Syntax: `objectPointer->member`

This expression is equivalent to

`(*objectPointer).member`

The operator `->` is made up of a minus sign and the greater than sign.

Example: `ptrAccount->display();`

This statement calls the method `display()` for the object referenced by `ptrAccount`, that is, for the object `savings`. The statement is equivalent to the statement in the previous example.

The difference between the class member access operators `.` and `->` is that the left operand of the dot operator must be an object, whereas the left operand of the arrow operator must be a pointer to an object.

☐ The Sample Program

Pointers to objects are often used as function parameters. A function that gets the address of an object as an argument can manipulate the referenced object directly. The example on the opposite page illustrates this point. It uses the function `getAccount()` to read the data for a new account. When called, the address of the account is passed:

`getAccount(ptr) // or: getAccount(&current1)`

The function can then use the pointer `ptr` and the `init()` method to write new data to the referenced object.

■ structs

Sample program

```
// structs.cpp
// Defines and uses a struct.
// --------------------------------------------------
#include <iostream>
#include <iomanip>
#include <string>
using namespace std;
struct Representative   // Defining struct Representative
{
  string name;          // Name of a representative.
  double sales;         // Sales per month.
};
inline void print( const Representative& v)
{
   cout << fixed << setprecision(2)
        << left  << setw(20) << v.name
        << right << setw(10) << v.sales << endl;
}
int main()
{
   Representative rita, john;
   rita.name    = "Strom, Rita";
   rita.sales   = 37000.37;
   john.name    = "Quick, John";
   john.sales   = 23001.23;

   rita.sales += 1700.11;                 // More Sales
   cout << "  Representative           Sales\n"
        << "-------------------------------" << endl;
   print( rita);
   print( john);
   cout << "\nTotal of sales: "
        << rita.sales + john.sales << endl;
   Representative *ptr = &john;           // Pointer ptr.
                                          // Who gets the
   if( john.sales < rita.sales)           // most sales?
     ptr = &rita;
   cout << "\nSalesman of the month: "
        << ptr->name << endl;   // Representative's name
                                // pointed to by ptr.

   return 0;
}
```

☐ Records

In a classical, procedural language like C, multiple data that belong together logically are put together to form a *record*. Extensive data such as the data for the articles in an automobile manufacturer's stocks can be organized for ease of viewing and stored in files.

From the viewpoint of an object-oriented language, a record is merely a class containing only public data members and no methods. Thus, you can use the `class` keyword to define the structure of a record in C++.

Example:
```
class Date
{ public:    short month, day, year; };
```

However, it is common practice to use the keyword `struct`, which is also available in the C programming language, to define records. The above definition of `Date` with the members `day`, `month`, and `year` is thus equivalent to:

Example:
```
struct Date { short month, day, year; };
```

☐ The Keywords `class` and `struct`

You can also use the keyword `struct` to define a class, such as the class `Account`.

Example:
```
struct Account {
    private:    //  . . .    as before
    public:     //  . . .
};
```

The keywords `class` and `struct` only vary with respect to data encapsulation; the default for access to members of a class defined as a `struct` is `public`. In contrast to a class defined using the `class` keyword, all the class members are `public` unless a `private` label is used. This allows the programmer to retain C compatibility.

Example:
```
Date future;
future.year = 2100;    // ok! Public data
```

Records in the true sense of the word, that is, objects of a class containing only `public` members, can be initialized by means of a list during definition.

Example:
```
Date birthday = { 1, 29, 1987};
```

The first element in the list initializes the first data member of the object, and so on.

■ UNIONS

An object of union WordByte **in memory**

Defining and using union WordByte

```cpp
// unions.cpp
// Defines and uses a union.
// --------------------------------------------------
#include <iostream>
using namespace std;
union WordByte
{
  private:
    unsigned short w;          // 16 bits
    unsigned char b[2];        // Two bytes: b[0], b[1]
  public:                      // Word- and byte-access:
    unsigned short& word()    { return w; }
    unsigned char&  lowByte() { return b[0]; }
    unsigned char&  highByte(){ return b[1]; }
};

int main()
{
    WordByte wb;
    wb.word() = 256;
    cout << "\nWord:       " << (int)wb.word();
    cout << "\nLow-byte:  " << (int)wb.lowByte()
         << "\nHigh-byte: " << (int)wb.highByte()
         << endl;
    return 0;
}
```

Screen output of the program

```
Word:       256
Low-Byte:  0
High-Byte: 1
```

☐ Memory Usage

In normal classes, each data member belonging to an object has its own separate memory space. However, a *union* is a class whose members are stored in the same memory space. Each data member has the same starting address in memory. Of course, a union cannot store various data members at the same address *simultaneously*. However, a union does provide for more versatile usage of memory space.

☐ Definition

Syntactically speaking, a union is distinguished from a class defined as a `class` or `struct` only by the keyword `union`.

Example:
```
union Number
{
    long   n;
    double x;
};
Number number1, number2;
```

This example defines the union `Number` and two objects of the same type. The union `Number` can be used to store either integral or floating-point numbers.

Unless a `private` label is used, all union members are assumed to be `public`. This is similar to the default setting for structures. This allows direct access to the members n and x in the union `Number`.

Example:
```
number1.n = 12345; // Storing an integer
number1.n *= 3;    // and multiply by 3.
number2.x = 2.77;  // Floating point number
```

The programmer must ensure that the current content of the union is interpreted correctly. This is normally achieved using an additional type field that identifies the current content.

The size of a union type object is derived from the longest data member, as all data members begin at the same memory address. If we look at our example, the union `Number`, this size is defined by the `double` member, which defaults to 8 == `sizeof(double)` byte.

The example opposite defines the union `WordByte` that allows you to read or write to a 16-bit memory space byte for byte or as a unit.

■ **EXERCISE**

Struct tm **in header file** ctime

```
struct tm
{
  int tm_sec;          // 0 - 59(60)
  int tm_min;          // 0 - 59
  int tm_hour;         // 0 - 23
  int tm_mday;         // Day of month: 1 - 31
  int tm_mon;          // Month: 0 - 11 (January == 0)
  int tm_year;         // Years since 1900 (Year - 1900)
  int tm_wday;         // Weekday: 0 - 6 (Sunday == 0)
  int tm_yday;         // Day of year: 0 - 365
  int tm_isdst;        // Flag for summer-time
};
```

Sample calls to functions time( ) **and** localtime( )

```
#include <iostream>
#include <ctime>
using namespace std;

  struct tm *ptr;          // Pointer to struct tm.
  time_t sec;              // For seconds.
  . . .
  time(&sec);              // To get the present time.
  ptr = localtime(&sec);   // To initialize a struct of
                           // type tm and return a
                           // pointer to it.

  cout << "Today is the "        << ptr->tm_yday + 1
       << ". day of the year " << ptr->tm_year
       << endl;
  . . .
```

Exercise

A program needs a class to represent the date.

■ Define the class `Date` for this purpose using three integral data members for day, month, and year. Additionally, declare the following methods:

```
void init( int month, int day, int year);
void init(void);
void print(void);
```

Store the definition of the class `Date` in a header file.

■ Implement the methods for the class `Date` in a separate source file:

1. The method `print()` outputs the date to standard output using the format `Month-Day-Year`.

2. The method `init()` uses three parameters and copies the values passed to it to corresponding members. A range check is not required at this stage, but will be added later.

3. The method `init()` without parameters writes the *current date* to the corresponding members.

NOTE

Use the functions declared in `ctime`

```
time_t   time(time_t *ptrSec)
struct tm *localtime(const time_t *ptrSec);
```

The structure `tm` and sample calls to this function are included opposite. The type `time_t` is defined as `long` in `ctime`.

The function `time()` returns the system time expressed as a number of seconds and writes this value to the variable referenced by `ptrSec`. This value can be passed to the function `localtime()` that converts the number of seconds to the local type `tm` date and returns a pointer to this structure.

■ Test the class `Date` using an application program that once more is stored in a separate source file. To this end, define two objects for the class and display the current date. Use object assignments and—as an additional exercise—references and pointers to objects.

■ **SOLUTION**

```cpp
// ----------------------------------------------------
// date.h
// First Definition of class Date.
// ----------------------------------------------------

#ifndef _DATE_              // Avoid multiple inclusion.
#define _DATE_

class Date
{
  private:                      // Sheltered members:
    short month, day, year;

  public:                       // Public interface:
    void init(void);
    void init( int month, int day, int year);
    void print(void);
};

#endif   //  _DATE_


// ----------------------------------------------------
// date.cpp
// Implementing the methods of class Date.
// ----------------------------------------------------

#include "date.h"

#include <iostream>
#include <ctime>
using namespace std;

// ----------------------------------------------------
void Date::init(void)    // Get the present date and
{                        // assign it to data members.
   struct tm *ptr;             // Pointer to struct tm.
   time_t sec;                 // For seconds.

   time(&sec);               // Get the present date.
   ptr = localtime(&sec);    // Initialize a struct of
                             // type tm and return a
                             // pointer to it.
   month = (short) ptr->tm_mon + 1;
   day   = (short) ptr->tm_mday;
   year  = (short) ptr->tm_year + 1900;
}
```

```
// --------------------------------------------------
void Date::init( int m, int d, int y)
{
   month = (short) m;
   day   = (short) d;
   year  = (short) y;
}

// --------------------------------------------------
void Date::print(void)              // Output the date
{
   cout << month << '-' << day << '-' << year
        << endl;
}


// ----------------------------------------------------
// date_t.cpp
// Using objects of class Date.
// ----------------------------------------------------
#include "date.h"
#include <iostream>
using namespace std;

int main()
{
   Date today, birthday, aDate;

   today.init();
   birthday.init( 12, 11, 1997);

   cout << "Today's date: ";
   today.print();

   cout << "\n Felix' birthday: ";
   birthday.print();

   cout << "--------------------------------\n"
           "Some testing outputs:" << endl;

   aDate = today;                  // Assignment ok
   aDate.print();

   Date *pDate = &birthday;        // Pointer to birthday
   pDate->print();

   Date &holiday = aDate;          // Reference to aDate.
   holiday.init( 1, 5, 2000);      // Writing to aDate.
   aDate.print();                  // holiday.print()

   return 0;
}
```

chapter 14

Methods

This chapter describes

- how constructors and destructors are defined to create and destroy objects
- how `inline` methods, access methods, and read-only methods can be used
- the pointer `this`, which is available for all methods, and
- what you need to pay attention to when passing objects as arguments or returning objects.

■ CONSTRUCTORS

Class Account **with constructors**

```cpp
// account.h
// Defining class Account with two constructors.
// --------------------------------------------------
#ifndef _ACCOUNT_
#define _ACCOUNT_
#include <string>
using namespace std;
class Account
{
   private:                     // Sheltered members:
      string name;              // Account holder
      unsigned long nr;         // Account number
      double state;             // State of the account
   public:                      // Public interface:
      Account( const string&, unsigned long, double );
      Account( const string& );
      bool init( const string&, unsigned long, double);
      void display();
};
#endif    //  _ACCOUNT_
```

Defining the constructors

```cpp
// Within file account.cpp:

Account::Account( const string& a_name,
                  unsigned long a_nr, double a_state)
{
   nr    = a_nr;
   name  = a_name;
   state = a_state;
}

Account::Account( const string& a_name )
{
   name = a_name;
   nr = 1111111;   state = 0.0;
}
```

☐ The Task of a Constructor

Traditional programming languages only allocate memory for a variable being defined. The programmer must ensure that the variable is initialized with suitable values.

An object of the class `Account`, as described in the previous chapter, does not possess any valid values until the method `init()` is called. Non-initialized objects can lead to serious runtime errors in your programs.

To avoid errors of this type, C++ performs implicit initialization when an object is defined. This ensures that objects will always have valid data to work on. Initialization is performed by special methods known as *constructors*.

☐ Declaration

Constructors can be identified by their names. In contrast to other member functions, the following applies:

- the name of the constructor is also the class name
- a constructor does not possess a return type—not even `void`.

Constructors are normally declared in the `public` section of a class. This allows you to create objects wherever the class definition is available.

Constructors can be overloaded, just like other functions. Constructors belonging to a class must be distinguishable by their *signature* (that is, the number, order, and type of parameters). This allows for different methods of object initialization. The example opposite shows an addition to the `Account` class. The class now has two constructors.

☐ Definition

Since a constructor has the same name as its class, the definition of a constructor always begins with

```
Class_name::Class_name
```

In the definition itself, the arguments passed can be checked for validity before they are copied to the corresponding data members. If the number of arguments is smaller than the number of data members, the remaining members can be initialized using default values.

Constructors can also perform more complex initialization tasks, such as opening files, allocating memory, and configuring interfaces.

■ CONSTRUCTOR CALLS

Sample program

```cpp
// account2_t.cpp
// Using the constructors of class Account.
// --------------------------------------------------

#include "account.h"

int main()
{
   Account giro("Cheers, Mary", 1234567, -1200.99 ),
           save("Lucky, Luke");

   Account depot;    // Error: no default constructor
                     //        defined.

   giro.display();         // To output
   save.display();

   Account temp("Funny, Susy", 7777777, 1000000.0);
   save = temp;            // ok: Assignment of
                           //     objects possible.
   save.display();

   // Or by the presently available method init():
   save.init("Lucky, Luke", 7654321, 1000000.0);
   save.display();

   return 0;
}
```

Unlike other methods, constructors cannot be called for existing objects. For this reason, a constructor does not have a return type. Instead, a suitable constructor is called once only when an object is created.

☐ Initialization

When an object is defined, initial values can follow the object name in parentheses.

Syntax: `class object( initializing_list);`

During initialization the compiler looks for a constructor whose signature matches the initialization list. After allocating sufficient memory for the object, the constructor is called. The values in the initialization list are passed as arguments to the constructor.

Example: `account nomoney("Poor, Charles");`

This statement calls the constructor with one parameter for the name. The other data members will default to standard values.

If the compiler is unable to locate a constructor with a suitable signature, it will not create the object but issue an error message.

Example: `account somemoney("Li, Ed",10.0); // Error!`

The class `Account` does not contain a constructor with two parameters.

If a constructor with only *one* parameter is defined in the class, the statement can be written with an equals sign =.

Example: `account nomoney = "Poor, Charles";`

This statement is equivalent to the definition in the example before last. Initialization with parentheses or the = sign was introduced previously for fundamental types. For example, `int i(0);` is equivalent to `int i =0;`.

☐ Default Constructor

A constructor *without* parameters is referred to as a *default constructor*. The default constructor is only called if an object definition does not explicitly initialize the object. A default constructor will use standard values for all data members.

If a class does not contain a constructor definition, the compiler will create a minimal version of the default constructor as a `public` member. However, this constructor will not perform initialization. By contrast, if a class contains *at least* one constructor, a default constructor must be defined explicitly, if it is needed. The definition of the `Account` class does not specify a default constructor; thus a new account object can be created with initialization only.

■ DESTRUCTORS

Sample program

```cpp
// demo.cpp
// Outputs constructor and destructor calls.
// -------------------------------------------------
#include <iostream>
#include <string>
using namespace std;
int count = 0;                          // Number of objects.
class Demo
{
   private:    string name;
   public:     Demo( const string& );    // Constructor
               ~Demo();                   // Destructor
};
Demo::Demo( const string& str)
{
   ++count;   name = str;
   cout << "I am the constructor of "<< name << '\n'
        << "This is the " << count << ". object!\n"
}
Demo:: ~Demo()                   // Defining the destructor
{
   cout << "I am the destructor of " << name << '\n'
        << "The " << count << ". object "
        << "will be destroyed " << endl;
   --count;
}
// -- To initialize and destroy objects of class Demo --
Demo globalObject("the global object");
int main()
{
   cout << "The first statement in main()." << endl;
   Demo firstLocalObject("the 1. local object");
   {
     Demo secLocalObject("the 2. local object");
     static Demo staticObject("the static object");
     cout << "\nLast statement within the inner block"
          << endl;
   }
   cout << "Last statement in main()." << endl;
   return 0;
}
```

☐ Cleaning Up Objects

Objects that were created by a constructor must also be cleaned up in an orderly manner. The tasks involved in cleaning up include releasing memory and closing files.

Objects are cleaned up by a special method called a *destructor*, whose name is made up of the class name preceded by ~ (tilde).

☐ Declaration and Definition

Destructors are declared in the `public` section and follow this syntax:

Syntax: `~class_name(void);`

Just like the constructor, a destructor does not have a return type. Neither does it have any parameters, which makes the destructor impossible to overload. Each class thus has *one* destructor only.

If the class does not define a destructor, the compiler will create a minimal version of a destructor as a `public` member, called the *default destructor*.

It is important to define a destructor if certain actions performed by the constructor need to be undone. If the constructor opened a file, for example, the destructor should close that file. The destructor in the `Account` class has no specific tasks to perform. The explicit definition is thus:

```
Account::~Account(){}        // Nothing to do
```

The individual data members of an object are always removed in the order opposite of the order in which they were created. The first data member to be created is therefore cleaned up last. If a data member is also a class type object, the object's own destructor will be called.

☐ Calling Destructors

A destructor is called automatically at the end of an object's lifetime:

- for local objects except objects that belong to the `static` storage class, at the end of the code block defining the object
- for global or `static` objects, at the end of the program.

The sample program on the opposite page illustrates various implicit calls to constructors and destructors.

■ INLINE METHODS

Sample class Account

```cpp
// account.h
// New definition of class Account with inline methods
// -------------------------------------------------------
#ifndef _ACCOUNT_
#define _ACCOUNT_

#include <iostream>
#include <iomanip>
#include <string>
using namespace std;

class Account
{
   private:               // Sheltered members:
     string name;              // Account holder
     unsigned long nr;         // Account number
     double state;             // State of the account
   public:               //Public interface:
                         // Constructors: implicit inline
     Account( const string& a_name = "X",
           unsigned long a_nr    = 1111111L,
           double  a_state       = 0.0)
     {
        name = a_name;  nr = a_nr;  state = a_state;
     }
     ~Account(){ }  // Dummy destructor: implicit inline
     void display();
};

// display() outputs data of class Account.
inline void Account::display()     // Explicit inline
{
   cout << fixed << setprecision(2)
       << "--------------------------------------\n"
       << "Account holder:   " << name  << '\n'
       << "Account number:   " << nr    << '\n'
       << "Account state:    " << state << '\n'
       << "--------------------------------------\n"
       << endl;
}
#endif   // _ACCOUNT_
```

A class typically contains multiple methods that fulfill simple tasks, such as reading or updating data members. This is the only way to ensure data encapsulation and class functionality.

However, continually calling "short" methods can impact a program's runtime. In fact, saving a re-entry address and jumping to the called function and back into the calling function can take more time than executing the function itself. To avoid this overhead, you can define `inline` methods in a way similar to defining `inline` global functions.

☐ Explicit and Implicit `inline` Methods

Methods can be explicitly or implicitly defined as `inline`. In the first case, the method is declared within the class, just like any other method. You simply need to place the `inline` keyword before the method name in the function header when defining the method.

Example:
```
inline void Account::display()
{
    . . .
}
```

Since the compiler must have access to the code block of an `inline` function, the `inline` function should be defined in the header containing the class definition.

Short methods can be defined within the class. Methods of this type are known as implicit `inline` methods, although the `inline` keyword is not used.

Example:
```
                // Within class Account:
    bool isPositive(){ return state > 0; }
```

☐ Constructors and Destructors with `inline` Definitions

Constructors and destructors are special methods belonging to a class and, as such, can be defined as `inline`. This point is illustrated by the new definition of the `Account` class opposite. The constructor and the destructor are both implicit `inline`. The constructor has a default value for each argument, which means that we also have a default constructor. You can now define objects without supplying an initialization list.

Example: `Account temp;`

Although we did not explicitly supply values here, the object `temp` was correctly initialized by the default constructor we defined.

■ ACCESS METHODS

Access methods for the `Account` class

```cpp
// account.h
// Class Account with set- and get-methods.
// --------------------------------------------------
#ifndef _ACCOUNT_
#define _ACCOUNT_

#include <iostream>
#include <iomanip>
#include <string>
using namespace std;

class Account
{
   private:              // Sheltered members:
     string name;        // Account holder
     unsigned long nr;   // Account number
     double state;       // State of the account
   public:              //Public interface:
                         // constructors, destructor:
     Account( const string& a_name = "X",
            unsigned long a_nr   = 1111111L,
            double   a_state     = 0.0)
     { name = a_name;  nr = a_nr;  state = a_state; }
     ~Account(){ }
                        // Access methods:
     const string& getName() { return name; }
     bool        setName( const string& s)
     {
       if( s.size() < 1)     // No empty name
         return false;
       name = s;
       return true;
     }
     unsigned long getNr() { return nr; }
     void        setNr( unsigned long n) { nr = n; }
     double getState() { return state; }
     void    setState(double x) { state = x; }
     void display();
};
// inline definition of display() as before.
#endif   // _ACCOUNT_
```

☐ Accessing Private Data Members

An object's data members are normally found in the `private` section of a class. To allow access to this data, you could place the data members in the `public` section of the class; however, this would undermine any attempt at data encapsulation.

Access methods offer a far more useful way of accessing the private data members. Access methods allow data to be read and manipulated in a controlled manner. If the access methods were defined as `inline`, access is just as efficient as direct access to the `public` members.

In the example opposite, several access methods have been added to the `Account` class. You can now use the

```
getName(), getNr(), getState()
```

methods to read the individual data members. As is illustrated in `getName()`, references should be read-only when used as return values. Direct access for write operations could be possible otherwise. To manipulate data members, the following methods can be used:

```
setName(), setNr(), setState().
```

This allows you to define a new balance, as follows:

Example: `save.setState( 2199.0);`

☐ Access Method Benefits

Defining access methods for reading and writing to each data member may seem like a lot of work—all that typing, reams of source code, and the programmer has to remember the names and tasks performed by all those methods.

So, you may be asking yourself how you benefit from using access methods. There are two important issues:

- ▨ Access methods can prevent invalid access attempts at the onset by performing sanity checks. If a class contains a member designed to represent positive numbers only, an access method can prevent processing negative numbers.
- ▨ Access methods also hide the actual implementation of a class. It is therefore possible to modify the internal structure of your data at a later stage. If you detect that a new data structure will allow more efficient data handling, you can add this modification to a new version of the class. Provided the public interface to the class remains unchanged, an application program can be leveraged by the modification without needing to modify the application itself. You simply recompile the application program.

■ const OBJECTS AND METHODS

Read-only methods in the `Account` class

```cpp
// account.h
// Account class with read-only methods.
// -------------------------------------------------
#ifndef _ACCOUNT_
#define _ACCOUNT_

#include <iostream>
#include <iomanip>
#include <string>
using namespace std;

class Account
{
   private:              // Sheltered members
     // Data members:  as before
   public:              // Public interface
      // Constructors and destructor
      . . .  // as before

     // Get-methods:
     const string& getName()  const { return name; }
     unsigned long getNr()     const { return nr; }
     double        getState() const { return state; }
     // Set-methods:
     . . .  // as before
     // Additional methods:
     void display() const;
};
// display() outputs the data of class Account.
inline void Account::display() const
{
   cout << fixed << setprecision(2)
        << "-----------------------------------\n"
        << "Account holder:   " << name  << '\n'
        << "Account number:   " << nr     << '\n'
        << "Account state:    " << state << '\n'
        << "-----------------------------------\n"
        << endl;
}
#endif   // _ACCOUNT_
```

☐ Accessing `const` Objects

If you define an object as `const`, the program can only read the object. As mentioned earlier, the object must be initialized when you define it for this reason.

Example: `const Account inv("YMCA, FL", 5555, 5000.0);`

The object `inv` cannot be modified at a later stage. This also means that methods such as `setName()` cannot be called for this object. However, methods such as `getName` or `display()` will be similarly unavailable although they only perform read access with the data members.

   The reason for this is that the compiler cannot decide whether a method performs write operations or only read operations with data members unless additional information is supplied.

☐ Read-Only Methods

Methods that perform only read operations and that you need to call for constant objects must be identified as read-only. To identify a method as read-only, append the `const` keyword in the method declaration and in the function header for the method definition.

Example: `unsigned long getNr() const;`

This declares the `getNr()` method as a *read-only method* that can be used for constant objects.

Example: `cout << "Account number: " << inv.getNr();`

Of course, this does not prevent you from calling a read-only method for a non-constant object.

   The compiler issues an error message if a read-only method tries to modify a data member. This also occurs when a read-only method calls another method that is not defined as `const`.

☐ `const` and Non-`const` Versions of a Method

Since the `const` keyword is part of the method's signature, you can define two versions of the method: a read-only version, which will be called for constant objects by default, and a normal version, which will be called for non-`const` objects.

■ STANDARD METHODS

Sample program

```cpp
// stdMeth.cpp
// Using standard methods.
// --------------------------------------------------
#include <iostream>
#include <iomanip>
#include <string>
using namespace std;

class CD
{   private:
      string interpret, title;
      long   seconds;                 // Time duration of a song
    public:
      CD( const string& i="", const string& t="", long s = 0L)
      {
         interpret = i;    title = t;    seconds = s;
      }
      const string& getInterpret() const{ return interpret; }
      const string& getTitle() const    { return title; }
      long  getSeconds() const          { return seconds; }
};
// Generate objects of class CD and output it in tabular form
void printLine( CD cd) ;            // A row of the table
int main()
{
   CD cd1( "Mister X", "Let's dance", 30*60 + 41),
      cd2( "New Guitars", "Flamenco Collection", 2772 ),
      cd3 = cd1,                     // Copy constructor!
      cd4;                           // Default constructor.
      cd4 = cd2;                     // Assignment!
   string line( 70,'-');   line += '\n';
   cout << line << left
        << setw(20) << "Interpreter" << setw(30) << "Title"
        << "Length (Min:Sec)\n" << line << endl;
   printLine(cd3);                   // Call by value ==>
   printLine(cd4);                   // Copy constructor!
   return 0;
}
void printLine( CD cd)
{   cout << left  << setw(20) << cd.getInterpret()
                  << setw(30) << cd.getTitle()
        << right << setw(5)  << cd.getSeconds() / 60
        << ':'   << setw(2)  << cd.getSeconds() % 60 << endl;
}
```

Every class *automatically* contains four standard methods:

- the default constructor
- the destructor
- the copy constructor and
- the assignment.

You can use your own definitions to replace these standard methods. As illustrated by the sample class `Account`, the compiler only uses the pre-defined default constructor if no other constructor is available.

The default constructor and the implicit, minimal version of a destructor were introduced earlier.

☐ Copy Constructor

The copy constructor initializes an object with another object of the same type. It is called automatically when a second, already existing object is used to initialize an object.

Example:
```
Account myAccount("Li, Ed", 2345, 124.80);
Account yourAccount(myAccount);
```

In this example, the object `yourAccount` is initialized by calling the copy constructor with the `myAccount` object. Each member is copied individually, that is, the following initialization process takes place:

```
yourAccount.name  = myAccount.name;
yourAccount.nr    = myAccount.nr;
yourAccount.state = myAccount.state;
```

The copy constructor is also called when an object is passed to a function by value. When the function is called, the parameter is created and initialized with the object used as an argument.

☐ Assignment

Assignment has been used in several previous examples. An object can be assigned to another object of the same type.

Example: `hisAccount = yourAccount;`

The data members of the `yourAccount` object are copied to the corresponding members of `hisAccount` in this case also. In contrast to initialization using the copy constructor, assignment requires two *existing* objects.

Later in the book, you will be introduced to situations where you need to define the copy constructor or an assignment yourself, and the necessary techniques will be discussed.

■ this POINTER

Sample class DayTime

```cpp
// DayTime.h
// The class DayTime represents the time in
// hours, minutes and seconds.
// ----------------------------------------------------
#ifndef _DAYTIME_
#define _DAYTIME_
class DayTime
{
  private:
     short hour, minute, second;
     bool overflow;
  public:
   DayTime( int h = 0, int m = 0, int s = 0)
    {
      overflow = false;
      if( !setTime( h, m, s))           // this->setTime(...)
        hour = minute = second = 0; // hour is equivalent
    }                                   // to this->hour etc.
    bool setTime(int hour, int minute, int second = 0)
    {
      if(    hour   >= 0  &&  hour < 24
          && minute >= 0  &&  minute < 60
          && second >= 0  &&  second < 60 )
      {
        this->hour   = (short)hour;
        this->minute = (short)minute;
        this->second = (short)second;
        return true;
      }
      else
        return false;
    }
    int getHour()   const { return hour;   }
    int getMinute() const { return minute; }
    int getSecond() const { return second; }

    int asSeconds() const       // daytime in seconds
    {   return (60*60*hour + 60*minute + second);   }

    bool isLess( DayTime t) const  // compare *this and t
    {
      return  asSeconds() < t.asSeconds();
    }        // this->asSeconds() < t.asSeconds();
};
#endif   // _DAYTIME_
```

☐ Accessing the Current Object

A method can access any member of an object without the object name being supplied in every case. A method will always reference the object with which it was called.

But how does a method know which object it is currently working with? When a method is called, it is passed a hidden argument containing the address of the current object.

The address of the current object is available to the method via the constant pointer this. Given that actObj is the current object of type Class_id, for which a method was called, the pointer this has the following declaration:

```
Class_id* const this = &actObj;
```

The name this is a keyword. As this is a constant pointer, it cannot be redirected. In other words, the pointer this allows you to access the current object only.

☐ Using the this Pointer

You can use the this pointer within a method to address an object member as follows:

```
Example:   this->data      // Data member: data
           this->func()    // Calling member function
```

The compiler implicitly creates an expression of this type if only a member of the current object is supplied.

```
Example:   data = 12;   // Corresponds to this->data=12;
```

Write operations of this type are permissible since the pointer this is a constant, but the referenced object is not. However, the above statement would be invalid for a read-only method.

The this pointer can be used explicitly to distinguish a method's local variables from class members of the same name. This point is illustrated by the sample method setTime() on the opposite page.

The this pointer is always necessary to access the current object, *this, collectively. This situation often occurs when the current object needs to be returned as a copy or by reference. Then the return statement is as follows:

```
return   *this;
```

■ PASSING OBJECTS AS ARGUMENTS

Calling methods `setTime()` **and** `isLess()`

```
#include "DayTime.h"
. . .
  DayTime depart1( 11, 11, 11), depart2;
  . . .
  depart2.setTime(12, 0, 0);
  if( depart1.isLess( depart2) )
    cout << "\nThe 1st plane takes off earlier" << endl;
  . . .
```

Global function `swap()`

```
#include "DayTime.h"
// Defines the global function swap():
void swap( DayTime& t1, DayTime& t2)          // Two
{                                             // parameters!
  DayTime temp(t1);  t1 = t2;  t2 = temp; // To swap
}                                             // t1 and t2.
// A call (e.g. in function main()):
  DayTime arrival1( 14, 10), arrival2( 15, 20);
  . . .
  swap( arrival1, arrival2);                  // To swap
  . . .
```

Implementing `swap()` **as a method**

```
// Defines the method swap():
class DayTime                  // With a new method swap()
{  . . .
  public:
  void swap( DayTime& t)       // One parameter!
  {                            // To swap *this and t:
    DayTime temp(t);  t = *this;  *this = temp;
  }
};
// A call (e.g. in function main()):
#include "DayTime.h"
  DayTime arrival1( 10, 10), arrival2( 9, 50);
  . . .
  arrival1.swap(arrival2);
  . . .
```

☐ Passing by Value

As you already know, passing by value copies an object that was passed as an argument to the corresponding parameter of a function being called. The parameter is declared as an object of the class in question.

Example: `bool isLess( DayTime t) const;`

When the method `isLess()` is called, the copy constructor executes and initializes the created object, `t`, with the argument.

```
depart1.isLess( depart2)    // Copy constructor
```

The function uses a copy of the object `depart2`. The copy is cleaned up when leaving the function, that is, the destructor is called.

☐ Passing by Reference

The overhead caused by creating and cleaning up objects can be avoided by passing arguments by reference. In this case, the parameter is declared as a reference or pointer.

Example: `bool isLess( const DayTime& t) const;`

This new declaration of the `isLess()` method is preferable to the previous declaration. There is no formal difference to the way the method is called. However, `isLess()` no longer creates an internal copy, but accesses directly the object being passed. Of course, the object cannot be changed, as the parameter was declared read-only.

☐ Methods Versus Global Functions

Of course, it is possible to write a global function that expects *one* object as an argument. However, this rarely makes sense since you would normally expect an object's functionality to be defined in the class itself. Instead, you would normally define a method for the class and the method would perform the task in hand. In this case, the object would not be passed as an argument since the method would manipulate the members of the current object.

A different situation occurs where operations with at least *two* objects need to be performed, such as comparing or swapping. For example, the method `isLess()` could be defined as a global function with two parameters. However, the function could only access the public interface of the objects. The function `swap()` on the opposite page additionally illustrates this point.

The major advantage of a globally defined function is its symmetry. The objects involved are peers, since both are passed as arguments. This means that conversion rules are applied to both arguments when the function is called.

■ RETURNING OBJECTS

Global function `currentTime()`

```
#include "DayTime.h"
#include <ctime>          // Functions time(), localtime()
using namespace std;

const DayTime& currentTime()      // Returns the
{                                 // present time.
  static DayTime curTime;
  time_t sec;  time(&sec);  // Gets the present time.
                            // Initializes the struct
  struct tm *time = localtime(&sec);   // tm with it.

  curTime.setTime( time->tm_hour, time->tm_min,
                   time->tm_sec );
  return curTime;
}
```

Sample program

```
// DayTim_t.cpp
// Tests class DayTime and function currentTime()
// ---------------------------------------------------
#include "DayTime.h"             // Class definition
#include <iostream>
using namespace std;

const DayTime& currentTime();    // The current time.

int main()
{
  DayTime cinema( 20,30);

  cout << "\nThe movie starts at ";
  cinema.print();

  DayTime now(currentTime());    // Copy constructor
  cout << "\nThe current time is ";
  now.print();

  cout << "\nThe movie has ";
  if( cinema.isLess( now) )
     cout << "already begun!\n" << endl;
  else
     cout << "not yet begun!\n" << endl;
  return 0;
}
```

A function can use the following ways to return an object as a return value: It can create a copy of the object, or it can return a reference or pointer to that object.

Returning a Copy

Returning a copy of an object is time-consuming and only makes sense for small-scale objects.

Example:
```
DayTime startMeeting()
{
    DayTime start;
    . . .      // Everyone has time at 14:30:
    start.setTime( 14, 30);
    return( start);
}
```

On exiting the function, the local object start is destroyed. This forces the compiler to create a temporary copy of the local object and return the copy to the calling function.

Returning a Reference

Of course, it is more efficient to return a reference to an object. But be aware that the lifetime of the referenced object must not be local.

If this is the case, the object is destroyed on exiting the function and the returned reference becomes invalid. If you define the object within a function, you must use a static declaration.

The global function currentTime() on the opposite page exploits this option by returning a reference to the current time that it reads from the system each time the function is called. The sample program that follows this example uses the current time to initialize the new object now and then outputs the time. In order to output the time, an additional method, print(), was added to the class.

Using Pointers as Return Values

Instead of returning a reference, a function can also return a pointer to an object. In this case too, you must ensure that the object still exists after exiting the function.

Example:
```
const DayTime* currentTime() // Read-only pointer
{                            // to the current time
    . . . // Unchanged
    return &curTime;
}
```

EXERCISES

Class Article

Private members:

	Type
Article number:	long
Article name:	string
Sales price:	double

Public members:

```
Article(long, const string&, double);
~Article();
void print();      // Formatted output
set- and get-methods for any data member
```

Output from constructor

```
An object of type Article . . . is created.
This is the . . .. Article.
```

Output from destructor

```
The object of type Article  . . . is destroyed.
There are still . . . articles.
```

Exercise 1

A warehouse management program needs a class to represent the articles in stock.

- Define a class called `Article` for this purpose using the data members and methods shown opposite. Store the class definition for `Article` in a separate header file. Declare the constructor with default arguments for each parameter to ensure that a default constructor exists for the class. Access methods for the data members are to be defined as `inline`. Negative prices must not exist. If a negative price is passed as an argument, the price must be stored as `0.0`.
- Implement the constructor, the destructor, and the method `print()` in a separate source file. Also define a global variable for the number of `Article` type objects.

  The constructor must use the arguments passed to it to initialize the data members, additionally increment the global counter, and issue the message shown opposite.

  The destructor also issues a message and decrements the global counter.

  The method `print()` displays a formatted object on screen. After outputting an article, the program waits for the return key to be pressed.

- The application program (again use a separate source file) tests the `Article` class. Define four objects belonging to the `Article` class type:

  1. A global object and a local object in the `main` function.
  2. Two local objects in a function `test()` that is called twice by `main()`. One object needs a static definition. The function `test()` displays these objects and outputs a message when it is terminated.

  Use articles of your own choice to initialize the objects. Additionally, call the access methods to modify individual data members and display the objects on screen.

- Test your program. Note the order in which constructors and destructors are called.

Supplementary question: Suppose you modify the program by declaring a function called `test()` with a parameter of type `Article` and calling the function with an article type object. The counter for the number of objects is negative after running the program. Why?

Methods for class Date

Public Methods:

```
Date();
Date( int month, int day, int year);
void setDate();
bool setDate( int mn, int da, int yr);

int getMonth() const;
int getDay() const;
int getYear() const;
bool isEqual( const Date&) const;
bool isLess( const Date&) const;
const string& asString() const;
void  print() const;
```

Converting a number to a string

The class stringstream offers the same functionality for reading and writing to character buffer as the classes istream and ostream do. Thus, the operators >> and << , just as all manipulators, are available.

```
// Example: Converting a number to a string.
#include <sstream>              // Class stringstream
#include <iomanip>              // Manipulators

  double x = 12.3;              // Number
  string str;                   // Destination string
  stringstream iostream;        // For conversion
                                // number -> string.
  iostream << setw(10) << x;    // Add to the stream.
  iostream >> str;              // Read from the stream.
```

Notices for exercise 3

■ A year is a leap year if it is divisible by 4 but not by 100. In addition, all multiples of 400 are leap years. February has 29 days in a leap year.

■ Use a switch statement to examine the number of days for months containing less than 31 days.

Exercise 2

In the exercises for chapter 13, an initial version of the Date class containing members for day, month, and year was defined. Now extend this class to add additional functionality. The methods are shown on the opposite page.

- The constructors and the method setDate() replace the init method used in the former version. The default constructor uses default values, for example, 1.1.1, to initialize the objects in question. The setDate() method without any parameters writes the current date to the object.
- The constructor and the setDate() method with three parameters do not need to perform range checking. This functionality will be added in the next exercise.
- The methods isEqual() and isLess() enable comparisons with a date passed to them.
- The method asString() returns a reference to a string containing the date in the format mm-dd-year, e.g. 03-19-2006. You will therefore need to convert any numerical values into their corresponding decimal strings. This operation is performed automatically when you use the << operator to output a number to the standard output cout. In addition to the cin and cout streams, with which you are already familiar, so-called *string streams* with the same functionality also exist. However, a string stream does not read keyboard input or output data on screen. Instead, the target, or source, is a buffer in main memory. This allows you to perform formatting and conversion in main memory.
- Use an application program that calls all the methods defined in the class to test the Date class.

Exercise 3

The Date class does not ensure that an object represents a valid date. To avoid this issue, add range checking functionality to the class. Range checking is performed by the constructor and the setDate() method with three parameters.

- First, write a function called isLeapYear() that belongs to the bool type and checks whether the year passed to it is a leap year. Define the function as a global inline function and store it in the header file Date.h.
- Modify the setDate() method to allow range checking for the date passed to it. The constructor can call setDate().
- Test the new version of the Date class. To do so, and to test set-Date(...), read a date from the keyboard.

Exercise 1

```
// ---------------------------------------------------
// article.h
// Defines a simple class, Article.
// ---------------------------------------------------
#ifndef _ARTICLE_
#define _ARTICLE_

#include <string>
using namespace std;

class Article
{
  private:
    long nr;                    // Article number
    string name;                // Article name
    double sp;                  // Selling price

  public:
    Article( long nr=0, const string& name="noname",
             double sp=0.0);
    ~Article();
    void print();

    const string& getName() const { return name; }
    long          getNr()   const { return nr; }
    double        getSP()   const { return sp; }

    bool setName( const string& s)
    {
      if( s.size() < 1)             // No empty name
        return false;
      name = s;
      return true;
    }
    void setNr( long n) { nr = n; }
    void setSP(double v)
    {                               // No negative price
      sp = v > 0.0 ? v : 0.0;
    }
};

#endif   // _ARTICLE_
```

```
// --------------------------------------------------------
// article.cpp
// Defines those methods of Article, which are
// not defined inline.
// Screen output for constructor and destructor calls.
// --------------------------------------------------------
#include "Article.h"           // Definition of the class
#include <iostream>
#include <iomanip>
using namespace std;

// Global counter for the objects:
int count = 0;

// --------------------------------------------------------
// Define constructor and destructor:
Article::Article( long nr, const string& name, double sp)
{
   setNr(nr);   setName(name);   setSP(sp);
   ++count;
   cout << "Created object for the article " << name
        << ".\n"
        << "This is the " << count << ". article!\n"
}
Article::~Article()
{
   cout << "Cleaned up object for the article " << name
        << ".\n"
        << "There are still " << --count << " articles!"
        << endl;
}
// --------------------------------------------------------
// The method print() outputs an article.
void Article::print()
{
   long savedFlags = cout.flags();      // To mark the
                                        // flags of cout.
   cout << fixed << setprecision(2)
        << "----------------------------------------\n"
        << "Article data:\n"
        << "  Number ....:  " << nr     << '\n'
        << "  Name   ....:  " << name   << '\n'
        << "  Sales price:  " << sp     << '\n'
        << "----------------------------------------"
        << endl;
   cout.flags(savedFlags);              // To restore
                                        // old flags.
   cout << "  --- Go on with return --- ";
   cin.get();
}
```

```cpp
// ------------------------------------------------------
// article_t.cpp
// Tests the Article class.
// ------------------------------------------------------
#include "Article.h"        // Definition of the class
#include <iostream>
#include <string>
using namespace std;

void test();

// -- Creates and destroys objects of Article class --
Article Article1( 1111,"volley ball", 59.9);
int main()
{
   cout << "\nThe first statement in main().\n" << endl;
   Article Article2( 2222,"gym-shoes", 199.99);
   Article1.print();
   Article2.print();
   Article& shoes = Article2;          // Another name
   shoes.setNr( 2233);
   shoes.setName("jogging-shoes");
   shoes.setSP( shoes.getSP() - 50.0);

   cout << "\nThe new values of the shoes object:\n";
   shoes.print();
   cout << "\nThe first call to test()." << endl;
   test();
   cout << "\nThe second call to test()." << endl;
   test();
   cout << "\nThe last statement in main().\n" << endl;
   return 0;
}

void test()
{
   Article shirt( 3333, "T-Shirt", 29.9);
   shirt.print();
   static Article net( 4444, "volley ball net", 99.0);
   net.print();
   cout << "\nLast statement in function test()"
        << endl;
}
```

Answer to the supplementary question:

The copy constructor is called on each "passing by value," although this constructor has not been defined explicitly. In other words, the implicitly defined copy constructor is used and of course does not increment the object counter. However, the explicitly defined destructor, which decrements the counter, is still called for each object.

Exercises 2 and 3

```
// --------------------------------------------------------
// Date.h
// Defining class Date with optimized
// functionality, e.g. range check.
// --------------------------------------------------------
#ifndef _DATE_    // Avoids multiple inclusions.
#define _DATE_
#include <string>
using namespace std;

class Date
{
  private:
    short month, day, year;
  public:
    Date()                          // Default constructor
    {   month = day = year = 1;   }

    Date( int month, int day, int year)
    {
        if( !setDate( month,  day, year) )
          month = day = year = 1;  // If date is invalid
    }
    void setDate();                 // Sets the current date
    bool setDate( int month, int day, int year);
    int getMonth() const { return month; }
    int getDay()   const { return day;   }
    int getYear()  const { return year;  }
    bool isEqual( const Date& d) const
    {
        return month == d.month && day == d.day
                      && year  == d.year ;
    }
    bool isLess( const Date& d) const;
    const string& asString() const;
    void print(void) const;
};
```

```cpp
inline bool Date::isLess( const Date& d) const
{
   if( year != d.year)            return year < d.year;
   else if( month != d.month)  return month < d.month;
   else                           return day < d.day;
}

inline bool isLeapYear( int year)
{
   return (year%4 == 0 && year%100 != 0) || year%400 == 0;
}
#endif   //  _DATE_


// ------------------------------------------------------
// Date.cpp
// Implements those methods of Date class,
// which are not defined inline.
// ------------------------------------------------------
#include "Date.h"                 // Class definition
#include <iostream>
#include <sstream>
#include <iomanip>
#include <string>
#include <ctime>
using namespace std;

// -----------------------------------------------------
void Date::setDate()       // Get the present date and
{                          // assign it to the data members.
   struct tm *dur;         // Pointer to struct tm.
   time_t sec;             // For seconds.

   time(&sec);             // Get the present time.
   dur = localtime(&sec);  // Initialize a struct of
                           // type tm and return a
                           // pointer to it.
   day   = (short) dur->tm_mday;
   month = (short) dur->tm_mon + 1;
   year  = (short) dur->tm_year + 1900;
}
```

```cpp
// ----------------------------------------------------
bool Date::setDate( int mn, int da, int yr)
{
   if( mn < 1 ||  mn > 12 ) return false;
   if( da < 1 ||  da > 31 ) return false;

   switch(mn)                   // Month with less than 31 days
   {
     case 2:  if( isLeapYear(yr))
              {
                if( da > 29)
                  return false;
              }
              else if( da > 28)
                return false;
              break;
     case 4:
     case 6:
     case 9:
     case 11:
              if( da > 30)  return false;
   }
   month = (short) mn;
   day   = (short) da;
   year  = (short) yr;
   return true;
}

// ----------------------------------------------------
void Date::print() const                 // Output a date
{
    cout << asString() << endl;
}

// ----------------------------------------------------
const string& Date::asString() const    // Return a date
{                                        // as string.
   static string dateString;
   stringstream iostream;                // For conversion
                                         // number -> string
   iostream << setfill('0')              // and formatting.
            << setw(2) << month << '-'
            << setw(2) << day   << '-' << year;

   iostream >> dateString;
   return dateString;
}
```

```cpp
// -------------------------------------------------------
// date_t.cpp
// Using objects of class Date.
// -------------------------------------------------------
#include "Date.h"
#include <iostream>
using namespace std;

int main()
{
   Date  today, birthday( 1, 29, 1927);
   const Date d2010(1,1,2010);

   cout << "\n Brigit's birthday: "
        << birthday.asString() << endl;

   today.setDate();
   cout << "\nToday's date: " << today.asString()
        << endl;;

   if( today.isLess( d2010))
      cout << " Good luck for this decade \n"
            << endl;
   else
      cout << " See you next decade \n" << endl;

   Date holiday;
   int month, day, year;    char c;

   cout << "\nWhen does your next vacation begin?\n"
        << "Enter in Month-Day-Year format: ";

   if( !(cin >> month >> c >> day >> c >> year) )
      cerr << "Invalid input!\n" << endl;
   else if ( !holiday.setDate( month, day,  year))
      cerr << "Invalid date!\n" << endl;
   else
   {
      cout << "\nYour first vacation: ";
      holiday.print();

      if( today.getYear() < holiday.getYear())
         cout << "You should go on vacation this year!\n"
               << endl;
      else
         cout << "Have a nice trip!\n" << endl;
   }
   return 0;
}
```

chapter 15

Member Objects and Static Members

The major topics discussed in this chapter are

- member objects and how they are initialized
- data members that are created once only for all the objects in a class.

In addition, this chapter describes constant members and enumerated types.

■ MEMBER OBJECTS

A class representing measurement results

```
// result.h
// Class Result to represent a measurement
// and the time of measurement.
// ---------------------------------------------------
#ifndef _RESULT_
#define _RESULT_
#include "DayTime.h"                    // Class DayTime
class Result
{
 private:
  double val;
  DayTime time;
 public:
  Result();                             // Default constructor
  Result(double w, const DayTime& z = currentTime());
  Result(double w, int hr, int min, int sec);
  double getVal() const { return val; }
  void    setVal( double w ) { val = w; }
  const DayTime& getTime() const  { return time; }
  void    setTime( const DayTime& z) { time = z; }
  bool    setTime(int hr, int min, int sec)
        {   return  time.setTime( hr, min, sec); }
  void print() const;        // Output result and time.
};
#endif  //  _RESULT_
```

A first implementation of constructors

```
#include "result.h"
Result::Result() { val = 0.0; }
Result::Result( double w, const DayTime& z)
{
   val = w;     time = z;
}
Result::Result( double w, int hr, int min, int sec)
{  val = w;
   time = DayTime(hr, min, sec);  // Assign a temporary
                                  // object of type
}                                 // DayTime to time.
```

☐ "Has-A" Relationship

Data members belonging to one class can be objects of a different class. In our example, the `Account` class, we already made use of this feature. The name of the account holder is stored in a `string` type data member. An object of the `Account` class therefore has a `string` type *member sub-object*, or *member object* for short.

If a class contains a data member whose type is of a different class, the relationship between the classes is referred to as a *"Has-A" relationship*.

☐ Calling Constructors

When an object containing member objects is initialized, multiple constructor calls are to be executed. One of these is the constructor for the complete object, and the others are constructors for the member objects. The *order of the constructor calls* is significant in this case. First, the member objects are created and initialized; this then allows the constructor to create the whole object. Unless otherwise stated, the default constructor will be called for each member object.

☐ The Constructors for the Sample Class `Result`

The example on the opposite page defines a sample class called `Result`. In addition to a `double` type measurement, the time of each measurement is recorded. For ease of reading, the constructors were defined separately, rather than as `inline`.

The default constructor only sets the value of the measurement to 0. However, initialization is complete since the default constructor is called for the member object `time`.

Example: `Result current;`

The default constructor for the member object `time` first sets the hours, minutes and seconds to 0. Then the constructor for the `Result` class is called and a value of `0.0` is assigned to `val`.

The other constructors can be used to initialize an object explicitly.

Example: `Result temperature1(15.9); // Current Time`
           `Result temperature2(16.7, 14, 30, 35);`

Since the compiler has no information on the relation of initial values and member objects, it first calls the default constructor for the member object `time`. Subsequently the instructions for the `Result` class constructor can be executed, and values are assigned to the data members.

■ MEMBER INITIALIZERS

New implementation of constructors

```
#include "result.h"
Result::Result() : val(0.0) { /* ... */ }

Result::Result( double w, const DayTime& z)
          : val(w), time(z)
{ /* ... */ }

Result::Result( double w, int hr, int min, int sec)
          : val(w), time(hr, min, sec)
{
  /* ... */
}
```

✓ **NOTE**

You can replace the comment /* ... */ with statements, if needed. However, in the case of the Result class there is nothing to do at present.

Sample program

```
// result_t.cpp
// Tests constructors of class Result
// ---------------------------------------------------
#include "Result.h"
#include <iostream>
using namespace std;

int main()          // Some air temperature measurements
{
   DayTime  morning(6,30);
   Result t1,                     // Default constructor
          t2( 12.5, morning),
          t3( 18.2, 12,0,0),
          t4(17.7);               // at current time

   cout << "Default values: ";   t1.print();

   cout << "\n Temperature    Time  \n"
        << "-------------------------" << endl;
   t2.print();
   t3.print();
   t4.print();
   cout << endl;
   return 0;
}
```

☐ Initializing Member Objects

Calling default constructors to create member objects raises several issues:

- A member object is initialized first with default values. Correct values are assigned later. This additional action can impact your program's performance.
- Constant objects or references cannot be declared as member objects since it is impossible to assign values to them later.
- Classes that do not have a default constructor definition cannot be used as types for member objects.

When defining a constructor, you can use *member initializers* to ensure general and efficient use of member objects.

☐ Syntax for Member Initializers

A member initializer contains the name of the data member, followed by the initial values in parentheses.

Example: `time(hr,min,sec)        // Member initializer`

Multiple member initializers are separated by commas. A list of member initializers defined in this way follows the constructor header and is separated from the header by a colon.

Example:
```
Result::Result( /* Parameters */ )
     : val(w), time(hr, min, sec)
     {  /* Function block  */ }
```

This ensures that a suitable constructor will be called for data members with member initializers and avoids calls to the default constructor with subsequent assignments. As the example shows, you can also use member initializers for data members belonging to fundamental types.

The argument names of the member initializers are normally constructor parameters. This helps pass the values used to create an object to the right member object.

 NOTE

Member initializers can only be stated in a constructor *definition*. The constructor declaration remains unchanged.

■ CONSTANT MEMBER OBJECTS

New version of class Result

```
// result2.h
// The class Result with a constant data member.
// ----------------------------------------------------
#ifndef  _RESULT_
#define  _RESULT_
#include "DayTime.h"              // Class DayTime
class Result
{
 private:
   double val;
   const DayTime time;

 public:
   Result(double w, const DayTime& z = currentTime());
   Result(double w, int hr, int min, int sec);
   double getVal() const { return val; }
   void   setVal( double w ) { val = w; }
   const DayTime& getTime() const  { return time; }
   void print() const;
};
#endif  //  _RESULT_
```

Using the new class Result

```
// result2_t.cpp  :     Tests the new class Result.
// ----------------------------------------------------
#include "result2.h"
#include <iostream>
using namespace std;
int main()
{
   DayTime   start(10,15);
   Result m1( 101.01, start),
          m2( m1),                // Copy constructor ok!
          m3( 99.9);              // At current time.
// m2 = m3;      // Error! Standard assignment incorrect.
   m2.setVal(100.9);             // Corrected value for m2
   cout << "\n Result     Time  \n"
        << "-------------------------" << endl;
   m1.print();    m2.print();   m3.print();
   return 0;
}
```

☐ Declaring const Member Objects

If a class contains data members that need to keep their initial values, you can define these members as const. For example, you could set the time for a measurement once and not change this time subsequently. However, you need to be able to edit the measurement value to correct systematic errors. In this case, the member object time can be declared as follows:

Example: const DayTime time;

Since the const member object time cannot be modified by a later assignment, the correct constructor must be called to initialize the object. In other words, when you define a constructor for a class, you *must* also define a member initializer for each const member object.

☐ The Sample Class Result

If the member object time is const, the first version of the constructors are invalid since they modify time by means of a later assignment.

Example: time = DayTime(st, mn, sk);   // Error!

However, the later versions of these constructors are ok. The member initializer ensures that the desired initial values are used to create the member object time.

One further effect of the const member object is the fact that the setTime(...) methods can no longer be applied. The compiler will issue an error message at this point and for any statement in the current program that attempts to modify the static member, time. This means that a programmer cannot accidentally overwrite a member declared as a const.

The new version of the Result class no longer contains a default constructor, since a default value for the time of the measurement does not make sense.

☐ Example with Fundamental Type

Data members with fundamental types can also be defined as const. The class Client contains a number, nr, which is used to identify customers. Since the client number never changes, it makes sense to define the number as const. The constructor for Client would then read as follows:

Example: Client::Client(/*...*/) : nr(++id)
          { /*...*/ }

The member initializer nr(++id) initializes the const data member nr with the global value id, which is incremented prior to use.

■ STATIC DATA MEMBERS

Class `Result` with static members

```
// result3.h
// The class Result with static data members.
// ---------------------------------------------------
#ifndef _RESULT_
#define _RESULT_
#include "DayTime.h"            // Class DayTime
class Result
{
 private:
   double val;
   const  DayTime time;
   // Declaration of static members:
   static double min, max;    // Minimum, maximum
   static bool first; // true, if it is the first value.
   void setMinMax(double w);  // private function
 public:
   Result(double w, const DayTime& z = currentTime());
   Result(double w, int hr, int min, int sec);
   // ...  The other member functions as before
};
#endif  // _RESULT_
```

Implementation and initialization

```
// result3.cpp
// Defining static data members and
// methods, which are not defined inline.
// ---------------------------------------------------
#include "result3.h"
double Result::min = 0.0;
double Result::max = 0.0;
bool   Result::first = true;
void Result::setMinMax(double w)    // Help function
{ if(first) {   min = max = w;   first = false; }
  else if( w < min)  min = w;
  else if( w > max)  max = w;
}
// Constructors with member initializer.
Result::Result( double w, const DayTime& z)
: val(w), time(z)
{  setMinMax(w);  }
Result::Result( double w, int hr, int min, int sec)
: val(w), time(hr, min, sec)
{  setMinMax(w);  }
// Implements the other member functions.
```

☐ Class-Specific Data

Every object has its own characteristics. This means that the data members of two different objects will be stored at different memory addresses.

However, sometimes it is useful to keep some common data that can be accessed by all the objects belonging to a class, for example:

- figures such as exchange rates, interest rates or time limits which have the same value for every object
- status information, such as the number of objects, current minimum or maximum threshold values, or pointers to some objects; for example, a pointer to an active window in a window class.

This kind of data needs to be stored *once only*, no matter how many objects exist. Since a programmer will also need to manage the data from within the class, it should be represented within the class rather than globally. *Static data members* can be used for this purpose. In contrast to normal data members, static data members occur only once in memory.

☐ Declaration

Static data members are declared within a class, that is, the keyword `static` is used to declare members of this type. On the opposite page, the following statement

Example: `static double min, max;   // Declaration`

defines two static data members called `min` and `max` that record the minimum and maximum values for the measurements.

☐ Definition and Initialization

Static data members occupy memory space even if no objects of the class in question have been created. Just like member functions, which occur only once, static data members must be defined and initialized in an external source file. The range operator `: :` is then used to relate the data members to the class.

Example: `double Result::min = 0.0;   // Definition`

As the example illustrates, the `static` keyword is not used during the definition. Static data members and member functions belonging to the same class are normally defined in one source file.

■ ACCESSING STATIC DATA MEMBERS

Class `Result` with static methods

```
class Result
{
 private:
   double val;
   const  DayTime time;
   static double min, max;     // Minimum, Maximum
   static bool first;          // true, if first result
   static void setMinMax(double w);  // Help function
 public:
   // ... Member functions as before, plus:
   static double getMin() { return min; }
   static double getMax() { return max; }
};
```

Application program

```
// result3_t.cpp
// Uses the new class Result.
// ----------------------------------------------------
#include "result3.h"
#include <iostream>
using namespace std;
int main()            //Some air temperature measurements
{
   DayTime  morning(6,45);
   Result temp1( 6.45, morning),
          temp2( 11.2, 12,0,0);
   double temp = 0.0;
   cout << "\nWhat is the air temperature now? ";
   cin >> temp;
   Result temp3(temp);          // At current time.
   cout << "\n Temperature   Time  \n"
        << "-------------------------" << endl;
   temp1.print();  temp2.print();  temp3.print();
   cout
    << "\n Minimum Temperature: " << Result::getMin()
    << "\n Maximum Temperature: " << Result::getMax()
    << endl;
   return 0;
}
```

☐ Static Data Members and Encapsulation

The normal rules for data encapsulation also apply to static data members. A static data member declared as `public` is therefore directly accessible to any object.

If the static data members `min` and `max` in the `Result` class are declared `public` rather than `private`, and given that `temperature` is an object belonging to the class, the following statement

Example: `cout << temperature.max;`

outputs the maximum measured value. You can also use the range operator:

Example: `cout << Result::max;`

This syntax is preferable to the previous example, since it clearly shows that a static data member exists independently of any objects.

☐ Static Member Functions

Of course, you can use class methods to access a static data member with a `private` declaration. However, normal methods can be used for class objects only. Since static data members are independent of any objects, access to them should also be independent of any objects. *Static member functions* are used for this purpose. For example, you can call a static member function for a class even though no objects exist in that class.

The `static` keyword is used to define static member functions.

Example: `static double getMin();    // Within class.`

As the `Result` class, which was modified to include the static member functions `getMin()`, `setMin()`, etc. shows, an `inline` definition is also permissible. Definitions outside of the class do not need to repeat the `static` keyword.

A static member function can be called using any object belonging to the class or, preferably, using a range operator.

Example: `temperature.setMax(42.4);    // Equivalent`
        `Result::setMax(42.4);        // Calls.`

Calling a static member function does not bind the function to any class object. The `this` pointer is therefore unavailable, in contrast to normal member functions. This also means that static member functions cannot access data members and methods that are not static themselves.

■ ENUMERATION

Sample program

```cpp
// enum.cpp
// Uses enum-constants within a class.
// ------------------------------------------------
#include <iostream>
using namespace std;

class Lights
{
  public:                     // Enumeration for class Lights
    enum State { off, red, green, amber };
  private:
    State state;
  public:
    Lights( State s = off) : state(s) {}
    State getState() const {   return state; }
    void setState( State s)
    { switch(s)
       { case off:     cout << "     OFF     ";  break;
         case red:     cout << "     RED     ";  break;
         case green:   cout << "     GREEN   ";  break;
         case amber:   cout << "     AMBER   ";  break;
         default:      return;
       }
       state = s;
    }
};

int main()
{
   cout << "Some statements with objects "
        << "of type Lights!\n";
   Lights A1, A2(Lights::red);
   Lights::State as;
   as = A2.getState();
   if( as == Lights::red)
   {
      A1.setState( Lights::red);
      A2.setState( Lights::amber);
   }
   cout << endl;
   return 0;
}
```

☐ Definition

An enumeration is a user-definable, integral type. An enumeration is defined using the enum keyword. A range of values and a name for these values are also defined at the same time.

Example: enum Shape{ Line, Rectangle, Ellipse};

This statement defines the enumerated type Shape. The names quoted in the list identify integral constants. Their values can be deduced from the list order. The first constant has a value of 0, and each subsequent constant has a value that is one higher than its predecessor.

In the previous example, Line thus represents a value of 0, Rectangle a value of 1, and Ellipse a value of 2. A Shape type variable can only assume one of these values.

Example:
```
Shape shape = Rectangle;   // Variable shape
// ...
switch(shape)              // To evaluate shape
{
   case Line:   // ...  etc.
```

However, you can also define the values of the constants explicitly.

Example: enum Bound { Lower = -100, Upper = 100};

You can leave out the type name, if you only need to define the constants.

Example: enum { OFF, OUT=0, ON, IN=1 };

This statement defines the constants OFF and OUT, setting their value to 0, and the constants ON and IN with a value of 1. The values for OFF and ON are implicit.

☐ Class-Specific Constants

Enumeration can be used to define integral symbolic constants in a simple way. In contrast to #define directives, which merely replace text strings, enum constants are part of a declaration and thus have a valid range. This allows you to define constants that are visible within a namespace or class only.

The example on the opposite page shows the enumerated type State, which was defined within the Lights class. This means that the type and enum constant are only available for direct use within the class. The enumeration itself is declared as public, however, and access from outside the class is therefore possible.

Example:
```
if(Lights.getState() == Lights::red)
// ...
```

exercises

▪ EXERCISES

Copy constructor of class `Article`

The copy constructor creates a copy of an existing object. The parameter is thus
a read-only reference to the object that needs to be copied. The copy
constructor in the `Article` class is thus declared as follows:

Declaration of copy constructor:

```
Article( const Article& );
```

The default copy constructor simply transfers the data members to the new
object.

The Member Class

Private Data Members	Type
Member Number	int
Name	string
Birthday	const Date
//Possibly more information, such as an address, telephone number, ...	

Public Methods

Constructor with one parameter for each data member

Access methods for each data member. The birthday is read-only.

A method for formatted screen output of all data members

Exercise 1

In the first exercise of the last chapter you defined a simple class called `Article`. This involved using a global counter to log object creation and destruction. Improve and extend the `Article` class as follows:

- Use a static data member instead of a global variable to count the current number of objects.
- Declare a static access method called `getCount()` for the `Article` class. The method returns the current number of objects.
- Define a copy constructor that also increments the object counter by 1 and issues a message. This ensures that the counter will always be accurate.

  Tip: Use member initializers.
- Test the new version of the class. To do so, call the function `test()` by passing an article type object to the function.

Exercise 2

A sports club needs a program to manage its members. Your task is to define and test a class called `Member` for this purpose.

- Define the `Member` class using the data members shown opposite. Use the `Date` class defined in the last chapter for your definition. Since a member's birthday will not change, the data member for birthdays must be defined as a `const`.

  Overload the constructor to allow for entering a date as an object as well as three values for day, month, and year.
- Implement the necessary methods.
- Test the new `Member` class by creating at least two objects with the data of your choice and calling the methods you defined.
- Add a static member called `ptrBoss` to the class. This pointer indicates the member who has been appointed as chairperson. If no chairperson has been appointed, the pointer should point to `NULL`.
- Additionally, define the static access methods `getBoss()` and `setBoss()`. Use a pointer to set and return the object in question.
- Test the enhanced `Member` class by reading the number of an existing member, making the member the new chairperson and displaying the chairperson using `getBoss()`.

Sample output

```
Simulation of two traffic lights!

Terminate this program with <Ctrl>+<C>!

  1. Light     2. Light
---------------------------
    RED           AMBER
                  GREEN
                  AMBER
    AMBER         RED
    GREEN
    AMBER
    RED           AMBER
                  GREEN
// . . .
```

Hints for implementing the function `wait()`

1. The function `time()` is declared in the header file `ctime`. The call `time(NULL)` determines the number of seconds of type `time_t` since 1.1.1970, 0:0 hours. The type `time_t` is defined as `long`.

2. Instead of calling the function `time()` in a loop, you can use the function `Sleep()` for Windows or the function `sleep()` for Unix. These system calls are not standardized, yet they are much more effective because they send a process to sleep instead of using a waiting loop.

Exercise 3

Create a program to simulate the signal positions for two sets of traffic lights at a junction. Use the class `Lights` as defined in this chapter for your program.

- Each set of lights is switched through the phases red, amber, green, amber, red, and so on. You must ensure that one set of lights can be only in the amber or green state when the other set of lights is red.
- The lights operate in an infinite loop that can be terminated by interrupting the program. You can use the key combination <Ctrl>+<C> for DOS and Windows and the Interrupt key, i.e., normally the <Del> key, for UNIX.
- The status of the lights is constant for a certain number of seconds. For example, the green phase can take 20 seconds and the amber phase 1 second. These values can be different for each set of lights. Define an auxiliary function

```
inline void wait( int sec)
```

The function returns after the stipulated number of seconds. To do so, you can call the standard function `time()` in a loop. Don't forget to read the notes on the opposite page.

SOLUTIONS

Exercise 1

```cpp
// ----------------------------------------------------
// article.h
// Defines a simple class - Article.
// ----------------------------------------------------
#ifndef _ARTICLE_H_
#define _ARTICLE_H_
#include <string>
using namespace std;

class Article
{
   private:
     long nr;                   // Article number
     string name;               // Article name
     double sp;                 // Sales price
     // Static data member:
     static int countObj;    // Number of objects

   public:
     Article( long nr=0, const string& name="noname",
              double sp=0.0);
     // Copy constructor:
     Article( const Article& anArticle);
     ~Article();
     void print();
     // Access methods:
     const string& getName() const { return name; }
     long          getNr()   const { return nr; }
     double        getSP()   const { return sp; }
     static int getCount() { return countObj; }
     bool setName( const string& s)
     {
        if( s.size() < 1)          // No empty Name
          return false;
        name = s;
        return true;
     }
     void setNr( long n) { nr = n; }
     void setSP(double v)
     {                                  // No negative price
        sp = v > 0.0 ? v : 0.0;
     }
};
#endif   // _ARTICLE_
```

```cpp
// --------------------------------------------------
// article.cpp
// Methods of Article, which are not defined as inline.
// Constructor and destructor output when called.
// --------------------------------------------------

#include "article.h"              // Definition of the class

#include <iostream>
#include <iomanip>
using namespace std;

// Defining the static data member:
int Article::countObj = 0;              // Number of objects

// Defining the constructor and destructor:

Article::Article( long nr, const string& name, double sp)
{
   setNr(nr);    setName(name);    setSP(sp);
   ++countObj;
   cout << "An article \"" << name
        << "\" is created.\n"
        << "This is the " << countObj << ". article!"
        << endl;
}
// Defining the copy constructor:
Article::Article( const Article& art)
:nr(art.nr), name(art.name), sp(art.sp)
{
   ++countObj;
   cout << "A copy of the article \"" << name
        << "\" is generated.\n"
        << "This is the " << countObj << ". article!"
        << endl;
}

Article::~Article()
{
   cout << "The article \"" << name
        << "\" is destroyed.\n"
        << "There are still " << --countObj << " articles!"
        << endl;
}

// The method print() outputs an article.
void Article::print()
{
    // As before! Compare to the solutions of chapter 14.
}
```

```cpp
// ------------------------------------------------------
// article_t.cpp
// Tests the class Article including a copy constructor.
// ------------------------------------------------------

#include "article.h"              // Definition of the class

#include <iostream>
#include <string>
using namespace std;

void test( Article a);                             // Prototype

Article article1( 1111,"tent", 159.9);      // Global

int main()
{
   cout << "\nThe first statement in main().\n" << endl;

   Article article2( 2222,"jogging shoes", 199.99);

   cout << "\nThe first call of test()." << endl;
   test(article1);                          // Passing by Value

   cout << "\nThe second call of test()." << endl;
   test(article2);                          // Passing by Value

   cout << "\nThe last statement in main().\n"
        << "\nThere are still " << Article::getCount()
        << " objects\n" << endl;

   return 0;
}


void test( Article a)          // Calls the copy constructor
{
   cout << "\nThe given object:" << endl;
   a.print();

   static Article bike( 3333, "bicycle", 999.0);
   cout << "\nThe static object in function test():"
        << endl;
   bike.print();

   cout << "\nThe last statement in function test()"
        << endl;
}
```

Exercise 2

The Date class from the last chapter (see files Date.h and Date.cpp) can be left unchanged. But it makes sense to define the function isLeapYear() as a static member function of class Date rather than globally.
The other files:

```
// -----------------------------------------------------
// member.h
// Defines the Member class containing a constant
// and a static member.
// -----------------------------------------------------
#ifndef _MEMBER_H_
#define _MEMBER_H_

#include "Date.h"
#include <string>
using namespace std;

class Member
{
  private:
    int nr;                      // Member number
    string name;                 // Name
    const Date birth;            // Birthday
    // ... more data

    static Member *ptrBoss;      // Pointer to boss,
                                 // NULL = no boss.
  public:
    Member( long m_nr, const string& m_name,
            const Date& m_birth)
    : nr(m_nr), birth(m_birth)
    {
        if( !setName(m_name))  name = "Unknown";
    }

    Member( long m_nr, const string& m_name,
            int day, int month, int year)
    : nr(m_nr), birth(day,month,year)
    {
        if( !setName(m_name))  name = "Unknown";
    }

    int          getNr()    const { return nr; }
    const string& getName() const { return name; }
    const Date&  getBirthday() const { return birth; }

    void setNr( int n) { nr = n; }
```

```cpp
      bool setName( const string& s)
      {
         if( s.size() < 1)                 // No empty name
            return false;
         name = s;
         return true;
      }
      void display() const;

      // static methods:
      static Member* getBoss()
      {
          return ptrBoss;
      }
      static void setBoss( Member* ptrMem)
      {
         ptrBoss = ptrMem;
      }
};


#endif    // _MEMBER_H_

// ---------------------------------------------------
// member.cpp
// Members of class Member not defined inline.
// ---------------------------------------------------

#include "member.h"                 // Class definition
#include <iostream>
using namespace std;

 // Pointer to the boss:
Member* Member::ptrBoss = NULL;

void Member::display() const
{
   string line( 50, '-');
   cout << line
        << "\n  Member number: " << nr
        << "\n  Member:        " << name
        << "\n  Birthday       " << birth.asString()
        << '\n' << line << endl;
}
```

```cpp
// ---------------------------------------------------
// member_t.cpp
// Using the class Member.
// ---------------------------------------------------
#include "member.h"                    // Class definition
#include <iostream>
#include <string>
using namespace std;

int main()
{
   Date today;  today.setDate();
   cout << "Date: " << today.asString() << endl;

   Member fran( 0, "Quick, Fran", 17,11,81),
          kurt( 2222, "Rush, Kurt", Date(3,5,77) );
   franzi.setNr(1111);
   cout << "\nTwo members of the sports club:\n" << endl;
   fran.display();
   kurt.display();
   cout << "\nSomething changed!" << endl;
   fran.setName("Rush-Quick");
   fran.display();
   Member benny( 1122,"Rush, Benny", 1,1,2000);
   cout << "The youngest member of the sports club: \n";
   benny.display();
   // Who is the boss?
   int nr;
   Member *ptr = NULL;
   cout << "\nWho is the boss of the sports club?\n"
        << "Enter the member number: ";
   if( cin >> nr)
   {
      if( nr == fran.getNr())
         ptr = &fran;
      else if( nr == kurt.getNr())
         ptr = &kurt;
      Member::setBoss( ptr);
   }
   cout << "\nThe Boss of the sports club:" << endl;
   ptr = Member::getBoss();
   if( ptr != NULL)
      ptr->display();
   else
      cout << "No boss existing!" << endl;
   return 0;
}
```

Exercise 3

The definition of class Lights from this chapter remains unchanged.

```cpp
// ----------------------------------------------------
// Lights_t.cpp : Simulates two traffic lights.
// ----------------------------------------------------
#include "lights.h"         // Definition of class Lights
#include <iostream>
#include <ctime>            // Standard function time()
using namespace hr;

inline void wait( int sec)            // Wait sec seconds.
{  time_t end = time(NULL) + sec;
   while( time(NULL) < end)    ;
}
// Alternative for Windows:
// #include <windows.h>
// inline void wait( int sec) {  Sleep( 1000 * sec); }
Lights A1, A2;                        // Traffic lights and
enum { greenTime1 = 10 , amberTime1 = 1,  // time to wait.
       greenTime2 = 14 , amberTime2 = 2  };
int main()
{  cout << "Simulating two traffic lights!\n\n"
        << "Terminate this program with <Ctrl>+<C>!\n"
        << endl;
   cout << "  1. Light      2. Light\n"
        << "--------------------------" << endl;
   while(true)
   {  A1.setState( Lights::red);            // A1 = red
      A2.setState( Lights::amber);   cout << endl;
      wait( amberTime2);
      cout << "              ";
      A2.setState( Lights::green);   cout << endl;
      wait(greenTime2);
      cout << "              ";
      A2.setState( Lights::amber);    cout << endl;
      wait(amberTime2);
      A1.setState( Lights::amber);           // A2 = red
      A2.setState( Lights::red);    cout << endl;
      wait(amberTime1);
      A1.setState( Lights::green);  cout << endl;
      wait(greenTime1);
      A1.setState( Lights::amber);    cout << endl;
      wait(amberTime1);
   }
   return 0;
}
```

chapter 16

Arrays

This chapter describes how to define and use arrays, illustrating one-dimensional and multidimensional arrays, C strings and class arrays.

■ DEFINING ARRAYS

The array `arr` in memory

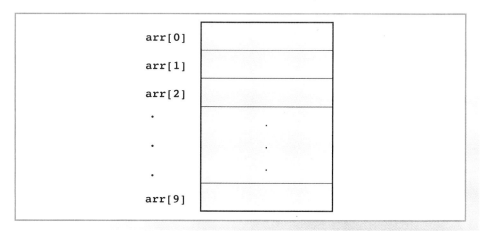

Sample program

```cpp
// array.cpp
// To input numbers into an array and output after.
// ----------------------------------------------------
#include <iostream>
#include <iomanip>
using namespace std;

int main()
{
    const int MAXCNT = 10;        // Constant
    float arr[MAXCNT], x;         // Array, temp. variable
    int i, cnt;                   // Index, quantity

    cout << "Enter up to 10 numbers \n"
         << "(Quit with a letter):" << endl;
    for( i = 0; i < MAXCNT  &&  cin >> x; ++i)
        arr[i] = x;
    cnt = i;
    cout << "The given numbers:\n" << endl;
    for( i = 0; i < cnt; ++i)
        cout << setw(10) << arr[i];
    cout << endl;
    return 0;
}
```

An *array* contains multiple objects of *identical types* stored sequentially in memory. The individual objects in an array, referred to as *array elements*, can be addressed using a number, the so-called *index* or *subscript*. An array is also referred to as a *vector*.

☐ Defining Arrays

An array must be defined just like any other object. The definition includes the *array name* and the *type* and *number* of *array elements*.

Syntax: `type name[count];`   `// Array name`

In the above syntax description, `count` is an integral constant or integral expression containing only constants.

Example: `float arr[10];`   `// Array arr`

This statement defines the array `arr` with `10` elements of `float` type. The object `arr` itself is of a *derived type*, an "array of `float` elements" or "`float` array."

An array always occupies a *contiguous* memory space. In the case of the array `arr`, this space is `10*sizeof(float) = 40` bytes.

☐ Index for Array Elements

The subscript operator `[]` is used to access individual array elements. In C++ an *index* always begins at zero. The elements belonging to the array `arr` are thus

`arr[0], arr[1] , arr[2], ... , arr[9]`

The index of the last array element is thus 1 lower than the number of array elements. Any `int` expression can be used as an index. The subscript operator `[]` has high precedence, just like the class member operators `.` and `->` .

No error message is issued if the index exceeds the valid index range. As a programmer, you need to be particularly careful to avoid this error! However, you can define a class to perform range checking for indices.

You can create an array from any type with the exception of some special types, such as `void` and certain classes. Class arrays are discussed later.

Example: `short number[20];`   `// short array`
              `for( int i=0; i < 20; i++ )`
                `number[i] = (short)(i*10);`

This example defines an array called `number` with 20 `short` elements and assigns the values `0, 10, 20, ... , 190` to the elements.

■ INITIALIZING ARRAYS

Sample program

```cpp
// fibo.cpp
// The program computes the first 20 Fibonacci
// numbers and the corresponding Fibonacci quotients.
// ------------------------------------------------------
#include <iostream>
#include <iomanip>
#include <cmath>                    // Prototype of sqrt()
#include <string>
using namespace std;

#define COUNT 20

long fib[COUNT + 1] = { 0, 1 };

string header =
" Index   Fibonacci number Fibonacci quotient  Deviation"
"\n                                       of limit "
"\n---------------------------------------------------";

int main()
{
  int i;
  double q, lim;

  for( i=1; i < COUNT; ++i )        // Computing the
    fib[i+1] = fib[i] + fib[i-1];   // Fibonacci numbers

  lim = ( 1.0 + sqrt(5.0)) / 2.0;   // Limit

  // Title and the first two Fibonacci numbers:
  cout << header << endl;
  cout << setw(5) << 0 << setw(15) << fib[0] << endl;
  cout << setw(5) << 1 << setw(15) << fib[1] << endl;
  // Rest of the table:
  for( i=2; i <= COUNT; i++ )
  {                                 // Quotient:
    q = (double)fib[i] / (double)fib[i-1];
    cout << setw(5)  << i << setw(15) << fib[i]
         << setw(20) << fixed << setprecision(10) << q
         << setw(20) << scientific << setprecision(3)
         << lim - q  << endl;
  }
  return 0;
}
```

☐ Initialization List

Arrays can be initialized when you define them. A *list* containing the values for the individual array elements is used to initialize the array:

Example: `int num[3] = { 30, 50, 80 };`

A value of `30` is assigned to `num[0]`, `50` to `num[1]`, and `80` to `num[2]`. If you initialize an array when you define it, you do not need to state its length.

Example: `int num[] = { 30, 50, 80 };`

In this case, the length of the array is equal to the number of initial values. If the array length is explicitly stated in the definition and is larger than the number of initial values, any remaining array elements are set to zero. If, in contrast, the number of initial values exceeds the array length, the surplus values are ignored.

Locally defined arrays are created on the stack at program runtime. You should therefore be aware of the following issues when defining arrays:

- Arrays that occupy a large amount of memory (e.g., more than one kbyte) should be defined as *global* or *static*.
- Unless they are initialized, the elements of a local array will not necessarily have a definite value. Values are normally assigned by means of a loop.

You cannot assign a vector to another vector. However, you can overload the assignment operator within a class designed to represent arrays. This topic will be discussed in depth later.

☐ The Sample Program Opposite

The example on the opposite page contains the first twenty Fibonacci numbers and their quotients. Fibonacci numbers are useful for representing natural growth. In computer science, Fibonacci numbers are used for things like memory management and hashing. Their definition is as follows:

- the first Fibonacci number is `0`, the second is `1`
- each subsequent Fibonacci number is the sum of its two immediate predecessors.

This results in the following sequence: `0, 1, 1, 2, 3, 5, 8, 13, ....`

The quotient of a Fibonacci number and its predecessor is referred to as a Fibonacci quotient. The sequence of Fibonacci quotients, `1/1, 2/1, 3/2, ...`, converges towards the threshold value `(1 + `$\sqrt{5}$`)/2`.

■ C STRINGS

☐ Initializing

```
char text[40] = "Hello Eve";
```

String text in memory:

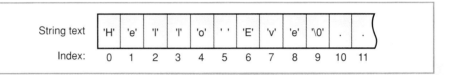

String text	'H'	'e'	'l'	'l'	'o'	' '	'E'	'v'	'e'	'\0'	.	.
Index:	0	1	2	3	4	5	6	7	8	9	10	11

✓ **NOTE**

The array `text` has length of `40`, whereas the string "`Hello Eve`" only occupies the first 9 bytes.

Sample program

```
// C-string.cpp  :  Using C strings.
// --------------------------------------------------------
#include <iostream>
#include <iomanip>
#include <cstring>
using namespace std;
char header[] = "\n    ***  C Strings  ***\n\n";
int main()
{
   char hello[30] = "Hello ", name[20], message[80];

   cout << header << "Your first name: ";
   cin  >> setw(20) >> name;    // Enter a word.
   strcat( hello, name);        // Append the name.
   cout << hello << endl;
   cin.sync();                  // No previous input.
   cout << "\nWhat is the message for today?"
        << endl;
   cin.getline( message, 80);   // Enter a line with a
                                // max of 79 characters.
   if( strlen( message) > 0)    // If string length is
   {                            // longer than 0.
     for( int i=0; message[i] != '\0'; ++i)
       cout << message[i] << ' ';   // Output with
     cout << endl;                  // white spaces.
   }
   return 0;
}
```

☐ char **Arrays**

Arrays whose elements are of char type are often used as data communication buffers.

Example: `char buffer[10*512];    // 5 Kbyte buffer`

However, their most common use is for string storage. One way of representing a string is to store the string and the terminating null character `'\0'` in a char array. When you define an array, you can use a string constant to initialize the array.

Example: `char name[] = "Hugo";`

This definition is equivalent to

```
char name[] = { 'H','u','g','o','\0' };
```

As you can see, the string name occupies five bytes, including an additional byte for the null character. If you need to allocate more memory, you can state the size of the array explicitly as shown opposite.

In the C language, strings are usually represented as char vectors with a terminating null character. In C++, strings of this type are referred to as C *strings* to distinguish them from objects of the string class.

☐ **C Strings and the** string **Class**

C strings are simple char arrays, which means that the functionality of the string class is not available for them. Thus, for example, assignments and comparisons are not defined.

Example:
```
char str1[20], str2[20] = "A string";
str1 = str2;                   // Error!
strcpy( str1, str2);           // ok!
```

The standard functions of the C language, such as strlen(), strcpy(), strcmp(), and others, are available for C strings. These global functions all begin with the str prefix.

As the program on the opposite page shows, I/O streams are overloaded for char arrays, too. Input and output are as easily achieved as with string class objects. However, the program must make sure not to overrun the end of the char array when reading data into the array. You can use the width() method or the setw() manipulator for this purpose.

Example: `cin >> setw(20) >> name; // 19 characters`

C strings are preferable to the string class if only a few operations are needed and you want to avoid unnecessary overheads.

■ CLASS ARRAYS

Sample program

```cpp
// AccountTab.cpp
// An array containing objects of class Account.
// -------------------------------------------------

#include "account.h"       // Definition of class Account
#include <iostream>
using namespace std;

Account giro("Lucky, Peter", 1234567, -1200.99 );
Account accountTab[] =
{
  Account("Tang, Sarah", 123000, 2500.0),
  Account("Smith, John", 543001),
  Account(),                      // Default constructor
  "Li, Zhang",                    // Account("Li, Zhang"),
  giro                            // Account(giro)
};

int cnt = sizeof(accountTab) / sizeof(Account);

int main()
{
   // To set some values:
   accountTab[1].setState( 10000.00);
                                   // Assignment ok:
   accountTab[2] = Account("Pit, Dave", 727003, 200.00);

   cout << "The accounts in the table:" << endl;
   for( int i = 0; i < cnt; ++i)
   {
      accountTab[i].display();
      if( i % 3 == 2)
      {
         cout << "Press return to go on!\n";
         cin.get();
      }
   }
   cout << endl;

   return 0;
}
```

☐ Declaring Class Arrays

Array elements can also be objects of a class type. The array is known as a *class array* in this case. When you declare an array of this type, you only need to state the type of the array elements.

Example: `Result temperatureTab[24];`

This statement defines the class array `temperatureTab` that stores 24 objects of type `Result`. This class was introduced at the beginning of the last chapter.

As the statement does not initialize the array explicitly, the default constructor is automatically called for each array element.

 NOTE

Class arrays can only be defined without explicit initialization if a default constructor exists for the class.

Thus, the previous example is only valid for the first version of the `Result` class as this class contains a default constructor.

☐ Explicit Initialization

A class array is initialized as usual by an *initialization list*. The list contains a constructor call for each array element.

Example:
```
Result temperatureTab[24] =
{
   Result( -2.5, 0,30,30),
   Result( 3.5),          // At present time
   4.5,                   // Just so
   Result( temp1),        // Copy constructor
   temp2                  // Just so
};
```

The first five array elements are initialized by the constructor calls implicitly contained in these statements. Instead of using a constructor with one argument, you can simply supply the argument. The default constructor is then called for the remaining elements.

If the size of an array is not stated explicitly, the number of values in the initialization list defines the size of the array.

The public interface of the objects in the array is available for use as usual.

Example: `temperatureTab[2].setTime( 2,30,21);`

No additional parentheses are needed in this statement since the subscript operator `[]` and the class member operator `.` are read from left to right, although they have the same precedence.

■ MULTIDIMENSIONAL ARRAYS

Sample program

```cpp
// multidim.cpp
// Demonstrates multidimensional arrays.
// ---------------------------------------------------
#include <iostream>
#include <iomanip>
using namespace std;

char representative[2][20] = {"Armstrong, Wendy",
                              "Beauty, Eve"};

        // Each representative has five different
        // articles available, having sold the following:
int articleCount[2][5] = { { 20,  51, 30,  17, 44},
                           {150, 120, 90, 110, 88}
                         };

int main()
{
   for( int i=0; i < 2; i++ )
   {
      cout <<"\nRepresentative:  " << representative[i];
      cout << "\nNumber of items sold: ";

      for( int j = 0; j < 5; j++ )
         cout << setw(6) << articleCount[i][j];
      cout << endl;
   }
    return 0;
}
```

Screen output:

```
Representative:  Armstrong, Wendy
Items sold:     20   51   30   17   44

Representative:  Beauty, Eve
Items sold:    150  120   90  110   88
```

☐ Defining Multidimensional Arrays

In C++ you can define multidimensional arrays with any number of dimensions. The ANSI standard stipulates a minimum of 256 dimensions but the total number of dimensions is in fact limited by the amount of memory available.

The most common multidimensional array type is the two-dimensional array, the so-called *matrix*.

Example: `float number[3][10];    // 3 x 10 matrix`

This defines a matrix called `number` that contains 3 *rows* and 10 *columns*. Each of the 30 (3 × 10) elements is a `float` type. The assignment

Example: `number[0][9] = 7.2;    // Row 0, column 9`

stores the value 7.2 in the last element of the first row.

☐ Arrays as Array Elements

C++ does not need any special syntax to define multidimensional arrays. On the contrary, an n-dimensional array is no different than an array with only one dimension whose elements are (n–1)-dimensional arrays.

The array `number` thus contains the following three elements:

`number[0]    number[1]    number[2].`

Each of these elements is a `float` array with a size of 10, which in turn forms the rows of the two-dimensional array, `number`.

This means that the same rules apply to multidimensional arrays as to one-dimensional arrays. The initialization list of a two-dimensional array thus contains the values of the array elements, that is, the one-dimensional rows.

Examples: `int arr[2][3] = { {5, 0, 0}, {7, 0, 0} };`
              `int arr[][3]  = { {5}, {7} };`

These two definitions are equivalent. When you initialize an array, you can only omit the size of the first dimension. It is necessary to define any other dimensions since they define the size of array elements.

☐ The Example on the Opposite Page

The program opposite defines the two-dimensional arrays `representative` and `articleCount`, which have two rows each. The `representative[i]` rows are `char` arrays used for storing the names of the representatives. You can also use a one-dimensional `string` array.

Example: `string representative[2] = {"La..","Fo.."};`

■ MEMBER ARRAYS

Class TelList

```cpp
// telList.h
// Class TelList to represent a list
// containing names and telephone numbers.
// -----------------------------------------------------
#ifndef _TelList_
#define _TelList_

#include <string>
using namespace std;
#define PSEUDO -1          // Pseudo position
#define MAX 100            // Maximal number of elements

// Type of a list element:
struct Element { string name, telNr; };

class TelList
{
  private:
    Element v[MAX];        // The array and the current
    int count;             // number of elements

  public:
    TelList(){ count = 0;}
    int getCount() const { return count; }
    Element *retrieve( int i )
    {
       return (i >= 0 && i < count)? &v[i] : NULL;
    }
    bool append( const Element& el )
    {
       return append( el.name, el.telNr);
    }
    bool append( const string& name,
                 const string& telNr);
    bool erase( const string& name);
    int  search( const string& name);
    void print();
    int  print( const string& name);
    int  getNewEntries();
};

#endif  // _TelList_
```

☐ Encapsulating Arrays

A programmer often needs to handle objects of the same type, such as company employees, bank accounts, or the articles in stock. A class designed to perform this task can use an array for ease of data management. An array allows you to access individual objects directly and perform searches.

A class that encapsulates an array will provide methods for simple array operations, such as inserting and deleting objects. When you design a class of this type, one aim will be to perform automatic range checking. This helps avoid overrunning the end of an array when performing read or write operations. The resulting class will contain a comfortable and safe interface for object data management.

☐ The Class `TelList`

The class `TelList` on the opposite page is designed to manage a simple telephone list.

Each entry in the list contains a dataset containing a name and a phone number. The `Element` type, which comprises two strings, was defined for this purpose. The array `v` can store up to `MAX` entries of the `Element` type. The data member `count` records the number of elements currently stored in the array. When a phone list is created, this number will initially be 0. When an element is inserted or deleted, the number is modified correspondingly.

The `TelList` class uses a single default constructor that sets the counter, `count`, to zero. It is not necessary to provide an initial value for the `MAX` elements in the array `v` since the default constructor of the `string` class is executed for all strings.

The tasks performed by the other methods are easily deduced from their names. The `retrieve()` method returns to a given index a pointer to the corresponding element. Using a pointer makes it possible to return a NULL pointer if the index is invalid.

The `append()` methods add a new entry to the list. The data passed to a method is copied to the next free array element and the counter is incremented. If there is no space available, the name field is empty, or the name is already in use, nothing happens. In this case, the method returns `false` instead of `true`.

The exercises for this chapter contain further details on these methods. You can implement the methods for the `TelList` yourself and go on to test them.

exercises

■ EXERCISES

Example of a bubble sort algorithm

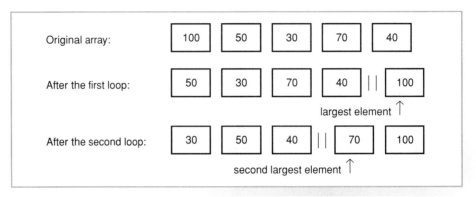

Sieve of Eratosthenes

For this task you can define an array of boolean values in which each element is initially `true`. To eliminate a number n you simply set the nth element in the array to `false`.

Result:

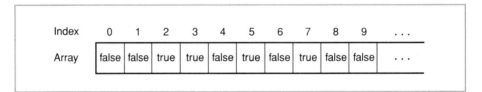

Screen shot of exercise 4

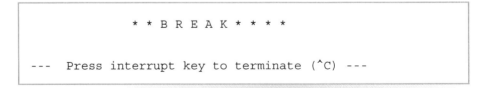

✓ **NOTE**

The output of a scrolling string has to be performed at the same cursor position. The screen control characters make it possible to locate the cursor, and that independent of the current compiler (see appendix).

Exercise 1

Write a C++ program that reads a maximum of 100 integers from the keyboard, stores them in a `long` array, sorts the integers in ascending order, and displays sorted output. Input can be terminated by any invalid input, such as a letter.

✓ **NOTE**

Use the *bubble sort algorithm* to sort the array. This algorithm repeatedly accesses the array, comparing neighboring array elements and swapping them if needed. The sorting algorithm terminates when there are no more elements that need to be swapped. You use a flag to indicate that no elements have been swapped.

Exercise 2

Chapter 14 introduced the sample class `DayTime` and the `isLess()` method. Define and initialize an array with four `DayTime` class objects.

Then write a `main` function that first uses the `print()` method to display the four elements. Finally, find the largest and smallest elements and output them on screen.

Exercise 3

Write a program that outputs all prime numbers less than 1000. The program should also count the number of prime numbers less than 1000. An integer >= 2 is a prime number if it is not divisible by any number except 1 and itself. Use the *Sieve of Eratosthenes*:

To find primary numbers simply eliminate multiples of any primary numbers you have already found, i.e.:

first eliminate any multiples of 2 (4, 6, 8, ...),
then eliminate any multiples of 3 (6, 9, 12, ...),
then eliminate any multiples of 5 (10, 15, 20, ..) // 4 has already been eliminated
and so on.

Exercise 4

Write a C++ program to create the screen output shown opposite. The following banner

```
*  *  *    B R E A K    *  *  *
```

is to be displayed in the center of the window and scrolled left. You can scroll the banner by beginning string output with the first character, then the second, and so on. Handle the string like a loop where the first letter follows the last letter and output continues until the starting position is reached.

You can use a wait loop to modify the speed of the banner after each string is output.

Exercise 5

Methods to be implemented for the TelList class

```
bool append( const string& name,
             const string& telNr);

bool erase( const string& name);

int  search( const string& name);

void print();

int  print( const string& name);

int  getNewEntries();
```

Menu of the application program

```
          *****  Telephone List  *****

          D = Display all entries

          F = Find a telephone number

          A = Append an entry

          E = Erase an entry

          Q = Quit the program

   Your choice:
```

Exercise 5

The sample class `TelList` was introduced in this chapter; however, some methods still need to be implemented and tested.

▪ Implement the `TelList` class methods shown opposite.
The name is used as an unambiguous key. This means the `append()` method can only be used to append an entry provided the name is neither blank nor already in use.

The method `erase()` deletes an array element. The position of the element to be deleted is first located using the `search()` method. If the element does not exist, `erase()` returns a value of `false`. In any other case, the last element in the array is used to overwrite the element that is to be deleted and the counter `count` is decremented.

The `search()` method finds the position in the array that contains the search name. If the search operation is unsuccessful, the value `PSEUDO` is returned.

The `print` method without parameters outputs all available entries. You can pass the first letter or letters of a name to the second method to output any entries beginning with these letters. Use the method `compare()` from the `string` class to help you with this task.

Example: `str1.compare( 0, 5, str2) == 0`

This expression is true if the five characters subsequent to position 0 in the strings `str1` and `str2` are identical.

The `getNewEntries()` method is used to read new phone list entries from the keyboard. Each new entry is appended using the `append()` method. Reading should be terminated if the user types an empty string. The method returns the number of new entries.

Write an application program that creates a phone list of type `TelList` and displays the menu shown on the opposite page.

▪ The menu must be placed in a function of your own that can return the command input. The menu must be called in the main loop of the program. Depending on the command input, one of the methods defined in the class `TelList` should be called. If the menu item "Erase" or "Search" is chosen, you must also read a name or the first letters of a name from the keyboard.

 NOTE

The phone list will not be stored permanently in a file. This is just one of the enhancements (another would be variable length) that will be added at a later stage.

solutions

SOLUTIONS

Exercise 1

```cpp
// ----------------------------------------------------
// bubble.cpp
// Inputs integers into an array,
// sorts in ascending order, and outputs them.
// ----------------------------------------------------
#include <iostream>
#include <iomanip>
using namespace std;

#define MAX   100                     // Maximum number
long number[MAX];

int main()
{
   int i, cnt;                        // Index, quantity

   cout << "\nS o r t i n g   I n t e g e r s \n"
        << endl;
   // To input the integers:
   cout << "Enter up to 100 integers \n"
        << "(Quit with any letter):" << endl;
   for( i = 0; i < MAX  &&  cin >> number[i]; ++i)
       ;
   cnt = i;
   // To sort the numbers:
   bool sorted = false;              // Not yet sorted.
   long help;                        // Swap.
   int  end = cnt;                   // End of a loop.

   while( !sorted)                   // As long as not
   {                                 // yet sorted.
     sorted = true;
     --end;
     for( i = 0; i < end; ++i)       // Compares
     {                               // adjacent integers.
       if( number[i] > number[i+1])
       {
          sorted = false;            // Not yet sorted.
          help     = number[i];      // Swap.
          number[i]  = number[i+1];
          number[i+1]= help;
       }
     }
   }
}
```

```cpp
    // Outputs the numbers
    cout << "The sorted numbers:\n" << endl;

    for( i = 0; i < cnt; ++i)
        cout << setw(10) << number[i];
    cout << endl;

    return 0;
}
```

Exercise 2

```cpp
// ------------------------------------------------------
// DayTime.h
// The class DayTime represents the time in hours,
// minutes and seconds.
// ------------------------------------------------------
#ifndef _DAYTIME_
#define _DAYTIME_
#include <iostream>
#include <iomanip>
using namespace std;

class DayTime
{
  private:
    short hour, minute, second;
    bool overflow;
  public:
    DayTime( int h = 0, int m = 0, int s = 0)
    {
      overflow = false;
      if( !setTime( h, m, s))          // this->setTime(...)
        hour = minute = second = 0;
    }
    bool setTime(int hour, int minute, int second = 0)
    {
      if(    hour   >= 0  &&  hour < 24
          && minute >= 0  &&  minute < 60
          && second >= 0  &&  second < 60 )
      {
        this->hour   = (short)hour;
        this->minute = (short)minute;
        this->second = (short)second;
        return true;
      }
      else
        return false;
    }
```

```cpp
        int getHour()   const { return hour;   }
        int getMinute() const { return minute; };
        int getSecond() const { return second; };

        int asSeconds() const        // Daytime in seconds
        {
          return (60*60*hour + 60*minute + second);
        }

        bool isLess( DayTime t) const  // Compares
                                       // *this and t.
        {
          return  asSeconds() < t.asSeconds();
        }        // this->sSeconds() < t.asSeconds();

        void print() const
        {
          cout << setfill('0')
               << setw(2) << hour     << ':'
               << setw(2) << minute   << ':'
               << setw(2) << second   << " Uhr" << endl;
          cout << setfill(' ');
        }
        void swap( DayTime& t)        // Just one parameter!
        {                             // Swaps *this and t:
          DayTime temp(t);  t = *this;  *this = temp;
        }
};

#endif    // _DAYTIME_

// -------------------------------------------------------
// TimeTab.cpp
// An array containing objects of class DayTime.
// -------------------------------------------------------
#include "DayTime.h"       // Definition of class DayTime
#include <iostream>
using namespace std;
char header[] =
"\n\n      ***  Table with Daytimes ***\n\n";

int main()
{
  DayTime timeTab[4] =
          { 18, DayTime(10,25), DayTime(14,55,30)};
  int i;
  timeTab[3].setTime( 8,40,50);           // Last element.
  cout << header << endl;
```

```
for( i = 0; i < 4; ++i)
{
    timeTab[i].print();
    cout << endl;
}

// To compute shortest and longest time:
int i_min = 0, i_max = 0;          // Indices for shortest
                                   // and longest elements.
for( i = 1; i < 4; ++i)
{
    if( timeTab[i].isLess( timeTab[i_min]) )
        i_min = i;

    if( timeTab[i_max].isLess( timeTab[i]) )
        i_max = i;
}

cout << "\nShortest time: ";  timeTab[i_min].print();

cout << "\nLongest time: ";   timeTab[i_max].print();

return 0;
}
```

Exercise 3

```cpp
// ---------------------------------------------------
// sieve.cpp
// Identifies prime numbers using the Sieve of
// Eratosthenes.
// ---------------------------------------------------
#include <iostream>
#include <iomanip>
using namespace std;
#define LIMIT   1000                    // Upper limit
bool flags[LIMIT] = { false, false};   // Array with flags

int main()
{
   register int i, j;                 // Indices
   for( i = 2; i < LIMIT; ++i)
      flags[i] = true;                // Sets flags to true
   // Sieving:
   for( i = 2; i < LIMIT/2; ++i)
   {
      if( flags[i])             // Is i a prime number?
      {                         // Yes -> Delete multiples.
         for( j = i+i; j < LIMIT; j += i)
            flags[j] = false;
      }
   }
   // To count:
   int count = 0;              // Counter
   for( i = 2; i < LIMIT; ++i)
      if(flags[i])             // If i is a prime number
         ++count;              // -> count
   // Output:
   cout << "There are"<< count <<" prime numbers less than"
        << LIMIT << endl;
   cout << "\nTo output prime numbers? (y/n) ";
   char reply;  cin.get(reply);
   if( reply == 'y' || reply == 'Y')
   { for( i = 2; i < LIMIT; ++i)
        if(flags[i])                 // If i is a prime number
        {                            // -> to output it.
           cout.width(8);  cout << i;
        }
   }
   cout << endl;     return 0;
}
```

Exercise 4

```cpp
// ----------------------------------------------------
// scroll.cpp
// Scrolling a message.
// ----------------------------------------------------
#include <iostream>
#include <iomanip>
using namespace std;
#define DELAY  10000000L                 // Output delay

inline void cls()                        // Clear screen
{
   cout << "\033[2J\n";
}

inline void locate(int z, int s)    // Put cursor in row z
{                                   // and column s
   cout << "\033[" << z << ';' << s << 'H';
}

char msg[] = "* * *  B R E A K  * * * ";

int main()
{
   int i, start = 0, len = strlen(msg);

   cls();  locate(24, 20);         // Row 24, column 20
   cout << "--- Press interrupt key to terminate (^C) ---";

   while( true )
   {
     locate( 12, 25);              // Row 12, column 25
     i = start;                    // Output from index start
     do
     {
        cout << msg[i++];
        i = i % len;               // if( i == len) i = 0;
     }
     while( i != start);
     cout << endl;                 // Outputs buffer to screen
     // Wait in short
     for( int count = 0; count < DELAY; ++count)
         ;
     ++start;                      // For next output
     start %= len;                 // start = start % len;
   }
   cls();
   return 0;
}
```

Exercise 5

```
// ---------------------------------------------------
// telList.h
// The class TelList representing a list
// with names and telephone numbers.
// ---------------------------------------------------
//
// As before in this chapter.


// ---------------------------------------------------
// telList.cpp
// Implements the methods of class TelList.
// ---------------------------------------------------
#include "telList.h"       // Definition of class TelList
#include <iostream>
#include <iomanip>
using namespace std;

bool TelList::append( const string& name,
                      const string& telNr)
{
    if( count < MAX                 // Space available,
        && name.length() > 1        // 2 characters at least
        && search(name) == PSEUDO) // not yet existing
    {
      v[count].name  = name;
      v[count].telNr = telNr;
      ++count;
      return true;
    }
     return false;
}

bool TelList::erase( const string& key )
{
    int i = search(key);
    if( i != PSEUDO )
    {                                 // Copies the last
      v[i] = v[count-1];  --count;  // element to position i
      return true;
    }
    return false;
}
```

```cpp
int TelList::search(const string& key )
{
   for( int i = 0; i < count; i++ )          // Searching.
     if( v[i].name == key )
       return i;                             // Found

   return PSEUDO;                            // Not found
}
// Functions to support the output:
inline void tabHeader()                      // Title of the table
{
   cout << "\n  Name                          Telephone #\n"
           "--------------------------------------------------"
        << endl;
}
inline void printline( const Element& el)
{
   cout << left << setw(30) << el.name.c_str()
        << left << setw(20) << el.telNr.c_str()
        << endl;
}

void TelList::print()            // Outputs all entries
{
   if( count == 0)
     cout << "\nThe telephone list  is empty!" << endl;
   else
   {
      tabHeader();
      for( int i = 0; i < count; ++i)
         printline( v[i]);
   }
}
int TelList::print( const string& name) const // Entries
{                                   // beginning with name.
   int matches = 0, len = name.length();

   for( int i = 0; i < count; ++i)
   {
      if( v[i].name.compare(0, len, name) == 0)
      {
        if( matches == 0) tabHeader();   // Title before
                                          // first output.
        ++matches;
        printline( v[i]);
      }
   }
   if( matches == 0)
     cout << "No corresponding entry found!" << endl;
   return matches;
}
```

```cpp
int TelList::getNewEntries()            // Input new entries
{
    int inputCount = 0;
    cout << "\nEnter new names and telephone numbers:"
            "\n(Terminate by empty input) "
         << endl;
    Element el;
    while( true)
    {
      cout << "\nNew last name, first name:  ";
      cin.sync(); getline( cin, el.name);
      if( el.name.empty())
        break;
      cout << "\nTelephone number: ";
      cin.sync(); getline( cin, el.telNr);
      if( !append( el))
      {
         cout << "Name has not been found!" << endl;
         if( count == MAX)
         {
            cout << "The Table is full!" << endl;
            break;
         }
         if( search( el.name) != PSEUDO)
            cout << "Name already exists!" << endl;
      }
      else
      {
         ++inputCount;
         cout << "A new element has been inserted!"
              << endl;
      }
    }
    return inputCount;
}

// ---------------------------------------------------------
// telList_t.cpp
// Manages a telephone list.
// ---------------------------------------------------------
#include "telList.h"        // Definition of class TelList
#include <iostream>
#include <string>
#include <cctype>
using namespace std;
inline void cls()
{  cout << "\033[2J\n";// Output only new-lines, if ANSI
}                          // control characters are not available.
```

```
inline void go_on()
{
   cout << "\n\nGo on with return! ";
   cin.sync();  cin.clear();              // No previous input
   while( cin.get() != '\n')
        ;
}

int menu();                              // Reads a command

char header[] =
"\n\n                     *****  Telephone List  *****\n\n";

TelList myFriends;                       // A telephone list

int main()
{
   int action = 0;                       // Command
   string name;                          // Reads a name

   myFriends.append("Lucky, Peter", "0203-1234567");

   while( action != 'B')
   {
     action = menu();
     cls();
     cout << header << endl;

     switch( action)
     {
       case 'D':                                // Show all
                 myFriends.print();
                 go_on();
                 break;

       case 'F':                                // Search
                 cout <<
                 "\n--- To search for a phone number ---\n"
                 "\nEnter the beginning of a name: ";
                 getline( cin, name);
                 if( !name.empty())
                 {
                   myFriends.print( name);
                   go_on();
                 }
                 break;

       case 'A':                                // Insert
                 myFriends.getNewEntries();
                 break;
```

```
         case 'E':                              // Delete
                cout <<
                "\n--- To delete a telephone entry. ---\n "
                "\nEnter the complete name: ";
                getline( cin, name);
                if( !name.empty())
                {
                  if( !myFriends.erase( name))
                    cout << name << " not found!"
                          << endl;
                  else
                    cout << "Entry for " << name
                          << " deleted!" << endl;
                  go_on();
                }
                break;

      case 'T':  cls();                    // To terminate
                break;
      }
   } // End of while

   return 0;
}

int menu()
{
   static char menuStr[] =
   "\n\n               D = Display all entries"
   "\n\n               F = Find a telephone number"
   "\n\n               A = Append a new entry "
   "\n\n               E = Erase an entry "
   "\n\n               Q = Quit the program"
   "\n\n Your choice:   ";

   cls();
   cout << header << menuStr;

   char choice;
   cin.sync(); cin.clear();      // No previous input
   if( !cin.get(choice))
      choice = 'B';
   else
      choice = toupper(choice);

   cin.sync();                         // Clear input buffer
   return choice;
}
```

chapter 17

Arrays and Pointers

This chapter describes the relationship between pointers and arrays. This includes:

- pointer arithmetic
- pointer version of functions
- pointers as return values and read-only pointers
- pointer arrays

Operations that use C strings illustrate how to use pointers for efficient programming. String access via the command line of an application program is used to illustrate pointer arrays.

■ ARRAYS AND POINTERS (1)

Sample program

```cpp
// textPtr.cpp
// Using arrays of char and pointers to char
// ----------------------------------------------------
#include <iostream>
using namespace std;

int main()
{
   cout << "Demonstrating arrays of char "
        << "and pointers to char.\n"
        << endl;

   char text[] = "Good morning!",
        name[] = "Bill!";
   char *cPtr = "Hello ";              // Let cPtr point
                                       // to "Hello ".
   cout << cPtr << name << '\n'
        << text << endl;

   cout << "The text \"" << text
        << "\" starts at address " << (void*)text
        << endl;

   cout << text + 6       // What happens now?
        << endl;

   cPtr = name;    // Let cPtr point to name, i.e. *cPtr
                   // is equivalent to name[0]
   cout << "This is the " << *cPtr << " of " << cPtr
        << endl;
   *cPtr = 'k';
   cout << "Bill can not " << cPtr << "!\n" << endl;
   return 0;
}
```

Sample output:

```
Demonstrating arrays of char and pointers to char.
Hello Bill!
Good morning!
The text "Good morning!" starts at address 00451E40
morning!
This is the B of Bill!
Bill can not kill!
```

☐ Name and Address of an Array

In C++ the name of an array is also the starting address for that array. To be more precise, an array name is a pointer to the first array element.

Example: `char town[] = "Beijing";`

In this case, `town` is a `char` pointer to `town[0]`, that is, a pointer to the memory address that stores the `'B'` character. Expressions `town` and `&town[0]` are thus equivalent.

Example: `cout << town; // or:  cout << &town[0];`

A pointer to the first character of the string `town` is passed. The characters forming the string are read and displayed from this point onward until the terminating null character, `'\0'`, is reached.

☐ Pointer Variables and Arrays

An array name is not a pointer variable but a constant that cannot be modified. However, you can assign this constant to a pointer variable.

Example:
```
char *cPtr;
cPtr = town;        // or: cPtr = &town[0];
cout << cPtr;       // To output "Beijing"
```

Now `cPtr` points to the array element `town[0]` just like `town`. But, in contrast to `town`, `cPtr` is a variable that can be moved.

Example: `cPtr = "Hello!";`

After this statement, `cPtr` points to the 'H' character. String constants such as "`Hello!`" are also `char` arrays and thus represent the address of the first array element.

☐ Typeless Pointers

If you need to display the address rather than the string, you should pass a `void*` type pointer rather than a `char` pointer.

Example: `cout << (void *)town;`

This casts the `char` pointer to a `void *` type pointer and passes it as an argument to the `<<` operator, which in turn outputs the address in hexadecimal format. The `<<` operator belongs to the `ostream` class and is overloaded for `void *` types for this purpose.

A `void *` pointer represents a memory address without establishing a certain type. `void *` pointers are also referred to as *typeless pointers* for this reason. When you use a typeless pointer for memory access, you must therefore name the type being accessed explicitly by means of type casting.

▪ ARRAYS AND POINTERS (2)

Sample program

```cpp
// arrPtr.cpp
// Outputs addresses and values of array elements.
// -------------------------------------------------

#include <iostream>
using namespace std;

int arr[4] = { 0, 10, 20, 30 };

int main()
{
   cout << "\nAddress and value of array elements:\n"
        << endl;

   for( int i = 0; i < 4; i++ )
      cout << "Address: " << (void*)(arr+i)    // &arr[i]
           << "    Value: " << *(arr+i)         // arr[i]
           << endl;

   return 0;
}
```

Interrelation between pointers and array elements

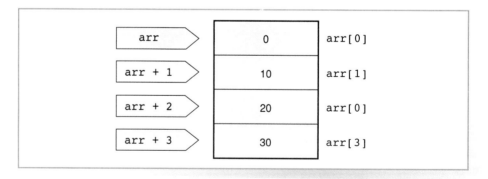

☐ Addressing Array Elements

Access to individual array elements in C++ is very closely related to pointer arithmetic. Now let's look at an `int` array to illustrate this point.

Example: `int arr[4] = { 0, 10, 20, 30 };`

As you already know, the name of the array `arr` is an `int` pointer to `arr[0]`.

Now it is possible to add or subtract pointers and integral values. The size of the object referenced by the pointer is automatically taken into consideration.

Since `arr` is an `int` pointer to `arr[0]`, `arr+1` points to the next array element `arr[1]`, i.e., to an address that is `sizeof(int)` bytes higher in memory. The memory space between the two entries will be two or four bytes, depending on the size of the type `int`. Thus the following applies to any given number, `i`:

`arr + i` points to the array element `arr[i]`,

`*(arr + i)` is the array element `arr[i]`,

This technique can also be used to address memory spaces outside of the array. Thus, `arr - 1` addresses the word that precedes `arr[0]`. But generally this does not make much sense, since you have no means of knowing what is stored at this memory address.

☐ Addressing with Pointer Variables

Array elements can also be addressed using pointer variables.

Example: `int *ptr = arr;    // ptr points to arr[0]`

In this case, both `ptr` and `arr` are pointers to the array element `arr[0]`. Thus, `ptr + 1, ptr + 2, . . .` point to the array elements `arr[1], arr[2], . . . .`

For any given integer, `i`, the following expressions are thus equivalent:

`&arr[i]`   `arr + i`   `ptr + i`

The following thus represent equivalent values:

`arr[i]`   `*(arr + i)`   `*(ptr + i)`   `ptr[i]`

At first it might seem surprising that you can use the array notation `ptr[i]` for pointers. The compiler translates `arr[i]` to `*(arr + i)`—in other words: "Start at address `arr`, move i objects up, and access the object!" This also applies to `ptr[i]`.

■ POINTER ARITHMETIC

Examples for arithmetic with pointers

```
float v[6] = { 0.0, 0.1, 0.2, 0.3, 0.4, 0.5 },
       *pv, x;

pv = v + 4;        // Let pv point to v[4].
*pv = 1.4;         // Assign 1.4 to v[4].
pv -= 2;           // Reset pv to v[2].
++pv;              // Let pv point to v[3].

x = *pv++;         // Assign v[3] to x and
                   // increment pv.
x += *pv--;        // Increment x by v[4] and let
                   // pv point to v[3] again.
--pv;              // Reset pv to v[2].
```

To step through an array of classes

```
// Searches for a given account number in a table of
// accounts and outputs the found account.
// ---------------------------------------------------
#include "account.h"     // Definition of class Account.

Account accountTab[100]; // Table containing accounts.

int main()
{
   int cnt;                // Actual number of accounts.
   Account *aPtr;          // Pointer to Account-objects.
   // To input data into accountTab and actualize cnt.
   // To search for the account number 1234567:
   bool found = false;
   for( aPtr = accountTab; aPtr < accountTab+cnt;++aPtr)
      if( aPtr->getNr() == 1234567 )
      {  found = true;
         break;
      }
   if( found)                     // Found?
      aPtr->display();            // Yes -> display.
   // To continue
}
```

In C++ you can perform arithmetic operations and comparisons with pointers, provided they make sense. This primarily means that the pointer must always point to the elements of an array. The following examples show some of your options with pointer arithmetic:

Example:
```
float v[6], *pv = v;   // pv points to v[0]
       int i = 3;
```

☐ Moving a Pointer in an Array

As you already know, the addition `pv + i` results in a pointer to the array element `v[i]`. You can use a statement such as `pv = pv + i;` to store the pointer in the variable `pv`. This moves the pointer `pv` `i` objects, that is, `pv` now points to `v[i]`.

You can also use the *operators* `++`, `--`, and `+=` or `-=` with pointer variables. Some examples are shown opposite. Please note that the indirection operator, `*`, and the operators `++` and `--` have the same precedence. Operators and operands thus are grouped from right to left:

Example:
```
*pv++    is equivalent to    *(pv++)
```

The `++` operator increments the pointer and not the variable referenced by the pointer. Operations of this type are not possible using the pointer `v` since `v` is a *constant*.

☐ Subtracting Pointers

An addition performed with two pointers does not return anything useful and is therefore invalid. However, it does make sense to perform a *subtraction* with two pointers, resulting in an `int` value that represents the number of array elements between the pointers. You can use this technique to compute the index of an array element referenced by a pointer. To do so, you simply subtract the starting address of the array. For example, if `pv` points to the array element `v[3]`, you can use the following statement

Example:
```
int index = pv - v;
```

to assign a value of 3 to the variable `index`.

☐ Comparing Pointers

Finally, *comparisons* can be performed with two pointers of the same type.

Example:
```
for( pv = v + 5; pv >= v; --pv)
        cout << setw(10) << *pv;
```

This loop outputs the numbers contained in `v` in reverse order. In the example on the opposite page, the pointer `aPtr` walks through the first `cnt` elements of the array `accountTab`, as long as `aPtr < accountTab + cnt`.

■ ARRAYS AS ARGUMENTS

Sample program

```cpp
// reverse.cpp
// Defines and calls the function reverse().
// reverse() copies a C string into another C string
// and reverses the order of characters.
// ----------------------------------------------------

#include <iostream>
using namespace std;
#include <string.h>        // Header-File for Cstrings,
                           // here for strlen().
void reverse( char str[], char umstr[]);   // Prototype

int main()                 // Read a word and
{                          // output in reversed order.
   const int CNT = 81;
   char word[CNT], revword[CNT];

   cout << "Enter a word: ";
   cin.width(CNT);         // maximal CNT-1 characters
   cin >> word;

   reverse( word, revword);                 // Call

   cout << "\nThe \"reversed\" word:    " << revword
        << endl ;

   return 0;
}

void reverse( char s1[], char s2[])        // Copies the
{                          // reversed C string s1 to s2
   int j = 0;

   for( int i = strlen(s1)-1; i >= 0; i--, j++)
      s2[j] = s1[i];

   s2[j] = '\0';                           // Terminating character
}
```

Sample output:

```
Enter a word: REGAL
The "reversed" word:    LAGER
```

If an array name is passed as an argument when calling a function, the function actually receives the address of the first array element. The called function can then perform read or write operations for any element in the array.

☐ Declaring Parameters

If the argument is an array, there are two equivalent methods of declaring parameters. This point is illustrated by the example using `strlen()` to return the length of a C string. For example, calling `strlen("REGAL")` returns a value of 5.

1. You can declare the parameter as an array.

   Example:
   ```
   int strlen( char str[])      // Compute length of
       {  int i;                 // str without '\0'.
          for( i = 0;   str[i] != '\0';   ++i)
             ;
          return (i);
       }
   ```

2. You can declare the parameter as a pointer.

   Example:
   ```
   int strlen( char *str)
       {   /*  as above  */  }
   ```

In both cases the parameter `str` is a pointer that stores the starting address of the array. Array notation is preferable if you intend to use an index to access the elements of an array. Calling `strlen("REGAL");` leads to the following situation:

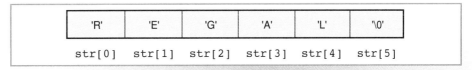

'R'	'E'	'G'	'A'	'L'	'\0'
str[0]	str[1]	str[2]	str[3]	str[4]	str[5]

As you can see, the length of a C string is equal to the index of the element containing the terminating null character.

The function `reverse()` on the opposite page copies the characters of a C string to a second `char` array in reverse order, first copying the last character in `s1`, that is, the character with the index `strlen(s1)-1`, to `s2[0]`, then the second to last character `s2[1]`, and so on.

☐ Array Length

A function to which an array is passed initially knows only the starting address of the array but not its length. In the case of C strings, the length is derived implicitly from the position of the terminating null character. In most other cases the length must be supplied explicitly.

Example:
```
void sort( Account aTab[], int len )
    { /* To sort array aTab of length len */}
```

■ POINTER VERSIONS OF FUNCTIONS

☐ Function strcpy

The standard function strcpy() copies C strings.

Example:
```
char dest[30], source[] = "A string";
strcpy( dest, source);
```

Here the string source is copied to dest "from left to right" just like an assignment.

The following function strcpy() is somewhat simpler than the standard function since it has no return value.

Index Version of strcpy()

```
void strcpy( char s1[], char s2[])     // Copies s2 to s1
{
   int i;                              // Index
   for( i = 0;  s2[i] != '\0';  ++i)   // Copy.
      s1[i] = s2[i];
   s1[i] = '\0';                       // Append terminating
}                                      // character.
```

Pointer version 1 of strcpy()

```
void strcpy( char *s1, char *s2)       // Copies s2 to s1
{
   for( ;  *s2 != '\0';  ++s1, ++s2)   // Copy
      *s1 = *s2;
   *s1 = '\0';                         // Append terminating
}                                      // character.
```

Pointer version 2 of strcpy()

```
void strcpy( char *s1, char *s2)       // Copy s2 to s1.
{
   while( (*s1++ = *s2++) != '\0' )    // Copy and append
      ;                                // terminating
}                                      // character.
```

☐ Using Pointers Instead of Indices

As we have already seen, a parameter for an array argument is always a pointer to the first array element. When declaring parameters for a given type `T`:

`T name[]`   is always equivalent to   `T *name`.

So far, in previous sample functions, the pointer has been used like a fixed base address for the array, with an index being used to access the individual array elements. However, it is possible to use pointers instead of indices.

Example: A new version of the standard function `strlen()`:

```
int strlen( char *str)       // Computes length
{                            // of str without '\0'.
   char* p = str;
   for( p = str;  *p != '\0'; ++p)   // Search
      ;                              // for  \0
   return (p - str);
}
```

In this case, the difference between two pointers results in the string length.

☐ The Sample Functions Opposite

The first version of the function `strcpy()` "string copy" opposite uses an index, whereas the second does not. Both versions produce the same results: the string `s2` is copied to `s1`. When you call the function, you must ensure that the char array referenced by `s1` is large enough.

As the parameters `s1` and `s2` are pointer variables, they can be shifted. The second "pointer version" of `strcpy()`, which is also shown opposite, uses this feature, although the function interface remains unchanged.

Generally, pointer versions are preferable to index versions as they are quicker. In an expression such as `s1[i]` the values of the variables `s1` and `i` are read and added to compute the address of the current object, whereas `s1` in the pointer version already contains the required address.

☐ Multidimensional Arrays as Parameters

In a parameter declaration for *multidimensional* arrays, you need to state every dimension with the exception of the first. Thus, a parameter declaration for a two-dimensional array will always contain the number of columns.

Example:
```
long func( int num[][10] );   // ok.
long func( int *num[10] );    // also ok.
```

■ READ-ONLY POINTERS

Sample program

```cpp
// accountFct.cpp
// Defines and calls a function, which outputs
// a list of overdrawn accounts.
// -------------------------------------------------
#include "account.h"      // Definition of class Account.

Account accountTab[] =    // Table with Account-objects.
{   Account("Twain, Mark", 1234567, -3434.30),
    Account("Crusoe, Robinson", 200000, 0.00),
    Account("Temple, Shirley", 543001, +777.70),
    Account("Valentin, Carl", 543002, -1111.10),
};
int cnt = sizeof(accountTab) / sizeof(Account);
                                        // Prototype:
int displayOverdraw( const Account *aTab, int cnt,
                     double limit);

int main()
{
    double limit = 0.0;
    cout << "Output the overdrawn accounts!\n"
         << "These are the accounts, which fell below \n"
         << "the limit, ex. -1000.00.\n" << endl;
    cout << "What is the limit? ";
    cin >> limit;

    cout << "Listing the overdrawn accounts:\n" << endl;
    if( displayOverdraw( accountTab, cnt, limit) == 0)
      cout << "\nNo account found!"
           << endl;
    return 0;
}

int displayOverdraw( const Account *aTab, int cnt,
                     double limit)
{   int count = 0;
    const Account* aPtr;
    for( aPtr = aTab;  aPtr < aTab + cnt;  ++aPtr)
      if( aPtr->getState() < limit ) // Below the limit?
      {
          aPtr->display();            // Yes -> display.
          ++count;
      }
    return count;
}
```

☐ Pointers to `const` Objects

You can use a normal pointer for both read and write access to an object. However, just like the definition used for a reference, you can also define a *read-only pointer*, that is, a pointer that can be used for read operations only. In fact, a read-only pointer is obligatory if you need to point to a constant object.

☐ Declaration

You use the keyword `const` to define a read-only pointer.

Example: `const int a = 5, b = 10,  *p = &a;`

This statement defines the constants `a` and `b`, and a pointer `p` to a constant object of type `int`. The referenced object `*p` can be read but not modified.

Example:
```
cout << *p;          // To read is ok.
*p = 1;              // Error!
```

The pointer itself is not a constant, so it can be modified:

Example: `p = &b;              // ok!`

The referenced object also does not need to be a constant. In other words, a read-only pointer can also point to a non-constant object.

Example:
```
Account depo("Twain, Mark", 1234, 4321.90);
const Account* ptr = &depo;     // ok!
ptr->display();                 // ok!
prt->setState( 7777.70);        // Error!
```

But `ptr` can only be used for read access to the non-constant object `depo`.

☐ Read-Only Pointers as Parameters

Read-only pointers are most commonly found in parameter lists. This guarantees that arguments cannot be modified.

Example: `int strlen( const char *s);`

In this example, the parameter `s` is a read-only pointer. This allows you to pass constant C strings to the standard function `strlen()`. You cannot remove the "write protection" by assigning the read-only pointer `s` to a normal pointer.

Example: `char *temp = s;              // Error!`

You need to declare a read-only pointer if a constant object may be passed as an argument.

▪ RETURNING POINTERS

Sample program

```cpp
// search1.cpp
// A filter to output all lines containing a given
// pattern. The function strstr() is called.
// Call:    search1  [ < text.dat ]
// ----------------------------------------------------
#include <iostream>
using namespace std;
#define MAXL  200               // Maximum length of line
namespace MyScope
{        // Self-defined version of function strstr():
 char *strstr( const char *str, const char *patt);
}
char line[500],                 // For a line of text.
    patt[] = "is";              // The search pattern.
int main()
{   int lineNr = 0; // As long as a line is left over:
   while( cin.getline( line, MAXL))
   {
      ++lineNr;
      if( MyScope::strstr( line, patt) != NULL)
      {                         // If the pattern is found:
         cout.width(3);
         cout << lineNr << ": "    // Output the line
             << line << endl;     // number and the line
      }
   }
   return 0;
}
```

```cpp
// strstr.cpp
// A self-defined version of the function strstr()
// ----------------------------------------------------
#include <string.h>          // For strlen() and strncmp()
namespace MyScope
{
 char *strstr( const char *s1, const char *s2)
 {            // To search for the string s2 within s1.
   int len = strlen( s2);
   for( ; *s1 != '\0'; ++s1)
      if( strncmp( s1, s2, len) == 0)   // s2 found?
         return (char *)s1;      // Yes -> return pointer
                                 // to this position, or
   return NULL;                  // else the NULL pointer.
 }
}
```

A function can return a pointer to an object. This makes sense for a function that searches for a particular object, for example. Such a function will return either a pointer to the required object or a NULL pointer if the object cannot be found.

The standard C library functions often use pointers as return values. For example, the functions `strcpy()`, `strcat()`, and `strstr()` each return a pointer to the first character in a C string.

☐ The Functions `strcpy()` and `strcat()`

In contrast to the example on the page entitled "Pointer versions of functions," the standard function `strcpy()` has a return value. The function returns its first argument, that is, a pointer to the target string and leads to the following:

Prototype: `char* strcpy( char* s1, const char* s2);`

The second parameter is a read-only pointer, since the source string is read-only.

The standard function `strcat()` concatenates two C strings, adding the C string passed as the second argument to the first argument. When you call this function, make sure that the `char` array for the first string is large enough to store both strings. The return value is the first argument. The following example shows one possible implementation.

Example:
```
char *strcat( char *s1, const char *s2 )
{
    char *p = s1 + strlen(s1); // End of s1
    strcpy(p, s2);
    return s1;
}
```

☐ Notes on the Sample Program

The program on the opposite page shows a self-defined version of the standard function `strstr()`. This version was placed in the `MyScope` namespace to distinguish it from the standard function.

The function `strstr()` searches for a given character sequence within a string. The standard function `strncmp()` is used to compare two strings. This function returns zero if the first n characters are identical.

The program uses the `strstr()` function to display all the lines in the text containing the letters "`is`" with line numbers. The exercises for this chapter contain a program called `search.cpp` where you can supply a search pattern.

■ ARRAYS OF POINTERS

Pointers in the array accPtr

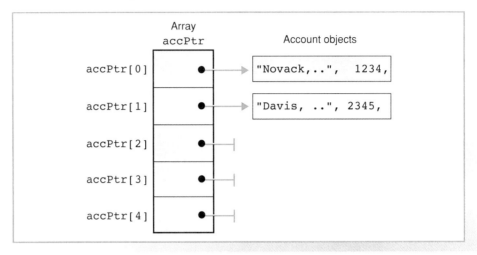

Sample function with pointers to char

```
// The function displayError() outputs an error message
// to a corresponding error number.
// --------------------------------------------------
#include <iostream>
using namespace std;
void displayError ( int errorNr)
{
    static char* errorMsg[] = {
                "Invalid error number",
                "Error 1: Too much data ",
                "Error 2: Not enough memory ",
                "Error 3: No data available "  };
    if( errorNr < 1 || errorNr > 3)
       errorNr = 0;
    cerr << errorMsg[errorNr] << endl;
}
```

✓ **NOTE**

A string literal, such as "Error..." is a char pointer to the first character in the string. Thus, such a pointer can be used to initialize another char pointer.

Due to its static declaration, the array is generated only once and remains valid until the program ends.

Pointers offer various possibilities for simple and efficient handling of large amounts of data. For example, when you are sorting objects it makes sense to define pointers to those objects and simply place the pointers in order, instead of rearranging the actual order of the objects in memory.

□ Defining Arrays of Pointers

Whenever you need a large number of pointers, you can define an array whose elements are pointers. An array of this type is referred to as a *pointer array*.

Example: `Account* accPtr[5];`

The array `accPtr` contains five `Account` pointers `accPtr[0]`, `accPtr[1]`, ... , `accPtr[4]`. The individual pointers in the array can now be assigned object addresses. Any pointers not currently in use should have the value NULL.

Example:
```
Account save("Novack, Kim", 1111, 9999.90);
Account depo("Davis, Sammy", 2222, 1000.);
accPtr[0] = &save;
accPtr[1] = &depo;
for( int i=2; i<5; ++i) accPtr[i] = NULL;
```

□ Initialization

As usual, an initialization list is used to initialize the array. In the case of a pointer array, the list contains either valid addresses or the value NULL.

Example: `Account* accPtr[5] = { &depo, &save, NULL};`

The value NULL is automatically assigned to any objects for which the list does not contain a value. This produces the same result as in the previous example.

□ Usage

The individual objects addressed by the pointers in an array do not need to occupy a contiguous memory space. Normally these objects will be created and possibly destroyed dynamically at runtime (this will be discussed in detail in a later chapter). This allows for extremely flexible object handling. The order is defined only by the pointers.

Example:
```
for( int i=0; i<5; ++i)
    if( accPtr[i] != NULL)
        accPtr[i]->display();  // To output
```

The function `displayError()` opposite displays the error message for a corresponding error number, using an array of `char` pointers to the error messages.

■ COMMAND LINE ARGUMENTS

Sample program

```cpp
// hello.cpp
// Demonstrates the command line arguments.
// Call:  hello name1 name2
// ---------------------------------------------------
#include <iostream>
using namespace std;

int main( int argc, char *argv[])
{
   if( argc != 3 )
   {
       cerr << "Use: hello name1 name2" << endl;
       return 1;
   }
   cout << "Hello " << argv[1] << '!' << endl;
   cout << "Best wishes \n"
        << "\tyours " << argv[2] << endl;
   return 0;
}
```

Example of calling the program:

```
hello Jeany Vivi
```

Screen output

```
Hello Jeany!
Best wishes
    Yours Vivi
```

Array argv in memory

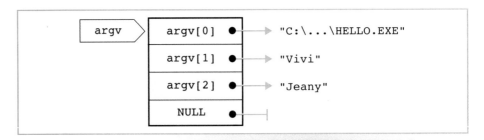

☐ Arguments for a Program

When you launch a program, you can use the command line to supply additional character sequences other than the program name. These *command line arguments* are typically used to govern how a program is executed or to supply the data a program will work with.

Example: `copy file1 file2`

In this case, the program `copy` is launched with the arguments `file1` and `file2`. The individual arguments are separated by spaces. Characters used for redirecting input and output (`>` or `<`) and a following word are evaluated by the operating system and not passed to the program. If an argument contains space or redirection characters, you must place it in double quotes.

☐ Parameters of the Function `main()`

So far we have only used the function `main()` without parameters. However, if you intend to process command line arguments, you must define parameters for `main()`.

Example:
```
int main(int argc, char * argv[] )
        {   . . . // Function block    }
```

`argc` contains the number of arguments passed via the command line. The program name is one of these, so `argc` will have a value of at least `1`.

The parameter `argv` is an array of `char` pointers:

`argv[0]`	points to the program name (and path)
`argv[1]`	points to the first real argument, that is, the word after the program name
`argv[2]`	points to the second argument
.....	
`argv[argc-1]`	points to the last argument
`argv[argc]`	is the NULL pointer

The parameters are traditionally named `argc` and `argv` although any other name could be used.

Various operating systems, for example WINDOWS 98/00/NT and UNIX, allow you to declare a third parameter for `main()`. This parameter is an array with pointers to environment strings. The exercises for this chapter contain a program that displays the program environment.

exercises

▦ EXERCISES

For exercise 3

Index version of the standard function `strcmp()`

```
// strcmp() compares two C strings lexicographically.
// Return value:        < 0, if str1 < str2
//                      = 0, if str1 == str2
//                      > 0, if str1 > str2 .
// ---------------------------------------------------------
int strcmp( const char str1[], const char str2[])
{
   int i;
   for( i=0; str1[i] == str2[i] && str1[i] != '\0'; ++i)
     ;
   return (str1[i] - str2[i]);
}
```

Notes on exercise 4

The selection sort algorithm

Method

First find the smallest element in the array and exchange it with the first element.

This procedure is repeated while `i > 0` for the remainder of an array containing array elements with an initial index of `i`.

Example

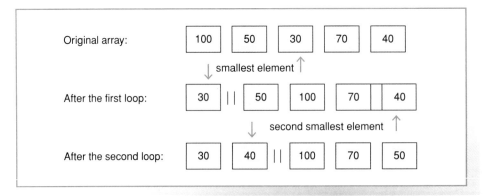

Exercise 1

Given an array v with the following definition:

```
int v[] = { 10, 20, 30, 40 }, i, *pv;
```

What screen output is caused by the following statements?

```
a.  for( pv = v;   pv <= v + 3;   pv++ )
        cout << "       *pv = "  <<   *pv;
b.  for( pv = v, i = 1;   i <= 3;   i++ )
        cout << "    pv[i] = "  <<   pv[i];
c.  for( pv = v, i = 0;   pv+i <= &v[3];   pv++,i++)
        cout << "   * (pv + i) = "  <<   * (pv + i);
d.  for( pv = v + 3;   pv >= v;   --pv )
        cout << "     v["  <<   (pv - v)   <<   "] = "
             << v[pv - v];
```

Exercise 2

Write a program that uses the cin method get() to read a line character by character and stores it in a char array. The line is then output in reverse order. Use a pointer, not an index, to address the array elements.

Exercise 3

The standard function strcmp() performs a lexicographical comparison of two C strings. The opposite page contains an index version of strcmp(). The return value is the difference between two character codes.

Write a pointer version of the function strcmp(). Call this function str_cmp() to distinguish it from the standard function.

To test the function, use a loop to read two lines of text and output the results of the comparison. The loop should terminate when both strings are empty.

Exercise 4

Define and test the function selectionSort() that sorts an array of int values in ascending order. The principle of the selection sort algorithm is shown opposite.

Arguments: An int array and its length
Return values: None

Develop both an index version and a pointer version. Test the functions with random numbers between -10000 and +10000.

Notes on exercise 5
Sample environment strings for DOS/Windows

```
   .  .  .
COMSPEC=C:\COMMAND.COM
PATH=C:\WINDOWS;C:\WINDOWS\COMMAND;C:\DOS;D:\TOOLS;
PROMPT=$p$g
TEMP=C:\TEMP
   .  .  .
```

Frequency table for exercise 7

Age \ Blood-pressure	<120	120–129	130–139	140–149	>= 160
20–29	25	34	26	12	8
30–39	19	27	24	11	4
40–49	6	15	35	36	18

Exercise 5

a. Write a program that outputs its own name and all command line arguments, each in a separate line.

b. Now extend the program to output its own environment. The environment is a memory area containing strings in the format

```
NAME=String
```

A third parameter for the function `main()` allows access to the environment. This parameter is an array of pointers just like `argv`. The array elements are `char` pointers to the environment strings, the last element being a NULL pointer.

Exercise 6

A sample filter program called `search1`, which outputs lines and the relevant line numbers for lines containing the search pattern `"ei"`, was introduced in this chapter.

Modify the program to produce a useful tool called `search`, to which you can pass any search pattern via the command line. The program should issue an error message and terminate if the command line does not contain a search string. Use the standard function `strstr()`.

Sample call:

```
search  Shanghai  < news.txt
```

Exercise 7

The following frequency was observed during an examination of the relationship between age and blood pressure for 300 males.

Write a function that calculates the sums of the rows and columns in an `int` matrix with three rows and five columns. Store the sums of the rows and columns separately in a one-dimensional row or column array.

Arguments: The matrix, the row array, and the column array.
Return value: The sum of all the matrix elements.

To test the function, output the matrix, as shown in the graphic opposite along with the computed sums in your `main` function.

■ SOLUTIONS

Exercise 1

Screen Output:

a.   *pv = 10   *pv = 20   *pv = 30   *pv = 40

b.   pv[i] = 20   pv[i] = 30   pv[i] = 40

c.   *(pv+i) = 10   *(pv+i) = 30

d.   v[3] = 40   v[2] = 30   v[1] = 20   v[0] = 10

Exercise 2

```
// -------------------------------------------------------
// reverse.cpp
// Exercise on pointer arithmetic:
// Reads a line and outputs the line in reverse order.
// -------------------------------------------------------
#include <iostream>
using namespace std;

#define MAXLEN 80

int main()
{
   char line[MAXLEN], *p;

   cout << "Enter a line of text: " << endl;

   // Input a line:
   for( p = line;
        p < line+MAXLEN  &&  cin.get(*p)  &&  *p != '\n';
        ++p )
     ;

   // Output the line in reverse order:
   while( --p >= line)
      cout << *p;

   cout << endl;

   return 0;
}
```

Exercise 3

```cpp
// --------------------------------------------------------
// str_cmp.cpp
// Define and test the pointer version str_cmp()
// of the standard function strcmp().
// --------------------------------------------------------
#include <iostream>
using namespace std;
#define MAXLEN 100        // Maximum length of C strings
// Prototype:
int str_cmp( const char* str1, const char* str2);
int main()                              // Test str_cmp()
{
    char text1[MAXLEN], text2[MAXLEN];
    cout << "Testing the function str_cmp()" << endl;
    while( true)
    {
        cout << "Enter two lines of text!\n"
                "End with two empty lines.\n" << endl;
        cout << "1. line: ";
        cin.sync();  cin.clear(); cin.get(text1,MAXLEN);
        cout << "2. line: ";
        cin.sync();  cin.clear(); cin.get(text2,MAXLEN);
        if( text1[0] == '\0' && text2[0] == '\0')
            break;                      // Both lines empty.
        int cmp = str_cmp( text1, text2);
        if( cmp < 0)
            cout << "The 1st string is smaller!\n";
        else if( cmp == 0)
            cout << "Both strings are equal!\n";
        else
            cout << "The 1st string is greater!\n";
        cout << endl;
    }
    return 0;
}
// --------------------------------------------------------
// Function str_cmp()
// Pointer version of the standard function strcmp().
// --------------------------------------------------------
int str_cmp( const char* str1, const char* str2)
{
    for( ; *str1 == *str2 && *str1 != '\0'; ++str1, ++str2)
      ;
    return (*str1 - *str2);
}
```

Exercise 4

```cpp
// --------------------------------------------------------
// selSort.cpp
// Implement the selection sort algorithm
// for int-arrays.
// --------------------------------------------------------

#include <iostream>
#include <iomanip>
#include <cstdlib>              // For srand(), rand()
#include <ctime>                // For time()
using namespace std;

// Prototype:
void selectionSort( int arr[], int len);

const int len = 200;
int intArr[len];                // int-array

int main()
{
   cout << "\n     ***  Selection Sort Algorithm  ***\n"
        << endl;

   // To initialize an int-array with random numbers:
   srand( (unsigned int)time(NULL));  // Initialize the
                                 // random number generator.
   for( int n=0; n < len; ++n)
      intArr[n] = (rand() % 20000)-10000;

   // To sort the numbers
   selectionSort( intArr, len);

   // To output the numbers
   cout << "The sorted numbers:" << endl;

   for( int i = 0; i < len; ++i)
      cout << setw(8) << intArr[i];
   cout << endl;

   return 0;
}

inline void swap( int& a, int& b)
{
   int temp = a;  a = b;  b = temp;
}
```

```
//  Index version:
/*
void selectionSort( int arr[], int len)
{
   register int j, mini;              // Indices

   for( int i = 0;  i < len-1;  ++i)
   {
      mini = i;                       // Search for minimum
      for( j = i+1; j < len; ++j) // starting with index i.
         if( arr[mini] > arr[j])
             mini = j;

      swap( arr[i], arr[mini]);     // Swap.
   }
}
*/

// Pointer version:
void selectionSort( int *arr, int len)
{
   register int *p, *minp;   // Pointer to array elements,
   int *last = arr + len-1;  // pointer to the last element

   for( ; arr < last;  ++arr)
   {
      minp = arr;                       // Search for minimum
      for( p = arr+1; p <= last; ++p) // starting with arr
         if( *minp > *p)
             minp = p;

      swap( *arr, *minp);               // Swap.
   }
}
```

Exercise 5

```
// --------------------------------------------------------
// args.cpp
// The program outputs the program name including the path,
// command line arguments and the environment.
// --------------------------------------------------------

#include <iostream>
using namespace std;

int main( int argc, char *argv[], char *env[])
{
   cout << "Program: " << argv[0] << endl;

   cout << "\nCommand line arguments:" << endl;

   int i;
   for( i = 1; i < argc; ++i)              // Arguments
     cout << argv[i] << endl;

   cout << "Type <Return> to go on";
   cin.get();

   cout << "\nEnvironment strings:" << endl;

   for( i = 0; env[i] != NULL; ++i)        // Environment
     cout << env[i] << endl;

   return 0;
}
```

Exercise 6

```
// --------------------------------------------------------
// search.cpp
// A filter that outputs all lines containing a certain
// pattern. The standard function strstr() is called.
//
// Call:    search  pattern [ < text.dat ]
//
// If no file name is passed the input is read from the
// keyboard. In this case end input with <Ctrl> + <Z>.
// --------------------------------------------------------
#include <iostream>
#include <cstring>        // Standard functions for C strings
using namespace std;
#define MAXL  200                 // Maximum length of line
char line[500];                   // For a line of text.
```

```
int main( int argc, char *argv[])
{
   if( argc != 2)
   {
     cerr << "Call:  search  pattern [ < text.dat ]"
          << endl;
     return 1;
   }

   int lineNr = 0;
                                // As long as a line exists:
   while( cin.getline( line, MAXL))
   {
     ++lineNr;
     if( strstr( line, argv[1]) != NULL)
     {                          // If the pattern was found:
       cout.width(3);
       cout << lineNr << ": "        // Output the line
            << line << endl;         // number and the line
     }
   }
   return 0;
}
```

Exercise 7

```
// -----------------------------------------------------
// matrix.cpp
// To compute the sums of rows and columns in a matrix.
// -----------------------------------------------------

#include <iostream>
#include <iomanip>
using namespace std;

// Define and initiate a two-dimensional array:

int matrix[3][5] = { { 25, 34, 26, 12,  8 },
                     { 19, 27, 24, 11,  4 },
                     {  6, 15, 35, 36, 18 } };

int rowsum[3];                 // For the sums of the rows
int colsum[5];                 // For the sums of the columns

// Prototype of function matrixsum():
int matrixsum( int arr2D[][5], int vlen,
               int rsum[], int csum[]);
```

```cpp
int main()
{
   cout << "Testing the function matrixsum().\n"
        << endl;

   // Compute sums:
   int totalsum =
       matrixsum( matrix, 3, rowsum, colsum);

   // Output matrix and sums:
   cout << "The matrix with the sums "
        << "of rows and columns:\n"
        << endl;

   int i,j;
   for( i = 0 ; i < 3 ; ++i)      // Output rows of the
   {                              // matrix with row sums.
     for( j = 0 ; j < 5 ; ++j)
       cout << setw(8) << matrix[i][j];
     cout << " | " << setw(8) << rowsum[i] << endl;
   }
   cout << " -------------------------------------------"
        << endl;
   for( j = 0 ;  j < 5  ;  ++j )
     cout << setw(8) << colsum[j];
   cout << " | " << setw(8) << totalsum << endl;
   return 0;
}

// -----------------------------------------------------------
int matrixsum( int v[][5], int len,
               int rsum[], int csum[])
{  int ro, co;                            // Row and column index
   for( ro = 0 ; ro < len ; ++ro)     // To compute row sums
   {
      rsum[ro] = 0;
      for( co = 0 ; co < 5 ; ++co)
        rsum[ro] += v[ro][co];
   }
   for(co = 0 ; co < 5 ; ++co)        // Compute column sums
   {
      csum[co] = 0;
      for( ro = 0 ; ro < len ; ++ro)
        csum[co] += v[ro][co];
   }
   return (rsum[0] + rsum[1] + rsum[2]);  // Total sum =
}                                         // sum of row sums.
```

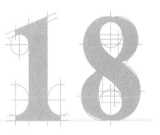

chapter

Fundamentals of File
Input and Output

This chapter describes sequential file access using file streams. File
streams provide simple and portable file handling techniques.

■ FILES

File operations

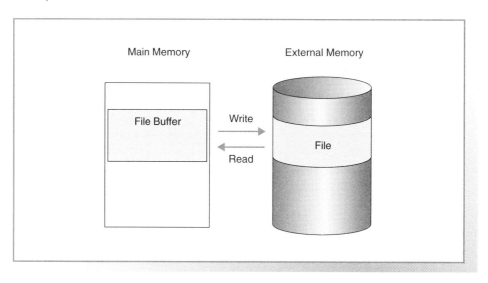

When a program is terminated, the program data stored in main memory is lost. To store data permanently, you need to write that data to a file on an external storage medium.

☐ File Operations

Single characters or character strings can be written to text files just like they can be output on screen. However, it is common practice to store records in files. A record contains data that forms a logical unit, such as the human resource information for a person. A *write operation* stores a record in a file, that is, the existing record in the file is updated or a new record is added. When you *read* a record, this record is taken from the file and copied to the data structure of a program.

Objects can be put into permanent storage using similar techniques. However, this normally involves more than just storing an object's data. You also need to ensure that the object can be correctly reconstructed when it is read, and this in turn involves storing type information and references to other objects.

External mass storage media, such as hard disks, are normally block-oriented—that is, data is transferred in blocks whose size is a multiple of 512 bytes. Efficient and easy file management thus implies putting the data you need to store into temporary storage in main memory, in a so-called *file buffer*.

☐ File Positions

From the viewpoint of a C++ program, a file is simply a long byte array. The structure of the file, using records for example, is entirely the programmer's responsibility, allowing for a maximum degree of flexibility.

Every character in a file occupies a byte position. The first byte occupies position 0, the second byte position 1, and so on. The *current file position* is the position of the byte that will be read or written next. Each byte that is transferred automatically increases the current file position by 1.

In the case of *sequential access*, the data is read or written byte by byte in a fixed order. The first read operation starts at the beginning of the file. If you need access to some piece of information in a file, you must read the file content from start to finish. Write operations can create a new file, overwrite an existing file, or append new data to an existing file.

Easy access to given data in a file implies being able to set the current file position as required. This technique is known as *random file access* and will be discussed in one of the following chapters.

■ FILE STREAMS

Stream classes for file access

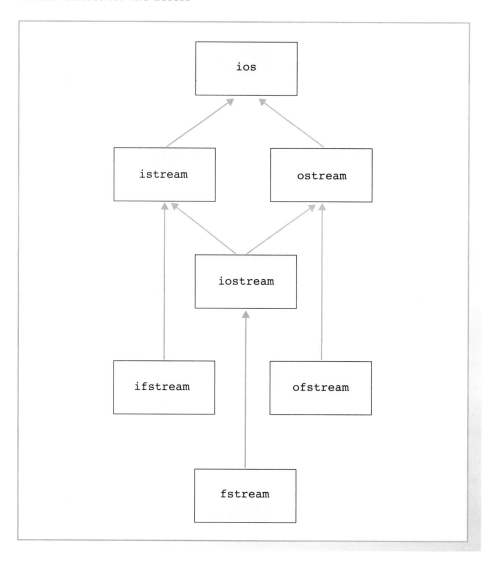

C++ provides various standard classes for file management. These so-called *file stream classes* allow for easy file handling. As a programmer you will not need to concern yourself with file buffer management or system specifics.

Since the file stream classes have been standardized, you can use them to develop portable C++ programs. One program can thus process files on a Windows NT or UNIX platform. You simply need to recompile the program for each platform you use.

☐ The File Stream Classes in the `iostream` Library

The class hierarchy on the opposite page shows that the file stream classes contain the stream classes, with which you are already familiar, as *base classes*:

- the `ifstream` class derives from the `istream` class and allows file reading
- the `ofstream` class derives from the `ostream` stream class and supports writing to files
- the `fstream` class derives from the `iostream` stream class. As you would expect, it supports both read and write operations for files.

The file stream classes are declared in the `fstream` header file. An object that belongs to a file stream class is known as a *file stream*.

☐ Functionality

The file stream classes inherit the functionality of their base classes. Thus, the methods, operators, and manipulators you have already used for `cin` and `cout` are also available here. Thus every file stream has:

- methods for non-formatted writing and reading of single characters and/or data blocks
- the operators `<<` or `>>` for formatted reading and writing from or to files
- methods and manipulators for formatting character sequences
- methods for state queries.

File handling methods, particularly methods for opening and closing files, round off the package.

▪ CREATING FILE STREAMS

Sample program

```cpp
// showfile.cpp
// Reads a text file and outputs it in pages,
// i.e. 20 lines per page.
// Call:  showfile  filename
// ----------------------------------------------------
#include <iostream>
#include <fstream>
using namespace std;

int main( int argc, char *argv[])
{
   if( argc != 2 )                  // File declared?
   {
       cerr << "Use: showfile filename" << endl;
       return 1;
   }
   ifstream file( argv[1]);   // Create  a file stream
                              // and open for reading.
   if( !file )                // Get status.
   {
     cerr << "An error occurred when opening the file "
          << argv[1] << endl;
     return 2;
   }

   char line[80];
   int cnt = 0;
   while( file.getline( line, 80))  // Copy the file
   {                                // to standard
     cout << line << endl;          // output.
     if( ++cnt == 20)
     {
       cnt = 0;
       cout << "\n\t ---- <return> to continue ---- "
            << endl;
         cin.sync(); cin.get();
      }
   }
   if( !file.eof() )            // End-of-file occurred?
   {
     cerr << "Error reading the file "
          << argv[1] << endl;
     return 3;
   }
   return 0;
}
```

☐ Opening a File

You need to open a file before you can manipulate it. To do so, you can

- state the *file name*, which can also contain a path
- define a so-called *file access mode*.

If the path is not explicitly stated, the file must be in the current directory. The file access mode specifically defines whether read and/or write access to the file is permitted.

Any files still open when a program terminates are automatically closed.

☐ File Stream Definition

You can open a file when you create a file stream—you simply state the file name to do so. In this case default values are used for the file access mode.

Example: `ifstream myfile("test.fle");`

The file name `test.fle` is passed to the constructor of the `ifstream` class, which opens the file for reading. Since the path was not stated, the file must be in the current directory. When a file is opened, the current file position is the beginning of the file.

If you create a file stream for write-only access, the file you state need not exist. In this case a new file is created.

Example: `ofstream yourfile("new.fle");`

This statement creates a new file called `new.fle` and opens the file for writing. But be careful! If the file already exists, it will be truncated to a length of zero bytes, or in other words deleted.

You can create a file stream which does not reference a specific file and use the `open()` method to open a file later.

Example: `ofstream yourfile;`
            `yourfile.open("new.fle");`

This example has the same effect as the previous example. More specifically, `open()` uses the same default values for file access when opening a file as the default constructor for the class.

It rarely makes sense to use fixed file names. In the case of the sample program on the opposite page, you state the file name in the command line when you launch the program. If no file name is supplied, the program issues an error message and terminates. Using interactive user input is another possible way to define a file name.

■ OPEN MODES

Flags for the open mode of a file

Flag	Effects
ios::in	Opens an existing file for input.
ios::out	Opens a file for output. This flag implies ios::trunc if it is not combined with one of the flags ios::in or ios::app or ios::ate.
ios::app	Opens a file for output at the end-of-file.
ios::trunc	An existing file is truncated to zero length.
ios::ate	Open and seek to end immediately after opening. Without this flag, the starting position after opening is always at the beginning of the file.
ios::binary	Perform input and output in binary mode.

 NOTE

1. These flags are defined in the baseclass ios, which is common to all stream classes, and are of the ios::openmode type.

2. By default a file is opened as a *text file* in so-called text mode. When you read from or write to a text file, control characters to indicate newlines or the end-of-file are interpreted separately and adapted to the current platform (so-called "cooked mode"). When a file is opened in binary mode, the file contents are left unchanged (the so called "raw mode").

Default settings when opening a file

The constructor and the method open() of all stream classes use the following default values:

Class	Flags
ifstream	ios::in
ofstream	ios::out | ios::trunc
fstream	ios::in | ios::out

To open a file in any but the default mode, you must supply both the file name and the open mode. This is necessary, for example, to open an existing file for write access without deleting the file.

☐ Open Mode Flags

In addition to the file name, you can pass a second argument for the open mode to the constructors and the open() method. The open mode is determined by using flags. A *flag* represents a single bit in a computer word. If the flag is raised, the bit in question will contain the value 1, with 0 representing all other cases.

You can use the bit operator, |, to combine various flags. Either the flag ios::in or ios::out must be stated in all cases. If the flag ios::in is raised, the file must already exist. If the flag ios::in is not used, the file is created, if it does not already exist.

Example: `fstream addresses("Address.fle", ios::out | ios::app);`

This opens a file for writing at end-of-file. The file is created, if it does not already exist. The file will automatically grow after every write operation.

You can use the default mode for the `fstream` class, that is, `ios::in | ios::out`, to open an existing file for reading and writing. This so-called update mode is used for updating the information in a file and is often seen in conjunction with random file access.

☐ Error Handling

Errors can occur when opening a file. A user may not have the required access privileges, or the file you want to read may not exist. The state flag `failbit` of the `ios` base class is raised in this case. The flag can either be queried directly using the `fail()` method, or indirectly by querying the status of a file stream in an `if` condition.

Example: `if( !myfile)          // or: if( myfile.fail())`

The `fail` bit is also set if a read or write error occurs. If a read operation fails, the end of the current file may have been reached. To distinguish this normal behavior from a read error, you can use the `eof()` method (eof = end-of-file) to query the `eof` bit:

Example: `if( myfile.eof())     // At end-of-file?`

The `eof` bit is set if you try to carry on reading at the end of a file. The sample program on the previous page illustrates the potential issues.

■ CLOSING FILES

Sample program

```cpp
// fcopy1.cpp  :  Copies files.
// Call: fcopy1  source  [ destination ]
// ----------------------------------------------------
#include <iostream>
#include <fstream>
using namespace std;
inline void openerror( const char *file)
{
  cerr << "Error on opening the file " << file << endl;
  exit(1);                    // Ends program closing
}                             // all opened files.
void copy( istream& is, ostream& os);     // Prototype

int main(int argc, char *argv[])
{
  if( argc < 2 || argc > 3)
  { cerr << "Call: fcopy1 source [ destination ]"
         << endl;
    return 1;                          // or: exit(1);
  }
  ifstream infile(argv[1]);          // Open 1st file
  if( !infile.is_open())
    openerror( argv[1]);

  if( argc == 2)                 // Just one sourcefile.
    copy( infile, cout);
  else                           // Source and destination
  {
    ofstream outfile(argv[2]);     // Open 2nd file
    if( !outfile.is_open() )
      openerror( argv[2]);
    copy( infile, outfile);
    outfile.close();                    // Unnecessary.
  }
  infile.close();                       // Unnecessary.
  return 0;
}

void copy( istream& is, ostream& os)  // Copy it to os.
{
  char c;
  while( is.get(c) )
      os.put(c);                        // or:  os << c ;
}
```

☐ Motivation

After you have completed file manipulation, the file should always be closed for the following reasons:

- data may be lost, if for some reason the program is not terminated correctly
- there is a limit to the number of files that a program can open simultaneously.

A program that terminates correctly will automatically close any open files before exiting. A file stream destructor will also close a file referenced by a stream. However, if the file is no longer in use before this point, you should close the file explicitly.

☐ Methods `close()` and `is_open()`

Each of the file stream classes contains a definition of a `void` type method called `close()`, which is used to close the file belonging to the stream.

Example: `myfile.close();`

However, the file stream continues to exist. It is therefore possible to use the stream to open and manipulate another file.

If you are not sure whether a file stream is currently accessing a file, you can always perform a test using the `is_open()` method . In the case of the `myfile` file stream, the test is as follows:

Example:
```
if( myfile.is_open() )
{ /* . . . */ }               // File is open
```

☐ The `exit()` Function

Open files are also closed when you call the global function `exit()`. The actual reason for using this function is to terminate a program in an orderly manner and return an error code to the calling process.

Prototype: `void exit( int status );`

The calling process, to which the `status` error code is passed for evaluation, will often be the command interpreter—a Unix shell, for example. Successful program execution normally produces the error code 0. The statement `return n;` is thus equivalent to the statement `exit(n);` when used in the `main()` function.

The program on the opposite page copies a file stated in the command line. If the user forgets to state a second (target) file, the source file is copied to standard output. In this case, the source file will need to be a text file.

■ READING AND WRITING BLOCKS

Sample program

```
// Pizza_W.cpp
// Demonstrating output of records block by block.
// ---------------------------------------------------
#include <iostream>
#include <fstream>
using namespace std;

char header[] =
"    * * *  P I Z Z A   P R O N T O  * * *\n\n";
// Record structure:
struct Pizza { char name[32];  float price; };
const int MAXCNT = 10;
Pizza pizzaMenu[MAXCNT] =
{
   { "Pepperoni", 9.90F },    { "White Pizza", 15.90F },
   { "Ham Pizza", 12.50F }, { "Calzone", 14.90F } };
int cnt = 4;
char pizzaFile[256] = "pizza.fle";

int main()                           // To write records.
{
   cout << header  << endl;

   // To write data into the file:
   int exitCode = 0;
   ofstream outFile( pizzaFile, ios::out|ios::binary );
   if( !outFile)
   {
      cerr << "Error opening the file!" << endl;
      exitCode = 1;
   }
   else
   {
      for( int i = 0; i < cnt; ++i)
        if( !outFile.write( (char*)&pizzaMenu[i],
                           sizeof(Pizza)) )
        {  cerr << "Error writing!" << endl;
           exitCode = 2;
        }
   }
   if( exitCode == 0)
     cout << "\nData has been added to file "
          << pizzaFile << "\n" << endl;
   return  exitCode;
}
```

The file stream classes can use all the `public` operations defined in their base classes. This means you can write formatted or unformatted data to a file or read that data from the file block by block or character by character.

☐ Formatted and Unformatted Input and Output

The previous sample programs illustrated how to use the methods `get()`, `getline()`, and `put()` to read or write data from or to text files. Formatted input and output of numerical values, for example, requires the `>>` and `<<` operators and appropriate manipulators or formatting methods.

Example:
```
double price = 12.34;
ofstream textFile("Test.txt");
textFile << "Price: " << price << "Dollar" << endl;
```

The file `Test.txt` will contain a line of text, such as `"Price  ...  "` that exactly matches the screen output.

Converting binary data to legible text is not practicable if you are dealing with large amounts of data. It makes sense to write the data for a series of measurements to a binary file in the order in which they occur in the program. To do so, you simply open the file in binary mode and write the data to the file, or read it from the file, block by block.

☐ Transferring Data Blocks

The `ostream` method `write()` transfers given number of bytes from main memory to a file.

Prototype:
```
ostream& write( const char *buf, int n);
```

Since `write()` returns a reference to the stream, you can check to ensure that the write operation was successful.

Example:
```
if( ! fileStream.write("An example ", 2) )
    cerr << "Error in writing!" << endl;
```

A warning is issued if an error occurs while writing the characters `"An"`. You can use the `read()` method to read data blocks from the file. The method transfers a data block from a file to a program buffer.

Prototype:
```
istream& read( char *buf, int n);
```

The methods `read()` and `write()` are often used for files with fixed length records. The block that needs to be transferred can contain one or more records. The buffer in main memory is either a structure variable or an array with elements belonging to the structure type. You need to cast the address of this memory area to `(char *)` as shown in the example opposite.

■ OBJECT PERSISTENCE

Class Account

```
// Class Account with methods read() and write()
// ------------------------------------------------
class Account
{
   private:
     string name;            // Account holder
     unsigned long nr;       // Account number
     double balance;         // Balance of account
   public:
      . . .    // Constructors, destructor,
               // access methods, ...
      ostream& Account::write(ostream& os) const;
      istream& Account::read(istream& is)
};
```

Implementing methods read() and write()

```
// write() outputs an account into the given stream os.
// Returns: The given stream.
ostream& Account::write(ostream& os) const
{
   os << name << '\0';          // To write a string
   os.write((char*)&nr, sizeof(nr) );
   os.write((char*)&balance, sizeof(balance) );
   return os;
}

// read() is the opposite function of write().
// read() inputs an account from the stream is
// and writes it into the members of the current object

istream& Account::read(istream& is)
{
   getline( is, name, '\0');    // Read a string
   is.read( (char*)&nr, sizeof(nr) );
   is.read( (char*)&balance, sizeof(balance));
   return is;
}
```

☐ Storing Objects

Objects are created during program runtime and cleaned up before the program terminates. To avoid this volatility, you can make an object *persistent*, that is, you can store the object in a file. However, you must ensure that the object can be reconstructed, as it was, when read. This means dealing with the following issues:

- Objects can contain other objects. You will generally not know how to store a member object.
- Objects can contain references to other objects. However, it does not make sense to store pointer values in a file, as the memory addresses will change each time you re-launch the program.

For example, the class `Account` on the opposite page contains the member object name, which is a `string` type. As `string` type objects are used to handle variable length strings, the object just contains a reference to the string. It therefore makes no sense to save the memory content of size `sizeof(name)` occupied by the object name in a file. Instead, you should write the string itself to a file.

One possible solution to this issue is to store the data to allow them to be passed to a constructor for the class when read. Another solution involves providing methods to allow the objects to write their own data members to files or read them from files. This technique is normally preferable since the class can now handle data storage itself, allowing it to write internal status data while simultaneously preventing external access to that data.

☐ Storing Account Class Objects

The opposite page shows the `Account` class, with which you are already familiar. File input and output methods have been added to the class. A file stream that references a file opened in binary mode is passed as an argument to the methods `read()` and `write()`. The return value is the stream in both cases, so the status can be queried when the function is called.

Example: `if( ! anAccount.write( outFile) )`
            `    cerr << "Error in writing!" << endl;`

When you read an account, you can simultaneously create an empty object that the `read()` method can access.

Example: `if( ! anAccount.read( inFile) )`
            `    cerr << "Error in reading!" << endl;`

The member object name is saved as a C string, that is, as a string terminated by the null character, `'\0'`. The `<<` operator and the function `getline()` are available for this task.

exercises

■ **EXERCISES**

For exercise 1
Possible calls to the program `fcopy`:

`fcopy file1 file2`

A file, `file1`, is copied to `file2`. If `file2` already exists, it is overwritten.

`fcopy file1`

A file, `file1`, is copied to standard output, that is, to the screen if standard output has not been redirected.

`fcopy`

For calls without arguments, the source and destination files are entered in a user dialog.

More details on the istream class method `read()`

If `is` is a file stream that references a file opened for reading, the following call

Example: `char buf[1024];`
               `is.read(buf, 1024);`

transfers the next 1024 bytes from file to the buffer `buf`. Provided that no error occurs, no less than 1024 bytes will be copied unless end-of-file is reached. In this case the `fail` and `eof` bits are set. The last block of bytes to be read also has to be written to the destination file. The method `gcount()` returns the number of bytes transferred by the last read operation.

Example: `int nread = is.gcount();`   `// Number of bytes`
                                          `// in last read op.`

Exercise 1

The sample program `fcopy1`, which copies a file to the screen or to a second file, was introduced in this chapter. Write a program named `fcopy` to enhance `fcopy1` as follows:

- If the program is launched without any arguments, it does not issue an error message and terminate but requests user input for the names of the source and target files. If an empty string is given as the name of the target file, that is, the Return key is pressed, the source file is displayed on screen.
- If the command line or the user dialog contains valid source and target file names, a *binary* copy operation is performed.
- Copy the data block by block with the `read()` and `write()` methods. The default block size is 1024 bytes.
- The `copy()` function returns `false` if an error occurs while copying and `true` in all other cases.

Also refer to the notes on the opposite page.

Exercise 2

a. Modify the sample program `Pizza_w.cpp` in this chapter to allow the user to add new pizza records to the four standard pizzas and store these records on file.

b. Then write a program called `Pizza_r.cpp`, which displays the pizza menu, that is, outputs the contents of the pizza file.

Exercise 3

Test the methods `read()` and `write()` in the `Account` class. To do so, write a program called `Account_rw.cpp` that

- initializes an array with account objects and stores the array in a file
- reads the contents of the file to a second array and displays the accounts in that array to allow you to check them.

Use binary mode for read or write access to the file.

For Exercise 4

New members of class `TelList`

```
New data members:
  string filename;  // File name
  bool dirty;       // true, if data is not
                    // stored yet.
New methods:
  const string& getFilename() const;
  bool setFilename( const string& fn);
  bool isDirty() const;

  bool load();    // Read data from the file
  bool save();    // Save data.
  bool saveAs();  // Save data as ...
```

Extended menu of the application program

```
        * * * * *  Telephone List  * * * * *


        S = Show all entries
        F = Find a telephone number
        A = Append an entry
        D = Delete an entry
        -------------------------------------------
        O = Open a file
        W = Save in the file
        U = Save as ...
        -------------------------------------------
        Q = Quit the program

Your choice:
```

Exercise 4

The program TelList, which was written as an exercise for Chapter 16, needs to be modified to allow telephone lists to be saved in a file.

To allow this, first add the data members and methods detailed on the opposite page to TelList. The string filename is used to store the name of the file in use. The dirty flag is raised to indicate that the phone list has been changed but not saved. You will need to modify the existing methods append() and erase() to provide this functionality.

The strings in the phone list must be saved as C strings in a binary file, allowing for entries that contain several lines.

Add the following items to the application program menu:

O = Open a file
  Read a phone list previously stored in a file.

W = Save
  Save the current phone list in a file.

U = Save as . . .
  Save the current phone list in a new file.

Choosing one of these menu items calls one of the following methods as applicable: load(), save() or saveAs(). These methods return true for a successful action and false otherwise. The user must be able to supply a file name for the save() method, as the list may not have been read from a file previously.

If the phone list has been modified but not saved, the user should be prompted to save the current phone list before opening another file or terminating the program.

solutions

■ **SOLUTIONS**

Exercise 1

```
// -----------------------------------------------------
// fcopy.cpp
// Copy files
// Call: fcopy  [ source  [ destination ] ]
// -----------------------------------------------------
#include <iostream>
#include <fstream>
using namespace std;

char usage[] = "Call: fcopy [source [destination]]}";

inline void openerror( const char *file)
{
  cerr << "Error opening the file " << file << endl;
  exit(1);
}

bool copy( istream& is, ostream& os),     // Prototype,
     ok = true;                           // ok flag.

int main(int argc, char *argv[])
{
  char source[256] = "", dest[256] = "";

  switch( argc )
  {
   case 1:                        // No file declared
                                  // ==> input file name.
     cout << "Copying source file to "
             "destination file!\n"
             "Source file: ";
     cin.getline( source, 256);
     if( strlen(source) == 0)
     { cerr << "No source file declared!" << endl;
       return 1;
     }
     cin.sync();                  // No previous input
     cout << "Destination file: ";
     cin.getline( dest, 256);
     break;
   case 2:                        // One file is declared.
     strcpy( source, argv[1]);
     break;
   case 3:    // Source and destination files are declared.
     strcpy( source, argv[1]);
     strcpy( dest, argv[2]);
     break;
```

```
    default:                // Invalid call to the program.
      cerr << usage << endl;
      return 2;             // or: exit(2);
  }

  if( strlen(dest) == 0)      // Only source file?
  {                           // yes ==> output to cout.
    ifstream infile(source);
    if( !infile )
        openerror( source);
    ok = copy( infile, cout);
    // The file is closed by the ifstream destructor.
  }
  else                        // Copy source to destination
  {                           // file in binary mode.
    ifstream infile( source, ios::in | ios::binary);
    if( !infile )
        openerror( source);
    else
    {
      ofstream outfile( dest, ios::out | ios::binary);
      if( !outfile)
          openerror( dest);
      ok = copy( infile, outfile);
      if( ok)
        cerr << "File " << source << " to file "
             << dest <<" copied!"<< endl;
    }
  }
  if(!ok)
  {  cerr << "Error while copying!" << endl;
     return 3;
  }
  return 0;
}

bool copy( istream& is, ostream& os)  // To copy
{                                      // is to os.
  const int BufSize = 1024;
  char buf[BufSize];
  do
  {
    is.read( buf, BufSize);
    if( is.gcount() > 0)
      os.write(buf, is.gcount());
  }
  while( !is.eof() && !is.fail() && !os.fail() );
  if( !is.eof() ) return false;
  else            return true;
}
```

Exercise 2

```cpp
// ----------------------------------------------------
// Pizza.h
// Header file for Pizza_W.cpp and Pizza_R.cpp.
// ----------------------------------------------------
#include <iostream>
#include <iomanip>
#include <fstream>
using namespace std;
// Structure of a record:
struct Pizza {  char  name[32];  float price;  };
#define MAXCNT    20              // Maximum number of pizzas
#define FILENAME  "pizza.fle"

inline void header()
{
   cout << "      * * *   P I Z Z A   P R O N T O   * * *\n\n"
        << endl;
}


// ----------------------------------------------------
// Pizza_w.cpp
// Demonstrating blockwise writing of records.
// ----------------------------------------------------
#include "Pizza.h"
Pizza pizzaMenu[MAXCNT] =
{
   { "Pepperoni", 9.90F },  { "White Pizza", 15.90F },
   { "Ham Pizza", 12.50F }, { "Calzone", 14.90F } };

int  cnt = 4;
char pizzaFile[256] = FILENAME;

int main()                              // Write records.
{
   int i;
   header();
   cout << "\nOur standard offer:\n" << endl;
   cout << fixed << setprecision(2);
   for( i = 0; i < cnt; ++i)
      cout << setw(20) << pizzaMenu[i].name
           << setw(10) << pizzaMenu[i].price << endl;
   cout << "\n-----------------------------------------\n"
        << endl;
```

```
    // Input more pizzas via keyboard:
    while( cnt < MAXCNT)
    {
      cin.sync(); cin.clear();
      cout << "What pizza should be added "
           << "to the menu?\n\n" << "Name:  ";
      cin.getline( pizzaMenu[cnt].name, 32);
      if( pizzaMenu[cnt].name[0] == '\0')
        break;

      cout << "Price: ";
      cin >> pizzaMenu[cnt].price;

      if( !cin)
        cerr << "Invalid input!" << endl;
      else
        ++cnt;

      if( cnt < MAXCNT)
        cout << "\n... and the next pizza!\n"
             << "Stop with <Return>.\n";
    }

    // Add data to the file:
    int exitCode = 0;
    ofstream outFile( pizzaFile, ios::out | ios::binary);
    if( !outFile)
    {
      cerr << "Error opening the file!" << endl;
      exitCode = 1;
    }
    else
    {
      for( int i = 0; i < cnt; ++i)
        if( !outFile.write( (char*)&pizzaMenu[i],
                             sizeof(Pizza)) )
        {
          cerr << "Error writing to file!"
               << endl;
          exitCode = 2;
        }
    }
    if( exitCode == 0)
      cout << "\nData added to file " << pizzaFile
           << ".\n" << endl;

    return exitCode;
}
```

```cpp
// ------------------------------------------------
// Pizza_r.cpp
// Demonstrating block by block reading of records.
// ------------------------------------------------

#include "Pizza.h"

char pizzaFile[256] = FILENAME;

int main()                   // Read and display records.
{
   header();

   ifstream inFile( pizzaFile, ios::in | ios::binary);
   if( !inFile)
   {
      cerr << "Pizza file does not exist!" << endl;
      return 1;
   }
   Pizza onePizza;
   int cnt = 0;

   cout << "\n----------------------------------------"
        << "\nThe available pizzas:\n" << endl;

   cout << fixed << setprecision(2);
   while( true)
      if( !inFile.read( (char*)&onePizza, sizeof(Pizza)) )
         break;
      else
      {
         cout << setw(20) << onePizza.name
              << setw(10) << onePizza.price << endl;
         ++cnt;
      }

   cout << "\n-----------------------------------------\n"
        << endl;

   if( !inFile.eof())
   {
      cerr << "Error reading file!" << endl;
      return 2;
   }
   else
      cerr << "These are " << cnt << " pizzas!\n" << endl;

   return 0;
}
```

Exercise 3

```cpp
// -------------------------------------------------------
// Account_rw.cpp
// Writes an array with objects of class Account to
// a file and feed the array into another array.
// -------------------------------------------------------

#include "Account.h"      // Definition of the class Account
#include <iostream>
#include <fstream>
using namespace std;

Account AccTab1[3] =
{
  Account("Lucky, Luke", 707070, -1200.99),
  Account("Mickey, Mouse", 123000, 2500.0),
  Account("Snoopy, Dog\n"         // String can contain more
          "Cell #: 01771234567", 543001)  // than one line.
};

Account AccTab2[3];      // Calls to default constructor

int cnt = 3;

char file[] = "account.fle";

int main()
{
   int i = 0;

   // --- Write accounts to file ---

   ofstream outFile( file, ios::out | ios::binary );
   if( ! outFile)
   {
     cerr << "Error opening file " << file
          << endl;
     return 1;
   }
   for( i = 0; i < cnt; ++i)
     if( !AccTab1[i].write(outFile) )
     {
       cerr << "Error writing to file " << file
            << endl;
       return 2;
     }
   outFile.close();
```

```
       // --- Reads accounts from file ---

       ifstream inFile( file, ios::out | ios::binary );
       if( ! inFile)
       {
         cerr << "Error opening file " << file
              << endl;
         return 3;
       }
       for( i = 0; i < cnt; ++i)
         if( !AccTab2[i].read(inFile) )
         {
           cerr << "Error reading file " << file
                << endl;
           return 4;
         }
       inFile.close();

       // --- Displays the accounts read ---

       cout << "The file " << file << " contains the "
            << "following accounts:" << endl;

       for( i = 0; i < cnt; ++i)
         AccTab2[i].display();

       cout << endl;

       return 0;
}
```

Exercise 4

```
// -------------------------------------------------------
// telList.h
// A class TelList to represent a list
// containing names and telephone numbers.
// The methods load(), save(), and saveAs() serve for
// loading and saving a telephone list.
// -------- ----------------------------------------------

#ifndef _TelList_
#define _TelList_

#include <string>
using namespace std;

#define PSEUDO -1          // Pseudo position
#define MAX 100            // Maximum number of elements
```

```cpp
// Type of a list element:
struct Element { string name, telNr; };

class TelList
{
  private:
    Element v[MAX];          // The array and the actual
    int count;               // number of elements.

    string filename;         // File name
    bool dirty;              // true if data has been changed
                             // but not yet saved.
  public:
    TelList() : count(0), filename(""), dirty(false)
    {}

    int getCount() { return count; }

    Element *retrieve( int i )
    {
       return (i >= 0 && i < count)? &v[i] : NULL;
    }
    bool append( const Element& el )
    {
       return append( el.name, el.telNr);
    }
    bool append( const string& name, const string& telNr);
    bool erase( const string& name);
    int  search( const string& name) const;
    void print() const;
    int  print( const string& name) const;
    int  getNewEntries();

    const string& getFilename() const { return filename; }
    bool setFilename( const string& fn)
    {  if( fn.empty()
          return false;
       else { filename = fn;  dirty = true; return true; }
    }
    bool isDirty() const { return dirty; }
    bool load();
    bool save();
    bool saveAs();
};
#endif  // _TelList_

// --------------------------------------------------------
// TelList.cpp
// Implements the methods of class TelList.
// --------------------------------------------------------
#include "telList.h"        // Definition of class TelList
#include <iostream>
#include <iomanip>
#include <fstream>
using namespace std;
```

```
bool TelList::append( const string& name,
                      const string& telNr)
{
    if( count < MAX               // Any space
        && name.length() > 1      // minimum 2 characters
        && search(name) == PSEUDO)  // does not exist
    {
      v[count].name  = name;
      v[count].telNr = telNr;
      ++count;
      dirty = true;
      return true;
    }
    return false;
}

bool TelList::erase( const string& key )
{
    int i = search(key);
    if( i != PSEUDO )
    {
      if( i != count-1)           // Copy the last element
          v[i] = v[count-1];      // to position i.
      --count;
      dirty = true;
      return true;
    }
    return false;
}
// ---------------------------------------------------
// Methods search(), print(), getNewEntries()
// are unchanged (refer to solutions of chapter 16).
// ---------------------------------------------------

// Methods for loading and saving the telephone list.

bool TelList::load()
{
    cout << "\n--- Load the telephone list "
         << "from a file. ---" << "\nFile: ";

    string file;                          // Input file name.
    cin.sync(); cin.clear();              // No previous input
    getline( cin, file);
    if( file.empty())
    {
      cerr << "No filename declared!" << endl;
      return false;
    }
```

```
// Open the file for reading:
   ifstream infile( file.c_str(), ios::in | ios::binary);
   if( !infile )
   {
      cerr << "File " << file
           << " could not be opened!" << endl;
      return false;
   }
   int i = 0;
   while( i < MAX)
   {
      getline( infile, v[i].name, '\0');
      getline( infile, v[i].telNr, '\0');
      if( !infile)
         break;
      else
         ++i;
   }
   if( i == MAX)
      cerr << "Max capacity " << MAX
           << " has been reached!" << endl;
   else if( !infile.eof())
   {
      cerr << "Error reading file " << file << endl;
      return false;
   }
   count = i;
   filename = file;
   dirty = false;
   return true;
}

bool TelList::saveAs()
{
   cout << "-- Save the telephone list in a file. --"
        << "\nFile: ";
   string file;                    // Input file name.
   cin.sync(); cin.clear();        // No previous input
   getline( cin, file);
   if( !setFilename(file))
   {
      cerr << "No file name declared!" << endl;
      return false;
   }
   else
      return save();
}
```

```cpp
bool TelList::save()        // Save the telephone list.
{
   if( filename.empty())
      return saveAs();
   if( !dirty)
      return true;

   ofstream outfile( filename.c_str(),
                     ios::out | ios::binary);
   if( !outfile )
   {
      cerr << "File " << filename
           << " could not be opened!" << endl;
      return false;
   }

   int i = 0;
   while( i < count)
   {
      outfile << v[i].name  << '\0';
      outfile << v[i].telNr << '\0';
      if( !outfile)
         break;
      else
         ++i;
   }
   if( i < count)
   {
      cerr << "Error writing to file " << filename << endl;
      return false;
   }
   dirty = false;
   return true;
}


// -------------------------------------------------------
// TelList_.cpp
// Organize a telephone list with class TelList.
// -------------------------------------------------------
#include "telList.h"       // Definition of class TelList
#include <iostream>
#include <string>
#include <cctype>
using namespace std;

inline void cls()
{
   cout << "\033[2J\n"; // If ANSI control characters are
}                       // not available, output new-lines.
```

```cpp
inline void go_on()
{
   cout << "\n\nGo on with return! ";
   cin.sync();  cin.clear();         // No previous input
   while( cin.get() != '\n')
         ;
}
int menu();                 // Enter a command
char askForSave();          // Prompt user to save.
char header[] =
"\n\n          * * * * *  Telephone List  * * * * *\n\n";
TelList myFriends;          // A telephone list

int main()
{
  int action = 0;           // Command
  string name;              // Read a name
  while( action != 'Q')
  {
    action = menu();
    cls();  cout << header << endl;
    switch( action)
    {
// --------------------------------------------------
//   case 'S':  case 'F':  case 'A':  case 'D':
//   unchanged (refer to the solutions of chapter 16).
// --------------------------------------------------
    case 'O':                           // To open a file
        if(myFriends.isDirty() && askForSave() == 'y')
           myFriends.save();
        if( myFriends.load())
           cout << "Telephone list read from file "
                << myFriends.getFilename() <<"!"
                << endl;
        else
           cerr << "Telephone list not read!"
                << endl;
        go_on();
        break;
      case 'U':                         // Save as ...
        if( myFriends.saveAs())
          cout << "Telephone list has been saved in file: "
               << myFriends.getFilename() << " !" <<endl;
        else
           cerr << "Telephone list not saved!" << endl;
        go_on();
        break;
```

```
      case 'W':                         // Save
         if( myFriends.save())
            cout << "Telephone list has been saved in "
                 << "the file "
                 << myFriends.getFilename() << endl;
         else
            cerr << "Telephone list not saved!"
                 << endl;
         go_on();
         break;

      case 'Q':                         // Quit
         if( myFriends.isDirty()  &&  askForSave() == 'Y')
            myFriends.save();
         cls();
         break;
      }
   } // End of while
   return 0;
}

int menu()
{
   static char menuStr[] =
// . . .
   "\n               ------------------------------------"
   "\n               O = Open a file"
   "\n               W = Save "
   "\n               U = Save as ..."
   "\n               ------------------------------------"
   "\n               Q = Quit the program"
 "\n\n Your choice:  ";

// ---------------------------------------------------
// everything else unchanged (cf. solutions in Chapter 16)
// ---------------------------------------------------
   return choice;
}

char askForSave()
{
   char c;
   cout <<  "Do you want to save the phone list(y/n)? ";
   do
   {  cin.get(c);
      c = toupper(c);
   }while( c != 'Y'  &&  c != 'N');
   return c;
}
```

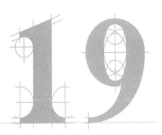

chapter

Overloading Operators

Overloading operators allows you to apply existing operators to objects of class type. For example, you can stipulate the effect of the + operator for the objects of a particular class.

This chapter describes various uses of overloaded operators. Arithmetic operators, comparisons, the subscript operator, and the shift operators for input and output are overloaded to illustrate the appropriate techniques.

The concept of friend functions, which is introduced in this context, is particularly important for overloading operators.

■ GENERALS

Overloadable operators

Operators	Meaning
`+  -  *  /  %` `++  --`	Arithmetic operators
`==  !=  <  <=  >  >=`	Relational operators
`&&  ||  !`	Logical operators
`=` `op=`	Assignment operators (`op` is a binary arithmetic or a binary bitwise operator)
`&  |  ^  ~  <<  >>`	Bitwise operators
`()  []`	Function call, subscript operator
`&  *  ->  ,` `new  delete`	Other operators

✓ **NOTE**

The assignment operator =, the address operator &, and the comma operator , have a predefined meaning for each built-in type. This meaning can be changed for classes by a definition of your own.

☐ Rules

An operator is always overloaded in conjunction with a class. The definition scope of an operator is simply extended—the characteristics of the operator remain unchanged. The following rules apply:

- You cannot create "new operators"—that is, you can only overload existing operators.
- You cannot redefine the operators for fundamental types.
- You cannot change the operands of an operator. A binary operator will always be binary and a unary operator will always be unary.
- The precedence and the order of grouping operators of the same precedence remains unchanged.

☐ Overloading

An operator is said to be overloaded if it is defined for multiple types. In other words, overloading an operator means making the operator significant for a new type.

Most operators are already overloaded for fundamental types. In the case of the expression:

Example: a / b

the operand type determines the machine code created by the compiler for the division operator. If both operands are integral types, an integral division is performed; in all other cases floating-point division occurs. Thus, different actions are performed depending on the operand types involved.

☐ Operators for Classes

In addition to defining methods, C++ offers the interesting possibility of defining the functionality of a class by means of operators. Thus, you can overload the + operator instead of, or in addition to, using the add() method. For the objects x and y in this class:

x + y   is equivalent to   x.add(y)

Using the overloaded operators of a class expressions of this type can be as easily defined as for fundamental types. Expressions using operators are often more intuitive, and thus easier to understand than expressions containing function calls.

Many operators belonging to the C++ standard library classes are already overloaded. This applies to the string class, with which you are already familiar.

Example:
```
string str1("Hello "), str2("Eve");
str1 += str2;              // Operator +=
if( str2 < "Alexa") ...    // Operator <
cout << str1;              // Operator <<
str2[2] = 'i';             // Operators [] and =
```

The tables on the opposite page show those operators that can be overloaded. Some operators cannot be overloaded, such as the cast operators, the sizeof operator, and the following four operators:

.   ::   .*   member access and scope resolution operators

?:   conditional operator

These operators either have a fixed significance in the classes for which they are defined, or overloading the operator makes no sense.

■ OPERATOR FUNCTIONS (I)

Operators < and ++ for class DayTime

```cpp
// DayTime.h
// The class DayTime containing operators < and ++ .
// --------------------------------------------------
#ifndef _DAYTIME_
#define _DAYTIME_
class DayTime
{
  private:
     short hour, minute, second;
     bool overflow;
  public:
  DayTime( int h = 0, int m = 0, int s = 0);
  bool setTime(int hour, int minute, int second = 0);
  int getHour()   const { return hour;   }
  int getMinute() const { return minute; }
  int getSecond() const { return second; }
  int asSeconds() const     // Daytime in seconds
  { return (60*60*hour + 60*minute + second);   }
  bool operator<( const DayTime& t) const // compare
  {                                       // *this and t
    return  asSeconds() < t.asSeconds();
  }
  DayTime& operator++()            // Increment seconds
  {
     ++second;                     // and handle overflow.
     return  *this;
  }
    void print() const;
};
#endif    // _DAYTIME_
```

Calling the Operator <

```cpp
#include "DayTime.h"
  . . .
  DayTime depart1( 11, 11, 11), depart2(12,0,0);
  . . .
  if( depart1 < depart2 )
    cout << "\nThe 1st plane takes off earlier!" << endl;
  . . .
```

☐ Naming Operator Functions

To overload an operator, you just define an appropriate *operator function*. The operator function describes the actions to be performed by the operator. The name of an operator function must begin with the `operator` keyword followed by the operator symbol.

Example: `operator+`

This is the name of the operator function for the + operator.

An operator function can be defined as a global function or as a class method. Generally, operator functions are defined as methods, especially in the case of unary operators. However, it can make sense to define an operator function globally. This point will be illustrated later.

☐ Operator Functions as Methods

If you define the operator function of a *binary* operator as a method, the left operand will always be an object of the class in question. The operator function is called for this object. The second, right operand is passed as an argument to the method. The method thus has a *single* parameter.

Example: `bool operator<( const DayTime& t) const;`

In this case the lesser than operator is overloaded to compare two `DayTime` objects. It replaces the method `isLess()`, which was formerly defined for this class.

The prefix operator ++ has been overloaded in the example on the opposite page to illustrate overloading unary operators. The corresponding operator function in this class has no parameters. The function is called if the object a in the expression ++a is an object of class `DayTime`.

☐ Calling an Operator Function

The example opposite compares two times of day:

Example: `depart1 < depart2`

The compiler will attempt to locate an applicable operator function for this expression and then call the function. The expression is thus equivalent to

`depart1.operator<( depart2)`

Although somewhat uncommon, you can call an operator function explicitly. The previous function call is therefore technically correct.

Programs that use operators are easier to encode and read. However, you should be aware of the fact that an operator function should perform a similar operation to the corresponding operator for the fundamental type. Any other use can lead to confusion.

■ OPERATOR FUNCTIONS(2)

Class Euro

```cpp
// Euro1.h : The class Euro containing arithmetic operators.
// ---------------------------------------------------------
#ifndef _EURO_H_
#define _EURO_H_
#include <sstream>                   // The class stringstream
#include <iomanip>
using namespace std;
class Euro
{
  private:
    long  data;                      // Euros * 100 + Cents
  public:
    Euro( int euro = 0, int cents = 0)
    {
      data = 100L * (long)euro + cents;
    }
    Euro( double x)
    {
      x *= 100.0;                                   // Rounding,
      data = (long)(x>=0.0 ? x+0.5 : x-0.5); //ex. 9.7 -> 10
    }
    long getWholePart() const { return data/100; }
    int  getCents() const { return (int)(data%100); }
    double asDouble() const { return (double)data/100.0; }
    string asString() const;         // Euro as string.
    void print( ostream& os) const   // Output to stream os.
    { os << asString() << " Euro" << endl;        }
    // ---- Operator functions ----
    Euro operator-() const           // Negation (unary minus))
    {
      Euro temp;
      temp.data = -data;
      return  temp;
    }
    Euro operator+( const Euro& e2) const    // Addition.
    {
      Euro temp;
      temp.data = data + e2.data;
      return  temp;
    }
    Euro operator-( const Euro& e2) const    // Subtraction.
    { /*  Analog just as operator +  */ }
    Euro& operator+=( const Euro& e2)        // Add Euros.
    {
      data += e2.data;
      return *this;
    }
    Euro& operator-=( const Euro& e2); // Subtract euros.
    { /*  Just as operator +=  */ }
};
// Continued on the next double page.
```

☐ Notes on the Sample Class Euro

The opposite page shows the Euro class, which represents the new European currency. The member data stores a given amount of euros as an integer in the format:

```
(integer part)*100 + Cents.
```

Thus data/100 returns the number of euros and data%100 the number of cents. This technique allows for easy implementation of the arithmetic operations needed for the Euro class.

In addition to a constructor that is passed whole euros and cents as arguments, there is a constructor that can process a double value of euros and a standard copy constructor.

Example: Euro e1(9,50), e2(20.07), e3(-e1);

☐ Negation, Addition, and Subtraction

The unary operator - does not change its operand. In the previous example, e3 is thus assigned a value of -9,50 euro, but e1 remains unchanged. The operator function is thus a const method that creates and returns a temporary object.

The binary operators + and - do not change their operands either. Thus, the operator functions also create temporary objects and return them with the correct values.

Example: Euro sum = e1 + e2;

The expression e1 + e2 results in e1.operator+(e2). The return value is used to initialize the new object, sum.

☐ The += and -= Operators

Although the operators + and - were overloaded for the Euro class, this does not automatically mean that the operators += and -= are overloaded. Both are distinct operators that require separate definitions. Of course, you should overload the operators to ensure that the statements

Example: sum += e3;   and   sum = sum + e3;

produce the same results.

The binary operators += and -= change the current object, that is, the left operand. A temporary object is not required! The expression sum += e3 represents the current object after modification. Thus, the operator function returns a reference to *this.

■ USING OVERLOADED OPERATORS

File `Euro1.h` **continued**

```cpp
// Continues file Euro1.h
// --------------------------------------------------------
inline string Euro::asString() const   // Euro as string
{
   stringstream strStream;           // Stream for conversion
   long temp = data;
   if( temp < 0 ) { strStream << '-';  temp = -temp; }
     strStream << temp/100 << ','
               << setfill('0') << setw(2) << temp%100;
     return strStream.str();
}
#endif   // _EURO_H_
```

Sample program

```cpp
// Euro1_t.cpp
// Tests the operators of class Euro.
// --------------------------------------------------------
#include "Euro1.h"                 // Definition of the class
#include <iostream>
using namespace std;

int main()
{
  cout << "* * *  Testing the class Euro  * * *\n" << endl;
  Euro wholesale( 20,50), retail;
  retail = wholesale;                // Standard assignment
  retail += 9.49;                    // += (Euro)9.49

  cout << "Wholesale price: ";   wholesale.print(cout);
  cout << "Retail price: ";   retail.print(cout);
  Euro discount( 2.10);          // double-constructor
  retail -= discount;
  cout << "\nRetail price including discount: ";
  retail.print(cout);
  wholesale = 34.10;
  cout << "\nNew wholesale price: ";
  wholesale.print(cout);
  Euro profit( retail - wholesale);    // Subtraction and
                                       // copy constructor
  cout << "\nThe profit: ";
  profit.print(cout);                  // Negative!

  return 0;
}
```

☐ Calling Operator Functions

The following expressions are valid for the operators in the Euro class.

Example:
```
Euro   wholesale(15,30),  retail,
        profit(7,50),  discount(1,75);
retail = wholesale + profit;
// Call:  wholesale.operator+( profit)
retail -= discount;
// Call:  retail.operator-=( discount)
retail += Euro( 1.49);
// Call:  retail.operator+=( Euro(1.49))
```

These expressions contain only Euro type objects, for which operator functions have been defined. However, you can also add or subtract int or double types. This is made possible by the Euro constructors, which create Euro objects from int or double types. This allows a function that expects a Euro value as argument to process int or double values.

As the program opposite shows, the statement

Example: `retail += 9.49;`

is valid. The compiler attempts to locate an operator function that is defined for both the Euro object and the double type for +=. Since there is no operator function with these characteristics, the compiler converts the double value to Euro and calls the existing operator function for euros.

☐ Symmetry of Operands

The available constructors also allow you to call the operator functions of + and – with int or double type arguments.

Example:
```
retail = wholesale + 10;        // ok
wholesale = retail - 7.99;      // ok
```

The first statement is equivalent to

```
retail = wholesale.operator+( Euro(10));
```

But the following statement is invalid!

Example: `retail = 10 + wholesale;      // wrong!`

Since the operator function was defined as a method, the left operand must be a class object. Thus, you cannot simply exchange the operands of the operator +. However, if you want to convert both operands, you will need global definitions for the operator functions.

▪ GLOBAL OPERATOR FUNCTIONS

Operators overloadable by methods only

The operator functions of the following operators have to be methods:

Operators	Meaning
=	Assignment operator
( )	Function call
[ ]	Subscript operator
->	Class member access

 NOTE

The function call operator () is used to represent operations for objects like function calls. The overloaded operator -> enables the use of objects in the same way as pointers.

The new Euro class

```cpp
// Euro.h
// The class Euro represents a Euro with
// global operator functions implemented for + and -.
// ----------------------------------------------------
#ifndef _EURO_H_
#define _EURO_H_
// ....
class Euro
{
  // Without operator functions for + and -.
  // Otherwise unchanged, specifically with regard to
  // the operator functions implemented for += and -=.
};
// ----------------------------------------------------
// Global operator functions (inline)
// Addition:
inline Euro operator+( const Euro& e1, const Euro& e2)
{
    Euro temp(e1);
    temp += e2;
    return  temp;
}
// Subtraction:
inline Euro operator-( const Euro& e1, const Euro& e2)
{
    Euro temp(e1);   temp -= e2;
    return  temp;
}
#endif   // _EURO_H_
```

☐ Operator Functions: Global or Method?

You can define an operator function as a global function instead of a method. The four operators listed opposite are the only exceptions.

```
+=    -=    *=    /=    %=
```

These operators always require a so-called *l-value* as their left operand, that is, they require an object with an address in memory.

Global operator functions are generally preferable if one of the following situations applies:

- ▧ the operator is binary and both operands are symmetrical, e.g. the arithmetic operators + or *
- ▧ the operator is to be overloaded for another class without changing that class, e.g. the << operator for the ostream class.

☐ Defining Global Operator Functions

The operands for a global operator function are passed as arguments to that function. The operator function of a unary operator thus possesses a *single* parameter, whereas the operator function of a binary operator has *two*.

The Euro class has been modified to provide a global definition of the operator functions for the operators + and -.

Example: `Euro operator+(const Euro& e1, const Euro& e2);`

Both operands are now peers. More specifically, conversion of int or double to Euro is performed for both operands now. Given a Euro object net, the following expressions are valid and equivalent:

Example: `net + 1.20   and   1.20 + net`

They cause the following function calls:

```
operator+( net, 1.20)    and
operator+( 1.20, net)
```

However, a global function cannot access the private members of the class. The function `operator+()` shown opposite therefore uses the += operator, whose operator function is defined as a method.

A global operator function can be declared as a "friend" of the class to allow it access to the private members of that class.

■ FRIEND FUNCTIONS

Class `Euro` with friend functions

```cpp
// Euro.h
// The class Euro with operator functions
// declared as friend functions.
// ----------------------------------------------------
#ifndef _EURO_H_
#define _EURO_H_
// ....
class Euro
{
  private:
    long  data;                // Euros * 100 + Cents
  public:
    // Constructors and other methods as before.
    // Operators -(unary), +=, -=  as before.
    // Division Euro / double :
    Euro operator/( double x)           // Division *this/x
    {                                   // =  *this * (1/x)
       return (*this * (1.0/x));
    }
    // Global friend functions
    friend Euro operator+( const Euro& e1, const Euro& e2);
    friend Euro operator-( const Euro& e1, const Euro& e2);
    friend Euro operator*( const Euro& e, double x)
    {
       Euro temp( ((double)e.data/100.0) * x) ;
       return temp;
    }
    friend Euro operator*( double x, const Euro& e)
    {
       return e * x;
    }
};
// Addition:
inline Euro operator+( const Euro& e1, const Euro& e2)
{
    Euro temp;   temp.data = e1.data + e2.data;
    return  temp;
}
// Subtraction:
inline Euro operator-( const Euro& e1, const Euro& e2)
{
    Euro temp;   temp.data = e1.data - e2.data;
    return  temp;
}
#endif   // _EURO_H_
```

☐ The Friend Concept

If functions or individual classes are used in conjunction with another class, you may want to grant them access to the `private` members of that class. This is made possible by a *friend declaration*, which eliminates data encapsulation in certain cases.

Imagine you need to write a global function that accesses the elements of a numerical array class. If you need to call the access methods of the class each time, and if these methods perform range checking, the function runtime will increase considerably. However, special permission to access the private data members of the class can dramatically improve the function's response.

☐ Declaring Friend Functions

A class can grant any function a special permit for direct access to its private members. This is achieved by declaring the function as a `friend`. The `friend` keyword must precede the function prototype in the class definition.

Example:
```
class A
{ // . . .
   friend void globFunc( A* objPtr);
   friend int  B::elFunc( const A& objRef);
};
```

Here the global function `globFunc()` and the method `elFunc()` of class `B` are declared as `friend` functions of class `A`. This allows them direct access to the private members of class `A`. Since these functions are not methods of class `A`, the `this` pointer is not available to them. To resolve this issue, you will generally pass the object the function needs to process as an argument.

It is important to note that *the class itself* determines who its friends are. If this were not so, data encapsulation could easily be undermined.

☐ Overloading Operators with Friend Functions

The operator functions for + and - in the `Euro` class are now defined as `friend` functions, allowing them direct access to the private member `data`.

In order to compute interest, it is necessary to multiply and divide euros by `double` values. Since both the expression `Euro*num` and `num*Euro` are possible, `friend` functions are implemented to perform multiplications. As the example shows, `friend` functions can also be defined `inline` in a class.

■ FRIEND CLASSES

Class Result

```cpp
// Result.h
// The class Result to represent a measurement
// and the time the measurement was taken.
// -------------------------------------------------
#ifndef _RESULT_
#define _RESULT_
#include "DayTime.h"            // Class DayTime
class Result
{
  private:
    double val;
    DayTime time;
  public:
    // Constructor and access methods

    friend class ControlPoint; // All methods of
};                             // ControlPoint are friends.
```

Class ControlPoint

```cpp
#include Result.h

class ControlPoint
{
    private:
      string name;              // Name of control point
      Result measure[100];      // Table with results
      // . . .
    public:
      // Constructor and the other methods
      // . . .
      // Compute static values of measurement results
      // (average, deviation from mean, ...).
      bool statistic();  // Can access the private
                         // members of measure[i].
};
```

☐ Declaring Friend Classes

In addition to declaring individual friend functions, you can also make entire classes "friends" of another class. All the methods in this "friendly" class automatically become friend functions in the class containing the friend declaration.

This technique is useful if a class is used in such close conjunction with another class that *all* the methods in that class need access to the private members of the other class.

For example, the class ControlPoint uses objects of the Result class. Calculations with individual measurements are performed repeatedly. In this case, it makes sense to declare the ControlPoint class as a friend of the Result class.

Example:
```
class Result
{
    // . . .
    friend class ControlPoint;
};
```

It is important to note that the ControlPoint class has no influence over the fact that it is a friend of the Result class. The Result class itself decides who its friends are and who has access to its private members.

It does not matter whether a friend declaration occurs in the private or public section of a class. However, you can regard a friend declaration as an extension of the public interface. For this reason, it is preferable to place a friend declaration in the public area of a class.

☐ Using Friend Functions and Classes

Using friend functions and friend classes helps you to create efficient programs. More specifically, you can utilize global friend functions where methods are not suited to the task in hand. Some common uses are global operator functions declared as friend functions.

However, extensive use of friend techniques diffuses the concept of data encapsulation. Allowing external functions to manipulate internal data can lead to inconsistency, especially if a class is modified or extended in a later version. For this reason, you should take special care when using friend techniques.

■ OVERLOADING SUBSCRIPT OPERATORS

A class representing arrays

```cpp
// Array_t.cpp
// A simple class to represent an array
// with range checking.
// -------------------------------------------------
#include <iostream>
#include <cstdlib>                    // For exit()
using namespace std;
#define MAX 100

class FloatArr
{
  private:
    float v[MAX];                     // The array
  public:
    float& operator[](int i);
    static int MaxIndex(){ return MAX-1; }
};

float& FloatArr::operator[]( int i )
{
   if( i < 0 || i >= MAX )
   {  cerr << "\nFloatArr: Outside of range!" << endl;
      exit(1);
   }
   return v[i];       // Reference to i-th element.
}

int main()
{
    cout << "\n An array with range checking!\n"
         << endl;
    FloatArr random;        // Create array.
    int i;                  // An index.
                            // Fill with random euros:
    for( i=0; i <= FloatArr::MaxIndex(); ++i )
       random[i] = (rand() - RAND_MAX/2) / 100.0F;
    cout << "\nEnter indices between 0 and "
         << FloatArr::MaxIndex() << "!"
         << "\n (Quit by entering invalid input)"
         << endl;
    while( cout << "\nIndex: " && cin >> i )
       cout << i << ". element:  " << random[i];
    return 0;
}
```

☐ Subscript Operator

The subscript operator [] is normally used to access a single array element. It is a binary operator and thus has two operands. Given an expression such as v[i], the array name v will always be the left operand, whereas the index i will be the right operand.

The subscript operator for arrays implies background pointer arithmetic, for example, v[i] is equivalent to *(v+i). Thus, the following restrictions apply to non-overloaded index operators:

- an operand must be a pointer—an array name, for example
- the other operand must be an integral expression.

☐ Usage in Classes

These restrictions do not apply if the index operator is overloaded for a class. You should note, however, that the operator function is always a class method with a parameter for the right operand. The following therefore applies:

- the left operand must be a class object
- the right operand can be any valid type
- the result type is not defined.

This allows for considerable flexibility. However, your overloading should always reflect the normal use of arrays. More specifically, the return value should be a reference to an object.

Since an index can be of any valid type, the possibilities are unlimited. For example, you could easily define *associative arrays*, that is, arrays whose elements are referenced by strings.

☐ Notes on the Sample Program

Range checking is not performed when you access the elements of a normal array. An invalid index can thus lead to abnormal termination of an application program. However, you can address this issue by defining your own array classes, although this may impact the speed of your programs.

The opposite page shows a simple array class definition for float values. The subscript operator [] has been overloaded to return a reference to the i-th array element. However, when the array is accessed, range checking is performed to ensure that the index falls within given boundaries. If an invalid index is found, the program issues an error message and terminates.

The class FloatArr array has a fixed length. As we will see, variable lengths are possible using dynamic memory allocation.

■ OVERLOADING SHIFT-OPERATORS FOR I/O

Declaration of the operator functions

```cpp
// Euro.h : Class Euro to represent an Euro
// ---------------------------------------------------
#ifndef _EURO_H_
#define _EURO_H_
// ....
class Euro
{ // The class is left unchanged.
  // The print() method is now superfluous.
};
// ---------------------------------------------------
// Declaration of shift operators:
ostream& operator<<(ostream& os, const Euro& e);
istream& operator>>(istream& is, Euro& e);
#endif    // _EURO_H_
```

Definition of operator functions

```cpp
// Euro_io.cpp
// Overload the shift operators
// for input/output of Euro type objects.
// ---------------------------------------------------
#include "Euro.h"
#include <iostream>
using namespace std;
// Output to stream os.
ostream& operator<<(ostream& os, const Euro& e)
{
    os << e.asString() << " Euro";   return os;
}

// Input from stream is.
istream& operator>>(istream& is, Euro& e)
{
    cout << "Euro amount (Format ...x,xx): ";
    int euro = 0, cents = 0;   char c = 0;
    if( !(is >> euro >> c >> cents))  // Input.
      return is;
    if( (c != ',' && c != '.')
        || cents>=100)                 // Error?
      is.setstate( ios::failbit);      // Yes => Set
    else                               // fail bit.
      e = Euro( euro, cents);          // No => Accept
    return is;                         // value.
}
```

When outputting a Euro class object, `price`, on screen, the following output statement causes a compiler error:

Example: `cout << price;`

`cout` can only send objects to standard output if an output function has been defined for the *type* in question—and this, of course, is not the case for user-defined classes.

However, the compiler can process the previous statement if it can locate a suitable operator function, `operator<<()`. To allow for the previous statement, you therefore need to define a corresponding function.

☐ Overloading the << Operator

In the previous example, the left operand of `<<` is the object `cout`, which belongs to the `ostream` class. Since the standard class `ostream` should not be modified, it is necessary to define a global operator function with two parameters. The right operand is a Euro class object. Thus the following prototype applies for the operator function:

Prototype: `ostream& operator<<(ostream& os, const Euro& e);`

The return value of the operator function is a reference to `ostream`. This allows for normal concatenation of operators.

Example: `cout << price << endl;`

☐ Overloading the >> Operator

The `>>` operator is overloaded for input to allow for the following statements.

Example: `cout << "Enter the price in Euros: "`
            `cin >> price;`

The second statement causes the following call:

`operator>>( cin, price);`

As `cin` is an object of the standard `istream` class, the first parameter of the operator function is declared as a reference to `istream`. The second parameter is again a reference to Euro.

The header file `Euro.h` contains only the declarations of `<<` and `>>`. To allow these functions to access the private members of the Euro class, you can add a `friend` declaration within the class. However, this is not necessary for the current example.

exercises

▪ EXERCISES

Prefix and postfix increment

To distinguish the postfix increment operator from the prefix increment operator, the postfix operator function has an additional parameter of type `int`.

Expression		Operator Function Call
++obj	(Prefix)	obj.operator++()
obj++	(Postfix)	obj.operator++(0)

✓ **NOTE**

The expression `obj++` represents a copy of `obj` before incrementing.

The prefix and postfix decrement operators `--` are distinguished in the same manner.

For exercise 2: Calculating with fractions

		a		c		a*d + b*c
Addition		–	+	–	=	--------------
		b		d		b*d
		a		c		a*d – b*c
Subtraction		–	–	–	=	--------------
		b		d		b*d
		a		c		a * c
Multiplication		–	*	–	=	--------------
		b		d		b * d
		a		c		a * d
Division		–	/	–	=	--------------
		b		d		b * c

✓ **NOTE**

Optimized error handling for the `Fraction` class will be discussed in Chapter 28, "Exception Handling"

Exercise 1

The < and ++ operators for the sample class DayTime were overloaded at the beginning of this chapter. Now modify the class as follows:

- Overload the relational operators

  <   >   <=   >=   == and !=

  and the shift operators

  >> and << for input and output

  using global operator functions. You can define these inline in the header file.

- Then overload both the prefix and postfix versions of the ++ and -- operators. The operator functions are methods of the class. The -- operator decrements the time by one second. The time is not decremented after reaching 0:0:0.

- Write a main function that executes all the overloaded operators and displays their results.

Exercise 2

You are to develop a class that represents fractions and performs typical arithmetic operations with them.

- Use a header file called fraction.h to define the Fraction class with a numerator and a denominator of type long. The constructor has two parameters of type long: the first parameter (numerator) contains the default value 0, and the second parameter (denominator) contains the value 1. Declare operator functions as methods for - (unary), ++ and -- (prefix only), +=, -=, *=, and /=. The operator functions of the binary operators +, -, *, / and the input / output operators <<, >> are to be declared as friend functions of the Fraction class.

- Implement the constructor for the Fraction class to obtain a positive value for the denominator at all times. If the denominator assumes a value of 0, issue an error message and terminate the program. Then write the operator functions. The formulae for arithmetic operations are shown opposite.

- Then write a main function that calls all the operators in the Fraction class as a test application. Output both the operands and the results.

■ **SOLUTIONS**

Exercise 1

```
// ---------------------------------------------------
// DayTime.h
// Class DayTime with all relational operators,
// the operators ++ and -- (prefix and postfix),
// such as the operators << and >> for input/output.
// ---------------------------------------------------

#ifndef _DAYTIME_
#define _DAYTIME_

#include <iostream>
#include <iomanip>
using namespace std;

class DayTime
{
  private:
    short hour, minute, second;
    bool overflow, underflow;

    void inc()                 // private function for ++
    {
      ++second;
      if( second >= 60)      // handle overflow.
          second = 0,  ++minute;
      if( minute >= 60)
          minute = 0,  ++hour;
      if( hour >= 24)
          hour = 0,  overflow = true;
    }
    void dec()                 // private function for --
    {
      --second;
      if( second < 0)        // handle underflow.
          second = 59,  --minute;
      if( minute < 0)
          minute = 59,  --hour;
      if( hour < 0)
          hour = 0,  underflow = true;
    }
  public:
    DayTime( int h = 0, int m = 0, int s = 0)
    {
      overflow = underflow = false;
      if( !setTime( h, m, s))
        hour = minute = second = 0;
    }
```

```
      bool setTime(int hour, int minute, int second = 0)
      {
        if(    hour   >= 0  &&  hour < 24
            && minute >= 0  &&  minute < 60
            && second >= 0  &&  second < 60 )
        {
          this->hour   = (short)hour;
          this->minute = (short)minute;
          this->second = (short)second;
          return true;
        }
        else
          return false;
      }
      int getHour()   const { return hour;   }
      int getMinute() const { return minute; };
      int getSecond() const { return second; };

      int asSeconds() const          // daytime in seconds
      {
        return (60*60*hour + 60*minute + second);
      }

      DayTime& operator++()          // ++Seconds
      {
        inc();
        return  *this;
      }
      DayTime operator++(int)        // Seconds++
      {
        DayTime temp(*this);
        inc();
        return temp;
      }

      DayTime& operator--()          // --Seconds
      {
        dec();
        return  *this;
      }
      DayTime operator--(int)        // Seconds--
      {
        DayTime temp(*this);
        dec();
        return temp;
      }
};
// --- Relational operators ---
//  t1 < t2
inline bool operator<( const DayTime& t1,
                       const DayTime& t2)
{   return  t1.asSeconds() < t2.asSeconds(); }
```

```cpp
//  t1 <= t2
inline bool operator<=( const DayTime& t1,
                        const DayTime& t2)
{   return  t1.asSeconds() <= t2.asSeconds(); }

//  t1 == t2
inline bool operator==( const DayTime& t1,
                        const DayTime& t2)
{   return  t1.asSeconds() == t2.asSeconds(); }

//  t1 != t2
inline bool operator!=( const DayTime& t1,
                        const DayTime& t2)
{   return !(t1 == t2); }

//  t1 > t2
inline bool operator>( const DayTime& t1,
                       const DayTime& t2)
{   return (t2 < t1); }

//  t1 >= t2
inline bool operator>=(const DayTime& t1,const DayTime& t2)
{   return !(t1 < t2); }

//  ---  Input and Output  ---
ostream& operator<<( ostream& os, const DayTime& t)
{
   os << setfill('0')
      << setw(2) << t.getHour()    << ':'
      << setw(2) << t.getMinute()  << ':'
      << setw(2) << t.getSecond()  << " Time";
   os << setfill(' ');
   return os;
}

istream& operator>>( istream& is, DayTime& t)
{
   cout << "Enter daytime in hh:mm:ss format: ";
   int hr = 0, min = 0, sec = 0;
   char c1 = 0, c2 = 0;
   if( !(is >> hr >> c1 >> min >> c2 >> sec))
     return is;
   if( c1 != ':' || c2 != ':' || ! t.setTime(hr,min,sec))
     is.setstate( ios::failbit);   // Error!
                                   //  => Set fail bit.
   return is;
}
#endif   // _DAYTIME_
```

```cpp
// -------------------------------------------------
// DayTim_t.cpp
// Testing the operators of class DayTime.
// -------------------------------------------------
#include "DayTime.h"          // Definition of the class
#include <iostream>
using namespace std;

int main()
{
  DayTime cinema( 20,30);
  cout << "\nThe movie starts at " << cinema << endl;

  DayTime now;
  cout << "What time is it now?" << endl;
  if( !(cin >> now) )
     cerr << "Invalid input!" << endl;
  else
     cout << "\nThe time is now" << now << endl;

  cout << "\nThe movie has ";
  if( cinema < now)
     cout << "already begun!\n" << endl;
  else
     cout << "not yet begun!\n" << endl;

  cout << "Now it is      " << now++ << endl;
  cout << "After 2 seconds: " << ++now << endl;

  DayTime depart(16,0);
  cout << "Let's go at " << --depart << endl;

  if( depart >= now )
     cout << "You can ride with us!" << endl;
  else
     cout << "We don't have room!" << endl;

  return 0;
}
```

Exercise 2

```
// -----------------------------------------------------
// Fraction.h
// A numerical class to represent fractions
// -----------------------------------------------------
#ifndef _FRACTION_
#define _FRACTION_

#include <iostream>
#include <cstdlib>
using namespace std;

class Fraction
{
  private:
    long numerator, denominator;

  public:
    Fraction(long n = 0, long d = 1);
    Fraction operator-() const
    {
        return Fraction(-numerator, denominator);
    }
    Fraction& operator+=(const Fraction& a)
    {
        numerator = a.numerator * denominator
                   + numerator * a.denominator;
        denominator *= a.denominator;
        return *this;
    }

    Fraction& operator-=(const Fraction& a)
    {
        *this += (-a);
        return *this;
    }

    Fraction& operator++()
    {
        numerator += denominator;
        return *this;
    }

    Fraction& operator--()
    {
        numerator -= denominator;
        return *this;
    }
```

```cpp
  friend Fraction operator+(const Fraction&, const Fraction&);
  friend Fraction operator-(const Fraction&, const Fraction&);
  friend Fraction operator*(const Fraction&, const Fraction&);
  friend Fraction operator/(const Fraction&, const Fraction&);
  friend ostream& operator<< (ostream& os, const Fraction& a);
  friend istream& operator>> (istream& is, Fraction& a);
};
#endif

// -----------------------------------------------------
// Fraction.cpp
// Defines methods and friend functions.
// -----------------------------------------------------
#include "Fraction.h"

// Constructor:
Fraction::Fraction(long n, long d)
{
  if(d == 0)
  { cerr << "\nError: Division by zero!\n";
    exit(1);
  }
  if( n < 0 ) n = -n, d = -d;
  numerator = n;    denominator  = d;
}
Fraction operator+(const Fraction& a, const Fraction& b)
{
   Fraction temp;
   temp.denominator = a.denominator * b.denominator;
   temp.numerator = a.numerator*b.denominator
                 + b.numerator * a.denominator;
   return temp;
}


Fraction operator-(const Fraction& a, const Fraction& b )
{
   Fraction temp = a;    temp += (-b);
   return temp;
}


Fraction operator*(const Fraction& a, const Fraction& b )
{
   Fraction temp;
   temp.numerator = a.numerator * b.numerator;
   temp.denominator  = a.denominator  * b.denominator;
   return temp;
}
```

```cpp
Fraction operator/(const Fraction& a, const Fraction& b )
{
   if( b.numerator == 0)
   {
     cerr << "\nError: Division by zero!\n";
     exit(1);
   }
   // To multiply a by the inverse of b:
   Fraction temp;
   temp.numerator = a.numerator * b.denominator;
   temp.denominator  = a.denominator   * b.numerator;

   if( temp.denominator < 0 )
     temp.numerator = -temp.numerator,
     temp.denominator  = -temp.denominator;

   return temp;
}

ostream& operator<<(ostream& os, const Fraction& a)
{
  os << a.numerator << "/" << a.denominator;
  return os;
}

istream& operator>>(istream& is, Fraction& a)
{
  cout << "Enter a fraction:\n"
          "  Numerator:       ";   is >> a.numerator;
  cout << "  Denominator != 0:  ";    is >> a.denominator;

  if( !is) return is;

  if( a.denominator == 0)
  {
     cout << "\nError: The denominator is 0\n"
             "  New denominator != 0: ";
       is >> a.denominator;

     if( a.denominator == 0)
     {
       cerr << "\nError: Division by zero!\n"; exit(1);
     }
  }
  if( a.denominator < 0 )
     a.numerator = -a.numerator,
     a.denominator= -a.denominator;
  return is;
}
```

```cpp
// -------------------------------------------------------
// Fract_t.cpp
// Testing the class Fraction.
// Modules: Fract_t.cpp   Fraction.cpp
// -------------------------------------------------------

#include "Fraction.h"

int main()
{
   Fraction a(1,3), b(4);

   cout << "\nSome test results:\n\n";

   cout << " a = " << a << endl;
   cout << " b = " << b << endl;

   cout << " a + b = " << (a + b) << endl;
   cout << " a - b = " << (a - b) << endl;
   cout << " a * b = " << (a * b) << endl;
   cout << " a / b = " << (a / b) << endl;

   cout << "  --a =  " <<  --a << endl;
   cout << "  ++a  = " <<  ++a << endl;

   a += Fraction(1,2);
   cout << " a+= 1/2;  a = " << a << endl;

   a -= Fraction(1,2);
   cout << " a-= 1/2;  a = " << a << endl;

   cout << "-b = " << -b << endl;

   cout << "\nAnd now an input\n";
   cin  >> a;
   cout << "\nYour input: " << a << endl;

   return 0;
}
```

chapter 20

Type Conversion for Classes

Implicit type conversion occurs in C++ when an expression cannot be compiled directly but can be compiled after applying a conversion rule. The programmer can stipulate how the compiler will perform implicit type conversion for classes by defining conversion constructors and functions.

Finally, we discuss ambiguity occurring due to type conversion and how to avoid it.

■ CONVERSION CONSTRUCTORS

Possible conversions

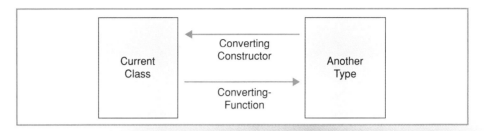

Converting constructors of class Euro

```
// The class Euro defined in the last chapter
// contains the following conversion constructors:
Euro::Euro( int );          // int -> Euro
Euro::Euro( double );       // double -> Euro

// The following declarations are now possible:
                            // Conversion constructors
Euro my(100),               // int-> Euro,
    your(321.41);           // double -> Euro.

my = 987.12;                // Implicit conversion:
                            //  double -> Euro

your += 20;                 // Implicit conversion:
                            //  int -> Euro

your = Euro(999.99);        // Explicit conversion
                            // (constructor style)

my = (Euro)123.45;          // Explicit conversion
                            // (cast style)

your = my;                  // No conversion
```

✓ NOTE

When the copy constructor performs a type conversion, a temporary object is first created and this object is used in the assignment. The temporary object is cleaned up later.

☐ Possible Type Conversions

Implicit and explicit type conversion is also performed for classes in C++. As a programmer, you decide what kind of conversion is permissible. You can allow type conversion between different classes or between classes and fundamental types.

Any type conversion involving a class is defined either

- by a *conversion constructor* or
- by a *conversion function*.

A conversion constructor performs type conversion by converting any given type to the type of the current class. A conversion function performs conversion in the opposite direction, that is, it converts an object of the current class to another type—a standard type, for example.

☐ Conversion Constructors

A constructor with a *single* parameter determines how to form an object of the new class from the argument passed to it. For this reason, a constructor with only one parameter is referred to as a *conversion constructor*. The copy constructor is an exception to this rule: it creates an object of the same class and does not perform type conversion.

Each conversion constructor is placed by the compiler on a list of possible conversions. The standard `string` class contains a constructor that creates a `string` object from a C string, for example.

Example: `string::string( const char* );`

This allows you to supply a C string as an argument wherever a `string` object is required.

☐ Calling a Conversion Constructor

Conversion constructors have already been used in several examples; for example, in the Euro class. The compiler uses them to perform implicit and explicit type conversion.

Examples:
```
Euro salary(8765.30);
salary += (Euro)897.1;        // explicit
salary += 897.1;              // implicit
```

The last statement initially causes a type mismatch. Addition is not defined for a euro and a `double` value. The compiler therefore activates the conversion constructor to create a temporary `Euro` type object from the `double` value. This object is then added to the value of the `salary` object.

▪ CONVERSION FUNCTIONS

A converting function for the Euro class

```
// Euro.h : The class Euro represents a euro.
// ----------------------------------------------------
// . . .
class Euro
{
  private:
    long  data;              // Euros * 100 + Cents
  public:
    Euro( int euro = 0, int cents = 0);
    Euro( double x);
    // For conversion from Euro to double:
    operator double() const { return (double)data/100.0; }

    // . . . other methods as before.
};
```

Testing conversions

```
// Euro_t.cpp : Testing conversions of class Euro.
// ----------------------------------------------------
#include "Euro.h"            // Definition of the class
#include <iostream>
using namespace std;
int main()
{
  cout << " * * *  Testing Conversions  * * * \n" << endl;
  Euro salary( 8888,80);
  double x(0.0);
  salary += 1000;            // implicit int -> Euro
  salary += 0.10;            // implicit double -> Euro
  x = salary;                // implicit Euro -> double
  x = (double)salary;        // explicit Euro -> double
  x = salary.operator double();    // also possible!
  // Constructor style is also safe for built-in types:
  x = double(salary);
  int i = salary;            // Euro -> double -> int
                                         // Output:
  cout << " salary = " << salary << endl;  // 9888,90 Euro
  cout << "      x = " << x << endl;        // 9888.9
  cout << "      i = " << i << endl;        // 9888
  return 0;
}
```

If you need to convert an object of the current class to another type, you must define a *conversion function* to do so. This is an operator function that defines how conversion is performed. Conversion functions are also automatically used by the compiler to perform implicit and explicit type conversion.

☐ Defining Conversion Functions

A conversion function is always implemented as a method of the current class. Its name is made up of the `operator` keyword and the target type to convert to.

Example: `operator int(void) const;`

The previous statement declares a conversion function where the target type is `int`. You may have noticed that the declaration of a conversion function does not contain a return type. This is because the return type is implicitly defined by the target type in the name of the conversion function. The target type can contain multiple keywords, such as `unsigned short` or `const float*`.

Thus, conversion functions must be written to construct a target type object from the current object, `*this`, and return the target object.

The `Euro` shown opposite contains a conversion function with a `double` target type. In other words, the function converts a `Euro` type object to a floating-point number.

Example: `double x = oneEuro;     // implicit`

☐ Conversion Function versus Conversion Constructor

The target type of a conversion function can also be a class. In this case, you must decide whether it is preferable to use a conversion constructor in the target class.

If you do not want to modify the target class—perhaps because it is a standard class—a conversion function will perform the task well.

☐ Standard Type Conversion

In addition to user-definable type conversions, the compiler also performs standard type conversions. In the previous example, an `int` variable is assigned to a euro object by this method.

Example: `int wholePart = oneEuro;`

This first converts a `Euro` object to `double` and then to `int`, that is, the cents are truncated.

■ AMBIGUITIES OF TYPE CONVERSIONS

Explicit type conversion for class Euro

```
// Euro.h : The class Euro represents a euro.
// -------------------------------------------------
// . . .
class Euro
{
 private:
   long  data;               // Euros * 100 + Cents
 public:
   explicit Euro( int euro = 0, int cents = 0);
   explicit Euro( double x);
   // Converting Euro to double:
   double asDouble() const { return (double)data/100.0;}
   // No conversion function operator double(),
   // or as previously seen.
};
```

Testing explicit conversions

```
// Euro_E_t.cpp
// Tests explicit conversion of class Euro.
// -------------------------------------------------
#include "Euro_Ex.h"        // Class definition
#include <iostream>
using namespace std;

int main()
{
  Euro salary( 8888.8);      // double constructor
  double x(0.0);
  /* Now impossible:
  salary += 1000;            // implicit int -> Euro
  salary += 0.10;            // implicit double -> Euro
  salary = 7777.77;
  x = salary;                // implicit Euro -> double
  x = (double)salary;        // There is no method
                             // operator double().
  // The following conversions are ok:
  salary = Euro( 7777.77);   // explicit double -> Euro
  salary += Euro(1000.10);
  x = salary.asDouble();     // explicit by method
                             // Euro -> double
  int i = salary.asDouble(); // Euro -> double -> int
  return 0;
}
```

☐ Type Conversion Failure

Defining a conversion function or conversion constructor can prevent you from compiling a program that is otherwise unchanged.

The `Euro` class contains a conversion constructor that converts a `double` value to euros. This means that the following statement is valid for two objects, `wholesale` and `retail`, of the `Euro` type.

Example: `retail = wholesale + 46.9;`

If you now additionally implement the conversion function

```
operator double()
```

that converts a euro to a `double` value, the previous statement can no longer be compiled. Since both conversion types `double -> Euro` and `Euro -> double` are defined, two possible conversions could be performed:

```
prov2 + Euro(546.9)        // To add euros
```

and

```
double(prov2) + 546.9;     // To add values
                           // of type double
```

However, the compiler can only perform implicit type conversion if the technique is not ambiguous. If more than one choice is available, the compiler issues an error message.

☐ Avoiding Implicit Type Conversion

You can prevent ambiguities by stating any desired conversions explicitly. This also has the advantage of highlighting type conversions in your source code. Moreover, undesirable type conversion, which can occur when classes are extended at a later date, can be avoided.

In order to ensure that some kinds of type conversion are only performed explicitly, you can use the following techniques:

- ▪ you can use an `explicit` declaration for the conversion constructor. As the example on the opposite page shows, only explicit calls to the constructor are possible in this case.

  Example: `wholesale + Euro(46.9)        // ok`

- ▪ implicit type conversions by conversion functions can be prevented by not defining the function, of course. Instead you can use a method of an appropriate name, for example `asType()`. Type conversion can only be performed by calling this function explicitly.

exercise

■ **EXERCISE**

Method simplify() **of class** Fraction

```cpp
// Fraction.cpp
// . . .

// To simplify fractions:
void Fraction::simplify()
{
    // Divide the numerator and denominator by
    // the greatest common divisor.

    if( numerator == 0)
    {
        denominator = 1;
        return;
    }

    // Calculating the greatest common divisor
    // using an algorithm by Euclid.
    long a = (numerator < 0) ? -numerator : numerator,
         b = denominator,
         help;

    while( b != 0)
    {
        help = a % b;  a = b;  b = help;
    }
    // a is the greatest common divisor
    numerator /= a;
    denominator  /= a;
}
```

Exercise

Enhance the numerical class `Fraction`, which you know from the last chapter, to convert both `double` values to fractions and fractions to `double`. In addition, fractions should be rounded after arithmetic operations.

- First declare the `simplify()` method for the `Fraction` class and insert the definition on the opposite page in your source code. The method computes the largest common divisor of numerator and denominator. The numerator and the denominator are then divided by this value.
- Add an appropriate call to the `simplify()` function to all operator functions (except `++` and `--`).
- Then add a conversion constructor with a `double` type parameter to the class.

  Example: `Fraction b(0.5);    // yields the fraction 1/2`

  `Double` values should be converted to fractions with an accuracy of three decimal places. The following technique should suffice for numbers below one million. Multiply the `double` value by `1000` and add `0.5` for rounding. Assign the result to the numerator. Set the value of the denominator to `1000`. Then proceed to simplify the fraction.

- You now have a conversion constructor for `long` and `double` types. To allow for conversion of `int` values to fractions, you must write your own conversion constructor for `int`!
- Now modify the class to allow conversion of a fraction to a `double` type number. Define the appropriate conversion function `inline`.

Use the function `main()` to test various type conversions. More specifically, use assignments and arithmetic functions to do so. Also compute the sum of a fraction and a floating-point number.

Output the operands and the results on screen.

■ **SOLUTION**

```cpp
// -------------------------------------------------------
// Fraction.h
// A numerical class to represent fractions.
// The class converts Fraction <--> double
// and simplifies fractions.
// -------------------------------------------------------
#ifndef _FRACTION_
#define _FRACTION_
#include <iostream.h>
#include <stdlib.h>
class Fraction
{
  private:  long numerator, denominator;

  public:
   Fraction(long z, long n);
   Fraction(double x);                  // double-constructor
   // Default  long- and int-constructor:
   Fraction(long z=0) : numerator(z), denominator(1) {}
   Fraction(int z)    : numerator(z), denominator(1) {}
   void simplify();
   operator double()                    // Fraction -> double
   {
       return (double)numerator / (double)denominator;
   }
   Fraction operator-() const
   { return Fraction(-numerator, denominator);    }
   Fraction& operator+=(const Fraction& a)
   {
      numerator = a.numerator * denominator
                 + numerator * a.denominator;
      denominator *= a.denominator;
      simplify();
      return *this;
   }
   Fraction& operator-=(const Fraction& a)
   {
      *this += (-a);       simplify();
      return *this;
   }
   // The rest of the class including methods
   //    operator++()   and   operator--()
   // and friend declarations are unchanged.
};
#endif
```

```
// -----------------------------------------------------
// Fraction.cpp
// Defines methods and friend functions
// that are not inline.
// -----------------------------------------------------

#include <iostream.h>
#include <stdlib.h>
#include "Fraction.h"

// Constructors:
Fraction::Fraction(long z, long n)
{
   // Unchanged! Same as in Chapter 19.
}

Fraction::Fraction( double x)
{
   x *= 1000.0;
   x += (x>=0.0) ? 0.5 : -0.5;      // Round the 4th digit.
   numerator = (long)x;
   denominator = 1000;
   simplify();
}

Fraction operator+(const Fraction& a, const Fraction& b )
{
   Fraction temp;

   temp.denominator = a.denominator * b.denominator;
   temp.numerator = a.numerator*b.denominator
                  + b.numerator * a.denominator;
   temp.simplify();
   return temp;
}

// The functions
//  operator-()    operator<<()      operator>>()
// are left unchanged.

// The functions
//  operator*()   and   operator/()
// are completed by a call to temp.simplify()
// just like the function operator+().
//

// The code of method Fraction::simplify(), as
// specified in the exercise, should be here.
```

```cpp
// ---------------------------------------------------------
// Fract_t.cpp
// Tests the class Fraction with type conversions.
// ---------------------------------------------------------
#include <iostream.h>
#include "Fraction.h"
int main()
{
   Fraction a, b(-1,5), c(2.25);
   double x = 0.5, y;
   a = x;                       // double -> Fraction
   cout << "\nSome test results:\n" << endl;
   cout << " a = " << a << endl;
   cout << " b = " << b << endl;
   cout << " c = " << c << endl;
   cout << "\nThe fractions as double values:\n" << endl;
                             // Fraction -> double:
   cout << " a = " << (double)a << endl;
   cout << " b = " << (double)b << endl;
   cout << " c = " << (double)c << endl;

   cout << "\nAnd calculate with:\n" << endl;
   cout << " a + b = " << (a + b) << endl;
   cout << " a - b = " << (a - b) << endl;
   cout << " a * b = " << (a * b) << endl;
   cout << " a / b = " << (a / b) << endl;

   cin  >> a;                 // Enter a fraction.
   cout << "\nYour input:    " << a << endl;
   a.simplify();
   cout << "\nSimplified:        " << a << endl;
   cout << "\nAs double value: " << (double)a << endl;
   cout << "\nEnter a floating point value: ";  cin >> x;
   cout << "\nThis is in fraction form:          "
        << (Fraction)x << endl;
// To calculate the sum b + x :
   cout << " b = " << b << endl;
   cout << " x = " << x << endl;
// a = b + x;                 // Error: ambiguous!
   a = b + Fraction(x);       // ok! To compute fractions.
   y = (double)b + x;         // ok! To compute doubles.
   cout << " b + x  as fraction:   " << a << endl;
   cout << " b + x  as double:     " << y << endl;
   return 0;
}
```

chapter **21**

Dynamic Memory Allocation

This chapter describes how a program can allocate and release memory dynamically in line with current memory requirements.

Dynamic memory allocation is an important factor in many C++ programs and the following chapters will contain several additional case studies to help you review the subject.

▪ THE OPERATOR new

Sample calls to new

```
// Dynamic objects of type long and double
// -----------------------------------------------------
   long *ptr_long;
   ptr_long = new long;              // No initialization
                                     // of the long object.
   *ptr_long = 1234567;              // Assign a value

   double *ptr_double;
   double z = 1.9;
   ptr_double = new double(z);       // With initialization

   ++(*ptr_double);                  // Increment the value
   *ptr_double += *ptr_long;         // ok to add long value

   ptr_long = new double(2.7);       // Error: ptr_long not
                                     // pointing to double!
```

On the heap

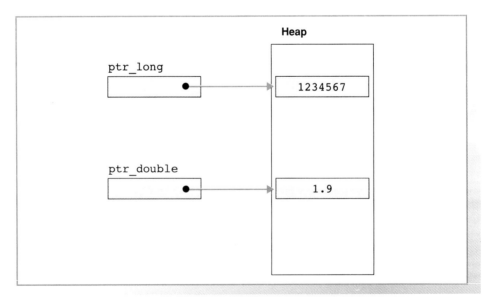

☐ Dynamic Memory Allocation

When a program is compiled, the size of the data the program will need to handle is often an unknown factor; in other words there is no way to estimate the memory requirements of the program. In cases like this you will need to allocate memory dynamically, that is, while the program is running.

Dynamically allocated memory can be released to continually optimize memory usage with respect to current requirements. This in turn provides a high level of flexibility, allowing a programmer to represent dynamic data structures, such as trees and linked lists.

Programs can access a large space of free memory known as the *heap*. Depending on the operating system (and how the OS is configured), the heap can also occupy large amounts of unused space on the hard disk by *swapping* memory to disk.

C++ uses the `new` and `delete` operators to allocate and release memory, and this means that objects of any type can be created and destroyed. Let's look at the scenario for fundamental types first.

☐ Calling `new` for Fundamental Types

The `new` operator is an operator that expects the type of object to be created as an argument. In its simplest form, a call to new follows this syntax

Syntax: `ptr = new type;`

Where `ptr` is a pointer to `type`. The `new` operator creates an object of the specified type and returns the address of that object. The address is normally assigned to a pointer variable. If the pointer belongs to a wrong type, the compiler will issue an error message.

Example: `long double *pld = new long double;`

This statement allocates memory for a `long double` type object, that is, `sizeof(long double)` bytes.

The previous call to new does not define an initial value for the new object, however, you can supply a value in parentheses to *initialize* the object.

Example: `pld = new long double(10000.99);`

Following this statement `pld` points to a memory address containing a `long double` type with a value of `10000.99`. The statement

```
cout << *pld << endl;
```

will output this value.

■ THE OPERATOR delete

Sample program

```
// DynStd.cpp
// The operators new and delete for built-in types.
// The program contains errors!
// ==> Save all data before starting.
// ---------------------------------------------------
#include <iostream>
using namespace std;
int main()
{
   cout << "\nTesting dynamic storage allocation! "
        << endl;
   // To allocate storage:
   double width = 23.78;
   double* ptrWidth  = &width;
   double* ptrLength  = new double(32.54);
   double* ptrArea = new double;

   // To work with ptrWidth, ptrLength, and ptrArea:
   *ptrArea = *ptrWidth * *ptrLength;
   delete ptrLength;        // Error: The object is still
                            // in use!
   cout << "\nWidth     : " << *ptrWidth
        << "\nLength    : " << *ptrLength
        << "\nArea      : " << *ptrArea << endl;

   // To free storage:
   delete ptrWidth;         // Error: The object has not
                            // been dynamically reserved
   delete ptrLength;        // ok
   delete ptrArea;          // ok

   delete ptrLength;        // Error: Pointer doesn't
                            // address any object.

   ptrLength = new double(19.45);      // ok
   // To give a name to a dynamic object:
   double& length = *ptrLength;        // Reference

   cout << "\nNew length      : " << length
        << "\nCircumference   : " << 2 * width * length
        << endl;
   return 0;             // On terminating the program
}                        // allocated storage will be freed.
```

A program should make careful use of available memory and always release memory that is no longer needed. Failure to do so can impact the performance of your computer system. Memory that is released is available for further calls to new.

☐ Calling delete

Memory that has been allocated by a call to new can be released using the delete operator. A call to delete follows this syntax

Syntax: delete ptr;

The operand ptr addresses the memory space to be released. But make sure that this memory space was dynamically allocated by a call to new!

Example: long *pl = new long(2000000);
           . . . .   // to work with *pl.
           delete pl;

If you do not call delete, the dynamically allocated memory space is not released until the program terminates.

You can pass a NULL pointer to delete when you call the operator. In this case nothing happens and delete just returns, so you do not need to check for NULL pointers when releasing memory.

A delete expression is always a void type, so you cannot check whether memory has been successfully released.

As the sample program illustrates, misuse of delete can be disastrous. More specifically

■ do not call delete twice for the same object
■ do not use delete to release statically allocated memory.

☐ Error Handling for new

If there is not enough memory available, the so-called *new handler* is called. The new handler is a function designed for central error handling. Thus, you do not need to design your own error handling routines each time you call new.

The new handler is activated by default and throws an exception. Exceptions can be caught by the program, allowing the error condition to be remedied (refer to Chapter 28, Exception Handling). Any exception that is not caught will terminate the program, however, you can install your own new handler.

If you are working with an older compiler, please note that new returns a NULL pointer if not enough memory is available.

■ DYNAMIC STORAGE ALLOCATION FOR CLASSES

Sample program

```cpp
// DynObj.cpp
// The operators new and delete for classes.
// ---------------------------------------------------
#include "account.h"
#include <iostream>
using namespace std;

Account *clone( const Account* pK);   // Create a copy
                                       // dynamically.
int main()
{
   cout << "Dynamically created objects.\n" << endl;

   // To allocate storage:
   Account *ptrA1, *ptrA2, *ptrA3;

   ptrA1 = new Account;        // With default constructor
   ptrA1->display();           // Show default values.

   ptrA1->setNr(302010);          // Set the other
   ptrA1->setName("Tang, Ming"); // values by access
   ptrA1->setStand(2345.87);     // methods.
   ptrA1->display();             // Show new values.

   // Use the constructor with three arguments:
   ptrA2 = new Account("Xiang, Zhang", 7531357, 999.99);
   ptrA2->display();           // Display new account.

   ptrA3 = clone( ptrA1);      // Pointer to a dyna-
                               // mically created copy.
   cout << "Copy of the first account: " << endl;
   ptrA3->display();           // Display the copy.

   delete ptrA1;               // Release memory
   delete ptrA2;
   delete ptrA3;

   return 0;
}

Account *clone( const Account* pK)   // Create a copy
{                                    // dynamically.
    return new Account(*pK);
}
```

The operators new and delete were designed to create and destroy instances of a class dynamically. In this case, in addition to allocating memory, a suitable constructor must be called. Before releasing memory, the destructor must be called to perform cleaning up tasks. However, the operators new and delete ensure that this happens.

☐ Calling new with a Default Constructor

A call to new for a class is not much different from a call for a fundamental type. Unless explicitly initialized, the default constructor is called for each new object, but you must make sure that a default constructor exists!

Example: `Euro* pEuro = new Euro;`

This statement allocates memory for an object of the Euro class. If enough memory is available, the default constructor for Euro is executed and the address of a new object returned.

☐ Explicit Initialization

To initialize an object explicitly, you can state its initial values in parentheses when you call new.

Syntax: `Type *ptr = new Type(initializing_list);`

The values in the initialization list are passed as arguments to the constructor. If the compiler is unable to locate a suitable constructor, an error message occurs.

Example: `Euro *pE = new Euro( -123,77);`

This statement assigns the address of a new Euro class object to the pointer pE. The object is initialized using the supplied values. The expression *pE thus represents the entire object.

Example: `*pE += 200;          // To add 200 euros.`

The public members are referred to via the member access operator ->.

Example: `cout << pE->getCents() << endl;    // 33`

☐ Releasing Memory

When an object that was created dynamically is destroyed, the delete operator makes sure that the object is cleaned up. The destructor is first called, and only then is the memory space released.

As previously discussed in the section on fundamental types, when you call delete you must ensure that the pointer is addressing a dynamic object or that you are dealing with a NULL pointer.

■ DYNAMIC STORAGE ALLOCATION FOR ARRAYS

Sample program

```cpp
// DynArr.cpp
// Operators new[] and delete[] for dynamic arrays.
// ----------------------------------------------------
#include <iostream>
#include <iomanip>
using namespace std;
int main()
{
   cout << "Using a dynamic array.\n" << endl;
   int size = 0, cnt = 0, step = 10,
       i;
   float x, *pArr = NULL;
   cout << "Enter some numbers!\n"
           "End with q or another character " << endl;
   while( cin >> x)
   {
     if( cnt >= size)               // Array too small?
     {                              // => enlarge it.
        float *p = new float[size+step];
                                    // Copy the numbers:
        for( i = 0; i < size; ++i)
           p[i] = pArr[i];
        delete [] pArr;            // Release old array:
        pArr = p;  size += step;
     }
     pArr[cnt++] = x;
   }
   // Work with the numbers:
   if( cnt == 0)
     cout << "No invalid input!" << endl;
   else
   {
     float sum = 0.0;
     cout << "Your input: " << endl;
     for( i = 0; i < cnt; i++)         // To output and
     {                                 // add.
       cout << setw(10) << pArr[i];
       sum += pArr[i];
     }
     cout << "\nThe average: " << sum/cnt << endl;
   }
   delete [] pArr;                 // To free the storage
   return 0;
}
```

Imagine you are compiling a program that will store an unknown quantity of elements in an array. Your best option is to let the program create the array dynamically. An array of this type is known as a *dynamic array*.

☐ The new[ ] Operator

The new[ ] operator is available for creating dynamic arrays. When you call the operator, you must supply the type and quantity of the array elements.

Syntax: `vekPtr = new Type[cnt];`

The pointer `vekPtr` will then reference the first of a total of `cnt` array elements. `vekPtr` has to be a pointer to `Type` for this reason. Of course, `Type` can also be a class.

Example: `Account *pk = new Account[256];`

This statement allocates memory for 256 `Account` type objects and uses the default constructor to initialize them. Those objects are

`pk[0], pk[1], . . . , pk[255],`

or in pointer notation:

`*pk, *(pk + 1), ....., *(pk + 255).`

If the array elements are of a class type, the class must have a *default constructor*, since you cannot supply an initialization list when calling new[]. Starting values for the array elements cannot be assigned until later.

☐ The delete[ ] Operator

It is always a good idea to release the memory space occupied by a dynamic array, if the array is no longer needed. To do so, simply call the `delete[]` operator. The braces `[]` tell the compiler to release the whole array, and not just a single array element.

Example: `delete[] pk;`

The operand for `delete[]`—the pointer `pk` in this case—*must* reference the place in memory that was allocated by a call to new[]! The destructor belonging to the current class is called for each array element. This shows the big difference to `delete`, which would merely call the destructor for `*pk`, i.e. for the first array element.

    The program on the opposite page stores numbers in a dynamic array. The size of the array is adjusted as required. To do so, a newer bigger array is created, the data is copied to the new array, and the memory occupied by the old array is released.

■ APPLICATION: LINKED LISTS

A simple linked list

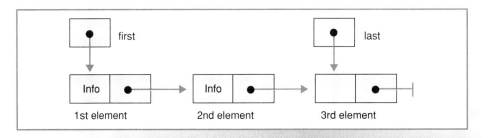

Appending a list element

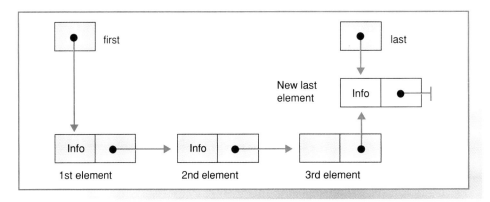

Deleting a list element

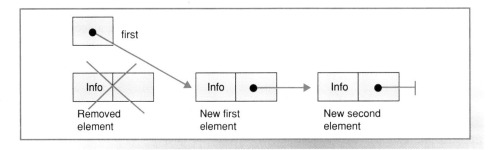

☐ Dynamic Data Structures

Now, let's implement a linked list as a sample application. A *linked list* is a dynamic data structure that allows easy insertion and deletion of data. A *data structure* defines how data can be organized in units, stored, and manipulated—as arrays, lists, or trees, for example.

The type of data structure you choose has a far-reaching effect on the amount of memory you need, the speed of access to the data involved, and the complexity (or simplicity) of the algorithms (data operations) you need.

In contract to a *static* data structure, whose size is known before a program is launched, a *dynamic* data structure can change size while a program is running. One example of this is an array whose size can be changed during runtime.

☐ Defining a Linked List

Another example is a linked list that is stored in main memory and has the following characteristics:

- each list element contains a data store for the live data and a pointer to the next element in the list
- each list element—except the first and last elements—has exactly one predecessor and one successor. The first element in the list has no predecessor and the last element no successor.

Some *elementary operations* are defined for linked lists, such as inserting and deleting list elements, or searching for and retrieving the information stored in a list element.

☐ Advantages

The storage used for the list elements need not be contiguous. The main advantage of linked lists is:

- memory for the list elements is only allocated when needed
- you only need to move a pointer when inserting or deleting list elements.

When an array element is inserted or deleted, the other array elements have to be moved to make room or fill up the "gap" in the array. If there is no room left, you need to allocate memory for a new array and copy the data to it before inserting a new element.

▪ REPRESENTING A LINKED LIST

Classes of header file `List.h`

```cpp
// List.h
// Defines the classes ListEl and List.
// --------------------------------------------------
#ifndef _LISTE_H_
#define _LISTE_H_
#include "Date.h"              // Class Date from Chapter 14
#include <iostream>
#include <iomanip>
using namespace std;

class ListEl                   // A list element.
{
  private:
    Date  date;                // Date
    double amount;             // Amount of money
    ListEl* next;              // Pointer to successor

  public:
    ListEl( Date   d = Date(1,1,1), double  b = 0.0,
            ListEl* p = NULL)
            : date(d), amount(b), next(p) {}
    // Access methods:
    // getDate(), setDate(), getAmount(), setAmount()
    ListEl* getNext()  const { return next; }
    friend class List;
};

// --------------------------------------------------
// Defining the class List
class List
{
  private:
    ListEl* first, *last;
  public:
    List(){ first = last = NULL; }  // Constructor
    ~List();                        // Destructor
    // Access to the first and last elements:
    ListEl* front() const { return first; }
    ListEl* back()  const { return last; }
    // Append a new element at the end of the list:
    void pushBack(const Date& d, double b);
    // Delete an element at the beginning of the list:
    void popFront();
};
#endif  // _LIST_H_
```

☐ Representing List Elements

You can use a recursive data structure to represent a linked list. A *recursive data structure* is a data structure containing a pointer to a data structure of the same type. Of course, the data structure cannot contain itself—that would be impossible—but it does contain a pointer to itself.

Now let's look at a linked list used to represent transactions in a bank account. A transaction is characterized by a date, a sum of money, and the reason for the transaction. Thus, the list element needed to represent a transaction will contain the transaction data in its data store and a pointer to the next element in the list.

The class shown on the opposite page, ListEl, was designed to represent list elements. To keep things simple, the data store contains only the date and a sum of money. The public declaration includes a constructor and access methods for the live data. Later, we will be overloading the << operator in order to output the list.

It is common practice to let the pointer for the last element in the list point to NULL. This also provides a termination criterion—the next pointer just needs to be queried for NULL.

☐ Representing a List

To identify a linked list, you just point a pointer at the first element in the list. You can then use the pointer to the successor of each element to address any element in the list. A pointer to the last element in the list is useful for appending new elements.

The opposite page shows the class definition for the List class. The private section comprises two pointers, which reference the first and last list elements respectively. The *constructor* has an easy job—it simply points both pointers to NULL, thus creating an empty list. The *destructor* has a more complex task: it has to release the memory occupied by the remaining list elements.

The pushBack() method is used to *append* a new element to the end of the list. To do so, memory is allocated dynamically and the new element becomes the successor of what was previously the last element and the last pointer is updated. In addition, the method must deal with a special case, where the list is empty.

The popFront() method deletes the first element in the list. This involves turning the pointer to the first element around to the second element and releasing the memory occupied by the first element. The special case with an empty list also applies.

■ EXERCISES

Notes on exercise 1

Effects of the `splice()` **function**

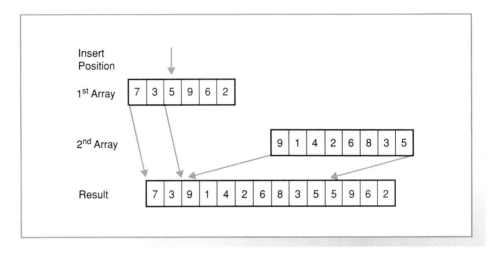

Exercise 1

Write a global function called `splice()` that "splices" two `int` arrays together by first allocating memory for a dynamic array with enough room for both `int` arrays, and then copying the elements from both arrays to the new array, as follows:

- first, the elements of the first array are inserted up to a given position,
- then the second array is inserted,
- then the remainder of the first array is appended.

Arguments: The two `int` arrays, their length, and the position at which they are to be spliced.

Return value: A pointer to the new array

Exercise 2

Write a global function called `merge()` that merges two sorted `int` arrays by first allocating memory for a dynamic array with enough room for both `int` arrays and then inserting the elements of both arrays into the new array in sequence.

Arguments: The two `int` arrays and their length.

Return value: A pointer to the new array

To test the function, modify the program used to sort arrays in Exercise 4 of Chapter 17.

Exercise 3

Complete and test the implementation of a linked list found in this chapter.

- First define the access methods shown opposite. Then overload the `<<` operator for the class `ListEl` to allow formatted output of the data in the list elements. You can use the `asString()` in the date class to do so.
- Then implement the destructor for the `List` class. The destructor will release the memory used by all the remaining elements. Make sure that you read the pointer to the successor of each element before destroying it!
- Implement the methods `pushBack()` and `popFront()` used for appending and deleting list elements.
- Overload the operator `<<` in the `List` class to output all the data stored in the list.
- Test the `List` class by inserting and deleting several list elements and repeatedly outputting the list.

■ SOLUTIONS

Exercise 1

```cpp
// ----------------------------------------------------
// Splice.cpp
// Implements the splice algorithm.
// ----------------------------------------------------
#include <iostream>
#include <iomanip>
#include <cstdlib>              // For srand() and rand()
#include <ctime>                // and for time().
using namespace std;

// Prototype:
int *splice( int v1[], int len1,
             int v2[], int len2, int pos);

int main()
{
    cout << "\n  * * * Testing the splice function * * *\n"
         << endl;
    int i, len1 = 10, len2 = 5;
    int *a1 = new int[len1],
        *a2 = new int[len2];
    // Initialize the random number generator
    // with the current time:
    srand( (unsigned)time(NULL));

    for( i=0; i < len1; ++i)     // Initialize the arrays:
       a1[i] = rand();           // with positive and
    for( i=0; i < len2; ++i)
       a2[i] = -rand();          // negative numbers.

    // To output the array:
    cout << "1. array: " << endl;
    for( i = 0; i < len1; ++i)
       cout << setw(12) << a1[i];
    cout << endl;
    cout << "2. array: " << endl;
    for( i = 0; i < len2; ++i)
       cout << setw(12) << a2[i];
    cout << endl;
    cout << "\n At what position do you want to insert "
            "\n the 2nd array  into 1st  array?"
            "\n Possible positions: 0, 1, ..., " << len1
         << " : ";

    int pos;  cin >> pos;
```

```
      int *a3, len3 = len1 + len2;
      a3    = splice( a1, len1, a2, len2, pos);

      if( a3 == NULL)
         cerr << "\n Invalid position!\n" << endl;
      else
      {
         cout << " The new spliced array: " << endl;
         for( i = 0; i < len3; ++i)
            cout << setw(12) << a3[i];
         cout << endl;
      }
      delete[] a1;   delete[] a2;   delete[] a3;
      return 0;
}

// -------------------------------------------------------
// Function splice() inserts the array v2 into v1
//  starting at position pos.
int *splice( int v1[], int len1,
             int v2[], int len2, int pos)
{
   if( pos < 0  ||  pos > len1)
      return NULL;

   int i = 0, i1 = 0, i2 = 0;
   int *v = new int[len1+len2];

   for( i = 0, i1 = 0; i1 < pos;  ++i, ++i1) // 1st part
       v[i] = v1[i1];

   for( i2 = 0; i2 < len2;  ++i, ++i2)       // 2nd part
       v[i] = v2[i2];

   for(  ; i1 < len1;  ++i, ++i1)            // 3rd part
       v[i] = v1[i1];

   return v;
}
```

Exercise 2

```cpp
// --------------------------------------------------
// merge.cpp
// Implements the merge algorithm.
// --------------------------------------------------
#include <iostream>
#include <iomanip>
#include <cstdlib>
#include <ctime>
using namespace std;

// Prototypes:
void selectionSort( int arr[], int len);
int *merge( int v1[], int len1, int v2[], int len2);

int main()
{
    cout << "\n  * * *   The Merge Algorithm  * * *\n"
         << endl;
    int i, len1 = 10, len2 = 20;
    int *a1 = new int[len1],
        *a2 = new int[len2];
    // Initialize the random number generator
    // with the current time:
    srand( (unsigned)time(NULL));
    for( i=0; i < len1; ++i)    // Initialized arrays:
       a1[i] = rand();
    for( i=0; i < len2; ++i)
       a2[i] = rand();
    selectionSort( a1, len1);        // To sort array a1.
    selectionSort( a2, len2);        // To sort array a2.
    // Output the arrays:
    cout << "The sorted arrays:" << endl;
    cout << "1st array: " << endl;
    for( i = 0; i < len1; ++i)
       cout << setw(12) << a1[i];
    cout << endl;
    cout << "2nd array: " << endl;
    for( i = 0; i < len2; ++i)
       cout << setw(12) << a2[i];
    cout << endl;
    int *a3, len3;
    a3   = merge( a1, len1, a2, len2);
    len3 = len1 + len2;
```

```
      cout << "The new merged array: " << endl;
      for( i = 0; i < len3; ++i)
         cout << setw(12) << a3[i];
      cout << endl;

      delete[] a1;   delete[] a2;   delete[] a3;
      return 0;
}
// -----------------------------------------------------
// Function selectionSort().
inline void swap( int& a, int& b)        // To swap.
{  int temp = a;   a = b;   b = temp;   }

void selectionSort( int *arr, int len)
{
   register int *p, *minp;   // Pointer to array elements,
   int *last = arr + len-1;  // Pointer to the last element
   for( ; arr < last;  ++arr)
   {
      minp = arr;                          // Search minimum
      for( p = arr+1; p <= last; ++p) // starting at
         if( *minp > *p)                   // position arr.
            minp = p;
      swap( *arr, *minp);                  // To swap.
   }
}
// -----------------------------------------------------
// merge() : Merges two sorted arrays to create
//           a new sorted array.
int *merge( int v1[], int len1, int v2[], int len2)
{
   int i = 0, i1 = 0, i2 = 0;
   int *v = new int[len1+len2];     // New int array.
   for( i=0; i1 < len1 && i2 < len2; ++i)
   {
      if( v1[i1] <= v2[i2])
         v[i] = v1[i1++];
      else
         v[i] = v2[i2++];
   }
   if( i1 < len1)          // Copy the rest of v1 or v2.
     while( i1 < len1)
       v[i++] = v1[i1++];
   else
     while( i2 < len2)
       v[i++] = v2[i2++];
   return v;
}
```

Exercise 3

```cpp
// ----------------------------------------------------
// date.h :    Defines the class Date.
// ----------------------------------------------------
// date.cpp
// Implements the methods of class Date,
// which are not inline defined.
// ----------------------------------------------------
//
// These files are left unchanged
// from Chapter 14 (solutions).
//


// ----------------------------------------------------
// List.h
// Defines the classes ListEl and List
// to represent a linked list.
// ----------------------------------------------------
#ifndef _LIST_H_
#define _LIST_H_
#include "Date.h"
#include <iostream>
#include <iomanip>
using namespace std;

class ListEl
{
  private:
    Date  date;          // Date
    double amount;       // Amount of money
    ListEl* next;        // Pointer to successor

  public:
    ListEl( Date    d = Date(1,1,1),
            double  b = 0.0,
            ListEl* p = NULL)
            : date(d), amount(b), next(p)  {}

    // Access methods
    const Date& getDate() const { return date; }
    void setDate()       // Sets the current date
    {
       date.setDate();
    }
    bool setDate( int day, int month, int year)
    {
       return setDate( day, month, year);
    }
```

```
      double   getAmount() const { return amount; }
      void     setAmount(double a) { amount = a; }
      ListEl* getNext()  const { return next; }
      friend class List;
};

// Output an element
ostream& operator<<( ostream& os, const ListEl& le);

// -----------------------------------------------------
// Defines the List class
class List
{
  private:
    ListEl* first, *last;
  public:
    List(){ first = last = NULL; }  // Constructor
    ~List();                        // Destructor

    // Access first and last elements:
    ListEl* front() const { return first; }
    ListEl* back()  const { return last; }
    // Appends a new element at the end of the list:
    void pushBack(const Date& d, double b);
    // Deletes an element at the beginning of the list.
    void popFront();
};

// Outputs the list
ostream& operator<<( ostream& os, const List& le);
#endif  // _LIST_H_

// -----------------------------------------------------
// List.cpp
// Implements the methods of class List,
// which are not previously defined inline.
// -----------------------------------------------------
#include "List.h"
// Destructor of the list:
List::~List()
{
   ListEl *pEl = first,  *next = NULL;
   for(  ; pEl != NULL;  pEl = next)
   {
      next = pEl->next;
      delete pEl;
   }
}
```

```cpp
// Appends a new element at the end of the list:
void List::pushBack(const Date& d, double b)
{
   ListEl *pEl = new ListEl( d, b);
   if( last == NULL)          // List empty?
      first = last = pEl;
   else
      last->next = pEl,  last = pEl;
}

// Deletes an element from the beginning of the list.
void List::popFront()
{
   if( first != NULL)         // Not empty?
   {
     ListEl *pEl = first;    // Save the first element.
     first = first->next;    // Move to the next element.
     delete pEl;             // Former first element
     if( first == NULL)      // Empty now?
        last = NULL;
   }
}

// --- Global functions for output ---
// Outputs an element:
ostream& operator<<( ostream& os, const ListEl& le)
{
    os << le.getDate().asString() << "  Amount: ";
    os << fixed << setprecision(2) << setw(10)
       << le.getAmount();
    return os;
}

// Outputs the list:
ostream& operator<<( ostream& os, const List& List)
{
   ListEl *pEl = List.front();
   if( pEl == NULL)
       os << "The list is empty!" << endl;

   for(   ; pEl != NULL;  pEl = pEl->getNext() )
      os << *pEl << endl;
   return os;
}
```

```cpp
// ---------------------------------------------------------
// List_t.cpp
// Tests the List class.
// ---------------------------------------------------------

#include "List.h"

int main()
{
   cout << "\n * * *  Testing the class list  * * *\n"
        << endl;

   List  aList;                  // A list

   cout << aList << endl;        // List is still empty.

   cout << "\nEnter account changes (Date and Amount)"
           "\n(Type invalid input to quit, e.g. q):\n";
   Date date;
   int month, day, year;   char c;
   double amount;

   while( true)
   {
     cout << "Date format Month-Day-Year : ";
     if( !(cin >> month >> c >> day >> c >> year)
         || ! date.setDate( month, day, year) )
     break;                                // Invalid date.

     cout << "Account change: ";
     if( !(cin >> amount) ) break;

     aList.pushBack( date, amount);
   }

   cout << "\nContent of the list:\n";
   cout << aList << endl;

   cout << "\nRemoving the first element of the list:\n";

   ListEl *ptrEl = ptrEl = aList.front();
   if( ptrEl != NULL)
   {
      cout << "Deleting:  " << *ptrEl << endl;
      aList.popFront();
   }

   cout << "\nContent of the list:\n";
   cout << aList << endl;

   return 0;
}
```

chapter 22

Dynamic Members

This chapter describes how to implement classes containing pointers to dynamically allocated memory. These include

- your own copy constructor definition and
- overloading the assignment operator.

A class designed to represent arrays of any given length is used as a sample application.

■ MEMBERS OF VARYING LENGTH

An object of class `FloatArr` **in memory**

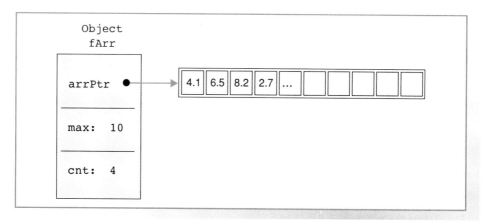

Data members of class `FloatArr`

```
// A class representing dynamic arrays of floats.
// -------------------------------------------------
class FloatArr
{
   private:
     float* arrPtr;     // Dynamic member
     int max;           // Maximum quantity without
                        // reallocating new storage.
     int cnt;           // Number of present elements

   public:

     // Public methods here

};
```

☐ Dynamic Members

You can exploit the potential of dynamic memory allocation to leverage existing classes and create data members of variable length. Depending on the amount of data an application program really has to handle, memory is allocated as required while the application is running. In order to do this the class needs a pointer to the dynamically allocated memory that contains the actual data. Data members of this kind are also known as *dynamic members* of a class.

When compiling a program that contains arrays, you will probably not know how many elements the array will need to store. A class designed to represent arrays should take this point into consideration and allow for dynamically defined variable length arrays.

☐ Requirements

In the following section you will be developing a new version of the `FloatArr` class to meet these requirements and additionally allow you to manipulate arrays as easy as fundamental types. For example, a simple assignment should be possible for two objects `v1` and `v2` in the new class.

Example: `v2 = v1;`

The object `v2` itself—and not the programmer—will ensure that enough memory is available to accommodate the array `v1`.

Just as in the case of fundamental types, it should also be possible to use an existing object, `v2`, to initialize a new object, `v3`.

Example: `FloatArr v3 (v2);`

Here the object `v3` ensures that enough memory is available to accommodate the array elements of `v2`.

When an object of the `FloatArr` is declared, the user should be able to define the initial length of the array. The statement

Example: `FloatArr fArr(100);`

allocates memory for a maximum of 100 array elements.

The definition of the `FloatArr` class therefore comprises a member that addresses a dynamically allocated array. In addition to this, two `int` variables are required to store the maximum and current number of array elements.

■ CLASSES WITH A DYNAMIC MEMBER

First version of class `FloatArr`

```
// floatArr.h : Dynamic array of floats.
// -------------------------------------------------
#ifndef _FLOATARR_
#define _FLOATARR_
class FloatArr
{
   private:
      float* arrPtr;      // Dynamic member
      int max;            // Maximum quantity without
                          // reallocation of new storage.
      int cnt;            // Number of array elements
   public:
      FloatArr( int n = 256 );      // Constructor
      FloatArr( int n, float val);
      ~FloatArr();                  // Destructor
      int  length() const { return cnt; }
      float& operator[](int i);     // Subscript operator.
      float  operator[](int i) const;
      bool append(float val);       // Append value val.
      bool remove(int pos);         // Delete position pos.
};
#endif    // _FLOATARR_
```

Creating objects with dynamic members

```
#include "floatArr.h"
#include <iostream>
using namespace std;
int main()
{
   FloatArr v(10);        // Array v of 10 float values
   FloatArr w(20, 1.0F);  // To initialize array w of
                          // 20 float values with 1.0.
   v.append( 0.5F);
   cout << " Current number of elements in v: "
        << v.length() << endl;                 //   1
   cout << " Current number of elements in w: "
        << w.length() << endl;                 //   20
   return 0;
}
```

The next question you need to ask when designing a class to represent arrays is what methods are necessary and useful. You can enhance `FloatArr` class step by step by optimizing existing methods or adding new methods.

The first version of the `FloatArr` class comprises a few basic methods, which are introduced and discussed in the following section.

☐ Constructors

It should be possible to create an object of the `FloatArr` class with a given length and store a `float` value in the object, if needed. A constructor that expects an `int` value as an argument is declared for this purpose.

```
FloatArr(int n = 256);
```

The number `256` is the default argument for the length of the array. This provides for a default constructor that creates an array with `256` empty array elements.

An additional constructor

```
FloatArr( int n, int val );
```

allows you to define an array where the given value is stored in each array element. In this case you need to state the length of the array.

Example: `FloatArr arr( 100, 0.0F));`

This statement initializes the 100 elements in the array with a value of `0.0`.

☐ Additional Methods

The `length()` method allows you to query the number of elements in the array. `arr.length()` returns a value of `100` for the array `arr`.

You can overload the subscript operator `[]` to access individual array elements.

Example: `arr[i] = 15.0F;`

The index `i` must lie within the range `0` to `cnt-1`.

The `append()` method can be used to append a value to the array. The number of elements is then incremented by one.

When you call the `remove()` method it does exactly the opposite of `append()` — deleting the element at the stated position. This reduces the current count by one, provided a valid position was stated.

■ CREATING AND DESTROYING OBJECTS

Effects of the declaration `FloatArr fArr( 10, 1.0F );`

First, memory is allocated for the data members:

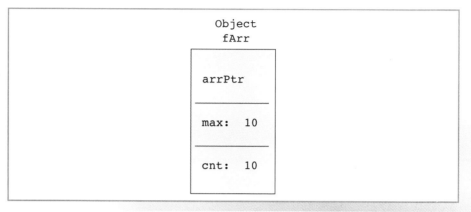

Then storage is allocated for 10 array elements and the variables `max` and `cnt` are set to 10:

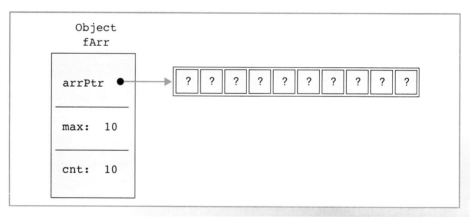

Finally, a value of 1.0 is used to initialize the array elements:

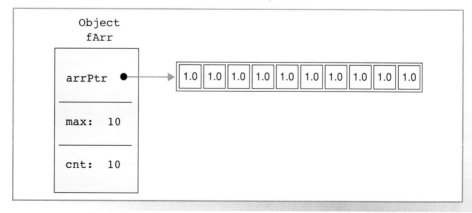

The memory for the array elements is not contained in a `FloatArr` object and must be allocated dynamically by the constructor. The object itself only occupies the memory required for the data members `arrPtr`, `max`, and `cnt`. Thus, `sizeof(FloatArr)` is a constant value that defaults to 12 bytes for 32 bit computers.

The additional dynamic memory allocation may need to be adjusted to meet new requirements, for example, if an assignment is made. Finally, the memory has to be released explicitly when an object is destroyed.

☐ Constructing an Object

The first constructor in the `FloatArr` class is defined as follows:

```
FloatArr::FloatArr( int n )
{
   max = n;    cnt = 0;
   arrPtr = new float[max];
}
```

This allocates memory for n array elements. The current number of array elements is set to 0.

The second constructor fills the array with the supplied value and is therefore defined as follows:

```
FloatArr::FloatArr(int n, float val)
{
   max = cnt = n;
   arrPtr  = new float[max];
   for( int i=0; i < cnt; ++i)
       arrPtr[i] = val;
}
```

The opposite page shows how memory is allocated for the object `fArr` and how this object is initialized.

☐ Destroying an Object

When an object is destroyed the dynamic memory the object occupies must be released. Classes with dynamic members will *always* need a destructor to perform this task.

The `FloatArr` class contains a dynamic array, so memory can be released by a call to the `delete[]` operator.

```
FloatArr::~FloatArr()
{
   delete[] arrPtr;
}
```

■ IMPLEMENTING METHODS

New version of class `FloatArr`

```cpp
// FloatArr.cpp:
// Implementing the methods of class FloatArr.
// ------------------------------------------------------
#include "floatArr.h"
#include <iostream>
using namespace std;

// Constructors and destructor as before.
// Subscript operator for objects that are not const:
float& FloatArr::operator[]( int i )
{
   if( i < 0 || i >= cnt )          // Range checking
   {
     cerr << "\n class FloatArr: Out of range! ";
     exit(1);
   }
   return arrPtr[i];
}

float FloatArr::operator[]( int i ) const
{
   // Else as before.
}

bool FloatArr::append( float val)
{
   if(cnt < max)
   {
      arrPtr[cnt++] = val;   return true;
   }
   else                             // Enlarge the array!
      return false;
}

bool FloatArr::remove(int pos)
{
   if( pos >= 0 && pos < cnt)
   {
      for( int i = pos; i < cnt-1; ++i)
         arrPtr[i] = arrPtr[i+1];
      --cnt;
      return true;
   }
   else
      return false;
}
```

IMPLEMENTING METHODS ▪ 485

☐ Read and Write Access Using the Subscript Operator

The subscript operator can be overloaded to allow easy manipulation of array elements.

Example:
```
FloatArr v(5, 0.0F);
v[2] = 2.2F;
for( int i=0; i < v.length(); ++i)
    cout << v[i];
```

The operator allows both read and write access to the array elements and cannot be used for constant objects for this reason. However, you will need to support read-only access to constant objects.

The `FloatArr` class contains two versions of the operator function `operator[]()` for this purpose. The first version returns a reference to the `i`-th array element and thus supports write access. The second, read-only version only supports read access to the array elements and is automatically called by the compiler when accessing constant objects.

The implementation of these versions is identical. In both cases range checking is performed for the index. If the index lies within the valid boundaries, an array element—or simply a value in the case of the read-only version—is returned.

☐ Appending and Deleting in Arrays

The `FloatArr` class comprises the methods `append()` and `remove()` for appending and deleting array elements.

In the first version, the `append()` only works if there is at least one empty slot in the array. In the exercises, `append()` is used to extend the array as required. This also applies for a new method, `insert()`, which you will write as an exercise in this chapter.

When the `remove()` method is used to delete an element, the elements following the deleted element move up one place, preserving the original order. The current count is decremented by one. What was formerly the last element in the array is not deleted but overwritten when a new element is inserted.

Another technique would be to copy the last element to the position of the element that needs to be deleted, simply overwriting that element. Of course, this technique is quicker and preferable for cases where the order of the elements is not significant.

▪ COPY CONSTRUCTOR

Effect of the standard copy constructor

```
FloatArr b(a);          // Creates a copy of a.
```

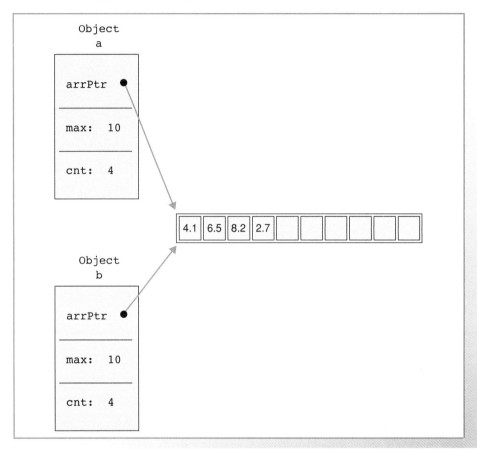

A self-defined copy constructor for class `FloatArr`

```cpp
//floatArr.cpp: Implementing the methods.
// ----------------------------------------------------
FloatArr::FloatArr(const FloatArr& src)
{
   max = src.max;      cnt = src.cnt;
   arrPtr = new float[max];

   for( int i = 0; i < cnt; i++ )
      arrPtr[i] = src.arrPtr[i];
}
```

☐ Initializing with an Object

The next step is to ensure that an existing object can be used to initialize a new object. Given an array, a, the following statement should be valid:

Example: `FloatArr b(a);`

The array b should now be the same length as the array a and the array elements in b should contain the same values as in a.

The `FloatArr` class needs a *copy constructor* to perform this task. The constructor has a reference to a constant array as a parameter.

Prototype: `FloatArr( const FloatArr& );`

☐ Standard Copy Constructor

If a class does not contain a copy constructor, the compiler will automatically create a minimal version, known as the *standard copy constructor*. This constructor copies the data members of the object passed to it to corresponding data members of the new object.

A standard copy constructor is normally sufficient for a class. However, simply copying the data members would serve no useful purpose for objects containing dynamic members. This would merely copy the pointers, meaning that the pointers of several different objects would reference the same place in memory. The diagram on the opposite page illustrates this situation for two `FloatArr` class objects.

This scenario would obviously mean trouble. Imagine releasing memory allocated for an object dynamically. The pointer for the second object would reference a memory area that no longer existed!

☐ Proprietary Version of the Copy Constructor

Clearly you will need to write a new copy constructor for classes with dynamic members, ensuring that the live data and not just the pointers are copied from the dynamically allocated memory.

The example on the opposite page shows the definition of the copy constructor for the `FloatArr` class. Calling `new []` creates a new array and the array elements of the object passed to the method are then copied to that array.

■ ASSIGNMENT

New declarations in class `FloatArr`

```
// FloatArr.h : Dynamic arrays of floats.
// ---------------------------------------------------
class FloatArr
{
  private:
   // . . . Data members as before
  public:
   // . . . Methods as before and
   FloatArr(const FloatArr& src);    // Copy constructor
   FloatArr& operator=( const FloatArr&); // Assignment
};
```

Defining the assignment

```
// In file floatArr.cpp
// The operator function implementing "=".
// ---------------------------------------------------
FloatArr& FloatArr::operator=( const FloatArr& src )
{
  if( this != &src )                // No self assignments!
  {
    max = src.max;
    cnt = src.cnt;
    delete[] arrPtr;               // Release memory,
    arrPtr = new float[max];       // reallocate and
    for( int i=0; i < cnt; i++)    // copy elements.
      arrPtr[i] = src.arrPtr[i];
  }
  return *this;
}
```

Sample calls

```
#include "FloatArr.h"
int main()
{
   FloatArr v;             // Default constructor.
   FloatArr w(20, 1.0F);   // Array w  - 20 float values
                           // with initial value 1.0.
   const FloatArr kw(w);       // Use copy constructor
                               // to create an object.
   v = w;                      // Assignment.
}
```

Each class comprises four implicitly defined default methods, which you can replace with your own definitions:

- the default constructor and the destructor
- the copy constructor and the standard assignment

In contrast to initialization by means of the copy constructor, which takes place when an object is defined, an assignment always requires an existing object. Multiple assignments, which modify an object, are possible.

☐ Default Assignment

Given that `v1` and `v2` are two `FloatArr` class objects, the following assignment is valid:

Example: `v1 = v2;`   // Possible, but ok?

Default assignment is performed member by member. The data members of `v2` are copied to the corresponding data members of `v1` just like the copy constructor would copy them. However, this technique is not suitable for classes with dynamic members. This would simply point the pointers belonging to different objects at the same dynamic allocated memory. In addition, memory previously addressed by a pointer of the target object will be unreferenced after the assignment.

☐ Overloading the Assignment Operator

In other words, you need to overload the default assignment for classes containing dynamic members. Generally speaking, if you need to define a copy constructor, you will also need to define an assignment.

The operator function for the assignment must perform the following tasks:

- release the memory referenced by the dynamic members
- allocate sufficient memory and copy the source object's data to that memory.

The operator function is implemented as a class method and returns a reference to the target object allowing multiple assignments. The prototype of the operator function for the `FloatArr` class is thus defined as follows:

```
FloatArr& FloatArr::operator=( const FloatArr& src)
```

When implementing the operator function you must avoid self assignment, which would read memory areas that have already been released.

■ EXERCISES

New methods of class List

```
// Copy constructor:
List::List(const List&);
// Assignment:
List& List::operator=( const List&);
```

New methods of class FloatArr

```
    // Methods to append a float or an
    // array of floats:
    void append( float val);
    void append( const FloatArr& v);
    FloatArr& operator+=( float val);
    FloatArr& operator+=( const FloatArr& v);

    // Methods to insert a float or an
    // array of floats:
    bool insert( float val, int pos);
    bool insert( const FloatArr& v, int pos );

// In any case, more memory space must be allocated
// to the array if the current capacity is
// insufficient.
```

Exercise 1

Complete the definition of the `List` class, which represents a linked list and test the class.

First, modify your test program to create a copy of a list. Call the default assignment for the objects in the `List` class. Note how your program reacts.

A trial run of the program shows that the class is incomplete. Since the class contains dynamic members, the following tasks must be performed:

- Define a copy constructor for the `List` class.
- Overload the assignment operator.

Exercise 2

Add the methods shown opposite to the `FloatArr` class. In contrast to the existing method

```
bool append( float val);
```

the new method must be able to allocate more memory as required. As this could also be necessary for other methods, write a private auxiliary function for this purpose

```
void expand( int newMax );
```

The method must copy existing data to the newly allocated memory.

Overload the operator `+=` so it can be used instead of calling the function `append()`.

The `insert()` method inserts a `float` value or a `FloatArr` object at position `pos`. Any elements that follow `pos` must be pushed.

Also overload the shift operator `<<` to output an array using the field width originally defined to output the array elements.

✓ **NOTE**

The `width()` method in the `ostream` class returns the current field width, if you call the method without any arguments.

Now add calls to the new methods to your test program and output the results after each call.

SOLUTIONS

Exercise I

```cpp
// --------------------------------------------------
// List.h
// Definition of classes ListEl and List
// representing a linked list.
// --------------------------------------------------
#ifndef _LIST_H_
#define _LIST_H_
#include "Date.h"
#include <iostream>
#include <iomanip>
using namespace std;

class ListEl
{
   // Unchanged as in Chapter 21
};
// ----------------------------------------------------
// Definition of class List
class List
{
  private:
    ListEl* first, *last;
  public:
    // New methods:
    List(const List&);                  // Copy constructor
    List& operator=( const List&); // Assignment
    // Otherwise unchanged from Chapter 21
};
#endif  // _LIST_H_

// ----------------------------------------------------
// List.cpp
// Implements those methods of class List,
// that are not defined inline.
// ----------------------------------------------------
#include "List.h"
// Copy constructor:
List::List(const List& src)
{
   // Appends the elements of src to an empty list.
   first = last = NULL;
   ListEl *pEl = src.first;
   for(  ; pEl != NULL;  pEl = pEl->next )
      pushBack( pEl->date, pEl->amount);
}
```

```cpp
// Assignment:
List& List::operator=( const List& src)
{
   // Release memory for all elements:
   ListEl *pEl = first,
          *next = NULL;
   for(   ; pEl != NULL;  pEl = next)
   {
      next = pEl->next;
      delete pEl;
   }
   first = last = NULL;

   // Appends the elements of src to an empty list.
   pEl = src.first;
   for(   ; pEl != NULL;  pEl = pEl->next )
      pushBack( pEl->date, pEl->amount);

   return *this;
}

// All other methods unchanged.


// -------------------------------------------------------
//  List_t.cpp
//  Tests the class List with copy constructor and
//  assignment.
// -------------------------------------------------------
#include "List.h"

int main()
{
   cout << "\n * * *  Testing the class List  * * *\n"
        << endl;
   List  list1;              // A list
   cout << list1 << endl;    // The list is still empty.

   Date date( 11,8,1999);    // Insert 3 elements.
   double amount( +1234.56);
   list1.pushBack( date, amount);

   date.setDate( 1, 1, 2002);
   amount = -1000.99;
   list1.pushBack( date, amount);

   date.setDate( 2, 29, 2000);
   amount = +5000.11;
   list1.pushBack( date, amount);
```

```
        cout << "\nThree elements have been inserted!"
                "\nContent of the list:" << endl;
        cout << list1 << endl;

        cout << "\nPress return to continue! "; cin.get();

        List list2( list1);
        cout << "A copy of the 1st list has been created!\n"
                "Contents of the copy:\n" << endl;
        cout << list2 << endl;

        cout << "\nRemove the first element from the list:\n";

        ListEl *ptrEl = ptrEl = list1.front();
        if( ptrEl != NULL)
        {
           cout << "To be deleted:  " << *ptrEl << endl;
           list1.popFront();
        }
        cout << "\nContent of the list:\n";
        cout << list1 << endl;

        list1 = list2;           // Reassign the copy.

        cout << "The copy has been assigned to the 1st list!\n"
                "Contents after assignment:\n" << endl;
        cout << list1 << endl;

        return 0;
}
```

Exercise 2

```cpp
// -----------------------------------------------------
// floatArr.h : Dynamic arrays of floating-point numbers.
// -----------------------------------------------------
#ifndef _FLOATARR_
#define _FLOATARR_

#include <iostream>
using namespace std;

class FloatArr
{
   private:
     float* arrPtr;      // Dynamic member
     int max;            // Maximum quantity without
                         // reallocating new storage.
     int cnt;            // Number of present array elements

     void expand( int newMax);   // Helps enlarge the array

   public:
     // Constructors , destructor,
     // assignment, subscript operator, and method length()
     // as before in this chapter.

     // Methods to append a floating-point number
     // or an array of floating-point numbers:
     void append( float val);
     void append( const FloatArr& v);
     FloatArr& operator+=( float val)
     {
         append( val);   return *this;
     }

     FloatArr& operator+=( const FloatArr& v)
     {
         append(v);   return *this;
     }

     // Methods to insert a floating-point number
     // or an array of floating-point numbers:
     bool insert( float val, int pos);
     bool insert( const FloatArr& v, int pos );

     bool remove(int pos);      // Delete at position pos.
     // To output the array
     friend ostream& operator<<( ostream& os,
                              const FloatArr& v);
};
#endif   // _FLOATARR_
```

```cpp
// --------------------------------------------------
// FloatArr.cpp
// Implements the methods of FloatArr.
// --------------------------------------------------

#include "floatArr.h"

//  Constructors, destructor, assignment,
//  and subscript operator unchanged.

//  ---  The new functions  ---

// Private auxiliary function to enlarge the array.
void FloatArr::expand( int new)
{
   if( newMax == max)
      return;
   max = newMax;
   if( newMax < cnt)
      cnt = newMax;
   float *temp = new float[newMax];
   for( int i = 0; i < cnt; ++i)
      temp[i] = arrPtr[i];

   delete[] arrPtr;
   arrPtr = temp;
}

// Append floating-point number or an array of floats.
void FloatArr::append( float val)
{
   if( cnt+1 > max)
      expand( cnt+1);

   arrPtr[cnt++] = val;
}

void FloatArr::append( const FloatArr& v)
{
   if( cnt + v.cnt > max)
      expand( cnt + v.cnt);

   int count = v.cnt;                 // Necessary if v == *this

   for( int i=0; i < count; ++i)
     arrPtr[cnt++] = v.arrPtr[i];
}
```

```
// Insert a float or an array of floats
bool FloatArr::insert( float val, int pos)
{
   return insert( FloatArr(1,val), pos);
}

bool FloatArr::insert( const FloatArr& v, int pos )
{
   if( pos < 0 || pos >= cnt)
      return false;                  // Invalid position

   if( max < cnt + v.cnt)
      expand(cnt + v.cnt);
   int i;
   for( i = cnt-1; i >= pos; --i)      // Shift up
      arrPtr[i+v.cnt] = arrPtr[i];     // starting at pos
   for( i = 0; i < v.cnt; ++i)         // Fill gap.
      arrPtr[i+pos] = v.arrPtr[i];
   cnt = cnt + v.cnt;
   return true;
}

// To delete
bool FloatArr::remove(int pos)
{
   if( pos >= 0 && pos < cnt)
   {
      for( int i = pos; i < cnt-1; ++i)
         arrPtr[i] = arrPtr[i+1];
      --cnt;
      return true;
   }
   else
      return false;
}

// Output the array
ostream& operator<<( ostream& os, const FloatArr& v)
{
   int w = os.width();              // Save field width.
   for( float *p = v.arrPtr; p < v.arrPtr + v.cnt; ++p)
   {
      os.width(w);    os << *p;
   }
   return os;
}
```

```cpp
// ---------------------------------------------------
// FloatV_t.cpp
// Tests the class FloatArr.
// ---------------------------------------------------
#include "FloatArr.h"
#include <iostream>
#include <iomanip>
using namespace std;

int main()
{
    FloatArr v(10);         // Array v for 10 float values
    FloatArr w(15, 1.0F);   // Initialize the array w of
                            // 15 float values with 1.0.
    cout << " Current total of elements in v: "
        << v.length() << endl;
    cout << " Current total of elements in w: "
        << w.length() << endl;

    float x = -5.0F;             // Append values.
    for( ; x < 6 ; x += 1.7F)
       v.append(x);

    v += v;                      // Also possible!

    cout << "\nThe array elements after appending:"
        << endl;
    cout << setw(5) << v << endl;

    const FloatArr cv(v);        // Copy constructor
                                 // creates const object.
    cout << "\nThe copy of v has been created.\n";
    cout << "\nThe array elements of the copy:\n"
        << setw(5) << v << endl;

    w.remove(3);            // Erase the element at
                            // position 3.
    w.append(10.0F);        // Add a new element.
    w.append(20.0F);        // And once more!

    v = w;
    cout << "\nAssignment done.\n";
    cout << "\nThe elements after assigning: \n"
        << setw(5) << v << endl;
    v.insert( cv, 0);
    cout << "\nThe elements after inserting "
            " the copy at position 0: \n"
        << setw(5) << v << endl;
    return 0;
}
```

chapter

Inheritance

This chapter describes how derived classes can be constructed from existing classes by inheritance. Besides defining derived classes, we will also discuss

- how members are redefined
- how objects are constructed and destroyed, and
- how access control to base classes can be realized.

■ CONCEPT OF INHERITANCE

Is relation

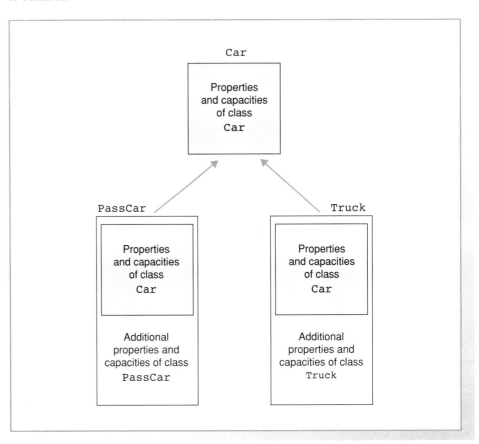

☐ Base Classes and Derived Classes

Inheritance allows new classes to be constructed on the basis of existing classes. The new *derived class* "inherits" the data and methods of the so-called *base class*. But you can add more characteristics and functionality to the new class.

A fleet management program used by a car hire company needs to handle all kinds of vehicles—automobiles, motorcycles, trucks, and so on. All of these vehicles have an identification number that indicates the vehicle, the manufacturer, and the vehicle status, such as "hired," "repair shop," and so on. Additionally, operations such as "modify status" are required for the class.

To differentiate between vehicle types, various classes are derived from the base class `Car`, such as `PassCar`, which is used to represent passenger-carrying vehicles. This class has additional attributes, such as the number of seats, type, sunroof (yes/no), and various additional operations.

☐ Is Relationship

An object of the `PassCar` type *is* a special object of the `Car` class. A passenger vehicle is a special kind of car. In cases like this we can say that the derived class establishes an *is* relationship to the base class.

We distinguish between this close relationship and a so-called *has* relationship. As already mentioned, a *has* relationship occurs between two classes when an member of one class has another class type. An `Account` object has a `string` object to represent the name of the account holder, for example.

☐ Data Abstraction and Reusability

Inheritance has a number of important benefits for software developers:

- *data abstraction*: General characteristics and abilities can be handled by generic (base) classes and specializations can be organized in hierarchical relationships by means of derived classes. This makes it easier to manage complex situations and relationships.
- *re-usability*: Classes that you have defined and tested can be reused and adapted to perform new tasks. The base class implementation need not be known for this purpose: only the public interfaces are required.

▪ DERIVED CLASSES

Defining a derived class

```
class C : public B
{
   private:
     // Declaration of additional private
     // data members and member functions
   public:
     // Declaration of additional public
     // data members and member functions
};
```

Direct and indirect derivation

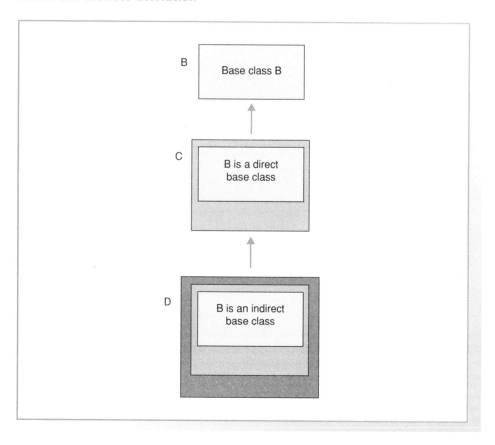

When you define a derived class, the base class, the additional data members and methods, and the access control to the base class are defined.

The opposite page shows a schematic definition of a derived class, C. The C class inherits the B class, which is defined in the public section following the colon. The private and public sections contain additional members of the C class.

☐ Access to Public Members in the Base Class

Access privileges to the base class B are designated by the public keyword that precedes the B. In other words,

- all the public members in base class B are publicly available in the derived class C.

This kind of inheritance ports the public interface of the base class to the derived class where it is extended by additional declarations. Thus, objects of the derived class can call the public methods of the base class. A public base class, therefore, implements the *is* relationship; this is quite common.

There are some less common cases where access to the members of the base class needs to be restricted or prohibited. Only the methods of class C can still access the public members of B, but not the users of that class. You can use private or protected derivation to achieve this (these techniques will be discussed later).

☐ Access to Private Members of the Base Class

The private members of the base class are protected in all cases. That is,

- the methods of the derived class cannot access the private members of the base class.

Imagine the consequences if this were not so: you would be able to hack access to the base class by simply defining a derived class, thus undermining any protection offered by data encapsulation.

☐ Direct and Indirect Base Classes

The derived class C can itself be a base class for a further class, D. This allows for class hierarchies. Class B then becomes an indirect base class for class D.

In the graphic on the opposite page, the arrow ↑ means directly derived from. That is, class D is a direct derivation of class C and an indirect derivation of B.

■ MEMBERS OF DERIVED CLASSES

Base class Car **and derived class** PassCar

```cpp
// car.h:   Definition of baseclass Car and
//          of the derived class PassCar
// -------------------------------------------------
#include <iostream>
#include <string>
using namespace std;

class Car                                 // Base class
{
  private:
    long    nr;
    string producer;
  public:                                 // Constructor:
    Car( long n = 0L, const string& prod = "");
                                          // Access methods:
    long  getNr(void) const { return nr; }
    void  setNr( long n ) { nr = n; }

    const string& getProd() const{ return producer; }
    void  setProd(const string& p){ producer = p; }

    void display( void ) const;    // Display a car
};

class PassCar : public Car          // Derived class
{
  private:
    string passCarType;
    bool    sunRoof;
  public:                                 // Constructor:
    PassCar( const string& tp, bool sd,
             int n = 0 , const string& h = "");
                                          // Access methods:
    const string& getType() const{ return passCarType; }
    void  setType( const string s) { passCarType = s; }
    bool  getSunRoof() const    { return sunRoof; }
    void  setSunRoof( bool b )  { sunRoof = b; }
    void  display() const;
};
```

Let's look at the example on the opposite page to illustrate how derived classes are defined. The `Car` class and a derived class `PassCar` are defined in the example.

☐ Data Members and Methods

The base class `Car` contains two data members, `nr` and `producer`, which are used to represent an identification number and the name of the manufacturer. The derived class `PassCar` inherits these data members. Thus, an object of the `PassCar` class also contains the data members `nr` and `producer`. The object includes a so-called *base subobject* of type `Car`.

The `PassCar` class additionally contains the data members `passCarType` and `sunRoof` to represent a passenger vehicle with or without a sunroof. So a `PassCar` type object has a total of four data members. For the sake of simplicity, we have omitted further data members, such as the number of seats, etc.

The base class `Car` contains a constructor, access methods, and the method `display()`, which is used for screen output. The methods are also inherited by the derived class `PassCar`.

In the `PassCar` class a constructor, additional access methods, and a second output function also called `display()` are declared. The derived class thus inherits a method called `display()` and declares a method with the same name. The `display()` method is said to have been redefined.

Every member function and every data member in a derived class can be redefined. The member assumes a new meaning for the derived class. The member inherited from the base class is also available in the derived class and will retain its original meaning. We will be looking at this point in more detail later.

☐ Public Interface

Since the `Car` class is a `public` base class of the `PassCar` class, all the `public` members of the base class are available in the derived class. For example, you can call the `getNr()` method for an object named `cabrio` in the `PassCar` class.

Example: `cout << "Car number: "<< cabrio.getNr();`

The public interface of the derived class thus comprises

- the `public` members of the base class and
- the `public` members additionally defined in the derived class.

■ MEMBER ACCESS

Accessing members of base class `Car`

```
class Car
{
  private:
    long nr;
    string producer;

  public:
    . . .
    long getNr(void);
    . . .
}
```
                                                    N
                                              not ok
                                              ok

```
class PassCar : public Car
{
  private:
    string passCarType;
    bool   sunRoof;
  public:
    . . .
}
```
                                              ok

```
void PassCar::display( void) const
{
  cout << "\nCar number: "
       << getNr();
  cout << "\nProducer: "
       << getProd();

  cout << "Type: "<< passCarType;
  cout << "Type: "<< passCarTyp
  if( sunRoof) cout << "yes";
  else         cout << " no";
  cout << endl;
}
```

☐ Access to Additional Members

The methods of derived classes can access any member additionally defined in the derived class.

Example: `const string& getType() const`
        `{   return passCarType;   }`

The `getType()` method directly accesses the private data member `passCarType` in the `PassCar` class in this example.

☐ Access to Private Members of the Base Class

However, a private member of the base class is not directly accessible for the methods of the derived class. The output function `display()` in the derived class `PassCar`, for example, cannot contain the following statement:

Example: `cout << "Producer: " << producer;`

As `producer` is a private data member of the base class `Car`, the compiler would issue an error message at this point.

Methods belonging to derived classes only have indirect access to the private data members of the base class. They use access methods in the `public` declaration of the base class for this purpose. The opposite page shows a version of the `display()` method that calls the `get` methods in its base class `Car`.

When you call an access method, you do not need to state the method's base class. The base class is identified by the `this` pointer, which is passed implicitly as an argument. The call to `getProd()` on the opposite page is thus equivalent to:

Example: `this->getProd();`

☐ Name Lookup

The following rules apply when searching for the name of a method:

- the compiler looks for the name of the method called in the derived class first
- if the name cannot be found, the compiler walks one step up the tree and looks for a *public* method with that name.

The above example thus calls the `getProd()` in the base class `Car`, as the method is not defined in the `PassCar` class.

■ REDEFINING MEMBERS

New version of method `display()`

```
// Within file Car.cpp
// This version of method PassCar::display() calls
// the method display() of the base class.
// ---------------------------------------------------

void PassCar::display( void) const
{
   Car::display();                // Method in base class

   cout << "Type:        " << passCarType;
   cout << "\nSunroof:   ";
   if(sunRoof)
       cout << "yes "<< endl;
   else
       cout << "no " << endl;
}
```

☐ Redefinition

There are two options for the names of data members or methods in derived classes:

1. The name does not occur in the base class → no redefinition.

2. The name already exists in the base class → redefinition.

In the second case, the member of the same name continues to exist unchanged in the base class. In other words, redefining members in a derived class has no effect on the base class.

However, the name lookup rules for the compiler lead to the following scenario:

- if a member is redefined in a derived class, it will mask the corresponding member in the base class.

This situation is similar to the one seen for local and global variables. A local variable will mask a previously defined global variable with the same name.

☐ Redefinition and Overloading

Normally, *methods* are redefined in derived classes. This adopts the methods to the new features of the class. When a method is redefined, the signature and the return type of the method can be changed. However, a redefinition does not overload functions since the derived class has a different scope.

Redefining a method will always mask a method with the same name in the base class. Of course, you can overload methods within the same class, and this means you can repeatedly redefine a base class method for a derived class.

☐ Access to the Members in the Base Class

If you redefine a method in a derived class, this does not alter the fact that the base class method still exists. If the method was declared in the `public` section of the base class, you can call it to redefine a method. The range `::` operator is used to access the base class method.

The new version of the `display()` method opposite illustrates this point. The `display()` method defined in the base class is used to output the data members of the base class. To do so, you must use the range operator with the name of the base class. Otherwise the `display()` method in the derived class will call itself and head off into an indefinite recursion.

■ CONSTRUCTING AND DESTROYING DERIVED CLASSES

First version of the constructor of PassCar

```
// First version of the constructor of PassCar
// -----------------------------------------------
PassCar::PassCar(const string& tp, bool sr, int n,
        const string& hs)
{
    setNr(n);               // Initial values for data
    setProd(hs);            // members of the base class.

    passCarType  = tp;      // Initial values for data mem-
    sunRoof = sr;           // bers of the derived class
}
```

Second version with base class initializer

```
// Second version of the constructors of PassCar
// -----------------------------------------------
PassCar::PassCar(const string& tp, bool sr, int n,
        const string& hs)  : Car( n, hs)
{
    passCarType  = tp;      // Initial values for data mem-
    sunRoof = sr;           // bers of the derived class
}
```

Third version with base class and member initializer

```
// Third version of the constructor of PassCar
// -----------------------------------------------
PassCar::PassCar(const string& tp, bool sr, int n,
        const string& hs)
    : Car( n, hs), passCarType( tp ), sunRoof( sr )
{
    // There remains nothing to do
}
```

☐ Constructor Calls

The constructor of a derived class is required to create an object of the derived class type. As the derived class contains all the members of the base class, the base sub-object must also be created and initialized. The base class constructor is called to perform this task. Unless otherwise defined, this will be the default constructor.

The order in which the constructors are called is important. The base class constructor is called first, then the derived class constructor. The object is thus constructed from its core outwards.

The first version of the constructor for `PassCar`, as shown opposite, sets initial values by calling the access methods of the base class. An implicit call to the default constructor of the base class occurs prior to this, and the base sub-object is initialized with default values. This process has the same drawbacks as the technique of creating objects with member objects. A default constructor must be available in the base class and initialization with incorrect values before assigning live values impacts the response of the program.

☐ Base Initializer

If the base class contains a constructor with parameters, it makes sense to call this constructor. This immediately initializes the data members with correct values. A *base initializer* for the constructor of the derived class can be defined for this purpose.

The second version of the constructor for `PassCar` contains a base initializer.

Example: `Car( n, hs )`

The syntax of the base initializer for base sub-objects is similar to that of the member initializer for member sub-objects. This means that you can state both the base and the member initializer in a list separated by commas. The third version of the `PassCar` constructor illustrates this point.

☐ Destroying Objects

When an object is destroyed, the destructor of the derived class is first called, followed by the destructor of the base class. The reverse order of the constructor calls applies.

You need to define a destructor for a derived class if actions performed by the constructor need to be reversed. The base class destructor need not be called explicitly as it is executed implicitly.

■ OBJECTS OF DERIVED CLASSES

Sample program

```
// car_t.cpp:  Testing the base class Car and
//             the derived class PassCar.
// ----------------------------------------------------
#include "car.h"

int main()
{
    const PassCar beetle("Beetle", false, 3421, "VW");
    beetle.display();
    cout << "\nAnd the passenger car number again: "
         << beetle.getNr() << endl;

    PassCar cabrio("Carrera", true);
    cabrio.setNr(1000);
    cabrio.setProd("Porsche");
    cabrio.display();
    cout << "\nOnly data of the base class: ";
    cabrio.Car::display();
    return 0;
}
```

Screen output

```
----------------------------------------------
Car number:    3421
Producer:      VW
Type:          Beetle
Sunroof:       no

And the passenger car number again: 3421

----------------------------------------------
Car number:    1000
Producer:      Porsche
Type:          Carrera
Sunroof:       yes

Only data of the base class:
----------------------------------------------
Car number:    1000
Producer:      Porsche
```

☐ Declaring Objects

The program opposite illustrates how objects of derived classes can be used. Two objects, `beetle` and `cabrio`, of the derived class `PassCar` type are declared. As the `PassCar` class does not contain a default constructor, both objects must be initialized. However, it is sufficient to state a `PassCar` type with or without a sunroof as default values exist for all other data members.

The object `beetle` is declared as `const` just to show that the `get` methods and the `display()` method can also be called for constant objects since they were declared as read-only methods.

However, the following call is invalid:

Example: `beetle.setNr( 7564 );`   `// Error`

This means you have to correctly define all the initial values for the object when you declare it.

☐ Calling Redefined Methods

When you call a redefined method, the object type determines what version of the method will be executed. In the `PassCar` class the method `display()` has been redefined. The statement

Example: `cabrio.display();`

also outputs the additional data members `passCarType` and `sunRoof`. However, in the case of the van object in the `Car` class, calling

Example: `van.display();`

will execute the method in the base class.

☐ Calling Methods in the Base Class

You may be wondering if a base class method can be called for an object of a derived class, if the method has been redefined in the derived class. This is possible using the scope resolution operator, `::`.

If you want to display the basic data of the `cabrio` object, you can use a direct call to the base class method `display()` to do so.

Example: `cabrio.Car::display();`

The name of the method is preceded by the name of the base class and the scope resolution operator in this case.

■ PROTECTED MEMBERS

Sample classes

```cpp
// safe.h : The classes Safe and Castle
// -------------------------------------------------
#include <iostream>
using namespace std;

class Safe
{
   private:
       int topSecret;
   protected:
       int secret;
       void setTopSecret( int n) { topSecret = n;}
       int  getTopSecret() const { return topSecret;}
       void setSecret( int n){ secret = n;}
       int  getSecret() const { return secret;}
   public:
       int noSecret;
       Safe()
       { topSecret = 100; secret = 10; noSecret = 0; }
};

class Castle : public Safe
{
   public:
    Castle()
    {
      // topSecret = 10;       // Error, because private
      setTopSecret(10);        // ok, because protected
      secret = 1;              // ok, because protected
      noSecret = 0;            // ok, because public
    }
    void test()
    {
    // top.Secret = 200;       // Error, because private
       setTopSecret(200);      // ok, because protected
       secret = 20;            // ok, because protected
       noSecret = 2;           // ok, because public
    }
};
```

Access to Sheltered Members

The private members of a base class are equally inaccessible for the methods and `friend` functions of a derived class.

When you create a class hierarchy you may want require the methods and `friend` functions of a derived class to communicate directly with the members of the base class. This would be particularly necessary if the base class contained members for use as building blocks for derived classes but not for general purpose use.

For example, a class used to represent a window on screen could contain the dimensions and other characteristics of a general windows. The characteristics need protecting; however, methods in derived classes will still need direct access.

Protected Members

To allow methods and `friend` functions access to the sheltered members of a base class, let's introduce an additional level of access control between `private` and `public`. This is achieved by means of *protected declarations*.

A member declared `protected` is sheltered from external access just like a `private` member. That means, a `protected` member is inaccessible for base class objects and any classes derived from the base class. However, in contrast to a `private` member, methods and `friend` functions of derived classes can access the member.

The classes defined opposite, `Safe` and `Castle`, show that `protected` members of the base class can be accessed directly in a derived class. In contrast to this, `protected` members are inaccessible to users of these classes.

Example:
```
Castle   treasure;
treasure.topSecret = 1;    // Error: private
treasure.secret = 2;       // Error: protected
treasure.setTopSecret(5);  // Error: protected
treasure.noSecret = 10;    // ok
```

`Protected` declarations should be used with caution. If you change the declaration of a `protected` member, every class derived from this class must be examined to ascertain whether additional modifications are necessary.

EXERCISES

For exercise 1

Class `Truck` being derived from class `Car`

Additional data members:

	Type
Number of axles	`int`
Load capacity	`double`

Additional methods:

```
void  setAxles( int a );
int   getAxles() const;
void  setCapacity( double cp );
void  getCapacity() const;

void display() const;
```

Exercise 1

The classes `Car` and `PassCar` are to modify to allow objects to be created and destroyed. In addition, the class `Truck` is to be added to the class hierarchy.

- Change the classes `Car` and `PassCar` to make the constructor issue the following message:

  `"Creating an object of type ... ."`
- Define a destructor for the `Car` and `PassCar` classes. The destructor should issue the following message:

  `"Destroying an object of type ...."`
- Then define the class `Truck`, which is derived from `Car`, using the data members shown opposite, a constructor, a destructor, and the additional methods shown opposite.
- Implement the constructor for the `Truck` class—the constructor should again issue a suitable message. Use the base initializer to initialize the data members of `Car`.
- Define a destructor for `Truck`—the destructor should again issue a suitable message for trucks.
- To test your class, create and display a `Truck` type object in your `main` function. If required by the user, enable your program to create and display objects of the types `PassCar` and `Car`.

Observe how the various objects and member objects are created and destroyed.

Exercise 2

Derive two classes, `DepAcc` and `SavAcc`, from the `Account` class, which was defined in Chapter 14, in the section titled "Const Objects and Methods." Additionally define an overdraft limit and an interest rate for the `DepAcc` class. The `SavAcc` contains the members of the base class and an interest rate.

- For both classes, define constructors to provide default values for all parameters, add access methods, and add a `display()` method for screen output.
- Test the new classes by initializing objects of the `DepAcc` and `SavAcc` types in the object declarations and outputting them. Then modify both a savings and a deposit account interactively and display the new values.

Exercise 3

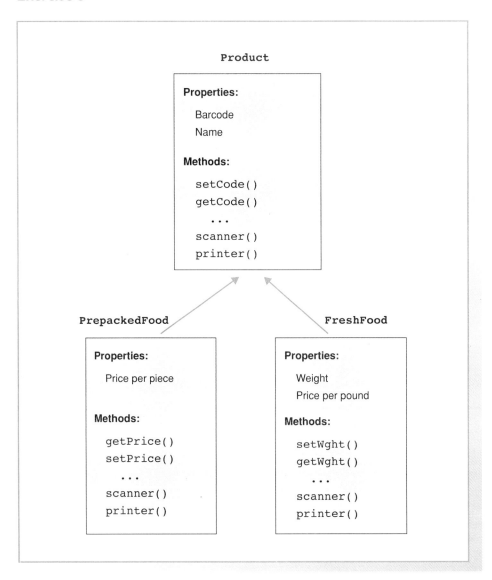

Exercise 3

A supermarket chain has asked you to develop an automatic checkout system. All products are identifiable by means of a barcode and the product name. Groceries are either sold in packages or by weight. Packed goods have fixed prices. The price of groceries sold by weight is calculated by multiplying the weight by the current price per kilo.

Develop the classes needed to represent the products first and organize them hierarchically. The `Product` class, which contains generic information on all products (barcode, name, etc.), can be used as a base class.

- The `Product` class contains two data members of type `long` used for storing barcodes and the product name. Define a constructor with parameters for both data members. Add default values for the parameters to provide a default constructor for the class. In addition to the access methods `setCode()` and `getCode()`, also define the methods `scanner()` and `printer()`. For test purposes, these methods will simply output product data on screen or read the data of a product from the keyboard.

- The next step involves developing special cases of the `Product` class. Define two classes derived from `Product`, `PrepackedFood` and `Fresh-Food`. In addition to the product data, the `PrepackedFood` class should contain the unit price and the `FreshFood` class should contain a weight and a price per kilo as data members.

  In both classes define a constructor with parameters providing default-values for all data members. Use both the base and member initializer.

  Define the access methods needed for the new data members. Also redefine the methods `scanner()` and `printer()` to take the new data members into consideration.

- Test the various classes in a `main` function that creates two objects each of the types `Product`, `PrepackedFood` and `FreshFood`. One object of each type is fully initialized in the object definition. Use the default constructor to create the other object. Test the `get` and `set` methods and the `scanner()` method and display the products on screen.

SOLUTIONS

Exercise 1

```cpp
// ----------------------------------------------------
// Car.h :   Defines the base class Car and
//           the derived classes PassCar and Truck
// ----------------------------------------------------
#ifndef _CAR_H_
#define _CAR_H_

#include <iostream>
#include <string>
using namespace std;

class Car
{
  // See previous definition in this chapter
};

class PassCar : public Car
{
  // See previous definition in this chapter
};

class Truck : public Car
{
  private:
    int    axles;
    double tons;

  public:
    Truck( int a, double t, int n, const string& hs);
    ~Truck();

    void   setAxles(int l){ axles = l;}
    int    getAxles() const    { return axles; }
    void   setCapacity( double t) { tons = t;}
    double getCapacity() const    { return tons; }

     void display() const;
};

#endif
```

```cpp
// -------------------------------------------------------
// car.cpp
// Implements the methods of Car, PassCar, and Truck
// -------------------------------------------------------
#include "car.h"
// -------------------------------------------------------
// The methods of base class Car:
Car::Car( long n, const string& prod)
{
    cout << "Creating an object of type Car." << endl;
    nr = n;   producer = prod;
}
Car::~Car()
{
    cout << "Destroying an object of type Car" << endl;
}
void Car::display() const
{
    cout << "\n-------------------------- "
         << "\nCar number:   " << nr
         << "\nProducer:     " << producer
         << endl;
}


// -------------------------------------------------------
// The methods of the derived class PassCar:
PassCar::PassCar(const string& tp, bool sd, int n,
        const string& hs)
    : Car( n, hs), PassCarTyp( tp ), sunRoof( sd )
{
   cout << "I create an object of type PassCar." << endl;
}
PassCar::~PassCar()
{
    cout << "\nDestroying an object of type PassCar"
         << endl;
}

void PassCar::display( void) const
{
   Car::display();              // Base class method
   cout << "Type:         " << passCarType
        << "\nSunroof:       ";
   if(sunRoof)
       cout << "yes "<< endl;
   else
       cout << "no " << endl;
}
```

```
// ----------------------------------------------------
// The methods of the derived class Truck:
Truck::Truck( int a, double t, int n, const string& hs)
        : Car( n, hs), axles(a), tons(t)
{
   cout << "Creating an object of type Truck." << endl;
}
Truck::~Truck()
{
    cout << "\nDestroying an object of type Truck\n";
}
void Truck::display() const
{
    Car::display();
    cout <<   "Axles:       " << axles
         << "\nCapacity:    " << tons << " long tons\n";
}

// ----------------------------------------------------
// Car_t.cpp : Tests the base class Car and
//             the derived classes PassCar and Truck.
// ----------------------------------------------------
#include "car.h"
int main()
{
    Truck toy(5, 7.5, 1111, "Volvo");
    toy.display();
    char c;
    cout << "\nDo you want to create an object of type "
         << " PassCar? (y/n) ";  cin >> c;
    if( c == 'y' || c == 'Y')
    {
       const PassCar beetle("Beetle", false, 3421, "VW");
       beetle.display();
    }

    cout << "\nDo you want to create an object "
         << " of type car? (y/n) ";   cin >> c;
    if( c == 'y' || c == 'Y')
    {
       const Car oldy(3421, "Rolls Royce");
       oldy.display();
    }
    return 0;
}
```

Exercise 2

```cpp
// ----------------------------------------------------
// account.h:
// Defines the classes Account, DepAcc, and SavAcc.
// ----------------------------------------------------
#ifndef _ACCOUNT_H
#define _ACCOUNT_H
#include <iostream>
#include <iomanip>
#include <string>
using namespace std;
class Account
{
  private:
    string name;   unsigned long nr;    double balance;
  public:
    Account(const string& s="X", unsigned long n
            = 1111111L, double st = 0.0)
    : name(s), nr(n), balance(st)
    { }
    const string& getName() const  { return name; }
    void  setName(const string& n) { name = n;}
    unsigned long getNr() const { return nr; }
    void setNr(unsigned long n) { nr = n; }
    double getBalance() const    { return balance; }
    void   setBalance(double st){ balance = st; }
    void display()
    {  cout << fixed << setprecision(2)
            << "----------------------------------------\n"
            << "Account holder:          " << name   << endl
            << "Account number:          " << nr     << endl
            << "Balance of the account:" << balance <<endl;
    }
};

class DepAcc : public Account
{
  private:
    double limit;                   // Overdraft limit
    double interest;                // Interest
  public:
    DepAcc(const string& s = "X",
           unsigned long n = 1111111L, double st = 0.0,
           double li = 0.0, double ra = 0.0)
    : Account(s, n, st), limit(li), interest(ra)
    { }
```

```
                                        // Access methods:
    double getLimit() const { return limit; }
    void    setLimit(double lt){ limit = lt; }
    double getInterest() const { return interest; }
    void    setInterest(double sl){ interest = sl; }

    void display()
    {
        Account::display();
        cout << fixed << setprecision(2)
            << "Overdraft limit: " << limit << endl
            << "Interest rate:   " << interest  << endl
            << "-------------------------------\n"
            << endl << endl;
    }
};

class SavAcc: public Account
{
  private:
    double interest;                 // compound interest
  public:
    SavAcc(const string& s = "X",
           unsigned long n = 1111111L, double st = 0.0,
           double in = 0.0)
    : Account(s, n, st), interest(in)
    { }

    // Access methods.
    double getInterest() const   { return interest; }
    void    setInterest(double in){ interest = in; }

    void display()
    {
        Account::display();
        cout << fixed << setprecision(2)
            << "Interest rate:    " << interest << endl
            << "-------------------------------\n"
            << endl << endl;
    }
};

#endif
```

```cpp
// ------------------------------------------------------
// account_t.cpp
// Tests the classes DepAcc and SavAcc
// derived from class Account
// ------------------------------------------------------
#include "account.h"

int main()
{
   string s;
   double db;

   SavAcc mickey("Mickey Mouse", 1234567,
                 2.40, 3.5);
   mickey.display();

   cout << "New name:            "; getline(cin, s);
   cout << "New interest rate: "; cin >> db;

   mickey.setName(s);
   mickey.setInterest(db);
   mickey.display();

   DepAcc dag("Donald Duck", 7654321,
              -1245.56, 10000, 12.9);
   dag.display();

   cout << "New limit:          "; cin >> db;
   dag.setLimit(db);
   dag.display();

   return 0;
}
```

Exercise 3

```cpp
// ---------------------------------------------------
// product.h : Defines the classes
//             Product, PrepackedFood, and FreshFood
// ---------------------------------------------------
#ifndef _PRODUCT_H
#define _PRODUCT_H
#include <iostream>
#include <iomanip>
#include <string>
using namespace std;

class Product
{
  private:
    long   bar;
    string name;

  public:
    Product(long b = 0L, const string& s = "")
    : bar(b), name(s)
    {  }
    void setCode(long b) { bar = b; }
    long getCode() const { return bar; }
    void  setName(const string& s){ name = s; }
    const string& getName() const { return name; }
    void scanner()
    {
       cout << "\nBarcode:    "; cin >> bar;
       cout <<   "Name:         "; cin >> name;
       cin.sync(); cin.clear();
    }
    void printer() const
    {
       cout << "\n------------------------------"
            << "\nBarcode:    " << bar
            << "\nName:        " << name
            << endl;
    }
};

class PrepackedFood : public Product
{
  private:
    double pce_price;
```

```
public:
  PrepackedFood(double p = 0.0,long b = 0L,
                const string& s = "")
    : Product(b, s), pce_price(p)
    {}
  void    setPrice(double p){ pce_price = p;}
  double getPrice()const    { return pce_price; }
  void scanner()
  {   Product::scanner();
      cout << "Price per piece:    "; cin >> pce_price;
  }
  void printer() const
  {   Product::printer();
      cout << fixed << setprecision(2)
           << "Price per piece:    " << pce_price << endl;
  }
};

class FreshFood : public Product
{
  private:
    double wght;
    double lbs_price;

  public:
    FreshFood(double g = 0.0, double p = 0.0,
              long b = 0L, const string& s = "")
      : Product(b, s), wght(g), lbs_price(p) {}
    void    setWght(double g) { wght = g;}
    double getWght()const    { return wght; }
    void    setPrice(double p) { lbs_price = p;}
    double getPrice()const    { return lbs_price; }
    void scanner()
    {   Product::scanner();
        cout << "Weight(lbs):  "; cin >> wght;
        cout << "Price/lbs:    "; cin >> lbs_price;
        cin.sync(); cin.clear();
    }
    void printer() const
    {
        Product::printer();
        cout << fixed << setprecision(2)
             << "Price per Lbs:   " << lbs_price
             << "\nWeight:       " << wght
             << "\nTotal:        " << lbs_price * wght
             << endl;
    }
};
#endif
```

```
// --------------------------------------------------------
// product_t.cpp
// Tests classes Product, PrepackedFood, and FreshFood.
// --------------------------------------------------------

#include "product.h"

int main()
{
    Product p1(12345L, "Flour"), p2;

    p1.printer();                 // Output the first product

    p2.setName("Sugar");          // Set the data members
    p2.setCode(543221);

    p2.printer();                 // Output the second product

                                  // Prepacked products:
    PrepackedFood pf1(0.49, 23456, "Salt"), pf2;

    pf1.printer();                // Output the first
                                  // prepacked product
    cout << "\n Input data of a prepacked product: ";
    pf2.scanner();                // Input and output
    pf2.printer();                // data of 2nd product

    FreshFood pu1(1.5, 1.69, 98765, "Grapes"), pu2;

    pu1.printer();                // Output first item
                                  // fresh food
    cout <<"\n Input data for a prepacked product: ";
    pu2.scanner();                // Input and output
    pu2.printer();                // data of 2nd product.

    cout << "\n-----------------------------"
         << "\n-----------------------------"
         << "\nAgain in detail: \n"
         << fixed << setprecision(2)
         << "\nBarcode:      " << pu2.getCode()
         << "\nName:         " << pu2.getName()
         << "\nPrice per Lbs: " << pu2.getPrice()
         << "\nWeight:       " << pu2.getWght()
         << "\nEnd price:    " << pu2.getPrice()
                                  * pu2.getWght()
         << endl;

    return 0;
}
```

chapter 24

Type Conversion in Class Hierarchies

This chapter describes implicit type conversion within class hierarchies, which occurs in the context of assignments and function calls.

In addition, explicit type casting in class hierarchies is discussed, in particular, upcasting and downcasting.

■ CONVERTING TO BASE CLASSES

Example for implicit conversion

```cpp
#include "car.h"

bool compare( Car&, Car&);

int main()
{
   PassCar beetle("New Beetle", false, 3421, "VW"),
           miata( "Miata", true, 2512, "Mazda");

   bool res = compare( beetle, miata);
   // ...
}
                              // ok!
                              // Implicit conversion
                              // to base class.
                              // Car& a = beetle;
                              // Car& b = miata;

bool compare( Car& a, Car& b)
{

   // Here a is the base part of beetle,
   // b is the base part of miata.
   // If this is inconvenient, an explicit
   // type cast to type PassCar has to be performed.

}
```

☐ Implicit Conversion

If a class is derived from another class by `public` inheritance, the derived class assumes the characteristics and features of the base class. Objects of the derived class type then become *special* objects of the base class, just like an automobile is a special type of vehicle.

You can utilize the *is* relationship when handling objects. It is possible to assign an object of a derived class to an object of the base class. This causes an *implicit type conversion* to a base class type.

The base class thus becomes a generic term for multiple special cases. Given that the classes `PassCar` and `Truck` were derived from the `Car` class, objects of the `PassCar` or `Truck` type can always be managed like objects of `Car` type.

☐ Assignments

Implicit type conversion in class hierarchies occurs in assignments to

- base class objects
- pointers or references to the base class.

☐ Function Calls

Additionally, a similar kind of implicit type conversion takes place for the arguments of function calls.

Given the function `compare()` with the following prototype

Example: `bool compare( Car& , Car& );`

and two objects of the derived `PassCar` class type, `beetle` and `miata`, the following statement is valid

Example: `compare( beetle, miata);`

The compiler performs implicit type conversion for the arguments `beetle` and `miata`, converting them to the parameter type, that is, to a reference to the base class `Car`.

Type conversion for arguments used in function calls is similar to the type conversion that occurs in assignments, as shown in the following section.

■ TYPE CONVERSIONS IN ASSIGNMENTS

☐ Effect of an assignment

```
Car    auto;
PassCar bmw("520i", true, 4325,
          "Bayerische Motorenwerke");
auto = bmw;
```

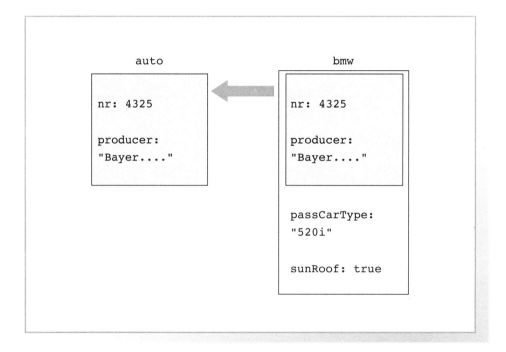

☐ Assignment to a Base Class Object

An object belonging to a derived class type can be assigned to an object of a base class.

Example:
```
Car    auto;
PassCar bmw("520i", true, 4325,
          "Bayerische Motorenwerke");
auto = bmw;
```

The object bmw, which belongs to the derived class PassCar, contains all the data members of the base class, Car, i.e. the vehicle id number and the manufacturer. During an assignment the object bmw is copied to the data members of the object auto step by step.

This makes the above statement equivalent to:

```
auto.nr       = bmw.nr;
auto.producer = bmw.producer;
```

The data members additionally defined in the derived class are not copied!

The following statement outputs the copied data members:

Example: auto.display();

The fact that you can assign an object belonging to a derived class to a base class object assumes that more will always fill less. The object on the right of the assignment operator will always contain a member object of the type on the left of the operator.

☐ Assignments to Derived Class Objects

This is not the case when you attempt to assign a base class object to an object of a derived class. The assignment

Example: bmw = auto;   // Error!

is therefore invalid, since the values for the additional data members passCarType and sunRoof are unknown.

An assignment in reverse order is only possible if you have defined an assignment of this type or a copy constructor with a parameter of the type "reference to base class." Both would be able to supply default values for the additional data members of the derived classes.

■ CONVERTING REFERENCES AND POINTERS

☐ Effect of a pointer assignment

```
PassCar cabrio("Spitfire", true, 1001, "Triumph");
Car* carPtr = &cabrio;
carPtr = &cabrio;
```

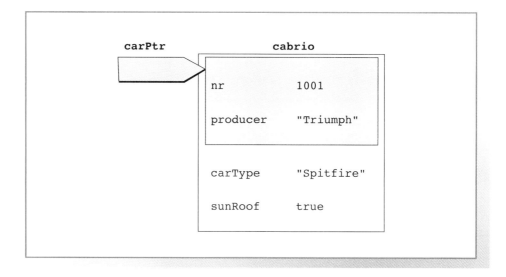

☐ Converting to Base Class Pointers

The *is* relationship between a derived class and a base class is also apparent when references and pointers are used. A pointer of the type "pointer to base class," or *base class pointer* for short, can reference an object of a derived class type.

Example: `Car* carPtr = &cabrio;`

In this case `cabrio` is an object of the class `PassCar`.
   The following rule applies for access to the referenced object:

> ■ a base class pointer can only access the public interface of the base class.

The additional members defined in the derived class are therefore inaccessible. To make this more clear:

Example: `carPtr -> display();`

calls the `display()` method in the base class `Car`. Although `carPtr` points to an object of the `PassCar` class in this case, it is impossible to call any methods additionally defined in the derived class.

Example: `carPtr->setSunRoof(false);     // Error`

The object `*carPtr` belongs to the `Car` class and only represents the generic part of `cabrio`. Thus, the following assignment is also invalid

Example: `PassCar auto;`
             `auto = *carPtr;        // Error!`

although `carPtr` is pointing at an object of the `PassCar` type in this case!

☐ Conversions in References to Base Classes

A similar situation arises when you are working with references. A reference of the type "reference to base class" can point to an object of a derived class. The reference will address only the generic part of the object in this case.

```
Example:    Car& carRef = cabrio;           // ok
            carRef.display();               // Output base members
            carRef.setSunRoof(true);        // Error
            PassCar auto;
            auto = carRef;                  // Error
```

Although the reference `carRef` points to an object of the `PassCar` type, it is impossible to assign the `PassCar` type object `auto` to this object.

■ EXPLICIT TYPE CONVERSIONS

Downcast

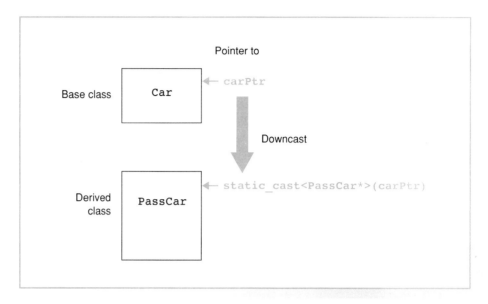

Upcast

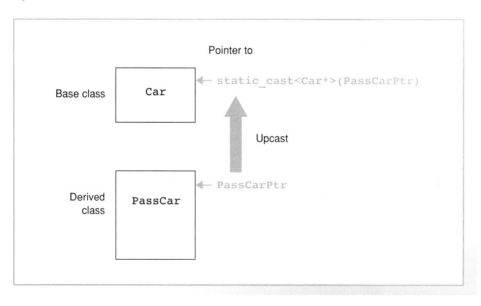

Upcasts and Downcasts

Type conversions that walk up a class hierarchy, or *upcasts*, are always possible and safe. Upcasting is performed implicitly for this reason.

Type conversions that involve walking down the tree, or *downcasts*, can only be performed explicitly by means of a cast construction. The cast operator (type), which was available in C, or the static_cast< > operator are available for this task, and are equivalent in this case.

Explicit Cast Constructions

Given that cabrio is again an object of the derived class PassCar, the following statements

Example:
```
Car* carPtr = &cabrio;
( (PassCar*) carPtr )->display();
```

first point the base class pointer carPtr to the cabrio object. carPtr is then cast as a pointer to the derived class. This allows you to access the display() method of the derived class PassCar via the pointer. Parentheses are necessary in this case as the member access operator -> has a higher precedence than the cast operator (type).

The operator static_cast< > conforms to the following

Syntax:
```
static_cast<type>(expression)
```

and converts the expression to the target type type. The previous example is thus equivalent to

Example:
```
static_cast<PassCar*>(carPtr)->display();
```

No parentheses are required here as the operators static_cast<> and -> are of equal precedence. They are read from left to right.

After downcasting a pointer or a reference, the entire public interface of the derived class is accessible.

Downcast Safety Issues

Type conversions from top to bottom need to be performed with great care. Downcasting is only safe when the object referenced by the base class pointer really is a derived class type. This also applies to references to base classes.

To allow safe downcasting C++ introduces the concept of *dynamic casting*. This technique is available for polymorphic classes and will be introduced in the next chapter.

exercise

EXERCISE

Class hierarchy of products in a supermarket

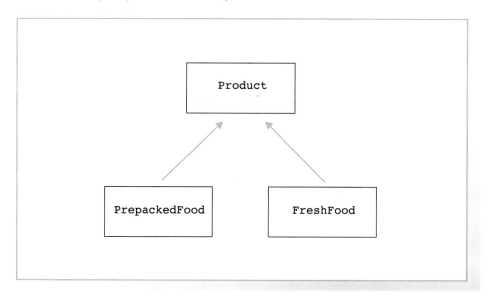

Exercise

The class hierarchy representing a supermarket chain's checkout system comprises the base class `Product` and the derived classes `PrepackedFood` and `FreshFood`. Your job is to test various cast techniques for this class (see also Exercise 3 in Chapter 23).

- Define a global function `isLowerCode()` that determines which one of two products has the lower barcode and returns a reference to the product with the lower barcode.
- Define an array with three pointers to the base class `Product`. Dynamically create one object each of the types `Product`, `PrepackedFood`, and `FreshFood`. The three objects are to be referenced by the array pointers.

  Additionally define a pointer to the derived class `FreshFood`. Initialize the pointer with the address of a dynamically allocated object of the same class.
- Now call the method `printer()` for all four objects. Which version of `printer()` is executed?
- Perform downcasting to execute the correct version of `printer()` in every case. Display the pointer values before and after downcasting.
- Use the pointer of the derived class `FreshFood` to call the base class version of `printer()`. Perform an appropriate upcast.
- Test the function `isLowerCode()` by multiple calls to the function with various arguments. Output the product with the lower barcode value in each case.

■ SOLUTION

```
// ---------------------------------------------------
// product.h : Defines the classes
//             Product, PrepackedFood, and FreshFood
// ---------------------------------------------------
//
// Unchanged! See the previous chapter's solutions.



// ---------------------------------------------------
// produc_t.cpp
// Tests up and down casts for the classes
// Product, PrepackedFood, and FreshFood.
// ---------------------------------------------------

#include "product.h"

const Product& isLowerCode(const Product& p1,
                           const Product& p2);

int main()
{
    Product* pv[3];
    FreshFood* pu;

    pv[0] = new Product(12345L, "Flour");
    pv[1] = new PrepackedFood(0.49, 23456, "Salt");
    pv[2] = new FreshFood(1.5, 1.69, 98765, "Grapes");

    pu =  new FreshFood(2.5, 2.69, 56789, "Peaches");

    cout << "\nA fresh product: ";
    pu->printer();

    cout << "\nThe generic data of the other products:";
    int i;
    for(i=0; i < 3; ++i)
        pv[i]->printer();
    cin.get();

    cout << "\nAnd now the downcast: " << endl;
    static_cast<PrepackedFood*>(pv[1])->printer();
    static_cast<FreshFood*>(pv[2])->printer();
    cin.get();

    cout << "\nAnd an upcast: " << endl;
    static_cast<Product*>(pu)->printer();
```

```
    cout << "\nNow compare the barcodes!" << endl;

    cout << "\nIs barcode for flour or salt smaller?";
    isLowerCode(*pv[0], *pv[1]).printer();

    cout << "\nIs barcode for salt or grapes smaller?";
    isLowerCode(*pv[1], *pv[2]).printer();

    return 0;
}

const Product& isLowerCode(const Product& p1,
                           const Product& p2)
{
    if(p1.getCode() < p2.getCode())
        return p1;
    else
        return p2;
}
```

chapter 25

Polymorphism

This chapter describes how to develop and manage polymorphic classes. In addition to defining virtual functions, dynamic downcasting in polymorphic class hierarchies is introduced.

■ CONCEPT OF POLYMORPHISM

Example

Classes with virtual methods:

```
Base:
```
    base class with virtual method `display()`.

```
Derived1 and Derived2:
```
    derived from `Base` with its own redefinitions
    of method `display()`.

Base class pointer and objects:

```
    Base*    basePtr;        // Base class pointer
    Derived1 angular;        // Objects
    Derived2 round;
```

Calling virtual methods:

When a virtual method is called, the corresponding version of the method is
executed for the object currently referenced.

```
    basePtr = &angular;
    basePtr->display();    // Calling
                           // Derived1::display()

    basePtr = &round;
    basePtr->display();    // Calling
                           // Derived2::display()
```

☐ Issues

If the special features of derived class objects are insignificant, you can simply concern yourself with the base members. This is the case when dynamic allocated objects are inserted into a data structure or deleted from that structure.

It makes sense to use pointers or references to the base class in this case—no matter what type of concrete object you are dealing with. However, you can only access the common base members of these objects.

However, you should be able to activate the special features of a derived class when

- ∎ the object is accessed by a pointer or reference to the base class and
- ∎ the concrete object type will not be known until the program is executed.

Given a base class pointer, `carPtr`, the statement

Example: `carPtr->display();`

should output *all* the data members of the object currently being referenced.

☐ Traditional Approach

Traditional programming languages solved this issue by adding a type field both to the base class and to the derived classes. The type field stored the type of the current class. A function that manages objects via the base class pointer could query the concrete type in a switch statement and call the appropriate method.

This solution has a disadvantage; adding derived classes at a later stage also meant adding a `case` label and recompiling.

☐ Object-Oriented Approach

The approach adopted by object-oriented languages is *polymorphism* (Greek for multi-form). In C++, *virtual methods* are used to implement polymorphic classes. Calling a virtual method makes the compiler execute a version of the method *suitable* for the object in question, when the object is accessed by a pointer or a reference to the base class!

■ VIRTUAL METHODS

Calling the virtual method `display()`

```cpp
// virtual.cpp : Tests the virtual method display()
//                of the classes Car and PassCar.
// ----------------------------------------------------

#include "car.h"
// The Car class with virtual method display():
// class Car
// {
//    ...
//    virtual void display() const;
// };

int main()
{
  Car* pCar[3];        // Three pointers to the base class.
  int i = 0;           // Index
  pCar[0] = new Car( 5634L, "Mercedes");
  pCar[1] = new PassCar("Miata",true,3421,"Mazda");
  pCar[2] = new Truck( 5, 7.5, 1234, "Ford");

  while( true)
  {
    cout << "\nTo output an object of type "
            "Car, PassCar or Truck!"
            "\n 1 = Car,  2 = PassCar,  3 = Truck"
            "\nYour input (break with 0): ";
    cin >> i;
    --i;
    if( i < 0  || i > 2)
      break;
    pCar[i]->display();
  }
  return 0;
}
```

☐ Declaring Virtual Methods

The `virtual` keyword is used to declare a virtual method in a base class.

Example: `virtual void display() const;`

The definition of a virtual method is no different from the definition of any other member function.

A virtual method does not need to be redefined in the derived class. The derived class then inherits the virtual method from the base class.

☐ Redefinition

However, it is common practice for the derived class to define its own version of the virtual method, which is thus modified to suit the special features of the derived class.

Creating a proprietary version of a virtual method means redefining that method. The redefinition in the derived class must have

1. the same signature and

2. the same return type

as the virtual method in the base class.

The new version of a virtual method is automatically virtual itself. This means you can omit the `virtual` keyword in the declaration.

When you redefine a virtual function, be aware of the following:

- if the return type is a pointer or reference to the base class, the new version of the virtual method can also return a pointer or reference to a derived class (Note: Not all compilers support this option.)
- constructors cannot have a virtual declaration
- a base class method does not become virtual just because it is declared as virtual in a derived class.

If you use a different signature or return type of a virtual base class method to define a method in a derived class, this simply creates a new method with the same name. The method will not necessarily be virtual!

However, the virtual method in the base class will be masked by the method in the derived class. In other words, only the non-virtual version of the method is available for a derived class object.

■ DESTROYING DYNAMICALLY ALLOCATED OBJECTS

Sample program

```cpp
// v_destr.cpp
// Base class with a virtual destructor.
// ------------------------------------------------------
#include <iostream>
#include <cstring>                 // For strcpy()
using namespace std;

class Base
{
  public:
    Base()
    {  cout << "Constructor of class Base\n"; }
    virtual ~Base()
    {  cout << "Destructor of class Base\n"; }
};
class Data
{
  private:
    char *name;
  public:
    Data( const char *n)
    { cout << "Constructor of class Data\n";
      name = new char[strlen(n)+1];  strcpy(name, n);
    }
    ~Data()
    { cout << "Destructor of class Data for "
           << "object: " << name << endl;
      delete [] name;
    }
};
class Derived : public Base
{
  private:
    Data data;
  public:
    Derived( const char *n) : data(n)
    {  cout << "Constructor of class Derived\n";  }
    ~Derived()              // implicit virtual
    {  cout << "Destructor of class Derived\n"; }
};

int main()
{
  Base *bPtr = new Derived("DEMO");
  cout << "\nCall to the virtual Destructor!\n";
  delete bPtr;
  return 0;
}
```

Dynamically created objects in a class hierarchy are normally handled by a base class pointer. When such an object reaches the end of its lifetime, the memory occupied by the object must be released by a `delete` statement.

Example:
```
Car *carPtr;
carPtr = new PassCar("500",false,21,"Geo");
    . . .
delete carPtr;
```

☐ Destructor Calls

When memory is released, the destructor for an object is automatically called. If multiple constructors were called to create the object, the corresponding destructors are called in reverse order. What does this mean for objects in derived classes? The destructor of the derived class is called first and then the destructor of the base class executed.

If you use a base class pointer to manage an object, the appropriate virtual methods of the derived class are called. However, non-virtual methods will always execute the base class version.

In the previous example, only the base class destructor for `Car` was executed. As the `PassCar` destructor is not called, neither is the destructor called for the data member `passCarType`, which is additionally defined in the derived class. The data member `passCarType` is a `string`, however, and occupies dynamically allocated memory—this memory will not be released.

If multiple objects are created dynamically in the derived class, a dangerous situation occurs. More and more unreferenced memory blocks will clutter up the main memory without you being able to reallocate them—this can seriously impact your program's response and even lead to external memory being swapped in.

☐ Virtual Destructors

This issue can be solved simply by declaring virtual destructors. The opposite page shows how you would define a virtual destructor for the `Car` class. Just like any other virtual method, the appropriate version of the destructor will be executed. The destructors from any direct or indirect base class then follow.

A class used as a base class for other classes should always have a virtual destructor defined. Even if the base class does not need a destructor itself, it should at least contain a dummy destructor, that is, a destructor with an empty function body.

■ VIRTUAL METHOD TABLE

VMT for the classes `Car` **and** `PassCar`

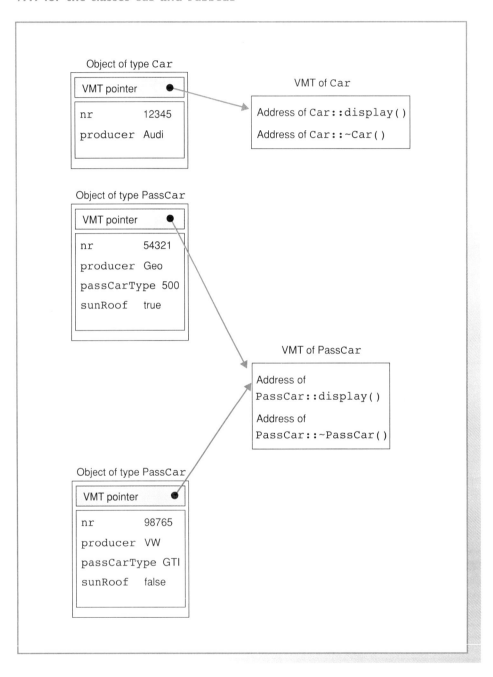

☐ Static Binding

When a non-virtual method is called, the address of the function is known at time of compilation. The address is inserted directly into the machine code. This is also referred to as *static* or *early binding*.

If a virtual method is called via an object's name, the appropriate version of this method is also known at time of compilation. So this is also a case of early binding.

☐ Dynamic Binding

However, if a virtual method is called by a pointer or reference, the function that will be executed when the program is run is unknown at time of compilation. The statement

Example: `carPtr->display();`

could execute different versions of the `display()` method, depending on the object currently referenced by the pointer.

The compiler is therefore forced to create machine code that does not form an association with a particular function until the program is run. This is referred to as *late* or *dynamic binding*.

☐ VMT

Dynamic binding is supported internally by *virtual method tables* (or VMT for short). A VMT is created for each class with at least one virtual method—that is, an array with the addresses of the virtual methods in the current class.

Each object in a polymorphic class contains a VMT pointer, that is, a hidden pointer to the VMT of the corresponding class. Dynamic binding causes the virtual function call to be executed in two steps:

1. The pointer to the VMT in the referenced object is read.

2. The address of the virtual method is read in the VMT.

In comparison with static binding, dynamic binding does have the disadvantage that VMTs occupy memory. Moreover, program response can be impacted by indirect addressing of virtual methods.

However, this is a small price to pay for the benefits. Dynamic binding allows you to enhance compiled source code without having access to the source code. This is particularly important when you consider commercial class libraries, from which a user can derive his or her own classes and virtual function versions.

■ DYNAMIC CASTS

Using dynamic casts

```cpp
// cast_t.cpp
// Dynamic casts in class hierarchies.
// ---------------------------------------------------
#include "car.h"
bool inspect( PassCar* ),        // Inspection of
     inspect(Truck* );           // car types.
bool separate(Car* );            // Separates cars
                                 // for inspection.
int main()
{
    Car* carPtr = new PassCar("520i", true, 3265, "BMW");
    Truck* truckPtr = new Truck(8, 7.5, 5437, "Volvo");
    // ... to test some casts and ...
    separate(carPtr);
    separate(truckPtr);
    return 0;
}
bool separate( Car* carPtr)
{
    PassCar* PassCarPtr = dynamic_cast<PassCar*>(carPtr);
    if( PassCarPtr != NULL)
       return inspect( PassCarPtr);
    Truck* truckPtr = dynamic_cast<Truck*>(carPtr);
    if( truckPtr != NULL)
       return inspect( truckPtr);
    return false;
}
bool inspect(PassCar* PassCarPtr)
{   cout << "\nI inspect a passenger car!" << endl;
    cout << "\nHere it is:";
    PassCarPtr->display();
    return true;
}
bool inspect(Truck* truckPtr)
{   cout << "\nI inspect a truck!" << endl;
    cout << "\nHere it is:";
    truckPtr->display();
    return true;
}
```

✓ **NOTE**

The compiler's option "Run Time Type Information (RTTI)" must be activated, for example, under Project/Settings. The GNU compiler activates these options automatically.

☐ Safety Issues in Downcasting

Downcasts in class hierarchies are unsafe if you use a C cast or the static cast operator. If the referenced object does not correspond to the type of the derived class, fatal runtime errors can occur.

Given that `carPtr` is a pointer to the base class `Car`, which is currently pointing to a `PassCar` type, the statement

Example: `Truck * truckPtr = static_cast<Truck*>(carPtr);`

will not cause a compiler error. But the following statement, `truckPtr->setAxles(10);` could cause the program to crash.

☐ The `dynamic_cast<>` Operator

You can use the cast operator `dynamic_cast<>` to perform safe downcasting in polymorphic classes. At runtime the operator checks whether the required conversion is valid or not.

Syntax: `dynamic_cast<type>(expression)`

If so, the expression `expression` is converted to the target type `type`. The target type must be a pointer or reference to a polymorphic class or a `void` pointer. If it is a pointer type, `expression` must also be a pointer type. If the target type is a reference, `expression` must identify an object in memory.

☐ Examples

Given a pointer `carPtr` to the base class `Car`, the statement

Example: `Truck* truckPtr = dynamic_cast<Truck*>(carPtr);`

performs a downcast to the derived `Truck` class, provided the pointer `carPtr` really identifies a `Truck` type object. If this is not so, the `dynamic_cast<Truck>` operator will return a NULL pointer.

Given that `cabrio` is a `PassCar` type object, the following statements

Example: `Car& r_car = cabrio;`
          `PassCar& r_passCar=dynamic_cast<PassCar&>(r_car);`

perform a dynamic cast to the "reference to `PassCar`" type. In any other case, that is, if the reference `r_car` does not identify a `PassCar` type object, an exception of the `bad_cast` type is thrown.

The dynamic cast can also be used for upcasting. The classes involved do not need to be polymorphic in this case. However, type checking is not performed at runtime. An erroneous upcast is recognized and reported by the compiler.

EXERCISES

Menu options

```
      * * * Car Rental Management * * *

          P = Add a passenger car

          T = Add a truck

          D = Display all cars

          Q = Quit

Your choice:
```

Different versions of method insert()

```
   Add a new passenger car:

   bool insert(const  string& tp, bool sr,
               long n, const string& prod);

   Add a new truck:

   bool insert(int a, double t, long n,
               const string& prod);
```

Exercise 1

Modify the vehicle management program to allow an automobile rental company to manage its fleet of automobiles. First, define a class called `CityCar` that contains an array of pointers to the 100 objects in the `Car` class. This also allows you to store pointers to objects of the derived class types `PassCar` and `Truck`. The objects themselves will be created dynamically at runtime.

■ Define a class `CityCar` with an array of pointers to the `Car` class and an `int` variable for the current number of elements in the array.

The constructor will set the current number of array elements to 0.

The destructor must release memory allocated dynamically for the remaining objects. Make sure that you use a virtual destructor definition in the base class `Car` to allow correct releasing of memory for trucks and passenger vehicles.

Implement two versions of the `insert()` method using the prototype shown opposite. Each version will allocate memory to an object of the appropriate type—that is of the `PassCar` or `Truck` class—and use the arguments passed to it for initialization. The method should return `false` if it is impossible to enter another automobile (that is, if the array is full), and `true` in all other cases.

The `display()` method outputs the data of all vehicles on screen. To perform this task it calls the existing `display()` method for each object.

■ Create a new function called `menu()` and store this function in a new source file. The function will display the menu shown opposite, read, and return the user's choice.

■ Additionally, write two functions, `getPassCar()` and `getTruck()`, which read the data for a car or a truck from the keyboard and write the data into the appropriate arguments.

■ Create an object of the `CityCar` type in your `main` function. Insert one car and one truck. These will be the first vehicles of the company's fleet.

If a user chooses "Add car" or "Add truck," your program must read the data supplied and call the appropriate version of `insert()`.

Dialog with the receptionist

In function `record()`

```
Please type next article?

        0 = No more articles

        1 = Fresh food

        2 = Prepacked article

    ?
```

Loop of `main()`

```
    Another customer (y/n)?

    If yes → to record
```

Exercise 2

An automatic checkout system for a supermarket chain needs to be completed.

- Declare the virtual methods `scanner()` and `printer()` in the base class `Product`. Also define a virtual destructor.

- Write the `record()` function, which registers and lists products purchased in the store in a program loop.

  The function creates an array of 100 pointers to the base class, `Product`. The checkout assistant is prompted to state whether a prepacked or fresh food item is to be scanned next. Memory for each product scanned is allocated dynamically and referenced by the next pointer in the array. After scanning all the available items, a sequential list is displayed. The prices of all the items are added and the total is output at the end.

- Now create an application program to simulate a supermarket checkout. The checkout assistant is prompted in a loop to state whether to define a new customer. If so, the `record()` function is called; if not, the program terminates.

■ **SOLUTIONS**

Exercise 1

```cpp
// ----------------------------------------------------
// car.h :  Defines the base class Car and
//          the derived classes PassCar and Truck
// ----------------------------------------------------
#ifndef _CAR_H_
#define _CAR_H_

#include <iostream>
#include <string>
using namespace std;

class Car
{
  private:
     long   nr;
     string producer;

  public:
     Car( long n = 0L, const string& prod = "");
     virtual ~Car() {}            // Virtual destructor.

     // Access methods:
     long  getNr(void) const { return nr; }
     void  setNr( long n ) { nr = n; }

     const string& getProd() const { return producer; }
     void  setProd(const string& p){ producer = p; }

     virtual void display() const;    // Display a car
};

// The derived classes PassCar and Truck are unchanged
// (see Chapter 23).

#endif

// ----------------------------------------------------
// car.cpp
// Implements the methods of Car, PassCar, and Truck
// ----------------------------------------------------

// Unchanged (see Chapter 23).
//
```

```
// ------------------------------------------------------
// city.h : Defines the CityCar class
// ------------------------------------------------------

#ifndef _CITY_H_
#define _CITY_H_

#include "car.h"

class CityCar
{
  private:
    Car* vp[100];
    int cnt;
  public:
    CityCar(){ cnt = 0;}
    ~CityCar();

    bool insert(const string& tp, bool sr,
                long n, const string& prod);
    bool insert(int a, double t,
                long n, const string& prod);

    void display() const;
};
#endif  // _CITY_H

// ------------------------------------------------------
// city.cpp : Methods of class CityCar
// ------------------------------------------------------
#include "city.h"

CityCar::~CityCar()
{
   for(int i=0; i < cnt; ++i)
     delete vp[i];
}

// Insert a passenger car:
bool CityCar::insert(const string& tp, bool sr,
                     long n, const string& prod)
{
    if( cnt < 100)
    {
       vp[cnt++] = new PassCar( tp, sr, n, prod);
       return true;
    }
    else
        return false;
}
```

```
// Insert a truck:
bool CityCar::insert( int a, double t,
                                  long n, const string& prod)
{
   if( cnt < 100)
   {
      vp[cnt++] = new Truck( a, t, n, prod);
      return true;
   }
    else
        return false;
}

void CityCar::display() const
{
   cin.sync(); cin.clear();    // No previous input
   for(int i=0; i < cnt; ++i)
   {
      vp[i]->display();
      if((i+1)%4 == 0)  cin.get();
   }
}

// -------------------------------------------------
// city_t.cpp : Test the CityCar class
// -------------------------------------------------
#include "city.h"
char menu(void);
void getPassCar(string&, bool&, long&, string&);
void getTruck(int&, double&, long&, string&);

int main()
{
   CityCar carExpress;
   string tp, prod; bool   sr;
   int    a;    long   n;  double t;

   // Two cars are already present:
   carExpress.insert(6, 9.5, 54321, "Ford");
   carExpress.insert("A-class", true, 54320, "Mercedes");
   char choice;
   do
   {  choice = menu();
      switch( choice )
      {
        case 'Q':
        case 'q': cout << "Bye Bye!"  << endl;
                  break;
```

```
             case 'P':
             case 'p': getPassCar(tp, sr, n, prod);
                       carExpress.insert(tp, sr, n, prod  );
                       break;
             case 'T':
             case 't': getTruck(a, t, n, prod);
                       carExpress.insert(a, t, n, prod);
                       break;
             case 'D':
             case 'd': carExpress.display();
                       cin.get();
                       break;
             default:  cout << "\a";      // Beep
                       break;
          }
      }while( choice != 'Q'  && choice != 'q');
      return 0;
}

char menu()                               // Input a command.
{
   cout << "\n  * * *  Car Rental Management * * *\n\n"
   char c;
   cout <<    "\n            P = Add a passenger car "
        <<    "\n            T = Add a truck "
        <<    "\n            D = Display all cars "
        <<    "\n            Q = Quit the program "
        << "\n\nYour choice: ";
   cin >> c;
   return c;
}

void getPassCar(string& tp, bool& sr, long& n,string& prod)
{
   char c;
   cin.sync(); cin.clear();
   cout << "\nEnter data for passenger car:" << endl;
   cout << "Car type:          "; getline(cin, tp);
   cout << "Sun roof (y/n):    "; cin >> c;
   if(c == 'y' || c == 'Y')
       sr = true;
   else
       sr = false;
   cout << "Car number:       "; cin >> n;
   cin.sync();
   cout << "Producer:        "; getline(cin, prod);
   cin.sync(); cin.clear();
}
```

```
void getTruck(int& a, double& t, long& n, string& prod)
{
   cout << "\nInput data for truck:" << endl;
   cout << "Number of axles:     "; cin >> a;
   cout << "Weight in tons:      ";  cin >> t;
   cout << "Car number:          ";    cin >> n;
   cin.sync();
   cout << "Producer:            "; getline(cin, prod);
   cin.sync();
}
```

Exercise 2

```
// --------------------------------------------------
// product.h : Defining the classes
//             Product, PrepackedFood, and FreshFood
// --------------------------------------------------
// . . .

class Product
{
  private:
    long    bar;
    string name;

  public:
    Product(long b = 0L, const string& s = "")
    : bar(b), name(s)
    {  }

// Access methods as previously used.

    virtual void scanner();       // Virtual now!
    virtual void printer() const;
};

// The classes PrepackedFood and FreshFood are unchanged!
// Refer to the solutions in Chapter 23.
```

```cpp
// ------------------------------------------------------
// counter.cpp : Simulates a checkout desk
// ------------------------------------------------------
#include "product.h"

void record();

int main()
{
   cout << "\nHere is a checkout desk!" << endl;
   char c;
   while(true)
   {
       cin.sync();
       cout << "\nAnother customer (y/n)?    ";
       cin  >> c;

       if(c == 'y' || c == 'Y')
           record();
       else
           break;
   }
   return 0;
}


// ------------------------------------------------------
// record() : Records the articles bought by a customer
//            and the total price.
void record()
{
   Product* v[100];
   int x, i, cnt = 0;
   double sum = 0.0;

   for (i = 0; i < 100; i++)
   {
      cin.sync();
      cout << "\nWhat is the next article?" << endl;
      cout << "  0 = No more article\n"
           << "  1 = Fresh Food\n"
           << "  2 = Prepacked article\n"
           << "? " ;
      cin  >> x;

      if( x <= 0 || x >= 3)
          break;
```

```
        switch(x)
        {
          case 2:
              v[i] = new PrepackedFood;
              v[i]->scanner();
              sum += ((PrepackedFood*)v[i])->getPrice();
              break;

          case 1:
              v[i] = new FreshFood;
              v[i]->scanner();
              sum += ((FreshFood*)v[i])->getPrice()
                      * ((FreshFood*)v[i])->getWght();
              break;
        }
    }
    cnt = i;
    for( i=0; i < cnt; i++)                // Output
       v[i]->printer();

    cout << "\n----------------------------"
         << fixed << setprecision(2)
         << "\nTotal price:   " << sum << endl;
}
```

chapter 26

Abstract Classes

This chapter describes how abstract classes can be created by defining pure virtual methods and how you can use abstract classes as a polymorphic interface for derived classes. To illustrate this we will be implementing an inhomogeneous list, that is, a linked list whose elements can be of various class types.

■ PURE VIRTUAL METHODS

The base class Coworker

```
// Coworker.h:  Defining the abstract class Coworker.
// ------------------------------------------------
#ifndef _COWORKER_H
#define _COWORKER_H

#include <string>
#include <iostream>
using namespace std;

class Coworker
{
   private:
     string name;
     // more information
   public:
     Coworker( const string& s = ""){ name = s; }
     virtual ~Coworker() {}      // Destructor

     const string&  getName() const{ return name; }
     void  setName( const string& n){ name = n; }

     virtual void display() const;

     virtual double income() const = 0;

     virtual Coworker& operator=(const Coworker&);
};
#endif
```

✓ NOTE

The virtual operator function for the assignment will be described in the section on "Virtual Assignments."

☐ Motivation

Virtual methods are declared in the base class to ensure that they are available in any derived classes via the common class interface. It may happen that they rarely perform any useful tasks in the base class. For example, a destructor in a base class does not need to perform any explicit cleaning-up operations.

In this case, of course, you can define a virtual dummy method whose address is entered in the VMT of the base class. However, this creates op-code for a function that should never be called. It makes more sense not to define a function like this. And this is where C++ steps in and gives you the opportunity of declaring *pure virtual methods*.

☐ Declaration

When a pure virtual method is declared, the method is identified by adding the expression = 0.

Example: `virtual void demo()=0;   // pure virtual`

This informs the compiler that there is no definition of the `demo()` method in the class. A NULL pointer is then entered in the virtual method table for the pure virtual method.

☐ The Base Class Coworker

The opposite page shows a definition of the `Coworker` class, which was designed to represent human resources data for a company. The class is used as a base class for various employees, blue-collar, white-collar, and freelancers.

To keep things simple the `Coworker` class has only a name as a data member. However, it could also contain the address of an employee, or the division where the employee works.

The `Coworker` class does not comprise data members to represent an employee's salary. It makes more sense to store data like this in derived classes where the hourly wage and number of hours worked by a blue-collar worker and the monthly salary for a white-collar worker are also defined. The `income()` method is therefore not defined for the base class and can be declared as a pure virtual method.

▪ ABSTRACT AND CONCRETE CLASSES

The derived class Laborer

```
// coworker.h:   Extending the headerfile.
// ------------------------------------------------
class Laborer : public Coworker
{
   private:
     double wages;                // Pay per hour
     int    hr;

   public:
    Laborer(const string& s="", double w=0.0, int h=0)
            : Coworker(s), wages(w), hr(h){ }

    double getWages() const { return wages; }
    void   setWages( double w ){ wages = w; }

    int    getHr() const { return hr; }
    void   setHr(int h ) { hr = h; }

    void   display() const;
    double income() const;

    Laborer& operator=(const Coworker&);
    Laborer& operator=(const Laborer&);
};
```

✓ **NOTE**

The operator functions for the assignments are discussed in the section "Virtual Assignments."

☐ Concrete or Abstract?

If a class comprises pure virtual methods, you cannot create objects of this class type.

Example: `Coworker worker("Black , Michael");`

The compiler will issue an error message here, as the `Coworker` class contains the pure virtual method `income()`. This avoids calling a method for `worker` that still needs to be defined.

A class that does not allow you to create any objects is referred to as an *abstract class*.

✓ NOTE

A class with pure virtual methods is an abstract class.

In contrast, a class that allows you to create objects is referred to as a *concrete class*.

☐ Deriving Abstract Classes

When a class is derived from an abstract class, it inherits all the methods the base class contains, particularly the pure virtual methods. If all of these pure virtual methods are implemented in the derived class, you can then create an object of the derived class type.

✓ NOTE

A class derived from a class containing pure virtual methods is a concrete class, if it contains a definition for each pure virtual function.

This means you need to implement the `income()` method in the `Laborer` class shown opposite. Since the hourly wage and the number of hours worked are both defined for blue-collar workers, it is possible to implement that method.

Example:
```
double Laborer::income()
{
    return ( wages * hr );
}
```

A class derived from a concrete class can again contain pure virtual methods, due to additional definitions in the derived class. In other words, an abstract class can be derived from a concrete class.

An abstract class does not necessarily need to contain pure virtual functions. If the class contains a `protected` constructor, objects of the class type cannot be created. The constructor can only be called then by methods in derived classes. A constructor of this type normally acts as base initializer, when an object of a derived class type is created.

■ POINTERS AND REFERENCES TO ABSTRACT CLASSES

The derived class Employee

```
// coworker.h:    Extending the headerfile.
// ------------------------------------------------
class Employee : public Coworker
{
  private:
    double salary;         // Pay per month
  public:
    Employee( const string& s="", double sa = 0.0)
                 : Coworker(s), salary(g){ }
    double getSalary() const { return salary; }
    void   setSalary( double sa){ salary = sa; }
    void   display() const;
    double income()const { return salary; }
    Employee& operator=( const Coworker& );
    Employee& operator=( const Employee& );
};
```

Sample program

```
// coworker_t.cpp : Using the Coworker classes.
// ------------------------------------------------
#include "coworker.h"

int main()
{
    Coworker* felPtr[2];
    felPtr[0] = new Laborer("Young, Neil",45., 40);
    felPtr[1] = new Employee("Smith, Eve", 3850.0);

    for( int i = 0; i < 2; ++i)
    {
      felPtr[i]->display();
      cout << "\nThe income of " << felPtr[i]->getName()
        << " :   " << felPtr[i]->income() << endl;
    }
    delete felPtr[0];  delete felPtr[1];
    return 0;
}
```

Although you cannot define objects for abstract classes, you can declare pointers and references to abstract classes.

Example: `Coworker *felPtr, &coRef;`

The pointer `felPtr` is a base class pointer that can address objects belonging to derived concrete classes. The reference `coRef` can also address objects of this type.

☐ References to Abstract Base Classes

References to base classes are often used as parameters in functions. The copy constructor in the `Coworker` class is just one of them.

Example: `Coworker( const Coworker& );`

The copy constructor expects an object belonging to a derived class, since the base class is abstract.

The assignment in the `Coworker` class has a reference as a parameter and returns a reference to the abstract class.

☐ Pointers to Abstract Base Classes

Pointers to base classes are generally used to address dynamically allocated objects. If the base class is abstract, you can only allocate memory for objects belonging to derived, concrete classes.

Example:
```
Coworker* felPtr;
felPtr = new Laborer("Young, Neil",45.,40);
cout << felPtr->income();
```

Since the `income()` method is virtual, a corresponding function found in the derived class `Laborer` is executed.

☐ Polymorphic Interface

Defining pure virtual methods also determines interfaces for general operations, although the interfaces still need to implemented in the derived classes. If a derived class contains its own definition of a virtual method, this version will also be executed if an object is referenced by a base class pointer or reference. Abstract classes are therefore also referred to as *polymorphic interfaces* to derived classes.

The opposite page shows the definition of the `Employee` class, which was also derived from the abstract class `Coworker`. The operator functions for the assignments are discussed and implemented in the following section.

■ VIRTUAL ASSIGNMENT

Assignment for class `Coworker`

```cpp
// Virtual Assignment in the base class
Coworker& operator=(const Coworker & m)
{
  if( this != &m )              // No self assignment
    name = m.name;

  return *this;
}
```

Assignments for class `Employee`

```cpp
// Redefinition: virtual
Employee& operator=(const Coworker& m)
{
  if( this != &m )             // No self assignment
  {
    Coworker::operator=( m );
    salary = 0.0;
  }
  return *this;
}

// Standard Assignment: not virtual
Employee& operator=(const Employee& a)
{
   if( this != &a )
   {
      Coworker::operator=( a );
      salary = a.salary;
   }
   return *this;
}
```

> ✓ **NOTE**
>
> Redefining the virtual operator function `operator=()`, which returns a reference to the derived class, is not yet supported by all compilers. In this case the return type must be a reference to the base class `Coworker`.

☐ Virtual Operator Functions

Operator functions implemented as methods can also be virtual. In this case, you can ensure that the right version of an operator function will be executed when using a pointer or reference to a base class to address a derived class object.

One example of this is the operator function for an assignment. If the function declaration is not virtual, and if the function is called via a base class pointer, only the base data of the object is overwritten. Any additional data members of the derived class remain unchanged.

☐ Using Virtual Assignments

The assignment was declared virtual in the Coworker base class. The derived classes Laborer and Employee both contain their own versions. Thus, in the following

Example:
```
void cpy(Coworker& a,const Coworker& b)
    { a = b; }
```

the assignment of the Employee class is executed, if an object of this class type is the first argument passed to it. If the object is a Laborer type, the assignment of the Laborer class is performed.

In the case of the cpy() function, you can therefore assign two objects of any class, including classes derived at a later stage, without having to modify the function itself! However, you definitely need to define a version of the assignment for each derived class.

☐ Redefining the Standard Assignment

When you define a new version for a virtual method in a derived class, this implies using the signature of the original method. Since the standard assignment of a derived class has a signature of its own, it is *not* virtual. The standard assignment for the Laborer class has the following prototype:

Example: `Laborer& operator=(const Laborer&);`

The type const Laborer& is different from the const Coworker& type of the parameter in the virtual operator function of the base class. The standard assignment thus masks the virtual assignment in the base class. This gives rise to two issues:

- ■ the virtual operator function for the assignment must be defined for every derived class
- ■ to ensure that the standard assignment is also available, the standard assignment must also be redefined in every derived class.

■ APPLICATION: INHOMOGENEOUS LISTS

The abstract base class `Cell` and derived classes

```cpp
// cell.h: Defining the classes Cell, BaseEl, and DerivedEl
// ---------------------------------------------------------
#ifndef _CELL_
#define _CELL_
#include <string>
#include <iostream>
using namespace std;

class Cell
{
  private:
    Cell* next;
  protected:
    Cell(Cell* suc = NULL ){ next = suc; }
  public:
    virtual ~Cell(){ }
    // Access methods to be declared here.
    virtual void display() const = 0;
};
class BaseEl : public Cell
{
  private:
    string name;
  public:
    BaseEl( Cell* suc = NULL, const string& s = "")
    :  Cell(suc), name(s){}
    // Access methods would be declared here.
    void display() const;
};
class DerivedEl : public BaseEl
{
  private:
    string rem;
  public:
    DerivedEl(Cell* suc = NULL,const string& s="",
              const string& b="")
    : BaseEl(suc, s), rem(b) { }
    // Access methods would be declared here.
    void display() const;
};
#endif
```

Terminology

Let's look into implementing an application that uses an inhomogeneous list. An inhomogeneous list is a linear list whose elements can be of different types. If the data you need to store consists of objects in a class hierarchy, one list element could contain an object belonging to the base class, whereas another could contain an object of a derived class.

Due to implicit type conversions in class hierarchies, you can use the base class pointers to manage the list elements, that is, you can manage the elements in a linked list. The following graphic illustrates this scenario:

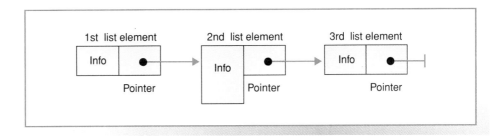

Representing List Elements

To separate the management of list elements from the information contained in the list, we have defined an abstract class called Cell as a base class for all list elements. The class contains a pointer of type Cell* as the data member used to link list elements. Since Cell type objects are not be created, the constructor in the Cell class has a protected declaration.

The Cell class does not contain any data that might need to be output. However, each class derived from Cell contains data that need to be displayed. For this reason, Cell contains a declaration of the pure virtual method display(), which can be modified for multiple derivations.

The classes BaseEl and DerivedEl, which are derived from Cell, represent list elements used for storing information. To keep things simple, the BaseEl class contains only a name, and the DerivedEl class additionally contains a comment. The public declaration section contains a constructor and access method declarations. In addition, a suitable version of the display() method is defined. Both classes are thus concrete classes.

■ IMPLEMENTING AN INHOMOGENEOUS LIST

Defining class `InhomList`

```
// List.h:  Defining the class InhomList
// -------------------------------------------
#ifndef _LIST_H
#define _LIST_H
#include "cell.h"
class InhomList
{ private:
    Cell* first;
  protected:
    Cell* getPrev(const string& s);
    void  insertAfter(const string& s,Cell* prev);
    void  insertAfter(const string& s,
                      const string& b,Cell* prev);
  public: // Constructor, Destructor etc....
    void  insert(const string& n);
    void  insert(const string& n, const string& b);
    void displayAll() const;
};
#endif
```

Inserting a list element in the middle

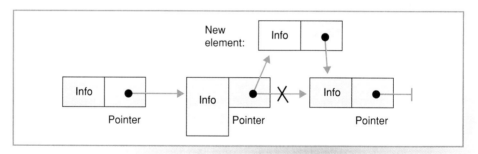

Definition of `insertAfter()` **version**

```
void InhomList::insertAfter(const string& s, Cell* prev)
{
  if( prev == NULL )    // Insert at the beginning,
    first = new BaseEl( first, s);
  else                  // middle, or end.
  {
    Cell* p = new BaseEl(prev->getNext(), s);
    prev->setNext(p);
  }
}
```

☐ The `InhomList` Class

The inhomogeneous list must allow sorted insertion of list elements. It is no longer suffi-cient to append elements to the end of the list; instead, the list must allow insertion at any given point. A pointer to the first element in the list is all you need for this task. You can then use the pointer to the next list element to access any given list element.

The definition of the `InhomList` class is shown opposite. A pointer to `Cell` has been declared as a data member. The constructor has very little to do. It simply sets the base class pointer to NULL, thus creating an empty list.

The list will be sorted by name. When inserting a new element into the list, the inser-tion point—that is the position of the element that will precede the new element—must first be located. In our example, we first locate the immediate lexicographical predeces-sor. The `getPrev()` method, shown opposite, performs the search and returns either the position of the predecessor or NULL if there is no predecessor. In this case, the new list element is inserted as the first element in the list.

☐ Inserting a New List Element

After finding the insertion position you can call the `insertAfter()` method that allo-cates memory for a new list element and inserts the element into the list. There are two cases that need to be looked at:

1. If the new element has to be inserted at the start of the list, what was originally the first element now becomes the second. The new element becomes the first element. The `first` pointer thus needs updating.

2. If the new element is inserted at any other position in the list, the `first` pointer is not affected. Instead, you have to modify two pointers. The pointer in the pre-ceding list element must be pointed at the new element and the pointer in the new element must be pointed at what was formerly the successor of the preceding element. This situation also applies in cases where the successor was a NULL pointer, in other words, when the new element is appended to the list.

Since the list contains objects of the `BaseEl` and `DerivedEl` types, the `insertAfter()` method has been overloaded with two versions. They differ only in different calls to the new operator.

The `insert()` method was overloaded for the same reason. Both versions first call the `getPrev()` method and the corresponding version of the `insertAfter()` method.

■ EXERCISE

The complete class InhomList

```
class InhomList
{
  private:
    Cell* first;

  protected:
   Cell* getPrev(const string& s);
   Cell* getPos(const string& s);

   void  insertAfter(const string& s, Cell* prev);
   void  insertAfter(const string& s,const string& b,
                      Cell* prev);
   void  erasePos(Cell* pos);

  public:
    InhomList(){ first = NULL; }
    InhomList(const InhomList& src);
    ~InhomList();

    InhomList& operator=( const InhomList& src);

    void  insert(const string& n);
    void  insert(const string& n, const string& b);
    void  erase(const string& n);

    void displayAll() const;
};
```

Exercise

Modify and complete the definition of the class `InhomList`, which represents an inhomogeneous list.

■ Write the destructor for the `InhomList` class. The destructor releases the memory occupied by the remaining list elements.

■ Implement the `getPrev()` method and both versions of the `insert()` and `insertAfter()` methods. The algorithm needed for inserting list elements was described in the section "Implementing an Inhomogeneous List."

■ Implement the `displayAll()` method, which walks through the list sequentially, outputting each element.

■ Test insertion and output of list elements. Check whether the comments on the objects are output, if present.

■ Define the `getPos()` method, which locates the position of an element to be deleted. If the element is in the list, its address is returned. Otherwise a NULL pointer is returned.

■ Write the `erasePos()` method, which deletes a list element at a given position. Pay attention to whether the element to be deleted is the first or any other element in the list. Since the destructor for `Cell` was declared virtual, only one version of the `deletePos()` method is necessary.

■ Define the `erase()` method, which deletes a list element with a given name from the list.

■ Test deletion of list elements. Continually display the remaining elements in the list to be certain.

■ Now implement the copy constructor and assignment. Use the `insert()` to construct the list, calling the applicable version of the method. You can call the `typeid()` operator to ascertain the type of the list element currently to be inserted. The operator is declared in the header file `typeinfo`.

Example: `if( typeid(*ptr) == typeid(DerivedEl)) ...`

The expression is true if `ptr` references a `DerivedEl` type object.

■ Then test the copy constructor and the assignment

■ **SOLUTION**

```cpp
// -------------------------------------------------------
// cell.h
// Defines the classes Cell, BaseEl, and DerivedEl.
// -------------------------------------------------------
#ifndef _CELL_
#define _CELL_

#include <string>
#include <iostream>
using namespace std;

class Cell
{
  private:
    Cell* next;

  protected:
    Cell(Cell* suc = NULL ){ next = suc; }

  public:
    virtual ~Cell(){ }
    Cell* getNext() const { return next; }
    void  setNext(Cell* suc) { next = suc; }

    virtual void display() const = 0;
};

class BaseEl : public Cell
{
  private:
    string name;

  public:
    BaseEl( Cell* suc = NULL, const string& s = "")
    :  Cell(suc), name(s){}

    // Access methods:
    void    setName(const string& s){ name = s; }
    const string& getName() const { return name; }

    void display() const
    {
        cout << "\n--------------------------------"
             << "\nName:        " << name << endl;
    }
};
```

```
class DerivedEl : public BaseEl
{
   private:
     string rem;

   public:
     DerivedEl(Cell* suc = NULL,
                 const string& s="", const string& b="")
     : BaseEl(suc, s), rem(b){ }
     // Access methods:
     void      setRem(const string& b){ rem = b; }
     const string& getRem() const { return rem; }
     void display() const
     {
         BaseEl::display();
         cout << "Remark:      " << rem << endl;
     }
};
#endif

// ------------------------------------------------------
// List.h : Defines the class InhomList
// ------------------------------------------------------
#ifndef _LIST_H_
#define _LIST_H_
#include "cell.h"
class InhomList
{
  private:
    Cell* first;
  protected:
    Cell* getPrev(const string& s);
    Cell* getPos( const string& s);
    void  insertAfter(const string& s, Cell* prev);
    void  insertAfter(const string& s,const string& b,
                       Cell* prev);
    void  erasePos(Cell* pos);
  public:
     InhomList(){ first = NULL; }
     InhomList(const InhomList& src);
     ~InhomList();
     InhomList& operator=( const InhomList& src);
     void  insert(const string& n);
     void  insert(const string& n, const string& b);
     void  erase(const string& s);
     void displayAll() const;
};
#endif
```

```
// ---------------------------------------------------
// List.cpp : The methods of class InhomList
// ---------------------------------------------------
#include "List.h"
#include <typeinfo>

// Copy constructor:
InhomList::InhomList(const InhomList& src)
{
   // Append the elements from src to the empty list.
   first = NULL;
   Cell *pEl = src.first;
   for(  ; pEl != NULL;  pEl = pEl->getNext() )
      if(typeid(*pEl) == typeid(DerivedEl))
            insert(dynamic_cast<DerivedEl*>(pEl)->getName(),
                   dynamic_cast<DerivedEl*>(pEl)->getRem());
      else
            insert(dynamic_cast<BaseEl*>(pEl)->getName());
}


// Assignment:
InhomList& InhomList::operator=(const InhomList& src)
{
   // To free storage for all elements:
   Cell *pEl = first,
        *next = NULL;
   while( pEl != NULL )
   {
      next = pEl->getNext();
      delete pEl;
      pEl = next;
   }

   first = NULL;                    // Empty list

   // Copy the elements from src to the empty list.
   pEl = src.first;

   for(  ; pEl != NULL;  pEl = pEl->getNext() )
      if(typeid(*pEl) == typeid(DerivedEl))
            insert(dynamic_cast<DerivedEl*>(pEl)->getName(),
                   dynamic_cast<DerivedEl*>(pEl)->getRem());
      else
            insert(dynamic_cast<BaseEl*>(pEl)->getName());

   return *this;
}
```

```
// Destructor:
InhomList::~InhomList()
{
   Cell *pEl = first,
        *next = NULL;
   while( pEl != NULL )
   {
      next = pEl->getNext();
      delete pEl;
      pEl = next;
   }
}

Cell* InhomList::getPrev(const string& n)
{
   Cell *pEl  = first,
        *prev = NULL;
   while( pEl != NULL  )
   {
      if( n > dynamic_cast<BaseEl*>(pEl)->getName() )
      {
         prev = pEl;   pEl  = pEl->getNext();
      }
      else
          return prev;
   }
   return prev;
}

Cell* InhomList::getPos( const string& n)
{
    Cell *pEl  = first;
    while( pEl != NULL  &&
           (n != dynamic_cast<BaseEl*>(pEl)->getName()))
       pEl  = pEl->getNext();
     if( pEl != NULL  &&
         n == dynamic_cast<BaseEl*>(pEl)->getName())
       return pEl;
     else
       return NULL;
}

void InhomList::insertAfter(const string& s, Cell* prev)
{
  if( prev == NULL )     // Insert at the beginning:
      first = new BaseEl( first, s);
  else                   // In the middle or at the end:
  {  Cell* p = new BaseEl(prev->getNext(), s);
     prev->setNext(p);
   }
}
```

```
void InhomList::insertAfter( const string& s,
                                const string& b, Cell* prev)
{
  if( prev == NULL )        // Insert at the beginning:
    first = new DerivedEl( first, s, b);
  else                      // In the middle or at the end:
  {
    Cell* p = new DerivedEl(prev->getNext(), s, b);
    prev->setNext(p);
  }
}

void InhomList::insert(const string& n)
{
  Cell* pEl = getPrev(n);
  insertAfter(n, pEl);
}

void  InhomList::insert(const string& n, const string& b)
{
  Cell* pEl = getPrev(n);
  insertAfter(n, b, pEl);
}

void  InhomList::erasePos(Cell* pos)
{
  Cell* temp;
  if( pos != NULL)
    if( pos == first )      // Delete the first element
    {
      temp = first;
      first = first->getNext();
      delete temp;
    }
    else           // Delete from the middle or at the end
    {                         // Get the predecessor
      temp = getPrev( dynamic_cast<BaseEl*>(pos)
                                        ->getName());
      if(temp != NULL)        // and bend pointer.
        temp->setNext(pos->getNext());
      delete pos;
    }
}

void  InhomList::erase(const string& n)
{
  erasePos( getPos(n));
}
```

```
void InhomList::displayAll() const
{
   Cell* pEl = first;
   while(pEl != NULL)
   {
       pEl->display();
       pEl = pEl->getNext();
   }
}

// ------------------------------------------------------
// List_t.cpp : Tests the sorted inhomogeneous list
// ------------------------------------------------------

#include "List.h"

int main()
{
   InhomList liste1;

   cout << "\nTo test inserting. " << endl;

   liste1.insert("Bully, Max");
   liste1.insert("Cheers, Rita", "always merry");
   liste1.insert("Quick, John", "topfit");
   liste1.insert("Banderas, Antonio");

   liste1.displayAll(); cin.get();

   cout << "\nTo test deleting. " << endl;

   liste1.erase("Banderas, Antonio");
   liste1.erase("Quick, John");
   liste1.erase("Cheers, Rita");

   liste1.displayAll(); cin.get();

   cout << "\n--------------------------------"
        << "\nGenerate a copy and insert an element. "
        << endl;

   InhomList liste2(liste1),     // Copy constructor
             liste3;             // and an empty list.

   liste2.insert("Chipper, Peter", "in good temper");
   liste3 = liste2;              // Assignment
   cout << "\nAfter the assignment:  " << endl;
   liste3.displayAll();

   return 0;
}
```

chapter 27

Multiple Inheritance

This chapter describes how new classes are created by multiple inheritance and explains their uses. Besides introducing you to creating and destroying objects in multiply-derived classes, virtual base classes are depicted to avoid ambiguity in multiple inheritance.

■ MULTIPLY-DERIVED CLASSES

The multiply-derived class MotorHome

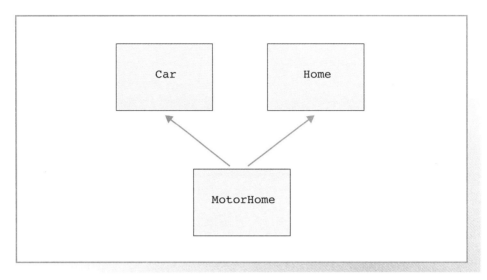

Definition scheme for class MotorHome

```
class MotorHome : public Car, public Home
{
   private:
     // Additional private members here
   protected:
     // Additional protected members here
   public:
     // Additional public members here
};
```

A class can contain not just one but several different base classes. In this case the class is derived from multiple base classes in a process known as *multiple inheritance*.

☐ The Multiply-Derived Class MotorHome

This class Car is used to represent vehicles and the class Home contains characteristic values for an apartment, such as floor space, number and type of rooms, and typical operations, such as building, selling, or renting.

Using these two classes you can then derive the MotorHome class. The opposite page shows the inheritance and definition schemes for the new class. An object of the MotorHome class contains both the members of Car and the members of Home. More specifically, the object contains two base sub-objects of type Car and Home.

☐ Accessibility of Base Classes

Since the MotorHome class has two public base classes, it assumes the public interfaces of both classes. A MotorHome type object not only allows access to the additional public members but to all the public members of the base classes Car and Home.

When defining a multiply-derived class, the accessibility, private, protected, or public, must be defined separately for each base class. The MotorHome class could have the public base class Car and the protected base class Home.

Example:
```
class MotorHome:public Car,protected Home
        {  . . . };
```

If the keyword is omitted, the base class will default to private.

Example:
```
class MotorHome : public Car, Home
        {  . . . };
```

This statement defines the public base class Car and the private base class Home. This makes all the public members in Home private members of the derived class.

In multiple inheritance each public base class establishes an *is relationship*. This is similar to simple inheritance. If the MotorHome class inherits two public base classes, a motor-home *is* a special kind of motor vehicle and a special kind of home.

■ MULTIPLE INDIRECT BASE CLASSES

The multiple indirect base class Car

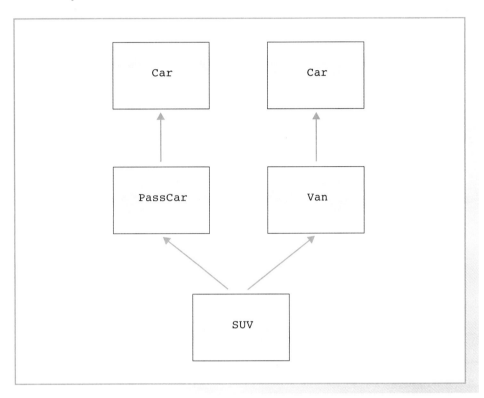

Definition scheme of class SUV

```
class SUV : public PassCar, public Van
{
   // Here are additional methods and data members
};
```

☐ Multiple Identical Base Classes

When multiply-derived classes are defined, a direct base class cannot be inherited more than once. The following statement

Example:
```
class B : public A, public A    // Error
    { . . . };
```

causes the compiler to issue an error message.

A class can be derived from several classes that have a common base class, however. This class is then referred to as a *multiple indirect base class*.

The inheritance graph on the opposite page shows the multiply-derived class SUV, which was derived from the classes PassCar and Van. Both base classes were themselves derived from the Car class. This makes Car a multiple indirect base class of the SUV class.

☐ Ambiguity

An object of the SUV class thus contains the members of Car *twice*. Access to members of the Car class results in *ambiguity*.

Example:
```
SUV mySUV(. . .);
cout << mySUV.getProd();    // Error
```

Both the base classes PassCar and Van contain a method called getProd(), which they both inherited from the Car class. In this case the compiler cannot decide which method is meant.

Ambiguity in the context of multiple inheritance is also possible when *several* base classes contain members with identical names. If both the Home class and the Car class contain a method called getNr(), the getNr() method cannot be correctly identified in the following statement.

Example:
```
MotorHome motorHome ( . . .);
motorHome.getNr();
```

To resolve ambiguity of this kind, you can use the scope resolution operator to determine which base class is meant.

Example:
```
cout << motorHome.Home::getNr();
cout << mySUV.PassCar::getProd();
```

The getNr() method in the Home class is called first, followed by the getProd() method inherited by PassCar from the Car class.

■ VIRTUAL BASE CLASSES

The virtual base class `Car`

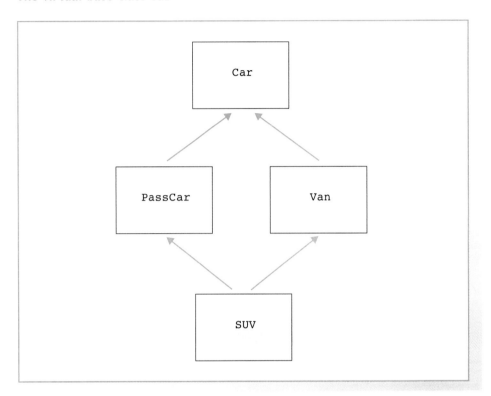

Definition scheme

```
class PassCar : public virtual Car
{
    // Here are additional members
    // of class PassCar
};

class Van : public virtual Car
{
    // Here are additional members
    // of class Van
};
```

☐ Issues

You will not normally want a class created by multiple inheritance to contain multiple instances of an indirect base class. Why should a station wagon contain two versions of the manufacturer's name or the chassis number for example? So you might be asking yourself whether you can define multiply-derived classes that will contain only one instance of an indirect base class.

C++ uses *virtual base classes* to do this. An object in a multiply-derived class contains only one instance of the members in a virtual base class. The inheritance graph on the opposite page uses the SUV class to illustrate this situation.

☐ Declaration

A direct base class is declared virtual when a derived class is defined. You can use the virtual keyword, which directly precedes the name of the base class.

In the definition scheme shown opposite, the Car class becomes the virtual base class of PassCar and Van. However, the fact that the base class Car is virtual has no significance at this point.

A virtual base class takes effect in cases of multiple inheritance. The following definition

Example:
```
class SUV
   : public PassCar, public Van
     { . . . };
```

ensures that the SUV class only contains one instance of the virtual base class Car. An object my of the SUV class gets sufficient memory for only one Car class sub-object. More specifically, the statement

Example:
```
cout<<"Producer: " << mySUV.getProd();
```

does not cause ambiguity.

The following items are important with respect to virtual base classes:

- a virtual base class stays virtual even if further derivations are built. Each class derived from PassCar also has the Car class as a virtual base class.
- you cannot change the declaration of an indirect base class to virtual.

You must therefore decide what classes are to be declared virtual when you design the class hierarchy. Later modifications will require modifications to the source code of any derived classes.

■ CONSTRUCTOR CALLS

☐ Building an inheritance graph

Class Definition

```
class multiDerived : public Base1, public Base2,
                     public Base3
{
  // Here are additional data members and methods
};
```

Inheritance graph

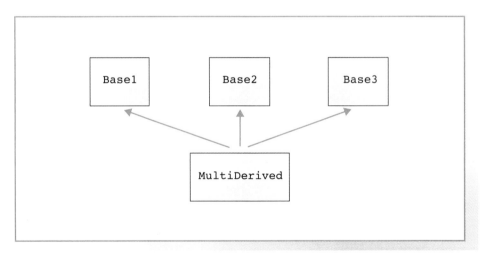

☐ Initialization

When an object is created in a simply-derived class, the sub-objects of the base classes are created first on all levels of the class hierarchy. The sub-object whose class is nearer to the top of the inheritance graph is created first.

The order of the constructor calls is "top down" and follows the inheritance graph. The activation order used for the constructors in simple inheritance has been generalized for multiple inheritance.

☐ Inheritance Graph

Again, the inheritance graph, also called *sub-object lattice*, has an important job to do. When a derived class is defined, the following rules apply:

■ In cases of multiple inheritance, base classes are entered into the inheritance graph from left to right in the order in which they were stated when the class was defined. The graph opposite illustrates this point.

If the class hierarchy does not contain any virtual base classes, the following applies to the activation order of the constructors.

■ The base class constructors are executed first, top-down and from left to right on each level.
■ Finally, the constructor belonging to the current class, which is at the bottom of the inheritance graph, is executed.

If we look at the example on the opposite page, this means that the sub-objects of the base classes `Base1`, `Base2`, and `Base3` are created in this order. Then the constructor of `MultiDerived` is executed.

☐ Base Initializers

The constructor for the class at the bottom end of the inheritance graph uses base initializers to pass the values to the direct and indirect base classes. If the base initializer definition is missing in a constructor definition, the default constructor of the base class is automatically executed.

Initial values are thus passed to the base class constructors "bottom up."

■ INITIALIZING VIRTUAL BASE CLASSES

Class SUV

```
class SUV : public PassCar, public Van
{
   private:
    // . . .
   public:
     SUV( ... ) : Car( ... )
     {
       // Initialize additional data members
     }

     void display() const
     {
       PassCar::display();
       Van::display();
       // Output additional data members
     }
};
```

Constructor Calls in Virtual Base Classes

When an object is created for a multiply-derived class, the constructors of the base classes are called first. However, if there is one virtual base class in the class hierarchy, the virtual base class constructor is executed *before* a constructor of a non-virtual base class is called.

 NOTE

The constructors of the virtual base classes are called first, followed by the constructors of non-virtual base classes in the order defined in the inheritance graph.

The constructor of the virtual base class nearest the top of the inheritance graph is executed first. This does not necessarily mean the top level of the class hierarchy, since a virtual base class can be derived from a non-virtual base class.

In our example with the multiply-derived class SUV (Sport Utility Vehicle) the constructor for the virtual base class Car is called first, followed by the direct base classes PassCar and Van, and last but not least, the constructor of the SUV class.

Base Initializers

You may be wondering what arguments are used to call the constructor of a virtual base class. A base initializer of the directly-derived class or any other derivation could be responsible. The following applies:

 NOTE

The constructor of a virtual base class is called with the arguments stated for the base initializer of the *last* class to be derived, i.e. class at the bottom end of the inheritance graph.

The example opposite shows SUV containing a constructor with *one* base initializer. Its arguments are passed to the constructor of the virtual base class Car.

For the purpose of initialization, it does not matter whether a class derived directly from Car contains a base initializer or not. Base initializers for virtual indirect base classes defined in the constructor of a direct base class are ignored. If the base classes PassCar and Van also contained base initializers for the virtual base class Car, these would be ignored too.

If the constructor for the last derived class does not contain a base initializer, the default constructor is executed for each virtual base class. Whatever happens, a default constructor must then exist in every virtual base class! Thus, base initializers that happen to exist in base classes are also ignored.

■ **EXERCISES**

The multiply-derived class MotorHome

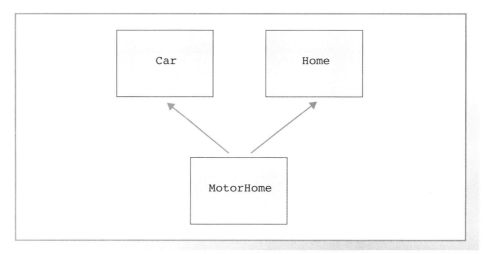

Additional members of class MotorHome

Data member: Type
   cat   CATEGORY

Methods:

   MotorHome(CATEGORY, long, const string&, int, double);

    void   setCategory(CATEGORY)
    CATEGORY getCategory() const ;

    void display() const;

Exercise 1

The multiply-derived class `MotorHome` needs to be fully implemented and tested.

- Define an enumeration type `CATEGORY` that represents the categories "Luxury," "First Class," "Middle Class," and "Economy".

- Develop a class called `Home` with two data members used to store the number of rooms and the size in square meters. Supply default values for your constructor definition to create a default constructor. In addition to access methods, also define the method `display()`, which outputs the data members of an apartment.

- Define a class derived from the `Car` and `Home` classes called `MotorHome`, which is used to represent motorhomes. Inheritance of `public` base classes is used. The `MotorHome` class contains a new data member used to store one value of the `CATEGORY` type. In addition to defining a constructor with default values, also define appropriate access methods and a `display()` method for output.

  Place your definitions of the `Home` and `MotorHome` classes in a separate header file, which includes the existing header file `car.h`.

- Write a `main` function that first fully initializes a `MotorHome` type object and then outputs the object.

  Then create a second instance of the `MotorHome` type without initial values and display the object on screen. Call all the set methods in the `MotorHome` class and its base classes to set your own values for the objects. Then output the object once more.

Class hierarchy for the multiply-derived class SUV

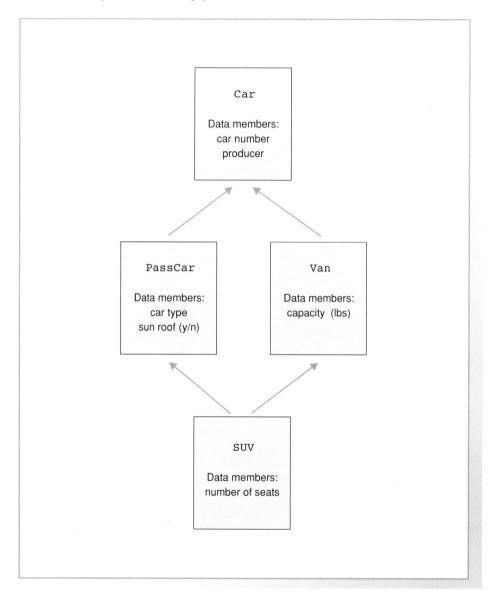

Exercise 2

Now fully define the SUV class for testing virtual base classes.

- Change the definition of the PassCar class in the car.h header file to make Car a virtual base class of the PassCar class.
- Then define the Van class using the Car class as a virtual base class. The new class should contain an additional data member used to represent the payload of the van in kilograms. A maximum of 750 kg applies to vans. The constructor should use default values to initialize the data members with defaults, thus providing a default constructor for the class. A maximum value of 750 applies for the payload. In addition to the access method display(), you still need to define methods for screen output.
- Create the class SUV, which is derived from PassCar and Van, to represent a station wagon. Store the number of seats available in the station wagon as a data member.

  The constructor in the SUV class should use the base initializer to set all the values of a station wagon using default values for every data member. Additionally, define access methods and a display() to define output.
- Use a main function to test the SUV class; the function should create station wagons with and without default values and display them on screen.

solutions

■ SOLUTIONS

Exercise 1

```
// -------------------------------------------------------
// car.h :  Definition of base class Car and
//          derived classes PassCar and Truck
// -------------------------------------------------------
// car.cpp
// Implementing methods of Car, PassCar, and Truck
// -------------------------------------------------------
//
// These files have been left unchanged
// from Chapters 23 and 25.
//


// -------------------------------------------------------
// motorHome.h : Definition of the class Home and the
//               multiply-derived class MotorHome
// -------------------------------------------------------
#ifndef _MOTORHOME_H_
#define _MOTORHOME_H_
#include "car.h"
#include <iomanip>
#include <iostream>
using namespace std;

enum CATEGORY {LUXURY, FIRSTCLASS, SECONDCLASS, ECONOMY};

class Home
{
   private:
      int room;
      double ft2;

   public:
      Home(int r = 0, double m2 = 0.0)
      { room = r; ft2 = m2;}
      void setRoom(int n){ room = n;}
      int  getRoom() const { return room; }
      void   setSquareFeet(double m2){ ft2 = m2;}
      double getSquareFeet() const { return ft2; }
      void display() const
      {
         cout << "Number of rooms:   " << room
              << "\nSquare feet: "
              << fixed << setprecision(2) << ft2 << endl;
      }
};
```

```cpp
class MotorHome : public Car, public Home
{
   private:
      CATEGORY cat;

   public:
      MotorHome(long n=0L, const string& prod="", int ro=0,
                double m2=0.0, CATEGORY k=ECONOMY)
      : Car(n, prod), Home(ro, m2), cat(k)
      {}

      void      setCategory(CATEGORY c){cat = c;}
      CATEGORY  getCategory() const { return cat;}

      void display() const
      {
         cout << "\nMotorHome:    ";
         Car::display();
         Home::display();
         cout << "Category:     ";
         switch(cat)
         {
            case LUXURY:        cout << "    Luxury";
                        break;
            case FIRSTCLASS:    cout << "    First class";
                        break;
            case SECONDCLASS:   cout << "    Second class";
                        break;
            case ECONOMY:       cout << "    Economy";
                        break;
         }
         cout << endl;
      }
};
#endif

// ----------------------------------------------------
// motorHome_t.cpp
// Testing the multiply-derived class MotorHome
// ----------------------------------------------------
#include "motorHome.h"

int main()
{
    MotorHome rv(12345L, "Texaco", 2, 40.5, LUXURY);
    rv.display();

    MotorHome holiday;
    holiday.display();          // Default values
    cin.get();
```

```
        holiday.setNr(54321);
        holiday.setProd("VW");
        holiday.setRoom(1);
        holiday.setSquareFeet(11.5);
        holiday.setCategory(SECONDCLASS);
        holiday.display();
        return 0;
}
```

Exercise 2

```
// ------------------------------------------------------
// car.h :  Definition of base class Car and
//          the derived classes PassCar and Truck
// ------------------------------------------------------
// car.cpp
// Implementing the methods of Car, PassCar, and Truck
// ------------------------------------------------------
//
// These files are carried over from Chapter 23 and 25,
// with the following changes:
//
// Class Car is a virtual base class now
class PassCar : public virtual Car
{
   // ...
};

class Truck : public virtual Car
{
   // ...
};


// ------------------------------------------------------
// suv.h : Defines the class Van and
//         the multiply-derived class SUV
// ------------------------------------------------------
#ifndef _SUV_H
#define _SUV_H

#include "car.h"

class Van : public virtual Car
{
  private:
    double capacity;
```

```cpp
public:
  Van(long n=0L, const string& prod="",
              double l=0.0)
  : Car(n,prod)
  {
      if(l > 750)  l = 750;
      capacity = l;
  }

  void setCapacity(double l)
  {
      if(l > 750)
          capacity= 750;
      else
          capacity = l;
  }
  double getCapacity() const { return capacity; }

  void display() const
  {
    cout << "Capacity:           "
         << capacity  << " kg" << endl;
  }
};

class SUV : public PassCar, public Van
{
  private:
    int cnt;           // Number of seats
  public:
    SUV(const string& tp="without type", bool sb=false,
        long n=0L, const string& prod=" none ",
        double l=0.0, int z = 1)
    : PassCar(tp,sb), Car(n,prod),
      Van(n,prod,l), cnt(z)
    { }

  void display() const
  {
     PassCar::display();
     Van::display();
      cout << "Number of seats:  " << cnt << endl;
  }
};

#endif
```

```cpp
// ----------------------------------------------------
// suv_t.cpp :  Tests the class SUV
// ----------------------------------------------------

#include "suv.h"

int main()
{
    SUV mobil("Bravada", true, 120345, "Oldsmobile",350,6);
    mobil.display();

    SUV trucky;
    trucky.display();

    trucky.setNr(543221);
    trucky.setProd("Renault");
    trucky.setCapacity(1000.);

    trucky.display();

    return 0;
}
```

chapter 28

Exception Handling

This chapter describes how a C++ program uses error-handling techniques to resolve error conditions. In addition to throwing and catching exceptions, we also examine how exception specifications are declared and exception classes are defined, additionally looking into the use of standard exception classes.

▪ TRADITIONAL ERROR HANDLING

Error checking after leaving a function

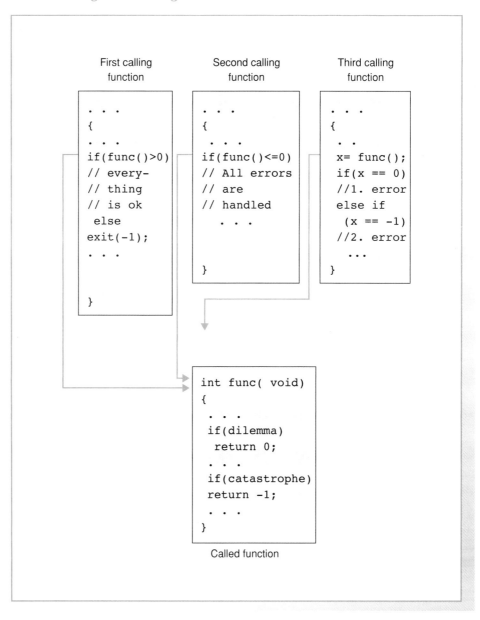

First calling function

```
. . .
{
. . .
if(func()>0)
// every-
// thing
// is ok
 else
exit(-1);
. . .


}
```

Second calling function

```
. . .
{
 . . .
if(func()<=0)
// All errors
// are
// handled
   . . .


}
```

Third calling function

```
. . .
{
 . .
 x= func();
 if(x == 0)
 //1. error
 else if
   (x == -1)
 //2. error
   ...
}
```

```
int func( void)
{
 . . .
 if(dilemma)
  return 0;
 . . .
 if(catastrophe)
 return -1;
 . . .
}
```

Called function

☐ Error Conditions

Errors that occur at program runtime can seriously interrupt the normal flow of a program. Some common causes of errors are

- division by 0, or values that are too large or small for a type
- no memory available for dynamic allocation
- errors on file access, for example, file not found
- attempt to access an invalid address in main memory
- invalid user input

Anomalies like these lead to incorrect results and may cause a computer to crash. Both of these cases can have fatal effects on your application.

One of the programmer's most important tasks is to predict and handle errors. You can judge a program's quality by the way it uses error-handling techniques to counteract any potential error, although this is by no means easy to achieve.

☐ Traditional Error Handling

Traditional structured programming languages use normal syntax to handle errors:

- errors in function calls are indicated by special return values
- global error variables or flags are set when errors occur, and then checked again later.

If a function uses its return value to indicate errors, the return value must be examined whenever the function is called, even if no error has occurred.

Example:
```
if ( func ()> 0 )
      // Return value positive => o.k.
   else
      // Treat errors
```

Error variables and flags must also be checked after *every* corresponding action.

In other words, you need to continually check for errors while a program is executing. If you do happen to forget to check for errors, the consequences may be fatal.

■ EXCEPTION HANDLING

Using the `throw` statement

```cpp
// calc_err.cpp: Defining the function calc(),
//                which throws exceptions.
// --------------------------------------------------

class Error
{
    // Infos about the error cause
};


double calc( int a, int b )
{
    if ( b < 0 )
        throw (string)"Denominator is negative!";

    if( b == 0 )
    {
        Error errorObj;
        throw errorObj;
    }

    return ((double)a/b);
}
```

☐ Exception Handling Concept

C++ introduces a new approach to error handling. *Exception handling* is based on keeping the normal functionality of the program separate from error handling. The basic idea is that errors occurring in one particular part of the program are reported to another part of the program, known as the *calling environment*. The calling environment performs central error handling.

An application program no longer needs to continually check for errors, because in the case of an error, control is automatically transferred to the calling environment. When reporting an error, specific information on the error cause can be added. This information is evaluated by the error-handling routines in the calling environment.

☐ The `throw` Statement

An exception that occurs is recorded to the calling environment by means of a `throw` statement; this is why we also say that an exception has been *thrown*.

Syntax: `throw fault;`

The expression `fault` is an *exception object* that is thrown to the calling environment. It can belong to any type except `void`.

Example: `throw "Fire!";`

In this example, the exception object is a string that is thrown to the calling environment.

☐ Exception Classes

Normally, you define your own exception classes to categorize exceptions. In this case you use the `throw` statement to throw an object belonging to a specific exception class.

An exception class need not contain data members or methods. However, the *type*, which is used by the calling environment to identify the error, is important. Generally, the exception class will contain members that provide more specific information on the cause of the error.

In the sample program on the opposite page, the `calc()` function throws exceptions in two cases, where the numerator is negative or has a value of `0`. In the first case, the exception thrown is a string. In the second case, the exception is an `Error` exception class object. Instead of creating a local exception object `errorObj`, a temporary object can be created:

Example: `throw Error();`   `// It is shorter`

■ EXCEPTION HANDLERS

Syntax of `try` **and** `catch` **blocks**

```
try
{

   // Exceptions thrown by this block will be
   // caught by the exception handlers,
   // which are defined next.

}
catch( Type1 exc1)
{

   // Type1 exceptions are handled here.

}

[ catch( Type2 exc2)
 {

    // Type2 exceptions are handled here.

 }
  . . .             //etc.
]
[ catch( ... )
 {

    // All other exceptions are handled here.
 }]
```

 NOTE

The brackets [...] in a syntax description indicate that the enclosed section is optional.

☐ How Exception Handling Works

The part of a program that performs central error handling in the calling environment is referred to as an *exception handler*. An exception handler catches the exception object thrown to it and performs error handling. The exception object type determines which handler will catch it and consequently be executed.

This means that you need to specify two things when implementing exception handling:

- the part of the program that can throw exceptions
- the exception handlers that will process the various exception types.

C++ provides language elements for this task, the keywords `try` and `catch`. Each keyword precedes a code block and thus they are often referred to as `try` and `catch` blocks. Syntactically speaking, each `try` and `catch` block is a statement, however.

☐ `try` and `catch` Blocks

A *try block* contains the program code in which errors can occur and exceptions can be thrown. Normally, a `try` block will consist of a group of functions that can produce similar errors.

Each *catch block* defines an exception handler, where the *exception declaration*, which is enclosed in parentheses, defines the type of exceptions the handler can catch. The `catch` blocks immediately follow the `try` block. A minimum of one `catch` block is required.

The exception handlers defined by the `catch` blocks catch the exceptions thrown within the `try` block. If there is no handler defined for a particular exception type, the program will not simply enter an undefined state but will be orderly terminated by a call to the standard function `terminate()`.

It is common practice to define specific handlers for certain types of errors and *one* generic handler for all other errors. This functionality is provided by a special syntax in the `catch` statement with an exception declaration consisting of just three dots.

Syntax:
```
catch( ... )
{   // General handler for
    // all other exceptions
}
```

Since the application program decides what reaction is applicable for certain error conditions, the `try` and `catch` blocks are formulated in the application.

■ THROWING AND CATCHING EXCEPTIONS

Demonstration program

```cpp
// calc_err.cpp:  Tests the function calc(),
//                which throws exceptions.
// ------------------------------------------------------
#include <iostream>
#include <string>
using namespace std;

double calc( int a, int b );

int main()
{
    int x, y;
    double res;
    bool flag = false;
    do
    {
      try                                   // try block
       {
         cout << "Enter two positive integers: ";
         cin >> x >> y;
         res = calc( x, y);
         cout << x << "/" << y << " = " << res << endl;
         flag = true;          // Then to leave the loop.
       }
       catch( string& s)               // 1st catch block
       {
         cerr << s << endl;
       }
       catch( Error& )                 // 2nd catch block
       {
         cerr << "Division by 0! " << endl;
       }
       catch(...)                      // 3rd catch block
       {
         cerr << "Unexpected exception! \n";
         exit(1);
       }
    }while( !flag);

    // continued ...
    return 0;
}
```

 NOTE

As the `Error` class contains no data members, the corresponding `catch` block declares only the type of exception, and no parameters. This avoids a compiler warning since the parameter is not used.

☐ Backing Out of an Error Condition

When the `throw` statement is executed, an exception object is thrown. That is, a temporary object of the same type and content as the `throw` expression is created.

Example: `throw "Cyclone!";`

This creates a string as an exception object and copies the string `"Cyclone!"` to it. Thus, if the `throw` expression is a class type, the copy constructor is executed.

The exception object is then thrown and the program control leaves the `try` block. Any changes to the stack that took place after entering the `try` block are unwound. This specifically involves destroying any local, non-static objects. *Unwinding the stack allow you to back out of the normal program flow in an orderly manner.*

☐ Searching for Handlers

After leaving the `try` block, the program control is transferred to an matching handler in the `catch` blocks that follow. This search operation is always performed sequentially beginning with the first `catch` block and the exception declaration of the handler determines whether the handler should be executed.

A handler is called when the type in the exception declaration is

- identical to the exception type thrown or
- a base class of the exception type or
- a base class pointer and the exception is a pointer to a derived class.

This is why the general exception handler `catch( ... )` always has to be defined last. Since the first suitable handler will be executed, and any exception thrown will be caught by the general handler, a handler defined after the general handler would never be called.

☐ Continuing the Program

After executing a handler, the program continues with the first statement following the `catch` blocks, unless the handler throws another exception or terminates the program. After completing exception handling, the exception object that was thrown is destroyed.

The first two `catch` blocks handle both exceptions that the `calc()` function can throw. In both cases a message is displayed and the program carries on prompting for input and computing values. If an unexpected exception occurs, a message is again displayed, but in this case the program then terminates.

■ NESTING EXCEPTION HANDLING

Nested `try` and `catch` blocks

```
try
{
    // Type1 exceptions are thrown here.
    try
    {
        // Type1 and Type2 exceptions are thrown here.
    }
    catch( Type2 e2)
    {
        // Type2 exceptions are pre-handled here
        throw;                  // and thrown again.
    }
        // Other Type1 exceptions
        // can be thrown.
}
catch( Type1 e1)
{
    // Type1 exceptions are handled here.
}
catch(...)
{
    // All remaining exceptions are handled here,
    // particularly Type2 exceptions.
}
```

NOTE

This scenario assumes that the error classes `Type1` and `Type2` are not derived one from another. If class `Type2` is derived from class `Type1`, any `Type2` exceptions thrown will be caught by the handler for the base class `Type1`.

☐ Nested `try` and `catch` Blocks

A program will normally contain multiple `try` blocks with appropriate exception handlers. This allows for various error handling in different parts of the program.

However, a `try` block can contain additional `try` blocks. This allows you to use the handlers in a nested `try` block for special purpose error handling, leaving the handlers in the surrounding `try` block to deal with remaining errors. Handlers in a nested `try` block can also pre-handle specific errors and then pass control to the `try` block wrapper for final handling.

☐ Re-throwing Exceptions

In the last of these cases an exception thrown by the nested `try` block has to be passed to the `try` block wrapper. This is achieved using a `throw` statement that does not expect an exception object.

Example: `throw;`   `// in a catch block`

This re-throws the pre-handled exception, which can then be processed by the handler in the surrounding `try` block. The statement is only valid within a nested `catch` block for this reason.

☐ Exception Specifications

The exceptions that a function can throw are features of that function. The application programmer must have knowledge of both the function prototype and the exceptions the function can throw to ensure that he or she will be capable of programming correct function calls and taking appropriate action in case of errors.

The exceptions a function can throw can be stated in a so-called exception specification list when you declare a function.

Example: `int func(int) throw(BadIndex, OutOfRange);`

The list `BadIndex, OutOfRange` states the exceptions that the function `func()` can throw. If the list is empty, that is, if the list contains only the `throw()` statement, no exceptions are thrown. If the `throw` statement is also missing, there is no specific information about possible exceptions and any exception can be thrown.

■ DEFINING YOUR OWN ERROR CLASSES

Exception handling for numeric operations

```cpp
// calc_new.cpp: New version of function calc(),
//               which throws exceptions of type
//               MathError.
// ----------------------------------------------------
#include <string>
#include <iostream>
using namespace std;
class MathError
{
   private:
     string message;
   public:
     MathError( const string& s) : message(s) {}
     const string& getMessage() const {return message;}
};

double calc( int a, int b ) throw(MathError);
int main()
{
   int x, y;  bool flag = false;
   do
   {
    try                                    // try block
     {
       cout << "Enter two positive integers: ";
       cin >> x >> y;
       cout << x <<"/"<< y <<" = "<< calc( x, y) << '\n';
       flag = true;        // To leave the loop.
     }
    catch( MathError& err)                 // catch block
     {
       cerr << err.getMessage() << endl;
     }
   }while( !flag);
   // continued ...
   return 0;
}
double calc( int a, int b ) throw (MathError)
{ if ( b < 0 )
     throw MathError("Denominator is negative!");
   if( b == 0 )
     throw MathError("Division by 0!");
   return ((double)a/b);
}
```

□ Exception Class Members

When an exception is thrown, the exception object type determines which exception handler will be executed. For this reason, an exception class does not need to have any members.

However, an exception class can contain data members and methods—just like any other class. This makes sense, as locally defined non-static objects are destroyed when an exception has been thrown and the stack is unwound. Thus, the exception handler can no longer access the previously existing objects.

You can use the data members of error classes to rescue data threatened by an error condition. For example, you can store data important for exception handling in an exception object.

□ The Exception Class `MathError`

The exception class `MathError` is defined opposite. The `calc()` function throws an exception when a number input by a user is negative or 0. When an exception is thrown,

Example: `throw MathError("Division by 0!");`

the error message is stored in the exception object. The exception handler can then use the `getMessage()` method to evaluate the message.

□ Exception Hierarchies

New exception classes can be derived from existing exception classes. A base class will normally represent a general error type and specific errors will be represented by derived classes.

Thus, the exception class `MathError` could be defined to represent general errors in mathematical computations, but it would make sense to define derived exception classes for special cases, such as "Division by 0" or "Arithmetic overflow." You could call these classes `DivisionByZero` and `OverflowError`, for example.

Be aware of the following rules for exception handlers in this context:

- given that T is a derived exception class, special errors of this type are handled by the exception handler
- if T is a base class, the handler will also catch the exception objects thrown by derived classes, thus providing similar handling for generic and specific errors.

■ STANDARD EXCEPTION CLASSES

Exception classes derived from `logic_error`

`invalid_argument`	Invalid argument
`out_of_range`	Argument value not in its expected range
`length_error`	Length exceeds maximum capacity
`domain_error`	Domain error reported by the implementation

Exception classes derived from `runtime_error`

`range_error`	Range error in internal computation
`underflow_error`	Arithmetic underflow error
`overflow_error`	Arithmetic overflow error

Using standard exception classes

```
// Subscript operator of class FloatArr throws
// exceptions with type of standard class out_of_range:
// ---------------------------------------------------
#include <stdexcept>
#include <iostream>
using namespace std;
double& FloatArr::operator[](int i) throw(out_of_range)
{  if( i < 0 || i >= anz )
      throw out_of_range("Invalid index!");
   else return arrPtr[i];
}
// -------------- Test Program ------------------
int main()
{
   try
   {
      // Uses arrays of type FloatArr
   }
   catch(out_of_range& err)
   {
      cerr << err.what() << endl;
   }
   // The program continues here.
}
```

☐ Hierarchy of Standard Exception Classes

The C++ standard library contains various exception classes, which are used in the string and container libraries, for example. However, the standard exception classes can be used just like exception classes of your own. Their definitions are to be found in the header file `stdexcept`.

The standard exception classes are organized in a hierarchy, the common base class being the `exception` class. In addition to a default constructor, a copy constructor, and an assignment, this class contains a virtual `public` method, `what()`, which returns a message on the error cause as a C string.

☐ Representing Logic Errors and Runtime Errors

The following exception classes are derived from the `exception` class:

`logic_error`   used to represent logic errors, caused by anomalies in the program's logic. These errors can be avoided.

`runtime_error`   used to represent runtime errors, such as under- or overflows occurring in internal computations. These errors are unpredictable.

The opposite page contains on overview of the exception classes derived from the `logic_error` and `runtime_error` classes. For example, the method `at()` in the `string` class throws an `out_of_range` type exception when an invalid string position is passed to it. If a string cannot be displayed because of its exceptional length, an exception of the `invalid_argument` type is thrown.

An exception of the `overflow_error` or `underflow_error` type is thrown if the value to be displayed is too large or too small for the type in use. The `range_error` class shows range errors, which can occur during internal computations.

A constructor with a string as a parameter is defined in every class derived from `exception`. This means you can initialize exceptions of these types with error messages. The `what()` method returns this error message as a C string.

■ EXERCISES

Exercise 1: Error messages of the exception handler

The first exception handler's message:

```
Error in reading:

Invalid index: ...
```

The second exception handler's message:

```
Error in writing:

Invalid index: ...
```

Exercise 1

The `FloatArr` class needs exception handling for cases where an invalid index is stated when accessing an array member.

- Define the exception class `BadIndex` for this purpose and store the class in the header file "`floatArr.h`". The exception class must contain a data member to store the invalid index. The constructor expects an index that it will copy to the data member. The `const` access method `getBadIndex()` returns the data member.

  Both subscript operators should be able to throw `BadIndex` type exceptions. Add an exception specification to the declaration of the subscript operators.

  The methods that expect the position as an argument, such as `insert()` and `remove()`, should also throw exceptions. Add appropriate exception specifications to the definitions and change the return types from `bool` to `void`.

- Change the definitions of the methods and operator functions to allow a `BadIndex` type exception to be thrown when the index passed to the function is outside the valid range.

- Write a `main` function where a constant vector is created and initialized with fixed values. Exception handling is required for the following scenarios. The array elements are displayed and an index is read until an invalid index value is input. The `catch` handler should output the information shown opposite for each invalid index.

  Then create a non-constant array. Add further exception handling to be performed. Elements are appended or inserted within a `try` block. Include an invalid element access attempt, which causes the `catch` handler to output the information shown opposite. Then finally output the array elements outside the `try` and `catch` blocks.

Exercises

For Exercise 2: Error messages of the exception handlers

Messages of the exception handlers
for an exception object of type DivisionByZero:

Error in initializing:

The denominator is 0!

Error in division:

No division by zero!

Error: Denominator is 0!

New denominator != 0: ...

Exercise 2

Implement exception handling for the `Fraction` class, which is used to represent fractions (see Exercise 2, Chapter 19). Dividing by 0 throws an exception that affects the constructor for the `Fraction` class and the operator functions / and `>>`.

- Define the exception class `DivError`, which has no data members, within the `Fraction` class. The exception class is of the following type

  ```
  Fraction::DivError
  ```

  Add an appropriate exception specification to the declarations of the constructor and the operator functions / and `>>`.

- Change the definition of the constructor in the `Fraction` class. If the value of the denominator is 0, a `DivisionByZero` type exception should be thrown.

- Similarly modify the operator functions.

- Now write a `main` function to test the various exceptions. You will need to arrange three different `try` and `catch` blocks sequentially.

  The first `try/catch` block tests the constructor. Create several fractions, including some with a numerator value of 0 and one with 0 as its denominator. The exception handler should issue the error message shown opposite.

  The second `try/catch` block tests divisions. Use a statement to attempt to divide by 0. The corresponding exception handler should send the second error message shown opposite to your standard output.

  The third `try/catch` block reads numerators and denominators of fractions in dialog. If the value of the denominator is 0, the denominator is read again. If the value is still 0, the third error message as shown opposite is output and the program terminates.

solutions

▪ SOLUTIONS

Exercise 1

```
// --------------------------------------------------------
// floatArr.h : Represents dynamic float arrays.
// Methods throw exceptions for an invalid index.
// --------------------------------------------------------
#ifndef _FLOATARR_
#define _FLOATARR_

#include <iostream>
using namespace std;

class BadIndex
{
  private:
   int index;
  public:
    BadIndex(int i){index = i;}
    int getBadIndex() const {return index;}
};

class FloatArr
{
   private:
     float* arrPtr;      // Dynamic member
     int max;            // Maximum number without
                         // reallocating more memory.
     int cnt;            // Current number of elements.

     void expand( int newSize);      // Function to help
                                     // enlarge the array.
   public:
     FloatArr( int n = 256 );        // Constructors
     FloatArr( int n, float val);
     FloatArr(const FloatArr& src);
     ~FloatArr();                        // Destructor
     FloatArr& operator=( const FloatArr&);   // Assignment

     int  length() const { return cnt; }

      // Subscript operators:
     float& operator[](int i) throw(BadIndex);
     float operator[](int i) const  throw(BadIndex);

     // Methods to append a float value
     // or an array of floats:
     void append( float val);
     void append( const FloatArr& v);
```

```
        FloatArr& operator+=( float val)
        {
            append( val);    return *this;
        }
        FloatArr& operator+=( const FloatArr& v)
        {
            append(v);    return *this;
        }

        // Methods to insert a float value
        // or an array of float values:
     void insert( float val, int pos) throw(BadIndex);
     void insert(const FloatArr& v,int pos) throw(BadIndex);
     void remove(int pos) throw(BadIndex); // Remove
                                            // at pos.
     // Output the array
     friend ostream& operator<<( ostream& os,
                                 const FloatArr& v)
     {
       int w = os.width();          // Save field width.
       for( float *p = v.arrPtr; p < v.arrPtr + v.cnt; ++p)
       {
           os.width(w);   os << *p;
       }
       return os;
     }
};
#endif   // _FLOATARR_

// ----------------------------------------------------
// floatArr.cpp
// Implementing the methods of FloatArr.
// ----------------------------------------------------
#include "floatArr.h"

// ---  Constructors  ---
FloatArr::FloatArr( int n )
{
    max = n;   cnt = 0;           // Sets max and cnt.
    arrPtr = new float[max];    // Allocates memory
}

FloatArr::FloatArr(int n, float val)
{
   max = cnt = n;
   arrPtr  = new float[max];
   for( int i=0; i < cnt; ++i)
       arrPtr[i] = val;
}
```

```
FloatArr::FloatArr(const FloatArr& src)
{
   max = src.max;
   cnt = src.cnt;
   arrPtr = new float[max];

   for( int i = 0; i < cnt; i++ )
     arrPtr[i] = src.arrPtr[i];
}

// --- Destructor ---
FloatArr::~FloatArr()
{
   delete[] arrPtr;
}

// Private functions to help enlarge the array.
void FloatArr::expand( int newSize)
{
   if( newSize == max)
      return;
   max = newSize;
   if( newSize < cnt)
      cnt = newSize;
   float *temp = new float[newSize];
   for( int i = 0; i < cnt; ++i)
      temp[i] = arrPtr[i];

   delete[] arrPtr;
   arrPtr = temp;
}

FloatArr& FloatArr::operator=( const FloatArr& src )
{
   if( this != &src )                 // No self assignment!
   {
      max = src.max;
      cnt = src.cnt;

      delete[] arrPtr;                // Release memory,

      arrPtr = new float[max];     // reallocate,

      for( int i=0; i < cnt; i++)  // copy elements.
         arrPtr[i] = src.arrPtr[i];
   }
   return *this;
}
```

```
float& FloatArr::operator[]( int i ) throw(BadIndex)
{
   if( i < 0 || i >= cnt )  throw BadIndex(i);
   return arrPtr[i];
}
float FloatArr::operator[]( int i ) const throw(BadIndex)
{
   if( i < 0 || i >= cnt )  throw BadIndex(i);
   return arrPtr[i];
}

// Append a float value or an array of floats.
void FloatArr::append( float val)
{
   if( cnt+1 > max)
       expand( cnt+1);
   arrPtr[cnt++] = val;
}
void FloatArr::append( const FloatArr& v)
{
   if( cnt + v.cnt > max)
       expand( cnt + v.cnt);
   int count = v.cnt;              // Necessary if
                                   // v == *this.
   for( int i=0; i < count; ++i)
     arrPtr[cnt++] = v.arrPtr[i];
}

// Inserts a float value or an array of floats.
void FloatArr::insert(float val, int pos) throw(BadIndex)
{
   insert( FloatArr(1, val), pos);
}

void FloatArr::insert( const FloatArr& v, int pos )
                                            throw( BadIndex )
{
   if( pos < 0 || pos > cnt)    // Append is also possible.
       throw BadIndex(pos);
   if( max < cnt + v.cnt)
       expand(cnt + v.cnt);
   int i;
   for( i = cnt-1; i >= pos; --i)    // Shift up from
       arrPtr[i+v.cnt] = arrPtr[i];  // position pos.
   for( i = 0; i < v.cnt; ++i)       // Fill the gap.
       arrPtr[i+pos] = v.arrPtr[i];
   cnt = cnt + v.cnt;
}
```

```
        // To delete
        void FloatArr::remove(int pos) throw(BadIndex)
        {
           if( pos >= 0 && pos < cnt)
           {
              for( int i = pos; i < cnt-1; ++i)
                 arrPtr[i] = arrPtr[i+1];
              --cnt;
           }
           else
             throw BadIndex(pos);
        }


        // --------------------------------------------------------
        // arr_h.cpp
        // Tests exception handling for float arrays.
        // --------------------------------------------------------
        #include <iostream>
        #include <iomanip>
        using namespace std;

        #include "floatArr.h"

        int main()
        {
            const FloatArr v(10, 9.9f);
            bool ok = false;

            while( !ok)
            {
              try
              {
                cout << "Here is the constant array v: \n";

                cout << setw(8) << v <<endl;

                int i;
                cout << "Index? "; cin >> i;
                cout << "\nThe value read: " <<  v[i] << endl;
                ok = true;
              }
              catch(BadIndex& err)
              {
                cerr << "Error in reading.\n"
                     << "\nInvalid index: "
                     << err.getBadIndex() << endl;
              }
            }
```

```
    FloatArr w(20);              // Array w
    try
    {
        w.insert(1.1F, 0);       // To write.
        w.insert(2.2F, 1);
//      w.insert(3.3F, 3);       // Error!
//      w[10] = 5.0;             // Error!
//      w.remove(7);             // Error!
    }
    catch(BadIndex& err)
    {
        cerr << "\nError in writing! "
             << "\nInvalid index: "
             << err.getBadIndex() << endl;
    }

    cout << "\nHere is the array: \n";
    cout << setw(5) << w << endl;
    return 0;
}
```

Exercise 2

```
// -------------------------------------------------
// fraction.h
// A numeric class to represent fractions,
// exception handling is included.
// -------------------------------------------------
#ifndef _FRACTION_
#define _FRACTION_
#include <iostream>
#include <cstdlib>
using namespace std;

class Fraction
{
  private:
    long numerator, denominator;

  public:
    class DivisionByZero
    {
        // No data members
    };
    Fraction(long z = 0, long n = 1) throw(DivisionByZero);
    Fraction operator-() const
    {
        return Fraction(-numerator, denominator);
    }
```

```
    Fraction& operator+=(const Fraction& a)
    {
        numerator = a.numerator * denominator
                 + numerator * a.denominator;
        denominator *= a.denominator;
        return *this;
    }

    Fraction& operator-=(const Fraction& a)
    {
        *this += (-a);
        return *this;
    }

    Fraction& operator++()
    {
        numerator += denominator;
        return *this;
    }

    Fraction& operator--()
    {
        numerator -= denominator;
        return *this;
    }
    friend Fraction operator+(const Fraction&,
                              const Fraction&);
    friend Fraction operator-(const Fraction&,
                              const Fraction&);
    friend Fraction operator*(const Fraction&,
                              const Fraction&);
    friend Fraction operator/(const Fraction&,
                              const Fraction&)
                        throw(Fraction::DivisionByZero);

    friend ostream& operator<<(ostream&, const Fraction&);
    friend istream& operator>>(istream& is, Fraction& a)
                        throw(Fraction::DivisionByZero);
};

#endif
```

```
// -------------------------------------------------------
// fraction.cpp
// Defines methods and friend functions.
// -------------------------------------------------------
#include <iostream>
#include <cstdlib>
using namespace std;
#include "fraction.h"
// Constructor:
Fraction::Fraction(long z, long n)
                         throw(Fraction::DivisionByZero)
{
  if(n == 0)  throw DivisionByZero();
  if( n < 0)  z = -z, n = -n;
  numerator = z;   denominator  = n;
}

Fraction operator+(const Fraction& a, const Fraction& b)
{
   Fraction temp;
   temp.denominator = a.denominator * b.denominator;
   temp.numerator = a.numerator*b.denominator
                 + b.numerator * a.denominator;
   return temp;
}

Fraction operator-(const Fraction& a, const Fraction& b )
{
   Fraction temp = a;   temp += (-b);
   return temp;
}

Fraction operator*(const Fraction& a, const Fraction& b )
{
   Fraction temp;
   temp.numerator = a.numerator * b.numerator;
   temp.denominator  = a.denominator  * b.denominator;
   return temp;
}

Fraction operator/(const Fraction& a, const Fraction& b )
                         throw(Fraction::DivisionByZero)
{
   if( b.numerator == 0)  throw Fraction::DivisionByZero();
   // Multiply a with the inverse of b:
   Fraction temp;
   temp.numerator = a.numerator * b.denominator;
   temp.denominator  = a.denominator  * b.numerator;
   if( temp.denominator < 0 )
     temp.numerator = -temp.numerator,
     temp.denominator  = -temp.denominator;
   return temp;
}
```

```cpp
ostream& operator<<(ostream& os, const Fraction& a)
{
   os << a.numerator << "/" << a.denominator;
   return os;
}

istream& operator>>(istream& is, Fraction& a)
                      throw(Fraction::DivisionByZero)
{
   cout << "Enter a fraction:\n"
           "  Numerator:       ";    is >> a.numerator;
   cout << "  Denominator != 0:  ";   is >> a.denominator;

   if( !is) return is;

   if( a.denominator == 0)
   {
     cout << "\nError: The denominator is 0\n"
          << "New Denominator != 0: "; is >> a.denominator;
   }
   if( a.denominator == 0)
      throw Fraction::DivisionByZero();
   if( a.denominator < 0 )
      a.numerator = -a.numerator,
      a.denominator  = -a.denominator;

   return is;
}


// --------------------------------------------------------
// fract_t.cpp : Testing the class Fraction.
// Modules: fract_t.cpp  fraction.cpp
// --------------------------------------------------------
#include <iostream.h>
#include "fraction.h"

int main()
{
   try        // Tests the exception of the constructor:
   {
     Fraction c(5,0);
   }
   catch(Fraction::DivisionByZero& )
   {
     cout << "\nError on initializing: "
          << "\nThe denominator is 0\n";
   }
```

```cpp
   Fraction a(1,3), b(3);

   try
   {
     cout << "\nSome test output:\n\n";

     cout << " a = " << a << endl;
     cout << " b = " << b << endl;

     cout << " a + b = " << (a + b) << endl;
     cout << " a - b = " << (a - b) << endl;
     cout << " a * b = " << (a * b) << endl;
     b = 0;
     cout << " a / b = " << (a / b) << endl;    // Error!
   }
   catch(Fraction::DivisionByZero& )
   {
     cout << "\nError on dividing: "
          << "\nNo division by zero! 0\n";
   }


   cout << "   --a =  " <<  --a << endl;
   cout << "   ++a  = " <<  ++a << endl;

   a += Fraction(1,2);
   cout << " a+= 1/2;  a = " << a << endl;

   a -= Fraction(1,2);
   cout << " a-= 1/2;  a = " << a << endl;

   cout << "-b = " << -b << endl;

   cout << "\nAnd now your input: \n";
   try
   {
     cin  >> a;
   }
   catch(Fraction::DivisionByZero&)
   {
     cerr << "\nError: The denominator is 0\n";
     exit(1);
   }

   cout << "\nYour input: " << a  << endl;

   return 0;
}
```

chapter **29**

More about Files

This chapter describes

- random access to files based on file streams
- options for querying file state
- exception handling for files.

We will also illustrate how to make objects in polymorphic classes persistent, that is, how to save them in files. The applications introduced in this chapter include simple index files and hash tables.

■ OPENING A FILE FOR RANDOM ACCESS

Combined open modes for read and write access

Open mode	Effects	Must the file exist?
ios::in | ios::out	To open the file for input and output.	yes
ios::in | ios::out | ios::trunc	Opens the file for input and output. If the file already exists, it will be truncated.	no
ios::in | ios::out | ios::app	Opens the file for input and output. If the file does not exist, it will be created. Before each writing access, a seek to end is performed.	no

 NOTE

1. If the flag ios::binary is additionally set, the file will be opened in binary mode.
2. If the flag ios::ate ("at end") is additionally set, the current seek position is set to end-of-file immediately after opening.

☐ Random File Access

So far we have only looked at sequential file access. If you need access to specific information in such a file, you have to walk through the file from top to tail, and new records are always appended at the end of the file.

Random file access gives you the option of reading and writing information directly at a pre-defined position. To be able to do this, you need to change the current file position explicitly, that is, you need to point the get/put pointer to the next byte to be manipulated. After pointing the pointer, you can revert to using the read and write operations that you are already familiar with.

☐ Open Modes

One prerequisite of random file access is that the position of the records in the file can be precisely identified. This implies opening the file in binary mode to avoid having to transfer additional escape characters to the file.

Example:
```
ios::openmode mode = ios::in | ios::out |
                     ios::app | ios::binary;
fstream fstr("account.fle", mode);
```

This statement opens the file "Account.fle" in binary mode for reading and *appending at end-of-file*. The file will be created if it did not previously exist. Random read access to the file is possible, but for write operations new records will be appended at the end of the file.

To enable random read and write access to a file, the file can be opened as follows:

Example:
```
ios::openmode mode = ios::in | ios::out |
                     ios::binary;
fstream fstr("account.fle", mode);
```

However, this technique can only be used for existing files. If the file does not exist, you can use the ios::trunc flag to create it.

The section "File State" discusses your error handling options if a file, such as "account.fle" cannot be found.

▪ POSITIONING FOR RANDOM ACCESS

The three access points in a file

Access point	Positioning flag	File
Beginning of the file	`ios::beg`	●
Current position	`ios::cur`	●
End of file	`ios::end`	●

☐ Discovering and Changing the Current Position

The file stream classes comprise methods to discover and change the current position in a file. The `tellp()` and `tellg()` methods return the current position of the put or get pointers as a `long` value.

Example: `long rpos = myfile.tellg();`

This statement queries the current position of the read pointer in the `myfile` stream. The current position is always returned as a byte offset relative to the beginning of the file.

The current file position can be modified using the `seekp()` or `seekg()` method. The position is stated as a byte offset, relative to either the beginning or end of the file, or relative to the current position in the file.

☐ Positioning Flags

Three `ios::seekdir` type positioning flags are defined in the `ios` class for this purpose; these are `ios::beg`, `ios::cur`, and `ios::end`.

Imagine you want to write the object `acc` to the file `"account.fle"` at offset `pos`. You can use the following statements to do so:

Example:
```
ofstream fstr("account.fle", ios::out |
                             ios::binary);

fstr.seekp(pos, ios::begin);
acc.write( fstr );
```

This calls the `write()` method in the `Account` class, which allows an object to write its own data members to a file (see Chapter 18).

If you do not specify a positioning flag, the position will be assumed to be relative to the beginning of the file. The statement used to position the write pointer in the last example can therefore be formulated as follows:

Example: `fstr.seekp(pos );`

The byte offset can also be negative for calls to the methods `seekp()` and `seekg()`. However, you cannot position the read/write pointer before the beginning of the file.

In contrast, it is possible to place the pointer at a position after the end of the file and then perform a write operation, which will create a gap with unknown content in the file. This only makes sense if all the empty slots in the file are of an equal length, as they can be overwritten later. This option is often used when programming hash tables.

■ POSITIONING FOR RANDOM ACCESS (CONTINUED)

Representing an index entry

```cpp
// index.h:  Defines the class IndexEntry
// ----------------------------------------------------
#ifndef _INDEX_H
#define _INDEX_H
#include <fstream>
#include <iostream>
using namespace std;

class IndexEntry
{
  private:
    long key;                   // Key
    long recNr;                 // Offset
  public:
    IndexEntry(long k=0L, long n=0L) { key=k; recNr=n;}
    // Access methods ... and:
    int recordSize() const
        { return sizeof(key) + sizeof(recNr); }
    fstream& write( fstream& ind) const;
    fstream& read(  fstream& ind);
    fstream& write_at(fstream& ind, long pos) const;
    fstream& read_at( fstream& ind, long pos);
};
#endif
```

The `read_at()` and `write_at()` methods

```cpp
// index.cpp:  Implements the methods
// ----------------------------------------------------
#include "index.h"
// . . .
fstream& IndexEntry::write_at( fstream& ind, long pos)
const
{
   ind.seekp(pos);
   ind.write((char*)&key, sizeof(key) );
   ind.write((char*)&recNr, sizeof(recNr) );
   return ind;
}

fstream& IndexEntry::read_at(fstream& ind, long pos)
{
   ind.seekg(pos);
   ind.read((char*)&key, sizeof(key) );
   ind.read((char*)&recNr, sizeof(recNr));
   return ind;
}
```

☐ Using Positioning Methods

The following statements are commonly used for random positioning

```
seekg( 0L);  and  seekp( 0L, ios::end );
```

They set the current position to the beginning or end of a file. You should be aware that the first argument is `0L` to indicate that `long` type is required.

If you need to determine the length of a file, you can point the `get` pointer to the end of the file and then query the position of the pointer:

Example:
```
fstr.seekg(0L, ios::end);
unsigned long count = fstr.tellg();
```

The `count` variable will then contain the number of bytes occupied by the file.

These positioning methods are useful for files opened in binary mode. However, it does not make much sense to use them for text files or particularly for devices. In text mode, conversions of LF <=> CR/LF prevent the methods from working correctly.

☐ Determining Positions in a File

The position of records in a files is easy to compute if all the records in the file are the same length. Given that `size` is the length of a record

```
0L,  size,  2*size,  ...
```

are the positions of the first, second, third records, and so on.

If you are working with variable length records, you cannot exactly compute their positions. To enable random access you therefore need to store the positions of the records in a separate structure, a so-called *index*.

The index stores pairs of keys and record positions, so-called *index entries* in a file. A key, a social security number, or customer id, for example, must uniquely identify a record. If the index is sorted, the position that correlates to the required key can be quickly found using the binary search algorithm.

☐ The `IndexEntry` Class

The `IndexEntry` class, used to represent an index entry, is shown opposite. The class comprises methods for reading and writing an index entry at the current file position or at any given position. The appropriate file stream is passed as an argument to the method.

■ FILE STATE

Representing an index

```
// index.h: (continued)
// Adds the definition of an index
// ------------------------------------------------
#include <string>

class IndexFile
{
   private:
    fstream index;
    string  name;                 // Filename of index

   public:
    IndexFile(const string& s);
    ~IndexFile() { index.close(); }

    void insert( long key, long pos);
    long search( long key);
    void retrieve(IndexEntry& entry, long pos );
  };
```

Constructor of class `IndexFile`

```
// index.cpp: (continued)
// Adds methods of class IndexFile
// ------------------------------------------------
IndexFile::IndexFile(const string& file)
{
   ios::openmode mode =  ios::in | ios::out
                                 | ios::binary;

   index.open(file.c_str(), mode);
   if(!index)                 // If the file does not exist
   {
      index.clear();
      mode |= ios::trunc;
      index.open(file.c_str(), mode);
      if(!index)
          return;
   }
   else
      name = file;
}

//. . .
```

☐ State Flags

A file stream can assume various states, for example, when it reaches the end of a file and cannot continue reading. A file operation can also fail if a file cannot be opened, or if a block is not transferred correctly.

The `ios` class uses *state flags* to define the various states a file can assume. Each state flag corresponds to a single bit in a *status-word*, which is represented by the `iostate` type in the `ios` class. The following state flags exist:

- `ios::eofbit`   end of file reached
- `ios::failbit`   last read or write operation failed
- `ios::badbit`   an irrecoverable error occurred
- `ios::goodbit`   the stream is ok, e.g. no other state flag is set.

The "flag" `ios::goodbit` is an exception to the rule since it is not represented by a single bit, but by the value 0 if no other flag has been set. In other words a status-word has the value `ios::goodbit` if everything is fine!

☐ Discovering and Changing the State

There are multiple methods for discovering and modifying the status of a stream. A method exists for each state flag; these are `eof()`, `fail()`, `bad()`, and `good()`. They return `true` when the corresponding flag has been raised. This means you can discover the end of a file with the following statement:

Example: `if( fstr.eof() ) ...`

The status-word of a stream can be read using the `rdstate()` method. Individual flags can then be queried by a simple comparison:

Example: `if( myfile.rdstate() == ios::badbit ) . . .`

The `clear()` method is available for clearing the status-word. If you call `clear()` without any arguments, all the state flags are cleared. An argument of the `iostate` type passed to `clear()` automatically becomes the new status-word for the stream.

☐ The `IndexFile` Class

The `IndexFile` class, which uses a file to represent an index, is defined opposite. The constructor for this class uses the `clear()` method to reset the `fail` bit after an invalid attempt to open a non-existent file. A new file can then be created.

The `IndexFile` class comprises methods for inserting, seeking, and retrieving index entries, which we will be implementing later in this chapter.

■ EXCEPTION HANDLING FOR FILES

Defining your own exception classes

```cpp
// exceptio.h : Exception classes for file access
// --------------------------------------------------
#ifndef _EXCEPTIO_H
#define _EXCEPTIO_H

#include <string>
#include <iostream>
using namespace std;

class FileError
{
  private:
    string filename;
  public:
    FileError( const string& file) : filename(file){ }
    string getName() const{ return filename; }
};
class OpenError : public FileError
{
  public:
    OpenError( const string& file):FileError(file){ }
};

class ReadError : public FileError
{
  public:
    ReadError( const string& file):FileError(file){ }
};

class WriteError : public FileError
{
  public:
    WriteError(const string& file):FileError(file){ }
};
#endif
```

☐ Implementing Your Own Exception Handling

You can exploit the error tracking options that state flags give you to implement your own exception handling for files. For example, a method that reads records from a file can throw an exception when the state flag `ios::eof` is raised, that is, when the end of the file is reached.

The opposite page shows typical exception classes organized in a hierarchy that can be used to represent error conditions on opening, reading from, and writing to a file. In each case the file name is saved for evaluation by the exception handler.

☐ Standard Exception Handling for Streams

C++ also provides standard exception handling for streams. You can use the `exceptions()` method to specify the flags in the status-word of a stream that will cause exceptions to be thrown.

The `exceptions()` method is defined in the `ios` stream base class. The method expects one or multiple state flags separated by the `|` sign. An exception is then thrown for the flags specified.

Example:
```
ifstream ifstrm("account.fle");
fstrm.exceptions(ios::failbit | ios::badbit);
```

On accessing the `fstrm` stream an exception is thrown if either one of the flags `ios::failbit` or `ios::badbit` is raised. The operation that caused the error is then terminated and the state flags are cleared by a call to `clear(rdstate());`.

The exception thrown here is of a standard exception class, `failure`. This type is defined as a `public` element in the `ios` base class and comprises the virtual method `what()` that returns a C string containing the cause of the error. The exception handler will normally send the string to standard error output.

You can call `exceptions()` without any arguments to discover the state flags in a status-word of a stream that can cause an exception to be thrown. If a bit is set in the return value of the `exceptions()` method, an appropriate exception will be thrown whenever this error occurs.

Example:
```
iostate except = fstrm.exceptions();
if( except & ios::eofbit) ...
```

This statement uses a bitwise AND operator to ascertain whether an exception is thrown when end-of-file is reached.

■ PERSISTENCE OF POLYMORPHIC OBJECTS

```cpp
// account.h :  Defines the classes
//              Account, DepAcc, and SavAcc
//              with virtual read and write methods.
// --------------------------------------------------
// . . .
enum TypeId { ACCOUNT, DEP_ACC, SAV_ACC };
class Account
{
  private:   // Data members: as previously defined.
  public:    // Constructor, access methods ...
    virtual TypeId getTypeId() const { return ACCOUNT;}
    virtual ostream& write(ostream& fs) const;
    virtual istream& read(istream& fs);
};
class DepAcc : public Account
{      // Data members, constructor, . . .
    TypeId getTypeId() const { return DEP_ACC; }
    ostream& write(ostream& fs) const;
    istream& read(istream& fs);
};
class SavAcc: public Account
{      // Data members, constructor, . . .
    TypeId getTypeId() const { return SAV_ACC; }
    ostream& write(ostream& fs) const;
    istream& read(istream& fs);
};
```

The methods `read()` and `write()` of class `DepAcc`

```cpp
// account.cpp:  Implements the methods.
// --------------------------------------------------
#include "account.h"
ostream& DepAcc::write(ostream& os) const
{
   if(!Account::write(os))
     return os;
   os.write((char*)&limit, sizeof(limit) );
   os.write((char*)&deb, sizeof(deb) );
   return os;
}
istream& DepAcc::read(istream& is)
{
   if(!Account::read(is))
     return is;
   is.read((char*)&limit, sizeof(limit) );
   is.read((char*)&deb, sizeof(deb));
   return is;
}
// . . .
```

☐ Storing Polymorphic Objects

Imagine you want to make the objects of a polymorphic class hierarchy persistent, that is, store them in a file. You need to ensure that an object can be reconstructed precisely when it is read. This gives rise to the fact that objects in polymorphic class hierarchies contain virtual methods. So it is not simply a case of making the data members of an object into records and writing them to a file.

 NOTE

1. You must write both the type and the data members of the object to a file.
2. If the objects contain dynamic members, you must save the referenced objects themselves along with information on the object type.

To allow the class to assume control over object storage, you need methods that allow the object to write its own data members to a file. The methods can have a virtual definition within the class hierarchy. Thus, if pointers are used to reference objects, the appropriate read/write operation for each object will be called.

☐ Storing Objects of the `Account` Hierarchy

The opposite page shows the `Account` class, with which you should already be familiar. Virtual file I/O methods have now been added. The implementation of the `read()` and `write()` methods was discussed earlier in Chapter 18, "Fundamentals of File Input and Output," and is unchanged.

The derived classes `DepAcc` and `SavAcc` also contain definitions of the `read()` and `write()` methods that read only their "own" objects and write them to files. The implementation first calls the appropriate base class method. If no errors occur, it is simply a question of transferring the additional data members of the derived class to or from a file.

At present, no type information will be written to file or read from file. This task will be performed by a special class whose features are used for file management. The following section contains more details on this topic.

■ PERSISTENCE OF POLYMORPHIC OBJECTS (CONTINUED)

```cpp
// account.h : (continued)
// Add definition of AccFile class
// --------------------------------------------------
// . . .
#include "exceptio.h"
class AccFile
{
  private:
    fstream f;              // Stream
    string  name;           // Filename
  public:
    AccFile(const string& s)  throw(OpenError);
    ~AccFile(){ f.close(); }
    long     append( Account& acc) throw(WriteError);
    Account* retrieve( long pos )  throw(ReadError);
};
```

The append() **method**

```cpp
// account.cpp: (continued)
// Implements methods of class AccFile.
// --------------------------------------------------
long AccFile::append( Account& acc) throw( WriteError)
{
    f.seekp(0L, ios::end);   // Seek to end,
    long pos = f.tellp();    // save the position.

    if( !f )
       throw WriteError(name);

    TypeId id = acc.getTypeId();  // To write the TypeId
    f.write( (char*)&id, sizeof(id));

    if(!f)
       throw WriteError(name);
    else
       acc.write(f);             // To write an object
                                 // to the file.
    if(!f)
       throw WriteError(name);
    else
       return pos;
}
// . . .
```

☐ A Scenario

Imagine you want to save the data for various account types, including current and savings accounts to a file. Since the objects you need to save belong to different types, you must save both the data members and the type of object. This is the only way to ensure that an object will be correctly reconstructed when read.

The methods in the class you are going to define should throw exceptions if errors occur. The exception type thrown by a method is stated in the exception specification.

☐ The `AccFile` Class

The `AccFile` class, which is used for random access to a file with account data, is defined opposited. The data members are an `fstream` type file stream and a string used for storing the file name.

The constructor saves the file name and opens a given file for reading and appending at end-of-file. If the file cannot be opened, the constructor throws an `OpenError` class exception.

The `append()` method writes an account passed to it as an argument at end-of-file and returns the position where the account was written into the file.

In order to get the current type of the argument, the virtual method `getTypeid()` is called. Depending on this type the `append()` method will write the appropriate type field to the file and then call the virtual method `write()`, allowing the current object to write itself to the file. If a write error occurs, the method will throw a `WriteError` type exception.

The `retrieve()` method first reads the type identifier and then determines the type of object it needs to allocate memory for. The data from the file is then transferred to the dynamically allocated object by a call to the virtual method `read()`. Here too, an exception will be thrown if a stream access error occurs.

■ APPLICATION: INDEX FILES

The `insert()` **method of class** `IndexFile`

```cpp
// index.cpp: (continued)
// Implements the methods of class IndexFile.
// ----------------------------------------------------
// . . .
void IndexFile::insert(long k, long n)
                       throw(ReadError, WriteError)
{
   IndexEntry entry;
   int size = entry.recordSize();    // Length of an
                                      // index entry.
   index.clear();
   index.seekg(0, ios::end);
   long nr = index.tellg();     // Get file length
                                // 0, if file is empty.
   if(!index) throw ReadError(name);

   nr -= size;                       // Last entry.
   bool found = false;
   while( nr >= 0 && !found )     // Search for position
   {                              // to insert
     if( !entry.read_at(index, nr))
       throw ReadError(name);

     if( k < entry.getKey())          // To shift.
     {
       entry.write_at(index, nr + size);
       nr -= size;
     }
     else
     {
       found = true;
     }
   }

   entry.setKey(k); entry.setPos(n);   // insert
   entry.write_at(index, nr + size);

   if(!index)
     throw WriteError(name);
}
```

It makes sense to organize data sequentially in files if you need to walk through all the records regularly. This is particularly true for files used to store salary data or phone bills.

However, most applications need to provide quick access to specific data. For example, a user would definitely prefer to be able to locate an account quickly by reference to an account number, rather than searching through a file from top to bottom. Index files can mean a real performance boost in cases like this.

☐ Index Files

An *index file* comprises a so-called *primary file* containing the live data, and an index. The *index* consists of pairs of keys and record positions for the primary file. A key stored in the index will identify a record in the primary file. This situation can be more easily explained by the following graphic:

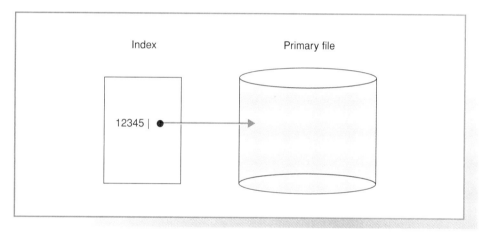

The index is sorted by reference to the keys for speed of access, allowing you to perform a binary search to locate the position of a record.

☐ Inserting into the Index

We can use the `IndexFile` class definition to represent an index. The `insert()` method, which correctly inserts a new record into the sorted index, is defined opposite.

The read pointer is first set to end-of-file for insertions. If the current position is 0, that is, the file is empty, the entry is inserted at offset 0. In all other cases, any entries whose keys are greater than the new key are shifted down to make room for the new entry.

■ IMPLEMENTING AN INDEX FILE

Representing the index file

```
// index.h:   Defines the class IndexFile
// --------------------------------------------------
class IndexFileSystem : public AccFile, public IndexFile
{
   private:
     string name;
   public:
     IndexFileSystem(const string s)
     : AccFile(s + ".prim"), IndexFile(s + ".ind")
     { name = s;   }

     void   insert  ( Account& acc );
     Account* retrieve( long key );
};
```

Methods `insert()` and `retrieve()` of class `IndexFileSystem`

```
// index.cpp:    Implementing the methods.
// --------------------------------------------------
void IndexFileSystem::insert(Account& acc)
{                           // No multiple entries:
  if(search(acc.getNr()) == -1)
  {
    long pos = append(acc); // Insert in primary file
    if(pos != -1)                          // Insert in
      IndexFile::insert(acc.getNr(), pos);   // index file.
  }
}

Account* IndexFileSystem::retrieve(long key )
{  long pos = search(key);    // Get the record address:
   if( pos == -1 )            // Account number found?
     return NULL;
   else
   {  IndexEntry entry;       // Read the index entry:
      IndexFile::retrieve(entry, pos);
                              // Read from primary file:
      return( AccFile::retrieve( entry.getPos() ));
   }
}
```

Index File for Account Management

Since an index file consists of a primary file and an index, it makes sense to derive the class used to represent an index file from the classes of the primary file and the index file. Let's now look at a sample index file, used for managing bank accounts.

The `IndexFileSystem` class, which is derived from the two previously defined classes `AccFile` and `IndexFile`, is defined on the opposite page. The only data member is a string for the file name. The constructor expects a file name as an argument and composes names for the primary file and the index by adding a suitable suffix. Base initializers are then used to open the corresponding files.

It is not necessary to define a destructor, since files are automatically closed when the base class destructors are called.

Inserting and Retrieving Records

The `insert()` method was defined to insert new records. It first calls the `search()` method to check whether the account number already exists in the index. If not, a new record is appended to the end of the primary file using the `append()` method. Then the key and the address of the record are inserted into the index.

The `IndexFileSystem` class also contains the `retrieve()` method, which is used to retrieve records from the primary file. The key, `key`, which is passed to the method, is used by the `search()` method to look up the address of the required record in the index. Then the record is retrieved from the primary file by the `AccFile` class `retrieve()` method.

Only the `retrieve()` methods for the `IndexFile` and `AccFile` classes and the `search()` method, which performs a binary search in the index, are needed to complete the index file implementation. It's your job to implement these three methods as your next exercise!

Using a sorted file to implement an index has the disadvantage that records need to be shifted to make room to insert new records. As shifting is time-consuming, an index is normally represented by a tree, which needs less reorganization.

■ EXERCISES

Exercise I

Class `IndexFile`

```
class IndexFile
{
   private:
     fstream index;
     string  name;              // Filename of the index

   public:
     IndexFile(const string s) throw(OpenError);
     ~IndexFile( ){ index.close(); }
     void insert( long key, long pos)
                             throw(ReadError, WriteError);
     long search( long key) throw(ReadError);
     void retrieve(IndexEntry& entry, long pos )
                             throw( ReadError);
};
```

Class `AccFile`

```
enum TypeId { ACCOUNT, DEPOSIT, SAVINGS };
class AccFile
{
  private:
    fstream f;
    string  name;            // Filename of primary file
  public:
      AccFile(const string s) throw(OpenError);
      ~AccFile(){ f.close(); }
      long   append( Account& acc)  throw(WriteError);
      Account* retrieve( long pos ) throw(ReadError);
};
```

Exercise 1

Complete and test the implementation of the `IndexFileSystem` class. The methods should throw exceptions of an appropriate `FileError` type if an error occurs.

a. Complete the constructor of the `IndexFile` class in order to throw an exception of the type `OpenError` if the file can not be opened.

b. Write the `retrieve()` method for the `IndexFile` class. The method retrieves a record at a given position in the index.

c. Define the `search()` method, which looks up an index entry for an account number passed to it as an argument. Base the method on the binary search algorithm.

    Return value: The position of the record found, or -1 if the account number is not found in the index.

d. Then define the `retrieve()` method for the `AccFile` class, which first evaluates the type field at a given position in the account file, then dynamically allocates memory for an object of the appropriate type, and finally reads the data for an account from the file.

e. Write a `main()` function that uses a `try` block to create an Index-FileSystem type object and to insert several accounts of various types into the index file. The subsequent user dialog reads a key and displays the corresponding record on screen. Write an exception handler to handle the various errors that could occur. The name of the file and the cause of the error must be output in any case of error.

Hash Files

Hash Files profit from random file access in localizing file records directly. Each file record must have the same length and it must be identified by a unique key, the so-called *hash key*.

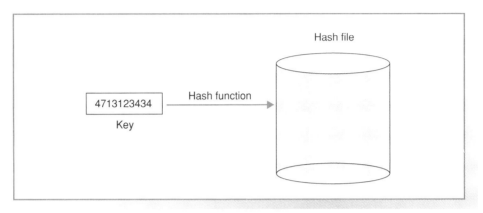

The idea behind hashing is to provide a function, the *hash function*, which is applied to the hash key of a record and yields the address of the file record. If the file records are numerated and if the hash key equals the record number, a simple hash function can be the identical function. However, hash keys, such as account or insurance numbers, consist of a fixed number of digits that do not start with 0.

The following example shows a frequently used hash function

Example: `Hash(key) = key % b;`

This hash function transforms the hash value `key` into a record number between `0` and `b-1`. The number `0` is the first record number and `b-1` is the last record number in the *address space* of the hash file. For a sufficiently large prime number `b`, the function `Hash()` yields a good distribution of file records in the address space.

However, the hash function maps the hash key values `key`, `key + b`, `key + 2*b`, etc. to the same record number. In this case *collisions* may occur, for example, when a new record being inserted hashes to an address that already contains a different record.

To solve this conflict, the new record must be inserted at some other position. The process of finding another position at which to insert the new record is called *collision resolution*.

Linear solution is a common collision resolution technique: Starting at the occupied position, subsequent positions are checked sequentially until an available position is found. The new file record is then inserted at this position.

Exercise 2

A hash file is required for speed of access to customer data. The concept of hash files is explained on the opposite page. To keep things simple, each record in the hash file contains only a customer id and a name. The customer id is the key used by the hash function opposite to compute the address of the record. Use linear solution as collision resolution technique.

Note: Linear solution provides for adequate access times if the address space is sufficiently large and not too full. It is also important to distribute the record numbers yielded by the hash function evenly throughout the available address space. The hash function opposite will guarantee a good distribution if b is a sufficiently large prime number.

- Develop the `HashEntry` class used to represent customer data. You need to store the customer id as an `unsigned long` value and the name of the customer as a `char` array with a length of 30. Supply default values for the constructor declaration and additionally declare the `read_at()` and `write_at()` methods that read customer information at a given position in a stream or write information at that position. Both methods expect the position and the stream as arguments.
- Define the `HashFile` class to represent a hash file. The `private` members of the class comprise an `fstream` type file stream, a string used to store the file name, an `int` variable used to store the number b, and the hash function shown opposite as a method. The `public` members comprise a constructor that expects a file name and a number b as arguments. It opens the corresponding file for read and write access. The destructor closes the file.

  Additionally declare the methods `insert()` and `retrieve()` to insert or retrieve single records. Both methods use a call to the hash function to compute the appropriate record number in the hash file. If a collision occurs, the methods perform a sequential search to locate the next free slot in the address space (mod of address space size), or the desired customer data.

- Test the `HashFile` by writing a `main` function that creates hash file with a small address space (e.g. b = 7). Add various customer information records to the hash file and then retrieve this data. Deliberately provoke collisions using the customer ids 5, 12, and 19, for example.

SOLUTIONS

Exercise 1

```
// -----------------------------------------------------
// exceptio.h : Error classes for file processing
// -----------------------------------------------------

// Unchanged (cf. earlier in this chapter).


// -----------------------------------------------------
// account.h :
// Defines the classes
//        Account, DepAcc, and SavAcc
// with virtual read and write methods as well as
// the class AccFile to represent account files.
// -----------------------------------------------------
#ifndef _ACCOUNT_H
#define _ACCOUNT_H

#include <fstream>
#include <iostream>
#include <iomanip>
#include <string>
using namespace std;

#include "exceptio.h"

enum TypeId { ACCOUNT, DEP_ACC, SAV_ACC };

class Account
{
  private:                      // Data elements:
    string name;
    unsigned long nr;
    double balance;

  public:                       // Constructor:
    Account( const string c_name   = "X",
             unsigned long c_nr     = 1111111L,
             double c_balance       = 0.0)
      : name(c_name), nr(c_nr), balance(c_balance)
      { }

    virtual ~Account() {}       // Virtual destructor
```

```
      // Access methods here:
      long getNr() const { return nr; }
      void setNr(unsigned long n){ nr = n; }
      // . . .

      // The other methods:
      virtual TypeId getTypeId() const { return ACCOUNT; }

      virtual ostream& write(ostream& fs) const;
      virtual istream& read(istream& fs);

      virtual void display() const
      {
         cout << fixed << setprecision(2)
              << "-------------------------------\n"
              << "Account holder:      " << name    << endl
              << "Account number:      " << nr      << endl
              << "Balance of account:  " << balance << endl
              << "-------------------------------\n"
              << endl;
      }
};

class DepAcc : public Account
{
  private:
    double limit;            // Overdrawn limit
    double interest;         // Interest rate

  public:
    DepAcc( const string s  = "X",
            unsigned long n = 1111111L,
            double bal = 0.0,
            double li  = 0.0,
            double ir  = 0.0)
      : Account(s, n, bal), limit(li), interest(ir)
      { }

    // Access methods:
    // . . .

    // The other methods are implicit virtual:
    TypeId getTypeId() const { return DEP_ACC; }

    ostream& write(ostream& fs) const;
    istream& read(istream& fs);
```

```
      void display() const
      {
          Account::display();
          cout << "Overdrawn limit:       " << limit << endl
               << "Competitive interest: " << interest
               << "\n--------------------------------\n"
               << endl;
      }
};

class SavAcc: public Account
{
  private:
    double interest;              // Compound interest

  public:
    // Methods as in class DepAcc.

};

// -------------------------------------------------
// The definition of class AccFile

class AccFile
{
  private:
    fstream f;
    string  name;          // Filename

  public:
      AccFile(const string& s) throw(OpenError);
      ~AccFile(){ f.close(); }

      long append( Account& acc)    throw(WriteError);
      Account* retrieve( long pos) throw(ReadError);

      void display() throw( ReadError);
};

#endif
```

```cpp
// --------------------------------------------------
// account.cpp
// Implement methods of the classes
// Account, DepAcc, SavAcc, and AccFile.
// --------------------------------------------------
#include "account.h"
#include <typeinfo>

ostream& Account::write(ostream& os) const
{
   os << name << '\0';
   os.write((char*)&nr, sizeof(nr) );
   os.write((char*)&balance, sizeof(balance) );
   return os;
}

istream& Account::read(istream& is)
{
   getline( is, name, '\0');
   is.read((char*)&nr, sizeof(nr) );
   is.read((char*) &balance, sizeof(balance));
   return is;
}

ostream& DepAcc::write(ostream& os) const
{
   if(!Account::write(os))
       return os;
   os.write((char*)&limit, sizeof(limit) );
   os.write((char*)&interest, sizeof(interest) );
   return os;
}

istream& DepAcc::read(istream& is)
{
   if(!Account::read(is))
       return is;
   is.read((char*)&limit, sizeof(limit) );
   is.read((char*)&interest, sizeof(interest));
   return is;
}

// ostream& SavAcc::write(ostream& os) const
// istream& SavAcc::read(istream& is)
// as in class DepAcc.
```

```
              // ---- Methods of class AccFile ----
              AccFile::AccFile(const string& s) throw( OpenError)
              {
                 ios::openmode mode = ios::in | ios::out | ios::app
                                         | ios::binary;
                 f.open( s.c_str(), mode);
                 if(!f)
                    throw OpenError(s);
                 else
                    name = s;
              }

              void AccFile::display() throw(ReadError)
              {
                 Account acc, *pAcc = NULL;
                 DepAcc depAcc;
                 SavAcc savAcc;
                 TypeId id;

                 if( !f.seekg(0L))
                    throw ReadError(name);


                 cout << "\nThe account file: " << endl;

                 while( f.read((char*)&id, sizeof(TypeId)) )
                 {
                    switch(id)
                    {
                       case ACCOUNT:  pAcc = &acc;
                                      break;
                       case DEP_ACC:  pAcc = &depAcc;
                                      break;
                       case SAV_ACC:  pAcc = &savAcc;
                                      break;

                       default: cerr << "Invalid flag in account file"
                                   . << endl;
                             exit(1);
                    }

                    if(!pAcc->read(f))
                       break;

                    pAcc->display();
                    cin.get();                // Go on with return
                 }
```

```
       if( !f.eof())
            throw ReadError(name);
       f.clear();
}

long AccFile::append( Account& acc) throw( WriteError)
{
    f.seekp(0L, ios::end);     // Seek to end,
    long pos = f.tellp();      // save the position.

    if( !f )
       throw WriteError(name);

    TypeId id = acc.getTypeId();
    f.write( (char*)&id, sizeof(id));  // Write the TypeId

    if(!f)
        throw WriteError(name);
    else
        acc.write(f);          // Add an object to the file.

    if(!f)
        throw WriteError(name);
    else
        return pos;
}

Account* AccFile::retrieve( long pos) throw(ReadError)
{
    f.clear();
    f.seekg(pos);                       // Set the get pointer

    if( !f )
       throw ReadError(name);

    TypeId id;
    f.read( (char*)&id, sizeof(id) );     // Get TypeId

    if(!f)
       throw ReadError(name);

    Account* buf;
    switch( id )
    {
      case ACCOUNT:  buf = new Account;
                     break;
      case SAV_ACC:  buf = new SavAcc;
                     break;
```

```cpp
        case DEP_ACC:  buf = new DepAcc;
                       break;
    }

    if( !(buf->read(f)))                    // Get data
       throw ReadError(name);

    return buf;
}

// -------------------------------------------------------
// index.h: Contains definitions of classes
//          IndexEntry representing an  index entry,
//          Index      representing the index and
//          IndexFile  representing an  index file.
// -------------------------------------------------------
#ifndef _INDEX_H
#define _INDEX_H

#include <fstream>
#include <iostream>
#include <string>
#include "account.h"
using namespace std;

class IndexEntry
{
  private:
    long key;                  // Key
    long recPos;               // Offset

  public:
    IndexEntry(long k=0L, long n=0L){ key=k; recPos=n; }


    void setKey(long k) { key = k; }
    long getKey() const { return key; }
    void setPos(long p) { recPos = p; }
    long getPos() const { return recPos; }

    int recordSize() const
    { return sizeof(key) + sizeof(recPos); }

    fstream& write( fstream& ind) const;
    fstream& read(  fstream& ind);

    fstream& write_at(fstream& ind, long pos) const;
    fstream& read_at( fstream& ind, long pos);
```

```cpp
      void display() const
      {   cout << "Account Nr: " << key
              << "   Position: " << recPos << endl;
      }
};

class IndexFile
{
   private:
     fstream index;
     string  name;                    // Filename of index

   public:
     IndexFile( const string& s)  throw (OpenError);
     ~IndexFile() { index.close(); }

     void insert( long key, long pos)
          throw(ReadError, WriteError);
     long search( long key) throw(ReadError);
     void retrieve(IndexEntry& entry, long pos )
          throw(ReadError);
     void display() throw(ReadError);
};

class IndexFileSystem : public AccFile, public IndexFile
{
   private:
     string name;                     // Filename without suffix
   public:
     IndexFileSystem(const string& s)
      : AccFile(s + ".prim"), IndexFile(s + ".ind")
      { name = s;   }

    bool     insert( Account& acc);
    Account* retrieve( long key);
};

#endif
```

```cpp
// -----------------------------------------------------
// index.cpp : Methods of the classes
//             IndexEntry, Index, and IndexFile
// -----------------------------------------------------
#include "index.h"

fstream& IndexEntry::write_at(fstream& ind, long pos) const
{
   ind.seekp(pos);
   ind.write((char*)&key, sizeof(key) );
   ind.write((char*)&recPos, sizeof(recPos) );
   return ind;
}

fstream& IndexEntry::read_at(fstream& ind, long pos)
{
   ind.seekg(pos);
   ind.read((char*)&key, sizeof(key) );
   ind.read((char*)&recPos, sizeof(recPos));
   return ind;
}

fstream& IndexEntry::write(fstream& ind) const
{
   ind.write((char*)&key, sizeof(key) );
   ind.write((char*)&recPos, sizeof(recPos) );
   return ind;
}

fstream& IndexEntry::read(fstream& ind)
{
   ind.read((char*)&key, sizeof(key) );
   ind.read((char*)&recPos, sizeof(recPos));
   return ind;
}

// -----------------------------------------------------
// Methods of class IndexFile
IndexFile::IndexFile(const string& file) throw (OpenError)
{
   ios::openmode mode =  ios::in | ios::out | ios::binary;
                         // Open file if it already exists:
   index.open( file.c_str(), mode);
   if(!index)           // If the file doesn't exist
   {   index.clear();
       mode |= ios::trunc;
       index.open( file.c_str(), mode);
       if(!index)
           throw OpenError(name);
   }
   name = file;
}
```

```
void IndexFile::display() throw(ReadError)
{
   IndexEntry entry;

   index.seekg(0L);
   if(!index)
     throw ReadError("IndexFile: Setting the get pointer");

   cout << endl << "The Index: " << endl;
   while( true)
   {
      if( !entry.read(index))
         break;
      entry.display();
   }
   if( !index.eof())
      throw ReadError(name);
   index.clear();
}

long IndexFile::search(long k) throw(ReadError)
{
   IndexEntry entry;
   long key;
   long  mid, begin = 0, end;   // Number of file records.
   int size = entry.recordSize();   // Length of an index
                                    // entry.
   index.clear();
   index.seekg(0L, ios::end);
   end = index.tellg() / size;

   if(!index)
       throw ReadError(name);

   if( end == 0)
      return -1;

   end -= 1;                       // Position of the last entry

   while( begin < end )
   {
      mid = (begin + end +1)/2 ;

      entry.read_at(index, mid*size);
      if(!index)
         throw ReadError(name);

      key = entry.getKey();
      if( k < key)
          end = mid - 1;
      else
          begin = mid;
   }
```

```
        entry.read_at(index, begin * size);
        if(!index)
            throw ReadError(name);

        if( k == entry.getKey() )        // Key found?
            return begin * size;
        else return -1;
}

void IndexFile::insert(long k, long n)
    throw(ReadError, WriteError)
{
    IndexEntry entry;
    int size = entry.recordSize();   // Length of an index
                                     // entry.
    index.clear();
    index.seekg(0, ios::end);
    long nr = index.tellg();         // Get file length
                                     // 0, if file is empty.
    if(!index) throw ReadError(name);

    nr -= size;                      // Last entry.
    bool found = false;
    while( nr >= 0 && !found )        // Search position
    {                                // to insert
        if(!entry.read_at(index, nr))
            throw ReadError(name);

        if( k < entry.getKey())       // To shift.
        {
            entry.write_at(index, nr + size);
            nr -= size;
        }
        else
        {
            found = true;
        }
    }

    entry.setKey(k); entry.setPos(n);  // Insert
    entry.write_at(index, nr + size);

    if(!index)
        throw WriteError(name);
}
```

```cpp
void IndexFile::retrieve( IndexEntry& entry, long pos)
     throw(ReadError)
{
    index.clear();
    if(!entry.read_at(index, pos))
        throw ReadError(name);
}

// ---------------------------------------------------
//  Implementing the methods of class IndexFileSystem.

bool IndexFileSystem::insert( Account& acc)
     throw(ReadError, WriteError)
{
  if(search(acc.getNr()) == -1)   // No multiple entries.
  {
    long pos = append(acc);        // Add to primary file.
    IndexFile::insert(acc.getNr(), pos); // Add to Index
    return true;
  }
  else
    return false;
}

Account* IndexFileSystem::retrieve(long key )
{
    // Get the record address from the index:
    long pos = search(key);       // Byte offset of
                                  // index entry.

    if( pos == -1 )               // Account number doesn't exist.
       return NULL;
    else                          // Account number does exist:
    {
       IndexEntry entry;          // To read the index eintry
       IndexFile::retrieve( entry, pos);
                                  // Get from primary file:
       return( AccFile::retrieve( entry.getPos() ));
    }
}

// ------------------------------------------------------
// index_t.cpp : Testing the index file
// ------------------------------------------------------
#include <iostream>
#include <string>
using namespace std;
#include "index.h"
#include "account.h"
```

```cpp
int main()
{
  try
  {
    IndexFileSystem database("AccountTest");

    Account acc1( "Vivi", 490UL, 12340.57);
    database.insert( acc1 );

    SavAcc acc2( "Ulla", 590UL, 4321.19, 2.5);
    database.insert( acc2 );

    DepAcc acc3( "Jeany", 390UL, 12340.20, 10000.0, 12.9);
    database.insert( acc3 );

    database.IndexFile::display();
    cin.get();

    database.AccFile::display();

    unsigned long key;
    cout << "Key? ";  cin >> key;
    if(database.search(key) != -1)
        cout << "Key " << key << " found" << endl;
    else
        cout << "Key " << key << " not found" << endl;

    Account* pAcc = database.retrieve(key);
    if( pAcc  != NULL )
    {
        pAcc->display();
        delete pAcc;
        pAcc = NULL;
    }
    else cout << "Retrieving failed" << endl;
  }
  catch(OpenError& err)
  {
      cerr << "Error on opening the file:" << err.getName()
          << endl;
      exit(1);
  }
  catch(WriteError& err)
  {
      cerr << "Error on writing into the file: "
          << err.getName() << endl;
      exit(1);
  }
```

```
    catch(ReadError& err)
    {
        cerr << "Error on reading from the file: "
             << err.getName() << endl;
        exit(1);
    }
    catch(...)
    {
        cerr << " Unhandled Exception" << endl;
        exit(1);
    }

    return 0;
}
```

Exercise 2

```
// -------------------------------------------------------
// exceptio.h : Error classes for file processing
// -------------------------------------------------------

// As seen previously in this chapter.


// -------------------------------------------------------
// hashFile.h
// Defines the classes
// HashEntry representing a record in a hash file and
// HashFile representing a hash file.
// -------------------------------------------------------
#ifndef _HASH_H_
#define _HASH_H_

#include <fstream>
#include <iostream>
#include <iomanip>
#include <string>
#include <string.h>
using namespace std;

#include "exceptio.h"

class HashEntry
{
  private:
    unsigned long nr;
    char name[30];
```

```cpp
  public:
    HashEntry(unsigned long n = 0L, const string& s = "")
    {
       nr = n;
       strncpy(name, s.c_str(), 29); name[30]='\0';
    }

    long    getNr() const { return nr; }
    void    setNr(unsigned long n){ nr = n; }
    string getName() const { return name; }
    void    setName(const string& s)
    {  strncpy(name, s.c_str(), 29); name[30]='\0'; }

    int getSize() const
    { return(sizeof(long) + sizeof(name)); }

    fstream& write(fstream& fs);
    fstream& read(fstream& fs);

    fstream& write_at(fstream& fs, unsigned long pos);
    fstream& read_at(fstream& fs, unsigned long pos);

    virtual void display()
    {
        cout << fixed << setprecision(2)
            << "---------------------------------\n"
            << "Client number:        " << nr     << endl
            << "Client:               " << name  << endl
            << "---------------------------------\n"
            << endl;
        cin.get();
    }
};

class HashFile
{
  private:
    fstream f;
    string  name;        // Filename
    unsigned long b;     // Size of address space

  protected:
    unsigned long hash_func(unsigned long key)
    { return key%b; }

  public:
    HashFile(const string s, unsigned long n )
                                   throw(OpenError);
```

```cpp
        void insert( HashEntry& rec)
                       throw( ReadError, WriteError );
        HashEntry& retrieve( unsigned long key )
                                      throw( ReadError );

        void display();
};

#endif

// --------------------------------------------------------
// hashFile.cpp : Methods of classes HashEntry and HashFile
// --------------------------------------------------------
#include "hashFile.h"

fstream& HashEntry::write(fstream& f)
{
    f.write((char*)&nr, sizeof(nr) );
    f.write( name, sizeof(name) );
    return f;
}


fstream& HashEntry::read(fstream& f)
{
    f.read((char*)&nr, sizeof(nr) );
    f.read( name, sizeof(name));
    return f;
}

fstream& HashEntry::write_at(fstream& f, unsigned long pos)
{
    f.seekp(pos);
    f.write((char*)&nr, sizeof(nr) );
    f.write( name, sizeof(name) );
    return f;
}

fstream& HashEntry::read_at(fstream& f, unsigned long pos)
{
    f.seekg(pos);
    f.read((char*)&nr, sizeof(nr) );
    f.read( name, sizeof(name));
    return f;
}
```

```
HashFile::HashFile(const string file, unsigned long n)
                                               throw(OpenError)
{
    ios::openmode mode =  ios::in | ios::out | ios::binary;
    f.open(file.c_str(), mode);    // Open file if it
                                   // already exists.
    if(!f)                         // If file doesn't exist:
    {
        f.clear();
        mode |= ios::trunc;
        f.open(file.c_str(), mode);
        if(!f)
            throw OpenError(name);
    }
    name = file;
    b = n;
    HashEntry rec(0L, "");
    f.seekp(0L);
    for( unsigned long i=0; i < b; i++) // Initialize
    {                                   // the address space
        rec.write(f);
        if(!f)
            throw WriteError(name);
    }
}

void HashFile::insert( HashEntry& rec)
    throw( ReadError, WriteError)
{
    HashEntry temp;
    int  size = temp.getSize();
    // Hash-Wert:
    unsigned long pos = hash_func(rec.getNr());

    temp.read_at(f, pos*size);            // Read a slot.
    if(!f)
        throw ReadError(name);
    else
    {
        if(temp.getNr() == 0L)            // Slot free?
            rec.write_at(f, pos*size);    // Yes => Add
                                          // to the file.
        else                              // No => Search for
        {                                 // a free slot.
            bool found = false;

            unsigned long p = (pos*size + size)%(b*size);
```

```
            while( !found && p!= pos*size  )
            {
               temp.read_at(f, p);
               if(!f)
                  throw ReadError(name);
               else
                  if(temp.getNr() == 0L)   // Free slot
                     found = true;         // found.
                   else
                      // Proceed to the next slot:
                      p = (p + size)%(b*size);
            }

         if( p == pos*size )         // Address space full.
             throw WriteError(name);

         if ( found == true )        // Add to file.
             rec.write_at(f,p);
      }

      if(!f)
          throw WriteError(name);
   }
}


HashEntry& HashFile::retrieve( unsigned long key )
                                           throw(ReadError)
{
   static HashEntry temp;
   int size = temp.getSize();

   unsigned long pos = hash_func(key);     // Hash value.

   temp.read_at(f, pos*size);              // Read a slot.

   if(!f) throw ReadError(name);

   if(temp.getNr() == key)                 // Found?
      return temp;                         // Yes  => finish
   else                                    // No   => search
   {
     unsigned long p = (pos*size + size)%(b*size);
     while( p!= pos *size )
     {
        temp.read_at(f, p);
        if(!f)
           throw ReadError(name);
```

```
                else
                   if(temp.getNr() == key)         // Record found.
                       return temp;
                   else
                       p = (p + size)%(b*size);     // Proceed to the
            }                                        // next slot.

             temp.setNr(0L); temp.setName("");     // Key doesn't
                                                    // exist.

             return temp;
        }
}

void HashFile::display()
{
    HashEntry temp;
    f.seekg(0L);

    for(unsigned int i = 0; i < b; i++)
    {
        temp.read(f);
        if(!f)
            throw ReadError(name);
        temp.display();
    }
    f.clear();
}

// -------------------------------------------------------
// hash_t.cpp : Tests hash files
// -------------------------------------------------------

#include <iostream>
#include <string>
#include "hashFile.h"
using namespace std;

int main()
{
  try
  {
    HashFile hash("Client.fle", 7);         // Address space
                                            // of length 7

    cout << "\nInsert: " << endl;
    HashEntry kde( 3L, "Vivi");
    hash.insert( kde );
```

```
   kde.setNr(10L); kde.setName("Peter");
   hash.insert( kde );

   kde.setNr(17L); kde.setName("Alexa");
   hash.insert( kde );

   kde.setNr(21L); kde.setName("Peter");
   hash.insert( kde );

   kde.setNr(15L); kde.setName("Jeany");
   hash.insert( kde );
   cout << "\nInsertion complete: " << endl;

   hash.display();

   unsigned long key;
   cout << "Key? ";  cin >> key;

   HashEntry temp = hash.retrieve(key);
   if(temp.getNr() != 0L)
      temp.display();
   else
      cout << "Key " << key
           << " not found" << endl;
}
catch(OpenError& err)
{
   cerr << "Error in opening the file:"
        << err.getName() << endl;
   exit(1);
}



catch(WriteError& err)
{
   cerr << "Error writing to file: "
        << err.getName() << endl;
   exit(1);
}
catch(ReadError& err)
{
   cerr << "Error reading from file: "
        << err.getName() << endl;
   exit(1);
}

return 0;
}
```

chapter 30

More about Pointers

This chapter describes advanced uses of pointers. These include pointers to pointers, functions with a variable number of arguments, and pointers to functions.

An application that defines a class used to represent dynamic matrices is introduced.

■ POINTER TO POINTERS

The function `accSort()`

```cpp
// accSort.cpp: Sorts an array of pointers to accounts
//              according to the account numbers
// -------------------------------------------------

#include "account.h"

void ptrSwap(Account**, Account** );

void accSort( Account** kptr, int n)
{
   Account **temp, **minp, **lastp;
   lastp = kptr + n - 1;    // Pointer to the last
                            // pointer in the array.

   for(  ; kptr < lastp; ++kptr )
   {
     minp = kptr;

     for( temp = kptr + 1; temp <= lastp; ++temp )
     {
       if( (*temp)->getNr() < (*minp)->getNr() )
          minp = temp;
     }
     ptrSwap( kptr, minp );
   }
}

void ptrSwap( Account **p1, Account **p2 )
{
   Account *help;
   help = *p1; *p1 = *p2; *p2 = help;
}
```

☐ Motivation

Pointer variables are objects that have an address in memory, and this means you can use pointers to address them. It is thus possible to create *pointers to pointers*. This is necessary if

- ▪ an array of pointers is to be dynamically allocated, or
- ▪ a function expects an array of pointers as an argument.

In both cases you need to declare a pointer variable that can access the first element in the array. Since each element in the array is a pointer, this pointer variable must be a pointer to a pointer.

☐ Generating Pointer Arrays Dynamically

Now let's look into creating a dynamic array of pointers to `Account` class objects.

Example: `Account** ptr = new Account*[400];`

The pointer `ptr` is now pointing at the first pointer in the array with a total of 400 `Account*` type pointers. The array elements can be addressed as follows:

```
*ptr           and   ptr[0]    (pointer to index 0)
*(ptr + i)     and   ptr[i]    (pointer to index i)
```

Access to objects managed by the array is achieved as follows:

```
**ptr          and   *ptr[0]    (object addressed by pointer at index 0)
**(ptr+i)      and   *ptr[i]    (object addressed by pointer at index i)
```

☐ Pointer Arrays as Arguments

When you define a function that expects an array of pointers as an argument, you must define parameters to match.

Example: `void accSort( Account **kptr, int len);`

You can use the `kptr` parameter to manipulate a pointer array whose length is stored in the second parameter, `len`. After calling

Example: `accSort( ptr, 100);`

`kptr` points to the first pointer `ptr[0]` in the pointer array `ptr`. Instead of `Account **kptr` you can also use the equivalent form `Account *kptr[]`.

   The opposite page shows an implementation of the function `accSort()`. The function uses the selection sort algorithm (which you have already worked with) for sorting. In this case it is important not to sort the accounts itself, but to sort the pointers instead. This saves time-consuming copying.

■ VARIABLE NUMBER OF ARGUMENTS

Fixed and varying arguments on the stack

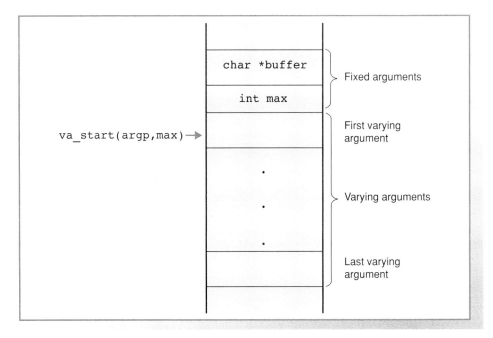

Scheme of a function with varying arguments

```c
#include <stdarg.h>

int func( char *buffer, int max, ... )
{
   va_list argptr;      // Declares argument pointer.
   long arg3;
    . . .
   va_start( argptr, max);          // Initialization.
   arg3 = va_arg( argptr, long );  // Read arguments.

   // To use argument arg3.
    . . . .

   va_end(argptr);      // Set argument pointer to NULL.
}
```

C++ allows you to define functions that allow a variable number of arguments. One example of a function of this type is the standard C function `printf()`, which requires at least one argument, a format string. The `printf()` function uses the conversion specifiers in the format string to compute the number and type of arguments that follow.

☐ Obligatory and Optional Arguments

Functions with a variable number of arguments always expect a fixed number of *obligatory* arguments and a variable number of *optional* arguments. At least one obligatory argument is required.

As you would expect, you need to define an appropriate parameter for each obligatory argument when you define a function of this type. The optional arguments are represented by three dots `...` in the parameter list. The function shown opposite, `func()`, expects two or more arguments. The prototype is, thus, as follows

Prototype: `int func( char *buffer, int max, ...);`

To allow functions with a variable number of arguments to be defined, C++ pushes the last argument onto the stack first. After calling the sample function `func()`, the stack looks like the diagram opposite.

The optional arguments are accessed via a pointer, the so-called *argument pointer*, which is designated by `argptr` here. The header files `cstdarg` or `stdarg.h` contain macros, which conform to ANSI standard, to manage the pointer and assure that the source code will be portable.

☐ Access to Arguments

The following steps are required to read the optional arguments:

1. The `va_list` type argument pointer `argptr` must be declared in addition to other local variables. The type `va_list` is defined in the header file `stdarg.h` as a typeless or `char` pointer.

2. The macro `va_start()` is then called to point the argument pointer `argptr` to the first optional argument. `va_start()` expects two arguments: the name of the argument pointer and the name of the last obligatory parameter.

Example: `va_start( argptr, max );`

■ VARIABLE NUMBER OF ARGUMENTS (CONTINUED)

The function `input()`

```cpp
// input.cpp: The function input() reads characters
//            from the keyboard and appends '\0'.
//            The input can be corrected with backspace.
// Arguments: 1. Pointer to the input buffer.
//            2. Maximum number of characters to be read
/             3. Optional arguments: Characters that
//               terminate the input.
//               This list has to end with CR = '\r'!
// Returns:   Character that breaks the input.
// --------------------------------------------------
#include <stdarg.h>
#include <conio.h>      // For getch() and putch()

int input(char *buffer, int max,... )
{
  int c, breakc;   // Current character, character to
                   // break with.
  int nc = 0;      // Number of characters read.
  va_list argp;    // Pointer to the following arguments.

  while(true)
  {
    *buffer = '\0';
    if( ( c = getch()) == 0)  // Read a character.
       c = getch() + 256;     // For special keys:
                              // Extended code + 256.
    va_start(argp, max);      // Initialize argp.
    do                 // Compare with break characters:
      if( c == (breakc = va_arg(argp,int)) )
         return(breakc);
    while( breakc != '\r');
    va_end( argp);
    if( c == '\b' &&  nc > 0)    // Backspace?
    {
        --nc,  --buffer;
        putch(c);  putch(' '); putch(c);
    }
    else if( c >= 32  &&  c <= 255  &&  nc < max )
    {               // Place character into the buffer
       ++nc,  *buffer++ = c;  putch(c);  // and output.
    else if( nc == max)    // Is end of buffer reached?
      putch('\a');         // Beep.
    }
  }
}
```

3. When the macro va_arg() is called, the optional argument pointed to by argptr is read from the stack. The arguments of va_arg() are the name of the argument pointer and the type of the optional argument:

Example: `arg3 = va_arg( argptr, long);`

Each call to the macro va_arg() sets the argument pointer to the next optional argument. The result of va_arg() has the type stated in the call. It must be identical to the type of the corresponding optional argument.

There is no special terminating condition for the last optional argument. A specific value (such as NULL, −1 or CR) can be used, or the current number of arguments can be defined by an obligatory argument.

4. After evaluating the arguments the argument pointer is set to NULL by the va_end() macro:

Example: `va_end( argptr);`

Optional arguments can also be read more than once. The procedure described above is repeated beginning at Step 2, that is, with the macro va_start().

☐ Notes on the Example Opposite

The sample function input() on the opposite page uses the getch() function to read character input from the keyboard and store it in the buffer addressed by the first argument. The second argument defines the maximum number of characters to be read. All other arguments are characters that can terminate keyboard input. The last argument *must* be a return character ('\r')!

Example:
```
#define ESC    27              // ESC key
#define F1    (256 + 59)       // F1 key
input( name, 20, ' ', ESC, F1, '\r');
```

This call to input() reads up to 20 characters and stores them in the array name. Input can be terminated by pressing the space, ESC, F1, or return keys. The return value is the corresponding character code. Non-printable characters are ignored unless stated as optional arguments.

Special keys, such as the function keys, return a value of 0 for the first call to getch() and the *extended code* for the second call. For function keys this code is within the range 59–68. To distinguish extended codes from normal ASCII codes (0–255), the value 256 is added to the extended code. A table of extended codes is available in the Appendix.

■ POINTERS TO FUNCTIONS

A jump table

```cpp
// funcptr.cpp:  Demonstrates the use of an array
//               of pointers to functions.
// -------------------------------------------------
#include  <iostream>
#include  <cstdlib>    // Prototype of atoi()
#include  <cctype>     // Macros  toupper(), tolower()
using namespace std;

void  error_message(char *), message(char *),
      message_up(char *), message_low(char *);

void (*functab[])(char *) = { error_message, message,
                              message_up, message_low };

char call[]="Input: 1,2, or 3";

int main()
{
   int n = 0;
   cout << "Which of the three functions "
        << "do you want call (1,2, or 3)?\n";
   cin >> n;

   if( n<1 || n>3)
     (*functab[0])( call );
    else
     (*functab[n])("Hello, world\n");
    return 0;
}

void error_message( char *s)  {  cerr << s << endl; }

void message( char *s)        {  cout << s << endl; }

void message_up( char *s)
{    int c;
     for( ; *s != '\0';++s) c = toupper(*s),cout.put(c);
}

void message_low( char *s)
{    int c;
     for( ; *s != '\0';++s) c = tolower(*s), cout.put(c);
}
```

☐ Using Pointers to Functions

In C++ the name of a function is a constant pointer to that function. It addresses the machine code for the function. This is a situation that we have already seen for arrays—the array name is also a constant pointer to the first array element.

There are many uses for pointers to functions. You can save them in an array to form a *jump table*. Individual functions are then accessible via an index.

A pointer to a function can also be passed as an argument to another function. This makes sense if the function you are calling needs to work with different functions depending on the current situation.

The standard function qsort() is an example of this. qsort() uses the *quick sort algorithm* to sort an array. Depending on the type of the array elements and the sort criteria, the qsort() function will expect as argument another comparison function.

☐ Declaring Pointers to Functions

A pointer to a function is declared as follows:

Syntax: type (* funcptr) (parameter_list);

This defines the variable funcptr, which can store the address of a function. The function has the type type and the parameter list stated. The first pair of parentheses is also important for the declaration. The statement type *funcptr(parameter_list); would declare a function funcptr that returned a pointer.

Now let's point funcptr to the function compare() and call compare() via the pointer.

Example:
```
bool compare(double, double); // Prototype
bool (*funcptr)(double, double);
funcptr = compare;
(*funcptr)(9.1, 7.2);
```

Calling (*funcptr)() is now equivalent to calling compare(). The declaration of compare() is necessary to let the compiler know that compare is the name of a function.

In the program shown opposite, functab is an array with four pointers to functions of the void type, each of which expects a C string as an argument. functab is initialized by the functions stated in its definition and thus functab[0] points to error_message(), functab[1] to message(), etc. When the program is executed, the function with the specified index is called.

■ COMPLEX DECLARATIONS

1st Example:

```
char (* strptr) [50]
     ⇧   ⇧      ⇧
     3.  1.     0.     2.
```

0. strptr is a
1. pointer to
2. an array with 50 elements of type
3. char.

2nd Example:

```
long   *   (* func ( ) )   [ ]
 ⇧     ⇧    ⇧  ⇧    ⇧        ⇧
 5.    4.   2. 0.   1.       3.
```

0. func is a
1. function with return value of type
2. pointer to
3. an array with elements of type
4. pointer to
5. long.

3rd Example:

```
char   *   (* (* funcptr )  ( ) )  [ ]
 ⇧     ⇧    ⇧ ⇧    ⇧          ⇧     ⇧
 6.    5.   3. 1.  0.         2.    4.
```

0. funcptr is a
1. pointer to
2. a function with return value of type
3. pointer to
4. an array with elements of type
5. pointer to
6. char.

☐ Operators and Complex Declarations

In the declaration and definition of a function or a variable the same operators that you find in expressions are used in addition to the base type and the name. These operators are:

Operator	Significance
[ ]	Array with elements of type
( )	Function with return value of type
*	Pointer to
&	Reference to

A *complex declaration* always uses more than one of these operators.

Example: `char *strptr[50];`

This declares `strptr` as an array of pointers to `char`. In a declaration, a combination of the three operators is permissible, however, the following exceptions apply:

- the elements of an array cannot be functions
- a function cannot return a function or an array (but it can return a pointer to a function or an array).

Operators have the same precedence in declarations as in expressions. You can use parentheses to redefine the order of precedence.

☐ Rules

When a complex declaration is evaluated, the following rules are applied:

0. Always start with the identifier being declared.

Then repeat the following steps until all the operators have been resolved:

1. If the parentheses/brackets () or [] are on the *right*, they are interpreted.

2. If there is nothing or just a right bracket on the right), the asterisk on the *left* is interpreted, if it exists.

At last the base type is interpreted.

This proceeding is demonstrated by the example opposite. The above rules apply to both the function and each of its arguments.

▪ DEFINING TYPENAMES

1st Example:

```
typedef DayTime FREETIME;
FREETIME timeArr[100];
```

2nd Example:

```
typedef struct { double re, im; } COMPLEX;
COMPLEX z1, z2, *zp;
```

3rd Example:

```
typedef enum { Mo, Tu, We, Th, Fr } WORKDAY;
WORKDAY day;
```

4th Example:

```
typedef enum { Diamonds, Hearts,
               Spades, Clubs } COLOR;
typedef enum { seven, eight, nine, ten ,
               jack, queen, king, ace } VALUE;
typedef struct
{
    COLOR f;
    VALUE w;
} CARD;

typedef CARD[10] HAND;

HAND player1, player2, player3;
```

☐ The typedef Keyword

C++ allows you to give types a new name using the keyword typedef.

Example: `typedef unsigned char BYTE;`

This defines the type name BYTE, which can then be used as an abbreviation of the unsigned char type. The statement

Example: `BYTE array[100];`

will then define an array array with 100 elements of the unsigned char type. Type names are normally uppercase, although this is not mandatory.

Examples: `typedef int* INTPTR;`
`typedef enum{ RED, AMBER, GREEN } Lights;`

Here, INTPTR identifies the type "pointer to int" and Lights is an enumerated type.

The new type name always assumes the position of a variable name in a typedef definition. Omitting the typedef prefix will define a variable name but not a new type name.

Type definitions do not allocate memory and do not create a new type. They simply introduce a new name for an existing type.

Example: `typedef char* (*PTR_TO_FUNC)();`

The type name PTR_TO_FUNC is an abbreviation for the type "pointer to a function that returns a pointer to char." The declaration

Example: `PTR_TO_FUNC search;`

is then equivalent to

`char* (*search)();`

☐ Advantages

The major advantage of using typedef is that it improves the readability of your programs, especially when complex types are named.

One additional advantage is that you can isolate platform dependent types. When a program is ported to another platform, you only need to change the platform dependent type once in the typedef definition.

■ APPLICATION: DYNAMIC MATRICES

Class Matrix

```cpp
// matrix.h:  Representing dynamic matrices.
// ---------------------------------------------------
#include <stdexcept>
#include <iostream>
using namespace std;

class Row
{
   double *ro;    int size;
 public:
  Row( int s) { size = s; ro = new double[s]; }
  ~Row(){ delete[]ro; }

  double& operator[](int i) throw(out_of_range)
  {if(i < 0 || i > size)
     throw out_of_range("Column index: Out of Range\n");
   else
     return ro[i];
  }
};

class Matrix
{
   Row **mat;             // Pointer to array of rows
   int lines, cols;       // Number of rows and columns
 public:
  Matrix(int ro , int co )
  { lines = ro; cols = co;
   mat = new Row*[lines];
   for(int i=0; i < lines; i++)
       mat[i] = new Row(cols);
  }

  ~Matrix()
  {   for(int i=0; i < lines; i++)
         delete mat[i];
     delete[] mat;
  }
  int  getLines() const { return lines; }
  int  getCols() const { return cols; }
  Row& operator[](int i) throw(out_of_range)
  { if(i < 0 || i > cols)
     throw out_of_range("Row index: Out of Range\n");
   else
     return *mat[i];
  }
};
```

Now let's develop an application that uses a class to represent dynamic matrices. Matrices are used for computing vectors needed to move, rotate, or zoom images in graphics programming, for example.

☐ The `Matrix` Class

Memory is to be allocated dynamically to a matrix m at runtime. Additionally, it should be possible to use the index operator to access the elements of the matrix.

Example: `m[i][j]   // Element in row i, column j`

The class will therefore need a dynamic member to reference the matrix. As you already know, a matrix is a single-dimensional array whose elements are single-dimensional arrays themselves.

The class Row, which can be used to represent single-dimensional arrays of `double` values, is defined opposite. The index operator is overloaded for the Row class to allow an exception of the `out_of_range` type to be thrown for invalid indices.

The `Matrix` class contains a dynamic member, mat, which can address an array of pointers to Row objects. mat is thus a pointer to a pointer.

☐ Constructor, Destructor, and Subscript Operator

The constructor in the `Matrix` class creates an array of `lines` pointers to objects of the Row type. A loop is then used to allocate memory to the rows dynamically.

In contrast, the destructor releases the memory occupied by the line arrays first, before releasing the space occupied by the pointer array `mat`.

The subscript operator in the `Matrix` class returns the line array i for a given index i. When the following expression is evaluated

Example: `m[2][3]`

the first call is to the subscript operator of the `Matrix` class, which returns a line array to index 2. Then the subscript operator of the Row class is called for the line array. It returns a reference to the `double` value at index 3.

You will be enhancing the `Matrix` class in the exercises to this chapter by overloading the copy constructor and the assignment, for example.

EXERCISES

Listing for exercise 1

```
#include <iostream>
using namespace std;

char* color[] = {"WHITE", "PINK", "BLUE", "GREEN" };
int main()
{
   cout << *color[1] << "   "
        << *color << "   "
        << *(color[3] + 3) << "   "
        <<  color[2] + 1 << "   "
        << *( *(color + 1) + 3)
        << endl;
   return 0;
}
```

For exercise 3

The standard function `qsort()`

```
#include <cstdlib>
void qsort( void* array, size_t n, size_t size,
            int (*compare)(const void*, const void*));
```

The function `qsort()`, "quick sort," sorts an array of n elements whose first element is pointed to by `array`. The size of each element is specified by `size`.

The comparison function pointed to by `compare` is used to sort the content of the array in ascending order. `qsort()` calls the function with two arguments that point to the elements being compared.

You will normally need to define the comparison function yourself. The function must return an integer less than, equal to, or greater than zero if the first argument is less than, equal to, or greater than the second.

✓ NOTE

Since the comparison function `compare` will be called as a C function, it should be declared and defined as

```
extern "C" int compare(....);
```

Refer to the Appendix "Binding C Functions."

Exercise 1

What does the program opposite output on screen?

Exercise 2

Write a function `min()` that computes and returns the minimum of two positive numbers. The function expects a *variable* number of `unsigned int` values as arguments. The last argument must be the number `0`.

Exercise 3

Write a C++ program that compares the speed of the quick sort and selection sort algorithms

Sort two identical sequences of random numbers of the type `int` to test the sort algorithms. Read the maximum number of random numbers from the keyboard and allocate the needed memory dynamically. Display the time in seconds required for the sort operation on screen after each sort operation.

 NOTE

You can use the `SelectionSort()` function defined in Exercise 4 of Chapter 17 as an algorithm for sorting the `int` values in this exercise.

Use the standard function `qsort()`, whose prototype is defined opposite, as quick sort algorithm for this exercise.

Exercise 4

Write additional methods to complete the `Matrix` class.

- Add a `const` version of the subscript operator to the `Row` and `Matrix` classes. Use an `inline` implementation.
- Define a constructor for the `Matrix` class. The constructor dynamically allocates a matrix with a given number of rows and columns, and initializes the matrix elements with a given value. Also write a copy constructor.
- Overload the assignment operator `=` and the compound assignment operator `+=`.

  Addition is defined for two n × n matrices, A and B, which have equal numbers of rows and columns. The sum C is a n × n matrix whose elements are computed by adding elements as follows

  ```
  C[i,j] = A[i,j] + B[i,j]        for  i, j = 0, ..., n-1
  ```

- Test the `Matrix` with a suitable `main` function that calls all the methods. Display the results of the calculations on screen.

SOLUTIONS

Exercise 1

Screen output: P WHITE E LUE K

Exercise 2

```
// -------------------------------------------------------
// minivar.cpp
// Defines and tests the function min(), which
// computes and returns the minimum of positive integers.
// The function expects a variable number of arguments
// with unsigned int types.
// The last argument must be 0!
// -------------------------------------------------------
#include <stdarg.h>

unsigned int min( unsigned int first, ... )
{
    unsigned int minarg, arg;
    va_list argptr;  // Pointer to optional arguments
    if( first == 0)
        return 0;
    va_start( argptr, first);
    minarg = first;
    while( (arg = va_arg(argptr, unsigned int) ) != 0)
        if( arg < minarg)
            minarg = arg;
    va_end (argptr);
    return minarg;
}

// ----- A small function main() for testing--------------
#include <iostream>
using namespace std;
int main()
{
    cout << "\nThe minimum of : 34 47 19 22 58 "
         << "is:   " << min(34, 47, 19, 22, 58, 0)
         << endl;
    return 0;
}
```

Exercise 3

```cpp
// -- --------------------------------------------------
// sort_t.cpp
// Compares the performances of sorting algorithms
//           quick sort  and  selection sort
// For this purpose, two identical arrays are dynamically
// generated and initialized with random numbers.
// The times needed for sorting are displayed.
// ----------------------------------------------------
#include <iostream>
#include <iomanip>
#include <cstdlib>
#include <ctime>
using namespace std;

void isort(int *v, int lenv);

// For qsort():
extern "C" int intcmp(const void*, const void*);

main()
{
   unsigned int  i, size;
   int  *numbers1, *numbers2;
   long time1, time2;

   cout << "\n   The performance of the sorting algorithms"
        << "\n         quick sort  and  selection sort"
        << "\n    is being compared.\n\n"
        << "\nHow many numbers are to be sorted?   ";

   cin >> size;
   numbers1 = new int[size];
   numbers2 = new int[size];
   cout << "\nThere are "
        << size << " random numbers to be generated.\n";
   srand((unsigned)time(NULL)); // Initialize the
                                // random number generator.
   for(i = 0 ; i < size ; ++i)
      numbers1[i] = numbers2[i] = rand(); // Random numbers

   cout << "\nSorting starts! Please wait.\n";
   time(&time1);                          // Length of time
                                          // for quick sort.
   qsort(numbers1, size, sizeof(int), intcmp);
   time(&time2);

   cout  << "\nTime taken by the quick sort algorithm: "
         << time2 - time1 << " seconds.\n";
```

```
        cout << "\nI am sorting again. Please wait!\n";

        time(&time1);                    // Length of time
        isort(numbers2, size);           // for selection sort
        time(&time2);

        cout << "\nTime taken by the insertion sort algorithm: "
             << time2 - time1 << " seconds.\n"
             << "\nOutput sorted numbers? (y/n)\n\n";

        char c;  cin >> c;
        if( c == 'Y' || c == 'y')
          for( i = 0 ; i < size ; ++i)
            cout << setw(12) <<  numbers1[i];

        cout << endl;
        return 0;
}


extern "C" int intcmp( const void *a, const void *b)
{
        return (*(int*)a - *(int*)b);
}

// ------------------------------------------------------
// isort()   sorts an array of int values
//           using the selection sort algorithm.

void isort( int *a, int len)    // Sort the array a of
{                               // length len in ascending
        register int *b, *minp;     // order
        int *last, help;

        last = a + len - 1;     // Points to the last element

        for( ; a <= last; ++a)   // Search for the smallest
        {                        // element starting at a.
          minp = a;              // minp points to the "current"
                                 // smallest array element.
            for( b = a+1; b <= last; ++b)     // Search for the
              if( *b < *minp )                // minimum.
                  minp = b;

            help = *a, *a = *minp, *minp = help;    // Swap.
        }
}
```

Exercise 4

```cpp
// -- ----------------------------------------------------
// matrix.h :  Represents dynamic matrices
// -------------------------------------------------------
#ifndef _MATRIX_H_
#define _MATRIX_H_

#include <stdexcept>
#include <iostream>
using namespace std;

class Row
{
    double *ro;
    int size;
  public:
    Row( int s) { size = s; z = new double[s]; }
    ~Row(){ delete[]ro; }

    double& operator[](int i)
    {
      if(i < 0 || i > size)
        throw out_of_range("Row index: Out of Range\n");
      return ro[i];
    }
    const double& operator[](int i)  const
    {
      if(i < 0 || i > size)
        throw out_of_range("Row index: Out of Range\n");
      return ro[i];
    }
};

class Matrix
{
  private:
    Row **mat;              // Pointer to array of rows
    int lines, cols;        // Number of rows and columns

  public:
    Matrix(int ro , int co)
    {
      lines = ro; cols = co;
      mat = new Row*[lines];
      for(int i=0; i < lines; i++)
        mat[i] = new Row(cols);
    }
    Matrix:: Matrix( int z, int s, double val);
```

```
  Matrix( const Matrix& );
 ~Matrix()
 {  for(int i=0; i < lines; i++)
        delete mat[i];
    delete[] mat;
 }
 int  getLines() const { return lines; }
 int  getCols()  const { return cols; }

 Row& operator[](int i)
 {
   if(i < 0 || i > cols)
      throw out_of_range("Row index: Out of Range\n");
   return *mat[i];
 }

 const Row& operator[](int i) const
 {
   if(i < 0 || i > cols)
      throw out_of_range("Row index: Out of Range\n");
   return *mat[i];
 }
                                      // Assignments:
 Matrix& operator=( const Matrix& );
 Matrix& operator+=( const Matrix& );
};
#endif


// -------------------------------------------------------
// matrix.cpp : Defines methods of class Matrix
// -------------------------------------------------------
#include "matrix.h"

Matrix:: Matrix( int ro, int co, double val)
{
    lines = ro; cols = co;
    mat = new Row*[lines];              // Array of pointers to
                                        // arrays of rows
    int i, j;
    for(i=0; i < lines; i++)           // Arrays of rows:
    {
       mat[i] = new Row(cols);         // Allocate memory
       for(j = 0; j < cols; ++j)
          (*this)[i][j] = val;         // and copy values.
    }
}
```

```
Matrix:: Matrix( const Matrix& m)
{
    lines = m.lines; cols = m.cols;   // Rows and columns

    mat = new Row*[lines];            // Array of pointers
                                      // to arrays of rows
    int i, j;
    for(i=0; i < lines; i++)          // Arrays of rows:
    {
        mat[i] = new Row(cols);       // To allocate
                                      // storage
        for( j = 0; j < cols; ++j)
            (*this)[i][j] = m[i][j];  // and copy values.
    }
}

Matrix& Matrix::operator=(const Matrix& m)
{
    int i, j;                         // Free "old" storage:
    for(i=0; i < lines; i++)
        delete mat[i];
    delete[] mat;

    lines = m.lines; cols = m.cols;   // Rows, columns

    mat = new Row*[lines];            // Array of pointers
                                      // to arrays of rows
    for(i=0; i < lines; ++i)          // Array of rows:
    {
        mat[i] = new Row(cols);       // Allocate space

        for( j = 0; j < cols; ++j)
            (*this)[i][j] = m[i][j];  // and copy values.
    }

    return *this;
}

Matrix& Matrix::operator+=( const Matrix& m)
{
    int i, j;
    if( cols == m.cols && lines == m.lines)
        for( i=0; i < lines; ++i)
            for( j=0; j < cols; ++j)
                (*this)[i][j] += m[i][j];

    return *this;
}
```

```cpp
// -------------------------------------------------------
// matrix_t.cpp : Tests dynamic matrices
// -------------------------------------------------------
#include "matrix.h"
void display( Matrix& m );          // Output a matrix.
int main()
{
    Matrix m(4,5);
    try
    {
      int i,j;
      for( i=0; i < m.getLines(); i++)
        for( j=0; j < m.getCols(); j++)
          m[i][j] = (double)i + j/ 100.0;

        cout << "Matrix created" << endl;
        display(m);

        Matrix  cop(m);
        cout << "Copy generated." << endl;
        display(cop);

        cop += m;
        cout << "Compute the sum:" << endl;
        display(cop);

        Matrix m1(4, 5, 0.0);
        cout << "Initializing a matrix with 0:" << endl;
        display(m1);
        m = m1;
        cout << "Matrix assigned:" << endl;
        display(m);
    }
    catch(out_of_range& err)
    {   cerr << err.what() << endl;    exit(1);  }
    return 0;
}

void display( Matrix& m)
{
    for(int i=0; i < m.getLines(); i++)
    {
      for(int j=0; j < m.getCols(); j++)
          cout << m[i][j] << "  ";
      cout << endl;
    }
    cin.get();
}
```

chapter 31

Manipulating Bits

This chapter describes bitwise operators and how to use bit masks. The applications included demonstrate calculations with parity bits, conversion of lowercase and capital letters, and converting binary numbers. Finally, the definition of bit-fields is introduced.

■ BITWISE OPERATORS

"True or False" table for bitwise operators

Bitwise AND	Result	Bitwise inclusive OR	Result
0 & 0	0	0 | 0	0
0 & 1	0	0 | 1	1
1 & 0	0	1 | 0	1
1 & 1	1	1 | 1	1
0 ^ 0	0	~0	1
0 ^ 1	1	~1	0
1 ^ 0	1		
1 ^ 1	0		

Examples

```
unsigned int a, b, c;
```

	Bit pattern
`a = 5;`	0 0 . . . . 0 0 1 0 1
`b = 12;`	0 0 . . . . 0 1 1 0 0
`c = a & b;`	0 0 . . . . 0 0 1 0 0
`c = a | b;`	0 0 . . . . 0 1 1 0 1
`c = a ^ b;`	0 0 . . . . 0 1 0 0 1
`c = ~a;`	1 1 . . . . 1 1 0 1 0

☐ Bit Coding Data

In cases where conservative use of memory is imperative, data often need to be bit coded, a technique to represent information as individual bits. Some examples of bit coded data can be found in file access rights or the status-word of a stream.

To access bit coded data, you need to be able to read or modify individual bits. C++ has six bitwise operators to perform these tasks:

- **Logical bitwise operators**

  | & | AND | | | inclusive OR |
  | ^ | exclusive OR | ~ | NOT |

- **Bitwise shift operators**

  << Left shift   >> Right shift

Operands for bitwise operators must have integral types. Operands belonging to `float` or `double` types are invalid.

The boolean tables on the opposite page show the effect of the *logical* bitwise operators for individual bits. If a bit is set, that is, if it has a value of 1, it will be interpreted as true. If the bit is not set, and thus has a value of 0, it will be interpreted as false. Examples for each bitwise operator follow.

The result type of a bitwise operation will be the integral type defined by the operand type. If, for example, both operands are `int` types, the result will also be of an `int` type.

☐ Arithmetic Type Conversions and Precedence

If the operands of a bitwise operator are of different types, normal arithmetic type conversion will occur. If one operand type is an `int` and the other a `long`, the `int` value will be converted to `long` before the operation is performed.

The logical bitwise operators & or | should not be confused with the logical && and || operators. The latter do not affect individual bits but interpret the whole value of their operands as boolean, returning a boolean value. The expression 1 && 2 returns the value `true`, whereas 1 & 2 has the value 0.

The *precedence* of the bitwise NOT operator ~ is high, since ~ is a unary operator. As you can see from the table of precedence in the appendix, both the binary operators &, ^, and | have low precedence. However, their precedence is higher than that of the logical operators && and ||.

■ BITWISE SHIFT OPERATORS

Right and left shift

	Bit pattern
`unsigned int a, b;`	
`a = 12;`	`0 0 . . . . 0 0 0 0 1 1 0 0`
`b = a << 3;`	`0 0 . . . . 0 1 1 0 0 0 0 0`
`b = a >> 2;`	`0 0 . . . . 0 0 0 0 0 0 1 1`

Using shift operators

```cpp
// getbin_t.cpp: Defines the function getbin(), which
//               reads a binary number (ex. 0101... )
//               from the standard input, and returns
//               a value of type unsigned int.
// ---------------------------------------------------
#include <iostream>
using namespace std;

unsigned int getbin()
{
   char c;
   unsigned int val = 0;

   while ( (c = cin.get()) == ' ' || c == '\t' )
      ;                  // Ignore leading blanks and tabs

   while( c == '0' || c == '1' )    // Read and convert
   {                                // the binary number
      val = (val << 1) | (c - '0');
      c = cin.get();
   }

   return val;
}
```

Left and Right Shift

The shift operators `<<` and `>>` shift the bit pattern of their left operand a certain number of bit positions. The number of positions is defined by the right operand. The examples opposite illustrate this point.

In the case of a *left shift*, 0 bits are padded. The bits dropped on the left are lost.

Example:
```
short x = 0xFF00;
x = x << 4;                 // Result: 0xF000
```

In the case of a *right shift*, 0 bits are padded from the left if the left operand is an unsigned type or has a positive value. In all other cases, the compiler determines whether to pad an expression with 0 bits (*logical shift*) or with the sign bit (*arithmetic shift*), although an arithmetic shift normally occurs.

Example:
```
short x = 0xFF00;
x = x >> 4;                 // Result: 0xFFF0
```

To ensure portable source code, you should use right shifts for positive values only.

Integral Promotion

Integral promotion is performed for the operands of a shift operator, that is `char` is extended to `int`. The result type in a shift operation is then the same as the type of the left operand after integral promotion.

The result of a shift operation is unpredictable if the value of the right operand is negative or larger than the length of the left operand expressed in bits.

Example:
```
char x = 0xFF;
x = x >> 9;                 // undefined result
```

Applications

Shift operators allow you to perform efficient multiplication and division with 2^n. Shifting a number n places left (or right) is equivalent to a multiplication (or division) by 2^n.

Examples:
```
unsigned res,number = 5;
res = number << 3;          // 5 * 2^3 = 40
res = number >> 1;          // 5 / 2^1 = 2
```

■ BIT MASKS

Bit positions

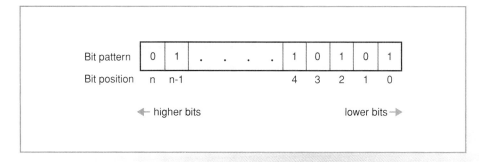

Example

```
#define MASK 0x20
char c = 'A';
c = c | MASK;
```

Current bit patterns:	0 1 0 0 0 0 0 1							'A' = 0x41
	| 0 0 1 0 0 0 0 0							MASK = 0x20
	0 1 1 0 0 0 0 1							'a' = 0x61

Deleting Bits

The *bitwise AND operator* is normally used to delete specific bits. A so-called *mask* is used to determine which bits to delete.

Example: c = c & 0x7F;

In the mask 0x7F the seven least significant bits are set to 1, and all significant bits are set to 0. This means that all the bits in c, with the exception of the least significant bits, are deleted. These bits are left unchanged.

The variable c can be of any integral type. If the variable occupies more than one byte, the significant bits in the mask, 0x7F, are padded with 0 bits when integral promotion is performed.

Setting and Inverting Bits

You can use the *bitwise OR operator* | to set specific bits. The example on the opposite page shows how to change the case of a letter. In ASCII code, the only difference between a lowercase and an uppercase letter is the fifth bit.

Finally, you can use the *bitwise exclusive OR operator* ^ to invert specific bits. Each 0-bit is set to 1 and each 1-bit is deleted if the corresponding bit in the mask has a value of 1.

Example: c = c ^ 0xAA;

The bit pattern for 0xAA is 10101010. Every second bit in the least significant eight bits of c is therefore inverted.

It is worthy of note that you can perform double inversion using the same mask to restore the original bit pattern, that is, (x ^ MASK) ^ MASK restores the value x.

The following overview demonstrates the effect of a statement for an integral expression x and any given mask, MASK:

- x & MASK   deletes all bits that have a value of 0 in MASK
- x | MASK   sets all bits that have a value of 1 in MASK
- x ^ MASK   inverts all bits that have a value of 0 in MASK.

The other bits are left unchanged.

■ USING BIT MASKS

Computing the parity of an integer

```cpp
// parity_t.cpp: Defines the function parity(), which
//               computes the parity of an unsigned
//               value.
// Returns:      0, if the number of 1-bits is even,
//               1  in all other cases.
// ----------------------------------------------------
inline unsigned int bit0( unsigned int x )
{
    return (x & 1);
}

int parity( unsigned int n)
{
    unsigned int par = 0;
    for( ; n != 0; n >>=1 )
      par ^= bit0(n);
    return (par);
}
```

☐ Creating Your Own Masks

You can use the bitwise operators to create your own bit masks.

Example: x = x & ~3;

In the bit pattern of 3, only the bits at positions 0 and 1 are set. The mask ~3 therefore contains a whole bunch of 1-bits and only the two least significant bits are 0. The above expression would thus delete the two least significant bits in x.

The mask ~3 is independent of the word length of the computer and is thus preferable to the mask 0xFFFC.

The next example shows masks that address exactly one bit in a word. They are created by left shifting 1.

Examples: x = x | (1 << 6);
           x = x & ~(1 << 6);

The first expression sets the sixth bit in x. The same bit is then deleted, as only the sixth bit in the mask ~(1 << 6) has a value of 0.

Of course, you can also use masks such as (1 << n) where n is a variable containing the bit position.

Example: int setBit(int x, unsigned int n)
          {
              if(n < sizeof(int))
                  return(x & (1 << n);
          }

☐ Bitwise Operators in Compound Assignments

The binary bitwise operators &, |, ^, <<, and >> can be used in compound assignments.

Examples: x >>= 1;
           x ^= 1;

Both statements are equivalent to

```
x = x >> 1;
x = x ^ 1
```

The function parity() shown opposite includes compound assignments with bitwise operators. Parity bit computation is used to perform error recognition in data communications.

■ BIT-FIELDS

Header of ATM cells

```
Byte
 1   ┌─────────────────┬─────────────────┐
     │ General Flow    │  Virtual Path   │
     │   Control       │   Identifier    │
 2   ├─────────────────┼─────────────────┤
     │  Virtual Path   │ Virtual Channel │
     │   Identifier    │   Identifier    │
 3   ├─────────────────┴─────────────────┤
     │          Virtual Channel          │
     │            Identifier             │
 4   ├─────────────────┬────────┬────────┤
     │ Virtual Channel │Payload │  CLP   │
     │   Identifier    │  Type  │        │
 5   ├─────────────────┴────────┴────────┤
     │          Header Error             │
     │            Control                │
     └───────────────────────────────────┘
```

General Flow Control	Controls the data stream
Virtual Path/Channel Identifier	Address of the virtual path/channel
Payload Type	Distinguish between payload and control data
CLP (Cell Loss Priority)	Mark cells with high priority
Header Error Control	Check sum for header

Representing an ATM cell

```c
struct ATM_Cell
{
   unsigned GFC : 4;      // General Flow Control
   unsigned VPI : 8;      // Virtual Path Identifier
   unsigned VCI : 16;     // Virtual Channel Identifier
   unsigned PT  : 3;      // Payload Type
   unsigned CLP : 1       // Cell Loss Priority
   unsigned HEC : 8;      // Header Error Control
   char payload[48];      // Payload
};
```

C++ lets you divide a computer word into *bit-fields* and give the bit-fields a name. Bit-fields offer major advantages; their uncluttered structure makes them preferable and less error prone than using masks and bitwise operators to manipulate individual bits.

☐ Defining Bit-Fields

Bit-fields are defined as data members of a class. Each bit-field is of `unsigned int` type with an optional *name* and *width*. The width is defined as the number of bits the bit-field occupies in a computer word and is separated from the bit-field name by a colon.

Example:
```
struct { unsigned bit0_4 : 5;
         unsigned        : 10;
         unsigned bit15  : 1; } word;
```

The member `word.bit0_4` designates the 5 least significant bits in a computer word and can store values in the range 0 to 31. The second data member does not have a name and is used to create a gap of 10 bits. The member `word.bit15` contains the value at bit position 15.

You cannot reference nameless bit-fields. They are used to align the subsequent bit-fields at specific bit positions.

The width of a bit-field cannot be greater than that of the computer word. The width 0 has a special significance; the subsequent bit-field is positioned on the next word boundary, that is, it begins with the next computer word. If a bit-field will not fit in a computer word, the following bit-field is also positioned on the next word boundary.

There are several special cases you need to consider when dealing with bit-fields:

- you cannot use the address operator for bit-fields. You cannot create arrays of bit-fields. Neither restriction applies to a class containing bit-field members, however.
- the order bit-fields are positioned in depends on the machine being used. Some computer architectures position bit-fields in reverse order. This is true of DEC Alpha workstations, for example.

☐ The Sample Program Opposite

The opposite page shows a class designed to represent ATM cells. Cells are used for data transportation in ATM (*Asynchronous Transfer Mode*) networks. Each cell comprises a 5 byte header with addresses and a checksum for error checking and 48 byte data section or *payload*. The header shown here is used to connect a computer to the network in the *User Network Interface*.

■ EXERCISES

Sample screen output for exercise 1

```
      ******  BITWISE OPERATORS  ******

Please enter two integers.

1st Number  -->  57
2nd Number  --> -3

The bit pattern of 57 = x :   0000 0000 0011 1001
The bit pattern of -3 = y :   1111 1111 1111 1101
The bit pattern of x & y :   0000 0000 0011 1001
The bit pattern of x | y :   1111 1111 1111 1101
The bit pattern of x ^ y :   1111 1111 1100 0100

How many bit positions is x to be shifted?
Count --> 4

The bit pattern of x << 4 : 0000 0011 1001 0000
The bit pattern of x >> 4 : 0000 0000 0000 0011

Repeat (y/n)?
```

Exercise 1

a. Write the function `putBits()` that outputs the bit pattern of a number as an `unsigned int` type. Only the 16 least significant bits are to be output no matter what the size of the computer word. The number is passed as an argument to the function, which has no return value.

b. Write a tutorial to demonstrate the effect of bitwise operators. First read two decimal integers from the keyboard and store them in the variables x and y. Then use the function `putBits()` to output the bit patterns of x, $x\&y$, $x \mid y$, x ^ y, and $\sim x$.

   To demonstrate the shift operators, shift the value of x a given number of bit positions right and left. Read the number of bit positions from keyboard input. Use the value 1 in case of invalid input.

The opposite page shows sample output from the program.

Exercise 2

Your task is to encrypt data to prevent spying during data communications. The sender uses a filter to encrypt the data in question, and the receiver uses the same filter to decrypt the transmission.

a. Define the function `swapBits()` that swaps two bits in an `int` value. The `int` value and the positions of the bits to be swapped are passed as arguments to the function. The return value is the new `int` value. If one of the positions passed to the function is invalid, the `int` value should be returned unchanged.

b. Write a filter that swaps the bits at bit positions 5 and 6, 0 and 4, and 1 and 3 in all characters except control characters (defined as ASCII Code >= 32).

Test the filter by writing the encrypted output to a file and then using the same filter to output the new file. The output must comprise the original unencrypted data.

solutions

■ SOLUTIONS

Exercise I

```cpp
// ------------------------------------------------------
// bits_t.cpp
// Demonstrates bitwise operators.
// ------------------------------------------------------
#include <iostream>
#include <iomanip>
using namespace std;

void putbits( unsigned int n);  // Prototype of putbits()

int main()                      // Learning bitwise operations
{
    int  x, y, count;
    char yn;

    do
    {
      cout << "\n\n   ******  BITWISE OPERATIONS  ******\n";

      cout << "\nPlease enter two integers.\n\n"
           <<  "1st number --> ";
      cin >> x;

      cout << "2nd number --> ";
      cin >> y;

      cout << "\nThe bit pattern of "
           << setw(6) << x << " = x  :     ";
      putbits(x);

      cout << "\nThe bit pattern of "
           << setw(6) << y << " = y  :     ";
      putbits(y);

      cout << "\nThe bit pattern of    x & y :    ";
      putbits(x&y);

      cout << "\nThe bit pattern of    x | y :    ";
      putbits(x|y);

      cout << "\nThe bit pattern of    x ^ y :    ";
      putbits(x^y);

      cout << "\n\nHow many bit positions"
              " is x to be shifted?"
           << "\nNumber --> ";
      cin >> count;
```

```cpp
        if( count < 0  ||  count > 15)
        {
           cout << "Invalid input!"
                << " Shifting by one bit position.\n";
           count = 1;
        }
        cout << "\nThe bit pattern of    x << "
             << setw(2) << count << " :    ";
        putbits( x << count);

        cout << "\nThe bit pattern of x >> "
             << setw(2) << count << " :    ";
        putbits( x >> count);

        cout << "\nRepeat (y/n)? ";
        cin >> yn;
        while( (yn | 0x20) != 'y'  &&  yn != 'n')
           ;

    }while( yn == 'y');

    return 0;
}

// --------------------------------------------------------
// Output the bit pattern of n (only the 16 lower bits).

void putbits( unsigned int n )
{
   int i;

   for( i = 15; i >= 0 ; --i)
   {
      cout << (char)( ((n>>i) & 1) + '0');    // i-th bit
      if( i % 4 == 0  &&  i > 0)       // and after 4 bits
         cout << ' ';                  // one blank.
   }
}
```

Exercise 2

```cpp
// --------------------------------------------------------
//  hide_t.cpp:  Filter to encrypt data.
//               Swap bits in bit positions 5 and 6,
//               0 and 4,  1 and 3 for all characters
//               except control characters.
//               Modules:  hide_t.cpp,  swapbits.cpp
//
//  Call:       hide_t [ < sourcefile ] [ > destfile ]
// --------------------------------------------------------
```

```cpp
#include <iostream>
using namespace std;

int swapbits( int ch, int bitnr1, int bitnr2); // Prototype

int main()                                      // Encrypt data
{
   int c;
   while( (c = cin.get()) != EOF)
   {
      if( c >= 32)                              // Control character?
      {
         c = swapbits(c, 5, 6);        // Swap bits
         c = swapbits(c, 0, 4);
         c = swapbits(c, 1, 3);
      }
      cout << c;
   }
   return 0;
}

// ------------------------------------------------------
// swapbits.cpp: The function swapbits() swaps two bits
//               within an integer.
// Arguments:    The integer and two bit positions.
// Returns:      The new value.
// ------------------------------------------------------

int swapbits( int x, int bitnr1, int bitnr2)
{                                    // To swap two bits in x.
   int newx, mask1, mask2;
   int msb = 8 * sizeof(int) - 1;   // Highest bit position

   if( bitnr1 < 0 || bitnr1 > msb ||
       bitnr2 < 0 || bitnr2 > msb)
     return x;         // Return, if bit position is invalid

   mask1 = (1 << bitnr1);    // Shift 1 to position bitnr1
   mask2 = (1 << bitnr2);    // Shift 1 to position bitnr2

   newx = x & ~(mask1 | mask2);           // Delete both bits

   if( x & mask1 )  newx |= mask2;    // Swap bits.
   if( x & mask2 )  newx |= mask1;

   return( newx);
}
```

Templates

Templates allow you to construct both functions and classes based on types that have not yet been stated. Thus, templates are a powerful tool for automating program code generation.

This chapter describes how to define and use function and class templates. In addition, special options, such as default arguments, specialization, and explicit instantiation are discussed.

■ FUNCTION AND CLASS TEMPLATES

Template and instantiation

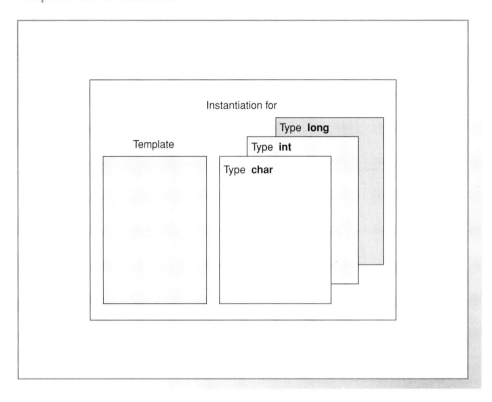

Motivation

As a programmer you will often be faced with implementing multiple versions of similar functions and classes, which are needed for various types.

A class used to represent an array of `int` values is very similar to a class representing an array of `double` values, for example. The implementation varies only in the type of elements that you need to represent. Operations performed with elements, such as search and sort algorithms, must be defined separately for each type.

C++ allows you to define *templates*—parameterized families of related functions or classes:

- a *function template* defines a group of statements for a function using a parameter instead of a concrete type
- a *class template* specifies a class definition using a parameter instead of a concrete type.

A class template can provide a generic definition that can be used to represent various types of arrays, for example. During *instantiation*, that is, when a concrete type is defined, an individual class is created based on the template definition.

Advantages of Templates

Templates are powerful programming tools.

- A template need only be coded once. Individual functions or classes are automatically generated when needed.
- A template offers a uniform solution for similar problems allowing type-independent code to be tested early in the development phase.
- Errors caused by multiple encoding are avoided.

Templates in the Standard Library

The C++ standard library contains numerous class template definitions, such as the stream classes for input and output, string, and container classes. The classes `string`, `istream`, `ostream`, `iostream`, and so on are instantiations for the `char` type.

The standard library also includes an algorithm library, which comprises many search and sort algorithms. The various algorithms are implemented as global function templates and can be used for any set of objects.

■ DEFINING TEMPLATES

Class template Stack

```cpp
// stack.h : The class template Stack with
//           methods push() and pop().
//-----------------------------------------------------
template<class T>
class Stack
{
  private:
    T* basePtr;        // Pointer to array
    int tip;           // Stack tip
    int max;           // Maximum number of elements
  public:
    Stack(int n){ basePtr = new T[n]; max = n; tip = 0;}
    Stack( const Stack<T>&);
    ~Stack(){ delete[] basePtr; }

    Stack<T>& operator=( const Stack<T>& );

    bool empty(){ return (tip == 0); }
    bool push( const T& x);
    bool pop(T& x);
};

template<class T>
bool Stack<T>::push( const T& x)
{
    if(tip < max - 1)          // If there is enough space
    {
        basePtr[tip++] = x;   return true;
    }
    else return false;
}

template<class T>
bool Stack<T>::pop( T& x)
{
    if(tip > 0)                // If the stack is not empty
    {
        x = basePtr{--tip};    return true;
    }
    else return false;
}
```

☐ Defining Function Templates

The definition of a template is always prefixed by

```
template<class T>
```

where the parameter T is a type name used in the definition that follows. Although you must state the class keyword, T can be any given type, such as an int or double.

Example:
```
template <class T>
void exchange(T& x, T&y)
{
    T help(x); x = y; y = help;
}
```

This defines the function template exchange(). The parameter T represents the type of variables, which are to interchange. The name T is common but not mandatory.

☐ Defining Class Templates

Example:
```
template <class U>
class Demo
{
    U elem;    . . .   // etc.
};
```

This defines the class template Demo<U>. Both U and Demo<U> are treated like normal types in the class definition. You simply need to state the name of the template, Demo, within the class scope.

The methods of a class template are also parameterized via the future type. Each method in a class template is thus a function template. If the definition is external to the class template, function template syntax is used. The method name is prefixed by the class template type and the scope resolution operator.

The example on the opposite page illustrates this point by defining a *stack* template. A stack is managed according to the last-in-first-out principle, *lifo-principle* for short; the last element to be "pushed" onto the stack is the first to be removed, or "popped," from the stack.

The methods of a class template are normally defined in the same header file. This ensures that the definition will be visible to the compiler, since it requires the definition to generate machine code for concrete template arguments.

■ TEMPLATE INSTANTIATION

Sample program

```
// stack_t.cpp: Testing a stack
// -----------------------------------------------------
#include <iostream>
#include <iomanip>
using namespace std;

#include "stack.h"

typedef Stack<unsigned> USTACK;   // Stack for elements
                                  // of type unsigned.
void fill(  USTACK& stk );
void clear( USTACK& stk );

int main()
{
    USTACK ustk(256);       // Create and fill
    fill( ustk);            // the original stack.
    USTACK ostk(ustk);      // Copy.
    cout << "The copy: " << endl;
    clear( ostk);           // Output and clear the copy.
    cout << "The original: " << endl;
    clear( ustk );          // Output, clear the original.

    return 0;
}

void fill( USTACK& stk )
{
    unsigned x;
    cout << "Enter positive integers (quit with 0):\n";
    while( cin >> x  && x != 0 )
      if( !stk.push(x) )
        {
            cerr << "Stack is full!"; break;
        }
}

void clear( USTACK& stk )
{
    if(stk.empty())
        cerr << "Stack is empty!" << endl;
    else
    {
        unsigned x;
        while( stk.pop(x))
          cout << setw(8) << x << "  ";
        cout << endl;
    }
}
```

Defining a template creates neither a concrete function nor a class. The machine code for functions or methods is not generated until instantiation.

☐ Instantiating Template Functions

A *template function* is instantiated when it is first called. The compiler determines the parameter type of T by the function arguments.

Example:
```
short a = 1, b = 7;
exchange( a, b );
```

The template is first used to generate the exchange() function machine code for the short type. The template functions can be called after this step.

This allows you to generate an exchange() template function for any type. Given that x and y are two double variables, the following statement

Example:
```
exchange( x, y );
```

creates a second template function for the double type.

☐ Instantiation of Template Classes

The instantiation of a *template class* is performed *implicitly* when the class is used for the first time, for example, when an object of the template class is defined.

Example:
```
Stack<int> istack(256);   // implicit
```

This statement first creates the template class Stack<int>, generating the machine code of all methods for the int type. After this step has been completed, an istack object of the Stack<int> type can be constructed.

If a further template class, such as Stack<float> is created, the machine code generated for the methods in this template class will be different from the machine code of the Stack<int> methods.

In other words, developing templates will not reduce the amount of machine code required for a program. However, it does spare the programmer's extra work required to develop multiple versions of functions and classes.

Templates are double checked for *errors* by the compiler—once when the template definition is compiled and again during instantiation. The first check recognizes errors that are independent of the template parameters. Errors in parameterization cannot be detected until instantiation if, for example, an operator for the template argument type has not been defined.

■ TEMPLATE PARAMETERS

The Stack **template with two template parameters**

```
// stackn.h: Class Template Stack<T, n>
// -------------------------------------

template <class T, int n>
class Stack
{
  private:
    T    arr[n];        // Array
    int tip;            // Tip of stack
    int max;            // Maximum number of elements
  public:
     Stack(){ max = n; tip = 0; };

     bool empty(){ return (tip == 0); }
     bool push( const T& x);
     bool pop(T& x);
};

template<class T, int n>
bool Stack<T, n>::push( const T& x)
{
   if(tip < max - 1)
   {
      arr[tip++] = x; return true;
   }
   else return false;
 }

template<class T, int n>
bool Stack<T, n>::pop(T& x )
{
   if(tip > 0)
   {
      x = arr{--tip];  return  true;
   }
   else return false;
}
```

☐ Multiple Template Parameters

You can also define templates with multiple parameters like the following class template,

Example:
```
template <class U, class V>
class Demo
{   // . . .      };
```

which has two parameters U and V. A class Demo<U,V> is defined for each pair of U, V types.

A template parameter need not always be a type name. Normal function parameters are also permissible, particularly pointers and references.

Example:
```
template<class T, int n>
class Stack{ . . . };
```

This defines the class template Stack<T, n> that is parameterized with the type T and an integer n.

The example on the opposite page uses the parameter n to specify the size of an array used to represent a stack. The major advantage is that the number of array elements is already known when an object of the template class is instantiated. Objects can then be created without allocating dynamic storage.

This simplifies the definition of the stack template. The copy constructor, the assignment operator, and the destructor no longer need to be defined!

☐ Restrictions

Two restrictions apply to template parameters other than type parameters:

- they cannot be modified
- they cannot be floating-point types.

The following expression would thus be invalid in the definition opposite:

Example: `++n; // Error: changing template parameter`

Even though double type template parameters are not permissible,

Example:
```
template<class T, double d>  // Error!
class Demo { . . . };
```

pointers and references to floating-point types are:

Example:
```
template<class T, double& ref>
class Demo { . . . };
```

■ TEMPLATE ARGUMENTS

Sample program

```cpp
// mini_t.cpp: Passing arguments to
//             function templates
// -------------------------------------------
#include <iostream>
using namespace std;

template <class T>
T min( T x, T y)
{
   return( (x < y) ? x : y);
}

int main()
{
   short x = 10, y = 2;

   cout << "x = " << x << "  y = " << y << endl;
   cout << "The smaller value is: "
        << min(x, y) << endl;       // Call is ok.

   double z1 = 2.2;
   float  z2 = 1.1F;

   cout << "\nThe smaller value is: "
        << min(z1, z2) << endl;    // Not ok!

   double z3 = 1.1;
   cout << "\nz1 = " << z1
        << "  z3 = " << z3 << endl;
   cout << "The smaller value is: "
        << min(z1, z3) << endl;    // Call is ok.

   return 0;
}
```

☐ Passing Arguments

A template is instantiated when a template argument is passed to it. The argument types must exactly match to the types of the template parameters.

Not even implicit type conversions, such as `float` to `double`, are performed. In the case of the template function `min()` this means that both arguments must be of the same type. The following call

Example:
```
float x = 1.1; double y = 7.7;
        min ( x , y );
```

would lead to an error message, since the template function cannot be defined by the

Prototype: `void min( float , double );`

☐ Restrictions

There are several restrictions for template arguments other than type names:

- ▪ if the template parameter is a reference, only a global or static object can be passed as a template argument
- ▪ if the template parameter is a pointer, only the address of an object or a function with global scope can be stated
- ▪ if the template parameter is neither a reference nor a pointer, only constant expressions can be used as template arguments.

Example:
```
int cnt = 256;                 // Error:
        typedef Stack<short, cnt> ShortStack;
```

Since only an `int` constant is permitted as a template argument, this statement provokes an error.

Strings, such as `"Oktoberfest,"` are also invalid as template arguments, as their scope is static and not global.

Example:
```
template<class T,char* s> class Demo{...};
```

Only globally defined strings can be used for instantiation, for example

```
char str[] = "Oktoberfest";  // global
Demo<double, str> income;    // ok
```

▪ SPECIALIZATION

Function template `min()`

```
template <class T>
T min( T x, T y)
{
    return( (x < y) ? x : y)
}
```

Specializing the function template for C strings

```
#include <cstring>

const char* min( const char* s1, const char* s2 )
{
    return( (strcmp(s1, s2) < 0 ) ? s1: s2 );
}
```

☐ ANSI specialization

The ANSI standard does not differ between template functions and "normal" functions. The definition of a function template and a function with the same name, which can be generated by the function template, causes the compiler to output an error message (ex. "duplicate definition ...").

That is why the ANSI standard provides its own syntax for defining specializations:

```
#include <cstring>

template<>
const char* min( const char* s1, const char* s2 )
{
    return( (strcmp(s1, s2) < 0 ) ? s1: s2 );
}
```

☐ Motivation

A template function can only be instantiated if all the statements contained in the function can be executed. If you call the template function exchange() with two objects of the same class, the copy constructor and the assignment must be defined for this class.

More specifically, all operators used in a template function must be defined for the current argument type. Thus, the function template min(), which determines the lesser of two arguments, can only be instantiated if the operator < is defined for the argument type.

Besides non-executable instructions there are other reasons to prevent a function template being instantiated for a particular type:

- the generic approach defined by the template does not return any useful results for a given type
- there are more efficient approaches for some types.

The statement

Example: minStr = min(, "VIVIAN", "vivian");

only returns the lower of the two addresses at which the C strings are stored.

☐ Defining Specialization

In cases like this, it makes sense to specialize the template function definition. To do so, you use a function with a separate definition to overload the template function. This technique is demonstrated on the opposite page using the function template min(), where a specialization has been defined for the char* type, both for older and more modern compilers that support the current ANSI standard.

If a template function is replaced by a specialization, the appropriate version must be executed when a call to the function is made. The order the compiler looks up a function guarantees that if both a function template and a specialization are defined for a specific type, the specialization will be called.

This also applies to the methods of a class template, which are function templates, of course. More specifically, a template class can only be created if all the methods in the appropriate function template can be instantiated without error.

■ DEFAULT ARGUMENTS OF TEMPLATES

A class template representing quadratic matrices

```cpp
// quadMat.h:  Defines the template QuadMatrix
//              to represent quadratic matrices
// -----------------------------------------------------
#include <iostream>
#include <stdexcept>
using namespace std;

template <class T, int cnt = 10>
class QuadMatrix
{
  private:
    T mat[cnt][cnt];
  public:
   int dim() const{ return cnt; }

   T*  operator[](int line) throw(out_of_range)
   {
     if( line < 0 || line >= cnt)
       throw out_of_range("Matrix: Index out of range");
     else
       return mat[line];
   }

   const T*  operator[](int line) const
                                     throw(out_of_range)
   {
     if( line < 0 || line >= cnt)
       throw out_of_range("Matrix: Index out of range");
     else
       return mat[line];
   }
   friend QuadMatrix& operator+(const QuadMatrix&,
                                const QuadMatrix&);
             // etc.
};
```

☐ Setting Defaults

You can define default arguments for template parameters, just as for function parameters. If an argument required to instantiate a template is missing, the default value is then used.

You can specify default values in the template definition or when you declare a template in a module.

☐ The Class Template `QuadMatrix<T, n>`

The class template defined opposite, `QuadMatrix<T, n>`, represents quadratic matrices. The subscript operator is overloaded to allow you to access a matrix element `m[i][j]` in a given matrix m. If the line index i is outside of the valid range, a standard `out_of_range` type exception is thrown.

The default values are chosen to create a matrix m for int values with 10 rows and 10 columns following this definition:

Example: `typedef QuadMatrix < > IntMat;`
            `IntMat m;`

You cannot omit the angled brackets since the `QuadMatrix` type does not exist. `QuadMatrix` is merely the name of a template.

The following definition

Example: `typedef QuadMatrix<double> DoubleMat;`
            `DoubleMat dm;`

defines a matrix dm of `double` values with 10 rows and 10 columns.

☐ Rules

The same rules apply to the default arguments of templates as to the default arguments of functions:

- if you declare a default argument for at least one parameter, you must define default values for all the remaining parameters
- if a template argument for which a default argument was declared is omitted during instantiation, all the remaining template arguments must be omitted.

■ EXPLICIT INSTANTIATION

Sample program for the class template QuadMatrix

```cpp
// expIns_t.cpp:  Tests explicit instantiation
// -------------------------------------------------------
#include <iostream>
#include <iomanip>
using namespace std;

#include "quadMat.h"
                              // Explicit Instantiation:
template class QuadMatrix<long double, 5>;

int main()
{
    QuadMatrix<long double, 5> m;

    try
    {
        for(int k=0; k < m.dim(); k++)
        {
            for( int l = 0; l < m.dim(); l++)
            {
                m[k][l] = k*l;
                cout << setw(2) << m[k][l] << " ";
            }
            cout << endl;
        }
    }
    catch(out_of_range& err )
    {
        cerr << err.what() << endl;
    }

    return 0;
}
```

In addition to implicit instantiation of templates, which occurs when a template function is called, for example, explicit instantiation is also possible. This is important when you design libraries that contain template functions and classes for application programs.

☐ Syntax

Explicit instantiation can be achieved by the following

Syntax: `template declaration;`

where `declaration` contains the name of the template and the template arguments.
   Explicit instantiation for the class template `Stack` would be performed as follows:

Example: `template class Stack<long double, 50>;`

This declaration creates the template class `Stack<long double, 50>` with a maximum of 50 `long double` type elements.
   Function templates can also be instantiated explicitly.

Example: `template short min( short x, short y);`

This creates a template function for the `short` type from the function template `min()`.

☐ ANSI Instantiation

The ANSI standard provides an additional technique for the explicit instantiation of function templates. Template arguments are stated in the angled brackets that follow the function name, when the function is first called.

Example: `min<long>(x, y);`

In this case, a template function `min()` for the `long` type is generated. This advanced syntax for function templates is not supported by all C++ compilers, however.
   Explicit instantiation of function templates extends their possible usage:

- ▪ function templates can be parameterized by types that cannot be derived from the function arguments—more specifically, function templates can be defined without function parameters
- ▪ function templates can be defined with function parameters that are not template parameters themselves.

exercises

■ EXERCISES

Interpolation search

The elements of a numerical array are assumed to be unique and sorted in ascending order.

The given value is compared with the array element at the position where the value is "expected" to be. For example, if the value searched for is two-thirds of the way from the lowest to the highest subarray element, the probe would be made two-thirds from the lowest to the highest index of the subarray. If the required value is lesser than that of the array element found at the expected position, the search is continued in the left part of the subarray, just like a binary search. Otherwise the search continues in the right part of the subarray.

The "expected" position exp in an array v can be calculated as follows: If key is the required value, $begin$ is the lowest, and end is the highest index of the corresponding subarray, the following applies:

```
double temp = (double)(key-vp[begin]);
temp /= (vp[end]-vp[begin]);
temp  = temp * (end - begin) + 0.5;
exp   = begin + (int)temp;
```

Insertion sort algorithm

The following technique is used to divide the array into a left, sorted part and a right, unsorted part:

Each subsequent element in the unsorted part of the array is selected and taken out from the array. As long as a greater array element can be found starting from the end of the left subarray, the element is shifted up by one position. If a smaller array element is found, the selected element is inserted at the vacant position.

✓ **NOTE**

> The left, sorted part originally consists of only one element, the first array element.

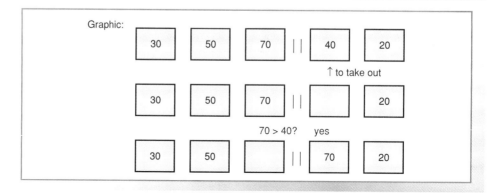

Graphic:

Exercise 1

■ Define a function template `interpolSearch()` that looks up a given element in a sorted, numeric array. The array elements are of the same type as the template parameter `T`.

The function template has three parameters—the value searched for of type `T`, a pointer to the first array element, and the number of array elements.

The function template returns the index of the first element in the array that corresponds to the searched for value, or −1 if the value cannot be found in the array.

Implement the function template. Use the technique described opposite as your algorithm for the interpolation search. Store the function template definition in the header file `search.h`.

■ Define a function template, `insertionSort()`, which sorts a numeric array in ascending order. The array elements are of the type of the template parameter `T`.

The function template has two parameters—a pointer to the first array element, and the number of array elements. There is no return value.

■ Define a function template `display()` to display a numeric array on screen.

The function template has two parameters—a pointer to the first array element and the number of array elements. There is no return value.

■ Use the function templates `interpolSearch()`, `insertionSort()`, and `display()` to define template functions for `double` and `short` types. To do so, define an array of `double` values and an array with `short` values.

Write a `main` function that creates and calls each template function `insertionSort()` for the `int` and `double` types. Then display the sorted arrays.

Add a call to each template function `search()` in your `main` function. Call `search()` passing values that exist and do not exist in the array.

Exercises

The class `FloatArr` **(as defined in Chap. 28, Ex. 1)**

```cpp
class FloatArr          // Without conversion functions
{
  private:
    float* arrPtr;      // Dynamic member
    int max;            // Maximum number, without having
                        // to reallocate storage.
    int cnt;            // Current number of elements

    void expand( int new Size);       // Function to help
                                      // enlarge the array.
  public:
    FloatArr( int n = 256 );
    FloatArr( int n, float val);
    FloatArr(const FloatArr& src);
    ~FloatArr();

    FloatArr& operator=( const FloatArr& );
    int  length() const { return cnt; }

    float& operator[](int i) throw(BadIndex);
    float operator[](int i) const  throw(BadIndex);

    void append( float val);
    void append( const FloatArr& v);
    FloatArr& operator+=( float val)
    {
        append( val);   return *this;
    }

    FloatArr& operator+=( const FloatArr& v)
    {
        append(v);   return *this;
    }

    void insert( float val, int pos) throw(BadIndex);
    void insert( const FloatArr& v, int pos )
                                      throw(BadIndex);

    void remove(int pos) throw(BadIndex);

    friend ostream& operator<<( ostream& os,
                                const FloatArr& v);

};
```

Exercise 2

Define a class template `Array<T, n>` to represent an array with a maximum of n elements of type `T`. Attempting to address an array element with an invalid index should lead to an exception of the `BadIndex` (defined previously) error class being thrown. If there is no space left to insert an element in the array, an exception of the `OutOfRange` type should be thrown.

- First define the error class `OutOfRange` without any data members. Use the error class `BadIndex`, which was defined in Exercise 1 of Chapter 28.
- Change the existing `FloatArr` class into a class template, `Array<T, n>`. Use `255` as the default value for the parameter n of the class template.

  This allocates memory for the array statically. Now define a default constructor and a constructor that initializes a given number of array elements with a given value. You do not need to define a copy constructor, a destructor, or an assignment operator.

  As access methods define the `size()` and the `length()` methods, the `size()` method returns the maximum number of array elements, that is, n; the `length()` method returns the current number of elements in the array.

  Also define methods for inserting and deleting elements like those defined for the `FloatArr` class. The methods have a `void` return type and can throw exceptions of type `BadIndex` and/or `OutOfRange`.

  Additionally overload the index and shift operators `<<`. The subscript operator throws `BadIndex` type exceptions.
- Test the class template `Array<T,n>` for `double` and `int` types first. Define arrays of the appropriate types, then insert and delete elements in the arrays. Output all the elements of the array.
- Modify the test program by adding an array for objects of a class type. Use the `DayTime` class from Exercise 1, Chapter 19 for this purpose.

  Test the array template by defining an array with 5 `DayTime` class objects and inserting a few objects. Then display all the objects on screen.

■ **SOLUTIONS**

Exercise 1

```cpp
// -----------------------------------------------------
// interpol.cpp : Template function interpolSearch()
// -----------------------------------------------------
#include <iostream>
using namespace std;

template <class T>
long interpolSearch(const T& key, T* vp, int len)
{
   int   expect, begin = 0, end = len - 1;
   double temp;

   if( end < 0                      // Array is empty or
       || key > vp[end]             // or key is out of
       || key < vp[begin] )         // range
      return -1;
   while( begin <= end )
   {
      if(key > vp[end] || key < vp[begin] ) // Key is not
         return -1;                         // in range.
      temp = (double)(key - vp[begin])
             / (vp[end]-vp[begin]);
      temp = temp * (end - begin) +0.5;
      expect = begin + (int)temp;
      if( vp[expect] == key )              // Key found?
         return expect;
      if( vp[expect] > key)
          end = expect - 1;
      else begin = expect+1;
   }
   return -1;
}

template <class T>
void insertionSort( T* vp, int len)
{
   T temp;
   for( int i=0; i < len; i++)
   {
      temp = vp[i];      // Take element out.
      int j;             // Shift greater elements up:
      for( j = i-1; j >= 0 && vp[j] > temp; j--)
         vp[j+1] = vp[j];
      vp[j+1] = temp;              // Insert.
   }
}
```

```cpp
template <class T>
void display(T* vp, int len)
{
   cout << "\n\nThe array: " << endl;
   for(int i = 0; i < len; i++)
   {
      cout << vp[i] << "   ";
      if( (i+1)%10 == 0)
         cout << endl;
   }
   cout << endl; cin.get();
}

// Two arrays for testing:
short  sv[5] = { 7, 9, 2, 4, 1};
double dv[5] = { 5.7, 3.5, 2.1, 9.4, 4.3 };

int main()
{
   cout << "\nInstantiation for type short: " << endl;
   display(sv, 5);

   insertionSort(sv, 5);
   cout << "\nAfter sorting: ";
   display(sv, 5);

   short key;
   cout << "\nArray element? ";  cin >> key; cin.sync();
   int pos = interpolSearch(key, sv, 5);
   if( pos != -1)
       cout << "\nfound!" << endl, cin.get();
   else
       cout << "\nnot found!" << endl, cin.get();
   // ------------------------------------------------
   cout << "\nInstantiation for type double: " << endl;
   display(dv, 5);

   insertionSort(dv, 5);
   cout << "\nAfter sorting: ";
   display(dv, 5);

   double dkey;
   cout << "\nArray element? "; cin >> dkey; cin.sync();
   pos = interpolSearch(dkey, dv, 5);
   if( pos != -1)
       cout << "\nfound!" << endl, cin.get();
   else
       cout << "\nnot found!" << endl, cin.get();

   return 0;
}
```

Exercise 2

```
// ---------------------------------------------------------
// array.h
// Use of class templates to represent arrays.
// ---------------------------------------------------------
#ifndef _ARRAY_H_
#define _ARRAY_H_

#include <iostream>
#include <iomanip>
using namespace std;

class BadIndex
{
  private:
    int index;
  public:
    BadIndex(int i):index(i){}
    int getBadIndex() const { return index; }
};

class OutOfRange {  /* Without data members*/ };

template <class T, int n = 256>
class Array
{
   private:
     T   arr[n];          // The array
     int cnt;             // Current number of elements

   public:
     Array( ){ cnt = 0;}
     Array(int n, const T& val );

     int  length() const { return cnt; }
     int  size()   const { return n; }

     T& operator[](int i) throw(BadIndex)
     {
        if( i < 0 || i >= cnt ) throw BadIndex(i);
        return arr[i];
     }
     const T&  operator[](int i) const throw(BadIndex)
     {
        if( i < 0 || i >= cnt ) throw BadIndex(i);
        return arr[i];
     }
```

```
        Array& operator+=( float val) throw(OutOfRange)
        {
            append( val);    return *this;
        }

        Array& operator+=(const Array& v)   throw(OutOfRange)
        {
            append(v);    return *this;
        }

        void append( T val) throw(OutOfRange);
        void append( const Array& v) throw(OutOfRange);

        void insert( T val, int pos)
                                throw(BadIndex, OutOfRange);
        void insert( const Array& v, int pos )
                                throw(BadIndex, OutOfRange);

        void remove(int pos) throw(BadIndex);
};

template <class T, int n >
Array<T,n>::Array(int m, const T& val )
{
    cnt = m;
    for(int i=0; i < cnt; i++ )
        arr[i] = val;
}

template <class T, int n >
void Array<T,n>::append( T val) throw(OutOfRange)
{
    if( cnt < n)
        arr[cnt++] = val;
    else
        throw OutOfRange();
}

template <class T, int n >
void Array<T,n>::append( const Array<T,n>& v) throw(OutOfRange)
{
    if( cnt + v.cnt > n)                // Not enough space.
        throw OutOfRange();

    int count = v.cnt;                  // Necessary if
                                        // v == *this
    for( int i=0; i < count; ++i)
        arr[cnt++] = v.arr[i];
}
```

```
template <class T, int n >
void Array<T,n>::insert( T val, int pos)
                                    throw(BadIndex, OutOfRange)
{   insert( Array<T,n>(1,val), pos);
}

template <class T, int n >
void Array<T,n>::insert( const Array<T,n>& v, int pos )
                                    throw(BadIndex, OutOfRange)
{
   if( pos < 0 || pos >= cnt)
      throw BadIndex();              // Invalid position.

   if( n < cnt + v.cnt)
      throw OutOfRange();

   int i;
   for( i = cnt-1; i >= pos; --i)    // Shift up
      arr[i+v.cnt] = arr[i];         // starting at pos.

   for( i = 0; i < v.cnt; ++i)       // Fill the gap.
      arr[i+pos] = v.arr[i];
   cnt = cnt + v.cnt;
}

template <class T, int n >
void Array<T,n>::remove(int pos) throw(BadIndex)
{
   if( pos >= 0 && pos < cnt)
   {
      for( int i = pos; i < cnt-1; ++i)
         arr[i] = arr[i+1];
      --cnt;
   }
   else  throw BadIndex(pos);
}

template <class T, int n >
ostream& operator<<(ostream& os, const Array<T,n>& v)
{
   int w = os.width();        // Save the field width

   for( int i = 0; i < v.cnt; ++i)
   {
      os.width(w);    os << v.arr[i];
   }
   os << endl;
   return os;
}
#endif
```

```cpp
// ----------------------------------------------------
// DayTime.h
// Class DayTime with relational operators,
// the operators ++ and -- (prefix and postfix),
// and the operators << and >> for I/O.
// ----------------------------------------------------

// The same as in Chapter 19.


// ----------------------------------------------------
// Array_t.cpp
// Testing class templates Array<T,n>.
// ----------------------------------------------------

#include "array.h"
#include "DayTime.h"
#include <cstdlib>
#include <iostream>
#include <iomanip>
using namespace std;

typedef Array<int, 100>   IntArr;
typedef Array<double>     DoubleArr;

typedef Array<DayTime, 5> DayTimeArr;

int main()
{
  try
  {
    const DoubleArr vd(10, 9.9);
    DoubleArr kd;

    cout << "\nThis is the constant array of doubles: \n";
    cout << setw(8) << vd;

    kd = vd;
    cout <<  "\nAn array of doubles after the assignment: "
         << endl;
    cout << setw(8) << kd;

    kd.remove(3);           // Delete the element at
                            // position 3.
    kd.append(10.0);        // Add a new element.
    kd.append(20.0);        // And repeat!

    cout <<  "\nThis is the modified array: "
         << endl;
    cout << setw(8) << kd;
```

```
        IntArr vi;

        int i;
        for(i=0; i < 10; i++)
            vi.append(rand()/100);

        cout << "\nThis is the array of int values: \n";
        cout << setw(12) << vi;

        vi += vi;
        cout << "\nAnd append: \n";
        cout << setw(12) << vi;

        IntArr ki(vi);
        cout << "\nThis is the copy of the array: \n";
        cout << setw(12) << ki;

        DayTimeArr vt;      // Array of DayTime objects.
        DayTime temp;

        for(i=0; i < 3; i++)
        {
            if( !(cin >> temp))
                break;
            vt.append(temp);
        }

        cout << "\nThe array with objects of type DayTime:\n";
        for(i=0; i < 3; i++)
            cout << setw(20) << vt[i] << endl;
    }
    catch(BadIndex& err)
    {
        cerr << "\nIndex " << err.getBadIndex()
                << " invalid";
        exit(1);
    }
    catch(OutOfRange& )
    {
        cerr << "\nArray is full!";
        exit(2);
    }

    return 0;
}
```

chapter 33

Containers

This chapter describes standard class templates used to represent containers for more efficient management of object collections. These include

- sequences, such as lists and double ended queues
- container adapters, such as stacks, queues, and priority queues
- associative containers, such as sets and maps, and
- bitsets.

Besides discussing how to manage containers, we will also be looking at sample applications, such as bitmaps for raster images, and routing techniques.

■ CONTAINER TYPES

Sequences and associative containers

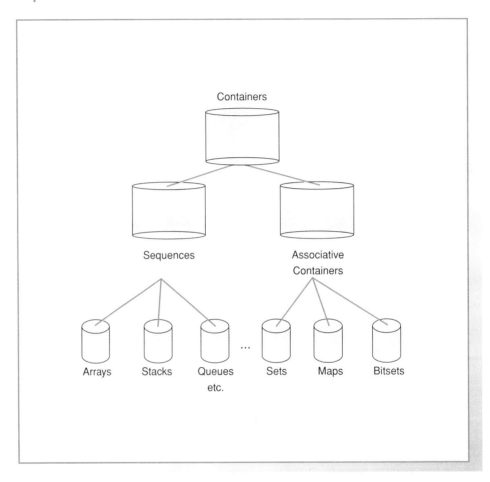

What is a Container?

Containers are used to store objects of the same type and provide operations with which these objects can be managed. These operations include object insertion, deletion, and retrieval. Memory is allocated for containers dynamically at runtime. Containers thus provide a safe and easy way to manage collections of objects.

The C++ standard library provides various class templates for container management in the *Containers Library*. These classes can be categorized as follows:

- **sequential containers,** or *sequences*, where the objects are arranged sequentially and access to an object can either be direct or sequential
- **associative containers,** where the objects are generally organized and managed in a tree structure and can be referenced using keys.

Sequences

Sequential containers are distinguished by the operations defined for them, which are either generic or restricted. Restricted operations, such as appending at the end of a container, have constant runtimes. That is, the runtime is proportional to a fixed period of time and does not depend on the number of objects in the container.

The following are sequential containers:

- **arrays,** which provide the same operations as C arrays but increase and decrease in size dynamically, in contrast to C arrays
- **queues,** which are managed on the FIFO (*First In First Out*) principle. The first element to be inserted is also removed first
- **stacks,** which are managed on the LIFO (*Last In First Out*) principle. The last element to be inserted is removed first.

Associative Containers and Bitsets

Associative containers comprise *sets*, which allow quick access to objects via sortable keys, and *maps*, which maintain efficient object/key pairs.

There are also so-called *bitsets*, which represent bit sequences of a given length and provide bitwise operators, with which bits can be manipulated.

■ SEQUENCES

Operations for sequences

Class Template	Time needed to insert or remove an object
`vector<class T, class Allocator` `= allocator<T> >`	At the end: constant. At the beginning or in the middle: linear.
`list<class T, class Allocator` `= allocator<T> >`	In all positions: constant.
`deque<class T, class Allocator` `= allocator<T> >`	At the beginning or end: constant. In the middle: linear

Container adapters

Class Template	Insertion	Deletion
`stack<class T, class Container` `= dequeue<T> >`	at the end	at the end
`queue<class T, class Container` `= dequeue<T> >`	at the end	at the beginning

`priority_queue<class T,`
`class Container = vector<T>,`
`Compare=less<T> >`
	priority based	at the beginning

Sequences and header files

Container	Header File
`vector<T, Allocator>`	`<vector>`
`list<T, Allocator>`	`<list>`
`deque<T, Allocator>`	`<deque>`
`stack<T, Container>`	`<stack>`
`queue<T, Container>`	`<queue>`
`priority_queue<T,` `Container, Compare >`	`<queue>`

☐ Representing Sequences

The Containers Library defines so-called *container classes* representing containers. These are class templates parameterized by the type `T` of the objects to be managed.

Three basic class templates are defined for sequences.

- The container class `vector<T, Allocator>` supports standard array operations, such as direct access to individual objects via the subscript operator `[]`, and quick appending and deletion at the end of the container. However, the runtime for insertion and deletion at the beginning or in the middle of the container is linear, that is, proportional to the number of objects stored in the container.
- The container class `list<T, Allocator>` provides functionality that is typical for double linked lists. This includes quick insertion and deletion at any given position. General list operations, such as sorting and merging, are also defined.
- The container class `deque<T, Allocator>` (*double ended queue*, pronounced "deck") provides direct access via a subscript operator, just like a normal array, but offers optimized insertion and deletion at the beginning and end of the container. The same operations in the middle of a container have a linear runtime.

The second template parameter is used for any storage allocation to be performed. The storage management is represented by a so-called *allocator class*, which is parameterized by an object of type `T`. It enables dynamic memory allocation for objects of type `T`. The default value of the template parameter is the *standard allocator class* `allocator<T>` that uses the `new` and `delete` operators to allocate and release memory.

☐ Adapter Classes

The basic sequence classes are used to construct so-called *adapter classes*. An adapter class expects a sequence as a template argument and stores the sequence in a `protected` data member.

The opposite page shows various adapter classes. The `priority_queue` template represents priority queues. The relationship between the keys used to manage the priorities is defined in the *comparator class*, `Compare`. The default value of the template parameter is the predefined comparator class, `less<T>`, which uses the lesser than operator `<` for type `T`.

■ ITERATORS

Iterating lists

```cpp
// Outputs a list containing integers.
// --------------------------------------------------
#include <list>
#include <iostream>
using namespace std;
typedef list<int> INTLIST;                    // int list

int display(const INTLIST& c)
{
   int z = 0;                                 // Counter
   list<int>::const_iterator pos;             // Iterator

   for( pos = c.begin(); pos != c.end(); pos++, z++)
     cout << *pos << endl;
   cout << endl;

   return z;
}
```

Iterating vectors

```cpp
// iterat_t.cpp: Outputs an array of accounts.
// --------------------------------------------------
#include <vector>
#include <iostream>
using namespace std;

#include "account.h"
typedef vector<Account> AccVec;        // Account vector

void display(const AccVec& v)
{
   AccVec::const_iterator pos;         // Iterator

   for( pos = v.begin(); pos < v.end(); pos++)
       pos->display();
   cout << endl;
}
```

☐ Positioning and Iterating in Containers

Each object in a container occupies the specific position where it was stored. To allow you to work with the objects in a container, the positions of the objects in the container must be accessible. There must therefore be at least one mechanism that allows:

- read and/or write access to the object at any given position and
- moving from the position of one object to the position of the next object in the container.

This situation should be familiar from your experience of working with pointers. Given that i is the index of an element in an array v, $(v+i)$ is its address, $*(v+i)$ the array element itself, and $(v + (++i))$ the address of the next array element.

Iterators were introduced in C++ to provide a uniform model for positioning and iteration in containers. An iterator can thus be regarded as an abstraction of a pointer.

☐ Iterator Types

Two types of iterators are important in this context:

- **bidirectional iterators**, which can be shifted up by the increment operator ++ and down with the decrement operator --, and use the operators * and -> to provide write or read access to objects
- **random access iterators**, which are bidirectional iterators that can additionally perform random positioning. The subscript operator [] was overloaded for this purpose, and the operations defined for pointer arithmetic, such as addition/subtraction of integers or comparison of iterators, are defined.

The container classes vector<T> and deque<T> have random access iterators and the container class list<T> has bidirectional iterators.

☐ Iterator Classes

The types iterator and const_iterator are defined in all the above classes to represent iterators. An iterator belonging to one of these classes can reference constant or non-constant objects.

The methods begin() and end() are also defined. The begin() method accesses the first position and end() accesses the position *after* the last container object.

Containers that belong to adapter classes offer only restricted access to the beginning or end. You cannot use iterators to walk through them.

■ DECLARING SEQUENCES

The derived container class sortVec<T, Compare>

```cpp
// sortVec.h: The Class Template SortVec representing
//            a sorted vector.
//------------------------------------------------------
#include <vector>       // For class template vector<T>
#include <functional>   // For comparator class less<T>
using namespace std;

template <class T, class Compare = less<T> >
class SortVec : public vector<T>
{
  public:
    SortVec()  { }
    SortVec(int n, const T& x = T());

    void insert(const T& obj);      // in sorted order
    int  search(const T& obj);
    void merge(const SortVec<T>& v);
};
```

Using the container class sortVec

```cpp
// sortv_t.cpp :   Tests the template SortVec.
//------------------------------------------------------
#include "sortVec.h"

typedef SortVec<int> IntSortVec;

int main()
{
    IntSortVec v, w;              // Default constructor

    v.insert(2);
    v.insert(7); v.insert(1);

    int n = v.search(7);

    w.insert(3); w.insert(9);

    v.merge(w);
    return 0;
}
// The array v then contains the elements: 1 2 3 7 9
```

☐ Constructors of vector, list, and deque

The container classes vector, list, and deque define three constructors and a copy constructor with which sequences can be created. Their functionality is similar for the various classes and is discussed in the following section using the vector class as an example.

The statement

Example:　vector<Account> v;

declares an empty container v for objects of the Account type. You can then insert individual objects into the container.

However, you can also declare a container and fill it with a predefined number of object copies.

Example:　Fraction x(1, 1);
　　　　　　vector<Fraction> cont(100, x);

This defines the container cont with 100 Fraction type objects, and fills it with the object x. If the second argument is not supplied, each of the 100 objects is initialized by the default constructor.

Finally, you can initialize a container with a part of another container. To do so, you must state a range of iterators.

Example:　vector<double> v(first,last);

The arguments first and last are iterators in an existing container. The new container, v, is initialized using objects in the range [first, last): this includes all the objects between the positions first (including first) and last (excluding last).

☐ Constructors for Adapter Classes

Only a default constructor and the copy constructor are defined for adapter classes. Given that wait is a predefined queue of the container class queue<double>, the following statement

Example:　queue<double> w(wait);

creates a new queue, w, and uses the object wait to initialize it.

The opposite page shows the derived container class sortVec, which is used to represent sorted, dynamic arrays. The class is parameterized by the type T of array elements. The second template parameter is a comparator class, which represents a comparison criterion for sorting.

▪ INSERTING IN SEQUENCES

Inserting methods

Method	Effect
`void push_back(const T&x);`	Adds x at the end of the sequence.
`void push_front(const T&x);`	Adds x before the first element of the sequence.
`iterator  insert(iterator   pos, const T&  x = T() );`	Inserts x after position pos and returns the position of the newly inserted element.
`size_type  insert(iterator  pos, size_type n, const T& x)`	Inserts n copies of x after position pos and returns the number of inserted elements.
`void insert(iterator pos, InputIterator first InputIterator last)`	Inserts all elements from range [first,last) after position pos into the sequence.

Method `insert()` of the derived container class `SortVec`

```
// Method insert() adds a new object at the end
// of the vector and reorganizes in ascending order.
//----------------------------------------------------
template <class T, class Compare >
void SortVec<T, Compare>::insert(const T& obj)
{
   SortVec::iterator  pos, temp;
   push_back(obj);                    // Add at the end.

   pos = end();  pos--;               // Last position

   while (pos-- > begin())            // Sort:
   {
     if( obj < *pos )                 // Swap:
     { temp = pos; *(++temp) = *pos;  *pos = obj; }
     else    break;
   }
}
```

☐ Insertion Methods

The following methods are defined in the container classes `vector`, `deque`, and `list`

- `push_back()`   insert at end
- `insert()`   insert after a given position.

Additionally, the following method is available in the `list` and `deque` classes

- `push_front()`   insert at beginning.

This method is not defined in the `vector` class.

The `insert()` method is overloaded in various versions, allowing you to insert a single object, multiple copies of an object, or object copies from another container. Given two containers v and w the following

Example: `w.insert(--w.begin(), v.begin(), v.end());`

inserts the objects from container v in front of all the other objects in w. A container can of course be assigned to another container of the same type. The assignment operator is overloaded for containers to allow this operation.

☐ Runtime Behavior

The `push_back()` and `push_front()` methods are preferable on account of their constant runtime. Insertion of *one* object with the `insert()` method also has a constant runtime in the `list` class. However, this is linear in the `vector` and `deque` classes, that is, the time increases proportionally to the number of objects in the container.

This dissimilar runtime behavior for methods can be ascribed to the implementation of various container classes. Normally, containers of the `list` type are represented by double linked lists in which each element possesses a pointer to the preceding and following element. This allows for extremely quick inserting at a given position.

The container classes `vector` and `deque` are represented as arrays. Inserting in the middle means shifting the objects in the container to make place for the new object. Therefore the runtime will increase proportionally with the number of objects the container holds.

☐ Insertion in Adapter Classes

There is only one insertion method for adapter classes: `push()`. In stacks and queues, `push()` appends an object with a constant runtime. Insertion of objects into priority queues depends on the priority of the object and the runtime is linear.

■ ACCESSING OBJECTS

Method `search()` **of container class** `sortVec`

```cpp
// sortvec.h
// Method search() seeks an object obj in the vector
// using the binary search algorithms:
// The object obj is first compared to the element in
// the middle of the vector. If obj is smaller than the
// "middle" element, it must belong to the left half or
// else to the right half of the vector. We repeat this
// process comparing obj with the "middle" element in
// the section where it is known to be, repeatedly
// halving the size of the interval until the interval
// consists of a single point, which is where obj
// belongs.
// This algorithm has logarithmic time and thus
// is very fast.
// ----------------------------------------------------
template <class T, class Compare >
int SortVec<T, Compare>::search(const T& obj)
{
  int first = 0, last = end() - begin() - 1, mid;

  while( first < last )
  {
      mid = (first + last + 1)/ 2;
                              // Search the left half,
   if( obj < (*this)[mid] )
        last = mid - 1;
   else first = mid;          // the right half.
  }

  if ( obj == (*this)[first] )  // Found?
        return first;           // Yes.
  else  return size();          // Not found.
}
```

☐ The `front()` and `back()` Methods

Access to individual objects in the container classes `vector`, `deque`, and `list` can be performed by the following methods

- `front()`   for access to the first element and
- `back()`   for access to the last element.

Both methods return a reference to the object in question.

Example: `double z = v.front();`
        `v.front() = 1.9;`

This saves the first object in container v in the variable z and then overwrites the object by `1.9`.

☐ Access via Indices

The subscript operator `[]` is overloaded in the `vector` and `deque` classes to permit the use of indices for access to the objects in a container. An index is a positive integer of the type `size_type`.

Example: `v[20] = 11.2;`   `// the 21st object`

Given that `pos` is an iterator that references the first object in a container v, the expression `v[20]` is equivalent to `pos[20]`.

When you use the subscript operator, you must ensure that the index does not exceed the valid range. You can use the access method `at()` to throw an exception if an index is out of range.

Example: `v.at(20) = 11.2;`

The `at()` method throws an exception of the standard error class `out_of_range` if an error occurs.

The subscript operator and the `at()` method are not defined in the `list` class. Before you can manipulate the tenth object in the container, for example, you need to walk through the container sequentially up to that position.

☐ Access to Objects in Adapter Classes

The method `top()` is defined for access to the element with the highest priority, or the element at the top of the stack, in the adapter classes `priority_queue` and `stack`.

The `queue` class comprises the `front()` method, which is used to access the first element.

■ LENGTH AND CAPACITY

Method `merge()` **of container class** `SortVec`

```
// sortvec.h:  Method merge() merges the argument vector
//             with the vector *this.
// ----------------------------------------------------
template <class T, class Compare >
void SortVec<T,Compare>::merge(const SortVec<T,
                                     Compare>& v)
{
  SortVec temp;                      // Temporary vector
  SortVec::iterator pos = begin(); // Iterator
  int n1 = 0, n2 = 0;

        // Copy the smaller object into vector temp:
  while(n1 < size() &&  n2 < v.size())
    if( pos[n1] <= v[n2] )
      temp.push_back(pos[n1++]);
    else
        temp.push_back(v[n2++]);
                             // Append the rest:
  while( n1 < size())
    temp.push_back(pos[n1++]);

  while( n2 < v.size())
    temp.push_back(v[n2++]);

  *this = temp;
}
```

The identifying features of a container are

- its *length*, that is, the number of objects held in the container, and
- the *capacity*, that is, the maximum number of objects the container can store.

The length of a container changes after every insertion or deletion—the capacity does not.

☐ Length of a Container

The length of a container is discovered by a call to the `size()` method. The method returns an integer of the `size_type` type.

Example:
```
Fraction x(1, 1);
vector<Fraction> v(100, x);
vector<Fraction>::size_type sz = v.size();
```

The variable `sz` contains the value `100` in this case.

The length of an empty container is always `0`. You can also use the `empty()` method to discover whether a container is empty. The method returns `true` in this case.

Example: `while( !cont.empty() )` ...

The methods `size()` and `empty()` are defined for all container classes. You can use the `resize()` method to change the length of a container.

Example: `cont.resize( n, x);`

The length is increased to n provided n `>` `size()` is true, or decreased for n `<` `size()`. If n `==` `size()`, nothing happens.

If the length is increased, n `-` `size()` copies of the object x are appended to the container. The second argument, x, can be omitted. In this case, the default constructor for a type `T` object is called as often as necessary.

☐ Capacity

The capacity of a container can be checked using the `max_size()` method.

Example: `size_type k = cont.max_size();`

The return value depends on the amount of memory available and the object size.

Only the `size()` and `empty()` methods are defined for adapter classes. You cannot discover the capacity of an object, nor can you call `resize()` to change its length.

▪ DELETING IN SEQUENCES

A priority queue

```cpp
// prior_t.cpp : Testing a priority queue
// ------------------------------------------------
#include <queue>
#include <string>
#include <iostream>
using namespace std;

class Parcel
{
  private:
   unsigned int prio;                      // Priority
   string info;
  public:
   Parcel(unsigned int p, const string& s)
                        :prio(p), info(s)  {}
   // Access methods, ... overloaded operators:
   friend bool operator<(const Parcel& x,const Parcel& y)
        { return (x.prio < y.prio); }
   friend ostream& operator<<(ostream& os,
                              const Parcel& x)
   { os << x.prio << "  "<<  x.info << endl; return os; }
};

int main()
{
   priority_queue<Parcel>  pq;

   pq.push(Parcel(7,"Bob"));    // Insert
   pq.push(Parcel(1,"Peter"));
   pq.push(Parcel(4,"Susan"));

   while( !pq.empty() )
   {
     cout << pq.top() << endl; // Output
     pq.pop();                 // and delete
   }
   return 0;
}
// Output:    7  Bob
//            4  Susan
//            1  Peter
```

☐ Deletion Methods

The following methods are available for deleting objects in the container classes `vector`, `deque`, and `list`:

- `pop_back()`   deletes the last object in the container
- `erase()`   deletes the object at a given position, or deletes all the objects in a given range
- `clear()`   deletes all the objects in a container.

The following method is additionally defined in the `deque` and `list` classes:

- `pop_front()` deletes the first object in the container.

The method does not have a return value, just like the `pop_back()` method.

The `pop_back()` and `pop_front()` methods are preferable on account of their constant runtimes. Using the `erase()` method to delete an object at the beginning or in the middle of a container also provides a constant runtime in the container class `list`. However, the runtime is linear in the `vector` and `deque` classes, since objects must be shifted within the container to fill the gap left by the deletion.

☐ Deleting Ranges of Objects

When you use the `erase()` method to delete the objects in a given range, the position of the first element to be deleted and the position *after* the last object to be deleted are required as arguments.

Example: `cont.erase(cont.begin() + 10, cont.end());`

This deletes all the remaining objects in the container, starting at position 11. The `erase()` method returns the new position of the object immediately after the range of objects deleted.

☐ Deletion in Adapter Classes

There is only one method of deletion for adapter classes, namely `pop()`. Given that `wait` is a queue of the queue type, the following statement

Example: `wait.pop();`

deletes the element at the beginning of the queue. In the case of a stack, `pop()` deletes the element at the top of the stack, and for priority queues, the object with the highest priority. The runtime is constant in all cases.

▪ LIST OPERATIONS

Sample program

```cpp
// list_t.cpp:  Tests list operations
// --------------------------------------------------
#include <list>
#include <cstdlib>
#include <iostream>
using namespace std;

typedef list<int>  INTLIST;
int display( const INTLIST& c);

int main()
{
  INTLIST ls, sls;
  int i;
  for( i = 1; i <= 3; i++)
    ls.push_back( rand()%10 );           // ex. 1 7 4

  ls.push_back(ls.front());              // 1 7 4 1

  ls.reverse();                          // 1 4 7 1

  ls.sort();                             // 1 1 4 7

  for( i = 1; i <= 3; i++)
    sls.push_back( rand()%10 );          // ex. 0 9 4

  // Insert first object of sls before the last in ls:
  INTLIST::iterator pos = ls.end();

  ls.splice(--pos, sls, sls.begin());   // 1 1 4 0 7

  display(sls);                          // 9 4

  ls.sort();                             // 0 1 1 4 7
  sls.sort();                            // 4 9
  ls.merge(sls);                         // 0 1 1 4  4 7 9
  ls.unique();                           // 0 1 4 7 9

  return 0;
}
```

The container class `list` comprises methods for list operations that are not defined in other container classes. These are

- sorting and inverting lists
- merging two sorted lists
- splicing lists.

Sorting, Inverting, and Splicing Lists

A container of the `list` type, or *list container* for short, can be sorted by a call to `sort()`. This assumes that the operator < is defined in class T. A call to `sort()` sorts the container in ascending order.

You can use the `reverse()` method to invert a list container, that is, to reverse the order of the objects in the container. What was originally the first element in the container becomes the last, and the second element becomes the second to last, and so on.

The `merge()` method is used to merge two list containers. Given that `ls1` and `ls2` are two sorted list containers, the following call

Example: `ls1.merge(ls2);`

creates the sorted list `ls1`, whose objects comprise the original objects of `ls1` and `ls2`. The `ls2` container is empty following this operation.

Splice Operations

Splice operations insert the objects from one list container at a given position in another list container and remove them from the original container. You can transfer either a whole container or just part of a container.

Example: `ls1.splice(pos, ls2);`

This inserts the whole of container `ls2` *in front of* position pos in `ls1`. `ls2` is emptied by this statement. The following statement

Example: `ls1.splice(pos1, ls2, pos2);`

Inserts the element at position pos2 in `ls2` *before* the element at position pos1 in `ls1` and deletes it from `ls2`. If you want to transfer part of a container, the third and fourth arguments must contain the starting and end position.

You cannot use a splice operation to insert at a position before `begin()` or after `end()`.

■ ASSOCIATIVE CONTAINERS

Container classes

Container Class	Representing

`set< class T,`
`    class Compare = less<T>,`
`    class Allocator = allocator<T> >`
	collections of objects with unique keys

`multiset< class T,`
`    class Compare = less<T>,`
`    class Allocator = allocator<T> >`
	collections of objects with equivalent keys, i.e. possibly multiple copies of the same key value

`map< class Key, class T,`
`    class Compare = less<T>,`
`    class Allocator = allocator<T> >`
	collections of objects/key pairs where the keys are unique

`multimap< class Key, class T,`
`    class Compare = less<T>,`
`    class Allocator = allocator<T> >`
	collections of objects/key pairs with possibly equivalent keys

Associative containers and header files

Container Class	Header File
`set< T, Compare, Allocator >`	`<set>`
`multiset<T, Compare, Allocator >`	`<set>`
`map< Key, T, Compare, Allocator >`	`<map>`
`multimap< Key, T, Compare, Allocator >`	`<map>`

Sequences store objects in linear order. Searching for a given object will thus require a linear runtime. If you have only a few objects to deal with, this will not cause any significant delay. However, it is a major disadvantage in large collections of objects.

☐ Representing Sets and Maps

Associative containers with different classes that represent sets and maps allow you optimize runtimes. They manage objects in so-called *heaps*, that is in trees with a minimum height. Operations are performed by sortable keys. One of the characteristics of a heap is that the object with the smallest key is always stored at the top of the heap.

Insertion, deletion, and search operations in sets and maps can be performed with logarithmic runtimes. That is, the response is proportional to $\log(n)$, where n is the number of objects in a container. Since a logarithmic function grows very slowly, response will be phenomenally quick.

☐ Unique and Ambiguous Keys

In a set, each object contains a key. This is why we refer to embedded keys. The relationship between the objects is defined by reference to this key. Besides sets, which have unique keys, you can also define *multisets*, where multiple objects can have the same key.

Maps are used to manage key/object pairs. In other words, the key is not embedded in the object but stored separately from it. The type of the key is Key, and T is the object type. The relationship between the objects is again defined by the keys.

Besides maps, which contain only unique keys, you can also define *multimaps*, where several objects can exist for a single key.

☐ Associative Container Classes

The opposite page shows various classes used to represent sets, multisets, maps, and multimaps. The template parameter Compare is a comparator class and Allocator is an allocator class. Both parameters have default values, which we already saw in the context of sequences.

The methods begin() and end() are defined for access to the positions in all associative container classes. They return the position of the first element or the position after the last element.

■ SETS AND MULTISETS

Sample sets and multisets

```cpp
// set_t.cpp:   Tests sets and multisets
// ----------------------------------------------------
#include <set>
#include <cstdlib>
#include <ctime>
#include <iostream>
using namespace std;

typedef set<int> IntSet;                // Define type and
typedef IntSet::iterator SetIter;       // iterator type

typedef multiset<int> IntMultiSet;      // Multiset and
typedef IntMultiSet::iterator MultiSetIter;  // iterator

int main()
{
   IntSet  lotto;                // Create a set.
   SetIter pos;                  // Bidirectional iterator

   srand((unsigned) time(NULL));
   while( lotto.size() < 6)    // Insert
     lotto.insert( rand()%50 );

   cout << "These are your lotto numbers: " << endl;
   for( pos = lotto.begin(); pos != lotto.end(); pos++)
      cout << *pos << "   ";
   cout << endl << endl;

   IntMultiSet  ms;              // Create a multiset.
   MultiSetIter mpos;            // Bidirectional iterator
   for( int i=0; i < 10; i++) // Insert
     ms.insert( rand()%10 );

   cout << "And now 10 random numbers "
        << " between  0 and 10: " << endl;
   for( mpos = ms.begin(); mpos != ms.end(); mpos++)
      cout << *mpos << "   ";
   cout << endl;

   return 0;
}
```

Sets and multisets are used for efficient management of object collections with sortable keys, that is, insertion, deletion, and search operations can be performed with logarithmic runtimes. Keys are always parts of objects, thus, keys are data members whose relationships to one another must be defined in the corresponding class. A lesser than relationship is normally defined for this purpose, that is, the operator < will be overloaded for the class.

☐ Declaring Sets and Multisets

The container classes `set` and `multiset` have two constructors each for creating containers. You can use the default constructor to create sets and multisets with a length of 0. The second constructor inserts objects from a range of iterators into the new set or multiset.

Example:
```
typedef set<Account> AccountSet;
        AccountSet mySet(first, last);
```

Here, [`first, last`) is a range of iterators in an existing container whose objects are of `Account` type.

The copy constructor is also defined, and this allows you to use an existing container of the same type to initialize a new container.

☐ Inserting and Deleting

The `insert()` method is available for insertions. This allows for insertion of individual objects or multiple objects from a given range of iterators.

Example:
```
mySet.insert(Account(1234,"May, Tom",100));
```

In contrast to multisets, a new object is only inserted in a set if it does not already exist in the container.

You can use the `erase()` method to delete objects. To do so, you can either specify the object itself or its position in the container.

Example:
```
mySet.erase(mySet.begin());
```

This deletes the first element in the `AccountSet` set.

You can delete all objects in a container with the following statement:

Example:
```
mySet.erase( mySet.begin(), mySet.end() );
```

For erasing a whole container you can also use the `clear()` method. Calling `empty()` will tell you whether the container is empty. The `size()` method returns the number of objects in the container.

■ MAPS AND MULTIMAPS

Using multimaps

```cpp
// mulmap_t.cpp:  Testing multimaps
// ----------------------------------------
#include <map>
#include <string>
#include <iostream>
using namespace std;

typedef multimap<int, string> MULTI_MAP;
typedef MULTI_MAP::iterator ITERATOR;

int main()
{
   MULTI_MAP  m;                // Create a multimap.
   ITERATOR pos;                // Iterator.
                                // To insert:
   m.insert(pair<int, string>(7, "Bob") );
   m.insert(pair<int, string>(3, "Sarah"));
   m.insert(pair<int, string>(1, "Diana"));
   m.insert(pair<int, string>(1, "Lisa"));

   cout << "This is the multimap: " << endl;
   for(pos = m.begin(); pos!= m.end(); pos++)
       cout << pos->first << "  "
            << pos->second << endl;
   cout << endl;

   pos = m.find(3);        // Search for the pair
                           // with the given key 3
   if( pos != m.end())     // and output the pair
   cout << pos->first << "  " << pos->second << endl;

   int key = 1;            // Determine the quantity of
                           // pairs with key value 1:
   cout << "There are " << m.count(key)
        << " pairs with key " << key << endl;

   return 0;
}
```

☐ Representing Pairs of Keys/Objects

Maps and multimaps store pairs of sorted keys and objects. The key is used again to identify the object but is stored separately from the object. The comparison criterion is applied to the keys.

The C++ Standard Library contains the class template `pair<const Key,T>` with two `public` data members `first` and `second`, a default constructor, and a copy constructor to represent key/object pairs. The first template parameter, `Key`, is the key type and the second is the object type `T`. The data member `first` is used to store the keys, and `second` stores the associated object.

Given that `pos` is the position of an object in a map or multimap, you can reference the key with `pos->first`, and the associated object itself with `pos->second`.

☐ Using Maps and Multimaps

The container classes `map` and `multimap` contain constructors with the same functionality as the `set` and `multiset` classes. Thus, you can create a container with a length of 0, or use the objects in an existing container to initialize a new container. The copy constructor is also defined.

The methods `insert()` for insertion, and `erase()` and `clear()` for deletion have the same interfaces as in the container classes `set` and `multiset`. The methods `size()`, which you can use to discover the length of the container, and `empty()`, which ascertains whether the container is empty, are also defined.

The `find()` method is used to look up key/object pairs and expects a key as an argument in the `map` and `multimap` classes. Its return value is the associated position in the container. In the case of multimaps where several objects can have the same key, it returns the first position with that key. If the search fails, the value `end()` is returned as a pseudo position.

You can use the `count()` method to discover the number of key/object pairs with a given key in the container. The method expects a key as an argument. The method returns 0 or 1 for maps, depending on whether a pair exists or not. In the case of multimaps, the return value can be greater than 1, of course.

■ BITSETS

Representing raster images with bitmaps

```cpp
//  bitmap.h : Defines the template Bitmap<N>
//             representing raster images.
// --------------------------------------------------
#ifndef _BITMAP_
#define _BITMAP_

#include <bitset>
#include <stdexcept>
using namespace std;

template <int N>
class Bitmap : public bitset<N>
{
   private:
        int lines, cols; // Number of rows and columns
        int ax, ay;      // Current cursor position
        int ai;          // Current index in the bitset
   public:
        Bitmap(int l, int c);
        void move(int x, int y);
        void draw(int x, int y);
};

template <int N>
Bitmap<N>::Bitmap(int l, int c)
{
  if (l*c <= N)
  {
   reset();                 // Set all bits to 0
   lines = l; cols = c;     // Rows and columns
   ax = 0; ay = 0; ai = 0;  // Current position
  }
  else throw invalid_argument("Invalid argument \n");
}

template <int N>
void Bitmap<N>::move(int x, int y)
{
  if( x >= 0 && x < lines && y >= 0 && y < cols)
  {   ax = x; ay = y;   ai = x * cols + y;  }
  else throw invalid_argument("Invalid argument\n");
}
// to be continued
```

☐ Declaring Bitsets

A bitset stores a bit sequence of a given length. This allows storage of mass bit coded data, such as raster images, with minimum memory used.

The container class `bitset<N>` provides the functionality needed to manage bitsets. The template parameter `N` is the length of bitset, that is the maximum number of bits stored.

You can use the default constructor to create a bitset with no initial values. However, you can also use a given bit-pattern to initialize a bitset. The bit-pattern is either defined as an `unsigned long` value or as a string.

Example:
```
string s = "10101010";
bitset<1024> b(s);
```

The string `s` can contain only the `'0'` or `'1'` characters. The last character in the string will be the first bit value (that is 0 or 1) at bit position 0, the second to last character in the string is the bit value at position 1, and so on. The remaining bits are padded with `0` up to a length of `N`. This also applies when an `unsigned long` value is used for initialization purposes.

☐ Notes on the Sample Program Opposite

The container class `Bitmap<N>`, which is defined opposite, can be used to represent simple monochrome raster images. A pixel (*picture element*) is represented by a bit in a bitset. If the bit is set, a pixel on screen will be illuminated (white) and otherwise turned off (black).

The number of pixels that can be represented horizontally and vertically is defined by the resolution. 480 by 800 is a typical screen resolution and 3300 by 2300 is a typical resolution for laser printers (at 300 dpi) for an $8\frac{1}{2} \times 11$ page size. The value of `N` is the product of the number of pixels in horizontal and vertical direction.

The container class `Bitmap<N>` is derived from `bitset<N>` by `public` inheritance. Thus, the class comprises a bitset and all the `public` bitset management methods it inherits. Additional data members are used to store the number of rows and columns of pixels, the current cursor position, and the current bitset index. The `move()` method moves the cursor to the position with the given coordinates. The `draw()` method draws a straight line from the current cursor position to the point with the given coordinates.

■ BITSETS (CONTINUED)

Bresenham algorithm

```cpp
// bitmap.h: In addition the Bresenham algorithm.
// -------------------------------------------------
template <int N>
void Bitmap<N>::draw(int x, int y)
{
  if( x >= 0 && x < lines && y >= 0 && y < cols)
  {
    int savex = x, savey = y;
    if(ax > x) // Draw in ascending x-direction
    {            // => possibly swap (ax,ay) and (x,y)
      int temp = ax; ax = x; x = temp;
      temp = ay; ay = y; y = temp;
    }
    int dx = x - ax, dy = y - ay;
    int xinc = 1, yinc;        // Increment

    if( dy < 0)                // Gradient < 0 ?
    { yinc = -1; dy = -dy;}    // Decrement y
    else yinc = 1;             // or else increment.

    int count = dx + dy;    // Number of pixels to be set

    int d = (dx - dy)/2;    // Measurement of deviation
                            // off the line.
    while( count-- > 0)
    {
      ai = ax * cols + ay;    // Index in the bitset
      set(ai);                // Set the bit

      if( d < 0)              // Next pixel in
      { ay += yinc;  d += dx; }    // y-direction
      else                         // or else in
      { ax += xinc;  d  -= dy; }    // x-direction
    }

    ax = savex; ay = savey; // Current cursor position
    ai = ax * cols + ay;    // Current index in bitset
  }
  else throw invalid_argument("Invalid argument\n");
}
#endif
```

Manipulating Bits

The container class `Bitset<N>` provides the `get()` and `set()` methods for reading and writing individual bits. These methods expect a bit position as an argument. You can additionally pass a value of `0` or `1` to the `set` method, which writes this value at the bit position stated. The default value here is `1`.

If you call the `set()` method without any arguments, *all* the bits in the bitset are set to 1. In contrast, the `reset()` method deletes all the bits. Bits can be inverted by a call to the `flip()` method. Each `0`-bit in the bitset is set then to `1` and each `1`-bit is set to `0`.

Bits at specific coordinates can be referenced by the subscript operator. The index is a bit position, that is a number between `0` and `N-1`.

As you would expect, bitwise operators can also be used for bit manipulation. The bit operators `&`, `|`, and `^` are globally overloaded for bitsets. The operator functions for the NOT operator `~`, the shift operators `<<` and `>>`, and the operators for compound assignments, `&=`, `|=`, `^=`, are implemented as methods of the container class.

The Bresenham Algorithm

The opposite page shows the `draw()` method that draws a line from the current cursor position pixel by pixel to the given coordinates. The Bresenham algorithm used here applies incremental techniques. Starting at the current cursor position, it sets the neighboring pixel in the x- or y-direction. To do this, you only need to increment or decrement the x- or y-coordinate by 1. This avoids time consuming floating-point arithmetic, which would be required to solve a linear equation.

To allow drawing to take place along a positive x-axis, the starting and target points of the straight line can be swapped. The difference between the y-coordinates of the starting and target points `dy = y - ay` then determines whether to increment or decrement by 1 along the y-direction.

Drawing neighboring pixels creates a "staircase" effect, which deviates from the straight line. The variable `d = (dx - dy)/2` represents this deviation. If the value of `d` is negative, the line is seen to be growing along y-direction and the next pixel is drawn along the y-direction. Then the deviation is corrected by adding `dx`. As soon as `d` becomes positive, the next pixel is drawn along the x-direction and the deviation is corrected with `dy`.

■ **EXERCISE**

Hot potato algorithm

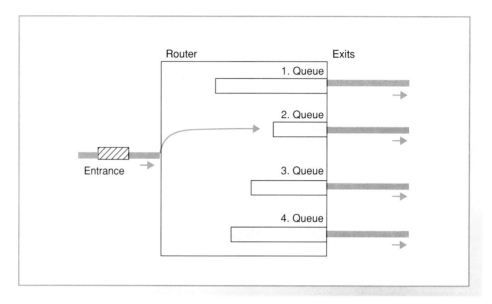

Test output

```
9 queues have been created.

The queues will now be filled
using the hot potato algorithm.

Some elements of randomly selected
queues are removed.

Output the queues:

1.queue: 28   88   70   60    6
2.queue: 64    6   54    1
3.queue:  2   88   64   30   66   29   11   74   49   41
4.queue: 17   25
5.queue: 96   97   47   27   71   34   87   58
6.queue: 77   82   54
7.queue: 35   65   23   40    5   83   92
8.queue: 32   23   54
9.queue: 28   55   54   73   28   82   21   99
```

Exercise

In data communications between two remote computers messages are transmitted via multiple subnets. En route to the target computers, so-called *routers* store these messages in queues before transmitting them towards the target via the next available line. The routers assume responsibility for route discovery, generally referring to complex address tables.

There are various routing techniques, including a simple algorithm that can do without address tables, the so-called *Hot Potato Algorithm*. The router simply tries to dispose of incoming messages as quickly as possible by sending each incoming message to the outgoing line with the shortest queue.

▪ Define a container class VecQueue<T>, which is parameterized with a message type T to represent this scenario. The class comprises an array of queues of type vector< queue<T> > and a data member used to store the current number of queues in the array.
The constructor creates the number of empty queues passed to it as an argument for the array. Additionally, you will need to declare the methods size(), empty(), push() and pop().
Overload the size() method in two versions: If no argument has been passed to the method, it returns the current number of messages in all queues. If an argument i of type int has been passed, the method returns the current number of messages in the i-th queue. Additionally, overload the empty() and empty(int i) methods, which return true, if all queues or the i-th queue are empty.
The push() method uses the hot potato algorithm to append a message passed to it at the end of the shortest queue.
The pop() and pop(int i) methods are used to simulate the assignment of messages to lines, that is retrieval and removal of messages from queues, in this exercise. The method pop() retrieves the message at the top of a randomly selected queue and deletes it, returning the message. The method pop(int i) retrieves the message at the top of the i-th queue and deletes it, returning the message.

▪ To test your class, declare a container of the type VecQueue<int> in your main function. A message is represented by a number. Use a loop to insert random numbers between 0 and 99 into the container and relay some of them to the outside lines. Then display the remaining messages on screen, as shown opposite, by calling the pop(int i) method.

Solution

```cpp
// -------------------------------------------------------
// vecQueue.h
// Defining the Class Template VecQueue<T>
// to represent a vector of queues.
// -------------------------------------------------------
#ifndef _VECQUEUE_H
#define _VECQUEUE_H

#include <vector>
#include <queue>
#include <cstdlib>                // For srand(), rand()
#include <ctime>                  // For time()
using namespace std;

template <class T>
class VecQueue
{
  private:
    vector< queue<T> > v;
    size_t sz;                    // Number of queues

  public:
    VecQueue(size_t n);

    size_t size() const;          // Current number of all
                                  // elements.
    size_t size(int i) const      // Number of elements in
    { return v[i].size(); }       // the i-th queue.

    bool empty() const       { return size() == 0; }
    bool empty(int i) const { return size(i) == 0; }

    void push(const T& a);   // Hot potato algorithm

    const T& pop();               // Removes the element at the
                                  // beginning of a randomly
                                  // choosen queue.
    const T& pop(int i);          // Removes the element at the
};                                // beginning of the i-th queue

template <class T>
VecQueue<T>::VecQueue( size_t n)        // Constructor
{
    if(n > 0)
      v.resize(n);

    sz = n;
    srand(time(NULL));
}
```

```
template <class T>          // Current number of all elements
size_t VecQueue<T>::size() const
{
    size_t count = 0;
    for( int i=0; i < sz; ++i)
      count += v[i].size();
    return count;
}

template <class T>          // To insert the argument into the
void VecQueue<T>::push(const T& a)          // shortest queue
{
    int small = 0;                          // To determine the
    for(int i = 0; i < sz; i++)      // shortest queue.
      if( v[i].size() < v[small].size())
          small = i;
    v[small].push(a);                       // and insert there.
}

template <class T>              // To retrieve and delete
const T& VecQueue<T>::pop()     // an element in a randomly
{                               // choosen queue.
    static T temp;
    int i, i0;

    i = i0 = rand() % sz;
    do
    {
      if(!v[i].empty())         // If i-th queue is not empty:
      {                         // To retrieve and delete the
        temp = v[i].front();    // element at the beginning.
        v[i].pop();
        break;
      }
      i = (i+1) % sz;      // Or else: Move to the next queue.
    }
    while( i != i0);
    return temp;
}

template <class T>                  // To retrieve and delete
const T& VecQueue<T>::pop(int i)  // an element in the
{                                   // i-th queue.
    static T temp;

    if( i >= 0 && i < sz)           // If the index is okay:
    {                               // To retrieve the element
        temp = v[i].front();        // at the beginning and
        v[i].pop();                 // to delete.
    }
    return temp;
}
#endif    // _VECQUEUE_H
```

Solutions (continued)

```
// -------------------------------------------------------
// hotpot_t.cpp : Simulates the hot potato algorithm
//                using a vector of queues.
// -------------------------------------------------------

#include <cstdlib>        // For srand(), rand()
#include <ctime>          // For time()
#include <iostream>
#include <iomanip>
using namespace std;

#include "vecQueue.h"

int main()
{
   const int nQueues = 9;
   VecQueue<int> vq(9);            // Vector of 9 queues

   cout << nQueues << " queues have been created."
        << endl;

   srand(time(NULL));

   cout << "\nThe queues will now be filled "
        << "using the hot potato algorithm."
        << endl;

   int i;
   for(i = 0; i < 100; i++)        // To insert 100 elements
     vq.push(rand()%100);

   cout << "\nSome elements of randomly selected "
           "queues are removed."
        << endl;
   for(i=0; i < 50; i++)           // To remove 50 elements
      vq.pop();

   cout << "\nTo output the queues:" << endl;
                                       // To retrieve, remove
   for( i = 0; i < nQueues; ++i)     // and display all
   {                                 // remaining elements.
      cout << "\n" << i+1 << ".Queue: ";
      while( vq.size(i) > 0 )
      {
         cout << setw(4) << vq.pop(i);
      }
      cout << endl;
   }

   return 0;
}
```

appendix

This appendix contains

- binary number representation
- preprocessor directives
- pre-defined standard macros
- binding C functions
- operator precedence table
- ASCII Code table
- screen control characters

■ BINARY NUMBERS

The numbers used by a program can be divided into two groups depending on their type:

- *integers* of the char, signed char, unsigned char, short, unsigned short, int, unsigned int, long, unsigned long types and
- *floating-point* numbers of the float, double, and long double types.

Both integral and floating-point numbers are represented internally as binary numbers, that is, as sequences of 0 and 1 values. However, the formats for representing integral and floating-point numbers differ. Thus, the bit-pattern of an integer will be interpreted differently from that of a floating-point number by the computer.

Representing Signed and Unsigned Integers

The binary format of integers is basically the same for the char, short, int and long types and differs only in

- the number of bytes available for each type and
- whether the number is interpreted as signed or unsigned.

The bit-pattern of a *positive integer* can be represented as a base 2 power series. The sign bit 0 additionally indicates that the number is positive in the case of signed types.

The number 4 can be represented by the following power series:

$$0*2^0 + 0*2^1 + 1*2^2 + 0*2^3 + 0*2^4 \ldots$$

The binary representation of the number 4 as signed char type value (8 bits) is thus as follows:

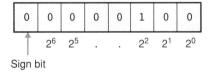

Two's complement is used to represent a *negative number*, for example -4:

First, *one's complement* of 4 is computed, that is, all the bits are inverted:

| 1 | 1 | 1 | 1 | 1 | 0 | 1 | 1 |

Then the number 1 is added:

| 0 | 0 | 0 | 0 | 0 | 0 | 0 | 1 |

Producing the bit pattern of −4:

| 1 | 1 | 1 | 1 | 1 | 1 | 0 | 0 |

You can also use two's complement to compute the absolute value of a negative number. Two's complement for -4 yields a value of 4.

Sign bits are not required for unsigned types. The bit can then be used to represent further positive numbers, doubling the range of positive numbers that can be represented.

The following table contains the binary formats of signed and unsigned integral 8 bit values:

Binary	Signed decimal	Unsigned decimal
0000 0000	0	0
0000 0001	1	1
0000 0010	2	2
0000 0011	3	3
.	.	.
.	.	.
0111 1101	125	125
0111 1110	126	126
0111 1111	127	127
1000 0000	−128	128
1000 0001	−127	129
.	.	.
.	.	.
1111 1100	−4	252
1111 1101	−3	253
1111 1110	−2	254
1111 1111	−1	255

If the bit-pattern of a negative number is interpreted as an unsigned number, the value of the number changes. The bit-pattern 1111 1100 of the number −4 will thus yield the following unsigned value:

$0*2^0 + 0*2^1 + 1*2^2 + 1*2^3 + 1*2^4 + 1*2^5 + 1*2^6 + 1*2^7$

that is, the decimal number 252.

Representing Floating-point Numbers

To represent a given floating-point number, x, the number is first broken down into a sign, v, a mantissa, m, and a power, exp, with a base of 2:

$x = v * m * 2^{exp}$

Memory for the values v, m, and exp is normally assigned in IEEE (Institute of Electronics and Electronical Engineers) format. The type float (32 bit) will thus be organized as follows:

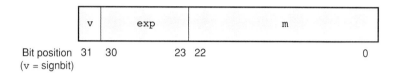

Bit position 31   30   23 22   0
(v = signbit)

In this "normalized" form, floating-point numbers are unambiguous. The mantissa, m, has a value that is greater than or equal to 1 and less than 2, the only exception being x == 0, where the mantissa is 0.

Example: -4.5 = -1 * 1.125 * 2²

The first digit of the mantissa is always 1 and need not be stored. The power is stored along with its *bias*. A bias of 127 applies for float types; thus a power e of a floating-point number is represented internally as e + 127.

The memory reserved for the mantissa defines the *accuracy*, and the memory reserved for the power defines the *range of values* for the floating-point number.

If platform-dependent ranges, such as the length of the mantissa or the smallest or largest value that can be represented, are significant in your programs, you can discover these ranges in the cfloat or climits header files.

You can use an instantiation of the numeric_limits class template for the type in question to query platform-dependent ranges by method calls.

■ PREPROCESSOR DIRECTIVES

The #define Directive

The #define directive is used to define symbolic constants and macros.

Syntax: #define name[(parameterlist)] [SubstituteText]

The preprocessor replaces name or name(parameterlist) with SubstituteText throughout the whole program. If SubstituteText is not stated, the preprocessor will delete the symbolic constant or macro throughout the program code (see also Chapter 7, "Symbolic Constants and Macros".)

Example: #define BUFSIZ   512 // Symbolic constant
          #define CLS   cout << "\033[2J" // Macro
          #define MAX(a,b) ((a)>(b) ? (a):(b))// Macro

The # Operator

A macro parameter in a substitute text can be preceded by the # operator (or *stringizing token*). When the macro is called, the argument is set in quotes, that is, a string constant is formed using the characters of the current argument.

Example: #define TITLE(s)   "**** " #s " *****"

The call

cout << TITLE(Catalog);

causes the preprocessor to expand the following string

"**** " "Catalog" " ****"

which is then concatenated to "**** Catalog ****".
    The characters " and \ are represented by \" and \\ within an argument.

Example: #define path(logid,subdir)
              "\\user\\" #logid "\\bin\\" #cmd

With   path(Smith, games)

the string "\user\Smith\bin\games " is produced.

The ## Operator

When a macro is defined, character sequences can be concatenated in the substitute text. The *past token operator*, ##, is used to this effect.
    When the macro is called, the parameter preceding or following the ## token is replaced by the appropriate argument. Then the token and any leading or trailing white-space character is removed.

Example: `#define debug(n) cout << "x" #n "=" << x ## n`

Calling

`debug(1);`

will generate the statement

`cout << "x1=" << x1;`

The arguments of a macro are not parsed for symbolic constants or macros. However, if the result of a concatenation is a symbolic constant or a macro, text replacement is again performed.

The #undef Directive

To change the definition of a symbolic constant or a macro at program runtime, you must first remove the original definition. To do so, the #undef directive is used.

Syntax: `#undef name`

Do not supply the parameter list for parameterized macros.
You can then use the #define directive to redefine the macro.

Example: `#define    BUFSIZE    512`
`              .`
`              .`
`              .`
`          #undef     BUFSIZE`
`          #define    BUFSIZE    1024`

The #include Directive

The #include directive copies a file to a program. The #include directive is replaced by the content of the file.

Syntax: `#include <filename>`
`              #include "filename"`

If the file name is surrounded by < and >, the file will only be looked up in the directories defined by the environment variable (usually INCLUDE).

If the file name is stated in quotes the file will also be looked up in the current directory first.

The name `filename` can include a path. In this case the file is only looked up in the directory stated.

You can also supply the file name as a symbolic constant. The substitute text must be in quotes or square brackets in this case.

Example:
```cpp
#include <iostream>
#include "project.h"
#if VERSION == 1
    #define MYPROJ_H "version1.h"
#else
    #define MYPROJ_H "version2.h"
#endif
#include MYPROJ_H
```

The #if, #elif, #else, and #endif Directives

You can use the #if, #elif, and #endif directives to compile certain parts of a source file and ignore others. The directives are known as *conditional compilation directives* for this reason.

Syntax:
```cpp
#if expression1
    [text1]
[#elif  expression2
    text2]
            .
            .
[#elif  expression(n)
    text(n)]
[#else
    text(n+1)]
#endif
```

Each #if directive must be terminated by an #endif directive. Multiple #elif directives can occur in between. The #else directive can occur once only.

The preprocessor evaluates expression1, expression2, ... in sequence. If an expression that yields "true" is found, that is its value is not 0, the corresponding code for this expression is processed.

If none of these expressions is true, the #else directive is executed. If this directive is omitted, no corresponding code is processed.

expression1, expression1, ... must be constant expressions of integral types and cannot contain the cast operator. Some compilers do not allow the use of the sizeof operator.

The corresponding text is a source text, that is, it comprises preprocessor directives, C++ statements, or whole C++ programs.

When a corresponding text is processed, the preprocessor may first execute directives before passing the expanded source code to the compiler for compilation. Code that the preprocessor has not processed is removed from the source.

The defined Operator

You can use the `defined` operator to check whether a symbolic constant or macro has been defined.

Syntax: `defined(name)`

The operator returns a value other than `0` if valid definition for `name` exists, and the value 0 in all other cases.

A definition created using the `#define` directive remains valid until it is removed by an `#undef` directive. If the substitute text following `name` in the `#define` directive is missing, the definition is still valid.

The `defined` operator is normally used in `#if` or `#elif` directives, for example

Example: `#if defined VERSION`

         `. . .`

Using the `defined` operator allows you to use its return value in a preprocessor expression.

The #ifdef and #ifndef Directives

You can also perform the same check using the `#ifdef` and `#ifndef` directives.

Syntax: `#ifdef    name`
         `#ifndef   name`

The `#ifdef` directive returns a value other than `0` if `name` is defined and otherwise 0.

In contrast, the `#ifndef` directive ensures that a value has not yet been defined, that is, that `name` is undefined, returning 0 if `name` has been defined, and a non-zero value in any other case.

Example: `#if defined(STATE) && defined(COND)`

         `. . .`

The #line Directive

The compiler uses line numbers and the name of a source file to display errors discovered on compilation. You can use the `#line` directive to change the line numbers and the file name.

Syntax: `#line new_number ["filename"]`

At this position a new line count begins by `new_number`. If `filename` is stated, it will become the new file name that the compiler refers to when issuing error messages.

The new file name must be in quotes and `new_number` must be an integral constant.

Example: `#line 170 "genprog1.cpp"`

The line number and the file name can also be stated as symbolic constants.

Example:
```
#if VERSION == 1
    #define NEWNUMBER 20
#else
    #define NEWNUMBER 25
#line NEWNUMBER
```

The `#line` directive is often used by program generators compiling code to produce a C++ program. In the case of error messages, the message can refer to the appropriate line and file name in the original code.

The current line number and file name can be accessed using the standard macros `__LINE__` and `__FILE__`.

Example:
```
cout << "Current line number: "
     << __LINE__ << endl
     << "File name: " << __FILE__ << endl;
```

The #error Directive

The `#error` directive can be used to show preprocessor errors.

Syntax: `#error errortext;`

The message `errortext` is issued and compilation is terminated.

Example:
```
#if defined  VERSION
    #if VERSION < 3
    #error VERSION too old.\n
    ##error Version 3 or better needed.
#endif
#include "version.h"
```

If the symbolic constant `VERSION` is defined and the value is less than 3, the following error message is output:

```
VERSION too old.
Version 3 or better needed.
```

The #pragma Directive

The `#pragma` directive is *compiler dependent* and allows you to define your own pre-processor commands for a specific compiler.

Syntax: `#pragma command`

Any other compiler that supports the `#pragma` directive but does not support the command following `#pragma` simply ignores the command.

Example: `#pragma pack(1)`

This directive causes a Microsoft compiler to align the components of a class bytewise, avoiding gaps. Other options are `pack(2)` and `pack(4)`.

■ PRE-DEFINED STANDARD MACROS

The ANSI standard provides for six pre-defined standard macros. Their names begin and end with two underscores:

`__LINE__`	Returns the number of the line containing the `__LINE__` macro. The first line in a source code is line 1. The numbering can be modified using the `#line` directive.
`__FILE__`	Returns the name of the source file that contains the `__FILE__` macro. The name can be modified using the `#line` directive.
`__DATE__`	Returns the date in the `mmm dd yyyy` format, where `mmm` is an abbreviation for the month, `dd` is the day of the month, and `yyyy` is the year, resulting in `Jul 17 2001`, for example.
	`__DATE__` refers to the point in time when the preprocessor started processing the source. Thus, the macro returns the same result at any position in the source code.
`__TIME__`	Returns the time as a string in the format `hh:mm:ss`, where `hh` refers to hours, `mm` to minutes, and `ss` to seconds, e.g., `15:23:47`.
	`__TIME__` refers to the point in time when the preprocessor started processing the source. Thus, the macro returns the same result at any position in the source code.
`__STDC__`	Is only defined if the source code contains ANSI keywords only.
`__cplusplus`	Is defined if the source code is compiled using a C++ compiler.

▪ BINDING C FUNCTIONS

Calling C Functions in C++ Programs

C functions from C libraries can be called in a C++ program. However, function calls are interpreted differently by the C++ compiler than you would expect from a C compiler. You must therefore supply additional binding information that is accessible via an `extern "C"` declaration.

Example: `extern "C" void oldfunc(int size);`

This informs the C++ compiler that a C compiler was used to compile the `oldfunc()` function.

If you need to declare multiple C functions, you can declare their prototypes after `extern "C"` within curved brackets. If you have already declared the functions in a header file, you can include the header file in an `extern "C"` block.

Example:
```
extern "C"
{
    #include "graphic.h"
}
```

It is common practise to declare `extern "C"` code in C header files. You can then include the C header both in C and in C++ programs.

Example:
```
#if defined _cplusplus
extern "C"
{
#endif

    // Prototypes for C functions here
#if defined __cplusplus
}
#endif
```

The symbolic constant `__cplusplus` is evaluated to discover whether the current compiler is a C or C++ compiler. If `__cplusplus` is defined, that is, a C++ compiler is active, the `extern "C"` block is inserted.

Defining C Functions in C++ Programs

It is also possible to define your own C functions for a C++ program. You need to do this if you call a function that expects a C function as an argument, such as the standard `qsort()` and `bsearch()` functions.

The definition for a C function in a C++ program must be encased in an `extern "C"` block. This instructs the compiler to compile the function as a C function.

Example:
```cpp
#include <string>
#include <iostream>
#include <cstdlib>
using namespace std;

static char* city[] = { "Paris", "London",
                        "Barcelona", "Hollywood"}
static char* key = "New York";

extern "C" int scmp(const void*, const void*);

int main()
{                               // Sort cities:
  qsort( city, 4, sizeof(char*), scmp);
                                // Find city:
  if( bsearch( &key, city, 4,
               sizeof(char*),scmp) == NULL)
  cout << "City" << (string) key
               << "not found.\n";
}

extern "C"
{
   int scmp(const void *s1, const void *s2)
   {
     return strcmp( *(const char**)s1,
                    *(const char**)s2 );
   }
}
```

The C function `scmp()` is passed to the standard functions `bsearch()` for binary searching and `qsort()` for sorting using the quick sort algorithm.

OPERATORS OVERVIEW ■ 795

■ OPERATORS OVERVIEW

Operator	Meaning
Arithmetical Operators:	
+ –	addition, subtraction
*	multiplication
/ %	division, modulus division
+ –	unary plus, minus operator
++ ––	increment, decrement operator
Relational Operators:	
== !=	"equal", "unequal"
< <=	"less", "less or equal"
> >=	"greater", "greater or equal"
Logical Operators:	
&& ||	AND, OR
!	NOT
Assignment Operators:	
=	simple assignment
op=	compound assignment (op is a binary arithmetical or binary bit-wise operator)
Bit-wise operators:	
& ~	AND, NOT
| ^	OR, exclusive-OR
<< >>	left shift, right shift

▪ OPERATORS OVERVIEW (CONTINUED)

Operator	Meaning
Access Operators:	
`::`	scope resolution operator
`[ ]`	subscript operator
`*`	indirection operator
`.` `->`	class member access operators
`.*` `->*`	pointer to member operators
Cast Operators:	
`(type)`	C cast operator
`dynamic_cast<>`	dynamic cast operator
`static_cast<>`	static cast operator
`const_cast<>`	const cast operator
`reinterpret_cast<>`	reinterpret cast operator
Operators for Storage Allocation	
`new` `new [ ]`	To allocate storage dynamically for an object, an array resp.
`delete` `delete [ ]`	To free dynamically allocated storage for an object, an array resp.
Other Operators:	
`?:` `,`	conditional expression and comma operator
`&`	address-of operator
`name()`	call to function `name`
`type()`	create a temporary object of type `type`
`sizeof()`	sizeof operator (size of type)
`typeid()`	typeid operator (type informations)

■ OPERATOR PRECEDENCE TABLE

Precedence	Operator	Grouping
1.	`::`	from left to right

2.	`.` `->` `[]`
	`++("postfix")` `--("postfix")`
	`name()` `typeid()` `type()`
	`dynamic_cast<>`
	`static_cast<>` `const_cast<>`
	`reinterpret_cast<>`
		from left to right

3.	`!` `~`
	`+ ("unary")` `- ( "unary")`
	`++ ("prefix")` `- ( "prefix")`
	`& ("address")` `* ( "indirection")`
	`new` `new[]` `delete` `delete[]`
	`(type)` `sizeof()`
		from left to right

4.	`.*` `->*`	from left to right
5.	`*` `/` `%`	from left to right
6.	`+ ("binary") - ("binary")`	from left to right
7.	`>>` `<<`	from left to right
8.	`<` `<=` `>` `>=`	from left to right
9.	`==` `!=`	from left to right
10.	`& ("bit-wise AND")`	from left to right
11.	`^`	from left to right
12.	`|`	from left to right
13.	`&&`	from left to right
14.	`||`	from left to right
15.	`?:`	from right to left

16.	`=` `+=` `-=` `*=` `/=`
	`%=`
	`&=` `^=` `|=` `<<=` `>>=`
		from right to left

17.	`,`	from right to left

■ ASCII CODE TABLE

decimal	octal	hex	character	decimal	octal	hex	character
0	000	00	(NUL)	32	040	20	(BLANK)
1	001	01	(SOH)	33	041	21	!
2	002	02	(STX)	34	042	22	"
3	003	03	(ETX)	35	043	23	#
4	004	04	(EOT)	36	044	24	$
5	005	05	(ENQ)	37	045	25	%
6	006	06	(ACK)	38	046	26	&
7	007	07	(BEL)	39	047	27	'
8	010	08	(BS)	40	050	28	(
9	011	09	(HT)	41	051	29	)
10	012	A	(LF)	42	052	2A	*
11	013	B	(VT)	43	053	2B	+
12	014	C	(FF)	44	054	2C	,
13	015	D	(CR)	45	055	2D	-
14	016	E	(SO)	46	056	2E	.
15	017	F	(SI)	47	057	2F	/
16	020	10	(DLE)	48	060	30	0
17	021	11	(DC1)	49	061	31	1
18	022	12	(DC2)	50	062	32	2
19	023	13	(DC3)	51	063	33	3
20	024	14	(DC4)	52	064	34	4
21	025	15	(DC5)	53	065	35	5
22	026	16	(SYN)	54	066	36	6
23	027	17	(ETB)	55	067	37	7
24	030	18	(CAN)	56	070	38	8
25	031	19	(EM)	57	071	39	9
26	032	1A	(SUB)	58	072	3A	:
27	033	1B	(ESC)	59	073	3B	;
28	034	1C	(FS)	60	074	3C	<
29	035	1D	(GS)	61	075	3D	=
30	036	1E	(RS)	62	076	3E	>
31	037	1F	(US)	63	077	3F	?

■ ASCII CODE TABLE (CONTINUED)

decimal	octal	hex	character	decimal	octal	hex	character
64	100	40	@	96	140	60	`
65	101	41	A	97	141	61	a
66	102	42	B	98	142	62	b
67	103	43	C	99	143	63	c
68	104	44	D	100	144	64	d
69	105	45	E	101	145	65	e
70	106	46	F	102	146	66	f
71	107	47	G	103	147	67	g
72	110	48	H	104	150	68	h
73	111	49	I	105	151	69	i
74	112	4A	J	106	152	6A	j
75	113	4B	K	107	153	6B	k
76	114	4C	L	108	154	6C	l
77	115	4D	M	109	155	6D	m
78	116	4E	N	110	156	6E	n
79	117	4F	O	111	157	6F	o
80	120	50	P	112	160	70	p
81	121	51	Q	113	161	71	q
82	122	52	R	114	162	72	r
83	123	53	S	115	163	73	s
84	124	54	T	116	164	74	t
85	125	55	U	117	165	75	u
86	126	56	V	118	166	76	v
87	127	57	W	119	167	77	w
88	130	58	X	120	170	78	x
89	131	59	Y	121	171	79	y
90	132	5A	Z	122	172	7A	z
91	133	5B	[	123	173	7B	{
92	134	5C	\	124	174	7C		
93	135	5D	]	125	175	7D	}
94	136	5E	^	126	176	7E	~
95	137	5F	_	127	177	7F	(DEL)

■ SCREEN CONTROL SEQUENCES

The following escape sequences reflect the ANSI standard for screen control. Replace the # sign by the appropriate decimal number in all cases.

ESC[#**A**	Cursor # lines up
ESC[#**B**	Cursor # lines down
ESC[#**C**	Cursor # characters right
ESC[#**D**	Cursor # characters left
ESC[z , s**H** or ESC[z ; s**f**	Put cursor in line z and column s
ESC[**s**	Save cursor position
ESC[**u**	Load saved cursor position
ESC[#**K**	# = 0: Delete from cursor position to line end
	# = 1:Delete from start of line to cursor position
	# = 2: Delete whole line
ESC[**2J**	Clear screen
ESC[#(;#...)$_{op}$**m**	# = 0: all attributes normal
	# = 1: switch double intensity on
	# = 4: Underline on (monochrome screens)
	# = 5: Blink on
	# = 7: Inverse on
	# = 3x: Foreground color
	# = 4x: Background color

        x = 0: black   x = 4: blue
        x = 1: red   x = 5: magenta
        x = 2: green   x = 6: cyan
        x = 3: yellow   x = 7:white

ESC[c1 ; c2**p**   Change key assignments: The key with decimal code c1 will then return code c2.

To enable these escape sequences, you must first load an appropriate screen device driver. To do so for Windows 9x, place the following line in your CONFIG.SYS file

DEVICE = C:\Windows\Command\Ansi.sys

Win NT and Win 2000 do not supply the ANSI screen control characters. Corresponding functions based on system calls are offered for download.

▪ LITERATURE

International Standard ISO/IEC 14882, *Programming Languages—C++*; published by American National Standards Institute, New York NY, 1998.

International Standard ISO/IEC 9899:1999(E), *Programming Languages—C*; published by ISO Copyright Office, Case postale 56, CH-1211, Geneva 20, 1999.

Stroustrup, Bjarne, *The C++ Programming Language*, Addison Wesley, 2000.

Josuttis, Nicolai, *The C++ Standard Library*, Addison Wesley, 1999.

index

Note: Italicized page locators indicate figures.